The Life of Stephen F. Austin

Published in cooperation with

The Texas State Historical Association

The Life of
Stephen F. Austin

FOUNDER OF TEXAS

1793-1836

*A Chapter in the Westward Movement of the
Anglo-American People*

By Eugene C. Barker

UNIVERSITY OF TEXAS PRESS, AUSTIN

INTERNATIONAL STANDARD BOOK NUMBER 0-292-78421-X

Preface

IT is just a hundred years since Stephen F. Austin began the transformation of the wilderness that Texas then was into an Anglo-American commonwealth. Measured by what he accomplished, he is one of the great figures of American history. But, although the period of Texas history to which he belongs—or, more properly, the period that belongs to him—has long been a fruitful field of study, for most readers of history the man has been obscured by the magnitude of his work. This is natural, and, moreover, is much as he would have had it. He was an unobtrusive, unassuming man, and both inclination and circumstances required him to do his work without the blare of trumpets. All that is written about him by his contemporaries could be printed in a few pages, and he has never been the subject of biographical study. That has determined the character of this treatment, which is primarily factual and direct rather than interpretative. It is in what he did and the manner of doing it that the admirable character and winning personality of the man must appear.

The materials for this study are found for the most part in several great collections of manuscripts. In the Library of the University of Texas are the papers preserved by Moses and Stephen F. Austin; the Bexar Archives; and transcripts obtained by the writer from many sources, but principally from the National Archives of Mexico and the State Archives of Coahuila, at Saltillo. Next to the Austin Papers, the most nearly indispensable collection—and a very voluminous one—is that of the General Land Office, at Austin. The Texas State Library has much Austin correspondence, and other manuscripts illustrating the period, in the collections known as the Nacogdoches Archives, the Lamar Papers, and Domestic Correspondence. And the Rosenberg Library at Galveston possesses an invaluable series of letters written by Austin to his confidential friend and secretary, Samuel M. Williams. The rich collections of printed Texana and Mexicana in the library of the University of Texas, the

Texas State Library, and the Bancroft Library of the University of California have supplemented the manuscript materials. And the newspaper files of many libraries have been searched, particularly those of the Library of Congress, the Wisconsin and Missouri Historical Societies, and the University of Chicago—but chiefly with negative results. Unless otherwise indicated, all manuscripts cited are in the Austin Papers.

Grateful acknowledgment is due the custodians of the collections enumerated for courteous and considerate assistance; to Mrs. Mattie Austin Hatcher, of the History Department of the University of Texas, for many kindnesses in locating material; to my friend L. W. Payne, Jr., Professor of English in the University of Texas, who generously read the galley proofs; and to Mrs. Hally Bryan Perry, Mrs. Edward W. Parker, and Mr. Guy M. Bryan, children of the late Colonel Guy M. Bryan, nephew of Stephen F. Austin, for the use of manuscripts in their possession. Finally, the research that has gone into the book, extending through many years, could not have been done without the uniformly cheerful and sympathetic cooperation of my wife.

EUGENE C. BARKER.

Austin, January, 1925.

Preface: Second Edition

THIS second edition of *The Life of Stephen F. Austin* is identical in text, except for a few technical differences here and there to adjust space. New make-up has reduced the number of pages from 551 to 477, but the Index is revised to fit the new paging. Some readers will be interested to know that after the first edition went to the printer the Austin Papers, on which the book is based, were published. Volumes I and II, containing respectively 1824 and 1184 pages, were issued by the American Historical Association in 1924 and 1928 as Volume II of its Annual Report for the years 1919 and 1922. Volume II, 494 pages, was published by The University of Texas Press in 1926. These volumes contained all of Stephen F. Austin's writings known at the time of publication, except a few somewhat lengthy documents previously published in relatively accessible works. The fundamental portion of this material, described in the Bibliography of this volume, page 451, passed on Austin's death to his nephew, Guy M. Bryan, and was donated to the University of Texas by Colonel Bryan's heirs—Mrs. Edward W. (Laura Bryan) Parker, Mrs. Emmet L. (Hally Bryan) Perry, and Mr. Guy M. Bryan, Jr. To these original Austin Papers were added, and included in the published collection, transcripts of Austin writings found in various Mexican government archives and elsewhere. Since publication of the three volumes of *The Austin Papers,* the University of Texas has acquired two other considerable collections of supplementary Austin material. The first of these is made up of a mass of letters written to Thomas F. Leaming of Philadelphia by Stephen F. Austin and other members of the Austin family. The other came to the University by gift of Mr. Thomas W. Streeter of Morristown, New Jersey, from the Beauregard Bryan estate. Beauregard Bryan was a grand-nephew of Stephen F. Austin, the son of Moses Austin Bryan.

EUGENE C. BARKER

The University of Texas
January 15, 1949

Contents

xi

Chapter VII

The Fredonian Rebellion 148

Chapter VIII

The Struggle for Stabilizing Laws 178

Its Beneficent Effect—Austin Dreams of a New Economic System in which Credit Rests Solely on Personal Character—Correspondence with Edward Livingston—Slavery—The Mexican Attitude—Austin's Changing Views on Slavery—The Federal Law of July, 1824—Austin Begs Exemption from Its Operation for the First Colony—He Outlines a Bill for the State Legislature Allowing Introduction from the United States until 1840—And Providing for Gradual Emancipation by Peonage Contracts with Slaves—Austin Petitions Legislature against Emancipation by State Constitution—Brown Austin Goes to Saltillo to Lobby—Article 13 Recognizes Existing Slavery, but Forbids Further Introduction—Machinery for Its Operation—Austin Moves to Legalize Peonage Contracts between Immigrants and Their Slaves—The Passage of the Law, and Its Operation—Austin Combines Defense of Slavery with Vision of Agricultural Progress—Guerrero's Emancipation Decree—The Political Chief Withholds Publication in Texas until Petition for Exemption Can Be Filed—Excitement of the Texans—Austin's Calm Determination—Guerrero Withdraws the Decree for Texas—Austin Urges William H. Wharton to Settle in Texas—Returning Confidence—Great Immigration—Austin's Reasons for Advocating Restriction of Slavery after Passage of the Law of April 6, 1830—Really Feared Slavery—Hope of European Immigration—But the Colonists Refused to Follow Him—Austin then Turned to Support Views of the Colonists—Explanation of His Apparent Instability—Want of Religious Toleration—Caused Little Active Discontent but an Obstacle to Immigration—Austin Expected Liberalization of the Government to Bring Toleration—His Cautious Treatment of the Subject—Austin's Personal Religion—His Promotion of Education—Efforts to Obtain Schools.

CHAPTER IX

Explanation of His Policy—His Love for Texas and His Faith in Its Future—His Feeling of Obligation to the Colonists and His Loyalty to Mexico—His Influence with the Settlers in Harmonizing Differences—His Defense of the Local Government against Ill-informed Criticism—The Wear and Tear of the Years—His Confidence in the Gratitude of the Colonists—The Policy of Loyalty and Aloofness toward Mexico—His Understanding of Mexican Character—Difficulty of Remaining Aloof after 1830—Silence and Tact—His Policy Arouses Criticism of the Impatient Radicals—Map of Texas—Payment of Old Debts—George Tennille Collects on New Madrid Speculations—Anthony Butler's Claims—The Hawkins Heirs—Lovelace and Wavell—Personal Philosophy.

CHAPTER X

Foundation of the Law in Fear of American Expansion—This Fear Sharpened by Boundary Negotiations of Adams and Jackson—And by Newspaper

Forecasts of the Purchase of Texas—Speculations in Texas Lands—Austin's Condemnation of the Speculators—Poinsett's Unpopularity in Mexico—Terán the Real Instigator of the Law of April 6—His Recommendations—Military Occupation of Texas—Counter-colonization by Mexicans—Alamán's *Iniciativa*—Articles Ten and Eleven—Terán Disapproves—Austin's Protest against the Law—Letters to Bustamante and Terán—His Argument that Immigrants to His Colony Were Not Excluded—The Government Accepts His Interpretation—Rapid Immigration—Austin's Efforts to Forestall Popular Excitement over the Law—His Editorials in the *Texas Gazette*—But He Warns the Government of Its Ill Effects—Military Commandant on the Frontier Checks Immigration—Austin's Efforts to Remove the Obstacle—Issues Certificates in Blank—Effect of the Law on Other Colonization Enterprises—The Galveston Bay and Texas Land Company—The Nashville Company or Robertson Colony—Austin Declines to Become Involved with These Companies—Neutrality—Execution of the Military Provisions of the Law—Garrisons in Texas—Failure of the Counter-colonization Feature.

Chapter XI

Preliminary Summary—The "Texas Association" or Nashville Company Sends Leftwich to Mexico to Apply for a Grant—Leftwich Gets the Contract in His Own Name—Location West of Austin's Colony—Welcomed by Austin—Leftwich Transfers the Grant to the Company—Felix Robertson Inspects the Territory—Sterling C. Robertson Accompanies Him—Another Inspection—The Company Seeks Recognition from the Government—Requests Austin's Assistance—H. H. League—Austin Presents the Company's Petition and Induces the Government to Grant It—But the Company Remains Inactive—Testimony of Amos Edwards—Of William H. Wharton—The Company Interested in Speculation, not Colonization—Sterling C. Robertson Obtains a Sub-Contract—Robertson's Arrival in Texas—Contract Annulled by the Law of April 6, 1830—Austin Intercedes for Robertson's Companions—Presents Robertson's Petition to Governor—Finds Governor Disposed to Re-grant the Territory to a French Company—History of the French Application—Austin in Partnership with Williams Applies for a New Grant Including the Annulled Nashville Company Grant—Robertson's Natural Resentment—But Austin Helpless to Aid Him and Acted for the Interest of Texas—Robertson Prepares to Attack the Validity of the Grant to Austin and Williams—*Ex Parte* Testimony to Prove the Contract Not Affected by the Law of April 6, 1830—Abuse of Austin during His Absence on a Mission to Mexico—Robertson Asks for Annulment of Austin's Grant and Reinstatement of His Own—Vituperative Statements to Governor and Legislature—Examination of the Facts—The Governor Reinstates Robertson's Contract, Austin Having Effected the Repeal of the Law of April 6, 1830—Williams's Ineffective Efforts to Combat Robertson—Robertson Announces Restoration of His Contract with Further Abuse of Austin—Williams Secures Reversal of the Case, but Robertson Refuses to Obey—The

Contents

The Life of Stephen F. Austin

CHAPTER I

In the Current of the Westward Movement

AMONG the thousands who sought religious liberty and spiritual if not bodily ease in the New World during the decade preceding the Great Rebellion a little family of four from the south of England landed at Boston in the spring of 1638—Richard Austin, his wife, and two sons, Richard and Anthony. They settled at Charlestown, and there the father soon died. He had been a tailor, and could hardly have left a considerable competence, but we can only guess at the vicissitudes of the bereaved family. Evidently poverty did not prevent the boys from obtaining a fair education, for in 1674 Anthony became the first town clerk of the new village of Suffield, Connecticut, held the office twenty-seven years—relinquishing it only to pass it on to his son—and in 1696 added to his other duties those of village schoolmaster, a position that he retained until his death in 1708. He had married in 1664 and had numerous sons and daughters, the eldest of whom was another Richard, born September 22, 1666. This Richard, like his father and his brother John, served his town in various honorable capacities, and reared a family of six sons and three daughters. The youngest were two boys, Moses and Elias, born respectively in 1716 and 1718. At the age of twenty-five Elias moved across the state and settled at Durham, where he was later joined by his brother Moses and a nephew, Jesse. Other members of the family were established at New Haven, near by. At his death in 1776 Elias Austin left five children; the youngest, Moses, born in October, 1761, became the father of Stephen Fuller Austin, the subject of this volume.[1]

---

[1] The date of Moses Austin's birth is from the baptismal record of the Rev. Elizur Goodrich, pastor of Durham, in William Chauncey Fowler, *History of Durham, Connecticut* (Hartford, 1856), 311. In a genealogical record prepared for his children Moses Austin dates his own birth "Ocbr 4th 1765." This misapprehension appears in several documents. See, for example, *The Austin Papers*, I, 1, 371, *Annual Report of the Ameri-*

"Of all the men who have figured in American history [said Professor Garrison] there are no other two who have attracted so little attention from their contemporaries and have yet done things of such vast and manifest importance, as Moses Austin and his son Stephen. Their great work consisted in the making of Anglo-American Texas, an enterprise planned and begun by the one and carried into execution by the other.

"The student will scarcely need to be reminded of the series of mighty effects, increasing in geometrical ratio in magnitude and historical significance, that followed directly therefrom. Thus it runs: the Texan Revolution, the annexation of Texas, the Mexican War, and the acquisition of the Southwest below the forty-second parallel from the Rio Grande to the Pacific—a territory almost equal in extent to the Louisiana Purchase and which contains the bulk of the mineral wealth of the United States. How far and in what way all this has permanently affected our national life, it would take volumes to tell; but the profound and far-reaching nature of the influences set in operation by the Austins is evident." [2]

Professor Garrison might have added with equal truth that until his day even historians did not perceive the importance of the Austins in American history. The reason was aptly expressed by Stephen F. Austin nearly a hundred years ago. "A successful military chieftain," he wrote, "is hailed with admiration and applause and monuments perpetuate his fame. But the bloodless pioneer of the wilderness, like the corn and cotton he causes to spring where it never grew before, attracts no notice. . . . No slaughtered thousands or smoking cities attest his devotion to the cause of human happiness, and he is regarded by the mass of the world as a humble instrument to pave the way for others." [3]

Only the barest outline of Moses Austin's early life is possible. [4] His mother died when he was ten, his father when he was fourteen, and it is probable that he spent his youth at Middletown with his sister who was married to Moses Bates. At any rate, he was at Middletown in 1782, engaged in some kind of business

can Historical Association, 1919, Vol. II. For the Austin genealogy the writer is further indebted to Mrs. Laura Bryan Parker of Germantown, Pennsylvania, and to Mr. J. M. Winterbotham of Galveston, Texas, for notes from the official records of Suffield and Durham.

[2] George P. Garrison, in *The Connecticut Magazine,* IX, 512.

[3] Austin to Mrs. Holley, December 29, 1831.

[4] Careful sifting of the local records of Connecticut, Philadelphia, and Virginia might glean important facts, but such a study might well appall any investigator and has been entirely beyond the means of this one.

with his brother-in-law.[5] Middletown was then the principal port of the Connecticut River, but trade could not have flourished during Austin's residence there, which was spanned almost exactly, in all probability, by the Revolutionary War. Nevertheless, the time and the place are significant. There was at Middletown an abandoned lead mine which the beginning of the war caused to be reopened,[6] and it is possible that the boy obtained there an introduction to the industry that in one way or another was to absorb most of his mature life.

With the settlement of the peace preliminaries in 1782, business activity revived and carried Moses Austin to the threshold of that long career on the western frontier that started forces, as Professor Garrison observed, which led to the acquisition of one-fourth the present area of the United States. The brief annals of the first stage of the momentous journey can be told in the terse words of the traveler himself:

"In 1783 [he wrote] Moses Austin removed from New Havin to Philadelphia and opened a dry goods store in Markett Street between front and Second street, and in Feby 1784 formed a partnership with Maning, Merril and commenced the importation of dry goods from England and in May opened a wholesale store in front street between Walnut and Chestnutt and in Augt of the same year extended the house to Richmond in Virginia and Moses Austin removed to that city in Sep^t and took charge of the business."

To this simple chronicle it may be added that Stephen Austin, the eldest brother of Moses, was also a member of Manning, Merrill and Company; that the Philadelphia house was later reorganized under his direction, with the firm name of Stephen Austin and Company; and that at the same time the Richmond branch was independently organized as Moses Austin and Company.[7]

[5] The Deed Records of Durham show that he was at Middletown in July, 1782; and Stephen Austin (an older brother) speaks of a "note I now hold of his given me when he was in Bussiness in Middletown with Mr. Bates."—To James Austin, July 9, 1800.

[6] On May 22, 1775, Titus Hosmer, member of the Connecticut assembly, wrote Silas Deane, in the Continental Congress: "The state of the Lead Mine in this town has likewise engaged our attention. Upon enquiry, we find the ore is plenty and reputed rich; . . . there can be no reasonable doubt, if we can succeed in refining, that this mine will abundantly supply, not only New England, but all the colonies with lead, in such plenty as to answer every demand of war or peace." On November 19 he wrote again that a stamping mill was going and that the furnace would begin next week.—*Collections of the Connecticut Historical Society* (Hartford, 1870), II, 238, 322.

[7] *The Austin Papers*, I, 1; agreement between M. and S. Austin to dissolve partnership, July 20, 1797; S. to M. Austin, February 23, July 25, 1801; M. Austin's reply, June, 1802.

At Philadelphia Moses Austin had met, and the following year returned to marry, Maria Brown, foster daughter and grandniece by marriage of Benjamin Fuller, one of the prominent merchants of his day. Through her mother she was descended from Isaac Sharp and Robert Turner, two of the Quaker proprietors of New Jersey.[8]

Of the business at Richmond we know next to nothing. For a time, at least, it must have prospered. Mrs. Austin writes of two house servants and of "haveing five or six men to find," indicating that so many were employed in the business. Besides, there is a tradition that the Austin home was "the most imposing structure of its day."[9] In 1789, or perhaps earlier, Moses Austin and Company took over by lease or purchase the lead mines on New River, in southwestern Virginia. The history of these mines is hard to arrive at. Colonel John Chiswell, who died in 1766, was reputed to own them, and at that time they were being extensively worked with slave labor. They were an indispensable resource during the Revolution, and great precautions were taken to protect them from Tories.[10] Of their output before and after the Austins obtained possession we are almost entirely in the dark. Writing to his brother in 1801 of the accumulation of slag, which they were then resmelting, Stephen Austin declared, "there still remains sufficient for your children and grandchildren." Lead was carted to Richmond in the form of pigs, bars, and shot; and a contract to roof the capitol with lead indicates that there was machinery at Richmond to convert the pigs into sheet metal. In 1796 Moses Austin, with his nephew, Parsons Bates, and Thomas Norvel, formed a subsidiary company for the manufacture of lead, or pewter, buttons, and Moses Austin and Company agreed to provide a storehouse and the stock. Work at the mines was done for the most part by slaves, and adjacent farms were cultivated to provide food for them and the animals. Stephen Austin, who was in England in 1795, had it

---

[8] The genealogy of the Sharps, "Sharpe of Wiltshire, Gloucestershire," etc. (MS.), is in the Library of the Pennsylvania Historical Society.

[9] *Austin Papers,* I, 7; S. T. Mordecai, *Richmond in By-Gone Days* (Richmond, 1856), 199.

[10] Original documents in *Virginia Magazine of History and Biography,* VI, 344; XI, 420; XVI, 206; XVII, 219; XXVI, 371; XXVII, 49. W. R. Ingalls, *Lead and Zinc in the United States* (New York and London, 1908), 90–91, varies greatly from this brief account of the mines. L. P. Summers, *History of Southwest Virginia,* etc. (Richmond, 1903), 69, is, in view of the known facts, unintelligible.

in mind to bring back several hundred men "bred to the Mining Business," but this plan was not realized.[11]

In 1791, without abandoning the business at Richmond, Moses Austin moved to the mines. This was a period of gigantic speculations in western lands, and Austin's acquaintance with the soil and character of southwestern Virginia was soon turned to account, speculators in Philadelphia buying Virginia warrants at twenty dollars a thousand acres and employing him to locate, survey, and patent lands to cover them. In addition to his other interests and activities Austin was captain of the Wythe County militia, being commissioned by Governor Brooke, on recommendation of the county court, March 23, 1796.[12]

Through the haze of scanty records, allowing only glimpses of this miscellaneous business at Philadelphia, Richmond, and the mines, one fact stands clear in the end—the Austins did not succeed. Why, we do not know. They did not lack industry, application, or enterprise. Perhaps, indeed, they had too much of the last. Currency was scarce in those days, business was conducted largely by credit and barter, and the most conservative merchants—which the Austins laid no claim to being—frequently found themselves suddenly beyond their depth.

In 1796 came the second stage of Moses Austin's momentous migration westward. Learning—from a chance traveler, says tradition—of the rich lead deposits in southeastern Missouri, known then as Upper Louisiana or Illinois, he determined to visit the country, make an inspection, and, if possible, obtain a grant. Probably his information was not so casual as tradition implies. Emigrants had been pouring into Kentucky and Tennessee for a quarter of a century, and many were now following the French inhabitants of the Old Northwest across the Mississippi. The Spanish policy of generous land donations to settlers, in contrast with the impecunious policy—as it seemed—of the United States, offered sufficient incentive for this, and Baron Carondelet, while governor of Louisiana, deliberately tried to capitalize the contrast. Austin says that

[11] Stephen to Moses Austin, February 23, 1801; William P. Palmer and Sherwin McRae, *Calendar of Virginia State Papers* (Richmond, 1885), V, 95, 224; *Austin Papers,* I, 21, 24, 28, 36, and, for an inventory of property at the Mines in 1801, pages 60–62.

[12] *Austin Papers,* I, 1, 10–28. For a graphic account of some Virginia land speculations of this period see James N. Granger, "Connecticut and Virginia a Century Ago," in *The Connecticut Quarterly,* III, 100, 190.

"hand Bills and Pamphlets, Printed in the English Language were circulated throughout the Western Country holding up great inducement to Emigrants, and in many parts of the Province Farming Utensils and Provisions, for one year, were granted to Emigrants." [13]

No man of his time had a keener appreciation than Carondelet of the menace to the Spanish empire in the westward thrust of American frontiersmen; and few have equaled in picturesque accuracy his description of their resistless energy, resourcefulness, and endurance.

"A carbine and a little cornmeal in a sack [he wrote] is sufficient for an American to range the forests alone for a month. With his carbine he kills wild cattle and deer for food, and protects himself from the savages. Having dampened the cornmeal, it serves in lieu of bread. He erects a house by laying some tree trunks across others in the form of a square; and even a fort impregnable to savages by building on a story crosswise above the ground floor. The cold does not fright him, and when a family grows tired of one place, it moves to another, and establishes itself there with the same ease." [14]

Carondelet's primary purpose in urging Americans to settle in Louisiana was to form a barrier against the British Canadians; but nothing, perhaps, could have reconciled him to building a dam of such material but his hope of gaining for Spain through Wilkinson's aid the whole of the Mississippi Valley, and his conviction that with or without permission the restless horde would swarm into the province anyway whenever fancy beckoned.

No doubt, then, Moses Austin knew more of Missouri than a chance traveler would be likely to impart. Aside from other means of information, the product of his Virginia mines met Missouri lead in Kentucky, and even such mild competition as then existed, when demand often exceeded supply, would beget interest and knowledge.

Starting December 8 with a lone companion, Josiah Bell, Austin went by Abingdon, Cumberland Gap, Danville, Frankfort, Louisville, and Vincennes to St. Louis, which he reached on January 15, 1797. Despite the intense cold—he crossed most of the streams on ice—the road through Kentucky was thronged with emigrants,

---

[13] *Austin Papers*, I, 116; Louis Houck, *A History of Missouri* (Chicago, 1908), II, 224–230.

[14] Louis Houck, *The Spanish Régime in Missouri* (Chicago, 1909), II, 13.

many in the most wretched condition. The night of the 17th Austin spent in a one-room cabin at Rock Castle with sixteen companions, and the next day recorded his reflections concerning "the many Distress.d families" that he passed—

"women and children in the Month of Decemb^r Travelling a Wilderness Through Ice and Snow, passing large rivers and Creeks, without Shoe or Stocking, and barely as maney raggs as covers their Nakedness, without money or provisions except what the Wilderness affords . . . to say they are poor is but faintly express'g there situation. . . . Can any thing be more Absurd than the Conduct of man, here is hundreds Travelling hundreds of Miles, they Know not for what Nor Whither, except its to Kentucky, passing land almost as good and easy obtain.d, the Proprietors of which would gladly give on any terms, but it will not do, its not Kentucky, its not the Promis.d land, its not the goodly inheratence, the Land of Milk and Honey."

From Vincennes the journey was over a waste of snow which obliterated all landmarks. Though he took the precaution to employ a guide, the road was soon lost and for five days the party, short of food and—strange to say—without guns, floundered in a general westward direction only to come out at Whitesides' Station, a day's march from St. Louis. The village of St. Louis Austin found to have "about two hundred Houses, most of which are of Stone, and some of them large but not Elegant." There was no tavern, and he had much difficulty in obtaining quarters, being finally indebted for a night's lodging to the hospitality of a "Mons. Le Compte." [15] Calling on the lieutenant governor and commandant general, Zenon Trudeau, he presented letters from the Spanish consul at Louisville, obtained others from the governor to François Vallé, commandant at St. Genevieve, and immediately departed for that place. On January 21, furnished by Vallé with a carryall drawn by two horses, he set out for the mines, forty miles to the west, made a hasty examination, and was back at St. Genevieve on the 26th.

The particular deposits that Austin inspected were known as Mine à Breton, or Burton. He recorded in his diary that he found them in every respect equal to his expectation, that they covered an area of forty acres, and that the ore was encountered within three feet of the surface "in great Plenty and better quality than any I

[15] This was very different from the dramatic entrance described by Austin in 1818. Henry R. Schoolcraft, *Travels in the Central Portions of the Mississippi Valley* (New York, 1825), 242.

have ever seen either from the Mines in England or America." He was informed that four hundred thousand pounds of lead had been taken from this mine the preceding summer, and estimated that the amount of mineral extracted, if properly smelted, would have yielded twelve hundred thousand pounds.[16]

Notwithstanding the volume of labor shown by the works at Mine à Burton, there were no inhabitants there. This was due to the hostility of the Osage Indians. The miners lived at St. Genevieve and went to the mines in a body from August to November, so that mining was limited to three or four months in the year. Moreover, Austin was told that the mines still belonged to the royal domain and were subject to grant. On January 26, therefore, he applied for a vast tract four leagues square around Mine à Burton.[17] At the same time he formed a partnership with John Rice Jones of Kaskaskia, François Vallé, and Pierre de Hault de Lassus de Luziere to exploit the mines, if his application was granted. Jones had long been a resident of the Northwest, knew the people and the language, and had been useful to Austin, whom he accompanied in his inspection of the mines. He was to have a one-fifth interest in the company, but what he was to contribute beyond his knowledge and local influence is not clear. Vallé took in effect merely an option on a one-fifth interest, reserving the right to withdraw without compensation upon Austin's return from Virginia to open the mine. De Luziere, who was commandant at New Bourbon, took a tenth interest, for which he was to pay from the profits of the enterprise. Obviously the function of these officials was to influence the governor general at New Orleans. De Luziere particularly was a person of consequence. His son, Charles de Hault de Lassus, was commandant at New Madrid, had served the king with distinction in Europe, and in 1799 succeeded Trudeau as lieutenant governor of Upper Louisiana. Austin's contribution to the business was explicitly defined. He was to establish machinery at the mine for the manufacture of sheet lead, shot, bars, and white lead; was to introduce as many skilled workmen as would be necessary to construct and operate the various works; and was to bring in merchandise

[16] The two preceding paragraphs are from Garrison (ed.), "A Memorandum of M. Austin's Journey," etc., *American Historical Review*, V, 518–542.

[17] Schoolcraft, *Travels*, etc., 243, says that Austin told him that the dimensions were inserted without instructions by the French secretary who drafted the application.

to the value of three thousand dollars. He was to superintend the work and receive therefor a salary of four hundred dollars a year.[18]

Returning through Tennessee, Austin arrived at home on March 9, having traveled, as he recorded in his diary, "upwards of two thousand Miles, 960 of which was a Wilderness and the Snow most of the way Two feet Deep."

Austin was assured, apparently, that his application would encounter no obstacle with the governor general. In practice grants recommended by the local commandants in Upper Louisiana were confirmed *pro forma,* and, having formed a partnership with two of these officials, his confidence seemed well founded.[19] Carondelet did, in fact, approve a grant of a square league in May, and Austin was informed of this before his return to Missouri; but he did not hold his preparations for this. In February he made with a practical iron worker of Frederick, Maryland, a contract—subsequently canceled—to exploit the iron deposits in his concession; in June he agreed with his brother upon the terms for dissolving their joint business in Philadelphia and Virginia; and in July he obtained from the Spanish minister a passport to St. Louis. In December he dispatched his nephew, Elias Bates, with a number of experienced workmen, to erect furnaces, sink a shaft, and build a saw mill at the mines and a factory at St. Genevieve. Finally, on June 8, 1798, to describe the exodus in his own words, "Moses Austin and Family, Consisting of Maria his wife, Stephen F. Austin his son, and Emily M. B. Austin his Daughter together with Moses Bates and family and Others Whites and blacks to the number of Forty persons,[20] and Nine Loaded Wagons and a Coach and four Horses, All left Austin Ville and took the Road for Morrises Boat Yard on the Great Kanhawa." There they loaded the contents of the wagons on a barge and began the tedious voyage down the Kanawha and Ohio and up the Mississippi to their destination. The incidents of the trip were such as must have been common to many similar parties. Mrs.

[18] *Austin Papers,* I, 29, 31, 47, 49. The partnership agreement lacks eight or ten lines on each of two pages, and the missing parts may have defined more fully the participation of the other partners.

[19] For brief statements of the land system in Upper Louisiana see Houck, *History of Missouri,* II, 224–230, and Amos Stoddard, *Sketches, Historical and Descriptive of Louisiana* (Philadelphia, 1812), 243–268.

[20] This evidently included drivers and helpers who were to return with the wagons. Apparently only twenty took the boat for Missouri.

Bates and her stepson, Parsons Bates, "paid the dept of Nature," and Henry Bates was drowned passing the falls of the Ohio—Austin losing thus two nephews during the voyage—and of the seventeen who on September 8 landed at Kaskaskia, opposite St. Genevieve, fifteen were too sick and debilitated to walk ashore.[21]

Missouri at the time of Austin's arrival was more primitive than western Virginia had been when he moved to the mines. Population was confined to half a dozen villages along the Mississippi and Missouri Rivers, and did not exceed four thousand. Most of the inhabitants, too, like Austin, were new arrivals, many having migrated from the Old Northwest after the Ordinance of 1787 prohibited slavery in that region. St. Genevieve contained, perhaps, a hundred houses and something more than six hundred inhabitants; New Bourbon, a mile to the south, had twenty houses; Cape Girardeau was just beginning; and New Madrid, the southernmost settlement in Upper Louisiana, contained in 1797 five hundred and sixty-nine whites and forty-six slaves; while St. Louis with its two hundred houses, as described by Austin the year before, had under a thousand.[22] American immigration was just beginning, so that the mass of the population was French Canadian, with a sprinkling of Spaniards from down the river. This fact is not without significance in the life of Stephen F. Austin, now an impressionable child of five. He was to grow to manhood with instinctive, sympathetic understanding of gentle, courteous, proud, and sensitive people whose friendship and good will depended upon the observance of social niceties that the Anglo-American too often dismisses with self-conscious embarrassment. It was among such people that his great work was to be done, and upon the harmonious cooperation of such that his success was to depend.

---

[21] *Austin Papers*, I, 2, 32–39.
[22] Austin's "Memorandum," as cited, in *American Historical Review*, V, 535–541; Houck, *Spanish Régime in Missouri*, II, 397; Stoddard, *Sketches*, etc., 209–218.

CHAPTER II

On the Missouri and Arkansas Frontier

TAKING the oath of allegiance and becoming by that simple ceremony a Spanish subject, Austin established his family at St. Genevieve and plunged into unexpected difficulties at the mines. These were due to the complex land system and the vagueness of his grant. He understood that the grant included the old workings at Mine à Burton, and a map accompanying his application showed, indeed, that he wished them included; but the governor's concession, which was essentially only a permit to have a survey made by the surveyor general, did not designate boundaries. Naturally the old inhabitants objected to having their diggings and crude furnaces taken in, and Vallé—and later De Lassus, when he became lieutenant governor—sustained them. For nearly two years the controversy went on, while the inhabitants of St. Genevieve and, as Austin declared, a band of vagabonds from the United States and elsewhere, without property or responsibility, ranged at will, digging his mineral and burning his woods. Finally the worst of the trouble was settled by running Austin's lines so as to exclude the old furnaces, and his title was then completed.[1]

[1] *Austin Papers*, I, 47, 49, 54–57, 67, 123. The statement that the title was complete is certainly true so far as Austin's interest is concerned, but may require some explanation for the investigator who cares to go into the subject exhaustively. In 1806 Will C. Carr, attorney for the United States in the prosecution of claims before the board of land commissioners, wrote Austin (*Austin Papers*, I, 107): "The comm^rs discover much anxiety to know whether you intend to have your title passed before them or not and from their suggestions they think it is not a complete title. On this subject you need not be uneasy, and I very well know you will not." The same year, it is inferred—the document is undated—Austin warning trespassers from his land said (*Ibid.*, 123): "I also think proper to notify the Public that I have a patent right to three Miles square of Land at the Mine à Burton and that said Title has been acknowledged Complete by the Government of the U States and as such transmitted by the secretary of the Treasury of the U states to William C. Carr Esq. Governmental Agent for Land Claims." This seems reasonably conclusive, but it is not final. The land commissioners evidently realized their desire to review Austin's claim and in 1811 reported it incomplete and unconfirmed because the final act of ratification by the Spanish intendant at New Orleans did not take place until after the retrocession of Louisiana by Spain to France. However, claimants who were in actual occupation, as Austin was, prior to the delivery of Missouri to the United States were not disturbed. In 1819 Austin's estate was taken over by his creditors, and I have not followed

This experience typifies Austin's life in Missouri. It was not at best an easy place to live in. Law was lax, and American frontiersmen were pouring in. Austin possessed many sterling virtues—uprightness, industry, perseverance, and the ability to mind his own business—but his little world required tact and adaptability, and, above all, a sense of humor; and besides having an impetuous temper, he was without a germ of either. As a result, he had racking controversies with unscrupulous neighbors and was subject to emotional turmoils that a more plastic spirit would have been spared. That he was nearly always right is clear from the fact that he enjoyed the cordial friendship of his most worthy contemporaries, as well as the confidence of American officials after Louisiana passed to the United States; but this only softens without obscuring one's impression of a choleric disposition that habitually met vexations somewhat more than half way.

Meanwhile, work at the mines did not wait on the adjustment of the disputes with the old miners. In July, 1799, Austin moved his family out, and by the beginning of the next year a saw mill, flour mill, furnace, and manufactory for shot and sheet lead were in operation, representing a capital investment of eight thousand dollars. Soon afterward he was asking permission to establish also a powder factory, but this seems not to have been allowed. These improvements developed lead mining in Missouri from an adventurous vacation sport, carried on between the end of harvest time and winter, to a permanent year-round industry. By 1802 all the native furnaces but one had been abandoned, and Austin was smelting the mineral from all the diggings. The old furnaces, little better than log fires, extracted barely thirty per cent of the ore, while Austin's furnace saved sixty-five per cent.[2]

In 1804 Austin made a report on the mines for Captain Amos Stoddard, the first American commandant of Upper Louisiana. This shows that besides his own, nine other mines were worked intermittently; and that the annual yield of all was valued at forty

---

his title further. In equity his case was certainly good, and the title was probably confirmed in 1834 by a second board of commissioners much more liberal than the first. See Lowrie and Clarke, *American State Papers, Public Lands* (Gales and Seaton, printers, Washington, 1834), III, 662, 671, 682, 703. Another edition of this series printed by Duff Green contains the same material but is paged differently.

[2] *Austin Papers*, I, 2, 51, 82.

thousand dollars, more than half of which was produced by Mine à Burton. The average price of pig metal was a hundred dollars a ton, but sheet lead and shot, of which Austin was manufacturing sixty tons a year, sold for a hundred and sixty dollars a ton. Only a hundred and fifty men were employed in all branches of the work, though Austin believed that a thousand could be profitably employed on his land alone. By this time a village of fourteen American and twelve French families had formed near the mines and been named Potosi after the famous silver mine in Bolivia, whose output it was fondly hoped Mine à Burton might soon rival.[3]

Transfer of the territory to the United States proved not to be an unmixed blessing to the inhabitants of Upper Louisiana. The change of government brought in its wake taxation, militia duty, and a meticulously rigid land system. The first Act of Congress for the government of Louisiana put Missouri under the jurisdiction of Governor Harrison and the territorial judges of Indiana. In October, 1804, these officers went to St. Louis and promulgated some legal regulations and established courts in the several districts, appointing Moses Austin presiding judge of the St. Genevieve district. The new government was unfamiliar and an object of suspicion to the French inhabitants. They did not trust it. And neither they nor the American settlers could be satisfied with the land system. Fortunately it is unnecessary to go deeply into this abstruse and exceedingly complex subject.[4] About a million and a half acres of land were claimed under French and Spanish grants. Very few titles were legally complete. Some of the claimants had gone so far as to have their lands surveyed, but had neglected to take the final step of having the title issued; some had the permit of a local commandant to settle, with his assurance of obtaining land; and some were squatters without even the verbal permit of the commandant. It would have been simpler and less expensive for the government, and in the end fairer to the inhabitants perhaps, to admit all claims and allow them to be located on vacant land, leaving it to the courts

[3] Austin's report was submitted to Congress by President Jefferson. It is in Lowrie and Clarke, *American State Papers, Public Lands* (printed by Gales and Seaton, Washington, 1832), I, 206–209. In October, 1816, Austin made another report on the mines for Josiah Meigs, commissioner of the General Land Office. This is in *Ibid.*, 707–712. For the naming of Potosi see Schoolcraft, *Travels,* etc., 244.

[4] It is excellently treated by Professor E. M. Violette, "Spanish Land Claims in Missouri," *Washington University Studies,* VIII, 167–200; see also Stoddard, *Sketches,* etc., 243–268, and Houck, *History of Missouri,* II, 224–230, III, 34–54.

to settle overlapping locations. Austin suggested substantially this in a forceful argument to the secretary of the treasury, in whose jurisdiction the matter lay; but Congress created a board to examine and adjudicate claims, and the result was years of suspense and strife.[5] Great disorder reigned at the mines in 1806, and Austin did not escape annoyance. John Smith T, a swashbuckling, quarrelsome man to whom he was indebted for many injuries, tried to locate a floating grant of a thousand acres in his Mine à Burton tract.[6]

The transfer to the United States nevertheless stimulated emigration to Missouri, and led to considerable business expansion. Moses Austin seemed to prosper. In addition to his other enterprises, he had from the beginning conducted a general store at the mines, where he sold clothing materials, household and kitchen furniture, hardware, and other manufactured goods for lead, peltry, and miscellaneous country produce. He exported these barter commodities to correspondents in New Orleans, Baltimore, Philadelphia, New York, and Boston and received his trade stock from them in exchange. He aspired at one time to establish a direct connection with London, but the clouds that were gathering to precipitate the War of 1812 were already smothering international trade and this plan failed. Money rarely changed hands in these far-flung transactions, which were characteristic, it may be said, of all Missouri commerce. In fact, there was no money, and both local and foreign, or interstate, trade was hampered by lack of it. This condition led Austin and certain associates in St. Louis and St. Genevieve to apply to the territorial legislature for authority to establish a bank. Their request was granted, but the bank, which after much delay was opened in December, 1816, rather aggravated than relieved the financial disorder. In view of what has been said, it is obvious that financial ratings of those days cannot be accurately determined. Austin was thought to be, and apparently considered himself, well to do,[7] but it is doubtful whether his wealth was not always specu-

[5] Austin to [Gallatin], *Austin Papers*, I, 115–122.
[6] *Ibid.*, I, 123, 136.
[7] In 1812 he estimated his property to be worth $160,000, the mines being valued at $150,000. In 1818 he reported that he had been offered $50,000 for the mine estate. *Austin Papers*, I, 333, 350. The first estimate is undated and is published out of its true chronological order. It was prepared in support of Austin's application to Congress for a charter for the Louisiana Lead Company, which was rejected April 13, 1812.—*Annals of Congress*, 12 Cong., 1 sess., 1318.

lative. The turnover in his various ventures was very slow, collections were uncertain, and his debts were chronically pressing.[8]

It is in his relations with his children that Moses Austin appears most happily. His son Stephen F. Austin was born at the mines in Virginia, November 3, 1793, and his daughter Emily two years later; his second son, James E. Brown Austin, was born in Missouri in 1803, after the purchase but before the transfer of Louisiana to the United States. In 1804 Stephen was eleven years old and it was time to think of his education. Naturally the father's thoughts turned to his own boyhood. By now a considerable New England colony was forming in Missouri, and a safe escort offering through a returning traveler, he sent the boy to friends in Connecticut with instructions to put him at a good school. Bacon Academy, the gift of Pierpont Bacon to the town of Colchester, had just opened. John Adams, its first preceptor, was one of the notable teachers of his day. It was said of him that he was "very near the same to America that 'Dr. Arnold of Rugby' was to England." The first board of trustees included some of the most distinguished men of the state —mostly graduates of Yale or Harvard—and the school as a consequence was widely patronized. Here Stephen was put and remained for three years, but all that we know of his course there is contained in the "certificate of scholarship and conduct" with which Dr. Adams discharged him: "This certifies that the bearer Stephen F. Austin has been a member of this Institution and a Boarder in my family, most of the time, for three years past. As a Scholar he has been obedient and studious; as a boarder, unexceptionable. Having passed acceptably the public examinations, and having during the whole period sustained a good Moral character, he is judged worthy of this honorary testimonial." In its six score years of honorable service many aspiring youths have no doubt gone with a similar testimonial from this celebrated school to contribute great and useful deeds to the life of the nation, but no other has so perceptibly influenced the history of his country as the little boy from the remote western wilderness.

Moses Austin's ideas of education were liberal for his day. Upon

---

[8] *Austin Papers*, I, 84–150, *passim*, affords glimpses of Austin's business life, and an interesting description of general commercial conditions is written by Breckenridge Jones, "One Hundred Years of Banking in Missouri," *Missouri Historical Review*, XV, 345–366.

learning that his son had been placed at the Colchester school, he wrote the principal:

"I have a disposition that Stephen should go through the Classicks. In short, I wish to make him a scholar. Yet I must confess I have for many years disapproved of spending months and years on the Greek and Hebrew. I never have thought either of those languages of much advantage to a man of business, and as I do not wish my son to make devinity his study, [I should like] as little time spent in Greek and Hebrew as is consistent with the regulations of the Academy. If his talents will justify I wish him for the Barr, but I have so many times in my life blamed Fathers for pressing on their sons a profession Nature never intended them for that I shall make of him what Nature has best calculated him to be. I want him to enter Yale as soon as he is prepared, ... I have a great desire he should write well, both as to the hand write and composition— practice will bring writing both easy and pleasing. A correct mode of thinking, both Religious and Political is of consequence and aught to be early implanted in the mind of man. I do not wish my son a Bigot in either, but correct Moral principles is of the first consequence. Such I trust you will impress on his mind."

He wished also to have his son trained in music, "if he has a turn that way."

At the same time he set out a code of social conduct for the boy:

"I do not expect you will expend money unwisely [he wrote], yet I do not wish you to render yourself Disagreeable to your young friends to avoid expending a few Dollars. When it appears necessary for you to forme company, pay readely your part of all expenses that may arise, but Never let yourself be imposed on by an improper Demand; and If you finde a Disposition in any of your young friends to do such an Act, I charge you, have nothing more to Do with them. Keep not there Company, and [here spake the characteristic Moses] promptly tell them the Cause, that is, that you will never keep Company with a Boy disposed to impose on you, nor allow yourself to make an improper Demand on your friends to save a Dollar. These are things many suppose of Small moment, but I do not. It's small things that stamp the disposition and temper of a man, and many times Boys lessen their greatness in life by small things which at the moment they think of little or no Consequence."

He pointed out such homely defects in his son's correspondence as lack of neatness and omitting to say how the new environment impressed him, and reminded him to sign his letters on the right-hand side of the page.[9]

---

[9] *Austin Papers*, I, 92–96, 144; Israel Foote Loomis, "Bacon Academy: Its Founder— and Some Account of its Service," *The Connecticut Quarterly*, II, 121–139.

Stephen Austin fulfilled his father's ideals. He developed ease of manner and social grace, with some appreciation of music and a liking for dancing; mastered a fluent and vigorous literary style; and grew into a man of liberal mind, unimpeachable integrity, and "correct moral principles" untouched by bigotry.

Contrary to his father's original plans, Stephen did not attend Yale, but crossed the mountains and entered Transylvania University at Lexington, Kentucky. This renowned school—the first "university" in the west—had resulted from the union of Transylvania Seminary and Kentucky Academy in 1799 and was now beginning its tenth session. His classmates here included some of the great names of Kentucky—Bowman, Todd, McCalla—and a few letters survive to show that they held him in high esteem. But again it is the certificate of discharge that tells most of the student: "It is hereby certified—that the bearer Stephen F. Austin has been a student —two sessions and a half—of the Transylvania University—during which time he studied various branches of the Mathematics—Geography—Astronomy—Natural and Moral Philosophy—read some History and conducted himself in an exemplary and praiseworthy manner." This is dated April 4, 1810, and is signed by James Blythe, Robert H. Bishop, and Ebenezer Sharpe, who constituted what would now be called the faculty of liberal arts. Young Austin was at the age when boys now finish high school—he had passed his sixteenth birthday the preceding November—but this was the end of his schooling. Two other children were coming on, and the expense of keeping him at college and sending him through the law school was too heavy, we may infer, for the family resources to stand. He returned to Missouri, therefore, to bear a hand in his father's scattered interests.[10]

Next spring Mrs. Austin went east with the other two children —the daughter to be put at a finishing school in New York, and the little boy, now eight years old, with the Rev. Samuel Whittlesy at Washington, Connecticut. The journey was down the Mississippi on a barge to New Orleans and thence in a "very Ellegant ship called the Masoury" (Missouri?) to Baltimore. They took a maid, and the passage for the party of four cost two hundred and fifty

<hr />

[10] *Austin Papers*, I, 171, 172, 174, 183, 188; Robert Peter, *Transylvania University* (Louisville, 1896), 1–110.

dollars. With them also went a consignment of fur, feathers, lead, and venison hams, in charge of one Elisha Lewis, which was expected to pay the cost of traveling and provide a fund for living expenses. What these articles yielded Mrs. Austin was never permitted to know—and therefore neither are we—Lewis, to her great exasperation, being "one of those kind of men that thinks women has nothing to do with men's Business."

No amount of description can portray so vividly as Mrs. Austin's letters to her husband the embarrassment and humiliation that were more or less inseparable from the system of uncertain transportation and inadequate currency that then existed. Though it seemed that reasonable provision had been made for her maintenance, there was not enough allowance for disappointed hopes, delayed collections, fluctuating prices, shipwreck, and losses from counterfeit banknotes. As a consequence, she was often short of money and compelled to borrow for indispensable necessities—a situation all the more embarrassing because her husband was thought to be wealthy. Her daughter's expenses, including board and what were called "the common branches of education"—reading, writing, spelling, arithmetic, grammar, history, geography "with the use of the globes," and plain needlework—were sixty-two dollars a quarter; and for the boy to be "instructed and provided with board, washing and mending, with wood and candles" cost three dollars a week. Besides, the ladies of the first circle, in which Mrs. Austin's friends moved, must wear everything "of the best, and of coars the highest price, in order that theay may be Distinguished from the common or midling sort of people." To have made "an appearance something like" those who called on her she must have spent, she wrote, all of two hundred and fifty dollars. These prices distressed her, for the reason—as she realized clearly enough herself—that she was used to different standards and a different economic system. "The bank bills," she explained, "melt down two fast for me that has lived so long in the country and had no occation for money." For the better part of 1812 she expected relief momentarily from the arrival of her son Stephen with a cargo of lead that, at eastern prices, would have put everything right, but, as so often happened in the early navigation of the Mississippi, his boat was sunk on the way to New Orleans; and, though he subsequently recovered most of the lead, successive delays at New Orleans eventually compelled the abandonment of the trip.

Thus deprived finally of the means of keeping the younger children at school, Mrs. Austin returned with them to Missouri in the spring of 1813, accepting the opportune escort of James Bryan, a friend and neighbor at the mines. The hand of romance was in this, for Bryan was the daughter's suitor, and part of his business in the east was to press his suit with the somewhat hesitant maiden. The monotonous journey homeward, floating for days down the beautiful Ohio, had its due effect, we may suppose, for shortly after the return she married him.[11]

It would be unnecessarily tedious to follow the Austin fortunes in detail from now on. The War of 1812 paralyzed all trade and industry—even lead mining—in Missouri, and before recovery they were again prostrated by the general depression of 1818–1819. For Moses Austin it was a period of energetic but steadily losing combat with adversity. During 1814 and 1815 he involved himself heavily trying to exploit the mines on a great scale with slaves leased from Colonel Anthony Butler, then of Kentucky—an ill-omened connection that was destined to plague Stephen F. Austin nearly all the rest of his life. The effort failed; but why, we do not know. The experiment with the bank of St. Louis, for whose organization he was largely responsible,[12] was no more successful; ending, in fact, in his total ruin. In 1817 Stephen F. Austin took charge of the mines and the business at Potosi, with the pleasing hope, as he expressed it, of being able to "free the family of every embarrassment"; but the task was beyond him.[13]

The territory in the meantime was forging ahead in population, at least, a fact that Congress recognized in 1812 by authorizing the erection of a territorial legislature. Moses Austin was among those nominated to President Madison for the first council, or senate, but he was not appointed. The younger Austin, however, was elected to the house of representatives in 1814 and served by successive re-

[11] *Austin Papers*, I, 190, 211–216; and twenty-five letters written by Mrs. Austin to her husband from Baltimore, Camden, Philadelphia, New York, and New Haven, the most important for this section being those of September 21 and December 30, 1811, and March 16 and August 4, 1812. These letters are held for her family by Mrs. Hally Bryan Perry, Mrs. Austin's great-granddaughter.

[12] *Austin Papers*, I, 232, 234, 260, 265.

[13] *Ibid.*, I, 299–350, *passim*.

elections until 1820, when Missouri was admitted to the Union.[14] The proceedings of the legislature are not available, so that it is not possible, even if it would be profitable, to follow Stephen F. Austin's legislative career. The important result for this study is that he was gaining invaluable experience for his future work in the practical government of a frontier state.

In 1819 Congress organized the territory of Arkansas, and thus sprang the signal for a rapid emigration from Missouri and other western states. More than a year before, James Bryan seems to have set up trading establishments in Louisiana and southern Arkansas, and perhaps to have opened a farm near Natchitoches. Stephen F. Austin now followed him in the summer of 1819. What disposition was made of the Potosi business we do not know; nor can we speak with assurance of the year that he spent in Arkansas. In partnership with William O'Hara, cashier of the Bank of St. Louis, he had acquired a number of New Madrid land certificates, one of which he located on the site of Little Rock. But the sardonic fate that dogged the Austin ventures subsequently proved his title incurably defective and robbed him of the fruit of his judgment. He took also from Missouri a stock of merchandise, left part of it at Little Rock, and carried the rest to Long Prairie on Red River, where he opened a farm.[15] In November, 1819, he narrowly missed election to represent Arkansas as the territorial delegate in Congress;[16] and in July, 1820, Governor Miller appointed him judge of the first judicial district of Arkansas.[17]

Austin was now at the beginning of a great career; and, although entirely unconscious of the fact, could hardly have been better fitted if he had prepared for it with premeditation and purpose. He was twenty-seven years old; well educated for his day; experienced in public service and in business; patient; methodical; energetic; and fair-spoken; and acquainted from childhood with the characteristic social types that mingled on the southwestern border. It was significant, too, that his family had unquenchable faith in the frontier. Virginia, Missouri, and Arkansas had failed them; but there was still Texas, and they were already at its threshold.

[14] *Ibid.*, I, 224; Houck, *History of Missouri*, III, 6–8.

[15] Austin had evidently made some sort of improvement at Long Prairie as early as the spring of 1818. See *Austin Papers*, I, 330, 333, 345.

[16] Dallas T. Herndon (ed.), *Centennial History of Arkansas* (Chicago, 1922), I, 156; J. H. Shinn, *Pioneers and Makers of Arkansas* (Little Rock, 1908), 54.

[17] *Austin Papers*, I, 365; and for the Arkansas period in general, 327–373, *passim*.

CHAPTER III

The Inauguration of Texan Colonization

HOW long Moses Austin had the Texas venture definitely in mind and what preliminary preparations he made for it cannot be clearly determined. In a memorandum written for his younger brother some time before 1829 Stephen F. Austin said that he and his father discussed the project in 1819 after the signing of the Florida treaty, and that the farm which he opened on Red River was intended as a resting place for emigrants and a base of supply until sufficient improvements could be developed to sustain them in the wilderness of Texas.[1] In a pamphlet which he published in 1829 he added that the location at Long Prairie proved unhealthful and investigation convinced him that the best route was through Natchitoches or New Orleans, and hence the farm was abandoned. He goes on to say that in the summer of 1820 it was agreed at Little Rock that his father should go to the capital of Texas and apply for permission to establish a colony, while he himself proceeded to New Orleans to prepare for the transportation of the families, if the petition was granted.[2] It is doubtful, however, whether the plan was thought out so deliberately as this would indicate. A letter from Moses Austin to his younger son in February, 1820, shows a good deal of uncertainty—"I shall go down the country in the spring," he wrote, "to see your brother and determine what I shall do." And Stephen F. Austin's own letters at the end of 1820 disclaim knowledge of his father's plans.[3]

Nevertheless, Moses Austin had had some thought of trading to Texas as early as 1813; in September, 1819, he was contemplating a trip to San Antonio;[4] and tentative consideration of some sort of

---

[1] In Wooten (ed.), *A Comprehensive History of Texas,* I, 442. J. E. B. Austin died in August, 1829, a date which to some extent fixes that of the memorandum.
[2] Gammel, *Laws of Texas* (Austin, 1898), I, 3.
[3] *Austin Papers,* I, 355, 373.
[4] *Ibid.,* I, 223; Schoolcraft, *Travels,* etc., 248.

operation in the "Spanish Country" is suggested in January, 1820, by Moses Austin's requesting a friend at Washington to obtain for him a copy of the passport that he carried to Missouri in 1797.[5] In October he was in conference with Stephen at Little Rock,[6] and some time the next month set out for Bexar with a gray horse, a mule, a negro man, and fifty dollars in cash—a total value of $850 —for which he was "to account to S. F. Austin or return them."[7] On November 27, he was at McGuffin's, a noted landmark about midway between Natchitoches and the Sabine.

He reached Bexar on December 23, in company with his servant Richmond and two companions whom he had encountered near Natchitoches, and was subjected to a searching examination. In answer to questions, he declared that he was fifty-three years old,[8] a Catholic, and a former subject of the King of Spain—as was proved by his passport of 1797; that with his family he wished to settle in Texas and cultivate cotton, sugar, and corn; and that he had brought with him no goods to trade, having only an *escopeta,* a pistol, two horses, some clothing for personal use, and the necessary traveling funds. In his application he added that he was a native of Connecticut and a resident of Missouri, that he was moved by the reestablishment of the liberal constitution in Spain to request permission to settle in the empire, and that he represented three hundred families who also desired to carry out the same object and thereby fulfill the King's intention at the time of the sale of Louisiana to allow his subjects to move to any part of his dominions.[9] The examination of his companions disclosed that one, Jacob Kirkham, was a farmer from Natchitoches searching for four runaway slaves, and that the other, Jacob Forsai (Forsythe), was a native of Virginia who came from Natchitoches to ask permission to settle in Texas.[10]

In his pamphlet of 1829 Stephen F. Austin gives some details of

---

[5] Meigs to Austin, March 9, 1820, enclosing passport of July 13, 1797. The interpretation given in the text seems to be the only reasonable explanation of this incident, but the letter does not clearly express it.

[6] E. A. Elliott to Bryan, October 29, 1820. Original with Mrs. Perry.

[7] Memorandum in "Common Place Book," in file of 1791.

[8] As we have seen, he was born in October, 1761. He had previously lifted four years from his age and he now relieved himself of two more.

[9] Examination, December 23, 1820, Nacogdoches Archives, Texas State Library; application (copy by Bastrop), December 26, 1820.

[10] Declarations in Nacogdoches Archives, Texas State Library.

his father's reception. Governor Martinez at first, without examining his papers, ordered him to leave Bexar "instantly and the province as soon as he could get out of it." Crossing the plaza to his lodgings, Austin met Baron de Bastrop, whom he had known years before in Louisiana, and Bastrop took his documents and intervened with the governor. A second interview was allowed, the ayuntamiento was consulted, and after three days' deliberation Martinez agreed to forward his application to the commandant general and recommend its approval.[11] It is evident that Austin's former Spanish citizenship carried the day.

Texas was in that administrative division of New Spain known as the Eastern Interior Provinces, including, besides Texas, Nuevo Leon, Coahuila, and Santander or Tamaulipas. At its head was the commandant general, Joaquin de Arredondo, with supreme civil and military jurisdiction over the four provinces, and it was to him that Martinez sent Austin's petition. Acting on the advice of the provincial deputation, a sort of federal council representing the provinces, Arredondo granted the application on January 17, 1821.[12]

In the meantime Austin had returned to the United States to await the answer to his petition. He was at McGuffin's again on January 15, where he recorded in his methodical way that the total expense of himself and his servant Richmond for the trip had been $25.78.[13] He had traveled at least part of the way back with Kirkham, whom he found to be both reckless and dishonest. Kirkham had told him before leaving San Antonio that some Spaniards wanted to return with them to Natchitoches. At the San Marcos, fifty miles eastward, he disclosed that these men would join the party on the Colorado with a drove of mules and horses, some of them stolen from the government corral, and that he had promised to buy them. To Austin's protest that such trade, even when the animals were not stolen, was contrary to the law and the orders of the governor, Kirkham blandly insisted that he had done nothing to encourage the Spaniards nor said anything "that would induce them to bring out mules except that if they should do so, he would

---

[11] Gammel, *Laws of Texas*, I, 4. Austin did not see his father after this meeting, but he could have obtained these details from his father's letters or from Bastrop.

[12] Ambrosio María de Aldasora, the Texan representative, to Martinez, January 17, 1821. For the government of the Eastern Interior Provinces at this time see *The Southwestern Historical Quarterly*, XXI, 223.

[13] Entry in "Common Place Book," in file for August, 1791.

purchase them." Austin was desperately anxious lest the governor should suspect him of complicity in the plot and begged the governor to examine the Spaniards, who he implies were captured, to discover the truth. At the same time he wrote Bastrop that Kirkham was talking promiscuously and declaring openly that he could take goods to San Antonio in any quantity and sell them to Lieutenant Sandoval, who had a store. "I cannot close this letter," he said, "without again reminding you that both Lieut. Sandival and yourself are in danger of being drawn into difficulty from the extreme imprudence of Kirkham." [14]

Expecting to return to Texas permanently in May, he asked Bastrop to obtain permission in the meantime for him to land tools and provisions at the mouth of the Colorado. He would be accompanied by twelve or fifteen hands, for whose good conduct he would be responsible, and thought that they could in a few days make themselves safe from the Indians. He seemed confident that the petition to settle three hundred families would be granted,[15] but implied that he would himself remove to the province whether or not the contract was allowed.[16]

There was a tradition in Austin's family that Kirkham deserted on the way back to Natchitoches, taking with him pack animals and provisions and leaving Austin and his servant to live on roots and berries and make their way to the settlements alone.[17] Stephen F. Austin declared that damage to his powder, which prevented him from killing game, compelled his father to subsist for the last eight days of the journey on roots and acorns, and that Moses Austin reached McGuffin's so ill from fatigue and exposure that he was in bed for three weeks.[18] As to the hardships of the trip there can be no doubt, for Austin himself wrote, "I have returned from St. Antonio in the Province of Texas . . . after undergoing everything but death";[19] and the negro, Richmond, was so exhausted that he had to be left at the Sabine with Douglass Forsythe.[20] But there are

[14] Austin to Martinez and to Bastrop, from Natchitoches, January 26, 1821, "Common Place Book," in file of August, 1791. Also to Trudeau, February 3, 1821.
[15] Austin to J. E. B. Austin, March 28, 1821.
[16] Austin to Bastrop, as cited, January 26, 1821.
[17] Note by Col. Guy M. Bryan, in "Common Place Book," in file of August, 1791.
[18] Wooten (editor), *A Comprehensive History of Texas,* I, 443.
[19] Austin to J. E. B. Austin, March 28, 1821.
[20] Austin to Forsythe, January 22, 1821.

evidently some inaccuracies in the tradition. Austin in the letters in which he tries to clear himself of responsibility for Kirkham does not mention Kirkham's desertion; and his return to Natchitoches consumed less time than the trip to San Antonio, so that he could not have lost much time from illness on the way. He was delayed after his arrival at Natchitoches, however, for he did not reach home until March 23.[21]

He wrote his son James, who was in school at Lexington, Kentucky, that he could settle his business in a few days, and expected to be in New Orleans in May. He already had applications which would fill his colony, if the petition was allowed, and from which he expected to obtain $18,000 in fees, but he gave no details of his plans. Ten days later he wrote, "I have made a visit to St. Antonio and obtained liberty to settle in that country. *As I am ruined in this,* I found nothing I could do would bring back my property again, and to remain in a Country where I had enjoyed wealth in a state of poverty I could not submit to." He explained that the governor had granted permission for him to settle the three hundred families on a tract of two hundred thousand acres on the Colorado, but that it must be confirmed by the commandant general before it would be effective. He wanted the land surveyed before parceling it out to families, and in order to attend to that and to make other preparations for planting the colony, he planned to take a force of twenty-five men to Texas immediately.[22] The form of contract which he made with the men of this advance guard shows the nature of the preparations that he had in mind. In return for transportation and subsistence until January 1, 1822, they were to build a house, enclosure, stockade, and block house, and to fence and cultivate "a piece of untimbered land in corn" and gather the crop into corn houses. Each "emigrant" should furnish himself with a good Spanish carbine for defense and should pledge himself to respect the king and constitution of Spain. Austin would provide farming tools, mules, and oxen, and at the end of his service would give each man six hundred and forty acres of land and five bushels of corn from the store houses.[23] It did not, apparently, occur to his sanguine mind that the season would be

[21] Austin to J. E. B. Austin, March 28, 1821.
[22] Austin to J. E. B. Austin, March 28, April 8, 1821.
[23] Form of Contract, April 22, 1821. It has seven signatures besides Austin's.

too far advanced when they reached Texas to raise a crop of corn. Another of his plans was to lay off at the mouth of the Colorado the town of Austina, which he thought would in a few years equal New Orleans "in consequence if not in wealth."[24]

During April and May he worked feverishly to arrange his tangled affairs. On May 22 he wrote Stephen F. Austin in New Orleans that he hoped to finish his business in a day or two, and instructed him, if possible, to obtain a vessel and prepare it for the voyage to the Colorado without delay. About the middle of the month he had received notice of the confirmation of his grant, and wrote with elation, "I now can go forward with confidence and hope and pray you will Discharge your Doubts as to the Enterprise . . . Raise your Spirits Times are changing a new chance presents itself."[25]

But he had never recovered from the exposure and exhaustion which he suffered on the return from Texas; and he had overtaxed himself in his efforts to get back. A few days after writing the letter just quoted, he went to Hazel Run, the home of his daughter, Mrs. James Bryan, and was stricken by pneumonia. He was attended by Dr. John M. Bernhisel, a youthful disciple of the celebrated Dr. Physic of the University of Pennsylvania, who "blistered and bled most copiously" and temporarily relieved him, but on June 10 he died. Almost his dying request was that Stephen F. Austin should carry out his vision. "He called me to his bedside," wrote Mrs. Austin, "and with much distress and difficulty of speech beged me to tell you to take his place and if god in his wisdom thought best to disappoint him in the accomplishment of his wishes and plans formed for the benefit of his family, he prayed him to extend his goodness to you and enable you to go on with the business in the same way he would have done." [26]

He was enterprising, industrious, and of indomitable energy, but it is doubtful whether he could have accomplished the task to which he set his hand. It required deliberateness, patience, tact, ability to make allowances, diplomacy of a high order. He was, as we have seen, impetuous, irascible, belligerent, even litigious in defense of his rights—all of which would, on the one hand, have

[24] Austin to J. E. B. Austin, April 8, 1821.
[25] Austin to S. F. Austin, May 22, 1821.
[26] Maria Austin to Stephen F. Austin, June 8, August 25, 1821.

kept him in a state of perpetual warfare with the frontiersmen of similar qualities who formed the colony, and on the other hand have rendered him entirely unfit to pilot the settlement successfully through the labyrinth of Mexican suspicion and jealousy.

Besides his father's injunction to discharge his doubts, there is a good deal of evidence to show Stephen F. Austin's hesitation to enter the Texas venture. In April, 1820, he wrote his brother-in-law from Arkansas: "I shall remain here this summer, and after that it is uncertain where I shall go. If my father saves enough to support him and you get through your difficulties, . . . I shall be satisfied." In June he wrote again: "If my father should come to Little Rock you may tell him that I wish to go to the mouth of White River to live if I can take anything there to begin with and if that cannot be done I shall go down the Mississippi and seek employ."[27] Though he accepted Governor Miller's appointment to the judicial bench in July,[28] at the end of August he was in Louisiana and apparently intended to remain there, for on December 2 a correspondent expressed the hope that Austin would soon be permanently settled in his new situation.[29] January 20, 1821, he wrote his mother that he knew nothing of his father's objects or prospects, though he understood that he was to return to Natchitoches in February. As to himself, he had gone to New Orleans to get employment: "I offered to hire myself out as a clerk, as an overseer, or anything else, but business is too dull here to get into business. There are hundreds of young men who are glad to work for their board." In this situation, he had met Joseph H. Hawkins, a lawyer, whose brother he had known at Lexington,[30] and Hawkins had offered to teach him law, boarding him and lending him books and money for clothes.

"An offer so generous [said Austin] and from a man who two months ago was a stranger to me, has almost made me change my opinion of the human race. There are however two obstacles in the way; one is that I

[27] Austin to James Bryan, April 30, June 2, 1820. Mrs. Perry's originals.
[28] Certified copy of Commission, *Austin Papers*, I, 365.
[29] Bates to Austin, December 2, 1820.
[30] Austin to J. E. B. Austin, May 10, 1823. Colonel Bryan erroneously says that Austin and J. H. Hawkins were classmates at Transylvania University.—*A Comprehensive History of Texas*, I, 445. Hawkins had been speaker of the Kentucky house of representatives, 1810–1813, and had succeeded Henry Clay in Congress in 1814, when Clay was appointed to the commission to negotiate the treaty of Ghent, closing the War of 1812.

shall earn nothing to help you with for at least 18 months; another is that perhaps those I owe in Missouri may prosecute here. . . . It will take me 18 months to become acquainted with civil law which is in force in this country and learn the French language—that once done I then shall have the means of fortune within my reach. I am determined to accept of Hawkins' offer."

In the meantime, he was assisting in editing the *Louisiana Advertiser*.[31]

This plan was changed by Moses Austin's success in Texas. His letter of May 22 indicates previous correspondence with Stephen, but none of it has survived. It is evident, however, that they understood each other, and we know that it was Moses Austin's proposal which brought Hawkins into the Texan undertaking.[32] On receipt of his mother's letter of June 8 telling of his father's desperate illness and one from James Bryan repeating his father's prayer that he would carry out the colonization contract,[33] Stephen on June 18 departed for Natchitoches on board the steamboat *Beaver*[34] to meet the escort which Governor Martinez had dispatched to accompany Moses Austin back to San Antonio. That his preparations were already made is shown by the fact that he took with him from New Orleans "eight or ten" men to explore the province,[35] and picked up another of his party, William Little, at the mouth of Red River on the 20th.[36] He anticipated the death of his father, and arranged with Hawkins to open his mail and notify him by special messenger if it should indeed occur.[37]

He arrived at Natchitoches on the 26th and found Josef Erasmo Seguin, J. M. Berramendi, and several other "Spaniards"—traders one suspects—waiting. His party set out on July 3, but he remained behind to attend to necessary business. On the 4th he wrote to his father, sending him a translation of Arredondo's permit to establish the colony, dined with Dr. John Sibley, and attended a ball. The next day he arranged for the sale of the negro

[31] Austin to his mother, January 20, 1821. Copy in Lamar Papers, Texas State Library.
[32] Hawkins to Mrs. Austin, June 27, 1821.
[33] *Ibid.* Bryan's letter has not survived.
[34] Austin's Journal, *Quarterly* of Texas State Historical Association, VII, 286.
[35] Hawkins to Mrs. Austin, June 27, 1821.
[36] Journal, as cited.
[37] Mrs. Austin to J. E. B. Austin, August 3, 1821, reciting a letter from Stephen which has not survived, written from Natchitoches, June 28, 1821.

Richmond whom his father had left to recuperate on the Sabine. On the 7th, leaving Seguin to follow, he joined his party in camp near McGuffin's, where they were delayed by strayed animals until the 9th. At daybreak on the 10th he learned of his father's death but continued on to Camp Ripley on the Sabine where, the messenger said, Dr. Sibley would send particulars and mail. Waiting there in vain through the 11th, he started back to Natchitoches on the 12th and reached it at breakfast the next morning only to find that the mail had been forwarded by Seguin, who was on the road. Writing his mother that he would continue the undertaking, he left Natchitoches again on the 14th, overtook Seguin, and was back at the Sabine on the 15th.[38] From here on his journal gives in detail his itinerary and observations upon the country that he traversed. At Nacogdoches the inhabitants to the number of thirty-six were collected to hear Seguin deliver the orders of the government, and appoint James Dill temporary head of the settlement. Several families there agreed to move into Austin's grant. The party left Nacogdoches July 21, was delayed several days on the way by sickness and by hunting for one of the men who lost himself in the woods, and arrived at San Antonio on August 12. Seguin wrote Governor Martinez from the Guadalupe that Austin's party then numbered sixteen. They impressed him as men of consequence with whom the governor would want to make a good showing, and he suggested that comfortable quarters be prepared for them.[39] A letter from Felix Trudeau, Spanish consul at Natchitoches, expressed also a very favorable opinion of Austin.[40]

Martinez received him, therefore, very cordially, recognized him without demur as heir to his father's concession, and entered into detailed arrangements for the establishment of the colony, authorizing him to explore the lands on the Colorado and sound the river to its mouth, and to introduce provisions, tools, and farming implements duty free through the port of San Bernard, which had just been legalized by the commandant general. Austin must be responsible for the good character of the immigrants, admitting none without letters of recommendation from their previous places

[38] Journal, as cited; and letters and documents of July 1, 4, 5, 13, 1821.
[39] Seguin to Martinez, August 10, 1821. Bexar Archives.
[40] Trudeau to governor and ayuntamiento of Bexar, July 12, 1821. General Land Office of Texas, Vol. 54, p. 65.

of residence; and until the government could organize the local administration they must "be governed by and be subordinate to" Austin.[41] On the 18th Austin presented a memorandum of a plan, no doubt previously discussed, for distribution of land to the colonists,[42] and, subject to slight modifications by the superior government, Martinez formally approved it the following day.[43]

The ten days spent at San Antonio were busy and full of interest. Besides his conferences with the governor, Austin entered into some tentative plans with Bastrop and Seguin to acquire control of the Indian trade;[44] engaged in a mustang hunt; and recorded in his journal an Indian raid in which one Indian was killed.[45] On the 21st he resumed the road, escorted for a time by the governor, Bastrop, and Berramendi. His route lay along the San Antonio River, and the first day's march took the party to the mission of San Juan de Capistrano. In his journal, which he kept very sketchily at this stage, he commented on the missions and the irrigation system. Arriving at La Bahía on Sunday, the 26th, he presented his credentials to the alcalde the next day and requested guides, as he had been instructed to do by the governor. The alcalde replied that the only competent guides were two soldiers whom he could not use without the governor's special order. The matter seemed so important that Austin decided to wait until the alcalde could receive instructions, and employed the time in writing letters and preparing six of his party to return to the United States with the surplus horses and mules, about sixty in number, which indicates that there was some licensed trading at San Antonio. On September 1 the messenger returned with information that the governor could not spare the soldiers for guide service, and on the alcalde's advice Austin engaged Manuel Becerra, one of the *regidores* of the town. He also employed two Jaraname Indians as "pilots," though just what was the distinction between pilots and guide is not clear. He was now delayed by Becerra's preparations, and did not get started until the 3d.[46]

[41] Martinez to Austin, August 14, 24, 1821, in *A Comprehensive History of Texas*, I, 471–2.

[42] Records of General Land Office of Texas, Vol. 54, pp. 67–8.

[43] Wooten (ed.), *A Comprehensive History of Texas*, I, 472.

[44] Seguin to Austin, August 30, and Bastrop to Austin, September 12, 1821.

[45] *Quarterly* of Texas State Historical Association, VII, 296.

[46] Writing from memory about 1829, Austin said that he left San Antonio the last of August and Goliad September 10.

Traveling along the Opelousas road about sixteen miles to Coleto Creek, the party turned down this to the Guadalupe, which it followed to the head of San Antonio Bay. From this point, on September 7, Austin told the guide to go to the old site of the mission and presidio of Bahía. Becerra struck due east, although the place he was seeking was near the mouth of Garcitas Creek almost directly north. After going fifteen miles he brought up on the shore of one of the inlets of Lavaca Bay. After wandering around the western shore of the bay for several days, Austin decided that his guide knew nothing about the country and dismissed him. It appears from Becerra's report on his return to Goliad, however, that his ignorance arose from the fact that while Austin's permit only authorized him to explore the Colorado, he seemed to be carefully mapping the valley of the Guadalupe and the coast.[47] Continuing northeastward, Austin struck the Colorado between the present towns of Columbus and Wharton, followed down the river some thirty miles, and turned northeastward again to the Brazos, which he reached on the 20th near the site of San Felipe, where he later established his capital. Here he divided the party for two days to explore both sides of the Brazos, and on the 22d set out for Natchitoches, where he arrived October 1.

In his trip to San Antonio and in his subsequent explorations he traversed the region now covered by twenty-three counties, and gained a very fair impression of the lower course of the San Antonio, Guadalupe, Colorado, and Brazos Rivers. In this vast region there were only two villages, with a total population, according to the governor, of 2,516 souls.[48] These were San Antonio and La Bahía, or Goliad. Nacogdoches had been, prior to the revolution and the filibustering expeditions which began in 1812, a town of nearly a thousand people,[49] but war and rapine scattered the inhabitants, and when Moses Austin passed through in the fall of 1820 it was entirely abandoned. A few stragglers and American squatters from the vicinity were collected by Seguin and given a local organization, as we saw, in the summer of 1821; and scat-

---

[47] Becerra's diary of the trip, Records, General Land Office of Texas, Vol. 54, p. 71.
[48] Martinez to López, February 6, 1822. The ayuntamiento of San Antonio estimated 3,000 in November, 1820.—*Southwestern Historical Quarterly*, XXIII, 61.
[49] Lester G. Bugbee, "The Texas Frontier, 1820–1825," in *Publications* of Southern History Association, March, 1900, p. 102.

tered here and there along the Sabine and Red Rivers were isolated families. Of the four missions near San Antonio, one was
deserted, three were occupied and the land cultivated by families
from the town, but all were in a state of dilapidation approaching
ruin. The two missions near La Bahía were still maintained, but
the priests had no real authority, and the Indians came and went
at will.[50] There were a few soldiers at La Bahía and a strong garrison at San Antonio, but the ayuntamiento complained that, un-
mounted, unclothed, and without supplies, they were useless in the
field and a nuisance in barracks, where they were compelled to
eke out a meager subsistence by thieving from the citizens.[51] The
pay of the soldiers furnished most of the specie in circulation at
San Antonio. The governor apparently winked at the departure
of an occasional drove of horses and mules for Natchitoches and
was equally blind when venturesome travelers arrived with pack
animals loaded with tobacco, flour, clothing, shoes, and other comforts of civilized life. Austin found money "tolerably plenty" at
La Bahía because of the trade "from Natchitoches to the coast,"
but the town was in a state of ruin, and the people lived very
poorly, owning a few cattle and horses which had escaped the
Indians and raising some corn—"little furniture or rather none at
all in their houses—no knives, eat with forks and spoons and their
fingers."[52] It was absolutely necessary for the nation to make some
effort to populate the province, Governor Martinez said, and the
easiest and least expensive way to do it was to offer sufficient in-
ducements to bring foreigners quickly to the country;[53] hence his
welcome to Austin.

From Natchitoches Austin made to Martinez a full report of
his reconnaissance, outlined the boundaries which he desired for
the colony, and submitted his final plan for distributing land to
the settlers. While he expected to confine the settlements to the
Colorado and Brazos valleys and the land between, the reservation
which he requested was much greater—from the mouth of the
Lavaca to its source, thence along the watershed between the Gua-

[50] Statement of ayuntamiento of Bexar to Martinez, November 15, 1820.—*Southwestern Historical Quarterly*, XXIII, 61.
[51] *Ibid.*. 66.
[52] Austin's Journal in *Quarterly* of Texas State Historical Association, VII, 298.
[53] Martinez to López, February 6, 1822. Bexar Archives.

dalupe and Colorado to a point six leagues above the Bexar-Nacogdoches road, then parallel with the road to the Brazos-San Jacinto watershed, down that to the sea, and along the shore to the point of beginning. He had given much thought to the method of distributing land and the quantity to be allowed settlers, and while in San Antonio proposed, as we saw, a scale that Martinez approved. Reflection now caused him to submit slight changes. He proposed to allow a man, whether married or single, six hundred and forty acres, and, in addition, three hundred and twenty acres for a wife, one hundred and sixty for each child, and eighty for each slave. The total for a man with wife, child, and slave did not differ greatly under the two plans, but the man's headright—and therefore the allowance to single men—was reduced from nine hundred and sixty to six hundred and forty acres. The original plan had contemplated a town lot for each settler, but he now decided to restrict the lots to mechanics, merchants, and professional men.[54] This method of division, he explained was better proportioned to the men of property and conformed to the section, half-section, and quarter-section grants to which the settlers were accustomed in the United States.

Fifty or more families from the vicinity of Nacogdoches had agreed to move to his grant in November and December, he said, and since he could not be there to receive them, he had appointed an agent to supervise them and prevent overlapping locations. He also appointed Josiah H. Bell, one of his former associates in Arkansas, to exercise temporarily in the settlement the duties of a justice of the peace.[55] He found at Natchitoches nearly a hundred letters from Missouri, Kentucky, and other western states, and was convinced that he could settle fifteen hundred families as easily as three hundred. Since Martinez desired the rapid settlement of the province, Austin proposed a plan which he thought would bring this about. Let the government appoint a commissioner, or superintendent, of immigration who knew conditions in the United States and the character of its inhabitants, as well as the quality and situation of the lands in Texas—himself in short—and a sur-

[54] Austin to Martinez, October 12, 1821. University of Texas transcripts from Fomento Archives, Mexico. The plan of August 18 is in Records of General Land Office, Vol. 54, pp. 67–68.
[55] *Ibid.*

veyor general, who, though independent of the commissioner, would act only on certificates furnished by him, and leave to these two officials the administration of such colonization regulations as the government might wish to prescribe. The distance to San Antonio, the expense of the journey, and the uncertainty and difficulty of dealing with the government in a language which they did not understand would deter the best class of immigrants from risking the venture. His proposal would meet this difficulty, and would at the same time be a convenient one for the government, which would have to deal only with the commissioner and the surveyor. The commissioner—and presumably his colleague as well—should be authorized "to exact from each settler a sufficient per cent on the land granted to compensate him for his trouble and expense in attending to the business."[56] Martinez approved the plan and recommended to his superior its adoption and the appointment of Austin, "because he is a subject already known and who during his stay in this city gave the impression of being a man of high honor, of scrupulous regard for formality, and of desiring to learn how to discharge faithfully the duties proposed by his late father."[57] As we shall see, however, the recommendation was rejected.

Two permits to settle in his colony that Austin issued while at Natchitoches add certain details of his plan which do not appear in his letter to the governor. To Josiah H. Bell, who on October 6 received a grant for himself, his wife, two sons, and three slaves according to the scale set forth in the letter to Martinez, Austin stipulated that the land must be occupied and cultivated within a year and that for the privilege of settling Bell should pay him $12.50 per hundred acres, half on receipt of title and the other half twelve months later. Austin obligated himself to obtain the title and to pay surveying charges and other fees. To William Kincheloe on the 16th he granted an extra six hundred and forty acres without payment of the twelve and a half cents an acre, in return for the erection of a mill. Thereafter it was a common practice, subsequently authorized by law, to augment grants in recognition of public service, and in proportion to ability to improve the land.

[56] Austin to Martinez, October 13, 1821.
[57] Martinez to López, November 18, 1821.

By November 10 Austin was back in New Orleans to make his final arrangements.[58] He bought a small vessel, the *Lively,* which Hawkins fitted out,[59] and engaged a number of emigrants to sail to Texas, sound the coast from Galveston Island to the Guadalupe, land at the mouth of the Colorado, build a stockade, plant and cultivate five acres of corn, and remain in his service until December, 1822, when he would give each of them six hundred and forty acres of land and half the yield of his crop. In the meantime, he agreed to furnish tools and work animals and to pay their living expenses while in his service.[60] He signed with Hawkins a contract formalizing their previous agreement, by which Hawkins pledged $4,000 to inaugurate the colony and Austin promised Hawkins half the land and other profits derived from the undertaking.[61] He had already written from Goliad in August the substance of the terms which he proposed to allow settlers, and his letters, appearing in the newspapers of the Mississippi Valley, had aroused great interest.[62] He now published his offer in final form. Settlers would receive the quantities of land indicated in his letter to Governor Martinez from Natchitoches—mechanics and men of capital being allowed additional land and privileges "in proportion to their capacity to be useful." In return they must take the oath of allegiance to the Mexican government, pay Austin twelve and a half cents an acre for the land, which he would deliver free of all other fees and expenses, and settle and cultivate a part of the grant by January, 1823. Nobody would be admitted who did not "produce satisfactory evidence of having supported the character of a moral, sober, and industrious citizen." In accordance with his instructions from Martinez, Austin signed himself Civil Commandant of the Colony.[63]

Details of the return to Texas are lacking. Austin probably left

---

[58] Austin to Bryan, November 10, 1821. Mrs. Perry's original.

[59] Austin to Martin, September 14, 1832.

[60] Agreement with Emigrants, November 22, 1821. It is signed by fourteen names. Austin said in 1832 (to Martin, September 14, as above) that the *Lively* carried out seventeen or eighteen men. William S. Lewis, one of the emigrants, names seventeen (*Quarterly* of Texas State Historical Association, III, 14) and says there were several others. Only six of those he mentions signed the agreement.

[61] Agreement between Austin and Hawkins, November 14, 1821. Austin acknowledged receipt of the $4,000, but it was not then nor later fully advanced—Austin to Martin, September 14, 1832.

[62] Parker to Austin, December 7, 1821.

[63] "General Regulations relative to the Colony," November 23, 1821.

New Orleans on November 25.[64] He was certainly back at Nacogdoches on December 17,[65] whence, no doubt, he proceeded immediately to the interior. During his absence a few families had moved into his grant, but our information concerning them is very scant. Evidently few of the "fifty or more" families of whom he wrote to Martinez from Nacogdoches in October had moved. Toward the end of November four families were camped on the west bank of the Brazos at the crossing of the La Bahía road, near the present site of Washington. The first to arrive was Andrew Robinson's; the others were those of three brothers, Abner, Joseph, and Robert Kuykendall. During December several other families joined them. About Christmas Robert and Joseph Kuykendall and Daniel Gilleland proceeded along the La Bahía road to the crossing of the Colorado and planted the first settlement on that river, near the present Columbus. The other Kuykendall brother and Thomas Boatright moved a few days later some ten miles west of the Brazos, and on January 1 established a settlement on New Year's Creek on land which they had previously explored. About the same time Josiah H. Bell settled on the Brazos some five miles below the La Bahía road.[66] During January and February the movement into the colony was very brisk. This was natural, of course, because it was necessary to leave the United States after gathering one crop and arrive in Texas, while it was still a wilderness, in time to plant another. Of Austin's own journey from Nacogdoches there is no record. He spent January and February searching for the party that the *Lively* was to land at the mouth of the Colorado, which, as it really landed at the Brazos, he did not find, and then he went to San Antonio to report to Governor Martinez. At the time of his departure, March 3, he said that there were fifty men on the Brazos and a hundred on the Colorado, building cabins and planting corn to be prepared for the coming of their families in the fall. He knew then of but eight families already arrived.[67]

[64] Austin to Bryan, November 23, 1821.

[65] James Gaines to Austin, January 5, 1822, acknowledges a letter of that date from Nacogdoches.

[66] "Recollections of Capt. Gibson Kuykendall" (son of Abner), written by J. H. Kuykendall in 1858, in *Quarterly* of Texas State Historical Association, VII, 29. Kuykendall wrote with truly critical sense, tried to verify verbal statements by contemporary notes, and there is strong probability that his account of these settlements, besides being more circumstantial, is more accurate than Yoakum's (*History of Texas*, I, 213).

[67] Memorial to Congress, May 13, 1822.

For several months the fate of the *Lively* was a subject of grave anxiety to Austin. He went to San Antonio and then to Mexico City still fearing that the vessel was lost. Rumor spread among the early colonists and later crystallized into a tradition that the ship was lost, and Yoakum records in his *History of Texas,* published in 1856, that after sailing from New Orleans "she was never heard of more." The essential facts in the history of the unfortunate little ship can be briefly told.[68] It was of thirty tons burden and cost Austin $600, most of which was provided by a loan from Edward Lovelace, one of the men who accompanied him in the exploration of the past summer.[69] It sailed toward the end of November, laden as we know with tools, provisions, seed, and seventeen or eighteen emigrants, instructed to sound the Texas coast and land in the Colorado. On December 3 it sailed past the mouth of the Brazos, and on the 23d returned there and landed the cargo and passengers.[70] What it had been doing in the meantime we do not know.[71] It then sailed southward to make soundings, and at least some of those left behind expected it to return, but they never saw it again. Instead, it arrived in New Orleans some time prior to February 6,[72] took on another cargo and more passengers, and returning was wrecked on the western shore of Galveston Island,[73] with the total loss of the cargo.[74] The passengers, among whom was Thomas M. Duke, were taken off the island by the schooner *John Motley* and landed at the mouth of the Colorado.[75] The party on the Brazos, disappointed at not finding Austin, divided into two groups, one commanded by Edward Lovelace and the other by William Little, both of whom knew something of the country through the exploration of the previous summer. While

[68] They are accurately presented by Lester G. Bugbee, "What Became of the Lively," in *Quarterly* of Texas State Historical Association, III, 141–148.

[69] Austin to Martin, September 14, 1832.

[70] Lovelace to Austin, June 26, 1822.

[71] William S. Lewis, one of the emigrants, wrote in 1873, evidently from contemporary notes, "Adventures of the 'Lively' Immigrants," *Quarterly* of Texas State Historical Association, III, 1–32, 81–107. He says that after leaving the Mississippi the vessel was driven far to the east and had to beat back against head winds and calms.

[72] Hawkins to Austin, February 6, 1822.

[73] The date is uncertain—probably some time in April (John Hawkins to Austin, April 29, 1822), but see Kuykendall, in *Quarterly* of Texas State Historical Association, VI, 247, who says May or June.

[74] Austin to Padilla, August 12, 1826.

[75] Kuykendall, "Recollections of Judge Thomas M. Duke," *Quarterly* of Texas State Historical Association, VI, 247.

Lovelace pursued a vain search up stream for a settlement,[76] Little remained below to watch the stores. When Lovelace returned, the reunited parties, living on game, tried to raise a crop of corn. The severe drought of 1822 defeated these efforts,[77] and finally discouraged, all but two or three drifted back to the United States.[78] Though the history of the *Lively* was well known to the early settlers, Austin's failure to find the first immigrants and the subsequent loss of the vessel became confused in the memory of later arrivals. This accounts for the legend of its mysterious disappearance with all on board.

At San Antonio, fresh from the disappointment at the mouth of the Colorado, another shock awaited Austin. Martinez had acted without consulting his superior in recognizing him to succeed his father; and having personal knowledge of the wilderness condition of Texas, of the difficulties of travel and communication, and realizing that immigrants must have permanent grants immediately in order to build shelters for their families and plant food crops, without which they would surely starve, he approved, as we have seen, Austin's schedule for distributing land and endorsed his suggestion for the appointment of an immigration commissioner. At Monterey, however, a hundred leagues to the south, the commandant general and the provincial deputation had no such conception of these practical problems, nor did they share the Texan executive's eager desire for the improvement of his province. They replied, therefore, to Martinez's report of what he had done that Austin must "not distribute lands, appoint judges, nor assume any authority whatever," but that in all cases he should make known his wishes to the superior government (themselves) and await its decisions, and in the meantime the immigrants must be settled provisionally on land designated by the nearest ayuntamiento.[79]

At the same time the new government in Mexico had begun the consideration of a colonization policy for Texas and the Cali-

[76] The news soon spread among the settlers, however, that the *Lively* had landed in the Brazos.—See Elliott, March 25, 1822, Hawkins, April 29, and Lovelace, June 26.

[77] Lovelace to Austin, June 26, 1822.

[78] Austin to Martin, September 14, 1832.

[79] López to Martinez, December 15, 1821, filed with November 18, 1821. The provincial deputation had in fact sent Martinez on May 1 a resolution of April 11 saying that the ayuntamiento should distribute the lands (see University of Texas transcripts from Fomento archives), but he apparently did not give it sufficient significance.

fornias.[80] Knowing the genius of his people for punctilio, Martinez could foresee occasion for infinite inquiry and delay concerning Austin's contract, and he advised him therefore to go to the capital and endeavor to get it confirmed. This was a totally unexpected and very distressing contingency. Besides feeling keen responsibility for the immigrants whom he had brought and was bringing to Texas and who it now appeared might suffer great delay in obtaining land, Austin's financial resources were far too limited to undertake such a trip lightly. With little hesitation, however, he set out, after appointing Josiah H. Bell to assume general direction of the incoming colonists. His passport was issued by Martinez on March 13, it was *viséd* at Monterey on April 10, and he arrived in the city on April 29. Between San Antonio and Monterey the Indians were a continual menace, and beyond Monterey the country swarmed with bandits. From San Antonio to Laredo he traveled with two companions, Dr. Robert Andrews and a man named Waters. Six miles west of the Nueces a band of fifty Comanches surrounded them and seized all their belongings, but upon learning that they were Americans released them and restored all their property except four blankets, a bridle, and—of all things—a Spanish grammar.[81] At Laredo Austin thought it prudent to await the departure of a considerable company which was traveling his road to La Punta, but from Monterey southward he had but one companion, a veteran of Mina's expedition going to Mexico to apply for a pension as a reward for service in the war for independence.[82]

From the Medina River to Laredo, Austin described the country as the "poorest I ever saw in my life, it is generally nothing but sand, entirely void of timber, covered with scrubby thorn bushes and prickly pear." Laredo was "as poor as sand banks, and drought, and indolence can make it." [83] For the rest of the journey, no one, he thought, who had read Humboldt could travel through it without great disappointment. A country more miserable than that between Monterey and the capital he hoped did

[80] December 7, 1821. *Diario . . . de la Soberana Junta,* 136 (Mexico, 1821).
[81] Austin to J. E. B. Austin, March 23, 1822. Their partiality for Americans is explained by their illicit trading relations with certain Americans.—See Austin to Bustamante, May 10, 1822, p. 54, below.
[82] Austin to Colonists, in Wooten (ed.), *A Comprehensive History of Texas,* I, 451.
[83] Austin to J. E. B. Austin, March 23, 1822.

not exist anywhere else in the world—the Choctaw Indians lived in luxury in comparison.[84] However, the country possessed great resources, and these combined with the enthusiasm growing out of the successful struggle for independence and the general harmony which prevailed, offered, in his judgment, "pledges of future greatness and prosperity."[85] Of the capital he wrote after a residence of ten weeks:

"This city is a truly magnificent one, as regards the external appearance of the buildings, and altho I at first thought it not larger than New York, I now think after a better examination that it is larger than any city in the U. S. and much more populous. The population however is very much mixed and a great proportion of them are most miserably poor and wretched, beggars are more numerous than I ever saw in any place in my life—robberies are frequent in the streets—the people are bigotted and superstitious to an extreem, and indolence seems to be the order of the day. In fact the City, Magnificent as it is in appearance is at least one century behind many others in point of intelligence and improvement in the arts and the nation is generally in the same situation."[86] "The clergy [he wrote a year later] have enslaved them to the last degree of oppression—fanaticism reigns with a power that equally astonishes and grieves a man of common sense."[87]

[84] Austin to J. E. B. Austin, June 13, 1822.
[85] Austin to Hawkins, May 1, 1822.
[86] Austin to J. E. B. Austin, July 8, 1822.
[87] To the same, July 13, 1823; and to Amigos Mios, May 28, 1823.

CHAPTER IV

Austin in Mexico

A GLANCE at the political situation in Mexico will explain the almost impossible task which Austin now faced. Iturbide had proclaimed the independence of Mexico in the Plan of Iguala, February 24, 1821, and General Juan O'Donojú, the highest Spanish authority in Mexico, had provisionally ratified it in the Treaty of Córdova, on August 24. These two documents offered the crown of Mexico to Ferdinand VII, or, in his default, to some other member of the Spanish royal family. Pending confirmation of this agreement by Spain, Iturbide and O'Donojú provided for a temporary government, consisting of a legislative junta and an executive regency which was to be chosen by the junta. The junta was also to frame a law for the election of a constituent congress and to pass other laws of an urgent nature.

The junta, nominated by Iturbide, organized on September 28. Its first work was the election of the regency, with Iturbide at its head. For the rest, it did not go smoothly. It spent much time discussing the status of certain religious orders, and more regulating the press, and passed into history on February 24, 1822, with the assembling of the national representative Congress which it had called.

The Congress, like the country, was divided into three parties —Bourbonists, national monarchists, and republicans. News soon arrived that the Spanish government rejected the Treaty of Córdova, and with this the Bourbon party disappeared. Republican sentiment grew rapidly in the Congress, but the city populace and the provinces turned strongly to Iturbide.

Austin, reached the city on April 29, and his own words give us the most graphic and accurate description of the situation and of his problem:

"I arrived in the City of Mexico in April without Acquaintances, without friends,—A Stranger in a City where untill very recently foreigners

43

were proscribed by the Laws and Discountenanced by the people, from prejudice—Ignorant of the Language, of the Laws, the forms, the dispositions and feelings of the Government, with barely the means of paying my Expences for a few months, and in fact I may say destitute of almost everything necessary to insure success in such a Mission as I had undertaken but the integrity of my intentions—Added to all this I found the City in an unsettled State, the whole people and Country still agitated by the revolutionary Convulsion which had just terminated in their emancipation, public opinion vacillating as to the form of Government which ought to be adopted—Party spirit raging with that Acrimony which political Collision is Calculated to excite and the recently established Government almost sinking under its efforts to preserve the public peace and order." [1]

To Hawkins Austin reported that he found the government fully informed, through Martinez, of the steps which he had taken and of the progress of the colony. He expected early approval of past actions and the passage of measures guaranteeing future prosperity. [2] Both the junta and Congress had, in fact, already under consideration a general colonization law. The subject first appeared, without introduction or explanation, in a report of the committee of foreign affairs on December 7, when it was tabled to await conclusion of the discussion on freedom of printing. [3] On the 24th a joint report of the committees on agriculture and foreign relations was read on the colonization of Texas and the Californias, but again was postponed because other committees considering related subjects had not reported. [4] The joint committee report again came up on January 2, and Señor Azcárate read from the committee of foreign relations that part of its report dealing with the settlement of Texas and the Californias. It was thought that the two should be considered together, and as General Anastacio Bustamante, captain general of the Provincias Internas, urged an early decision concerning Texas, which was in his jurisdiction, the report was made the order of the day for January 7. [5]

Bustamante's anxiety was due to pressure of Austin's move-

[1] Austin to his Colonists, June 5, 1824.
[2] Austin to Hawkins, about May 1, 1822.
[3] *Diario . . . de la Soberana Junta*, 136. A committee report of February 22, 1822, says that the regency submitted the subject of colonization on November 26, 1821.
[4] *Ibid.*, 173.
[5] *Ibid.*, 188; Mateos, *Historia Parlamentaria de los Congresos Mexicanos*, (Mexico, 1877), I, 167.

ments in Texas. He wrote Iturbide on January 5 that he had examined all the documents which he could collect on Austin's colony, with the result that he recommended the location of the settlement around the abandoned missions of Concepción and San José. In this way the colonists would have the protection of the garrison at San Antonio, and would, in time, intermarry with the native citizens. He favored a liberal policy of encouragement to immigrants, but they should not be allowed to settle far from San Antonio. The United States before this, he said, had advanced its boundaries by dubious means, and Mexico should not assist a further extension by establishing an Anglo-American colony in the immediate line of march.[6]

On the 7th Azcárate was ill. On the 11th he had not been able to assemble the necessary documents to conclude his work with Bustamante. On the 18th communications from Iturbide and the minister of foreign affairs were read and referred to the joint committee of agriculture and foreign affairs. On the 24th the president of the junta urged the prompt dispatch of the business of Texas and the Californias, and Azcárate replied at length. It was a grave subject, he said. He was working upon it without ceasing and would report at the earliest possible moment. On February 7 the ministry of foreign affairs sent in various documents concerning the "settlement of the Anglo-American Moses Austin," and with their reference to the committee the subject of Texas took its leave of the sessions of the junta, which gave place to the Congress on February 24.[7]

The committee felt keenly, however, the pressing necessity of settling the colonization policy for the frontier provinces, and did finish its report on February 22, but the junta was then so absorbed in preparations for installing Congress that it could not be presented. The committee acknowledged its indebtedness to a colonization law passed by the Spanish Córtes in 1821, and some sections of the report were suggested by direct requests from Martinez in Texas and from Gaspar López, commandant general of the Eastern Provinces, for instructions. It invited Europeans and

---

[6] Bustamante to Iturbide, January 5, 1822. University of Texas Transcripts from Department of Fomento, Mexico.

[7] *Diario . . . de la Soberana Junta*, 203, 220, 239, 261, 283; Mateos, *Historia Parlamentaria de los Congresos Mexicanos*, I, 206, 209, 222.

Americans of the Catholic religion and good character to settle in Texas, Coahuila, Tamaulipas, New Mexico, and the Californias; but the idle and vicious were not desired. Good character and Catholic faith must be attested by certificates from qualified officials, and persons not usefully employed within three months after arrival should be expelled. Families introduced by a contractor (*capitulante*) received a hundred and sixty acres of land, those who came at their own expense three hundred and twenty acres. The land was free, but each settler must pay the state an acknowledgment of fifty cents at the end of six years. Married men could introduce household goods and tools to the value of $5,000 free of duty; single men to the value of $2,000. They would be exempt from all taxes and tithes for the first six years after settlement, and for the next six years would pay only half rate. Contractors would receive a premium of a league of land for each thirty families that they introduced. The public welfare demanded first the settlement of Coahuila, but the peopling of Texas should not be abandoned, and to this end ayuntamientos should be instructed to send two-thirds of the foreign families applying to them to Coahuila and the other third to Texas. The poor of the empire and the soldiers of the Army of Independence should be settled in Texas for its protection against invasion or injury.

In several of its sessions the junta had discussed a bill concerning slavery,[8] and Martinez on December 1, in a letter which Iturbide transmitted to the junta early in January, had written that colonists wanted to know the legal status of their slaves, since they would undoubtedly be ruined if the slaves were freed;[9] but the committee had found the subject beyond its abilities to settle, and passed it on to the constituent Congress.[10]

Before Austin's arrival in Mexico several petitions had been referred to the congressional committee on colonization, among them one of March 20, 1822, from "Benjamin Mailan [Milam] and three companions," asking for land in Texas.[11] And soon after

[8] October 18, 24, November 20, 21, *Diario . . . de la Soberana Junta*, 47, 56, 125.

[9] Martinez to Commandant General, December 1, 1821, University of Texas transcripts from Department of Fomento, Mexico.

[10] Report of the Committee, February 22, 1822, in *Ibid*.—"The constituent congress shall determine whether the slaves which they bring with them shall be admitted."

[11] *Actas del Congreso Constituyente Mexicana* (Mexico, 1822), 1ª folio, 67, 89. 2ª folio, 36, 37; Mateos, *Historia Parlamentaria de los Congresos Mexicanos*, I, 312. T. (or

his arrival Austin wrote Hawkins that applications were before Congress from Andrew Erwin and Robert Leftwich, of Tennessee, and from two Europeans, one of whom wished to settle five thousand Irish and the other eight thousand German colonists.[12] A few weeks later General James Wilkinson, late of the United States army, became an applicant. Indeed, a friend wrote Hawkins, "the Austin Grant will have as much to fear from the encroachment of new grantees as from any other cause."[13]

Austin expressed the hope of being able to return to Texas, with his business satisfactorily arranged, in ten or twelve days, but he had yet to learn something of the Mexican refinements of the art of procrastination. On May 13 he presented to Congress an elaborate memorial, outlining the history of his enterprise to the time of his departure from Texas. He stated the boundaries which he desired—between the Brazos and the Lavaca, and from the Gulf to the Bexar-Nacogdoches road—and explained the plan which he and Martinez had agreed upon for the division of land among the settlers. He hoped to have ere now a map of the region, with soundings of the coast, but the loss of the *Lively* prevented that and he could show only a rough map of the interior. He begged that these boundaries be fixed, that the amount of land which he had promised immigrants be confirmed, and that he be allowed to put them in possession and give them titles; that he be permitted to place other families from the United States on any lands that might remain after the settlement of the three hundred; that he be granted such land for his own family, consisting of mother, brother, and a brother-in-law who was the father of four children, as the government might consider a just compensation for his pains, expenses, and labors; that he be authorized to found one or more towns in his grant and select for himself and give also to useful artisans building places free of charge; and, finally, that he

---

J.) Reilly, writing J. H. Hawkins from Mexico on April 26, 1822, said that General Trespalacios had been appointed Governor of Texas. "His second in command is a Mr. Mileham, formerly of Kentucky, now a colonel in the Mexican Service, he will be also accompanied by a Colonel Burns (English) and a Captain Austin of New York—These two last were with General Long." Were these Milam's associates in the application for land?

[12] Austin to Hawkins (about May 1, 1822). Erwin and Leftwich wanted a grant in Texas. The European applicants have not been identified, but probably wanted to colonize that province.

[13] Reilly to Hawkins, April 26, 1822.

be granted letters of citizenship. In return for these concessions he offered to explore the coast and present to the government a map and description of the bays and channels; remove the raft which obstructed navigation at the mouth of the Colorado; and to organize, arm, and equip the settlers and hold them at all times ready to march against Indians or other enemies of the province. When he left Texas there were already, he said, fifty men on the Brazos and a hundred on the Colorado, building houses, planting corn, and getting ready to remove their families in the fall. Eight families, including women and children, had arrived in the province, and he had information that others were on the road to it.[14]

At the same time Austin presented to General Bustamante a plan for establishing lasting peace with the Comanches and Lipans. These Indians, he said, had been used by the insurgents as allies in 1812, and after Arredondo's defeat of Toledo's army some of the American soldiers of fortune who were serving with him had settled around Natchitoches. There they connected themselves with unscrupulous traders, and, through their acquaintance with the Comanches and Lipans, established an extensive commerce with them, exchanging store goods for horses and mules, which they sold in the United States. As long as this market was open, the Indians would continue to war on the Mexican border provinces to obtain their stock in trade. This illicit traffic followed according to Austin, three principal channels, one through Nacogdoches, one through Pecan Point, on Red River above Natchitoches, and the third far to the west by way of the Kansas and Missouri Rivers. The first two channels could be blocked by garrisons at Nacogdoches and on Red River opposite Pecan Point. The third, which was used almost altogether by Indians, who passed the stolen animals from nation to nation until they reached Missouri, he thought might be closed by an appeal to the United States. In effect, citizens of the United States, with which Mexico was at peace, by purchasing these stolen animals were instigating in that country hostile expeditions against Mexico. This was contrary to international law and to the neutrality law of the United States. "I therefore have no doubt that if this subject was represented to the Government of the United States, that a law would

[14] Austin to Congress, May 13, 1822.

be passed which would effectually stop this iniquitous traffic."
Two things would then remain to be done to insure permanent
peace with the Indians. One of these was to establish systematic
trade with the Indians under government regulation, and the
other was "to strengthen the province of Texas by fostering the
settlement which is already formed on the Colorado and Brazos
by me, and encouraging the introduction of more settlers." Of various methods of regulation, he favored granting a monopoly of
the Indian trade to a chartered company, which he thought might
find its capital in the United States. "The welfare of the new settlers which I have brought into Texas is closely connected with
these subjects. We are all equally interested in procuring a peace
with the Indians. I therefore offer my services in any way that the
Government may want them towards effecting this desirable object." [15]

These two documents well illustrate Austin's ability to grasp an
administrative problem and urge the advancement of his own
enterprise as the obvious means of its solution. The Comanches
were a scourge to the frontier provinces. Ever since his own arrival in Texas in May, 1817, Governor Martinez had consistently
begged for the increase of the garrisons and population and for
the establishment of licensed trade with the Indians to maintain
peace with them and break their connection with American
traders.[16] But the difficulties were beyond the slender and always
over-strained resources of the government.[17] What more reasonable, therefore, than the prompt acceptance of Austin's proposal?
Under proper restrictions, every branch of the government did,
in fact, wish to accept it.

On May 15, the regency sent to Congress the file of documents
concerning Texas received from the commandant general, and
on the 18th listened to Austin's memorial.[18] Elated at the progress
of his affairs, Austin saw himself already on the road to Texas.
But the party divisions in Congress, and between Iturbide and
Congress, had now reached a crisis. Convinced that the republi-

[15] Austin to Bustamante, May 10, 1822.
[16] Martinez to López, December 1, 1821, University of Texas Transcripts from Department of Fomento, Mexico.
[17] López to Iturbide, December 28, 1821, in *Ibid*.
[18] *Actas del Congreso Constituyente*, 2ª folio, 253, 275.

cans intended to strip Iturbide of power, a few soldiers, headed by a sergeant and accompanied by a mob, went shouting through the streets on the evening of the 18th proclaiming Iturbide emperor. The next morning Congress assembled at seven o'clock, with the mob filling the halls and interrupting its deliberations by continual demands for the election of Iturbide. In the hope of quieting the disorder, the Congress begged Iturbide to attend the session, and after demurring that it was not fitting for him to be present at debates which so greatly concerned himself, he yielded to persuasion and appeared, escorted by his generals, and, literally, as the journals of Congress declare, "In the arms of the people who proclaimed him." [19] They had unhitched his mules and themselves drawn his coach through the streets. At the invitation of the president he addressed the crowd, exhorting them to let Congress deliberate in peace, but they would be content with nothing less than his immediate election. Some of the deputies who declared themselves personally in favor of the election of the generalissimo, begged for delay until the provinces could express their wishes, but the mob could not be controlled, and that staunch patriot Valentin Gómez Farías indicated the surrender of Congress by a resolution signed by himself and forty-six other members calling for the election of Iturbide, "with the definite and indispensable condition that he shall pledge himself, in the oath which shall be presented, to obey the constitution, laws, orders, and decrees which emanate from the sovereign Mexican Congress." [20] Many speeches followed, plainly tempered by the spirit of the galleries, and at the end the vote showed seventy-seven for the election of Iturbide and fifteen for delay until instructions from the provinces could arrive. The recorded vote was short of a quorum, but the journal explains that some of the deputies had left the chamber after signing Farías's resolution, thinking their vote sufficiently expressed in it, while others were scattered through the hall and prevented from voting by the disorder that reigned. [21]

[19] *Ibid.*, 2ª folio, 282.

[20] *Ibid.*, 285.

[21] *Ibid.*, 331–332. For other accounts of Iturbide's elevation, see H. H. Bancroft, *History of Mexico*, IV, 757–778; Lorenzo de Zavala, *Ensayo Histórico de las Revoluciones de Mégico* (Paris, 1831), I, 164–175; Lúcas Alamán, *Historia de México* (Mexico, 1852), V, 447–458.

Austin wrote an account of this revolution to his brother at San Antonio on May 22:

"Some great events have transpired since my arrival here, and this great city is now in a State of Commotion and rejoicing—on the 17 the Generalissimo Iturbide resigned, and sent his resignation to Congress,[22] this produced much sensation which broke out on the night of the 18, by firing of Musketry and cannon in the air loaded with Balls, and loud shouts from the soldiers and citizens proclaiming Iturbide Emperor under the title of Augustin 1st—the next day the Congress met at 7 and at 12 elected Iturbide Emperor, this was Sunday, on Monday the form of the oath was agreed on and on Tuesday which was yesterday it was administered in Congress Hall by the President amidst the Shouts of the Multitude, this day has been a constant scene of rejoicing, the army paraded and the Bells have kept a constant roar since daylight. I hope this event will be a fortunate one for the country. The Emperor I believe is a very good man as well as a great one, and has the happiness of the nation much at heart. I shall return as soon as I can, but it is uncertain when that will be, everything is now at a stand, my prospects are very good and I think everything will be right." [23]

There can be no doubt that the army and the masses of the city were happy, and Zavala believed that a plebiscite of the provinces would have resulted in the free election of Iturbide,[24] but, as Austin wrote his brother, "there are some dark clouds hanging over this part of the Country, many are dissatisfied and disappointed at the election of Iturbide, and the Republican party is still restless, tho I hope there will be no difficulty, but I fear it much." [25]

On May 25 Austin, through the Minister of Foreign Affairs, congratulated Iturbide on his elevation to the throne, offered his services and his loyalty, professed his desire to be a citizen of the empire, and begged Iturbide's support for his memorial of the 13th.[26] By now, however, there were numerous other applicants for land in Texas, and it was one of these that gave rise to the first important debate in Congress. Diego Barry, Tadeo Ortiz, and Felipe O'Reilly had asked for six thousand leagues of land,

[22] The journals do not mention this, and I have seen no other reference to a resignation.
[23] Austin to J. E. B. Austin, May 22, 1822.
[24] Zavala, *Ensayo Histórico de las Revoluciones de Mégico*, I, 173.
[25] Austin to J. E. B. Austin, May 22, 1822.
[26] Austin to Iturbide, May 25, 1822, University of Texas Transcripts from Department of Fomento, Mexico.

in which to settle ten thousand Irish and Canary Island families. The committee on colonization made a special report on June 3, recommending that they be allowed two thousand leagues for introducing fifteen thousand "persons, of both sexes, old enough to be heads of families"—that is, of marriageable age. The report does not make the details of administration clear. It was evidently intended that the proprietors should grant or sell lands on their own terms in these two thousand leagues to the immigrants whom they introduced, and that lands remaining after the fifteen thousand were settled should belong to the proprietors. The colonists must be settled within two years,[27] lands must be occupied and improved—or forfeited—within six years, and the proprietors must sell one-third of their residuary lands within ten years and another third in the next ten years to at least ten different purchasers.

Fear of encroachment from the United States was strongly expressed in the committee's report. It declared: "The situation of Texas, its fertility, and its abundant waters make it superior to any other province of the Empire . . . These advantages and its proximity to the United States aroused sometime ago (*tiempo ha*) the desire of the United States to possess it—a desire which they will satisfy if we do not take steps to prevent it. . . . The committee cannot conceal from Congress that our neglect in this matter would bring upon Texas the fate of the Floridas." No better protection against such a calamity could be adopted than the settlement there of an industrious population, attached to the Empire by the ties of religion and interest in its lands. The Irish had given striking proofs of their industry in the cultivation of extensive tracts in the United States; and the Canary Islanders had demonstrated the same virtue in many places, especially in Cuba. "It cannot be doubted, then," the committee continued, "that with such colonists the population will increase rapidly, or that the wealth of Texas will develop proportionally; nor that this population and this wealth will be the bulwark against which any attempt of the neighboring nation must shatter itself." [28]

[27] No penalty was named, however, for failure to introduce the full number, nor compensation for partial fulfillment of the contract.
[28] The committee report, June 3, 1822, is in University of Texas Transcripts from Department of Fomento, Mexico.

Considerable opposition to the committee's report developed in the debate on June 5. Some members thought it a prodigal waste of the nation's lands; two thousand leagues could not possibly be improved by fifteen thousand inhabitants; the proprietors would exploit and oppress the immigrants; and their residuary rights would make them dangerously powerful landlords. The minister of foreign affairs, who had been invited to participate in the discussion, advised the prompt passage of a general colonization law in order to systematize the business and relieve Congress of the burden of considering individual cases. This was in fact the opinion of Congress, and the report was recommitted to await the draft of a general law.[29] In the course of the debate on the 3d J. B. Arizpe, the deputy from Monterey, had reminded members of the grant to Moses Austin, with whose terms his son had "religiously complied, having already conducted some families to the land conceded to him, and having begun considerable labors."[30] This was significant of progress by Austin. Arizpe was a man of force, and Austin had won his support.

After the debate, which he must have followed with anxious interest, Austin filed another memorial with the Foreign Office: 'The families which he had brought to Texas under the authority and guarantee of the former government were in a most critical situation during his absence, without chief or head in a country until now a wilderness and in the vicinity of Indians alike fierce and warlike.' He implied, without directly stating it, that his mother and sister were already in Texas exposed to these dangers and privations, and hoped that the minister and the colonization committee would dispose of his application and enable him to return to his settlement. This, he pointed out, was of great importance to the whole plan of colonization, because the failure of his colony "would incredibly hinder, or perhaps, for want of a rallying point and a base of provisions, make the establishment of other colonies impossible for many years." In return for the concession he would obligate himself: (1) to settle within two years two-thirds of the territory bounded by the Brazos, the Lavaca, the Bexar-Nacogdoches road, and the sea with ten in-

---

[29] *Actas del Congreso Constituyente*, II, 7, 8, 21–24 (Mexico, 1822).
[30] *Ibid.*, 7.

habitants to the square league of farming land (provided there remained enough land in the other third for his three hundred families); (2) to make at his own expense and present to the government an accurate map of the coast; (3) to remove, with the aid of the colonists, the obstacles to navigation at the mouth of the Colorado; (4) to arm and organize in rifle companies all the men capable of bearing arms, for the purpose of repelling Indian incursions in Texas—provided always that the government needed their assistance; and (5) to be responsible for the good conduct of every individual who with his permission settled in the province.[31]

Though disappointed and disillusioned, Austin did not let his feelings influence his letters. To his brother he wrote on July 8: "The Colonization law is still pending and as the Emperor's Coronation is deferred until the middle or last of this month I expect nothing will be done for some time yet—I have only to wate with patience and have no doubt that in the end all will be right. . . . I shall probably not be in Bexar before the 1 of September, but do not be discouraged at my detention."[32] On July 26 he wrote to the settlers on the Brazos and Colorado: the Emperor had been crowned on the 21st; the government was now firmly established, he thought; and, as Iturbide had sworn to support the constitution which Congress was to make, there was every reason to believe that the government would be "as free and liberal as any man could wish." He hoped to find them on his arrival "in peace and happiness, with *Bread* in abundance, and contentment in every breast— . . . tell them [the settlers] not to be discouraged at the gloomy prospect which wild woods present to them on their first arrival, a short time will change the scene, and we shall enjoy many a merry dance and wedding frolic together."[33]

The colonization committee had, in fact, read its report to Congress on July 16 and it had been ordered to the printer.[34] It did not again appear until August 20. In a flowery speech introducing the bill, José Antonio Gutierrez de Lara declared that the in-

[31] Austin to "Ministro de Estado" (G. Calderon), June 6, 1822. University of Texas Transcripts from Department of Fomento, Mexico.

[32] Austin to J. E. B. Austin, July 8, 1822.

[33] Austin to "Josiah H. Bell, A. Robinson and other settlers on the Rivers Brazos and Colorado," July 26, 1822.

[34] *Actas del Congreso Constituyente*, II, 309.

fluence of Mexican independence was about to be felt from the rising of the sun to the place of its going down; and Mexico would become the center of the commerce of the world, connecting Europe and Asia. Impressed with the importance of peopling and developing the country, the committee had labored to frame a law for "producing those beneficent effects which we have admired in a neighboring nation, whose advancement in population and in territorial and commercial wealth has no example in the annals of the world." The passage of this law would be like the breaking of an over-strained dyke, and colonists would inundate the country to plant settlements, towns, and cities in the plains now roamed by wild beasts and savage Indians. Much could wisely be left to the intelligence and self-interest of the colonists, and the committee had thought it best to confine its bill to the most general regulations, such as prescribing the maximum and minimum holdings, the definition of land measures, and establishment of a contract system for the introduction of settlers by empresarios. The committee deplored the existence of slavery and the slave trade in the world, "which dishonors the human race," and it proposed to prohibit the slave trade in Mexico, but it could not disregard the rights of property, unjust though they were, and settlers must be allowed to introduce their own slaves, with the understanding that children born in the empire to those who arrived after the publication of the law should become free at the age of fourteen.[35]

The first article of the committee's bill limited its privileges to Catholics. To such it guaranteed liberty, property, and all other civil rights. Heads of families engaged in farming would receive a *labor* (a hundred and seventy-seven acres) of land; those who raised cattle a *sitio* (4,428 acres); and those who followed both occupations—as all farmers did—a *labor* and *sitio*. They must improve the land within six years. They could bring in for their own use tools, machinery, and other implements; and each family could introduce household goods to the value of two thousand dollars. For the first six years from the date of a concession the colonists would pay no tax nor tithe whatever, and for the next six years only a half rate. The committee thought that it would

[35] *Actas del Congreso Constituyente*, II, 15–21.

be necessary at the beginning to promote colonization by the use of immigration agents, and authorized the government to make contracts with such agents to introduce not less than two hundred families each, for which they should receive a premium of three *haciendas* (fifteen square leagues) and two *labors* of land, up to a maximum of nine *haciendas* and six *labors* for six hundred families. But the contractor, or empresario as the law called him, should forfeit his right to the premium lands if he had not settled and cultivated them within twelve years from the date of the contracts, and at the end of twenty years he must sell or otherwise alienate two-thirds of them. Article 30 tersely stated the provision concerning slavery: "After the promulgation of this law there shall be neither sale nor purchase of slaves in the empire. Children born in the empire to those introduced after its publication shall be free at the age of fourteen." The actual administration of an empresario contract was left vague. The government was to indicate the province to be settled and the lands which the settlers were to have, but no procedure was laid down for granting titles to them. Individual immigrants, not members of an empresario colony, should apply to the ayuntamiento, or local government, nearest to the place they wished to settle, and that body would distribute lands to them in accordance with orders from the superior government. In all cases the government would give preference in the distribution of land to natives, and especially to ex-soldiers who had fought in the Army of Independence and in the first period of the revolution.[36] The committee which signed the bill consisted of Antonio Cumplido of the province of Valladolid, Lorenzo de Zavala of Yucatan, Carlos Espinosa de los Monteros of Mexico, Salvador Porras of Durango, José Antonio Gutierrez de Lara of Santander (Tamaulipas), Refugio de la Garza of Texas, and Manuel Teran of Chiapa.

Notwithstanding his presentation of the committee bill, Gutierrez de Lara believed that in some respects it should be more explicit. His experience as a surveyor convinced him, he said,[37] of the necessity of fixing definitely the unit of land and water measurement, because the *vara* varied in different provinces. Moreover,

---

[36] *Actas del Congreso Constituyente Mexicana*, III, 21–25; Mateos, *Historia Parlamentaria de los Congresos Mexicanos*, I, 812–814.
[37] *Ibid.*, III, 35; Mateos, as cited, I, 820.

observation had shown him that great evils accompanied the unlimited subdivision of landed estates. He thought it almost as
necessary to fix the minimum as the maximum holding. He therefore offered a bill containing forty-two articles regulating these
two subjects with great minuteness. The smallest subdivision of
farming land he fixed at a quarter of a *labor,* and the smallest
unit of grazing land at a square league, or *sitio.* He appended a
number of charts to illustrate the various possibilities in laying
off grants and establishing towns, and sought to make of his bill,
as he himself said, a manual for the guidance of surveyors. It did
not touch the general features of the committee bill, and could
have been combined with it, as he may have intended it to be,
without affecting its fundamental provisions. He thought that the
Indians should be assigned adequate lands, and that slaves should
be transformed into indented servants with the privilege of buying
their freedom.[38]

Gómez Farías, too, offered a bill which differed in details from
the committee bill. He proposed to allow empresarios a premium
of one *labor* for each family introduced at their expense—which
would amount to about half the premium proposed by the committee; fixed the maximum holding at ten leagues and required
empresarios whose premiums exceeded that to sell the excess
within twelve years; and declared uncompromisingly against
slavery.[39]

All of these bills contemplated free headrights to individual
families not members of an empresario contract; and nobody
seems to have reflected that in the midst of a world of free land
the empresario would have small chance to compensate himself
for labor and expenses by sale of premium land.

Discussion of the committee bill brought out various objections
and suggestions. The restriction of settlement to Catholics, it was
thought, should be stated more emphatically; provision should
be made for civilizing the Indians; the imaginary distinction between grazing and farming land should be abandoned; empre-

[38] *Ibid.,* III, 25–45; Mateos, as cited, I, 814–817.
[39] *Ibid.,* III, 46–52; Mateos, as cited, I, 827–831. Farías had been a member of the
committee on colonization on June 5 (*Actas del Congreso Constituyente Mexicana,* II,
8), but all committees were renewed and some shifts occurred on July 1 (*Actas,* III,
134). The committees were not listed then, so that it is not known whether he continued on the committee.

sarios should be allowed to make contracts for fewer than two hundred families and should obtain their compensation from the colonists instead of from premium lands; each settlement should be required to maintain a school; and safeguards should be provided against immigrants who, "under the pretext of colonization, settled on the coast and in the very doors of our houses for the purpose of seizing the country." [40] Señor Godoy could not brook the defense of slavery in connection with the rights of property. It might be that for practical reasons slavery must be tolerated, but let us have in that connection no more talk of the rights of property. [41]

Zavala defended the bill. The committee, he said, had protected the Church, and objection to the article limiting settlement to Catholics was merely verbal. The same family might engage in both farming and stock raising and obtain a league and a *labor* of land; the committee had not intended to prescribe rigidly the use of the land, and pasture land might be tilled if the owner desired. Contracts for introducing fewer than two hundred families could be made with the provincial deputation of each province. The ayuntamientos could provide for local schools. And the Indians would, in the end, be civilized by the settlement of the country. As to slavery, the laws recognized it, and the committee could only try to harmonize with them in some degree the abstract principle of liberty. What would the Gentleman from Guanajuato do if he owned a thousand slaves and a philosopher tried to persuade him that, having no legitimate right to hold them, he must liberate them or suffer the maledictions of humanity? In his own opinion, it was better to pass good laws, such as the Gentleman acknowledged this colonization law to be, and to pay no attention to declamations, which led in the end to revolutions. [42]

Having approved the bill as a whole, the house ordered its reading by articles. The first article read: "The government of the Mexican nation protects the liberty, property and civil rights of all Catholic foreigners who settle in its empire." This aroused a veritable tornado of hair-splitting argument. Did "government"

[40] *Ibid.*, III, 52–67; Mateos, as cited, I, 831–839.
[41] *Ibid.*, III, 57; Mateos, as cited, I, 834.
[42] *Ibid.*, III, 58–61, 65–66; Mateos, as cited, I, 834–836, 838.

mean only the executive department or all the branches of government? Did not the laws also protect? Was it foreigners only who were protected, and not citizens also who wished to form a settlement? Were liberty and property the only political rights which were to be protected, and were they guaranteed only to foreigners? In any case, since the law recognized slavery, the guarantee of liberty was false and that of property was unjust. Nevertheless, the article passed. The next day was without a quorum. The second article was taken up on the 22d and discussed for hours in the same way. On the 23d a motion prevailed to send the bill back for general revision in the light of all that had transpired. Some of the committee resented this action, and Porras and Zavala asked to be excused, but the president replied that the time was near for renewing all committees, when their requests would be considered.[43]

Austin had written Hawkins on August 6, "The colonization law is now printing and will be finally discussed and disposed of in eight or ten days. . . . There is a section in it which embraces my case,[44] and without some unexpected opposition or difficulty, I hope to have my claim fully confirmed, and be on the way to the settlement at all events in fifteen or twenty days. I shall however, not leave this until my land claim is finally adjusted; and although I am aware the settlers have experienced much inconvenience by my absence, still in the end my visit here will not be without advantages to the settlement."[45]

Further work on the colonization law, as indeed upon the constitution and all other projects of Congress, was now interrupted by a violent political storm. In the letter just quoted Austin wrote that alarming rumors had recently upset public confidence, but that he thought conditions had become more settled. This, however, was not the case. On August 26 the emperor precipitated tremendous excitement by the arrest of fifteen deputies who were charged with conspiracy to overthrow the government. Congress demanded their trial or release within forty-eight hours, in accord-

---

[43] *Ibid.*, III, 66–88; Mateos, as cited, I, 838–849.

[44] Article 10: "The settlements made by the former government shall be regulated by this law in all matters which develop in future and in those still pending; but those already finished remain in their present status."

[45] From (Cincinnati) *Western Spy and Literary Cadet,* October 19, 1822.

ance with a provision of the Spanish constitution, and the emperor replied that the evidence against them was too voluminous to be examined in so short a time. On August 29 the rumor spread that an absolute monarchy was to be established and Congress dissolved. For ten days the tempest raged and then subsided, but the deputies remained in prison.

Despairing now of early action by Congress, Austin appealed to Iturbide for a special decree investing him provisionally with the powers necessary to get the settlement started on a secure basis and encourage the settlers to improve their lands. Specifically, he wanted the boundaries of the colony fixed as previously described, and authority to assign lands and maintain order and to exclude undesirables.[46] But Iturbide was no more able than Congress to attend to the needs of a handful of foreigners in a wilderness twelve hundred miles away.

On September 26 the colonization law again emerged from the murk of confusion that enveloped it. We are entirely in the dark concerning the deliberations of the committee after the bill was recommitted a month before. Whether Zavala had retired or other changes of personnel had been made, the journal does not show. Gómez Farías was again a member,[47] however, and it was his bill, first read on August 20, which the committee now reported. It was discussed intermittently article by article until October 10, when, with the amendments and suggestions which had been made in debate, it was again sent back to the committee.[48]

Meantime the political horizon was growing darker. On September 25, Zavala read an address reviewing the failures of the present Congress, paralyzed by feuds and jealousies, and proposing its dissolution after providing for the election of a new one to sit in two houses and with more equitable representation of the provinces.[49] "Everybody who had the least ability to think," said Zavala, "saw that that Congress could no longer save the nation, and that if Iturbide had committed great errors, Congress was not

[46] Austin to Iturbide, September 8, 1822. University of Texas Transcripts from Department of Fomento, Mexico.

[47] Mateos, *Historia Parlamentaria de los Congresos Mexicanos*, I, 1009.

[48] *Ibid., passim*, I, 991–1010.

[49] *Ibid.*, 991; Zavala, *Ensayo Histórico de las Revoluciones de Méjico*, I, 190. Bancroft (*History of Mexico*, IV, 784) misinterprets this proposal, representing Zavala's plan to have been to reduce the membership of the existing Congress and then organize in two houses.

free from them." [50] But Congress, naturally, did not take kindly to his proposal. Instead, it adopted a resolution from Gómez Farías for a committee of three to prepare a circular setting forth what Congress had actually accomplished, the measures that were on the point of completion and the causes that had retarded others, and promising the completion of the committee's report on the constitution within twenty days.[51] Zavala complained that his motion was regarded by the ignorant as a new blow aimed at Congress by one of its most distinguished members. This view was strengthened by the action of Iturbide. He heartily concurred in that part of the proposal which advised the dissolution of Congress, and on October 16–18 held informal meetings with his Council, some generals, and about forty deputies, in which it was decided to request Congress to reduce itself to seventy members. On its refusal to do so, he sent one of his generals to the assembly on October 31 with a degree ordering it to adjourn within half an hour, which it did.[52] Iturbide's defense for this action was that he could not allow the "nation to fall into anarchy at the hands of men who, some from inexperience and others from evil intention, had proposed a system of opposition to the progress of my administration." Nearly eight months had passed, he said, "not only without a single step's being taken in the formation of the Constitution, the principal purpose for which Congress was called, but also without the passage of a general revenue law or a law concerning the army." [53]

The financial situation was really at the bottom of the government's troubles. Zavala paints it in vivid colors—no order in the fiscal system nor effort to regulate it; revenues enormously reduced and expenses correspondingly increased; foreign commerce prostrate, with Spanish trade stopped and that with other nations not yet begun; the mines closed and no capital to reopen them; old revolutionists flocking to the capital to demand employment, pensions, indemnities, and rewards for services; scarcity on the one hand and cruel exigencies on the other. Even the deputies were not regularly paid, and some were not able at times to take their

[50] Zavala, *Ensayo Histórico de las Revoluciones de Méjico,* I, 190.
[51] Mateos, *Historia Parlamentaria de los Congresos Mexicanos,* I, 991.
[52] Zavala, *Ensayo Histórico de las Revoluciones de Méjico,* I, 191.
[53] Quoted by Zavala, *Ibid.,* I, 191.

letters from the mail for lack of postage.[54] To this add party intrigues and personal plots, and the result is a somber picture of public distress and mutual distrust.

In place of Congress Iturbide selected forty-five of the members to form what he called the *junta nacional instituyente*. This was to continue the work on the constitution, frame pressing laws concerning the treasury department and the army, pass a law for the election of a new Congress, and exercise general legislative power until the meeting of the Congress.[55] Among those chosen by the emperor for the junta were at least five who had served on the colonization committee—Zavala, Gutierrez de Lara, Refugio de la Garza, Monteros, and Porras. The junta formally organized on November 2. On the 6th Austin presented another memorial to the emperor, urging prompt action on his application. He had been in the capital, he repeated, since April, awaiting orders and instructions. His colony, if fostered, would become in a few years one of the firmest supports of the empire, but its advancement was paralyzed by his absence. Colonists already there were discouraged and depressed by the uncertainty of their position, and some of the most worthy and industrious would return to Louisiana if the emperor did not extend his paternal hand to protect them. He begged approval of the plan for distribution of the land agreed upon with Martinez, and asked authority to settle an additional two hundred Catholic families on the land remaining in his grant after the first three hundred should be placed. It would be necessary to organize a militia force and to establish temporary regulations for the civil government of the colony, subject to the emperor's ultimate approval, and for this also he asked authority. Otherwise the colony on the common border of two nations and beyond the active supervision of either would become the haven of criminals and refugees from both countries. There ought to be a judicial officer in the colony, he said, with power to inflict corporal punishment for thefts and assaults, and to punish with the death penalty murder or collusion with the Indians in robbing or making war on the whites. For himself, he asked permission to select land for his compensation. It was characteristic of Austin

[54] Zavala, *Ibid.*, I, 179–180; Alamán, *Historia de Mégico* (Mexico, 1849–1852), V, 468–478.

[55] Mateos, *Historia Parlamentaria de los Congresos Mexicanos*, II, 13–15; *Gaceta Imperial*, III, 925–927.

in all his future relations with Mexico and Mexicans that there was no tone of complaint or fault-finding in this long document. He did not even refer to the previous petitions that he had addressed to Iturbide. He reviewed the whole situation *de novo,* emphasizing the benefits of a flourishing settlement in Texas, not to himself nor to the colonists, but to Mexico by providing a buffer for the interior provinces against marauding Indians.[56]

The next day (November 7) the minister of foreign relations sent to the junta a request for the prompt passage of a colonization law.[57] One is tempted to see in this the answer to Austin's memorial of the 6th, but acquaintance with the deliberate movements of Mexican officials warns that this was probably not the case. Action followed too closely on the heels of the request. In response to the minister's message Zavala moved that the junta consider the bill of the late Congress, thirty-odd articles of which, he said, had been approved, leaving only a few to be discussed. Without opposition this was accordingly referred to a committee for revision in connection with the government's suggestion of military premiums. The committee was appointed on the 9th, and consisted of Zavala, Porras, Garza, Gutierrez de Lara, and Monteros. All of them had served on the colonization committee of the old Congress, and we may therefore presume that Austin was already in close relation with them. On the 14th Zavala moved that the remaining articles of the old bill be adopted, but on reading the bill it appeared that the articles would have to be renumbered. The committee agreed to have this done by the next day, Saturday, but there was no session Saturday, and on Sunday the committee reported that "various difficulties" would arise in the execution of the law as framed, and for that reason it preferred to offer the original bill presented on August 20. After a slight discussion the committee was instructed to put itself in accord with the government on the subject and the matter went over. The government agreed, and on November 23 the original committee bill was presented, discussed, and twenty-eight articles were passed with slight changes. On the 26th the three remaining articles were passed, and the bill went to the emperor.[58]

Austin wrote on November 22: "My business relative to the set-

[56] Austin to Iturbide, November 6, 1822.
[57] Mateos, *Historia Parlamentaria de los Congresos Mexicanos,* II, 18.
[58] *Ibid.,* II, 19, 21, 22, 25, 28, 29.

tlement is now acting on and in less than ten days I shall be dispatched with everything freely arranged. The principal difficulty is slavery, this they will not admit—as the law is all slaves are to be free in ten years, but I am trying to have it amended so as to make them slaves for life and their children free at 21 years—but do not think I shall succeed in this point, and that the law will pass as it now is, that is, that the slaves introduced by the settlers shall be free after 10 years—As regards all other matters there will be no difficulty." [59] There is no record of the discussions of the committee, but Austin evidently succeeded beyond his expectations, for the slavery article was presented as it came from the original committee on August 20, and passed, with only verbal changes, to read: "After the promulgation of this law there shall be neither sale nor purchase of slaves who are brought to the empire; their children born in the empire shall be free at the age of fourteen." [60]

But, in the words of Austin, "a General Santana" proclaimed a republic at Vera Cruz on December 2, and for a time the emperor was too busy to spare any attention to the colonization law. On December 25 Austin wrote his brother, "the Emperor has not yet approved it, and it will not be finished for at least three weeks more . . . do not be discouraged at my long delay and inform the settlers that I will not leave here until *all* is well arranged— 'Blessed is he that holdeth out to the end' and I am determined to persevere." [61] The political tension was lessened by Santa Anna's crushing defeat at Jalapa on December 21, and ten days later the emperor returned the law to the junta with minor objections to two articles. These were quickly amended and the bill was signed on January 4, 1823, and published on the 7th. [62] Except for unimportant verbal changes in three articles and reduction of the term allowed for improvement of land from six to two years in a fourth, the law is literally identical with the bill introduced on August

[59] Austin to [Edward Lovelace,] November 22, 1822. Copy. Endorsed by Colonel Guy M. Bryan, "Received from Mrs. Bell and I presume was addressed to her husband Josiah H. Bell." Reference in the letter to an application for land on Galveston Bay indicates that it was written to Lovelace.

[60] Mateos, *Historia Parlamentaria de los Congresos Mexicanos*, II, 28. Was it Austin's influence that brought about the substitution of the original committee bill for the Farías bill with its less favorable slavery article?

[61] Austin to J. E. B. Austin, December 25, 1822.

[62] Mateos, *Historia Parlamentaria de los Congresos Mexicanos*, II, 57, 58; Austin to Trespalacios, January 8, 1823.

20.[63] At no stage in the passage of the bill did any opposition to a liberal immigration policy appear. The only feature which caused difficulty—and that did not appear in the debates—was the slavery article. One wonders, therefore, if it would not have been passed early in October had Gómez Farías not succeeded then in substituting his own bill for the committee bill.

Austin wrote Trespalacios, the new governor of Texas:

"I am certain that if I had not remained at the capital to agitate this subject and to importune continually the members of the junta, and particularly the members of the colonization committee, the law would never have been passed.... With the greatest effort, I succeeded in obtaining an article concerning slaves, and although it is very different from what I wished, it is better than nothing.... This article passed with much difficulty. Never would an article have been passed by the Congress permitting slavery in the empire for a moment in any form whatever. After the dissolution of Congress, I talked to each individual member of the junta of the necessity which existed in Texas, Santander, and all the other unpopulated provinces for the new colonists to bring their slaves; and in this way I procured the article." [64]

Though Austin now hoped to be able to return to his colony at once,[65] there was still a weary time ahead of him. The law was a general act, fixing the rights and privileges of immigrants and the terms upon which the executive might make contracts with empresarios. It did not confirm his grant, and he must now look to the emperor for that. The first step in this direction was reasonably expeditious. On January 14 the council of state reported on his petition of May 13. Taking this up article by article, it declared: (1) that Austin had not been authorized to stipulate the quantity of land that settlers should receive, and that he should conform in this respect to the more liberal provisions of the law—a *labor* of farming land and a league of grazing land to heads of families engaged in both farming and stock raising; (2) that there was not sufficient information available concerning the area between the Brazos and the Lavaca and the San Antonio road and the Gulf to warrant fixing the boundaries of the grant as Austin desired, but that this was not essential, since the land actually owned in fee by

[63] The bill in Mateos, *Ibid.*, I, 812–814; translation in Gammel, *Laws of Texas*, I, 27–30.

[64] Austin to Trespalacios, January 8, 1823.

[65] Andrews to J. E. B. Austin, January 25, 1823.

the colonists would constitute the limits of the colony; (3) that Austin, in union with the governor of the province or a commissioner appointed by him, should be authorized to partition the lands, put colonists in possession, and extend titles; (4) that immigrants beyond the three hundred families of the contract must settle in the interior, near existing native settlements, as the law required; (5) that Austin should receive premium lands, subject to the provisions of the law; (6) that he should be permitted to found a town and dispose of lots conformably to the law and his petition; (7) that he should organize the colonists into a body of national militia, reporting to the governor and acting under his orders and those of the captain general; and (8) that until the government of the colony could be established Austin should be "charged with the administration of justice, settling all differences which may arise among the inhabitants, and preserving good order and tranquillity." The council believed that he merited the boon of citizenship for which he asked, but said that this could only be granted by the legislative department. This report required only the formal approval of the emperor to make it effective and Austin's business would be done. But the revolution launched by Santa Anna in December had spread, and Iturbide was fighting for his throne, so that it was not until February 18 that he found breathing space to sign the decree.[66]

New occasion for delay now appeared in the vagueness of one paragraph of the decree. The fifth article of Austin's petition asked "That authority be granted him to found one or more towns; . . . to take for himself and family sufficient lots for their uses; and to grant lots to useful mechanics free; but that others should pay for them at the price fixed by the government and the proceeds be applied to the building of churches and other establishments of public utility." [67] The report of the council and the imperial decree disposed of this in general terms, authorizing the establishment of a town and providing for its government, and "as to the other details (*pormenores*) contained in this article, they are granted as

[66] Certified copies of the documents used for this paragraph are in the Austin Papers and in the General Land Office of Texas, Vol. 54, pp. 81–86. The essential parts are translated in Wooten (ed.), *A Comprehensive History of Texas*, I, 473–474, and in Gammel, *Laws of Texas*, I, 31–32.
[67] Austin's memorial, May 13, 1822.

Austin requests." To clarify this Austin immediately asked for a certified copy of the fifth article of his petition, in which the "details" were set forth.[68] By March 10 the copy had been made but was not signed; and, begging to be pardoned for his importunities, Austin again addressed the state department. He reminded the minister that he had been awaiting the settlement of his business since April and that in his absence the colony, deprived of his influence and direction and abandoned by the government, had been retarded and all but ruined by attacks of the Indians and the suspense of the colonists. He was sure that the minister needed only to understand the situation to act. The business could be finished in half an hour. Travelers were leaving for the north in a few days; if he could not accompany them, it might be necessary for him to sail to New Orleans and return to Texas from there by land, for it was not safe for a man to travel alone. Would His Excellency not sign the document at once?[69] This obtained the desired result; Valle signed the next day.[70]

But the imperial bark was now on the rocks, and conjectures were rife that the new government, when it was established, would annul all that had been done since the election of Iturbide. Austin sought the advice of lawyers and other well-informed men. Some thought that a contract such as his would not be affected by the coming change; others that it would be safer to get the approval of Congress.[71] Although he had already obtained his passport[72] to return to Texas, he decided to wait. Pressure of the revolution drove Iturbide to try to restore the old Congress, which he had dissolved on October 31. Fifty-eight members, including those of the *junta instituyente,* met on March 7. On the 19th Iturbide offered his abdication. The Congress did not obtain a quorum until the 29th. It then provided for the maintenance of the executive department by the appointment of a commission of three generals,

[68] Austin to Juan Miguel Riezgo, Chief Clerk of the State Department, no date (about February 19, 1823). University of Texas Transcripts from Department of Fomento, Mexico.

[69] Austin to José del Valle, March 10, 1823. There are two drafts of this document, differing slightly and supplementing each other. They illustrate the care with which Austin prepared his official communications.

[70] "Sobre el Establecimiento Colonial," etc., file of March 20, 1823. *Austin Papers,* I, 590.

[71] Austin to his Colonists (1829), in Gammel, *Laws of Texas,* I, 11.

[72] Bustamante to Austin, March 3, 1823.

and on April 8 declared that Iturbide's election had been forced by violence, that he had had no legal right to the throne, that it was unnecessary therefore to consider his abdication, and that all the acts of his administration were subject to revision by Congress to be either confirmed or revoked.[73] Without waiting for this final act, Austin on April 5 had applied to Congress for confirmation of his grant.[74] His dignified persistency, his acquaintance with most of the members of Congress, particularly with those of the *junta instituyente,* and the strength of his cause finally won. On the 11th Congress passed his application on to the executive department with a recommendation to approve, which it did on the 14th.[75] At the same time Congress suspended the imperial colonization law, so that Austin's was the only concession granted according to that law.

An article dated in New Orleans on March 4, 1823, by a writer who said that he left Mexico on February 23, emphasized Austin's popularity and influence with the government: "He has effected more with that government than other foreigners have ever been able to do; and a man of less energy, patience, and perseverance could never have succeeded." [76] Besides what has already appeared to support it, this estimate is borne out by a good deal of additional evidence. For example, Bustamante commended Austin for his conduct during his long detention at the capital "for his personal qualities and for the desires which animated him to be useful to the empire." [77] Other applicants recognized Austin's position of influence and besought his assistance.[78] And J. B. Arizpe told Austin that in considering his application for citizenship both the ex-

[73] A good summary of events of this period is in Bancroft, *History of Mexico,* IV, 790–855. The official decrees are in Dublan y Lozano, *Legislación Mexicana,* I, 632–634. See also contemporary notes by Austin, March 4–10, 1823, and his address to his colonists (1829) in Gammel, *Laws of Texas,* I, 10–12.

[74] Translations of Records of Austin's First Colony, I, 10–11. MS., General Land Office of Texas.

[75] Translation of the decrees in Wooten (ed.), *A Comprehensive History of Texas,* I, 475; Gammel, *Laws of Texas,* I, 32–33.

[76] The article is signed C. G., and my notes are from the Lexington *Kentucky Reporter,* May 5, 1823. It probably appeared in other western papers.

[77] Bustamante to Gaspar López, March 3, 1823.

[78] On March 6, 1823, General James Wilkinson, in Mexico since the preceding May, asked help in obtaining a contract to settle three hundred families. On April 30, Robert Leftwich, who arrived about the same time as Austin, thanked him for advice and influence with J. B. Arizpe, member of Congress from Monterey. "This is adding one more favor to the many hundreds already received."

ecutive and Congress expressed the most complimentary opinions of his character and deserts.[79]

Austin left the City of Mexico on his return to Texas on April 18, lacking just ten days of a year from the date of his arrival.[80] He had still to settle some troublesome administrative details with the commandant general at Monterey, but there yet remain to be noticed some phases of his work at the capital. Years later in a remarkable letter to his confidential friend and secretary Austin briefly stated the controlling principle of his relations with the government and people of Mexico. From the day of his arrival, he said, "I bid an everlasting farewell to my native country, and adopted this, and in so doing I determined to fulfill rigidly all the duties and obligations of a Mexican citizen." [81]

One essential duty of citizenship is to know the language of one's country. Austin applied himself industriously to this task, and by the beginning of August was writing his own letters and memorials to the government in intelligible if not idiomatic or grammatical Spanish. This was the key which opened to him a sympathetic but very accurate understanding of Mexican racial qualities that served him through all the rest of his life. It also enabled him to win the confidence of officials and was no doubt the secret of his ultimate success in obtaining approval of his contract.

To a man of Austin's acute intellect and training in the world of affairs the political situation in Mexico was a fascinating, even if somewhat exasperating, subject of study. One of the fundamental provisions of the Plan of Iguala had been the establishment of a constitutional monarchy, and all of the rapidly shifting legislative bodies of 1821–1823, whether qualified or not to frame a constitution, tried to do something to shape its character. The *junta provisional gubernativa* reluctantly contented itself with reiterating the declarations of the Plan of Iguala concerning the government, but there were no restrictions on the power of the

[79] Arizpe to Austin, May 24, 1823. Though Congress voted citizenship to Austin on May 22, 1823, the certificate was not issued until March 9, 1824. See original of that date and Mateos, *Historia Parlamentaria de los Congresos Mexicanos,* II, 269, 358, 368.

[80] Austin to J. E. B. Austin, April 23, 1823.

[81] Austin to Williams, February 5, 1831. Rosenberg Library.

Constituent Congress which assembled on February 24, 1822, and it proceeded at once to appoint a committee on the constitution. The members of the committee were, however, overworked on other committees and had made little progress when Iturbide's *coup d'état* of May 19 established the empire. But the one essential condition of Gómez Farías's motion to elect Iturbide was that he must swear to support the constitution which Congress should form. Work on the constitution therefore continued, but went very lamely on account of the inexperience of most of the deputies and the growth of the republican party, which, of course, was inclined to limit the imperial power more severely than Iturbide was willing to admit and caused him to resort to obstructive tactics. Austin believed that the clashing interests could be harmonized by what an American knows as "checks and balances" in the organization of Congress, and in August, 1822, he outlined such a plan, to become a part of the constitution. The object, he explained, was to "regulate the legislative department so that its deliberations may be free and independent, and at the same time controlled, so as to be incapable of exceeding its authority, or clashing with that of another." He proposed to accomplish this by a congress of two houses. The "Chamber of Commons" should be popularly elected by districts and should represent the provinces of the empire on the basis of one representative for each seventy thousand inhabitants; while the "Senate" should consist of three members from each province, two chosen by the provincial deputation and one appointed by the emperor. Since the emperor appointed the captain general and the governor of the province and these were members of the provincial deputation, the senate could be expected to guard the imperial prerogative securely. Members of commons and senate must have been citizens of the empire three and five years respectively and must reside in the provinces which they represented. The commons were elected for two years and the senate for eight, one-fourth retiring every two years. "The Government would then be composed," said Austin, "of a Chamber of Commons as purely democratic as a representative body can be, —of a Senate, independent of the other branch, and united by interest to the Emperor, but whose legal existence at the same time would depend on sustaining the Chamber of Commons in the event of any attempt to destroy it by the Executive; for if one branch of the Government was to be annihilated, the whole must fall, and a new organization be made. This chamber then would serve as a barrier to prevent the mutual encroachment of the Executive and Commons upon the authority of each other." The resemblance of this system to that of the United States, he thought, would probably satisfy the republicans, while its actual operation would in fact be measurably under the control of the emperor, who, by prudent management, could soon confirm public confidence in it.[82] This document is in English, and there is no evidence that Austin ever submitted it to any member of Congress, though Zavala, with whom he was acquainted through his work on the colonization committee, did, as we have seen, on September 25 propose a reorganization of Congress in two houses.[83] The subject is approached by Austin through a very tactful introduction expressing the hope that his motives might excuse his presumption, and explaining that he would be wanting in his duty as a citizen of the empire if he did not feel that anxiety for the common welfare of the country "which ought to animate the bosom of every good man." It illustrates thus early his ability to combine with an implication that all is not perfect in Mexico and a suggestion for its improvement a deferential style that could not but soothe the most sensitive chauvinist.

Again on January 16, 1823, Austin addressed—whether it was ever delivered we do not know—a very remarkable document to the *junta nacional instituyente*. Two of the chief functions which Iturbide had assigned this rump parliament were the passage of a law for the election of a new congress and the formation of a project of a constitution for this congress to adopt.[84] Little progress was made on either, and the revolt proclaimed by Santa Anna on December 2 spread rapidly. It was this situation that called forth "Reflections addressed to the junta Instituyente."[85] In this Austin assumed the prevailing contract theory of government: the people were sovereign and government was instituted by them for their

[82] Plan for Organization of Congress, "City of Mexico, August, 1822."
[83] Zavala, *Ensayo Histórico de las Revoluciones de Mégico*, I, 190; Mateos, *Historia Parlamentaria de los Congresos Mexicanos*, I, 991.
[84] Mateos, as cited, II, 13–14.
[85] MS., January 16, 1823.

common welfare. The Constituent Congress which assembled on February 24, 1822, had been freely elected and therefore legally represented the people. With full authority it had declared a constitutional hereditary monarchy and had freely elected Iturbide to the office of emperor. But the constitution, "the foundation, the soul of all free political institutions," was still lacking, though Mexico had now been independent for nearly two years. This was the cause of the revolution and the civil war which threatened and which could only be cured by the prompt adoption of a constitution. But the junta was not chosen by the people and did not represent them, so that it had no authority to form a constitution. Only a constituent congress could do that. Let the junta, therefore, pass the election law without further delay, and, to reassure all parties, publish a statement declaring: (1) "That all Government of right originates from the people, is founded in consent, and is instituted for the general good"; (2) that the people, through their legal representatives, the old Congress, had declared the government to be a constitutional monarchy, so that the form of government was legally elected; (3) that the people must send to the capital a new Congress to frame the constitution; and (4) since this body could not "execute the duties entrusted to them by the people without the secure and inviolable guarantee of liberty of speech and personal security, that . . . all the troops within the city where Congress sits ought to be under their direction, and commanded by a general of their nomination."

This document is no doubt an example of practical politics. It is not likely that Austin believed very strongly in the legality of the emperor's election, but he did believe a monarchy to be the most suitable form of government for Mexico, and had a very favorable opinion of Iturbide's ability and good intentions.[86] The essential thing was to find a basis of agreement acceptable to the emperor and the more moderate of his opponents, so as to check thereby the defections that were now daily taking place and put an end to the revolution. It is significant that the Plan of Casa Mata, which was the platform upon which the various shades of revolutionists united on February 1, demanded the assembling of a new Congress and its support by the army; that Iturbide on March 4 recalled the old Congress in the hope of staying the revo-

[86] Austin to [Edward Lovelace], November 22, 1822.

lution; and that this body refused to begin its deliberations until the few troops which remained loyal to the emperor were withdrawn from the city. It would be rash to imagine that Austin's "Reflections" shaped these events, but they illustrate his keen power of analyzing a complex political problem and of selecting the only practicable compromise which might unlock it.

With the abdication of Iturbide on March 19 it was evident that monarchy was at an end, but the republicans were divided into federalists and centralists and it was not clear which would win. Austin thought "a Central Republic . . . the worst Gov't in the world—for all the power will be in the hands of a few men in Mexico and instead of a Republic it will in effect be an aristocracy which is worse than a monarchy, for in it we shall have 100 Tyrants instead of one." [87] He busied himself, therefore, in framing a federal constitution, with the hope, no doubt, that the first party to offer a concrete program would gain the advantage. His draft,[88] which is dated March 29, is a combination of the Constitution of the United States and the Spanish constitution of 1812 adapted to general and local conditions in Mexico, with the addition of some provisions which are not found in either and which may therefore be ascribed to Austin himself. These independent touches are for the most part in the first twenty-nine articles, which constitute a bill of rights. All the familiar provisions are here, except religious toleration—the contract theory of government; sovereignty of the people; the right to life, liberty, property, and the pursuit of happiness; taxation by consent; freedom of speech and press; the right to be secure against search and seizure by general warrants; the declaration against entail and primogeniture, titles of nobility, retroactive laws, and quartering troops. Austin's contribution to this section is in Articles 26 and 27.

"Despotic Governments [he says] have endeavored to keep the minds of the people in darkness by prohibiting the introduction of books proscribed for their liberal principles. Free Governments on the contrary have thrown open the door for the admission of all without exception, and experience has fully proved the beneficial effects of this liberal policy in enlightening the people. . . . All restrictions or prohibitions therefore on the introduction, sale or reading of books, are calculated to prevent the

[87] Austin to J. E. B. Austin, May 20, 1823.
[88] "Project of a Constitution for the Republic of Mexico, formed by Stephen F. Austin of Texas. City of Mexico, March 29, 1823."

diffusion of intellectual light and knowledge; to retard the improvement of the Nation by perpetuating ignorance, superstition and servile principles; and are at variance with the genius of free institutions, and shall never be imposed under any pretext whatever. A nation can only be free, happy and great in proportion to the virtue and intelligence of the people; the dissemination of useful knowledge and of the arts and sciences is therefore of primary importance to national liberty and prosperity, and to effect this great object, it shall be the duty of Congress to provide by every means in their power for the speedy establishment of schools, academies and colleges throughout the whole nation for the instruction of youth and children."

Congress was to have the American form of two houses, instead of the single house of the Córtes, and all the powers of the Congress of the United States, with a few important additions. For example, it not only declared war but dictated the instructions for peace commissioners and ratified treaties. To avoid some of the constitutional problems that were then disturbing the United States, Austin declared that Congress had the right to make appropriations for internal improvements "in roads, canals, or other works of public utility"; to grant charters to banking companies and other corporations; and to establish and maintain a general system of education. Although the Catholic religion was established and no other was tolerated, Congress could define the pope's authority over the clergy and property of the Mexican church, could annul or prohibit excommunications or other ecclesiastical censures, establish and abolish religious orders, and exclude ecclesiastics from Congress. The executive and judiciary departments presented no notable features.

Besides his indebtedness to the Spanish constitution and to the Constitution and constitutional history of the United States, Austin probably drew on the labors of the committees that had worked on the imperial constitution since 1821, but the reports of these committees are not available for comparison. Nor again is it possible to trace any influence of this document upon the subsequent development of the federal constitution, though there is an indication that Austin furnished a copy to some member of Congress.[89]

---

[89] For example, Austin noted in the margin of articles 141–145 that they were "omitted in the copy."

But Austin's connection with the *Acta Constitutiva*, the first form of the federal republican constitution, is very close. Besides urging the great advantages of the federal over the central system in his correspondence of the period,[90] on his arrival at Saltillo in May he formed the acquaintance of Miguel Ramos Arizpe, with whose brother Juan, the deputy from Monterey, he was already intimate. Ramos Arizpe was a man of great learning and experience. He had represented Coahuila in the Spanish Córtes (1810–1814) and had only returned to Mexico at the beginning of 1822. He was a liberal and a federalist. The refusal of the restored Congress to undertake the formation of a constitution after the banishment of Iturbide aggravated the contest between the federalists and the centralists and threatened to plunge the country into anarchy before the new Congress could be elected and assembled. In the hope of averting this and at the same time giving the federalists a concrete program, Austin at the end of May submitted to Ramos Arizpe an outline of a federal government which he had condensed and adapted from the Constitution of the United States. Except in brevity and in the omission of the detailed machinery of local government taken over from the Spanish constitution, this document does not differ notably from that prepared by him in March. His plan was to have it approved, in substance, by the different states, which would then notify their representatives in the old Congress and authorize them to put it into temporary effect for the nation. Arizpe was much impressed, made changes and corrections in the copy preserved in the Austin Papers, recommended that it be printed, and said that he would send it to his friends. Whether it was printed is not known, but manuscript copies were pretty widely distributed,[91] and Austin believed that it "had much influence in giving unity of intention and direction to the Federal party." As a matter of fact, the pressing importance of circulating such a plan was somewhat lessened by the declaration of the old Congress on June 12 for the federal republican form of government.[92] Arizpe was elected to the new Congress in Sep-

[90] See, for example, a very strong letter to "amigos mios," May 28, 1823.
[91] Austin noted on his manuscript, "Mercado took a copy of this plan to Guadalaxara in June, 1823, Rafael Llanos and Sendejas kept copies of it in Monterey, and also Juan Guerra, Genl Garza's secretary."
[92] Dublan y Lozano, *Legislación Mexicana*, I, 651.

tember, and on November 14, a few days after its organization, offered, with the assistance of a competent committee, to prepare within three days a provisional constitution.[93] He was taken at his word and appointed chairman of a committee on the constitution, which reported the *Acta Constitutiva* on November 20. It was discussed intermittently for two months and finally adopted with little change and published on January 31, 1824.[94] Its verbal similarity to Austin's plan is not more marked than is likely to be the case with two documents drawn independently from a common source, but in substance it is very nearly parallel.[95] Arizpe was much too positive a character to accept any plan without subjecting it to his own analysis, and it is evident that Austin's draft was thoroughly assimilated and coordinated with his own study of the Constitution of the United States, the Spanish constitution, and the political history of Mexico, but that the plan should influence him was inevitable.

Though Austin dwelt upon the beneficent effects of federal government, "proved by the happy experience of many years" in the United States, he saw clearly enough the differences between the people of the two nations which might prevent the system from yielding the same results in Mexico. He probably expressed his real opinion when he wrote, "these people will not do for a Republic," [96] but a republic in some form they were now going to have, and between the federal and the centralized system he thought there was no room for hesitation. The first would no doubt work badly, with much confusion and inefficiency, but at least the provinces might preserve under it a degree of local freedom, and it would certainly remove one obstacle to the rapid settlement of his colony by reassuring those who feared to enter a monarchy. On the other hand, the central system would be a "perfect aristocracy," composed of clergy and capitalists supported by the army, and appointing provincial governors and local officials; and "the City of Mexico would become in effect what Rome

---

[93] Bustamante, Carlos María, *Historia del Emperador Iturbide,* 188; Alamán, *Historia de Mégico,* V, 588.

[94] For the passage of the *Acta,* see W. A. Whatley, "The Formation of the Mexican Constitution of 1824" (MS.), University of Texas.

[95] For a Spanish copy see Dublan y Lozano, *Legislación Mexicana,* I, 693–97; translation in Gammel, *Laws of Texas,* I, 61–66.

[96] Austin to Edward Lovelace, November 22, 1822.

was in the days of the Republic—the absolute mistress of the provinces and consequently of the nation." [97]

Austin's mission in Monterey was to consult the commandant general of the Eastern Interior Provinces about some of the details of administering his colony. That office was now held by Felipe de la Garza, whom Austin had met in Mexico City[98] and claimed as a particular friend.[99] On his arrival, Austin submitted his questions. First, Iturbide's decree of February 18, confirmed later by Congress and the provisional executive, authorized him to administer justice, settle disputes, and maintain order in his settlement until the organization of the local government. Did this extend to the punishment of the capital offenses of murder, piracy, robbery, and aiding hostile Indians in war against the whites; or did it mean that he was merely to arrest such criminals and send them to Bexar for trial? If he himself had jurisdiction, what were the laws to which he should conform; if he was to send them on to Bexar, from what fund should he draw for traveling expenses? Second, did his authority to organize the militia and maintain interior and exterior order empower him to wage war against hostile Indians, and what should be his rank in the militia? Third, might he be authorized, in cooperation with a commissioner appointed by the governor, to designate a port in Texas for the introduction of provisions, tools, and household furniture of the colonists, and grant clearances to vessels transporting such goods? [100] Garza submitted this letter to the provincial deputation of Nuevo Leon, Coahuila, and Texas, and on June 16 replied that Austin's judicial power was supreme except in capital cases, in which he should conduct an examining trial and send a transcript to the governor, condemning the accused meanwhile to labor on the public works of his settlement; that he should organize a battalion of militia under the regulations recently passed by Congress, appoint corporals, sergeants, and superior officers, and command it with the rank of lieutenant-colonel; and that he might designate a port and issue clearances as requested.[101]

[97] Austin to amigos mios, May 28, 1823; Plan of Federal Government, May [31], 1823.
[98] Alamán, *Historia de Mégico*, V, 499.
[99] Austin to J. E. B. Austin, May 10, 1823.
[100] Austin to Garza, May 27, 1823. Translation of Records of Austin's First Colony, I, 12–13. MS., General Land Office of Texas.
[101] Garza to Austin, June 16, 1823, in file of March 20, 1823.

A month later Governor Luciana García appointed Bastrop commissioner of the colony,[102] and together he and Austin set out for the settlements to put the settlers in possession, choose a port and town-site, and establish Austin's administration. While at Bexar, Austin made use of the printing press there to publish an address to the settlers. Nothing but their interest, he said, could have detained him so long. He had felt in honor bound to protect those who embarked with him, and had finally been completely successful. The conditions announced by him at the beginning of the settlement must be observed, and no one who could not furnish "the most unquestionable testimony of good character and industrious and moral habits" would be allowed to remain in the colony longer than was absolutely necessary to prepare for removal. All good citizens had a common interest in this, and he besought their assistance in carrying out the extraordinary civil, judicial, and military powers with which he was invested.[103] At the beginning of August he and Bastrop reached the settlement on the Colorado to begin the work of issuing titles.

Austin had set forth from Bexar in March, 1822, with four hundred dollars. For expenses in Mexico he had sold his watch, drawn on Hawkins, and borrowed from General Wavell, an English gentleman and soldier of fortune with whom he formed a connection to be mentioned later.[104] He lived very meagerly—even felt unequal to the postage on a letter to his brother in every mail—and totally exhausted his wardrobe.[105] The year in the city was filled with privation, disappointment, and anxiety, but the proverbial uses of adversity were probably never better justified by their fruit. He learned the language, won the confidence of the men who controlled the government for the next decade, acquired a knowledge of individual and national character and susceptibilities which enabled him to work effectively for his colony with remarkably little friction or suspicion, and laid the political course of keeping aloof from the Mexican family quarrels

[102] García to Bastrop, July 16, 1823, in file of March 20, 1823.
[103] The University of Texas has a proof copy of this proclamation, loaned by Mr. T. W. Streeter of New York City. There is a copy in the Franklin *Missouri Intelligencer*, October 14, 1823.
[104] Austin to ——— Martin, September 14, 1832; Wavell to Austin, January 14, 1826; and other authorities cited below, page 253.
[105] Austin to J. E. B. Austin, July 8, 1822, and May 10, 1823.

which was to save his settlers a thousand anxieties. It is not too much to say that the experience of these twelve months gave him half of the elements of success in his undertaking—the ability to work pleasantly and efficiently with the government and people. The other half of his problem, no less difficult, was at home—to manage and direct the colonists.

CHAPTER V

The Establishment of the First Colony

THE colonization of Texas began at an auspicious time. As Professor Turner has so effectively described in his illuminating studies,[1] the current of population set westward with the establishment of the first English settlement on the Atlantic coast. For a century and a half the movement was necessarily slow, up the rivers beyond tide-water, into the piedmont. The broad parallel ranges of the Appalachian Mountains served as a dam to hold venturesome frontiersmen back from the country beyond. By the beginning of the American revolution, however, they had begun to trickle across the barrier into Kentucky and Tennessee, and the first census of the United States showed in 1790, 277,000 people west of the mountains. The next, in 1800, found 386,000 spread over Kentucky, Tennessee, Ohio, Indiana, and Mississippi. In 1810 the number just topped a million, and the area of settlement had increased to include Michigan, Illinois, Louisiana, Arkansas, and Missouri. Ten years later there were 2,218,000 west of the mountains; all of the territory east of the Mississippi and south of the Lakes had been admitted to the Union; and there were two states, Louisiana and Missouri, west of the great river.

The lure which drew people to the west was, of course, the cheap and fertile land that could be bought from the federal government on easy terms. From 1800 to 1820 the minimum price in the government auctions was $2 an acre, and after having been once offered at auction it could be bought in private sale at the same price. Payment could be made, one-fourth cash with application and the balance in two, three, and four years. Higher prices, with easier terms, were offered by the land companies and indi-

[1] Frederick J. Turner, *The Frontier in American History* (New York, 1920), particularly "The Significance of the Frontier" and "The Old West."

vidual speculators. The credit system naturally stimulated speculation, and after the War of 1812, with wildcat banking unrestrained and paper money plentiful, a veritable frenzy swept the country. From 1815 to 1819 the government sales alone were nearly twelve million acres, of which more than five million were sold in 1819. The evils of the credit system were obvious enough, but the politicians managed to retain it until 1820, when Congress passed a law, effective July 1, reducing the minimum quantity of land that could be purchased to eighty acres and the price to $1.25 an acre, which must be paid in cash. Partly from the effect of this, sales fell from 5,110,000 acres in 1819 to 1,098,000 in 1820 and 781,000 in 1821. They did not again reach a million acres until 1829.[2] Then, with seventy-two million acres surveyed and on the market, Benton railed at Senator Foot's suggestion of discontinuing surveys as a scheme to limit sales "to the refuse of innumerable pickings," to break and destroy "the magnet which was drawing the people of the Northeast to the blooming regions of the West."[3] The western states were extremely sensitive to any measure that might check immigration in the slightest degree, and the frontiersman demanded virgin land of well nigh limitless area upon which to fix his location.

Operating with the introduction of the cash system to check the sale of public lands, the panic of 1819 carried distress and bankruptcy throughout the west, and coincidently the inauguration of sound management in the Second United States Bank put an end to wildcat banking and cheaper paper money. Even now the monotonous, pitiful story of debt, court judgments, and dispossessions carried by the letters and newspapers of 1820–1825 burdens and depresses a sympathetic reader.[4]

Comments of contemporary newspapers vividly illustrate the

---

[2] For this paragraph, P. J. Treat, *The National Land System* (New York, 1910), Chapters 5, 14; and A. B. Hart, "Disposition of the Public Lands," in *Quarterly Journal of Economics*, I, 253.

[3] *Debates in Congress*, 24 Cong., 1 Sess., p. 24.

[4] Jefferson, for example, writes of Virginia in 1820, "This State is in a condition of unparalleled distress. The sudden reduction of the circulating medium from a plethory to all but annihilation is producing an entire revolution of fortune. In other places I have known lands sold by the sheriff for one year's rent; beyond the mountain we hear of good slaves selling for one hundred dollars, good horses for five dollars, and the sheriff generally the purchaser." Jefferson to Nelson, March 12, 1820. Jefferson's *Works*, Memorial Edition, XV, 238.

restless movement into the west just before the opening of Texas. In February, 1817, an Illinois paper[5] quoted from a Georgia paper saying that emigration to Alabama was "immense," between three and four thousand having settled at Fort Claiborne in the fall of 1816. In October[6] the same paper declared that families from nearly every state in the Union were moving to Illinois and Missouri—that "the roads from Shawneetown to this place [Kaskaskia] and from Vincennes to St. Louis are almost crowded with people; as many as thirty or forty wagons" traveling within sight of one another. An observer at St. Charles, Missouri, reported an average of a hundred and twenty vehicles a week passing that point during the fall of 1819, from which the editor of the *St. Louis Enquirer*[7] estimated an immigration of ten or twelve thousand by that route alone. They came almost exclusively, he said, from the states south of the Ohio and the Potomac, brought many slaves and large herds of cattle, and were "even more valuable for respectability than for numbers." In the same issue "a Missourian" reported as passing one point on the Missouri River during October two hundred and seventy-one wagons and carriages, fifty-five two-wheeled carts, and many pack horses bound for Boone's Lick, Salt River, and other settlements.

The dissatisfaction with the federal land system after 1820 is reflected in the plaint from St. Louis that "The difference is too great not to produce its effect, between a republic which gives first rate land gratis, and a republic which will not sell inferior land for what it is worth."[8] "Mexico," this paper remarks with a sneer at the United States, "does not think of getting rich by *land speculations,* digging for lead, or boiling salt water, but by increasing the number and wealth of her citizens."[9]

The stage was well set therefore for the migration to Texas. The stream of population flowing westward with resistless momentum had reached the borders of the province. From Louisiana one need only step across the more or less imaginary boundary and "squat" on Spanish soil. For the rest of the west it was but

[5] *The Western Intelligencer* (Kaskaskia), February 5, 1817.
[6] *Ibid.*, October 23, 1817.
[7] Issue of November 10, 1819.
[8] *Missouri Advocate* (St. Louis), August 27, 1825.
[9] *Ibid.*, October 15, 1825.

three days' sail from the mouth of the Mississippi or a ten days' trek from Natchitoches on Red River. With many pinched by the hard times following the panic, others who had bought land from individuals dispossessed and ruined by creditors desperately seeking to avert from themselves a similar fate, and government lands obtainable for a new start only by the cash payment of $1.25 an acre in real money, is it strange that Austin's announcement of generous grants at nominal price and easy terms opened to their imaginations new visions of hopeful opportunity?

Two weeks after his return from Texas, and before learning that his application to settle three hundred families was granted, Moses Austin wrote, "I have been offered as many names of respectable families as will make up the number." [10] "Everyone has the highest opinion of his plans," wrote Mrs. Austin, "and many only waiting till they know he has made the establishment, when they mean to follow him." [11] From Natchitoches in October, 1821, Stephen F. Austin, returning from his reconnaissance of Texas, wrote Governor Martinez that he had found there nearly a hundred letters of inquiry from Missouri and many from Kentucky. "I am convinced," he said, "that I could take on fifteen hundred families as easily as three hundred if permitted to do so." [12] On November 3 a member of the territorial legislature of Arkansas wrote, "The Spanish Country is all the rage in the southern end of the Territory and if I could wait two months I have no doubt that my company would consist of fifty persons, most of whom would intend making corn before their return. If no interruption in government takes place, a great many of the most respectable farmers in this country will certainly move immediately on to your grant." [13] From Opelousas one wrote, "I would be glad to know at what time you will be at Natchitoches. There some of my neighbors and me will meet you and if you will grant us land we will proceed on and make corn." [14] Another, from St. Francisville, Louisiana, "It is probable there will be several small families of us will go together, if I like the prospect." [15] An inquirer from Mis-

[10] Moses Austin to J. E. B. Austin, April 8, 1821.
[11] Mrs. Austin to Stephen F. Austin, June 8, 1821.
[12] Austin to Martinez, October 13, 1821.
[13] Robert Andrews to Austin, November 3, 1821.
[14] Henderson to Austin, November 1, 1821.
[15] Montgomery to Austin, November 22, 1821.

souri wrote, "I expect, Sir, if I can hear from you shortly, that
early next Spring I can leave Cape Girardeau County with Several respectable families together with several young men Mechanics of almost every description for that country, and will endeavor to be there in time to make a Crop." [16] James Bryan, Austin's brother-in-law, wrote from Missouri, "I can assure you that
a great number will move from this State, as also from other
States and the Arkansas Territory. I received at Herculaneum a
number of letters addressed to you . . . the most of them from
Kentucky, Ohio, Illinois, and Missouri." [17] At the same time Mrs.
Austin wrote that nothing was talked of but the province of Texas,
and she thought a third of the population of Missouri would move
in another year, if reports continued favorable.[18] Observers at
Little Rock reported many families passing that place for Texas,
and forecast an "immense emigration" the following spring.[19]
Austin's partner, J. H. Hawkins, wrote from New Orleans on
February 6, 1822, that four vessels had recently sailed for the
Colorado, and declared that if the *Lively* had returned from its
first voyage with a good report, the province would be crowded
to overflowing. One man had offered him three hundred families
from Tennessee. Indeed, he said, hundreds were already on the
way and thousands were ready to go at the first encouraging word
from Austin.[20] From another angle, Governor Martinez wrote his
superior as early as December 1, that the permit to Austin was
considered in the United States as opening the door to all and
had already resulted in the entrance of five hundred families—
the worst, he added, that the United States could produce.[21] All
of these estimates were exaggerations, of course, but they indicate
truly a great interest in the new outlet to the southwest.

Many families took the road with no other knowledge of Texas
than they could obtain from the papers that published Austin's

---

[16] Ellis to Austin, November 23, 1821.

[17] Bryan to Austin, December 15, 1821.

[18] Mrs. Austin to Austin, December 15, 1821, January 19, 1822; Brickey to Austin,
January 18, and Bryan to Austin, April 15, and to J. E. B. Austin, January 15, 1822.

[19] Elliott to Bryan, December 26, 1821; Woodruff to Austin, January 18, 1822.

[20] See also Hawkins to Austin, May 31, 1822: "I have received very many letters to
you all of which I have opened and read . . . and shall answer in the most laconic manner
to be civil—The business is becoming too weighty to be prolix."

[21] Martinez to López, December 1, 1821, University of Texas Transcripts from Department of Fomento, Mexico.

letters and announcements. Others, with more to lose by an unfortunate change, perhaps, paused to inquire further. Was the country independent of Spain? Was it already settled or a wilderness? What was the form of government? How were land titles obtained? What facilities for commerce did the country afford? How far was it from New Orleans? Was the settlement on the coast? How deep were the river entrances? What was the climate, and was the country healthy? A few before 1827 asked about the status of slavery and many about religious toleration. For example, James T. Dunbar, of Baltimore, representing a considerable group of prospective emigrants, declared that "The idea of an established church of any particular creed would forever banish from our minds the design of leaving our natal soil." [22] Elijah Noble, representing a similar group in Lexington, Kentucky, wanted to know whether the settlers would be "allowed to worship their god agreeable to the dictates of their own minds etc. or will they be comp.ᵈ to acknowledge the Catholic religion as the supreme religion of the land." [23] Charles Douglas, of Murfreesboro, Tennessee, thought that three or four hundred families could be enlisted there to move at once to Texas, but he was "sorry to see that the roman catholic is the established religion and none other tolerated. This will have a bad effect upon the minds of many good but weak people in the U. S. and (I am afraid) will very much discourage emigration to your country." [24] Few could rise to the philosophical indifference of Colonel John Hawkins, Austin's old neighbor in Washington County, Missouri, weighed down with debt and pursued by executions. He had five sons of an age to work on a farm, with another growing up, and the religious restriction did not deter him—"I know I can be as good a Christian there as I can here. It is only a name anyhow." [25]

The wave of enthusiasm for Texas broke against the events of 1822 and 1823. Austin's long absence in Mexico, the confusion and disorders of government, delay in the passage of the colonization law and the suspense about land titles, Indian hostilities, the severe drought which destroyed the corn crop and drove many of the

---

[22] To Austin, December 13, 1821.
[23] To Austin, June 29, 1822; also Ayers to Austin, June 6, 1822.
[24] To Austin, February 20, 1824.
[25] John Hawkins to Austin, September 21, 1824.

first adventurous emigrants to a steady diet of lean deer and mustang horses; all these were reported in the United States and magnified by rumor as the story passed from mouth to mouth. A few examples will illustrate the character and discouraging influence of the reports that continued to circulate long after Austin returned from Mexico with all legal obstacles to the settlement of his colony removed. Hugh McGuffin from his home in Natchitoches parish, a famous landmark on the principal highway to Texas, wrote Austin in September, 1822: "We have had several reports respecting you since you have left St. Antonio. Some was that you were Drowned others killed by Indians and some affirmed that you were actually dead, all of which I have endeavored to silence as soon as possible, I haveing heard better by some fiew who wished to tell the truth—the emigration is considerably stoped to that country for the present in consiquence of the badness of the crops on the Brazos and Colorado Rivers still there appears to be a considerable number who wishes to go on." [26] From Mobile in November, 1823, a correspondent quoted a Mexican passenger on a vessel driven to that port for repairs: "the general says to me that all negrows in the Provances of Mexico are free, and that slavery will not be permited and that you have no author[ity] to grant land nor to invite settlers to the Provance." [27] And from Missouri a hardy old gentleman who had visited Texas and seen the Promised Land with his own eyes wrote in 1824: "I have done Every thing in my power to Cause the people to Emigrate to that Country, but so many fals Reports Comes from there that If a man has not been there he is too apt to believe such Reports and Decline going . . . It is hard to make people believe the Truth; the Merchants in particular are more opposed to people moving to that Country or any other than Ever I saw . . . It is very hard for the Truth [to] git as far as here; it scearcely can git on this side Red River before it is Detected and stoped." [28] For a time the *Arkansas Gazette* played Cassandra to the inexplicable folly which dragged worthy families from assured comfort and prosperity in Arkansas and the rising city of Little Rock to the insecure wilderness of Texas, and its prophecies and insinuations

[26] McGuffin to Austin, September 13, 1822.
[27] Nixon to Austin, November 14, 1823.
[28] John Hawkins to Austin, September 21, 1824.

spread widely through exchanges in other papers.[29] As early as April, 1823, Joseph H. Hawkins declared that nothing but Austin's speedy return and some publications by him in the newspapers of the United States would restore interest to its early intensity,[30] but even when such publications appeared they were discounted; and it became more and more the practice for representatives of neighborhood groups to visit Texas and make a personal inspection before venturing to move.

Some of the discouraging accounts of Texas were merely the inevitable expansion of unfavorable impressions of dissatisfied visitors. Others were the malicious fabrications and distortions of bad characters banished from the colony. A single instance from a goodly number will illustrate this. In January, 1824, charges were laid before John P. Coles, alcalde of the settlement on the Brazos River, against William Fitz Gibbon and his two step-sons for stealing hogs and horses. The two young men were arrested, tried before a jury of six men, and convicted. The evidence also proved the guilt of the older man, but he had escaped to the United States.[31] In February a friend at Nacogdoches wrote Austin: "As I feel much interested in the welfare of your settlement I give you the following report spread here and gone to the United States—that the people are much dissatisfied with Austin, think he has no right to sell the lands, that [he] compels every man to take a league at $700 half down, that many would leave the settlement and that Austin will about abandon the settlement." The name of the man so reporting, he added, was Gibbon.[32]

Of the number of immigrants who reached Texas before Austin's return from Mexico we cannot be very certain. He reported a hundred and fifty, including eight families, at the beginning of March, 1822. By September, 1824, the Baron de Bastrop had issued two hundred and seventy-two titles to settlers in the first colony,

[29] For example, *The Tennessee Gazette* (Jackson), August 20, 1825, quoting the *Arkansas Gazette,* commenting on a report that General Wilkinson had been granted a contract to establish a colony in Texas, "And, although we have always been opposed to the blind infatuation which has led hundreds of American citizens to emigrate to Texas, we hope that those who may join him may meet with better success than has fallen to the lot of a large majority of those who have gone before them." Austin's younger brother attributed personal motives to the editor of the *Arkansas Gazette* (see his letter to Mrs. Perry, October 28, 1825); but in general the "boom town" spirit would account for him.
[30] J. E. B. Austin to Austin, May 4, 1823.
[31] Coles to Austin, January 31, 1824.
[32] Clark to Austin, February 3, 1824.

of which seventeen were issued to "families" of single men, but it is not likely that all the other recipients, who were married men, had already brought their families to Texas. An official census of the colony, taken in the fall of 1825, but reported in March, 1826, showed 1,800 souls, of whom 443 were slaves.

Governor Martinez had told Austin during his first visit to San Antonio that he had no means of extending local administration to the colony and that Austin must for a time be responsible for its government. Acting on this authority, Austin in October, 1821, appointed Josiah H. Bell to be a sort of provisional justice of the peace to the settlers whom he expected to proceed at once from Nacogdoches to the Brazos;[33] and on his hasty departure for Mexico City in the spring of 1822 he arranged for Bell to continue in authority.[34] By the end of the year the increase of population in the two widely separated settlements on the Brazos (now Washington County) and on the Colorado near the present town of Columbus caused Governor Trespalacios, who had succeeded Martinez, to order the election of an alcalde and a military commandant in each.[35] Bastrop convened the settlers on the Colorado on November 20. Most of them, he reported, were preparing to return to the United States, as some had already done, on account of the uncertainty about their land titles and the continued hostility of the Tonkawa and Karankawa Indians. Bastrop, in the name of the governor, assured them of the protection of the imperial government, said that they would receive the lands they were occupying as soon as the colonization law was passed, took their oath of allegiance, and left them in good spirits, pledged to remain. They elected John Tumlinson alcalde, Robert Kuykendall captain, and Moses Morrison lieutenant. Bastrop was unable to go to the Brazos, but authorized Bell, who was elected alcalde, to carry out his mission.[36] Andrew Robinson was elected there to command the militia.[37] There was a constable in each district, either elected or appointed by the alcaldes, but no other civil officers. The alcaldes were given no instructions, and when a case came before them

[33] Austin to Martinez, October 12, 1821.
[34] Austin's statement in Gammel, *Laws of Texas,* I, 8.
[35] Trespalacios to Bastrop, November 10, 1822, in Records of General Land Office of Texas, Vol. 54, p. 75.
[36] *Ibid.,* 76–78.
[37] Bastrop to Robinson, August 5, 1823.

they seem to have handled it according to a rough system of their own, conforming in general, no doubt, to the procedure of the justice's court in the United States. The office was not a comfortable one. Tumlinson begged Bastrop to furnish him a "rule" for his guidance, and Bell anxiously reported his decisions to the governor and waited in suspense for approval. Their authority was both too little and too great. Without the sustaining prestige of formal laws their decisions had only the capricious force of public opinion to support them, and there was always the fear of unwittingly contravening some unfamiliar Mexican custom.[38]

Austin and Bastrop reached the settlements on the Colorado on August 4, and the second half of Austin's education as a colonial proprietor began upon which success for the colony depended, namely, learning the art of managing the colonists. Bastrop issued a proclamation explaining his own position as commissioner and certifying Austin's authority as supreme civil, judicial, and military officer until constitutional administration could be established.[39] Two days later Austin issued a statement similar to the one which he had printed at San Antonio. The legality of his grant was now unquestionable, he said, and the titles which he and Bastrop were empowered to issue would be secure forever; but in the end success depended on the hardihood, unity, determination, and willingness of the colonists to be guided by him in their relations with the government. His opportunity for knowing what was best for them in this was infinitely better than theirs, and his desire for their prosperity was almost as great as for that of his own family— "in fact," he added, "I look upon them as one great family who are under my care." In this connection he needed at present only to warn them that the Catholic religion was established by law and must be scrupulously respected. He was endeavoring to secure the appointment of Father Francisco Maynes to be curate of the colony because he had formerly been stationed at Natchitoches and knew Americans and the English language.[40]

Those already in the colony had come on the faith of Austin's announcements in the fall of 1821 that they should receive a certain

[38] See by the writer, "The Government of Austin's Colony," *Southwestern Historical Quarterly*, XXI, 225–227.
[39] Bastrop to Colonists, August 4, 1823.
[40] See Austin to García, August 10, 1823.

quantity of land and pay him an acknowledgement of twelve and a half cents an acre. Turning now to this subject, the tone of Austin's statement suggests that he may already have heard murmurs of dissatisfaction with these terms, though this is uncertain. He reminded them that the enterprise had cost him much time and money, and must continue to do so. Surveyors and chain bearers must be employed, the commissioner's expenses must be paid, there was much clerical labor to be done in writing and recording titles, and a moment's reflection must convince the settlers that some assistance from them was necessary. They could expect the greatest indulgence possible, but—

"Those who have the means must pay me a little money on receipt of their titles; from those who have not money I will receive any kind of property that will not be a dead loss to me, such as horses, mules, cattle, hogs, peltry, furs, bees wax, home made cloth, dressed deer-skins, etc. Only a small part will be required in hand, for the balance I will wait one, two, and three years, according to the capacity of the person to pay.... I will sacrifice my own interest rather than distress them for one cent of money. But I have many sacred duties to attend to which cannot be executed without money. The most of what I receive from the settlers will be applied for their own benefit, and I think they must all agree that it is also my duty to provide for my own family, and that in justice I ought to be compensated for the losses and fatigues I have sustained."

The amount of land obtainable had been changed by the law to a minimum of a hundred and seventy-seven acres, but that could be increased without limit, he said, in proportion to the size of a family. The family was the unit of distribution, and single men must unite in arbitrary groups, take a title in the name of one, and then subdivide the land.[41] In a personal letter of the same date to Josiah H. Bell he expressed the hope that his statement would satisfy the settlers—"Surely there ought to be no difficulty on this subject. Can any man doubt that in less than three or even two years he cannot sell a part of his land for cash at 50 cents or one dollar p^r. acre?"

Except to make plain his ultimate authority and responsibility under the extraordinary powers vested in him by Congress and the commandant general, Austin made no change in the civil organization already established. Indeed, he had no desire to be occupied in

[41] Austin to Bell, *et al.*, August 6, 1823.

settling "neighborhood disputes about cows and calves," [42] and consistently sought to avoid even appellate judicial duty. Two problems were, however, pressing in order to restore the confidence of the settlers and assure the permanency of the colony. One of these was to start surveys and begin issuing titles, and the other was to put the fear of the white man into the mind of the Indians. He made a contract immediately with Seth Ingram to begin the surveys on the Colorado, [43] and leaving Bastrop to supervise this work, he made a hasty trip to the mouth of the river to see what settlements had been made during his absence, [44] and to gather also information for action against the Indians.

Despite numerous accounts of individual encounters, robberies, murders, raids, and expeditions, there is no systematic history of the early relations between the colonists and the Indians, and the records are hardly complete enough to write one. In general, there were three groups that gave the first settlers trouble, the Karankawas along the coast, the Tonkawas in the interior, ranging from the San Antonio River to the Brazos east of the San Antonio road, and the Wacos and Tahuacanos on the Brazos, west of the San Antonio road. The Karankawas were fiercely hostile, and occupying the lower course of the Colorado and Brazos, they were in a position to harass all who came to Texas by sea. Parties just landed frequently found it necessary to leave their goods near the coast, concealed or under light guard, while they proceeded to the settlements to get boats or wagons, and the Indians made a practice of preying on these stores, and sometimes they killed the guards. [45] When Bastrop reported the discouragement of the settlers in the fall of 1822, Governor Trespalacios ordered the enlistment of a sergeant and fourteen men for their protection. They entered service in May, 1823, [46] and were stationed near the mouth of the Colorado. They were poorly equipped and unpaid, [47] but gave some relief. Austin begged General Garza to pay them and continue them in service, but their subsequent history is not revealed by the

[42] Austin to Bell, April 16, 1830.
[43] Austin to Bastrop, August 12, 1823.
[44] Austin to García, August 8, 1823.
[45] For such an instance see Kuykendall's "Recollections of Capt. Horatio Chriesman," *Quarterly* of Texas State Historical Association, VI, 237.
[46] Austin to Guerra [about November 30, 1823].
[47] García to Garza, October 20, 1823, and Austin to Guerra as above.

records. One of Austin's first steps after arriving in the settlements was to offer employment to ten men, to be paid by him, to serve as rangers attached to the command of Lieutenant Moses Morrison,[48] but again the documents fail, and we do not know whether the force was organized. It was probably in his mind to shift the cost as soon as possible to the government, for in letters to both the governor and the commandant general he dwelt on the necessity of enlisting a sergeant and ten additional men.[49]

On the Colorado Austin lodged at Sylvanus Castleman's, where just a few days before his arrival unidentified Indians had stolen the *cavalladas* of Castleman and Aylett C. Buckner and killed one Mexican. All the animals were recovered except a mule belonging to Buckner, but two weeks later, during Austin's absence at the mouth of the river, the Tonkawas got away with Castleman's *cavallada,* which included now the horses of Austin and Bastrop; and the few animals still left in the neighborhood from the daily thefts of the Indians were too exhausted to pursue.[50] Bastrop wrote at this time that the people were so harassed by the continual depredations—murder, robbery, horse stealing, cattle killing, destruction of hogs and crops—that it was difficult to find anybody to assist the surveyors.[51] Some time in September, however, when a party of Tonkawas made a raid on the Brazos, Austin followed with about thirty men and compelled the chief to give up the horses and whip the particular braves who had stolen them. He ordered him at the same time to leave the settlements alone and threatened to shoot instead of whipping thieves apprehended in future.[52] This was the beginning of better relations with these Indians. They were a small tribe, numbering less than a hundred and fifty warriors,[53] and

---

[48] Austin's proclamation is undated. It is on the reverse of a proclamation of August 4, 1823, by Bastrop.

[49] Austin to García, August 11, 1823, and to Guerra (Garza's secretary), [November 30, 1823].

[50] Austin to García, August 28, 1823.

[51] Bastrop to García, August 28, 1823, Records of General Land Office of Texas, Vol. 54, p. 97.

[52] Austin to García. October 20, 1823. Also "Recollections of Capt. Gibson Kuykendall" *Quarterly* of Texas State Historical Association, VII, 31–32. Kuykendall says that the punishment inflicted on these Indians was fifty lashes, one-half by the chief and the other half by Captain Abner Kuykendall. "The lash," he says, "was very lightly laid on by Carita who frequently paused to ask Austin 'cuantos' [how many?]. Before he had inflicted his moity of the stripes the culprits pretended to swoon; but as soon as father began to apply the lash they were roused to the most energetic action."

[53] Kuykendall, as cited in preceding note, page 40.

though they continued to hang around the settlements, begging, pilfering, and sometimes, when in force, threatening and frightening isolated families, they were too weak to risk hostilities. In May, 1824, greatly to the relief of the settlers on the Colorado, Carita signed a treaty with Austin by which he agreed to keep his band out of the settlement.[54] Judging from an undated order which Austin issued to Captain Amos Rawls—presumably in the summer of 1824—the Tonkawas higher up the Colorado, under the Chief Sandía, continued to be troublesome.[55] The order instructed Rawls to demand stolen horses and the thieves from Sandía. If the thieves were surrendered, he was to whip them and shave their heads; if the horses were not restored, he was to seize enough horses, mules, and other property to reimburse the losses, hold them as hostages for ten days, and then, if the lost animals were not restored, sell them and compensate the owners. From time to time during 1825 there were petty annoyances from Tonkawas, and in April, 1826, a considerable number of them were killed in what seems to have been a somewhat unprovoked attack by the settlers on the lower Colorado.[56]

Austin recorded in his diary on September 17, 1821, after meeting a squad of Coaques, or Cokes, as they were commonly called, "These Indians and the Karanquas may be called universal enemies to man—they killed of[f] all nations that came in their power, and frequently feast on the bodies of their victims—the [approach of] an American population will be the signal of their extermination for there will be no way of subduing them but extermination."[57] This very nearly proved true prophecy. The Karankawas and their allies were apparently little more numerous than the Tonkawas,[58] but were much more warlike, and rarely failed to fight when the odds favored them. One gathers the impression from the episodal accounts available that probably nine-tenths of the fatal encounters

---

[54] Cummins to Austin, May 3, 1824. "I read the Treaty to the people at our meeting the other day at Rossen alleys they were all well pleased with it—I do think a good one for which some of us gives you our thanks—"

[55] I have arbitrarily placed this order about June 22, 1824.

[56] Affidavits of April 27–May 2, 1826. Also Kuykendall, "Extracts from a Biographical Sketch of Capt. John Ingram," *Quarterly* of Texas State Historical Association, VI, 326–328.

[57] *Quarterly* of Texas State Historical Association, VII, 305.

[58] A report by J. A. Padilla in 1820 estimated the "Cocos," including apparently the Karankawas, at about four hundred.—*Southwestern Historical Quarterly*, XXIII, 51.

during the first three years of the colony were with these Indians. But for their blood-thirstiness, they would not have been a serious nuisance, because, as they neither rode nor traded, they had no use for horses and only stole for food.[59]

The first movement with the appearance of an organized campaign against the Karankawas took place at the end of June, 1824. About the middle of the month a band had penetrated the settlements on the Colorado to a point near the present town of Columbus and had been discovered in the act of skinning a calf belonging to Captain Robert Kuykendall. A detachment of militia under Captain Amos Rawls pursued them and fought a skirmish in which an Indian was killed and one of the settlers was permanently crippled by an arrow through the elbow. The Indians then took to the canebrakes, and Rawls called on Austin for reinforcements to follow them to the coast and attack the main tribe. The only report of the rest of the campaign is a laconic sentence in a letter from Austin to the political chief at San Antonio: "As soon as I received the notice I ordered the militia against them and they killed five Indians at the mouth of the Colorado." The Indians evidently planned retaliation in force, for James Cummins wrote Austin on August 25 that "it appears that about fifty of the Keronkiweys are coming on to attact the lower settlement of this river and have said they would divide into two Companys and perhaps one Company may Come up the River as high as this Settlement." Austin immediately took the field with sixty-two men, but though he divided his force and reconnoitered both sides of the Colorado and, uniting again at the mouth of the river, marched westward to the Lavaca, he did not encounter the Indians. Supplies being nearly exhausted on September 7, he ordered the men home to refit, and resumed the campaign about the middle of the month with ninety men, of whom some thirty were negroes belonging to Colonel Groce. The Indians, realizing that they were in for trouble, took refuge in the mission at La Bahía, to which they nominally belonged, and proposed peace. When Austin came within a few miles of the town, the priest and the municipal officers met him as mediators and ar-

[59] For relations with the Karankawas see *Quarterly* of Texas State Historical Association, VI, 239–247, 324; VII, 35, 47; and letters of Austin, April 20, June 14, August 6, 1824.

ranged a treaty by which the Karankawas agreed not to set foot east of the San Antonio River; but, finding that this too greatly restricted their hunting and fishing grounds, they appealed for an extension of the deadline to the Lavaca, and Austin consented. The treaty was limited to one year.[60]

The Wacos and Tahuacanos were more numerous than either the Tonkawas or the Karankawas, numbering in 1824 according to the estimate of an intelligent observer, between two hundred and three hundred warriors.[61] But their villages were two hundred miles from the frontier, and they did not often disturb the settlers. They were suspected of killing John Tumlinson, alcalde of the Colorado district, in the summer of 1823, but later denied it. In March, 1824, nearly two hundred warriors, hunting for the Tonkawas, caused a good deal of anxiety in the settlement near the present town of La Grange, but they committed no depredations, professed friendship for the Americans, and expressed a desire for a treaty.[62] In response to this, or using it as a pretext, Austin in June, 1824, dispatched a commission to negotiate a treaty with them.[63] The party found the principal village, on the site of the present city of Waco, almost deserted, a part of the tribe being engaged in a buffalo hunt and a war party having gone against the Osages. The village consisted of "about sixty" lodges and was surrounded by well-tended fields of corn, beans, pumpkins, and melons. The commissioners remained between two and three weeks and concluded the treaty, though the Indians pleaded a general demurrer to all charges of depredation against the whites. There was a small Tahuacano village on the east bank of the Brazos a few miles below the Wacos, but their main settlement was some distance away on the Trinity. The Tahuias Indians, with whom the Wacos and Tahuacanos were

[60] Other terms of the treaty do not appear. For this paragraph see Rawls to Austin, June 13, 1824, and Austin's reply of the 14th; Cummins to Austin, August 25; Austin to Saucedo, August 26 (Blotter, No. 6); Austin's Diary, August 30–September 7; Coles to Dimmit, September 14; Austin to authorities of La Bahía, about November 1, replying to letter of October 28; Kuykendall's "Reminiscences" in *Quarterly* of Texas State Historical Association, VII, 35, 47–48. These "Reminiscences" supplement the documents and can be checked by them. They are astonishingly accurate.

[61] Thomas M. Duke in *Quarterly* of Texas State Historical Association, VI, 249.

[62] Cummins to Austin, March 3, 1824, and *Quarterly* as cited, VI, 321.

[63] An autograph copy of Austin's "talk" is endorsed by him as having been sent by Thomas M. Duke and William Selkirk, but Judge Duke's recollection in 1857 was that Aylett C. Buckner was the head of the mission.—*Quarterly*, VI, 249.

frequently associated, lived six days' travel up the Brazos from the Wacos and were not included in this treaty.

In a report to the governor at the close of 1824, Austin very accurately described the Indian situation with one brief sentence: "The Indians are now beginning to fear us, but we cannot for some time yet hope for complete peace with them." [64]

Step by step in the defense against the Indians went, of course, the organization of the militia. In the fall of 1822, as we have seen, Bastrop by Trespalacios's orders had created one military district including all the settlers on the Brazos and another including all on the Colorado. By December, 1823, settlement was so extended that Austin thought it desirable to subdivide the Colorado district. He accordingly ordered an election for the 15th to choose a lieutenant for the lower district of the Colorado, east of Eagle Lake, to be independent in local matters but subject to the captain of the upper district in other affairs. At the same time, Captain Robert Kuykendall being on the point of removing from the Colorado, Austin appointed James Ross to succeed him. By March 31, 1824, the same conditions made it advisable to subdivide the Brazos district, and Austin appointed Josiah H. Bell, who had moved down the river from the present Washington County, to be lieutenant on the lower Brazos. [65] Both these changes were suggested by the need of strengthening the defense against the coast Indians, and they were at first provisional, but sectional jealousy was soon to make them permanent. On May 3 James Cummins wrote Austin that they had been unable to elect officers because of the division between the upper and lower district on the Colorado and suggested that, as each section could muster about thirty men, they be permanently divided and each allowed to elect a full corps of officers, a step which Austin took, either because of this suggestion or on his own motion, the next day. [66] On June 22, 1824, still another company was created on the Brazos and a battalion of five companies was organized. [67] In

---

[64] Austin's Blotter, December 20, 1824, in file of August 26, 1824.

[65] Austin's proclamations of December 3, 1823, and March 31, 1824. Bell was to command "on the Brazos and Oyster Creek from the Fort and on the Bernard from the Mound to the sea shore."

[66] Austin to Cummins, May 4, 28, 1824; Cummins to Austin, May 3, 15, 25.

[67] Battalion order, June 22, 1823 [1824]. Failure to interpret this date correctly led the writer into some errors in an article in *The Southwestern Historical Quarterly*, XXI, 232–233. Captains of the five companies first elected after the organization were Andrew Robinson, Horatio Chriesman, Randal Jones, Jesse Burnam, and Amos Rawls.

November, after annexing a settlement of twenty-three families on the San Jacinto, a sixth company was organized.[68]

While there is some evidence of the operation, both before and after the arrival of the colonists, of organized bands of horse thieves trading with Natchitoches, this was in fact not a serious nuisance even at the beginning, and it quickly disappeared.[69]

Naturally, Austin's most immediate and continuous attention was required by various aspects of the land business. For several reasons the surveys went unexpectedly slowly. Some preliminary inspection of the country and crude maps of the streams were necessary before instructions could be given to the surveyors so as to avoid waste and to take the maximum advantage of water frontages. Some of the colonists were slow to select land and others were quick to change. Austin himself urged the thin string of families on the Brazos and Colorado to concentrate for protection, and, though the settlers on the Colorado refused to move, some on the upper Brazos responded.[70] Competent surveyors were scarce. It was difficult to get assistants for them. And Indian attacks in the field were of common occurrence. Bastrop remained in the settlements until the end of January, and was then, before issuing any titles, recalled to San Antonio to discharge his duty as a member of the ayuntamiento.[71]

In the meantime, serious dissatisfaction developed about the fee of twelve and a half cents an acre which Austin charged for land. The beginning of the feeling cannot be traced. The plan, as we know, was well advertised in the newspapers of the United States, and there can be little doubt that every immigrant arrived in Texas in 1822–1823 with full knowledge and approval of it. But the imperial colonization law, under which Austin's contract was finally approved, allowed the empresario a premium of more than sixty-five thousand acres of land for the introduction of each two hundred families, and was that not intended by the government to compensate the empresario fully for all expenses and responsibilities? It requires very small knowledge of human nature to under-

---

[68] Austin to Flores, November 6, 1824.

[69] Kirkham's relations with such a gang (Moses Austin to Martinez, January 21, 1821) have already been noticed. See also "Recollections of Capt. Gibson Kuykendall," *Quarterly of Texas State Historical Association*, VII, 32.

[70] Austin to Bell, September 28, 1823.

[71] Bastrop to Austin, January 20, 1824.

stand how the suspicion germinated and rapidly hardened into conviction that Austin designed to charge for land which the government freely bestowed and for a service which the government liberally compensated.

It is impossible to determine with any degree of certainty what was the intent of the law, because the subject was never directly discussed by Congress, and no clear line of inference appears. In June, 1822, as we have seen, the committee on colonization recommended that James Barry, Thaddeus Ortiz, and Philip O'Reilly be granted two thousand leagues of land on which to settle fifteen thousand Irish and Canary Island Catholics, and that, in order to avoid the accumulation of large estates, they should be required to sell within twenty years two-thirds of the surplus that might remain from the settlement. Martinez de los Rios thought that this would still leave the proprietors too much land; but Gómez Farías pointed out that without improvement the land was practically useless, and in proof of this he asserted that owners of land in Texas let it for several years rent free in return for cultivation. Nothing was said about compensation of the proprietors (or empresarios) except by the premium lands, but would such lands in fact yield a compensation? It is apparent enough to us that they would not, but was it also clear to Congress? [72] In discussing the first colonization bill on August 20, one of the speakers declared that it would require a great outlay of capital to transport settlers, many of whom would have to be supported until they could establish themselves, and that

"in view of this it is necessary that the empresario should treat freely with them concerning the method of indemnifying himself for his advances, for which reason it seems to me that the law ought to be so framed that, while fixing a minimum for the property of each family . . . it should for the rest confine itself to assigning a grant according to the number of families, leaving its distribution to the empresario, because this is the only way in which he can indemnify himself freely for his advances. It should not be left to assign him separately a grant of land for this as a premium for his contract." [73]

[72] *Actas del Congreso Constituyente*, II, 7–8, 21–24.

[73] "En vista de esto es necesario que el empresario trate libremente con ellas sobre el modo de indemnizarse en sus adelantos, por lo que me parece que la ley debe estar concebida en terminos, que fijando un *minimum* a la propriedad de cada familia para evitar arbitrariedades, se reduzca en lo demas a asignar un terreno por familia, dejando al empresario la reparticion de esto terreno, por que es el unico medio que puede indemnizarlo libremente de sus anticipaciones; sin que por esto se deje de asignarle separadamente un terreno, que sea el premio de su solicitud."—Mateos, *Historia Parlamentaria de los Congresos Mexicanos*, I, 832.

Zavala took no notice of this in his general defense of the bill,[74] and no light is shed by the subsequent discussion of the imperial law.

It seems evident, then, that members of Congress realized that empresarios might be subjected to heavy expense, that they should be reimbursed, and that Texas lands were of small immediate value; but they did provide for premium lands. The emperor's decree validating Austin's contract in accordance with this law declared that there was granted to Austin "for the expenses which he has been at, a quantity of land in proportion to his families, agreeably to the provisions of the 19th article of said law."[75] Since the law prescribed a minimum free grant of a *labor* for farming and a league and a *labor* for farming and stock-raising combined, and since the empresario could earn the premium only by settling at least two hundred families on this free land, how could the premium lands be expected to yield him any considerable compensation?[76]

Certainly Austin did not understand the provision to abrogate the contracts which he had already made with the colonists, nor to forbid others of the same kind. While at San Antonio, on his return from Mexico, before reaching the colony, he wrote to a correspondent in the United States: "My grant is approved by the Sovereign Congress and Supreme Executive power. . . . The smallest quantity of land which a family that *farms* and *raises stock,* both, will receive is one league square . . . the cost will be 12½ cents p^r. acre."[77] And we have already noticed his announcement to the settlers upon his arrival at the Colorado.[78]

Criticism and suspicion passed from mouth to mouth and left no written record, but it is easy to imagine its course. A colonist is denied the land which he selects, and thinks himself the victim of unfair discrimination. Another sees his neighbor obtain from two to five leagues, while he can get but a paltry league and *labor*. Bastrop, it is true, says that Austin has authority to exclude any settler from his colony and that all in excess of his contract, or who are ex-

---

[74] *Ibid.,* I, 834–836.
[75] Gammel, *Laws of Texas,* I, 31.
[76] The puzzle is increased by the provision that free grants might be greatly enlarged at the discretion of the authorities, and that all families in excess of the three hundred which the contract admitted must settle in the interior—thereby reducing the market for the premium lands.
[77] Austin to Caldwell, July 17, 1823.
[78] Austin to Colonists, August 6, 1823; and to Bell, same date.

cluded from the colony, must leave the country or settle in the interior; but Austin and Bastrop are as hand in glove—Austin writes proclamations and Bastrop signs them, or Bastrop writes in Spanish and Austin translates. Who knows truly that Austin has this power to bind and loose, to command the militia, and govern the colony? Why are titles delayed? The law set aside Austin's plan of distribution and quadrupled the amount of land which he intended to allow a family; it granted him a generous premium for his services, and made no mention of fees to be paid either to the empresario or the government; was it not the purpose of the law to prohibit such fees, and were Austin and Bastrop not conspiring to defraud the colonists?

Now and then we glimpse the rising tide. On March 18, 1824, the acting political chief, José Antonio Saucedo, issued from San Antonio an address to the colonists reminding them of benefits already received, assuring them that the government, though slow in completing its organization, would not neglect their interest, and enjoining them to be obedient to Austin: "It is . . . necessary that you should listen with attention and confidence to your immediate chief (Col. Austin) whose authority is from the Supreme powers of the nation . . . and that you should disregard and despise all those idle slanders and vague stories which are put in circulation by the enemies of good order for the sole purpose of creating confusion and discontent." [79] On April 7, Bastrop wrote Austin, enclosing some proclamations which the political chief had directed to the inhabitants of the Brazos and Colorado. Probably this of March 18 was one of them. Another evidently sought to reassure the colonists about the certainty of obtaining titles. "If," said Bastrop, "they are not fully convinced by the reasons that he gives them that there is no necessity for being uneasy about the validity of their possessions, they will never be quieted, and it is useless to insist on saying anything more to them about the matter." [80]

In the same letter he told of one "Peeq" (probably Pike) who had been talking in San Antonio of the large sums which Austin was collecting for lands. Already a hundred and fifty families were established, he said, from whom Austin had received $75,000. The

[79] Saucedo to Castleman, March 18, 1824. Translation by Austin.
[80] Bastrop to Austin, April 7, 1824.

political chief, Saucedo, had answered this by pointing out that the value of the lands on the Brazos and Colorado made it necessary to have them surveyed by competent surveyors, which occasioned heavy expense, and that in addition, Austin had to provide stamped paper for the deeds and to pay the commissioner, besides having been at heavy expense in Mexico obtaining a fortune for the colonists which they need only hold out their hands to receive. Another correspondent spoke of a man named Price and a Lieutenant Branom as purveyors of complaints against Austin.[81]

Despite Saucedo's defense of Austin in April, he evidently succumbed to the malcontents, because while visiting the colony the next month he ruled that Austin had no right to enforce his schedule of charges, and substituted a fee bill which he said conformed to the prevailing tariff and customs of the country. According to this, colonists were required to pay for each league "judicial fees" of $127 to the commissioner, $27 to the surveyor, $8 for stamped paper and clerical work, and $30 to the state.[82] At the same time Saucedo found it necessary to issue a proclamation denying that he had come to remove Austin from office. On the contrary, he said, "I now positively assure you that said Austin is completely authorized by the Supreme Government to found this colony and unless he forfeits the good opinion that is now entertained of him he will continue to exercise the Civil and Military powers he now has until the organization of this colony is completed."[83]

This, of course, brought the subject squarely to an issue, and on June 5 Austin issued an address to the colonists reviewing his services and expenses in behalf of the colony, pointing out some of the consequences which must follow a strict observance of Saucedo's order, and leaving finally to them to decide whether they should carry out their contracts with him. It is a long and able document, which loses somewhat by condensation. It should be read in full. He reviewed his father's journey to Texas in 1820, which indirectly caused his death; his own reconnaissance in 1821 and his agreements with Governor Martinez; his public advertisements of the terms to immigrants; his long and expensive detention in Mexico

---

[81] Dimmit to Austin, June [15?], 1824.

[82] Saucedo to the Colonists, May 20, 1824. I have been unable to verify the statement that this conformed to prevailing and customary charges.

[83] Saucedo to the Colonists, May 21, 1824. Translation by Austin.

obtaining confirmation of the grant; and reminded them that never before, nor as yet since, had such permission to settle in Texas been allowed, and that only in his own colony and for three hundred families could titles be obtained.

"Consider the advantages which you will receive from my labors [he urged] and then let your unbiassed Judgement decide upon my motives, and say whether I have been right or wrong in the measures which I have adopted.... Ask yourselves whether any of you would in 1821 have taken upon you the weight of responsibility which I then did? Whether you would have jeopardized your property, hazarded your health, your lives, your all to make the fortunes of others and been content to do so without the hope of any greater compensation than you could give to an individual who joined you as a settler and who would have no responsibility, labor or expense to encounter more than the care of his own family. Would you have been content I ask to do it; or would it have been just that you should have done so? If not can you blame me for making the public declaration in the beginning of the Settlement that the Settlers must aid me by paying a specific sum for the benefits I secured to them; and was there then anything unjust or improper in such an arrangement in its Origin? If not let us proceed to examine whether anything occurred in the progress of the business which rendered an adherence to the original terms of the contract with the Settlers improper."

Conceding for a moment that the law could have annulled these private contracts, and remembering that in such case he as well as the settlers would have been relieved of his obligations, Austin asked what would have been the resultant situation. Without some authority to direct surveys, each settler would have run his lines as he pleased, would have marked them or not by real or imaginary boundaries; he and the Baron de Bastrop would have made deeds accordingly; and a foundation would have been laid for endless litigation like that which had ruined thousands in Kentucky, Tennessee, and other states where grants were made without actual surveys.

"To comply therefore with my part of the contract with the Settlers in full and at the same time to save them from even the possibility of difficulty hereafter relative to their lines I determined to survey the lands regularly and accurately and to continue upon myself the responsibility which my original contract with the Settlers imposed on me of being personally responsible for the expence of surveying, for the expences due to the Govern^t, and for all other expenses whatever; expecting that the Settlers would comply with their part of the contract by paying the sum originally stipulated."

He thought the plan advantageous to the first settlers, because with the fees of the newcomers he intended to meet the pressing expenses of administration and allow those who had endured the early privations more time. In it was also involved a well-conceived and far-reaching program for financing important public improvements.

"From those who did not pay money or some other property that could be used I intended [he said] to have taken notes payable in Cotton in yearly installments of one, two, or six years according to the situation of the person. This would not have been oppressive for every one could have paid two or three hundred pounds of Cotton annually without ever feeling it—these notes would have insured a certainty of receiving a specific quantity of Cotton annually and this certainty would have given me credit with some Merchant in New Orleans to advance me Cotton Gins and a Vessel to prepare and transport to market this as well as all other Cotton made in the country, and thus in one year the Cotton trade would have been in full operation, which is the principal thing that is to raise us from poverty. Besides, another branch of my plan was to hire as many workmen as I could to build Mills, Cotton Gins and any other improvements that would have advanced the country and thus enable those who did not wish to clear their farms immediately and raise Cotton to pay for their land in that way.... The operation of this plan would have been to save the old settlers from being harrassed in any way relative to their lands for a portion of that part of the expenses which they would have been compelled to advance under a different system would have been paid by the New Settlers. The land would have all been accurately and regularly run off, whereby difficulties both immediate and remote would have been avoided. The Cotton trade would have been established at once. The country would have been improved by Mills and machinery without delay, and by these means would have advanced more during the next year than under a different system it probably could have done in four or five."

As to the charge that he was speculating and exploiting the poor, Austin asked them to look at the facts. For surveying and various government fees on three hundred leagues of land he became responsible for the payment of $70,600.50, and against this he stood to collect by the terms of his contracts $555 a league, or a total of $166,500, "payable in property at a distant period and in small installments and that property received at double or treble what it

would bring in cash." Would the balance of $96,000 be an exorbi-
tant remuneration, even in real money, for his enterprise and three
years' labor? Or, from another point of view, was the land not
worth the price? Could they get titles even now except in his
colony? Would they have undertaken the labor and expense incurred by his father and himself without hope of compensation?
Would the premium of twenty-two and a half leagues, half of
which under his contract went to Hawkins, reimburse him for his
actual expenditures, when every man who came could obtain all
the land he could use at nominal cost? "Whatever may be the determination of the Settlers ... I hope they will do me the justice to take
a full and impartial view of the whole subject and not be too ready
to condemn me as a speculator on the poor, a charge which I am
told a few discontented men have made against me and one which
I think is unmerited and which I do hope the reflecting and sound
part of the colony will pronounce to be unjust."

He thought the contracts with the colonists reasonable and did
not concede the right of the political chief to set them aside. If he
could annul these private contracts, Austin asked, could he not
annul others? Where was the stopping place? There was a very
important principle and a dangerous precedent involved. Even if
the government could annul the contracts, ought not every honorable man to feel himself in equity bound to fulfill them? There
Austin left the matter.[84] Writing later to a Mexican friend he said:
"The colonists ... say that I ought to do everything for them free,
because the government has already paid me in the lands which
came to me as empresario. But they do not reflect that I can not live
on lands; that I cannot eat them, make clothes of them, nor sell
them; and that I have spent all that I had in their service." [85]

What proportion of the settlers were disaffected there is no means
of knowing. John P. Coles, a man of convictions who sometimes
spoke his mind, declared that every candid man admitted his obligation, and he thought that Austin had weakened confidence in his
authority and integrity by recognizing Saucedo's decree.[86] Erasmo
Seguin, now representing Texas in the federal Congress, wrote that

[84] The document is published in full in *The Austin Papers,* I, 811–824. On this incident
see further: Clark to Austin [about June 15]; Gaines, June 18; Cox, August 8, 1824.
[85] Austin to Padilla, August 12, 1826.
[86] Coles to Austin, July 7, 1824.

Saucedo had no right to abrogate the contracts and informed Austin that the national colonization law, then on the eve of passage, contained an article specifically guaranteeing agreements between empresarios and colonists, which in fact it did.[87] This, of course, did not affect Saucedo's decision concerning the first colony. It would have been difficult under any circumstances to obtain a judicial determination of the question, and at that time it was no doubt impossible. Austin petitioned the state congress in 1827 to recognize the validity of his contracts as a vindication of his character, without reinstating them;[88] and there is among his papers the draft of a bill by the committee on colonization proposing such action,[89] but of its legislative history no record is available.[90]

Saucedo's action was not merely a blow to Austin's personal fortunes but raised, in fact, a very real menace to the maintenance of the colony. Certain public and semi-public services upon which the welfare and security of all depended must be performed. In virtue of his leadership and of the authority with which the government had invested him, Austin discharged these services—directed the administration of the local government; translated official documents and circulated them among the settlers; maintained a secretary, and conducted all the business connected with obtaining and recording titles; received Indian deputations; provided presents to keep the Indians in good humor, and sometimes bore much of the cost of campaigns against them; entertained travelers who came to view the country, so that, as he said, his place was more like a public inn than a private house; furnished them translations of laws and documents; and exerted himself to promote immigration for the mutual benefit of all. How could these services be continued without means, and could the colony exist, not to say prosper, without them? Austin turned to Bastrop, who, as we have seen, by Saucedo's tariff was entitled to $127 a league, and together they agreed that Austin should receive one-third of this fee.[91] Collections, however, were very difficult. Few had money and some

---

[87] Seguin to Austin, August 11, 1824. Article 14 of the law of August 18, 1824: "This law guarantees the contracts, provided they are not contrary to the laws, which the empresarios may make with the families which they introduce at their expense."

[88] Austin to State Congress, October 11, 1827.

[89] The document is in Austin's writing, and may be a copy of the committee's bill or a bill which Austin drew hoping to get the committee to introduce it.

[90] The *actas* or journals of the legislature give no light on the bill.

[91] Austin to Martin, September 14, 1832.

had nothing to pay with. Others accepted Saucedo's decree as a release from their obligation to Austin but considered the fees it imposed illegal. In a way, it is true, the game was in Austin's hand, because a settler could not obtain a title without his approval, and he could have withheld it until payment was made, but in practice he had to accept notes. Some of these were never paid and most that were paid were paid in horses, cattle, and produce.[92]

The administration of the land system affected immediately and obviously the interest of every family in the settlement. Envy, avarice, and a sense of injury are easily excited amid privation and distress, and from the beginning Austin recognized this as the most sensitive problem in his relations with the settlers. "The task before me is a very terrible one," he wrote to his confidential friend Bell. "I cannot expect to please all, nor shall I try to do it. I will try to satisfy myself by doing justice to all."[93] Some of the settlers, unable to obtain the particular location that they desired, suspected Austin of reserving it for himself or a favorite. Others, as we have seen, could not understand the excessive grants which a few received in recognition of special equipment to develop them—such as Groce with his hundred slaves—or as compensation for the establishment of public utilities, like mills, gins, and saw mills. Bastrop's regulation requiring unmarried men to take title in pairs swelled the murmur through their inability to agree upon private division of the land after it was obtained. Several of the colonists had served in the early filibustering movements for the liberation of Mexico and felt that they were entitled to preferential treatment in the choice of land. James Gaines, for example, on the Sabine, had served with Gutierrez in 1813 and had certificates from that chief for four hundred and sixty-six leagues of land which he thought Austin should recognize. Aylett C. Buckner, on the Colorado, had fought with Mina, Gutierrez, Trespalacios, and Long and nursed a deep sense of injury because Austin interfered with his selection of a league and a half. Finally, squatters in East Texas attributed the government's efforts to remove them to the interior to machinations of Austin and Bastrop, who, they thought, would gain from their settlement on the Brazos and Colorado.

[92] Austin to Padilla, August 12, 1826; to Governor and to Congress, October 11, 1827; to Martin, September 14, 1832.
[93] Austin to Bell, August 29, 1823.

A few extracts will illustrate the various aspects of this trouble-some problem and the spirit of resentment that harassed Austin. Gaines wrote that steps were being taken to secure from Congress recognition of the deserts of the Gutierrez veterans: "I Expect you Don't Believe in this Business But rely on It Business will Take a Great Change in the Course of the Next Year, when Likely the first will be Last and the Last first, the Great Small and the Small Great." 'You have more education than I,' he said, 'but I am older and wish to offer you a bit of advice':

"Wind up your Colony Business as soon as you can, You certainly can by this Time form an opinion of a Majority of your people now and well know by what Tye you Govern them, Whenever that Tye is Removed by accident or otherwise what Treatment do you suppose you will Re-ceive from them ... It will be curses and abuse, this you may Rely on, as they accuse you of Everything bad and threaten continually Revenge, They say they bore the heat and Burthen of the Day, and you slight them By Reserving to yourself all the Good Land they say you are never Gov-ernd Two days by the Same Rule nor Law You give some young men ¼ League of Land and others one and more Leagues Some men of wealth and Respectability you wont Give but one League Others of Less wealth Get Two three or four Leagues, now when they have obtained their Titles, and the Teror of being Drove out of the Country is Removed and they have whiskey plenty then look for the Revenge so long threatened."[94]

Buckner had earlier located two bodies of land amounting to a league and a half. He had understood that Austin approved his selection but now learned that Austin had taken some of the land from him. Besides his service in the early wars for independence, he thought that he had other grounds for consideration. 'He was one of the first to build a cabin on the Colorado, the first to put a plough in the ground, he had lost more property by Indian depredations than any one else on the Colorado, had kept open house ever since he came to the colony, had never asked nor received a cent from any man eating under his roof, and had entertained more people than any one else in the colony, Austin not excepted. He knew that some got a league and paid no fees because they transferred half of it to Austin or to his brother; he knew that lands were unequally divided. He was not a simpleton and he was not blind; his eyes were open and he used them. He hoped that Austin would allow

[94] Gaines to Austin, November 10, 1824.

him the lands which he promised; if not, he would appeal to the government for the amount which he thought himself entitled to.'[95] Again, Jacob Betts had spent three years in poverty and misery, "looking forerd for better times part of the thime fed with soft words and fair promises," which had not been fulfilled. "I am now offerd one half of what some others are that have just arrive in the country . . . reaping the reward of my Laber." He had lost all confidence in Austin and was prepared to meet the worst. He would accept the half league that Austin offered him but would not be satisfied, and "If I am not satesfyed you will find I can do you or the Colony as mutch Injury as any other man though it is not my wish."[96]

These complaints are typical of the discontented element, and it is significant of Austin's strength, understanding, judgment, and tact that, in time, he quieted them all.[97] In an interesting letter to Benjamin W. Edwards, later notorious in the Fredonian rebellion, Austin analyzed very objectively the cause of his difficulties. To begin with, his task was complicated, and the protracted absence of Bastrop threw all responsibility upon him, unaided by laws or definite instructions from the government. In some respects his power was too great and had brought censure, jealousy, and envy upon him. No human being could have avoided errors, and in some instances he had deliberately sacrificed his own judgment for what seemed to be best for the immediate welfare of the colony. The colonists were ignorant of Spanish, and he and his secretary were the only interpreters. This exposed him to embarrassment and suspicion.

"You know [he continued] that it is innate in an American to suspect and abuse a public officer whether he deserves it or not. I have had a mixed multitude to deal with, collected from all quarters, strangers to each other, to me, and to the laws and language of the country. They

[95] Buckner to Austin, April 20, 1825.
[96] Betts to Austin, May 13, 1825.
[97] Buckner attempted in June, 1825, to hold a convention to protest against Austin and the political chief, but after a show of firmness from Austin he accepted explanations and became thereafter, until his death in 1832, a faithful supporter of Austin's. Betts admitted in June that perhaps Austin had been right and himself wrong, and asked for the half league that Austin offered him. Besides the documents already cited on this subject, see letters of J. E. B. Austin and of Anthony Clark, May 15, 22, 1824; of Austin, June 6, 7, 13, 18, 1825; of Buckner, June 10, August 10, September 7; of Groce and of Rabb, June 11, 1825.

come here with all the ideas of Americans and expect to see and understand the laws they are governed by, and many, very many of them have the licentiousness and wild turbulence of frontiersmen. Added to this, when they arrive here the worst of the human passions, avarice, is excited to the highest extent and it directs the vanguard in their attacks on me, jealousy and envy direct the flanks and maliciousness lurks in the rear to operate as occasion may require. Could I have shown them a law defining positively the quantity of land they were to get and no more and a code of written laws by which they were to be governed I should have had no difficulty."

On the whole, however, "considering the temper and dispositions of the people" with whom he had to deal, he thought that he had fared very well, "for to the ignorant part of the Americans independence means resistance and obstinacy, right or wrong. This is particularly true with frontiersmen." [98]

To a considerable degree Austin succeeded in relieving himself of the tedium of judicial duties. As we have already seen, he found the settlements on his return from Mexico organized in two districts with an alcalde over each, assisted by a constable. In December, 1823, he subdivided the Brazos district, making a third, which he called the San Felipe district; [99] and by the incorporation of a settlement on the San Jacinto into his colony in the fall of 1824 a fourth district was created there. [100] In January, 1826, he established the district of Mina, on the Colorado; [101] and perhaps at the same time subdivided the San Felipe district to create the district of Victoria. [102] By the beginning of 1828, when the constitutional régime went into operation and Austin's extraordinary powers ceased, there was still another district, making seven in all. [103]

Neither the officers nor the people were acquainted with the Mexican laws—if, in fact, the general laws extended to the settle-

[98] Austin to Edwards, September 15, 1825.

[99] Austin's proclamation, December 2, 1823. The boundaries of this district were defined as extending from Chocolate Bayou on the east to the San Bernard on the west, and from the coast to the Coshatti road in the interior. By a proclamation of January 1, 1825, Austin changed the name of the Brazos district, above this line, to Bravo in honor of General Nicolas Bravo.

[100] Austin to Flores, August 26, 1824, Flores to Austin, September 21, and Austin to Flores, November 4.

[101] Austin to Morrison and Buckner, January 4, 1826.

[102] The authority for this surmise is a note without date on the letter to Morrison and Buckner above.

[103] Austin's statement to his colonists (1829), in Wooten (ed.), *A Comprehensive History of Texas*, I, 458; and Gammel, *Laws of Texas*, I, 15.

ments—and to supply this deficiency and relieve the procedure of the alcaldes of the appearance of arbitrariness, Austin, on January 22, 1824, promulgated a set of "Instructions and Regulations for the alcaldes." This constituted a brief civil and criminal code, which he apologetically explained he had drawn up without the aid of form-books or precedents. The civil code provided for the appointment by Austin of a sheriff to execute his own processes as judge, and constables to execute those of the alcaldes; fixed the jurisdiction of the alcaldes; and prescribed definite judicial procedure. The alcalde acting alone had final jurisdiction under ten dollars; acting with arbitrators, he had final jurisdiction up to twenty-five dollars, and primary jurisdiction, subject to appeal, up to two hundred dollars.

As the first step in settling a case the alcalde must try to bring the litigants to an agreement by "conciliation"—a sort of settlement out of court. If this failed, he proceeded to try the case alone or with the help of arbitrators, as the parties to the suit determined. The first four articles of the criminal code dealt with offenses of Indians —such as violence to the settlers, rambling through the colony without a license, and stealing. Anybody was authorized to arrest and conduct such Indians, without the use of arms, if possible, to the nearest alcalde or captain of militia. If, upon examination by this official, the Indians proved to be guilty, they might suffer a maximum penalty of twenty-five lashes. On the other hand, colonists who abused Indians incurred heavy fines. Several articles covered offenses by and against slaves and provided for the recovery of fugitive and stolen slaves by their owners. The rest of the code dealt with various crimes—some suggested by anticipation, no doubt, and some by actual experience in the colony: murder, theft, robbery, gambling, profane swearing and drunkenness, counter-feiting or passing counterfeit money. All such cases must be investigated by the alcalde and tried by a jury of six and the record and verdict transmitted to Austin for approval. Capital cases, as we know, had to be submitted by Austin to the superior authorities, first at Monterey and later at Saltillo. Fines were the usual penalties prescribed by the "Regulations"—to be applied to schools and other public purposes—but whipping and banishment from the colony were allowed. For theft the penalty was a fine of three times the value of the stolen property, and hard labor on public works "until the superior government decides on the case." Alcaldes were required to keep and pass on to their successors a record of all cases tried by them. When Saucedo visited the settlements in May Austin submitted the "Regulations" to him and obtained his cordial approval.[104] The civil code carried a schedule of moderate fees for issuing and serving writs and executing judgments, but made no provision for court charges in trying a suit. Later Austin asked the political chief's approval for such fees, but his answer is not available.[105] The "Regulations" were very welcome to the alcaldes, who, there is abundant evidence to show, did not enjoy the privilege of administering common law of their own choosing.

In the early years of the colony the judicial duties of the alcaldes were not heavy, but the officers were important agents in Austin's system, serving as his local correspondents, receiving, promulgating, and executing his orders, and keeping him informed of local opinions and conditions; supervising militia elections; keeping their districts free of prowling Indians and vagabonds; settling quarrels; attesting contracts; and performing what passed in effect, until the arrival of a priest, as a civil marriage ceremony. The alcaldes occupied, in fact, a sort of patriarchal relation to their respective communities.

With the rapid influx of immigrants after 1825, judicial business increased, and Austin found himself unable to spare the time from other pressing demands to attend to appeals from the alcalde courts. On July 6, 1826, he issued a proclamation ordering each of the six districts then existing to elect a representative to meet with him to form a new judicial system and to adopt an equitable system of taxation for its support and for the defense of the settlements from hostile Indians. The result of this conference was the creation of a superior court composed of any three alcaldes. This might hear appeals from Austin himself, but it is evident that in most cases the appeal was directly from a single alcalde to this body without resort to Austin. This "court of alcaldes" held three sessions a year at San Felipe.

---

[104] The "Regulations" may be found conveniently in Wooten (ed.), *A Comprehensive History of Texas*, I, 481–492.

[105] Austin's blotter, August 26, 1824. The rates suggested were: cases involving from $25 to $40 six *reales*, $40 to $70 eight *reales*, $70 to $100 twelve *reales*, and above $100 two dollars.

Austin suffered some embarrassment from the political chief's inability to understand the judiciary's independence of his own executive decrees. A particularly trying instance of this in which the Mexican empresario Martin de Leon was the defendant occurred in 1826. The case illustrates Austin's respectful but fearless bluntness with officials when no other course would serve. One Thomas Grey had bought a *burro* from De Leon and paid for it, but left it for a time to run with the herd. When he sent for it De Leon claimed twenty-five dollars or a cow and calf for the expense of keeping it on his range, and declined to deliver it. Some time later De Leon sent a load of corn to the Colorado, and Grey seized the opportunity to attach the corn, cart, and yoke of oxen. De Leon went to San Antonio and complained to the political chief that his dignity as an empresario, sole judge of his own district, had been maliciously violated; and Saucedo instructed Austin to have the alcalde of the Colorado district return the attached property, at his own expense, to De Leon at his home, and to order him to refrain in future from issuing "illegal writs," especially of the "scandalous character" of this one. In his reply Austin reminded Saucedo that the only laws in the colony were the provisional regulations approved by himself two years before and sanctioned by the governor. He was convinced, from a thorough examination, that the alcalde had acted according to these regulations. De Leon's driver, who was his son, could have released the attachment by giving bond for his father's appearance before the alcalde to answer Grey's complaint, but had not chosen to do it.

Therefore, Austin continued,

"considering all the features of the transaction between Grey, De Leon, and the Alcalde of the Colorado, I find myself in an exceedingly delicate and embarrassing situation. I presume that my conduct, since I entered Texas, has been a proof of my obedience and submission to the lawful authorities, and this is the first order which I have not executed as soon as circumstances permitted, without hesitation, or delay. Like the Alcalde of the Colorado, I am between two fires. On the one hand duty, as well as honor and inclination, urge me to obey faithfully the orders of the superior authority; on the other, the same considerations cause me to doubt if my compliance will not amount to an injustice, or produce fatal consequences. Our people, thus far, have been contented to live under the existing provisional rules, convinced that they were approved by the

Superior Authority; but your Lordship's order causes them to doubt their legality, and whether they are bound to obey them. Thus I run the hazard of finding the only rules and laws by which I could hope to succeed in preserving good order in the Colony, and keeping bad men in subjection, destroyed and annulled by the very authority that sanctioned them and this without supplying their places by any others. It will be believed that if the rule under which the Alcalde of the Colorado attached De Leon's property is not lawful, no other rules are so, since they were established by the same authority.

"The amount of money in litigation with De Leon is nothing, nor ought the ruin of the Alcalde of the Colorado, or any other person, to have any weight if they are guilty. The difficulty lies in the disorganizing principles that may be created, and also, in the belief that cannot fail to exist in the minds of the settlers, that the Executive, or political officers unite in their person all the executive and military political and judiciary powers that were formerly vested in the Governors and the Spanish Government.

"Therefore I beseech your Lordship to decide that De Leon's case shall follow the course prescribed by the existing provisional rules, and to excuse my hesitation in executing your orders to the effect that the Alcalde shall return, at his expense, the attached property to De Leon on the Guadalupe; considering that my delay has been caused by the doubt herein submitted, and not by a want of respect for the Superior authority." [106]

The judicial system was never satisfactory, even after the inauguration of constitutional government in Texas. It was the subject of much thought and of voluminous correspondence by Austin, and really constituted the background for much of the feeling of neglect and mal-administration that led to the revolution in 1835. [107]

In the fall of 1823 the colonists first began to feel themselves in the current of national political responsibilities. Erasmo Seguin sat

[106] Austin to Saucedo, March 18, 1826. Translation in Nacogdoches Archives. Saucedo's reply is not available. In the same mail Austin answered a complaint of Edmund Mc-Locklin that he had refused to deliver a negro for whom McLocklin had shown a bill of sale: "In answer to this complaint," Austin wrote, "I have to say first that it is false." McLocklin had presented a paper without any of the formalities or requisites necessary in other countries to a legal bill of sale. Four different persons had presented bills of sale to the same negro, each protesting that his was legal, and in Austin's opinion all were forged by the bearers or their friends. McLocklin was a man of infamous character whom he had driven from his colony, and De Leon was now harboring him. De Leon was protecting also a mulatto named Drake whom Austin had punished and ordered from the colony for a theft. Perhaps, Austin suggested, he, too, had complained.—Austin to Saucedo, March 18, 1826.
[107] This discussion of the judicial system is taken substantially from a paper by the writer on the government of Austin's colony, published in *The Southwestern Historical Quarterly*, XXI, 223–252 (January, 1918). Many references are cited there which are not repeated here.

in the new constituent Congress, representing Texas. Each province was required to support its own deputies, and Governor García requested the new citizens to contribute. The republican constitution and the national colonization policy, both vital to Texas, were to be shaped by this assembly, and it was important that Texas should be ably represented. Besides having great confidence in Seguin, Austin wished to give the authorities proof of the readiness of the colonists to recognize their civic obligations, and urged the settlers to respond liberally, which they did in the form of subscriptions of corn from the new harvest. There was not enough money in the colony to make up a respectable collection, but corn had brought famine prices at Bexar the year before, and might still be used to maintain the garrison there. In 1823, however, the San Antonio valley yielded a bountiful crop, and, after suitable acknowledgment of the generosity of the colonists, the governor decided that the market would not bear the cost of transporting the contribution to San Antonio.[108]

At the same time steps were being taken to organize republican government in the provinces to supplant the Spanish system, which had remained substantially unchanged during the Iturbide régime. Bastrop wrote Austin on March 18, 1824, that Texas was to send a deputy to the provincial congress at Monterey, which was to be made up of representatives of Nuevo Leon, Coahuila, and Texas, and that his friends at San Antonio were talking of electing him. He would go, too, he said, if he had the means to sustain himself, because he believed that one with his knowledge of Texas and of the business of the colony could greatly benefit the province. In the meantime, he suggested that the settlers authorize him to represent them in the electoral assembly at San Antonio on April 25, which they did. He plainly wished Austin to understand that the colony as the chief beneficiary of his service must be willing to pay the bill. On April 7 he wrote that the Texan representative must be a man of *mundo,* acquaintance with the world; able to hold his own with the other deputies, who would try to dominate him; and astute enough to turn to the advantage of his own province the rivalry between Coahuila and Nuevo Leon; in short, he implied,

---

[108] García to Austin, September 24, 1823; subscription list, November 16, 28; Austin to García, December 2, 1823; Austin to Cummins, February 26, and Saucedo to Austin, May 25, 1824.

himself. Finally, on May 10, he wrote that he had been elected, but that if Austin wished him to serve, he must provide two good horses of easy gait, a pack mule, and some money on account of the commissions which would be due him. Nuevo Leon, he reported, objected to the proposed union with Coahuila and Texas and would probably set up as a separate state. This he considered fortunate for Texas, because Nuevo Leon had several clerical deputies, its people were accustomed to the ecclesiastical yoke, and it would be difficult to obtain concessions to religious toleration from such a legislature. The federal Congress had already, in fact, three days before united Coahuila and Texas. Even this was resented by the Mexicans of Texas because they foresaw that the state government would be controlled by Coahuila. Seguin wrote from Mexico, however, that the union was only an experiment; that it was absurd to talk of maintaining a state organization with the thin population and undeveloped resources of Texas; but that the province might be made into a federal territory if the connection with Coahuila proved unworkable.[109]

Saucedo invited suggestions from the colonists for the instruction of the Texan deputy, and Austin called a mass meeting to prepare a suitable statement. Various precinct gatherings proposed subjects for legislation—for example, laws requiring registration of cattle marks and brands, protecting deer and wild horses, regulating the burning of grass on the prairies, and provision for trial by jury—but the general meeting confined itself to two resolutions, one requesting permission to raise tobacco in the province and the other asking the legislature not to prohibit the continued immigration of slaves with their owners.[110]

Bastrop's protracted absence caused the settlers considerable uneasiness, because they could not get titles without his signature. After his election, delay still followed delay, and he did not arrive in the colony until July, when Saucedo wrote that he must return to Bexar by August 20 to take up his journey to Saltillo.[111] During his short stay he issued two hundred and seventy-two titles, leaving

[109] Bastrop to Austin, March 18, April 7, May 10, 1824; Austin to Saucedo, April 20; Seguin to Bastrop, March 24, April 21, 1824.
[110] Austin's proclamation, May 25; resolutions of the meeting, June 5; report of committee, June 10, 1824.
[111] Austin to Saucedo, June 20, 1824; Saucedo to Austin, June 22, July 10, 1824; Bastrop to Austin, March 18, 1824.

only twenty-eight lacking to fill Austin's contract. Seventeen were issued to artificial "families," that is, unmarried men in partnership. "The lands chosen by the settlers were the rich bottoms of the Brazos, the Colorado, and the Bernard, each *sitio* having a frontage on the river equal, in theory at least, to about one-fourth of its length; the east bank of the Brazos was wholly occupied from the Gulf as far up as the present county of Brazos." [112]

Among the powers granted to Austin was the authority, with the commissioner, to establish a town. Soon after his return from Mexico in 1823 he wrote Josiah H. Bell that he thought he had found a satisfactory location on the Colorado, but he wished to hear of sites on the Brazos with a good water supply independent of the river. Governor García had already christened the unborn town San Felipe de Austin, and a militia proclamation of December 2, 1823, indicates that Austin by that time was applying the name to the settlement founded by John McFarland at the lower Atascosito crossing of the Brazos. The town was formally "established" by Austin and Bastrop in July, 1824. [113]

By September 21 Bastrop was back in San Antonio, hurrying to the Legislature. His immediate necessities had been satisfied by the collection of $2,821.56¼ from the colonists, $1,000 of which went to the treasury of the provincial administration. This took most of the specie in the settlements, and he was compelled to allow two years for the payment of the balance of his own and the government fees. Before leaving for Saltillo he assigned to Austin and to Saucedo each one-third of his own fees in the event of his death. He retained the office of commissioner, which in the end was an inconvenience to Austin because it delayed the closing of the first contract. He expected to return after one term in the legislature, but was re-elected and served until his death in February, 1827. He was a man of very considerable ability, and all contemporary testimony agrees that his service was of the greatest importance to Texas. [114]

[112] Bugbee, "The Old Three Hundred," in *Quarterly* of Texas State Historical Association, I, 109.

[113] García to Bastrop, July 26, 1823, in Gammel, *Laws of Texas,* I, 34; Austin to Bell, August 29, September 28, 1823; plat and official creation of the town in Translation of Record . . . of Austin's First Colony, 22–23, General Land Office of Texas. In recognition of his rights as the original settler, McFarland was given a life tenure of the ferry at San Felipe, subject to regulations framed by Austin and Bastrop. (See copy of his charter, July —, 1824.)

[114] Bastrop to Austin, August 30, September 22, 1824; Saucedo to Austin, September 21, 1824.

With the growth of the colony, Austin realized the need of a public recorder, and in February, 1824, asked authority to appoint such an officer to record deeds, transfers, and other legal documents; but Saucedo replied that this was the duty of the district alcaldes until the organization of an ayuntamiento in the colony, when each should deposit the records of his office with the secretary of the ayuntamiento. Subsequently he instructed Austin to act in the same way as custodian of the general archives of the colony until he could surrender them to the secretary of the ayuntamiento. Why, then, Austin asked, could he not in the meantime appoint a secretary for the colony with substantially the same duties that a secretary of ayuntamiento would have? Saucedo replied that he might, and Austin appointed Samuel M. Williams, who arrived in Texas in May, with a fluent command of Spanish and French, a fine Spencerian hand, and an insatiable capacity for work. He immediately assumed the duties which Austin had outlined for the recorder, charging fees approved by the political chief, and for the next eleven years was Austin's confidential and indispensable assistant in labors which taxed to the utmost the patience and industry of both.[115]

The first colony was now established, and before the end of 1824 Austin was applying for a new contract to settle another three hundred families.[116] The conquest of the wilderness was well begun; the Indians were becoming respectful; food crops were abundant; comfortable cabins were building; and the tense, anxious memories of 1822–1823, when the fate of the colony hung in the balance, were receding into the heroic past to be recalled only to point a moral or beguile the half-incredulous traveler.

Austin's personal world had narrowed. His mother died after he had despatched his brother to remove her to Texas, and his widowed sister remarried and remained with her three small children in Missouri. Austin had declared years before that he himself would never marry until the family was free of debt, and he now settled down to a very busy but rather lonely life. His letter of instruction to mother and sister when he expected them to join him in Texas reveals much of his simple wisdom and homely philosophy of life:

---

[115] Austin to Bastrop, February 3, and to Saucedo, August 26, 1824; Saucedo to Austin, March 16, June 22, July 10, September 21, 1824. The last letter is in the Bexar Archives.
[116] Austin to Supreme Executive Power, October 1, 1824; to Arizpe, October 1, 1824.

"After many delays and disappointments [he wrote] I am at length enabled to start brother to you, there are two modes of moving to this country, one down the Mississippi to the mouth of Red River and up that to Natchitoches, and thence through by land a distance of about two hundred and fifty miles—the other route is to go to Orleans and thence round by sea to the mouth of the Brazos River, I am yet undecided which of these two routes will be the best. . . .

"We have all had a good Schooling in the best School in the World, that of Adversity and I hope have profited by it. Our prospects now are beginning to look up, but we must still remember our past troubles and not forget that wealth is hard to acquire and easily lost—let our motto be *economy* and *plain living*. It is my wish that nothing should be worn in the family but homespun, at least for several years. It is the cheapest but what is of much more importance it will set an example to the rest of the Settlers that will have a good effect.

"Also I wish everything about the house to be plain and pretty much like the rest of our neighbors—we are all poor in this country and therefore all on an equality and so long as this continues we shall all go on well and harmoniously as regards good neighborship, and our industry will soon remidy our poverty if we have the proper economy with it. The situation I am placed in here will cause all the acts of any of my family to be observed and it will require a uniform affible deportment to all, without regarding their appearances or poverty to prevent giving offences, the only distinction that must be known here is between the *good* and the *bad* and that must be very marked and decissive. I make these observations that you may have a better idea of the course that will be necessary to adopt here—for you know how easy it is to give offence to a certain class of mankind."

To his brother Austin wrote at the same time, as a guide to his conduct on the trip to Missouri, "Do not make any display or noise, treat all who make enquiries politely, [answer] them as well as you can, and put nothing in the newspapers." [117]

[117] Austin to Mother and Sister, and to J. E. B. Austin, May 4, 1824; Saucedo to Austin, September 22; McGuffin to Austin, November 12, and Cable to Austin, November 20, 1824.

CHAPTER VI

The Extension of Anglo-American Colonization

OPPONENTS of a federal government for Mexico shrewdly argued that while the constitution of the United States united independent states into a nation, the *acta constitutiva* dissolved the union in Mexico and made separate nations of the provinces.[1] They might have illustrated the inverse operation of the federal system in the two countries by the administration of the public lands. Claimed by the states in the north, the lands were surrendered to the national government as the price of union; while in Mexico they were owned by the central government and turned over to the states for administration.

The new constituent Congress held its first session on November 5, 1823. Less than half of its members had served in the earlier body, and so lacked experience. The first ten weeks were devoted largely to the passage of the *acta constitutiva,* and thereafter the constitution absorbed much attention. When the committee on colonization was created we do not know.[2] On December 11 Erasmo Seguin was seated as deputy from Texas, and became appropriately a member of the committee.[3] On June 12 Covarrubias of Guadalaxara moved the completion of what remained to be done on the colonization law, and from time to time thereafter one catches a glimpse of the committee, but it is not until August 3, when discussion of the law began by articles, that the journals afford any information about its work. The law as issued on August 18, 1824, was very general. It authorized the states, subject to a few restrictions, to provide for the administration of the public domain and prescribe regulations for immigration. The state laws must, of

---

[1] Alamán, *Historia de Mégico,* V, 589.
[2] Mateos, *Historia de los Congresos Mexicanos,* is for this period very fragmentary. The journals for April, May, and June, as originally published, are in the García Library of the University of Texas, but are lacking for November-March and July-August, 1824.
[3] Mateos, *Ibid.,* II, 614; Seguin to Austin, January 14, 1824.

course, conform to the *acta constitutiva* and the constitution; must not, without the approval of the federal executive, permit foreigners to settle within twenty leagues of the international boundary nor within ten leagues of the coast; must not permit more than eleven leagues of land to be held by one person; must forbid transfers of land to religious orders; and must not grant titles to non-residents of the republic. The federal government reserved the right to erect forts, arsenals, and other public works on vacant lands, with the consent of Congress; and to prohibit immigration from any particular nation whenever in its judgment the general interest so required. Finally the law guaranteed contracts that were not contrary to the laws between empresarios and the families which they introduced at their expense.[4] An amendment to admit only "Roman Apostolic Christians" was rejected, with only the vote of the mover in its favor.[5]

As early as May 15 Congress had passed a resolution offered by Seguin and Ramos Arizpe, instructing the colonization committee to collect all documents concerning concessions in Coahuila and Texas and transmit them to the state for action when its government should be formed.[6] The two provinces had been united by statute on May 7 until Texas should acquire sufficient population for separate organization. We have already noticed the election of Bastrop to represent Texas. The state congress was installed on August 15, but Bastrop did not take his seat until October. The first act affecting Texas created the office of political chief and defined his duties (February 1, 1825). The next was the colonization law, March 24, 1825.[7] These, as Bastrop said, were the only things of consequence that the legislature had done down to that time; and they were largely the result of his perseverance and skillful management.[8] For a time there was great opposition to the settlement of Americans in Texas lest they should rise and deliver the province to the United States; and a bill drawn by General Wilkin-

[4] Mateos, *Ibid.*, II, 807, 868–85, *passim;* translation of the law in Gammel, *Laws of Texas,* I, 97–98.

[5] Mateos, *Ibid.*, II, 873, declares that the amendment was "admitted," but it does not appear in the law, and Seguin to Austin, August 11, 1824, gives the vote.

[6] *Diario de las Sesiones del Congreso Constituyente,* II, 526.

[7] These laws are in Gammel, *Laws of Texas,* I, 121–133. Their passage is described in "Bastrop in the Legislature," MS., November 16, 1824, January 1, 1825, February 9, 1825; and in Bastrop to Austin, March 19, 1825.

[8] Bastrop to Austin, March 19, 1825.

son and forwarded from Mexico by Ramos Arizpe gave Bastrop much trouble. "This cursed plan threatened to upset everything," he complained.[9]

The colonization law invited immigrants who fulfilled the requirements of the federal law to settle in Coahuila and Texas. Foreigners already in the state who desired land must go before the local ayuntamiento of the district and take the oath to observe the federal and state constitutions and the Catholic religion; others must on arrival prove their "Christian and good moral character" by testimonials from the place of their emigration. Wishing to increase the population of the state as rapidly as possible, the framers of the law provided both for the settlement of individual families and for colonies introduced by empresarios, or contractors. Families introduced by an empresario were entitled normally to a *labor* of land (one hundred and seventy-seven acres) for farming and twenty-four *labors* for cattle raising, making a total of a league (4,428 acres) in all. For this they must pay the state an acknowledgment in three installments, four, five, and six years from the date of the grant—$30 for a league, $3.50 for a *labor* of irrigable, and $2.50 for a *labor* of non-irrigable land. Families immigrating independently, without the agency of an empresario, were entitled to one-fourth more than others. Unmarried men with an empresario could obtain a quarter of a league and others a third, which could be augmented to a league after marriage. To encourage inter-marriage, an additional quarter-league was allowed to those who married Mexican women. All grants could be augmented by the governor, as the law said, for "family, industry, and activity"—meaning in proportion to the size of the household and its ability to utilize the land—and for the construction of improvements of semi-public utility. Lands must be "cultivated" or "occupied" within six years, but these terms were not defined, and in practice a very small improvement was sufficient to satisfy the legal requirements. Settlers could bequeath but not sell land before it was improved, and the heir inherited the obligation to cultivate. None could hold title after leaving the republic.

An empresario was one who settled at least one hundred families,

---

[9] Bastrop to Austin, April 27, May 6, 1825. He does not indicate the nature of Wilkinson's plan.

for which he was entitled to a premium, or compensation, of five leagues of grazing land and five *labors* of farming land. But he could not obtain the premium for more than eight hundred families. The empresario contracts were limited to six years and were declared absolutely null, without obligation of compensation, if a hundred families had not been settled before the expiration of the term. This provision became important in determining the validity of certain contracts after the passage of a federal act in 1830 excluding immigrants from the United States. The state law tracked the federal act in guaranteeing contracts between the empresario and the colonists.

Various miscellaneous provisions of the law were important. It recognized specifically the reservations of the federal act, prohibiting grants in the coast and border reserve without the approval of the superior government, forbidding grants in mortmain, limiting permanent holdings to a maximum of eleven leagues,[10] and admitting the right of the federal government to regulate immigration, even to the extent of excluding settlers from a particular nation. It authorized sales to Mexicans, up to eleven leagues, for a hundred, a hundred and fifty, and two hundred dollars a league respectively for grazing, non-irrigable, and irrigable land—a provision which speculators used to considerable advantage some years later; declared that for six years there should be no essential change in the law; and granted exemption from general taxes for ten years. Indians were to have free markets in the settlements, and when they were sufficiently advanced in civilization were to receive land on the terms of other settlers. "In respect to the introduction of slaves," the law declared, "the new settlers shall subject themselves to the laws that are now, and shall be hereafter established on the subject." And partly, perhaps, in anticipation of the labor shortage which would result from the exclusion of slaves, the governor was instructed to send to the political chief of Texas all vagrants and criminals sentenced in other parts of the state to military service, for work on the public roads and to be hired to individuals. This needs to be remembered in considering the indignation caused by a similar provision in the federal law of April 6, 1830.

While the intention of the legislature was certainly to encourage

---

[10] Empresarios who earned more than eleven leagues in premiums must dispose of the excess within twelve years.

settlement of individuals, it proved in practice all but impossible to obtain land except through becoming a member of an empresario's colony. Families coming in without the agency of an empresario were expected to apply to the nearest ayuntamiento, which would indicate the land on which they were to settle and take steps to obtain title; but there were a number of difficulties in the way. First was the barrier of language. The immigrant could not deal with the ayuntamiento. Moreover the procedure was complicated, and the ayuntamiento had neither the knowledge nor the means necessary to carry it out. Finally, the greater portion of the habitable area of the province was soon covered with empresario grants, valid for six years, and no settlement could be made in them without the consent of the empresario. The difficulty of negotiating directly with the government under such conditions is well illustrated by the experience of settlers in East Texas, whose titles remained in suspense until the end of 1835. It is evident, therefore, that the empresarios gave their colonists a very real service in obtaining titles for them and relieving them of the burden of individual application to the ayuntamiento and the government.

Robert Leftwich and Haden Edwards had remained in Mexico City after Austin's return to Texas, and had from time to time during 1823 and 1824 renewed their petitions. They were thus instrumental perhaps in furthering the passage of the national colonization law.[11] After its passage interest shifted to Saltillo, and six weeks after the passage of the state law Bastrop wrote Austin that contracts had been made for the settlement of twenty-four hundred families in Texas.[12] These were with Leftwich for eight hundred families, with Green DeWitt and Frost Thorn for four hundred each, and with Edwards for eight hundred—all on April 15. Besides additional grants to Austin, contracts were approved in 1826 for the settlement of fourteen hundred families, in 1827 for one hundred, in 1828 for nine hundred, and in 1829 for six hundred and fifty—fifteen contracts in all. None of these was entirely fulfilled, and in some not a single family was ever settled.

Before seeing the national colonization law, Austin had, on

---

[11] For the activity of Leftwich and Edwards see Mateos, *Historia Parlamentaria de los Congresos Mexicanos*, II, 377, 379, 477, 482, 648—May 23, 26, June 10, August 18, 22, 1823, January 13, 1824. There were others, however. On June 10, 1823, the minister of foreign relations transmitted to Congress nine petitions for land in Texas.

[12] Bastrop to Austin, May 6, 1825.

October 1, 1824, and again on November 6, applied to the federal provisional executive for permission to settle two or three hundred families on the vacant land in and adjoining his first settlement, particularly on the shores of Galveston Bay. He foresaw the development of a great cotton trade from Texas and asked at the same time for the legalization of the port of Galveston—which he declared best suited to large vessels—and for authority to found a town on the island. He had letters, he said, from more than two hundred families who wished to move to Texas, and his knowledge and experience would enable him to distribute land to them with the minimum disturbance of existing locations. His appeal was partly personal. Never again, he pointed out, would an empresario have to face the difficulties which he had overcome. His colonists had made the first dent in the wilderness, withstood the first shock of the Indians, suffered hunger and privation which, because of their hardihood and industry, new settlers would not encounter. Yet after three years of absorbing labor in bringing this to pass he found himself, through Saucedo's annulment of his contracts with the colonists, poorer than when he began, and he hoped by a new grant to recoup his losses.[13] Answering a query from Seguin, Austin outlined a plan for directing colonization like the one he proposed to Martinez in 1821. This was the appointment of two commissioners, a Mexican and an American with an interest in the country, with full power to direct surveys and issue titles. Under such an arrangement, with the admission of slaves and the opening of the port of Galveston for the shipment of cotton, "which is the principal product that must raise us from poverty," the rapid and systematic settlement of the province with well to do families from Louisiana, Mississippi, Alabama, and Arkansas would be simple.[14]

Control of colonization in Texas had now, however, passed to Coahuila, and on February 4, 1825, Austin forwarded a petition to the governor, asking permission to settle three hundred families. Many industrious farmers had already crossed the boundary of the province and stopped in East Texas, where there was no local

---

[13] Application to Supreme Executive, October 1, 1824, and argument to support it (undated); to same November 6, and petition to state congress (same date) to reinforce his application.

[14] Flores to Austin, December 6, 1824, and Austin's reply, undated.

organization, and where they could obtain neither titles nor protection from bad characters who infested this No Man's Land. By settling them on the Brazos and Colorado above his colony, he would be able to take the offensive against the Indians and put a stop to the raids of the Tahuacanos, while the nation would gain the benefit of their enterprise and industry. At the same time he memorialized the legislature for a port on Galveston Bay, without which, he said, commerce would be paralyzed and agriculture strangled. After the passage of the colonization law, the governor granted the request to make the additional settlement, and on May 20, in response to a later application, extended the number to five hundred families.[15] This was Austin's first contract with the state. He made another in 1827 for one hundred families and one in 1828 for three hundred, besides a contract for himself and Williams in 1831 for the settlement of eight hundred families of Mexicans and Europeans.

The executive council had deliberately refused to define the boundaries of Austin's first colony in 1823, saying that in the first place it lacked sufficient knowledge of the geography of the country and in the second that it was unnecessary, because the land actually occupied by the settlers would constitute the colony. Something more definite, however, seemed desirable in fixing Austin's judicial authority, and on May 20, 1824, Saucedo by proclamation declared that his jurisdiction extended from the sea-shore to the San Antonio road and from the Lavaca to Chocolate Bayou, which was substantially what Austin had requested of the executive council. This was enlarged in November to take in the west bank of the San Jacinto, when the settlers on that stream were incorporated into Austin's colony. The numerous contracts after the passage of the state law made an official demarcation of the colony necessary to prevent confusion, and on March 7, 1827, the governor fixed the limits as commencing at a point on the west bank of the San Jacinto ten leagues from the coast; thence up the river to its source; and north from there to the San Antonio road; along the road westward "to a point from whence a line due south will strike the head of the La Baca"; down this line and the east bank of the

---

[15] Austin to Governor, February 4, April 4, 1825; to Legislature, February 4, 1825; Governor to Austin, April 27, May 20, and Bastrop to Austin, May 6, 1825.

Lavaca to the ten league reserve; and then along this to the place of beginning.[16] It was on the vacant land left in this area after the location of the first three hundred that Austin was to settle his new contract of five hundred families.

The "Little Colony," as it was called—one hundred families— began at the San Antonio road and ascended the east bank of the Colorado fifteen leagues; running thence eastward, parallel with the road, to the watershed between the Colorado and the Brazos, which was also the boundary of the Leftwich grant; southward along this to the road; and thence with the road to the Colorado. In his application Austin declared that citizens of San Antonio had requested him to make a settlement there for the protection of travelers and to check Comanche and Tahuacano raids on the town. Miguel Arciniega was appointed commissioner of this colony in 1830, and on June 8, 1832, he formally established the town of Bastrop at the Colorado crossing of the San Antonio road.[17]

The reservations of the federal law did not apply to the first settlers, and some of them had located within ten leagues of the sea. Austin called attention to this in a petition of June 5, 1826, and asked for the inclusion of the reserved land between the Lavaca and the San Jacinto in his first contract with the state. This was strongly endorsed by the governor, and was approved by the president, after which, on July 17, 1828, the state granted him a contract to introduce three hundred additional families in this territory. At the same time the governor appointed him commissioner to extend titles to these settlers, so that the land business in this colony was officially wholly in Austin's hands, as it was in fact in the others.[18]

Four other contracts, on account of their subsequent relation to this story, should be mentioned here. In December, 1826, David G. Burnet received a grant to settle three hundred families. At the same time Joseph Vehlein, a German merchant of Mexico City, obtained a grant for three hundred, and in 1828 another for one hundred. The first two covered a large part of the territory previously granted to Edwards, whose contract had just been vacated by the

[16] Translations of Empresario Contracts, p. 52. General Land Office of Texas. There is a somewhat ambiguous translation by Austin in Gammel, *Laws of Texas,* I, 50.
[17] The documents for this paragraph are in Translations of Empresario Contracts, pp. 131–133. General Land Office of Texas.
[18] The documents are in Gammel, *Laws of Texas,* I, 51–55.

governor, and the third extended Vehlein's boundaries through the coast reserve to the Gulf. The fourth grant was to Lorenzo de Zavala, March 12, 1829, to settle five hundred families in the border reserve east of Nacogdoches. The four grants formed a compact territorial unit, and in 1830 the empresarios pooled them with certain New York and Boston capitalists in the Galveston Bay and Texas Land Company and prepared to promote colonization on a great scale from the United States and Europe.

All contracts were granted in stereotyped form, differing generally only in the boundaries designated for each. They were expressly subject to all the provisions of the colonization law, were limited to six years, and recognized legal titles already existing in the grant; settlers must be Catholic, and of industrious and good moral character, attested by the authorities of the place from which they emigrated; and the empresario was obligated to exclude criminals and bad characters, organize and command the militia, and to notify the government when a hundred families were settled so that a commissioner could be appointed to issue titles and establish a town. When the town was established a school must be maintained to teach the Spanish language and a church must be built and properly furnished and requisition made for the necessary priests.[19]

Before this the uneasiness produced in the United States by the discouraging reports of 1822–1823 had passed, and a strong, steady, and wide-spread interest in Texas revived. Francis P. Wall, one of the men landed at the mouth of the Brazos from the unfortunate *Lively* on its first trip, wrote in September, 1824, that great numbers were going from Louisiana and Mississippi to view the country; in January, 1825, a correspondent from Alexandria wrote that many travelers passed that settlement on their way to Austin's colony; and from Mississippi, Alabama, and Tennessee similar reports reached Austin, so that the confidence with which he applied for his second contract was not without foundation.[20]

Two deterrents, however, still checked the flow of immigration to some extent—Mexico's known hostility to slavery, and the want of religious toleration. Letter after letter sought assurance

---

[19] A copy of these terms may be conveniently found in Gammel, *Laws of Texas*, I, 48.
[20] Wall to Austin, September 16, 1824; Holstein to Austin, January, 1825.

on these subjects. James A. E. Phelps, who had visited Texas, wrote
Austin on his return to Mississippi:

"The emigrating, or Texas fever prevails to an extent that your wishes
would no more than anticipate—It has pervaded all classes of the citizens
of this state and the adjoining; from the man with capital, to the man that
wishes to acquire a living. Nothing appears at present to prevent a portion of our wealthy planters from emigrating immediately to the province
of Texas but the uncertainty now prevailing with regard to the subject
of slavery. There has been a parragraph that has gone the round of the
nuse paper publication in the Middle States, perporting to be an extract
from a Mexican paper, which precludes the introduction of negro property into the Mexican Republic, without exception; subjecting the persons so offending to the severest penalties, and also an immediate emancipation of those slaves now belonging to the citizens of the province of
Texas, and fredom to the *slave* that *touches* the soil of Mexico.
"If this be a fact it will check the tide of emigrating spirits at once, and
indeed it has had its influence already.... I have ventured to contradict so
much of the report and publication as relates to your colony, upon the authority of yourself, so far as guaranteeing the right of that species of property under consideration. That portion of the Mexican Republik is becoming every day more and more an object of interest with this portion
of the United States. There is not a day passes that I am not call^d on to
give (the superficial) information that I am in possession of as regards
your country, and have to regret that I am not able to satisfy the eager, yet
not idle, curiosity of my friends. If slavery is tolerated by the new constitution I could wish, for the benefit of yourself and others, that you would
petition the government for extension of territory, and colonial location,
so as to comprise the Trinity and its waters. Three Hundred familys more
can be settled in less than two years.
"A very considerable number of Gentlemen of fortune will visit the
colony this Spring from this section of the Country with a view of becoming citizens." [21]

Another, writing from Franklin County, Alabama, declared that
great interest was aroused there about Austin's settlement. He
wished to know the attitude of the government toward religion.
Would it "wink at liberty of conscience"? Uncertainty on this score,
he said, had a powerful effect in preventing the emigration of good
colonists. "You may depend upon it that your exclusive system has
a most discouraging effect upon emigration, particularly among
the more respectable classes of the community. If that first and most

[21] Phelps to Austin, Pinckneyville, Mississippi, January 16, 1825.

obnoxious article could be blotted from your constitution, my word for it, families of respectability and influence would flock to your country from every part of the United States." The matter of slavery, too, presented difficulties, said this writer. Well to do planters would not remove to Texas unless they could be assured that their slaves would be secured to them under the laws. Could they be introduced, he asked, "as the laboring servants of emigrants"; and, if so, when would they be free?[22]

From Logan County, Kentucky, came the query whether toleration would be allowed immigrants,

"so far as to be exempted from the payment of tithes to the established Church, if they should desire it. And to think and act for themselves in matters of conscience? Provided they do not interfere with the Catholic Religion, and with fidelity support the laws of the land, as citizens ought to do? and thereby to enjoy as much Religious liberty as the Protestants have in France and some other Catholic countries? Or as the Catholics have in the United States? Or should these privileges in their full extent be refused, we ask for the Privilege of exercising the rights of private judgement in our own houses and neighbourhood? Provided, nevertheless, that our difference in opinion with the Catholics be a silent one?"[23]

Though a writer from Washington County, Alabama, expressed the opinion that exclusion of slavery might prevent fewer than was expected from moving to Texas and that it might be a positive inducement to some who would not otherwise have thought of going,[24] these letters are typical of many received by Austin during 1825–1829, and explain in part his anxiety to remove these two obstacles to immigration. Slavery he made the subject of long and frequent petitions until a working arrangement was established in May, 1828, by a state law recognizing labor contracts which, in effect, allowed immigrants to indent their slaves for life after nominally liberating them; but toleration was too delicate a matter for formal representation, and Austin rarely permitted himself to mention it even in semi-personal correspondence with officials in whom he had the greatest confidence.[25] In practice, though the settlers were deprived of the ministrations of Protestant preachers, they

[22] Douglas to Austin, February 15, 1825.
[23] Smith to Austin, December 25, 1825.
[24] Rankin to Austin, December 14, 1825.
[25] For full discussion of these subjects see below, pages 201–228.

were seldom subjected to those of the Catholic clergy, and, so far as one may judge from the documents that have come down to us, they reconciled themselves to the situation with very little complaint. And despite the anxiety of prospective immigrants, Austin's mail continued to bring such expressions as, "Your country is much spoken of here [in Alabama] and much more in Tennessee and Kentucky";[26] "there is to be a large meeting of citizens at Versailles, Woodford County [Kentucky], on the subject of going to your settlement";[27] and "such is the mania for Emigrating to your country that nothing but a positive prohibition from the Government will stop them."[28] One enthusiastic traveler on his return from Texas, "found agriculture fast declining in all the Middle and Southern region of our country, oppressed with heavy duties on imports from abroad and taxes at home, and the people burthened with debts"; thousands of families were without a foot of soil or any hope of owning any; and he could not but contrast their condition with those whose "happy star had conducted them to a country blessed with the finest soil in North America, with plenty, health, peace and happiness."[29]

As was natural, emigrants looking toward Texas fixed their eyes on Austin's settlements rather than on those of other empresarios. He had already the prestige of success, of knowing and getting on with the Mexican authorities. His colonists were actually receiving titles and making improvements. They had taught the Indians the first lessons of respect for the white man, and in their growing strength there was security. Society among them had passed from the individualistic to the cooperative stage; and newcomers need no longer hazard all the hardships of the primitive wilderness. Moreover, Austin's boundaries included the fairest part of the province then known—land of exhaustless fertility, abundantly watered and accessible to the sea, timber and prairie interspersed in convenient proportions, and a well nigh perfect climate for eight months of the year, with the unpleasant heat of the remaining four tempered by the steady breeze from the Gulf. All who visited Texas and returned to the United States advertised its su-

[26] Royall to Austin, Tuscumbia, February 21, 1825.
[27] Hawkins to Austin, Lexington, August 6, 1826.
[28] League to Austin, Nashville, January 18, 1827.
[29] Ellis to Austin, Tuscumbia, January 3, 1828.

perior natural advantages, and men who had themselves no intention of emigrating wrote to Austin for reliable information which they might detail to others.[30] The cancellation of Edwards's contract, DeWitt's troubles, and the delay of other empresarios in beginning to carry out their contracts emphasized the apparently smooth-running machinery of Austin's colony.

The census of March 31, 1828, gave Austin's settlements 2,021; that of June 30, 1830, 4,248; and that of a year later 5,665.[31] Before the end of 1833 seven hundred and fifty-five titles had been issued in Austin's various grants from the state,[32] besides three hundred and ten in the original grant from the national government.

There is no precise record to indicate the origin of the first three hundred families, though it is evident that a larger proportion were from Missouri than were in the later colonies; but for the contracts with the state Austin kept a register and required those who applied for permission to settle to register the state from which they came, together with much other statistical information. In a tabulation of eight hundred[33] applicants from the United States between July, 1825, and July, 1831, two hundred came from Louisiana, a hundred and eleven from Alabama, three hundred from Arkansas, Tennessee, Missouri, and Mississippi, and most of the others from New York, Kentucky, Ohio, Georgia, Pennsylvania, and Virginia. Twenty registered from all New England, and probably every Atlantic state had at least one representative.[34] A total of one hundred were from the Atlantic and seven hundred from the trans-Appalachian states. But the place of immediate emigration affords little indication of the real origin of the colonists. The population of the United States west of the mountains had increased from 386,000

[30] Sheldon to Austin, October 15, 1825; Hawkins, August 6, 1826. "We keep continually published in the Papers some interesting descriptions of the Country and shall continue to do so. The best description of the Country has been lately published in the Argus signed by Smith also a good description signed by Lewis."—Hawkins to Austin, Lexington, Kentucky, September 6, 1826.

[31] Nacogdoches Archives, Texas State Library. These totals probably include slaves, since they are not particularly mentioned.

[32] *Abstract of Original Titles in the General Land Office,* printed by act of Congress, May 24, 1838 (Houston, 1838). Some of these titles were issued to augment previous grants, so that the total is somewhat in excess of the individual headrights and does not indicate the number of families introduced.

[33] This does not represent the total number of registrants for the period, but only those conveniently listed.

[34] The figures are in round numbers. For a more detailed statement see "Notes on the Colonization of Texas," *Southwestern Historical Quarterly,* XXVII, 117.

in 1800 to 3,676,000 in 1830, so that few adults who arrived in Texas prior to 1831 could have been born in the west.[35]

The formal procedure for an immigrant seeking admission to Austin's colony varied little under any of his contracts. Immediately upon arrival he presented himself to Austin; registered his name, "whether married or single, his family, specifying their number and sex, the place of his nativity, his age, where from last, and his occupation"; deposited recommendations attesting "his Christian morality and good habits"; and took the oath to support the federal and state constitutions. He became thereupon an applicant, and Austin or his representative, Williams, gave him a permit to select land. He must notify the empresario of his choice within thirty days, and petition for the land in due form on stamped paper and in Spanish. Instructions were then issued to the surveyor to survey and plat the land, and upon payment of certain fees the commissioner issued the title. The stamped paper cost two dollars, the commissioner's fee was fifteen dollars, Williams received ten dollars—which he abundantly earned—for clerical work, and Austin required, under his contracts with the state, the payment of sixty dollars to himself until the end of 1829, and thereafter of fifty dollars. Such an arrangement, as we have seen, was authorized by both federal and state laws, but Austin carefully explained its justification. "The Empresario," he said, "as the general Agent of the Colonists has procured at his own expense and labor the privilege of enabling them to obtain complete titles to land without the delay and expense and perplexities of personal applications at the seat of Govt. by each individual. He has all the labor of the translations, the examination of the surveyor's returns and translating them, the receiving, registering, and locating of Colonists, also heavy responsibilities and much labor of a complicated and perplexing nature—and as his whole time must necessarily be devoted to the service of the Colonists, and under heavy expenses, he in justice and equity has a right . . . to receive from the settlers a small

---

[35] Apparently this was a problem which interested Austin for a few months, and before other details crowded it from his mind he listed forty-seven applicants, of whom thirty-six recorded previous residence in two states. Of the thirty-six, twenty-seven had moved originally from the Atlantic States (and fourteen of them from north of Maryland), three from Europe, and six from Kentucky and Tennessee, to states farther west. Of the remaining eleven, one was from Germany and apparently ten were natives of trans-Appalachia. There appears to be no reason for doubting that these figures are a fair index to the previous migrations of Texan immigrants.

recompense in comparison with the benefits he procures and the labor he undergoes for them." This fee was to be paid in three installments, ten dollars on receipt of permission to select land and twenty and thirty dollars six and eighteen months later, the deferred payments being secured by a note and lien on the land. Unmarried men, who received but a quarter-league, paid only half this fee to the empresario.[36] Other fees, however, were the same. "No one was turned away, or ever waited for his title, because he was poor," said Austin. He accepted cows, horses, mules, hogs, corn, and other produce at prices far above the market and often lent money to pay the surveyor and the commissioner.[37]

On his return from Mexico in 1823, Austin wrote that owing to the difficulty of making a beginning some men were admitted when he embarked in his enterprise "who would have been rejected under different circumstances," but that this difficulty no longer existed. Shortly after this, in stating the terms upon which immigrants would be received he wrote, "No one will be rec^d as a settler or be permitted to remain in the Province who does not bring the most unequivocal evidence from the highest authority and most respectable men of the state and neighborhood where he resides that his character is *perfectly unblemished,* that he is a moral and industrious man, and absolutely free from the vice of intoxication." Others would be ordered from the province, and, if necessary, escorted to the boundary. The substance of this was embodied, as we have seen, in the terms which he advertised to settlers. It was subsequently enjoined upon all empresarios by their contracts with the state; and there is much evidence that Austin tried scrupulously to enforce it.[38] One case in which he was imposed

---

[36] "Regulations" (May, 1825) for settlement in Austin's colony "dated April, 1825, being the second Colony of said Austin." The fee after 1829 was fixed by a notice which Austin published on November 20 of that year, payable ten dollars on receipt of title and forty dollars a year later. See a broadside pasted in "Applications for land in Austin's Colony," Book A, General Land Office of Texas. There are a great many unpaid notes in the Austin Papers signed in accordance with this agreement.

[37] Austin to the Colonists, November 1, 1829, in Gammel, *Laws of Texas,* I, 18–19: "The mass of the settlers who have paid anything, paid it in cows, at twenty to twenty-five dollars a head, corn at two or three dollars a bushel, etc., etc.; which property thus received, has been sold for two-thirds less than it was received at to raise cash, it being necessary to resort to all manner of shifts, to raise the means of keeping up the local government, and managing along the settlers, so as to prevent them from running headlong into anarchy and confusion." See also his address to the colonists, June 5, 1824.

[38] Austin to Caldwell, July 17, 1823; to ——— October 20, 1823; Terms, October 30, 1823.

upon by the good appearance of a man who came without credentials and whom he later had to flog from the colony convinced
him that the rule should be rigidly observed.[39] He banished several
from the colony in 1823 and 1824, and others occasionally thereafter, and the news spread that it was not a comfortable refuge
for evil-doers. Some of these established themselves on the borders
of Louisiana and Arkansas and told tales of violence and anarchy
in Texas to account for their own inability to live there; and some
resorted to the neighboring settlement of the Mexican empresario
De Leon and annoyed Austin by making false reports about him
to the government.[40] As population increased, immigrants who
arrived without certificates of character could usually find some
settler to vouch for them, and now and then Austin admitted one
on probation and withheld his title until he proved himself.[41]

Aside from the requirements of the law, common sense and self-
protection dictated such a policy. All Austin's material interests,
all his hopes of a future competence and relief from debt—not to
mention his strong feeling of responsibility for his colonists—depended upon the steady, permanent development of Texas, which
only a law-abiding population of sterling character could assure.
In reply to an inquiry in 1829 he wrote, "The settlers of this colony
taken en masse are greatly superior to any new country or frontier
I have ever seen and would lose nothing by a comparison with some
of the oldest counties of many of the southern and western states
... in proportion to our numbers, we are as enlightened, as moral,
as good, and as 'law abiding' men as can be found in any part of
the United States, and greatly more so than ever settled a frontier." [42]
This, of course, is *ex parte* testimony, but historical judgment
formed by study of all available contemporary records confirms it.
The great majority, especially of the earlier colonists, were men
of family seeking homes, not speculators or adventurers.

[39] Austin to Bell, December 6, 1824.
[40] See for example, White to Austin, January 31, 1829; Austin to Saucedo, March 18,
1826, and to White, March 31, 1829.
[41] See "Register of Families in Austin's Colony," General Land Office of Texas: "John
H. Jones, single man, wants a place . . . and as he is an entire stranger I have required
him to produce me satisfactory evidence of his moral conduct" (p. 16); "Henry Martin,
Mary his wife, 1 male child, 3 female children . . . has presented no recommendations—
his reception as a colonist is to be subject to future evacuation—no certificate is issued to
him, and it is entirely optionary with the empresario to receive him or not" (p. 18, June
17, 1831).
[42] Austin to White, March 31, 1829.

This is not to say that the province was a pastoral elysium. There was some petty thieving, some litigation about contracts, some suits to collect notes, some gambling, and, judging from Austin's occasional outbursts of exasperation against drunkards, too much drinking. These were vices of the age, and of all places. Austin wrote in 1829, "When you come here, you will be astonished to see all our houses with no other fastening than a wooden pin or door latch, even stores are left in this state—there is no such thing in the colony as a stable to lock up horses nor pens to guard them in." [43] The *Texas Gazette,* reporting a burglary the next year, declared it the first that had ever occurred in Austin's colony. [44] A high proportion of the early settlers owed debts in the United States, which after 1829 were not collectable in Texas by suit until the defendant had been twelve years a resident. This was probably the basis of a story published in a Louisiana paper by a returned traveler from "that land of milk and honey toward which many longing eyes are turned." He said he was surrounded at every turn by the inhabitants of Texas, inquiring what he had done in the United States that made it necessary for him to seek refuge among them. This was their custom with all newcomers, they explained, and said that if one had "ran away from his creditors only, he was regarded as a gentleman of the first water and welcomed on all hands," but if guilty of murder or high misdemeanor, they could assure him only of their protection. [45] Debt, however, was universal in the United States in the decade of the twenties, and though there are not wanting cases of absconders fleeing to Texas with property to escape creditors, so far as the records show, they are very few.

The strictly local administrative problems of the empresario continued much the same as during the establishment of the first colony. Austin remained officially responsible for the government of the settlers until the inauguration of the ayuntamiento of San Felipe in 1828, and thereafter he was for several years the buffer between that inexperienced body and the political chief, who requested him not to withhold from it his guiding hand. He continued to be commander-in-chief of the militia. The direction of the land system became more burdensome as the volume of busi-

[43] *Ibid.*
[44] Issue of August 14, 1830.
[45] *Texas Gazette,* August 21, 1830.

ness enlarged, entailing preparation of instructions for surveyors, examining and filing field notes, preventing conflicts between applicants, recording titles, and collecting and remitting land dues to the political chief. And withal, as population increased, the difficulty of preserving harmony among the settlers, between them and himself, and between them and the authorities became more complex. It would be hard to exaggerate Austin's labors during these years. A letter to the political chief gives a clue to the character and variety of his routine. He had left San Felipe on April 4, he said, to point out some land recently conceded to the secretary of state and had been detained by excessive rains until the 29th. On May 1 he had begun the trial of a case that lasted seven days; at the same time he had had to entertain a delegation of Tonkawa Indians, and to make preparations for a campaign against another tribe; to talk to and answer questions of many "foreigners" who had come to look at the country, explaining and translating the federal constitution and some of the laws for them; to receive and pass upon applications for land, hear reports and issue instructions to surveyors; and to correspond with the superior civil and military authorities. This was his excuse for not answering promptly some of the political chief's letters.[46]

He was frequently given special commissions by state and federal officials desiring information about Texas which involved long and tedious investigations and a great deal of labor: a survey of

---

[46] Austin to Saucedo, May 8, 1826. Austin wrote the governor, October 11, 1827: "According to the law and my contract with the government, I, as empresario, am obligated to introduce the families and present them to the commissioner, and to do nothing else. But experience has demonstrated that my labors do not stop with this. In the first place, I have to receive in my house most of those who come to see the country preparatory to moving, entertain them, spend days and weeks going over the land to instruct and inform them as newcomers of their situation, to furnish them translations of the laws and to explain them, etc., etc. After all this, when the colonist arrives with his family to settle, the law requires him to present a certificate of character from the authority of his former place of residence. All of these documents are in English or French, and I have the labor of translating them. After the new colonist is received and has selected his land, the surveyor must survey it so that he can be put in possession of it by the commissioner; and none of the surveyors understand a word of Spanish, nor does the commissioner understand a word of English or of the exact and scientific measurement of land, and consequently I of necessity have to supervise everything—examine the measurements, calculations, and plats made by the surveyors and certify that they are accurate, translate all into Spanish and give them to the commissioner in due form to be incorporated in the title. Thus the labor of the commissioner is reduced to signing his name and the empresario has to do the work of a pack mule who carries all the load and receives none of the benefit."

Galveston Bay; a report on immigrant Indians from the United States; the purchase of a vessel for the military commandant; or a report on the natural history of the province with reference to the collection of specimens for the national museum. His friends at San Antonio used him as purchasing agent and banker. Seguin writes him for a *calesa* or phaeton, which he can get in New Orleans; Saucedo for a strong cot and some low-heeled shoes; Padilla, from Saltillo, for a light wagon to transport his family to Texas; Bastrop must have easy saddle horses and a pack animal to take him to the legislature. Other empresarios sought his advice and begged his intervention to untangle snarls with superior officers. The colonists called on him to arbitrate disputes, make contracts for them, assume debts, cash drafts, reprimand the ayuntamiento, and curb the lawyers. From the United States, in addition to the staple inquiries of prospective emigrants, came a variety of requests: to act as guardian for an untried youth, to settle the estate of a deceased traveler, to trace missing persons, collect debts, or apprehend fugitives. To the early settlers he was the fountain of knowledge, the source of authority, the safe, if sometimes tiresome, counsellor and guide. If they grew restive under his direction when tranquil and at ease, they unburdened their anxieties to him with childlike irresponsibility when in trouble.

The civil organization remained as it was described in the preceding chapter, the precinct alcaldes taking care of petty disputes and the court of alcaldes settling most appeals. This system was broadly legal, since Austin's authority was ample, and was acquiesced in, but it was not satisfactory either to Austin or to the colonists. Nor did it become satisfactory when, with the organization of the ayuntamiento of San Felipe, the constitutional alcalde assumed Austin's judicial responsibility and *comisarios* supplanted the provisional precinct alcaldes, all administering duly enacted laws instead of Austin's "Regulations." For ten years the defects of the judiciary system were the subject of complaint and petition from Austin to the governor and legislature, and to them he attributed the growth of much of the exasperation that led to the revolution in 1835.

Getting titles for the settlers was, of course, the primary business of the empresario, and occupied much of his attention. Bastrop's absence embarrassed him, preventing the closing of the first contract, which still wanted twenty-eight titles when Bastrop set out to Saltillo in the fall of 1824, and delaying the appointment of a commissioner for the second colony, because Austin was anxious for Bastrop to have that, too.[47] Work on the constitution, however, dragged in the legislature, and Bastrop could not be spared. In April (1826) the governor designated Gaspar Flores, of San Antonio, to seat the settlers of the second contract,[48] and the following February, Bastrop being on his death bed, authorized him to finish the first colony. Various delays occurred. Soon after the arrival of Flores in the colonies the Fredonian rebellion took Austin, without whose presence he was helpless, to East Texas, and detained him for several months. Hardly had work begun upon Austin's return before illness overtook the commissioner, and when he recovered the season was so advanced that he determined to go home and await the cooler weather of the autumn. Thus 1827 passed. He returned in March, 1828, but again withdrew with the advance of the hot season. He probably spent November and December in the colony, but in January, 1829, he was recalled, despite Austin's protest, to assume the office of alcalde to which he had been elected.[49] Miguel Arciniega succeeded Flores in November, 1830, and though official duties sometimes held him also in San Antonio, he resided in the colonies a good part of the next three years and signed more than five hundred titles. As commissioner for the Coast Colony, Austin himself during the same period issued one hundred and eighty-four titles.

Duties of the commissioner were fixed by executive instructions of September 4, 1827.[50] He was to examine the character certificates of immigrants, assuring himself thereby that they were "of the Christian religion" and possessed good moral character; to administer the oath of allegiance; appoint and instruct surveyors; keep a record of titles in a bound volume, giving certified copies to the settlers; establish towns and install ayuntamientos as they

[47] Austin to Saucedo, May 8, 1826.
[48] Saucedo to Austin, May 17, 18, 1826.
[49] Saucedo to Flores, March 19, 1827; Austin to Colonists, March 16, 1828; Flores to Austin, December 2, 1828. Flores's Letter Book and Vol. 54 of General Land Office Records, pp. 124, 126. Altogether Flores issued seventy-six titles during 1827–1828.
[50] Gammel, *Laws of Texas*, I, 180–182.

were established. A law of May 16, 1828, fixed the commissioner's fee, which was to be paid by the colonist, at fifteen dollars for a league of pasture land and two dollars for a *labor* of arable land.[51] The provision for a permanent bound record was probably suggested by Austin. The titles for the first settlers were issued on separate sheets, the original being preserved by the empresario and a copy given to the grantee. Realizing the danger of loss or destruction of these loose sheets, Austin early petitioned the political chief for the establishment of a record office where not only patents but transfers, liens, and other documents could be recorded, as in the United States.[52] Saucedo could not be made to see the necessity for this, but in 1827 the governor authorized Flores to validate, under very minute regulations, copies of the titles of the first colony in a massive volume which still bears mute testimony to Austin's assiduous industry in safeguarding the interests of his settlers.[53]

The ideal tract, whether for farming or pasturage, must front on running water, and to economize and prevent monopoly of riparian privileges surveyors were instructed to limit such frontages to one-fourth the depth of the survey and not to include both banks of rivers and permanently flowing creeks in a single tract. While topographical conditions sometimes compelled variation from part of this rule, causing a line to cross fairly large streams, surveyors in general studiously observed it, and frontage on water is a universal characteristic of original patents of this period.

For a few years Austin continued to incur abuse and malicious misrepresentation from an occasional dissatisfied applicant denied, for reasons which he did not know or care to understand, the particular parcel of land that he wanted. Such a man would gather fuel for the conflagration that he sought to kindle from memories of the old controversy about the twelve and a half cent fees. He would remind his auditors of Austin's opportunity, as the sole channel of communication between the government and the settlers, to suppress laws and information advantageous to them and detrimental to himself; and would prove Austin's cupidity and corruptness by his intimacy with the local authorities at San Antonio,

[51] *Ibid.,* I, 216.
[52] Austin to Saucedo, August 16, 1825.
[53] The governor's instructions, Gammel, *Laws of Texas,* I, 37. The volume of transcripts, made by Austin and Samuel M. Williams, is in the General Land Office of Texas.

whom—it was assumed—he must therefore have bribed.[54] There is little of this after 1827. The effect of Austin's labor had become by then too plain for misrepresentation. He alone of all the empresarios save DeWitt was settling colonists and procuring titles, and it was only through his assistance and his standing at Bexar that De Witt was able to make a precarious beginning, harried by Indians and persecuted by his quarrelsome neighbor, the Mexican empresario De Leon. Squatters on the San Jacinto, to their great relief, were incorporated in his colony, as we have seen, and got titles to their lands; others on the Trinity begged to be taken in and were denied.[55] Whatever the motives of this man Austin, the benefits which he obtained for his settlers at so little cost and annoyance to them were palpable, greatly desired, and apparently could be obtained by none but him.

One feels, too, that his tireless application, accuracy, and assurance in everything that concerned the land system must have had their effect. He had the records and he knew the facts, and a reasonable man could rarely maintain a dispute with him. His thoroughness, as well as his ability to clear up a complex misunderstanding in direct and unmistakable language without a superfluous word, can be best illustrated by one of the typical letters which from time to time it was necessary for him to write explaining why a newcomer could not have the land he had set his heart on, even though it appeared to be vacant—for example, the following, which he wrote to Elias R. Wightman on April 7, 1829:

"Dr Sir,
    "When you spoke to me relative to the league of land on the Bernard next above Mr. G. Huffs I informed you that the place was entered for Mr. Elisha Moore on the 1st of January last—I was willing that Mr. Griffith for whom you applied should have the place, provided Mr. Moore would relinquish, but if Moore does not relinquish his right of prior entry no other person can get it. I have this day recd. information from Mr. Moore that he will not relinquish his entry—in this state of the business Mr. Moore's right [will] hold good in preference to any other, and the labor or improvements made by Mr. Griffith or any other person will be lost by him unless Mr. Moore voluntarily chuses to pay for them.

[54] For the activity of two such agitators, Lewis B. Dayton and George A. Nixon, see *Quarterly* of Texas State Historical Association, VII, 49; Grant to Austin, May 13, 1826, and Arciniega to Austin, August 25, 1827.
[55] See below, 324–327.

"In order that this subject may be fully understood by you and all others I will give you a correct statement of what has passed relative to this League of land.

"About two years ago it was promised to J. H. Bell for his mother in law provided she removed to the country by the 1st of May last, she did not come, and for Mr. Bell's accomodation the time was extended to the 1st of January last and the land was reserved for her until then. Mr. Bell paid the commissioner's fees to him, as I understood;—he paid nothing towards the surveying nor any office fees—

"On the 1st day of January Mr. T. M. Duke called on me with a letter from Mr. Moore and applied for the same land for Mr. Moore, and on that day it was entered for him—Mr. Bell afterwards made arrangements at this place with Mr. Duke (as they both informed me) for Moore to pay him, Bell, the amt. he had paid to the Commissioner, and I thought the matter was all finally settled and understood by all parties. In this state of the business you called on me about three weeks ago and stated that you had removed two families on to this same league and applied for it, for Mr. Griffith—I informed you what had passed, and that the place had been entered for Mr. Moore since the 1st day of January last, and that I had written to Mr. Bell early in January that the place was entered for Moore, and that Bell and Duke had made an arrangement relative to the fees that were paid by the former to the Commissioner, and that I could not give you any permission to occupy the place, and if the families that were then on it continued, it would be at their own risk, and that Mr. Moore's prior entry would entitle him to the place unless he relinquished it—As I before observed Moore informs me through his agent T. M. Duke that he will not relinquish—*This settles the question at once*—

"I shall return the league to the Commissioner as entered for Mr. Moore on the 1st day of Jany. last which is the day it was entered as you can convince yourself by reference to my letter to Mr. Bell before referred to, and the title will be made to Mr. Moore and all improvements made by you or the families who are on it, or by any others who go on it without permission from Moore will be lost.

"I have always given the preference to actual settlers when they occupied places not promised to others previously, tho agreeably to law no such settlement can give any person any right to demand a title, as a *matter of right,* unless the settlement was made after having first obtained a regular permission from the Empresario or Commissioner—In this case Mr. Griffith has gone on to a place that was [entered] by Moore before Griffith came to the country, and you as the agent of Griffith was fully informed of the true situation of the land before he went on to it— you informed me that Mr. Bell told you to go on to it and that he relinquished his claim to you—Mr. Bell had no right to tell you any thing of the kind, for he had no claim to relinquish—The promise to him expired on the 1st of January, and Moore's entry was made on that day and Bell was informed of that fact some time between the 5th and 10th of January by my letter to him.

"After taking a candid view of the whole matter you cannot fail to be convinced that Mr. Moore's right is a good one, and I expect that you will cause the families you have placed there to move off immediately, unless they remain with Moore's permission—If they do not remove— Mr. Moore can compel their removal immediately after the arrival of the Commissioner."

Whatever his disappointment at losing a chosen location, one could not long doubt Austin's fairness after reading such a statement.

Until 1827 the attitude of the Indians was doubtful and vital. The treaty with the Karankawas in September, 1824, was limited to one year. That with the Wacos and Tahuacanos, though not restricted in duration, was precarious at best. West of them were the Comanches, fiercely hostile to the Mexicans and a menace to the settlers, who must inevitably become involved in their feud with the Mexicans. Among the settlements were the Tonkawas, pilferers and beggars, and a good deal of a nuisance. Their presence gave the Wacos, Tahuacanos, and Comanches a pretext for entering the colonies. Avowedly they came to punish the Tonkawas for raids upon themselves, but they rarely failed to collect involuntary tribute from the settlers. In East Texas were the partially civilized Cherokees, Choctaws, and Caddos, generally desiring peace, but uneasy about their lands, and on the defensive against the encroachment of the whites. Surrounding them were odds and ends of many nations who could sometimes be organized by the Wacos and Tahuacanos.

The desperate situation can be inferred from the embarrassing proposal which Austin made to the political chief for avoiding Comanche hostility in 1825. Rumor reported these Indians to be raiding San Antonio and Goliad, robbing and killing, but the settlers still profited from their partiality to Americans and were not disturbed. Though it shamed him to the soul, Austin suggested that they take advantage of this circumstance until they were strong enough to carry on an effective campaign. His colonists were widely scattered and it took time to mobilize them; he could not maintain a standing force, because the men could not be spared from the fields; the government had no means to protect or aid them; and prudence, therefore, "suffocating the purest sentiments of sympathetic fraternity," counseled the selfish policy of *sauve qui peut* until the settlement was on its feet.[56]

Shortly after this, Austin received in the same mail two letters from Colonel Ahumada, the superior military officer in Texas. The first, dated August 21, ordered him to march immediately against the Wacos, Tahuacanos, and Tahuiases on the Brazos, and the second, written on the 26th, countermanded the order, because the Comanches were thought to be at the Waco villages in force.[57] Anticipating a renewal of the order, while still hoping that Ahumada would leave its execution to his discretion, Austin took counsel of the colonists in an elaborate questionnaire. If the expedition were ordered in positive terms, would it be necessary to defend the frontier with blockhouses, should they be paid for by a general contribution, and should all the frontier settlers be compelled to abandon their homes and gather in the forts? With the Karankawas active on the coast, would it be safe to draw the men of the lower settlements into the interior, or could peace be made with them, so that two frontiers need not be defended at the same time? Should they invite the Lipans and Tonkawas to join them, remembering that such an alliance would establish in their minds the right to live on the country permanently, "to steal our hogs and corn and kill some of our cattle"? On the other hand, if he were left with discretionary authority, should he attack at once or parley in the effort to make a satisfactory treaty? It is evident that there was a strong demand for an aggressive movement and that Austin was trying indirectly to discourage it. A war now would check immigration to all the colonies and more particularly would delay settlement of the Leftwich grant which he expected to be well under way by the following spring and which, when formed, would be a protective buffer between his settlements and these Indians. "True," he admitted, "we have received repeated insults from the Indians which merit punishment, and great excitement and thirst for revenge exists in many persons; this is a correct feeling, but whether this is the proper time to seek revenge or not is a question which cool judgment and not passion should decide."[58]

---

[56] Austin to Saucedo, August 20, September 8, 1825.
[57] Austin to Ahumada, September 10; to Colonists, September 28, 1825.
[58] Austin to Colonists, September 28, 1825.

The questionnaire was to be discussed in the various militia districts. The answer was probably in accordance with Austin's wishes. He subsequently wrote John P. Coles, one of his confidential aids, that the government was displeased because they had not gone to war with the Wacos and Comanches, to which Coles philosophically replied that he was sorry, "but, sir, we had better be driven out of the country by the Government than by the Indians"—the fate which he apparently believed would be the consequence of a war.[59] The virtue of resignation, however, did not sit so comfortably upon the inhabitants of the exposed Colorado frontier. At almost the same time, one of these was writing Austin: "I wish to inform you that in my absence the Waco Indians came to my House and plundered and carried off the following articles, two sheets two Quilts and Wagon Cover and nearly all our wearing Clothing and Table Furniture. It appears from the Conduct of those Indians that we cannot settle the frontiers of this Colony unless we can have an understanding with them, for if they are allowed to Rob and plunder it will be impossible . . . I am determined to kill the first one that undertakes to Rob me again, which will commence a war." He thought peace could be made with them, and he desired peace on honorable terms.[60]

During the winter and early spring the Tahuacanos and Choctaws at different times raided the Tonkawas, killing a number of them, but they left the colonists undisturbed.[61] On April 4, however, Captain James J. Ross, with thirty-one men attacked a party of sixteen Tahuacanos who had entered the Colorado settlements to steal horses, killing eight and wounding five.[62] Austin sent spies to their villages to see how the tribe would take this loss, and, though they reported that there seemed to be no disposition for a general war, he expected retaliatory raids from small parties and determined to anticipate them by a decisive campaign. He ordered the militia to be prepared by the middle of May, and without waiting to consult Ahumada proposed an alliance to the Cherokees, Shawnees, and Delawares. His plan was for the militia to attack the main villages

[59] Coles to Austin, January 7, 1826.
[60] Castleman to Austin, January 17, 1826.
[61] Austin to Ahumada, March 27, 1826.
[62] Austin to Ahumada, April 6, 1826, quoting Ross's report. The Indians were a-foot, and each carried a leather lariat.

of the Wacos and Tahuacanos on the Brazos at daybreak May 25, while the Indian allies at the same hour stormed the Tahuacano town at the head of the Navasota, about thirty miles east of the Brazos. He intended before ending the campaign to destroy the Tahuias village on Red River. The allies could thus prove their loyalty to the government, and might hope to be rewarded by a legal grant of the land which they were occupying.[63] They were willing, but Ahumada vetoed the alliance, because he thought it bad policy to let the Indians feel that the whites were dependent upon them, and ordered Austin to suspend the campaign until he himself could obtain reinforcement and supplies from Tamaulipas.[64]

When this order arrived Austin had just received information that led him to believe that the Wacos had organized a formidable confederation, and, though he notified the Cherokees that they would not be needed, he thought it best to keep the militia, which was already embodied, under arms. A detachment under Captain Buckner reconnoitered as far as the villages on the Brazos, but found them deserted, with much corn, beans, and melons growing in the fields.[65] At the end of July Austin notified Ahumada that the Indians had returned to harvest their crops, but that they would be gone again by August 15 or 20, which would not allow time enough to organize a campaign against them. To protect the frontier from their intermittent visits until the Mexican forces could take the field, Austin called a meeting of representatives of the six militia districts to devise a plan of defense. The result of this conference was an arrangement to keep from twenty to thirty mounted rangers in service all the time, each land owner being required to serve a month, or furnish a substitute, for every half league that he owned.[66] Whether the plan was ever put into operation we do not know.

The suppression of the Fredonian rebellion took a large Mexican force to Texas in the spring of 1827, and General Bustamante was preparing for a campaign of extermination when peace overtures came from all the marauding tribes. On May 13, after conferring

[63] Austin to Fields, April 24, and to Ahumada, April 30, 1826.
[64] Ahumada to Austin, May 4, 18, 1826; Austin to Ahumada, May 8, 18, and to Cherokees, May 8, 1824.
[65] Austin to Ahumada, June 6, 16 (quoting Buckner's report of the 11th), 1826; Austin to Saucedo, May 19, 1826.
[66] Austin to Ahumada, July 31, and to Saucedo, August 14, 28, 1826.

with Austin, Bustamante signed a treaty with the principal Karan-kawa chief, Antoñito. This renewed the treaty of September, 1824; fixed the eastern range of the Indians at the Lavaca River; pledged Antoñito to bring all the Karankawas and Cokes into the peace or to abandon them to their fate in war with the colonists; and allowed Austin to keep as a hostage a Karankawa woman and some children who had been captured, until convinced of the good faith of the Indians.[67] At the same time a delegation of Wacos and Tahua-canos assured Colonel Francisco Ruiz at Nacogdoches of their desire for peace, and he seems to have accompanied them to San Antonio, where Bustamante concluded a treaty with them and also with the Comanches.[68] This did not, of course, remove the menace of the Indians, but it ameliorated it; and for Austin's settlement it marked the passing of the crisis. In the summer of 1829 the political chief called on the ayuntamiento of San Felipe for a hundred and fifty men for a campaign against the Wacos and Tahuacanos, but before they could be assembled Colonel Ruiz notified Austin that the campaign was postponed.[69] DeWitt's settlement on the Guadalupe and the Mexicans of San Antonio and Goliad were the chief sufferers. A report of the ayuntamiento of San Antonio in December, 1832, declared that these places had lost ninety-seven men, not including soldiers, since 1821, and this notwithstanding the fact, as it reminded the government, that except during 1825–1827 the Indians were nominally at peace.[70]

The letters of Austin and his brother to their sister give intimate glimpses of Austin and of what each thought of his work during this period. Austin, sober and self-contained, immersed in a thousand cares, seemed at first afraid to claim the success that others awarded him, lest he invite reverses which he saw always on the horizon; the brother, on the other hand, cheerful and exuberant, was confident that Austin had "accomplished an enterprise that will perpetuate our name and place it with honor on the page of

[67] An official copy of the treaty made at Goliad, May 27, 1827, is signed by Bustamante, Martin and Fernando de Leon, Manuel Becerra, Father Miguel Muro in behalf of Antoñito and other chiefs, Brother Antonio Valdez, Jacob Betts, representing Austin's colony, and Estevan F. Austin. Austin, however, was not present.—See Bustamante to Austin, May 14, 1827.

[68] Ruiz to Austin, May 28, June 2, 1827; Bustamante to Austin, June 19. The treaties are not available.

[69] Músquiz to Austin, June 11, 1829; Ruiz to Austin, July 23, 1829.

[70] Filisola, *Memorias para la Historia de la Guerra de Texas*, I, 273.

history." Thus we read from Austin: "The colony progresses very well, though not very rapidly. We have but little commerce as yet, though must have a great deal in a few years . . . in the woods and poor. The enterprise I undertook is better calculated to enrich those who come after me than to benefit myself. I have the labor to perform and the seed to sow, but my successors will reap the harvest." A year later: "The affairs of the colony are going on tolerably well tho immigration is not very rapid. . . . My prospects of making a fortune are *bad,* I shall be but poorly compensated, tho expect to pay my debts and make a comfortable support for my old age." In 1828 there were nearly three thousand settlers in his colony, but he himself was "poor as to disposable means." "It is a troublesome business and requires much more perseverance and patience than any one can imagine who has not tried it." [71] But cares sat lightly on the younger brother. The country would soon be settled, he wrote in 1825. The next year there was prospect of overflowing immigration. Later, "the period cannot be far distant when our fullest anticipations will be realized." But the strenuous years were taking their toll of Austin. The brother wrote in 1829, "He begins to look quite old and the wrinkles are becoming plainer daily." [72]

[71] Austin to Mrs. Perry, December 12, 1825; August 21, 1826; July 24, October 25, 1828.
[72] J. E. B. Austin to Mrs. Perry, October 28, 1825; February 28, 1826; May 26, 1829.

CHAPTER VII

The Fredonian Rebellion

HADEN EDWARDS was one of the crowd of anxious applicants who waited at Mexico through 1823 and 1824 for the passage of the national colonization law. After its enactment the scene of his vigils shifted to Saltillo, where, on April 15, 1825, he obtained under the state law a contract to settle eight hundred families. From the intersection of the coast and border reservations, ten leagues from the sea and twenty from the Sabine, the eastern boundary of his grant ran north to a point fifteen leagues from Nacogdoches; from there the northern line ran at right angles westward to the Navasota River; thence the western boundary followed in an irregular line the Navasota, the San Antonio road, and the San Jacinto to the coast reserve line, which formed the southern boundary to the point of beginning. Along the San Jacinto the grant touched Austin's colony.[1] It included the site of one of the oldest Spanish settlements in Texas and adjoined on the east a twilight zone occupied by squatters, which neither Spanish nor American jurisdiction had reached for years. This was at the bottom of Edwards's disaster.

Founded in 1716 as a barrier against the French, Nacogdoches and the surrounding missions were officially abandoned in 1773, when France no longer menaced. But two generations of settlers had planted themselves too firmly in the soil to be uprooted, and after an effort to withdraw them to San Antonio had failed, these Spanish pioneers were allowed to return to their beloved *ranchos* in 1779.[2] The population of the district in 1806 was nearly a thousand,[3] but the savage, undiscriminating warfare of *gachupinos* and

[1] Copy of the contract in Translations of Empresario Contracts, 37–38, General Land Office of Texas.

[2] Bolton, "The Spanish Abandonment and Reoccupation of East Texas, 1773–1779," in *Quarterly* of Texas State Historical Association, IX, 67–137.

[3] Bugbee, "The Texas Frontier, 1820–1825," in *Publications* of Southern History Association, IV, 102.

republicans during the Mexican revolution devastated the country and drove the neutral inhabitants across the border for protection, so that when Moses Austin journeyed to San Antonio in 1820 the region was deserted. Part of Seguin's mission to Natchitoches in 1821, when he met Austin, was to proclaim the king's pardon to those who had fled and invite them to return.[4] Doubly reassured by the success of the revolution, many did return within the next three years and reoccupy what was left of their former homes. Preceding and accompanying them went certain Americans. Some were the sediment left by the waves of revolutionary invasions. Others claimed to have been driven from Louisiana by floods in the Mississippi and stopped on the frontier by exaggerated rumors of Austin's difficulties and reports of drought and famine on the Brazos. Intending at first, perhaps, to move to the interior, they settled down to make a crop and ended by erecting cabins, clearing farms, and building gins and school houses.[5]

Of these squatters, some of whom were men of considerable means, there were four well-defined groups besides those around Nacogdoches. Three were within the border reservation around San Augustine, Tenaha, and Sabinetown, outside Edwards's grant. The other was on the lower Trinity and San Jacinto. The first three were outside any empresario grant; the fourth was partly in Austin's and partly in Edwards's territory.

None of the immigrants save those whom fortune favored by inclusion in Austin's colony had a shadow of title to their holdings; nor had many of the natives completed their titles before their exodus to the United States.

Seguin reported from Natchitoches in June, 1821, that the news of Moses Austin's concession had caused a rush to Texas and that families in the most destitute condition were already scattered from the Sabine to Nacogdoches and beyond. On his return, he collected thirty-six men in Nacogdoches, as we saw, and gave them a provisional organization under James Dill as alcalde and commandant, but told them that the government did not want them to remain in

---

[4] Austin to ———, July 1, 1821.
[5] Petition of Settlers to Saucedo, February 10, 1824, General Land Office of Texas, Vol. 53, p. 197; Petition to the President, March 10, 1827, and Ahumada to Bustamante, April 1, 1827, Transcripts from Department of Fomento, Mexico; Settlers on Trinity and San Jacinto to Saucedo, November 26, 1827, General Land Office, Translations, 135–137.

the province.[6] Nevertheless they did not leave; others came.[7] By 1825 the population of this border district was estimated at sixteen hundred.[8] Dill continued to act as alcalde through 1822 and possibly through 1823. Juan Seguin was elected to the office in 1824, with subordinate alcaldes for the neighboring district,[9] an arrangement made necessary by the increasing population. In 1825 Pedro Procela seems to have been elected at Nacogdoches, but upon his death a few months later the duties of the office devolved, in some way not recorded, on his son Luis, who signed himself alcalde *"interino,"* or *pro tem.* This, Edwards protested, was "acting as alcalde by *proxy,* a thing unheard of in a republican country"; [10] but his status raised no question with the political chief at San Antonio. The whole local government was irregular, like that established by Trespalacios on the Brazos and Colorado during Austin's detention in Mexico. There was no ayuntamiento.

The situation, then, was one which would call for a high order of understanding, judgment, self-control, tact, and mingled firmness and conciliation on the part of the empresario. Such a motley mixture of races, social classes, and good and bad characters has never since jostled elbows on the stage of American history except in the mining camps of California and Arizona—criminals of the old Neutral Ground, Spanish and French creoles, rough American frontiersmen, substantial planters accustomed to a gentler environment, and fragments of a dozen Indian tribes in varying degrees of civilization. Months before Edwards obtained his contract, the contemporary records are filled with accounts of conflicting land claims and crimes and violence ranging from murder through robbery, theft, and personal assault to the comparatively minor misdemea-

---

[6] Seguin to Martinez, June 23 (Nacogdoches Archives), August 19, 1821 (Bexar Archives); Austin's Journal in *Quarterly* of Texas State Historical Association, VII, 288–289.

[7] Governor Martinez wrote Gaspar López, December 1, 1821 (Fomento Transcripts), that five hundred families had crossed the boundary. Dill complained, January 21, 1822 (Nacogdoches Archives), that families continued to pour into the territory between Nacogdoches and the Sabine, making no report of themselves and asking no questions about the privileges that immigrants might claim.

[8] Bugbee, "The Texas Frontier," *Publications* of Southern History Association, IV, 105.

[9] Election return, January 16, 1824. Nacogdoches Archives.

[10] Yoakum, *History of Texas,* I, 238. Saucedo wrote the Governor, November 27, 1825 (Bexar Archives) an unverified report that Luis Procela was deposed by the Americans, that Dill was appointed and then deposed, and that at the time of writing he did not know who held the office. Documents in the Nacogdoches Archives do not, however, indicate any breach in Procela's tenure.

nor of kidnapping slaves from the United States for sale in Texas.[11]

Edwards's contract was in the stereotyped form, but three of its provisions were to give him trouble, and must be examined: (1) Article 2 provided that "all possessions with proper titles which may be found in Nacogdoches, and throughout its vicinity, shall be respected by the colonists under this contract. The empresario is charged with this duty; and in all cases wherein claims may be made by the original owners he is bound to protect their rights." (2) To enable Edwards to maintain order and exclude undesirables, he was authorized to organize and, until further orders, command the militia. And (3) after the introduction of one hundred families he was to ask for the appointment of a commissioner who should have authority to grant titles and establish towns. These provisions in Austin's grant, a primitive wilderness where white men had never settled, could cause no friction, but for Edwards the situation was fraught with difficulty. With the greatest prudence—and he was not prudent—he could hardly have avoided trouble in the administration of the first requirement; and he seems to have misinterpreted his powers—or the authorities understood that he did —under the other two.

Edwards and Leftwich returned from Saltillo through Texas in May, 1825, and one or the other, probably Leftwich, wrote Austin on the 12th [12] suggesting an agreement of the empresarios upon a uniform price for land and a uniform mode of local government. "I presume," the writer proceeded, "that you still adhere to your first price established, viz., 12½ cts. per acre, the exp^s of surveying and making the title [included], which I am of opinion is low enough when we take into consideration the trouble and hardships we have to undergo in settling a wilderness." Later, in the summer, Benjamin W. Edwards, brother of Haden, spent some time with Austin at San Felipe. It is evident from the correspondence which followed that their relations were frank and cordial and that they talked about many phases of the colonization business. Austin interpreted the colonization law to Edwards, and it is scarcely pos-

---

[11] There is an abundance of manuscripts in the Nacogdoches and Bexar Archives through 1822–25 to support this paragraph. See also Lester G. Bugbee's striking paper already cited, "The Texas Frontier, 1820–1825."

[12] The letter is unsigned, but the two men had been companions in suspense for nearly three years, and it no doubt represents the opinions of both.

sible that he did not recite the controversy settled the year before concerning the land fees.[13]

Haden Edwards, with his family, arrived at Nacogdoches in September[14] and within a month had that community seething with resentment. The cause of this was a notice posted at the principal street corners.

"To all who shall see the present [it read] know that I, Haden Edwards, empresario and military commandant of that portion of the state of Coahuila and Texas which has been conceded to me by the authorities of said state, and in virtue of the powers which have been delegated to me by those authorities, have decreed, and by the present do decree and order, that every individual, or family, resident within the limits of the specified territory and all those who claim to have a right to any part or parts of the land or lands of said territory shall immediately present themselves to me and show me their titles or documents, if any they possess, so that they may be received or rejected, according to the laws; and if they do not do this, the said lands will be sold, without distinction, to the first person who occupies them. Those who have valid titles will be obliged to bear the cost of proving them.[15] And by this notice I order that no person shall settle within the limits of my territory without my permission." [16]

Another proclamation on November 12 repeated this and warned squatters that the law recognized no preference to them and that if they did not immediately arrange with Edwards, their holdings would be sold to the first applicant.[17]

Now, the government's record on the claims of the old settlers is a consistent one and antedates the contract with Edwards, and even the national colonization law, so that it is not open to the charge of having shaped its policy, whether unreasonable or not, for Ed-

---

[13] Austin to B. W. Edwards, September 15, and Edwards's reply, October 1, 1825. Foote (*Texas and Texans*, I, 226), who wrote from a manuscript prepared by B. W. Edwards, says that he and Austin agreed that a breach with Mexico was ultimately inevitable and that they must go softly until they had introduced enough settlers to assure the success of a revolution, but there is much reason to question Edwards's statement.

[14] B. W. Edwards to Austin, October 1, 1825.

[15] "Quedando obligados los que tengan sus titulos competentes a pagar los gastos hechos para su mejora." This has usually been misinterpreted, "Those who have valid titles will be required to pay the cost of improvements [made on their lands by innocent purchasers]." See Yoakum, *History of Texas*, I, 239; Bancroft, *North Mexican States and Texas*, II, 100. Another form of the notice published by Edwards on November 12, 1825 (appendix to Empresario Contracts, Vol. 3, p. 145, General Land Office of Texas) reads, "y aquellos q^e puedan tener justos titulos, seran obligados a pagar la perfecion que se debe haser en estos."

[16] Appendix to Empresario Contracts, Vol. 3, p. 130, General Land Office of Texas. This is from a Spanish translation of the original English.

[17] *Ibid.*, Vol. 3, p. 145.

wards's undoing. In February, 1824, thirty-six squatters in the Ais
Bayou district complained to the political chief at San Antonio that
a certain Edmund Quirk claimed under a Spanish grant a hundred
and four sections, which swallowed all their improvements. They
were informed, they said, that his legal title did not exceed half a
league, the rest of the claim being based on purchase from the
Indians. They asked protection and relief, but Saucedo replied that
old claims must be presumed to be good until the government
could assemble the inhabitants of Nacogdoches, hold an inquest,
and determine the merits of all; and that in the meantime they
should evacuate their settlements.[18] A year later—and still before
the grant was made to Edwards—the old claimants sent a delegation to SanAntonio to request the return of the local archives, taken
there for safe-keeping in 1810, which they thought contained their
titles. Saucedo reported this to the governor, and was instructed by
him to furnish certified copies on request.[19] Writing the political
chief in June about Edwards's contract, the governor told him that
a commissioner would be appointed to seat the old settlers, whose
possessions Edwards was required to respect, as soon as the legislature defined the powers of such an officer.[20] The trouble was, of
course, as Saucedo explained, that the record often showed the titles
to be defective. In some instances the government had not been paid
for the land; in others the final decree of possession was lacking.
Some who no doubt believed themselves in good faith owners of the
land that their ancestors occupied found that they had nothing.[21]

While it is obvious enough that Edwards was justified in wanting to know as soon as possible what previous claims must be respected in his grant, his ultimatum shows unwarranted precipi-
tancy and entire lack of sympathy with equitable pretensions of the
wretched old settlers. In mitigation, it must be remembered that

[18] The petition is in Records, Vol. 53, p. 197, General Land Office; the answer, April 3,
1824, Nacogdoches Archives.
[19] Petition to Legislature, November 7, 1825, reciting visit to San Antonio in March,
Records of Land Office, Vol. 3, pp. 152–156; Saucedo to Governor, August 21, and
Governor's reply, October 7, 1825, Bexar Archives.
[20] Saucedo to Procela, July 6, 1825, quoting the governor's letter of June 17. Nacogdoches
Archives.
[21] Samuel Norris wrote Saucedo on receipt of a list of the papers at San Antonio, "Some
must have been extracted during the revolution, because there are many old settlers here
who formerly had titles and now they neither have them in their own possession nor are
they in that capital, though they delivered them in 1810 to the governor of the province."
May 16, 1826, Bexar Archives.

he had fretted away three years in Mexico under heavy expense waiting for his contract and that his impatience to recoup his losses quickly was natural and human. In further explanation of his proclamation, a tradition has developed in the history of Texas that a thriving business in forged land titles was being carried on at Nacogdoches; but if this is true, no contemporary documentary evidence of it is available.[22]

The first response of the old inhabitants to Edwards's proclamation was a petition to the legislature. They were Mexican citizens; they had served the country with arms in hand, defending its most sacred liberty; they did not want Edwards, a foreigner whom they did not know, and whose opinions they did not know, to command them or deprive them of their lands; and they asked therefore that they be granted the land in the coast and border reservations and twenty-five leagues around Nacogdoches besides, and be relieved of his interference.[23] A glimpse of the rising excitement and further evidence of Edwards's intemperateness is seen in a letter from Edwards to Austin two months later.

"I found on my return from your place [he wrote] that there had a considerable storm arisen, heavy threats to send me over the Sabine: but I came out in a Herricane and promised to send in irons any man who dared acknowledge the threat to Saltillo. Sounded the trump all around bidding defiance to all their threats and bidding them to leave the lands or come forward and make arrangements to pay for them. They are now all friendly, promise to pay me for their lands and spend their lives in my defence." [24]

The letter is noticeably cordial to Austin, the writer anticipating "some happy hours united with yourself and the Baron," and "wishing you every prosperity and happiness." At the same time, for

[22] Yoakum, *History of Texas*, I, 238; Bancroft, *North Mexican States and Texas*, II, 100; Brown, *History of Texas*, I, 132. These writers name José Antonio Sepúlveda as the chief offender, but even a superficial acquaintance with his deficient education and illiterate writing shows the impossibility of his forging such documents. It is significant that Foote, who had access to a long account written by Benjamin Edwards, does not mention this charge. Its foundation probably lies in the fact that Sepúlveda was commissioned by the old inhabitants to go to Bexar and get the proofs of their ownership supposed to be there. See Norris to Saucedo, January 1, 1826, Nacogdoches Archives.

[23] Petition to Legislature, November 7, 1825, Appendix to Empresario Contracts, Vol. 3, pp. 152–156, General Land Office. The reply, if there was any, is lacking. A somewhat similar suggestion was made by the political chief, that fifteen leagues square be granted to the town of Nacogdoches; but the governor told him that the law restricted municipal common lands to four square leagues, and in fact only one league was allowed. Saucedo to Governor, April 29, Arizpe to Saucedo, May 20, Torres to Saucedo, June 13, 1826. Bexar Archives.

[24] Haden Edwards to Austin, January 9, 1826.

some reason which does not appear, B. W. Edwards, traveling through Austin's settlement, was consumed with anger at Austin. "I am convinced he was Rong," wrote John P. Coles, "and I believe I satisfied him that he was Rong. For the want of paper I doo not Relate the particulars but we will speak of it when I see you." [25]

In the meantime, Edwards had begun to put his program into operation, collecting from a number of settlers on the Trinity the first payment on lands that they occupied, and taking at least one claim from a Mexican (Ignacio Sertuche) who could not produce his deed, and selling it to an American.[26] The price or fee, which he was reported to have fixed was $520 a league.[27] But for the fact that Austin had relinquished the contracts with his colonists for similar fees and substituted nominal charges under the colonization law, there would probably have been no opposition to this, for the squatters were anxious to obtain titles and would have considered this a reasonable charge for such security as Edwards had authority to give them. Edwards justified the charge with rare lack of passion in a letter to Austin of February 28. The colonization law recognized the right of the empresario to charge the colonists for his services and did not prescribe the amount; his own settlers and the better class of squatters approved his fee as a means of excluding the idle and vicious; so that, he declared, "I feel myself more than doubly justified in asking what I do for the good of the colony, and of the government in general, as you must admit as a candid man that one colonist who is willing and able to pay for the lands as offered is worth fifty of those indolent Idlers who barely live to exist and have no ambition or enterprise further." He was constantly being told, he said, that "Judge Austin gives land at Congress prices and says we have no right to ask or receive more"; but he had paid no attention to this, thinking that Austin no doubt heard many falsehoods about him from those who wished to set the empresarios at variance in the hope of reaping a benefit for themselves. He had been told, but did not credit it, that Austin had called a

[25] Coles to Austin, January 7, 1826.

[26] Edwards to Nathaniel Trammel, November 26, 1825, Nacogdoches Archives: receipt for $120, first payment on a league of land, lying half on each side of the Trinity and including the ferry. This was Sertuche's claim.

[27] Edwards to George Orr, receipt for $120, March 4, 1826, Appendix to Empresario Contracts, Vol. 3, p. 148, General Land Office; Saucedo to Governor, February 19, April 16, 1826; Norris to Saucedo, May 2, 20, 1826, Torres to Saucedo, June 27, 1826, all in Bexar Archives.

meeting of the settlers on the San Jacinto for March 4 to adopt a memorial to the government against him.

Austin explained in reply to this that he had called militia elections throughout his colony for March 4; that he had visited the San Jacinto district on his way home from an inspection of Galveston Bay and found the people there greatly inflamed by threats attributed to Edwards that he would drive them from their lands unless they paid him his price—although they had by special permission of the political chief already received titles from Austin; that he had reassured them about their titles; and had told them that it would be both undesirable and improper to address the government on the subject, so long as Edwards went no farther than threats. He then recounted in the bluntest possible language current reports—some of them, perhaps, untrue—of Edwards's imprudences and gave sage advice tested by his own knowledge and experience.

"I will here, with perfect candor and in friendship [he wrote] remark that your observations generally are in the highest degree imprudent and improper, and such as are calculated to ruin yourself and materially to injure all the American settlements; for example, you have publicly stated that you could have procured a grant for all the land on the east side of the Brazos, and taken it from the settlers, as you intended to do on the east side of the San Jacinto; that Saucedo was not governor or political chief of Texas and had no right to act, and that his orders were illegal; that the Spaniards around Nacogdoches were a set of 'Washenangoes,' and that you would put them all over the Sabine; that you had the absolute right of disposing of the land within your colony as you pleased, and the government would not make any grants, nor in any way interfere with you for six years; that you despised the class of people who were now settlers in the country, and only wanted rich men, and would drive away all the poor devils who had been the first to settle, unless they paid you your price. One moment's sober reflection will show you the imprudence and impropriety of such declarations as those above mentioned. . . .

"The truth is, you do not understand the nature of the authority with which you are vested by the government, and it is my candid opinion that a continuance of the imprudent course you have commenced will totally ruin you, and materially injure all the new settlements.

"These remarks are made in perfect friendship, although with blunt candor, and as such I hope will be received. I have taken no steps to injure you in any way, nor will I unless you interfere with the vested rights of the settlers of this colony. I have made no representations, nor ever had an idea of making any.

"I have not said, even to my brother, as much about you as I have now stated in this letter. If you will ask Mr. Orr to show you a letter I wrote him some time since, in answer to one of his letters requesting a copy of the colonization laws, you will see that, instead of fermenting discontent against you, I said all I could to promote harmony.[28] . . .

"You may, perhaps, think that I am too blunt and candid in my remarks, but there is one thing you must believe, or else do me an injustice, my candor proceeds from friendship and not from any desire to censure or wound your feelings, and I advise you to be more prudent in your remarks and observations generally. You have an extremely difficult and laborious task to perform; you will be watched with a jealous eye by every one, and the most innocent expression will be misunderstood or wilfully perverted, and nothing will injure you more than direct collisions with the old Spanish settlers in your colony, and I would advise the utmost prudence with them in particular." [29]

With trouble enough brewing over his land policy to ruin him, Edwards became involved in an election contest. On December 15, 1825, an alcalde for Nacogdoches was to be elected. Samuel Norris, one of the old inhabitants and a citizen, was opposed by Chichester Chaplin, Haden Edwards's son-in-law. The civil jurisdiction of Nacogdoches covered a vast area from the Neches River to the Sabine.[30] Chaplin received the votes of the squatters in the border reserve, and took possession of the local archives and assumed the powers of the office. Norris received the unanimous vote of the old inhabitants, who appealed to the political chief on the ground that the squatters, being foreigners, had no right to vote.[31] At the

[28] Austin to George Orr, March 10, 1826: "I very much regret that there should have arisen any discontent among the settlers on the Trinity in regard to the manner of procuring their lands; everything of this nature has a tendency to injure the progress of the new settlements generally, and I would with due respect to those settlers, and as their friend, and the friend of all the new settlements, recommend to them to be extremely cautious not to do anything of a violent or disorderly character towards the persons intrusted by the government with the superintendence of the new settlements. The utmost harmony should be cultivated, the agents of the government should be treated with respect, and, if cause of complaint exists against them, representations should be made to the proper authority in a mild manner, and without anything like passion or abuse. These ideas are respectfully suggested to you in friendship. They proceed from a sincere desire to see harmony prevail, and not from any disposition or desire on my part to intrude my advice or censure on any person. . . . I can have no object in wishing harmony but the prosperity of the country, for my own conduct in regard to receiving settlers will not be regulated or in any manner influenced by what the other empresarios may do."

[29] Austin to Haden Edwards, no date (about March 15, 1826). Edwards's interference in the San Jacinto district is further evidenced by an order of March 3 (Nacogdoches Archives) removing the captain of militia from office and calling a new election.

[30] Saucedo to Governor, August 2, 1825. Bexar Archives.

[31] Procela to Saucedo, January 1, 1826, Nacogdoches Archives; Edwards, proclaiming Chaplin elected, January 1, Chaplin to Saucedo, January 5, and Procela to Saucedo, January 5, 1826, Bexar Archives.

same time they recited all their other complaints against Edwards. This document reached the political chief with a letter from Edwards telling of his various troubles, charging them principally to Sepúlveda and to Luis Procela, the outgoing acting alcalde, and hinting "very delicately," says Yoakum,[32] "that if these turbulent characters had been citizens of the United States, he would have dealt with them in a summary manner, as he [would in that case have] had a right to do under his contract." Remembering that this was written when Edwards was riding the "Herricane" and "sounding the trump all around,"[33] the delicacy of his hinting is questionable. Saucedo's reply annulled the election of Chaplin; confirmed that of Norris and instructed him to demand the archives; declared that Edwards had no authority to demand a showing of titles by the old settlers, or to sell any land; and ordered Norris to inform Trammel that he had no title to Sertuche's land, which he had bought from Edwards, and must restore it.[34]

It seems likely that Chaplin's supporters voted for him with no sense of impropriety, for in the final clash most of them stood by the government; nor is it certain that either Chaplin or Edwards wanted to usurp the office. When notified by Norris on March 19 that the chief had ratified his election and ordered him to take possession of the archives, Chaplin responded with the perfectly proper and natural request to see the order. Norris replied that Chaplin could come to his house and examine it, and Chaplin insisted that it should be formally presented and that he be given time to list the documents in the archives so that Norris could receipt for them. This passion for propriety was not consistent with the record of the Edwards party as the old settlers viewed it, and Norris believed that Chaplin was simply quibbling for time. He therefore called for assistance, and Sepúlveda, recently elected captain of a company of eighty-two, had detailed a force to take the

---

[32] Yoakum, *History of Texas*, I, 238.

[33] See above, 154. Yoakum had Edwards to Saucedo, January 5, 1826, but it is not now accessible.

[34] Saucedo to Norris, February 13, 1826. Bexar Archives. Yoakum (*History of Texas*, I, 240) tells a somewhat circumstantial story about Sertuche's case, for which he cites no authority. One suspects that it was based on oral tradition. While no effort has been made here to examine the claim, a casual reading of the documents indicates that Sertuche had at least a shadow of title and that Edwards sold the land to Nathaniel Trammel (see receipt from Edwards to Trammel, for $120, November 26, 1825, Nacogdoches Archives), who, contrary to Yoakum's account, was trying to oust Sertuche.

papers when Chaplin announced his readiness to give them up.[35] In a report to the political chief Chaplin denied any intention of disobedience and made an effort at conciliation. "It was at the solicitation of many good citizens that I took this office [he said] I have never asked for it, and I have written this communication solely to justify my conduct as a good Mexican citizen, and not to accuse any one. Norris is a man of substance, very capable of pleasing all, and I hope that he will continue with much honor in the exercise of his office." [36]

By the same mail Edwards wrote, not so tactfully perhaps, questioning the chief's ruling and complaining of Sepúlveda, James Gaines, and others as disturbers of the peace. Saucedo replied that Norris had received the majority of the legal votes and was entitled to the office, but that if he was not qualified to hold it, Edwards might appeal to the government; that his complaints against individuals should be investigated by the alcalde and the appropriate penalties assessed if they were guilty; that in the matter of the land claims nothing could be done until the appointment of a commissioner, who would proceed according to his instructions and the law; that the law itself gave a preference to Mexicans until forfeited by bad conduct, and that he considered Sepúlveda and Sertuche entitled to the preference. In conclusion he warned Edwards that some charges were pending against himself, growing out of his proclamation of October 25, one for declaring himself military commandant of that section and the other for ordering old settlers to produce titles.[37]

From this point Edwards was doubtless to some extent the victim of persecution. The record for the next few months reads like the bickering of quarrelsome children. The old inhabitants had been much alarmed by Edwards's threats of confiscation. The news spread that he was in the shadow of the chief's displeasure, and they had many scores against him which it now seemed safe to pay. They poured their tales into the ears of the alcalde, ignorant and officious, and he relayed them to Saucedo, offended and suspicious over Ed-

---

[35] Norris to Saucedo, March 22, 1826, Nacogdoches Archives, gives a circumstantial account. The correspondence that passed on the 19th is in the Bexar Archives.
[36] Chaplin to Saucedo, April 3, 1826, Bexar Archives.
[37] Saucedo to Haden Edwards, May 1, 1826, Bexar Archives. The contents of Edwards's letter of April 3 can be inferred from Saucedo's reply.

ward's lack of deference. Saucedo's rulings, in turn, shaped to fit conditions that he did not fully understand, reached Edwards more or less distorted, to be further misapprehended by him.

Besides contumacious persistency in selling land, the principal offenses charged to Edwards were that he never presented his credentials officially to the alcalde; that he had a larger supply of arms at his house than innocence of purpose required; that with his approval Chaplin tried unsuccessfully to enlist the inhabitants of the border in a plan for revenge after his removal from office; that he denied the authority of the political chief and said that his orders must come from Saltillo; that he had gone to New Orleans to sell the colony; that he had sold it for $120,000; that he was inciting a revolution; and, finally, that he was returning to Nacogdoches with seven hundred men prepared for war. Other charges were: abusing Sepúlveda, selling salines, founding a town without authority and upon the claim of an old inhabitant, and opposing the slavery article of the state constitution.[38]

Saucedo's response to most of these reports has been noticed—that the commissioner, when appointed, would determine the validity of titles and that Edwards had no authority to disturb the old inhabitants; that the commissioner alone had power to found towns; that money paid Edwards for land could be recovered, because he had no right to sell it; and that if Edwards, in the face of all warnings, continued to be guilty of punishable offences, he should be arrested and sent, if necessary, to San Antonio for trial.[39]

Haden Edwards went to the United States in May to interest "men of influence and capital in his grant" [40]—which was probably at the bottom of the report that he went to sell the colony—and left Benjamin W. Edwards in charge at Nacogdoches. Benjamin Edwards did not understand Spanish. There was no publication of official documents; and everything reached him by rumor and gossip. Neither he nor his brother seems ever to have understood the injunction that the empresario could not sell land. Saucedo had

[38] Authority for these statements is too voluminous to cite conveniently. Most of them are covered in: Norris to Saucedo, April 4, May 2, 16, 30, September 14, 1826, Appendix to Empresario Contracts, Vol. 3, pp. 134, 137, 138, 140, 160; and in Nacogdoches Archives, Norris to Saucedo, May 16, September 5, October 17, 1826.

[39] Saucedo to Norris, February 13, May 17, 18, 1826, Bexar Archives and Nacogdoches Archives.

[40] B. W. Edwards to Austin, July 21, 1826.

ruled thus against Austin in 1824—arbitrarily and illegally, Austin thought, though he accepted the ruling—but Edwards paid no attention to this, and made no attempt even to sustain the fee allowed by the provision of the colonization law which recognized contracts between empresario and colonist.[41] The immigrants, to whom the ruling was in fact favorable, understood it to mean that they could not obtain land from Edwards at all. The governor's decision that the civil jurisdiction of Nacogdoches should extend to its ancient limits, from the Neches to the Sabine, was misrepresented to mean that only the alcalde and ayuntamiento could grant land there, though most of it lay in the twenty league reserve and could not be acquired without the concurrent approval of the state and federal governments. Taking his stand on the nominal fact that the government was republican, and assuming that its institutions and procedure must perforce conform to those of the United States, Benjamin Edwards was surprised that no formal indictment of his brother was presented, no investigation made, and no defense heard. He was honestly bewildered, and suspected forgery of some of the documents of which he was told. "It cannot be," he wailed, "that the fundamental principles of a free constitution, cemented by the blood of thousands, is thus trampled under foot, and its most sacred principles violated in the persons of Americans, after being invited into this country with a guarantee of their rights and liberties." In addition to the uneasiness caused by the uncertainty over titles, the alcalde, controlled by James Gaines, a mean and spiteful man, made a travesty of justice, he said, administering it in a way that was conducive alone "to the *interest* of the *officers* and subservient to their private feelings against those who are obnoxious to them." They charged twenty and twenty-five dollars as costs in a single suit, he said, and Sepúlveda, who had evidently become the local revenue collector, was charging exorbitant fees for stamped paper.[42] He was alarmed at the danger of an explosion, and threw himself upon

[41] In 1837 or 1838 Edwards told Mirabeau B. Lamar, who was collecting historical materials, that it was well understood at Saltillo when the colonization law was passed that the empresarios would charge twelve and a half cents an acre for land, and quotes Bastrop as saying that the governor thought the price too low. Lamar Papers, Texas State Library.

[42] Since the colonists were by law exempt from taxation for six years, Edwards questioned the validity of any charge for stamped paper for legal documents. He was, of course, in error. Whether the court costs which he mentions were excessive, would depend on the time consumed in the case and whether or not the sub-alcaldes of the neighboring districts went to Nacogdoches to participate in the trial.

Austin for "every information and advice as to what steps had best be taken." [43]

The situation was, indeed, as Edwards thought, approaching a crisis. Sepúlveda's company at Nacogdoches was supported by two large companies in the frontier settlements, composed for the most part of men of substance and character, though directed, apparently, by Gaines. [44] Seizing the pretext of Austin's preparation for a campaign against the Waco and Tahuacano Indians, one of Edwards's supporters offered to organize a company of a hundred men, which the alcalde, Norris, naturally forbade. [45] Nevertheless, some organization did take place, which aggravated the danger of brawls.

Austin's reply to Edwards's request for advice has not survived. Foote [46] quotes part of it. He expressed sympathy for Edwards and anxiety over the inevitable influence of the unfortunate situation upon immigration and progress.

"The subject [he said] has caused me great unhappiness, but I had determined not to interfere with it in any way—*it is a dangerous one to touch, and particularly to write about.* You wish me to advise you. I scarcely know what course will be best. The uncertainty as to the precise nature of the charges against you renders it difficult, nay impossible, to make a regular defence. I think, however, I would write directly to the Governor of the State. Give him a full statement of facts and a very minute history of the acts of your principal enemies, and their opponents, and their manner of doing business in every particular, both in regard to your brother as well as all others. State the general situation of the country, the confusion and difficulties which exist, and the causes of them, etc., in order that the government may have the whole subject fully before them, and be enabled to judge of the motives that have influenced those who have been most clamorous against you. Write in *English,* and make an apology for doing so, as that it is impossible to procure translators, etc. I advise the utmost caution and prudence on your part and that of all your friends as to your expressions, for every word you utter will probably be *watched and reported if considered exceptionable.*"

[43] B. W. Edwards to Austin, July 21, 1826.

[44] Sepúlveda to Saucedo, March 23, Norris to Saucedo, March 22, April 11, Muster Roll of Captain Theodore Dorset's Company of Ayish Bayou (seventy-one men), April 1, 1826, all in Nacogdoches Archives.

[45] Thompson to Austin, July 22, 1826; Austin to Saucedo, August 11; Saucedo to Norris, August 23 (Nacogdoches Archives); Norris to Austin, September 5. Theodore Dorset wrote Norris (Nacogdoches Archives), September 4, that Thompson wished to get a company of vagabonds organized so as to prevent the expulsion of bad characters from the country.

[46] Foote, *Texas and Texans,* I, 269–270.

The advice to write to the governor, Edwards followed—no doubt to the best of his ability. But that the tone of the letter would offend a Mexican official can be inferred from Yoakum's observation that it "was worthy of a freeman, and in a free country would have been applauded." [47]

The decree of the government was already written, however, and this letter did not affect it. When Saucedo wrote Norris on February 13 telling him to inform Edwards that he had no authority to interfere in the town's public business, to elect an alcalde, or to appoint militia officers, he added the warning that "if he continues such proceedings, the political chief will be compelled to make an energetic representation to the supreme government for annulling his contract and expelling him from that territory." Luckily, he said, the government had already turned its attention to that frontier, and he expected a permanent military force to be established there. Reporting Edwards's offenses to the governor, Saucedo observed that it would be difficult to correct them after a considerable number of colonists were settled; and "who knows," he asked, "that they will not try to separate from the state and unite all the territory that they occupy to their native country?" [48]

Meantime, Edwards's hasty proclamation of October 25 had reached the eyes of the federal authorities, and the war department was writing at the request of the president to inquire what office Haden Edwards held and whether he had authority to command the militia as he claimed. Saucedo in reply recited the terms of the contract, which empowered Edwards to organize his colonists to exclude bad characters and maintain order, but explained that this gave him no right to interfere at Nacogdoches and assume the title of military chief. Colonel Mateo Ahumada, commanding at San Antonio, offered the curious interpretation that Edwards's authority would not begin until after he had settled the eight hundred families of his contract, when one would naturally expect it to end. Edwards belonged to the class of men [said Saucedo] who knew no law but that of the rifle and who looked upon the Mexican with contempt; he feared that Edwards would attempt to make himself independent as soon as he found himself in force; and to guard

---

[47] Yoakum, *History of Texas*, I, 243. The letter, which was dated September 5, is not available.
[48] Saucedo to Norris, February 13, and Gonzales, February 19, 1826, Bexar Archives.

against this he urged the establishment of a permanent garrison at Nacogdoches.[49] Saucedo continued to din his fears into the ears of the governor, who passed them on to the federal government. On May 20 the governor instructed him to apprise Edwards of the displeasure with which his proceedings were viewed and tell him that if they were not corrected he would lose his contract. Before this warning reached Nacogdoches the president had issued an order for the immediate expulsion of Edwards.[50]

This summary command assigned for its justification a report from the governor on March 13 recounting the procedure of Edwards, and Saucedo's fears of secession. The governor's decree recited three reasons for annulment of the contract and expulsion: (1) Edwards's insulting the dignity and usurping the authority of the state by the proclamation of October 25, "falsely styling himself military commander," and requiring the inhabitants to show titles or have "their lands sold to the highest bidder"; (2) despoiling some of the inhabitants and giving their lands to others; (3) selling part of the land intended for the colony and appropriating the money, as if he were "absolute Lord and Master of those lands." Colonists introduced by Edwards, however, if they fulfilled the legal qualifications, would be admitted.[51] The first charge was literally true, though it should be said for Edwards that he was probably entirely sincere in believing that his contact authorized him to command the militia of the region. He did "despoil" some of the old inhabitants, though he would not have admitted that term. The third charge apparently has no better foundation than the reports that he had gone to the United States to sell the colony.

It seemed a simpler matter, however, to issue such a decree than to execute it. By the president's order the secretary of war instructed the commandant of the Eastern Interior Provinces to put it into

[49] Pedraza to Elosua, February 25, 1826, Appendix to Empresario Contracts, Vol. 3, p. 129, General Land Office; Ahumada to Elosua, April 2, 1826, Nacogdoches Archives; Saucedo to Elosua, April 16, 1826, Bexar Archives.

[50] Saucedo to Governor, April 30, 1826, Appendix to Empresario Contracts, Vol. 3, p. 135, General Land Office. Governor to Saucedo, May 20, 1826, transmitted by him to Norris, June 1, Nacogdoches Archives; Same to same, March 3, August 23 (quoting president's order of June 3), Translations of Empresario Contracts, 105, 108, General Land Office.

[51] Preceding note; and Governor to Saucedo, August 23, 1826, Translations of Empresario Contracts, 105.

effect. That officer, having no regular troops at Nacogdoches, begged to be excused; and the governor passed the order to the political chief, to be carried out by the alcalde of Nacogdoches with the local militia. This seemed to Saucedo a very large undertaking, and he "pocketed" the order until the end of November.

This was the situation, though Benjamin Edwards did not know it, when he wrote the governor. His letter was received by the vice-governor, Victor Blanco, who thought it "disrespectful," "sarcastic," "exceedingly absurd," and "offensive to the dignity of the government." The case was already closed, Blanco said, but since Edwards pretended not to know the reasons for the government's action, he would enlighten him. He then recited the various charges against Haden Edwards and commented upon them. Edwards had no right of property in his grant, he had not bought it; he had no right to exact a price for settlement in it; he was not commander of the militia, and could not become such until he had settled the full eight hundred families contracted for;[52] he had no right to enter the country dictating laws as a sovereign, and if now, in his weakness, he was so arrogant, what might the government not expect when he grew strong? In short, Blanco concluded, "He has lost the confidence of the government. I doubt his fidelity, and it is imprudent to admit men who begin their career by dictating laws as if they were sovereigns." If Edwards objected to the decree, he added, he could first leave the country and then appeal to the national government for redress.[53]

This letter is an instructive example of the psychology of suspicion and misunderstanding. The bald facts alleged were in the main true—though their spirit was at least to some extent misconstrued—but the procedure was wholly *ex parte,* and Edwards had no opportunity to question or explain. His course was certainly impetuous and imprudent, but it probably did not occur to him that he was transcending the authority of his contract or injuring the dignity of the state. On the other hand, it is entirely possible that Blanco was sincere and that he never realized the arbitrariness

---

[52] This, of course, was a palpably unreasonable interpretation of the contract.

[53] Blanco to B. W. Edwards, October 20, 1826, Translations of Empresario Contracts, 106–108, General Land Office. Blanco repeated this in substance on November 3 to Haden Edwards, who, after returning from the United States, wrote the governor on October 2. See Translation of Empresario Contracts, 108.

of his decree or its cruel disproportion to the gravity of the offense. It is futile to inquire whether a contract could be annulled by executive proclamation without judicial process. Edwards had spent three years in Mexico to little purpose if he expected the legal and constitutional standards of the United States to control that inexperienced and groping republic. Nor was his own course clear of the charge of autocracy.

On November 22 a curious incident was enacted at Nacogdoches. The official record reads like burlesque, but the actors seemed to take it seriously. Some forty men rode into town, seized Norris and Sepúlveda, built fortifications, took possession of the alcalde's archives and read them at ease, organized a "court martial," proclaimed a reward of a hundred dollars for James Gaines—dead or alive—brought Haden Edwards into court and vainly invited complaints against him, tried Norris and Sepúlveda, convicted them, and declared them deserving of death, but commuted the sentence to removal from office and perpetual disbarment from office in future. The charges against Norris were corruption and oppression, extortion, "treachery to the people," murderous intent, and other offenses; those against Sepúlveda were forgery, treachery, inciting to theft, swindling, and being a person of notorious and infamous character. Having deposited the archives with Joseph Durst, whom they declared temporary alcalde, the band liberated the prisoners on the 25th and quietly dispersed.[54] Some of the specifications against Norris were serious enough; some were for the simple discharge of official duty, as, for example, validating stamped paper for legal documents, which the plaintiffs erroneously believed to be contrary to the law exempting them from taxation; and some are amusing now but were irritating, of course, to the sufferers, as, that Norris imprisoned Leonard Dubois thirty days "for ironically calling Hosea Sepulver an honest man," and that he wrote the governor "volumes of slanderous falsehood" about the people, and incessantly called on the governor for troops to put down rebellion "which he falsely states exists here." One of the counts against Sepúlveda was that of requesting a man to steal a

[54] Minutes of the Court Martial, November 23–25; Torres to Saucedo, November 22, and Proclamation of Reward for Gaines, November 25, Bexar Archives; Reports of Torres, Sepúlveda, and Norris to Saucedo, November 28, and Durst to Saucedo, November 29, 1826, Nacogdoches Archives.

mule for him and promising that if prosecuted, "he would clear him with his pen, as he had done many a one before." To some of the participants the proceeding could have meant no more than a huge frolic, but the authorities were in no mood to regard it charitably.

Austin, who knew that troops were on the point of marching from San Antonio, wrote to two of the men with whom he was on cordial terms:

"I have heard with the deepest regret and astonishment of the late proceedings against the authorities of Nacogdoches. It appears as tho the people in your quarter Have run mad or worse. They are destroying themselves, building up the credit of their enemies with the Gov^t and jeopardising the prospects of hundreds of innocent families who wish to live in peace and quietness in the country. The new colonies are yet in their infancy and the Gov^t will either protect or crush them according to the opinion it may form as to the character they will assume when arrived at full maturity. . . . These measures were in the highest degree imprudent and illegal, for the law points out the mode of punishing officers in this Gov^t from the president down to an alcalde or a corporal. . . .

"There is one way for you all to save yourselves and *only one,* and that is to go in person and present yourselves to the chief of the department of Texas. State your grievances, and acknowledge at once and without any reserve or stiff and foolish republican obstinacy that wrong steps were taken, that the attack on the alcalde was totally wrong—that you were misled by passion or something else (for it puzzles me to frame excuses for such conduct) and petition the Governor to order a general court of inquiry in which the conduct of the alcalde and Gain[e]s and all others and your own should be fully and fairly and openly investigated, and that their punishment should fall on the heads of those who merited it without respect of persons. . . . Let the Americans put aside their rifles and be guided by more prudence and reason than they have been. Let them submit to the Gov^t and be obedient to the laws and only seek redress in the legal mode. . . . No matter what Norris may have done, the party who entered Nacogdoches have done as bad and are liable to heavy punishment. . . .

"You may think this letter severe. My object is to befriend you as far as I can consistent with my duty and so far as I believe you merit it and no farther. You want strong medicine. You may deem the course I have pointed out an unpleasant one or make a thousand imaginary objections, *but you may* rely on it that it is the only one that can save you. You *must* humble yourselves before the Government and that *immediately.*" [55]

[55] Austin to John A. Williams and B. J. Thompson, December 14, 1826.

At the same time Austin wrote reassuringly to Saucedo: "It appears from information just received from Nacogdoches that there is no party in that district opposed to the government and that the movements there proceeded from private and personal feelings against some individuals, and particularly against Gaines, Sepúlveda, and Norris; but the reports vary and it seems to me that the surest way to learn the truth is to investigate both sides of the matter in the place where the movements took place." [56] Austin's object is obvious. It was to avert a clash and get a judicial investigation launched which would have disclosed that all the annoyances were not on one side, and that the apparent disobedience and disrespect on the part of the immigrants were largely the effect of ignorance. The game was, in fact, not yet irretrievably lost. General Bustamante had just written Ahumada that he knew the reports from Nacogdoches were grossly exaggerated,[57] and Saucedo was a kindly man and not beyond the reach of reason.[58]

Saucedo and Colonel Ahumada with a considerable force set out from San Antonio on December 13.[59] They arrived at San Felipe on January 3, 1827, and were delayed there three weeks by rain and bad weather.[60] On December 16, with a handful of men, Benjamin Edwards rode into Nacogdoches; paraded through the village under a red and white flag, inscribed, "Independence, Liberty, and Justice"; seized and fortified the "stone house"; and proclaimed the Republic of Fredonia. It is doubtful whether Edwards could at any time command thirty men,[61] and subsequent state-

[56] Austin to Saucedo, December 16, 1826.

[57] Bustamante to Ahumada, November 29, 1826, Translations of Empresario Contracts, 110, General Land Office.

[58] Foote says (*Texas and Texans*, I, 231) that Saucedo was "represented to have been a beastly sot, altogether hostile in his feelings towards the settlers from the United States." This is probably the basis for Yoakum's statement (I, 232) followed by Brown (I, 118), that he was greatly prejudiced against the Americans.

[59] J. A. Navarro to Inhabitants of Nacogdoches, December 28, 1826, Nacogdoches Archives. They had expected to march on the 2d (Saucedo to Blanco, December 1, Bexar Archives), but were delayed by a Comanche raid on San Antonio. On the 10th they expected to march the next day with a hundred and ten infantry and fifty cavalry (Ahumada to Elosua, December 10, 1826, Nacogdoches Archives).

[60] Saucedo to Blanco, January 9, 1827, Bexar Archives.

[61] The point cannot be discussed here in detail. Foote (*Texas and Texans*, I, 251, 252) implies that he had but fifteen when he entered Nacogdoches, but says that "In a day or two their ranks were swelled by nearly two hundred colonists residing in remote neighborhoods." He then goes on to explain how they were reduced again to "not more than fifteen" on January 4 (p. 258). Patricio de Torres wrote Austin from Nacogdoches on December 16 that they did not number more than fifty when all were united and that the force then was only thirty. John C. Morrison found the town on December 20 in possession of "thirty or forty men" (see his declaration of January 11, 1827).

ments from some of the participants indicate that they had little heart in the movement.[62] The inhabitants of the border were almost to a man against the insurrection, but, over-estimating its strength and fearing the Indians that Edwards had attached to his party and others who might take advantage of the general confusion to ravage and plunder, their first feeling was one of helplessness and dismay. Neutrality or flight seemed to them the only alternatives, and many began to move across the Sabine.[63]

The Indians were, in fact, the chief danger in the situation. Richard Fields, the principal leader of the Cherokees, smarting under a sense of personal wrong and disappointed in the effort to obtain from the government land which he believed had been promised his people in 1822, and Dr. John Dunn Hunter, an enigmatic philanthropist who had interested himself in the fortunes of the Cherokees, made a treaty of alliance with the Fredonians on December 21, 1826. The substance of the agreement was that the Indians should have the territory west of the Bexar-Nacogdoches road from Red River to the Rio Grande and that the whites should have the rest of the province. Premium lands of empresarios and individual possessions in either district should be recognized, provided the owners did not forfeit them by opposing independence. Fields, however, evidently acted without authority of the tribe and in opposition to the war chiefs, Bowl and Mush. He and Hunter were never able to muster more than thirty warriors, and half of those withdrew upon finding the few Fredonians in Nacogdoches engaged in a drunken brawl.[64]

It is possible that the Edwards brothers had not counted on support from the Cherokees, and that they regarded the treaty as a gift of the gods.[65] But it was perfectly obvious that they had no

[62] Thomas Hastings testified, February 5, 1827, that when the Fredonians entered Nacogdoches he was keeping a store there. They told him that they were going to compel all the Americans to join, and in order to save his property he did join them, making preparation, however, as fast as possible to leave the place (Nacogdoches Archives). Burril J. Thompson, February 17, said that he never favored independence; that he was driven to resist the tyranny of Norris, but did not wish to oppose the government.

[63] Bean to Austin, December 31, 1826, quoting Elisha Roberts of Ais Bayou. Also "Life of A. Horton," *Quarterly* of Texas State Historical Association, XIV, 305–308.

[64] For this treaty and the history of the Cherokees in Texas see the article by E. W. Winkler in *Quarterly* of Texas State Historical Association, VII, 95–165, and the documents there quoted and cited. In all its relations to the Indians the writer of this study used his material critically, forcefully, and accurately, but for the Fredonian insurrection, which was merely incidental to his study, he was influenced by Foote's flatulent oratory.

[65] According to Foote, *Texas and Texans*, I, 247–251, the overture came from Hunter,

chance of success unless they could get assistance from the United States and from Austin's colony. For this they relied on Benjamin Edwards's oratory and the readiness of the American frontiersmen to respond to the cry of oppression and dash into a fight with a despised "foreigner" without asking questions. The first flood of eloquence was directed, on Christmas day, to the inhabitants of Pecan Point, on Red River. "Enticed" from their native country by fair promises and a guarantee of rights and liberties, said Edwards, the insurgents found themselves basely deceived. They had obtained no land, their slaves were about to be liberated by the adoption of the state constitution, military despotism was substituted for freedom, citizens had been seized by a brutal soldiery, bound hand and foot, and dragged into exile or incarcerated in dungeons at the will of a petty tyrant. Their fathers had poured out their blood in willing torrents upon the altar of liberty to resist oppression; should the sons of such fathers do less? No! They had embarked in the glorious cause with a determination to be freeman or to perish under the flag of liberty. They were able and willing to carry on the struggle alone, but would welcome assistance.[66] During the next two days similar addresses went to various inhabitants of Austin's colony;[67] and, finally, one "To the citizens of the United States of North America." [68] The settlers need not hazard much, said Edwards to Austin's colonists: "We can send you an ample force to secure the people of that colony, and will do it the moment we ascertain they are for Independence. Our friends in the United States [he added] are already in arms, and only waiting for the word." [69]

In the meantime, Austin was exerting every effort to pacify the insurgents and induce them to throw themselves on the mercy of the government; and, failing that, to keep the hot-headed members of his own colony from making a false step while he persuaded

---

who had found the Indians on the verge of war with the settlers and diverted them to war against the government in alliance with the Fredonians. But Foote was not above manufacturing this explanation to avert from his hero, Benjamin Edwards, the odium of inciting the Indians.

[66] B. W. Edwards and H. B. Mayo to Inhabitants of Pecan Point, December 25, 1826.

[67] On December 26 to James Ross, Aylett C. Buckner, and Jesse Thompson, and on the 27th to Bartlett Sims. The letters are published in Wooten (ed.), *A Comprehensive History of Texas*, I, 518–521.

[68] Foote, *Texas and Texans*, I, 272–276. The document is undated.

[69] Edwards to Buckner, December 26, 1826.

the local officials to deal leniently with the offenders at Nacogdoches. No better examples can be found of Austin's tact, plausibility, straight-forward firmness, and uncommon good sense than some of his utterances at this time. To Burril J. Thompson, supposed to be the captain of a company and therefore an important man, he wrote on December 24: "We are now in a distant and new country from that of our first acquaintance, and in another Gov^t with which you are almost as much a stranger as you are to its language, and every tie that can bind former friends and acquaintances together certainly ought to operate with renewed force here. We were friends in Missouri, we ought to be friends in Texas, and I have taken up my pen to write you as a friend who takes an interest in your welfare and I will therefore speak with the frankness of friendship." He then proceeded, in substance: You have committed a great error, and made the words of your enemies true. The government was ready to investigate the conduct of Norris and to punish him if guilty; it annulled Edwards's contract because it was convinced that he was speculating at the expense of the settlers, whom it wished to protect. You think that the government has no force to move against you. That is a delusion that will ruin you. You think this colony will join you; some think that the people of the United States will aid you. Absurd! The government can march five thousand men into Nacogdoches in two months, and every man in this colony will join them. There is talk of your calling out the Indians from Red River to the Rio Grande—unbelievable of Americans! However, the situation can still be saved; disband your company, call a meeting of the honest and honorable men of your community, and address a statement to the political chief, expressing entire submission and obedience to the government. "I do not wish any person basely to submit to oppression, but it is not submitting to oppression to submit to the laws, more especially when we have voluntarily pledged ourselves to obey those laws by removing to the country."

"Do not let designing men deceive you as to the part the people of this colony will take [Austin concluded]. They are *unanimous* in disapproving all such violent proceedings and they will all be faithfull to the Gov^t of their adoption, and if necessary take up arms in its defense. . . . I will befriend you all so far as I can consistent with my duty to the Gov^t but I am a Mexican citizen and officer and *I will sacrifice my life before I will violate my duty and oath of office."*

Reiterating this to Thompson on January 1, Austin then turned to the task of shaping the attitude of his own colonists. In an address to the different districts of his settlement he pointed out the unreasonableness of the insurgent leaders and the duty of the colonists to support the government, and asked for thirty volunteers to accompany Saucedo and Ahumada, who were approaching San Felipe.[70] A few days later, after the arrival of these officers, he issued a particularly strong address.

"Put the question to your own bosoms and ask what would you as citizens of the U. S. of the north living in that nation think or say, should a few foreigners settled without legal authority on the frontier immagine that the local subordinate officers who had charge of them had done them an injustice, and should for that cause without first seeking the legal remidy, condemn, abuse, and vilify the whole American people and rise in open rebellion against the Gov^t, calling in the aid of savage allies and desperados to wage a war of desolation and massacre against the inhabitants of the frontier? What would you think of such foreigners? What would you do if called on by your Gov^t to march against them? As patriots, as friends to the cause of liberty and virtue and justice you would say reclaim them, convince them of their delusions by reason and persuasion, and should these fail put them down by force of arms and expel them [from] the country. You are now placed precisely in the situation above indicated—you are now Mexicans, and you owe the same duties to the Government of your adoption that you once owed to that of your nativity."

The Mexican government was still in its infancy, he continued, the state government just beginning, incipient and provisional, so that delays in the administration of justice were to be expected; those who looked back to the organization of state government in the United States would "probably find more collision, and as much cause of complaint arising out of the delays necessarily produced by overturning one Gov^t and establishing another," than could be found in Mexico.[71]

The colonists responded promptly with resolutions of loyalty.

[70] Austin to Inhabitants of Victoria, January 1, 1827. The document indicates that the same went to other districts.
[71] Austin to the colonists, about January 5, 1827.

How sincere they may have been, it would be impossible to determine. This was the course that Austin advised, and they trusted his judgment. All could unite, without violence to any conviction, in condemning alliance with the Indians, and all dwelt strongly upon that.[72]

Colonel Bean, Indian agent and guardian in general of the government's interests in East Texas, from his *rancho* on the Neches had already been doing yeoman service to prevent the spread of the insurrection; and with the arrival of the troops at San Felipe Saucedo began, perhaps with Austin's advice and certainly with his active cooperation, a campaign of conciliation to divide and pacify the insurgents. In an address of January 4 he explained that his object in going to Nacogdoches was to restore order, preserve the integrity of the territory, avoid if possible the disasters of war, and hear complaints of those unjustly treated by the local authorities. Edwards's contract was annulled, he said, on account of mismanagement, and on the faith of the government he assured them that none who had settled in the territory with the object of colonizing would be disturbed. The same day he and Ahumada wrote Fields, inviting him to a conference and assuring him that the Cherokees would certainly obtain lands as soon as the government was informed of what they wanted; while Austin wrote to Hunter, arguing the folly of his hoping to establish an independent Indian state between Mexico and the United States which both nations would think it necessary in self-defense to crush. On the 6th, finally, Saucedo wrote to Haden Edwards offering pardon to all who would lay down arms. Transmitting this to Edwards, Bean wrote, "It is not too late, and we have it in our power to forget past errors. More can be gained by prudence and conciliation than by war." To the governor, Saucedo justified the offer of amnesty by the weakness of his force, the distance from reinforcement, and the widespread ruin that might follow a general Indian rising. But Fields felt himself too deeply involved to retire, and the Edwards brothers declared that they "never would concede one inch, short of an acknowledgement on the part of the government of

[72] Duke to Austin, January 3, 4, 1827; Jones to Austin, January 3; Orr to Austin, January 17; resolutions of San Felipe, January 6, of Bravo, January 9, and of DeWitt's Colony, January 27.

their entire, free, and unmolested independence from the Sabine to the Rio Grande."[73]

This was the bluster of desperation. Fields and Hunter could not deliver the support of the Indians which they promised, though they eventually lost their lives in the attempt; the inhabitants of the border turned from neutrality to active hostility; and the insignificant number of Fredonians in Nacogdoches dwindled instead of increasing. On the night of the 28th, learning that troops and militia from Austin's colony were on the march, the insurgents abandoned the town and fled across the Sabine.[74]

The militia, requested by the political chief and called by Austin on January 22, including some men from the Atascosito settlement on the lower Trinity, reached the number of two hundred and fifty. Another hundred and fifty organized in the Ais Bayou district. Austin contributed a four-pounder to batter the fortifications of the "stone house." But except for an insignificant skirmish with the local government party on January 4, the "rebellion" passed without the firing of a shot. The main force arrived at Nacogdoches February 8, but a detachment of thirty-five men under Laurence Richard Kenny had preceded it, and, united with a small force that Colonel Bean had gathered, had done some scout duty and captured nine prisoners. To save expense the militia was now disbanded and sent home. Austin remained, serving as interpreter and by his influence with the Americans doing much, said Ahumada, to restore order.[75]

Reading between the lines of a letter to his secretary on March 4, one appreciates the importance of Austin's work as a peace maker —on the one side, against the vengeful efforts of James Gaines and the local patriots, persuading Saucedo and Ahumada to continue the policy of amnesty and conciliation, and, on the other, guarding

[73] Bean to Austin, December 28, 30, 1826; Ahumada to Fields, Saucedo to Fields, and Austin to Hunter, January 4, 1827; Ellis *et al.*, to Austin, January 22; Saucedo to inhabitants of Nacogdoches, January 4, to Edwards, January 6, and to Blanco, January 9, Bexar Archives; Bean to Edwards, January 6, Nacogdoches Archives.

[74] One's impatience with Foote's betrayal (I, 276–285) of the historian's obligation to tell the truth as he knows it gives way to amusement at the ingenuity of his grandiose distortions to conceal the *opéra bouffe* character of this exit.

[75] For this and the preceding paragraph: Norris to Ahumada, January 2, 1827, Bean, February 7, and Henry, February 9, to same, Nacogdoches Archives; Torres to Seguin, January 14, Saucedo to Blanco, February 12, and especially Ahumada's report to Bustamante, February 13, Bexar Archives; Saucedo to Austin, January 22, and Austin to Militia, January 22.

the anxious settlers in the border zone from making a false step which might upset this plan.

"I expected [he said] to have started home this day, but Ahumada has determined to visit the country as far as to the Sabine and insists on my accompanying him. I go with great reluctance for my thoughts and feelings are all in the colony and I am heartily tired of this country.

"It is perhaps a fortunate thing for me that I have learned patience in the hard School of an Empresario for I assure you that in this place I have had full use for all I possessed. Things are all settled here and I think tranquility is fully and firmly established but matters were in a dreadfull and a critical situation, and nothing but the greatest prudence has prevented the most serious disturbances. Gain[e]s and a few others blamed Ahumada and me, and me in particular, for the course I have advised, but I have a consolation that to me is worth more than the approbation of any man,—in the consciousness that I have done right. Fields and Hunter are certainly killed by the Cherokees and all the other leaders of the party have escaped over the Sabine and I advised a mild course with those who were compromitted in a secondary degree and Ahumada himself was in favor of such a course and adopted it and for this a few men blame me, but they are but few, for the whole country in general are gratified, and the Mexican character stands higher now than it ever did before. I hope the people of the Colony will be satisfied with me, for next to the approbation of my own conscience, *theirs* is worth more to me than all the world besides." [76]

Ahumada wrote General Bustamante that he had unfortunately found the opinion almost unanimous on the frontier that the government was arbitrary. He had tried to be as lenient as possible in restoring order and believed that he had been successful. He had released the prisoners, after an examination; and had refused to confiscate the property captured from the insurgents. [77]

By reconnaisance and investigation Ahumada learned that there were a hundred and sixty-eight families in the border strip between the Atoyac and Sabine. [78] Most of them, he thought, had settled there in good faith before the establishment of the border reserve, expecting to get land under the imperial colonization law. They had cleared farms and made many improvements—roads, ferryboats, mills and gins, and houses ranging in value from $200

[76] Austin to Samuel M. Williams, March 4, 1827, Rosenberg Library.
[77] Ahumada to Bustamante, February 13, 27, 1827, Bexar Archives.
[78] Saucedo to the Governor, March 19, 1827 (Bexar Archives) gives this number. A transcript of the letter from the Department of Fomento, Mexico, says 178. Another transcript from the same collection (Governor to Minister of Relations, March 18, 1828) says 144 families and 38 bachelors.

to $800. Each of the five gins could gin two bales of cotton a day, and the past year the district had marketed two hundred bales in Natchitoches. He thought that the present occupants should be recognized and given titles. They were being annoyed by old claimants, most of whom he was sure had themselves no legal rights, and to put an end to this friction he recommended the appointment of a commissioner to examine claims and exact payment for improvements when occupants were dispossessed. Grudgingly Saucedo concurred, though he believed it would be better to require the squatters to move to the interior. In 1828 both state and federal governments approved the settlement, but various disappointments followed and the settlers did not obtain titles until 1835.[79]

The Edwardses made some futile efforts to enlist support in Louisiana and continue the "rebellion," and for several months Fredonian sympathizers annoyed their loyal neighbors with taunts and threats, but the establishments of a permanent military force at Nacogdoches ended that.[80] As a matter of fact, the movement had attracted little attention in the United States, and Dr. John Sibley tersely summed up the opinion of the Louisiana border where it was best understood: "There never was a more silly, wild quicksotic scheme than that of Nacogdoches, and all sober honest thinking people here view it in the same light."[81]

To fervent souls who must fly to the relief of distress regardless of its cause or of the consequent suffering of innocent dependents there is no defense for Austin's course; but to others it needs no defense. The facts are simple. The government acted arbitrarily, and the punishment of the Edwardses exceeded their offense; but they also had acted with extreme imprudence. They were impetuous, stubborn, impractical, and inconsiderate, and brought their trouble upon themselves. Austin's advice, which would have avoided it, they disregarded; and the amnesty which his influence obtained from the political chief they rejected. Force alone was left. Austin and his colonists were Mexican citizens. Austin was a military officer. Their first duty was to the government; their

[79] Ahumada to Bustamante, April 1, 1827, Transcripts from Department of Fomento, Mexico; Saucedo to Blanco, April 18, 1827, Bexar Archives.

[80] Nicolas Flores to Francisco Ruiz, May 9, 1827; Ruiz to Ahumada, May 13; Norris to Saucedo, June 26; Saucedo to Ahumada, July 9; and many other documents—all in Bexar Archives.

[81] Sibley to Austin, Natchitoches, February 18, 1827; also Slocum to Austin, March 27.

second to themselves; and there was no conflict. Duty both to the government and to themselves demanded their cooperation in the suppression of the insurrection. Austin, with the happiness of four hundred families dependent upon him, naturally realized this. Expediency pointed in the same direction, for Mexico in 1827 could have mustered force to drive the Americans out of the province, but there is too much evidence to doubt that in addition to his desire to save his people Austin was sincerely and honestly loyal to Mexico.

CHAPTER VIII

The Struggle for Stabilizing Laws

AUSTIN compared his work to that of a farmer starting improvements in a virgin forest.

"Such an enterprise as the one I undertook in settling an un-inhabited country must necessarily [he said] pass through three regular gradations. The first step was to overcome the roughness of the wilderness, and may be compared to the labor of the farmer on a piece of ground covered with woods, bushes, and brambles, which must be cut down and cleared away, and the roots grubbed out before it can be cultivated. The second step was to pave the way for civilization and lay the foundation for lasting productive advancement in wealth, morality, and happiness. This step might be compared to the ploughing, harrowing, and sowing the ground after it is cleared. The third and last and most important step is to give proper and healthy direction to public opinion, morality, and education . . . to give tone, character, and consistency to society, which, to continue the simile, is gathering in the harvest and applying it to the promotion of human happiness. In trying to lead the colony through these gradations my task has been one of continued hard labor. I have been clearing away brambles, laying foundations, sowing the seed. The genial influences of cultivated society will be like the sun shedding light, fragrance, and beauty." [1]

Austin was now in the second stage of this analogy. His contracts were filling satisfactorily, and population was flowing also into DeWitt's colony. The Indians were no longer an extreme menace. The outcome of the Fredonian rebellion had placed the colonists high in the confidence of Mexican officials. The ground was cleared and the planting going on, but much cultivating remained to be done to assure the prosperity and happiness of the settlements. (1) Ports must be opened and shipping laws modified to promote trade with the Mexican coast and with Europe. (2) Constitutional local government and a convenient and efficient judicial system had to be established. (3) The colonists must be pro-

[1] Austin to Mrs. M. A. Holley, January 14, 1832.

tected from prosecution for debts incurred before immigration until they could get a new start and pay without beggaring their families anew. (4) The slavery question must, if possible, be settled so that well to do planters could feel secure in moving to Texas. (5) Toleration must be obtained, or provision made for the ministration of Catholic clergy in the colony. (6) Provision must be made for public education.

The early history of Mexico's fiscal administration has been neglected by writers of its political history, so that it is very difficult for foreign students to obtain an intelligent conception of it. In general outline the tariff system was like that of the United States, prohibiting the importation of certain commodities, and providing for the collection of *ad valorem* duties on others at maritime and frontier custom houses. Partly to economize cost of administration, the government kept the number of legal ports at a minimum and was always reluctant to create a new one. The policy was to some extent, no doubt, inherited from the Spanish system of commercial restriction and concentration. The tariff act of 1827[2] fixed a tonnage duty of seventeen *reales* ($2.12½) a ton on all foreign vessels entering a Mexican port, and forbade them to engage in the coasting trade, which, in face of the deficiency of Mexican shipping, was all but equivalent to prohibiting coastwide traffic.

The imperial colonization law, allowing colonists entering Mexico to introduce for their own use household utensils, tools, and merchandise without paying duty was annulled, as we have seen, with the other legislation of Iturbide's reign; but on September 29, 1823, Congress passed a special act for the relief of the inhabitants of Texas. This allowed all goods imported for their consumption to enter Texas free of duty for seven years.[3] Strictly administered, this would have benefited the Texans very little, because the only port legally established in the province—and there seemed to be doubt of that at times—was that of Espíritu Santo or San Bernard Bay.[4] This

[2] November 16. See *Colección de Órdenes y Decretos . . . de la Nación Mexicana* (Second edition), 97 (Mexico, 1829).

[3] *Colección de los Decretos y Órdenes del Soberano Congreso Mexicano*, etc., II, 196–197 (Mexico, 1825).

[4] The port was established by royal order in 1805, and the representative of Texas in the deputation of the Eastern Interior Provinces wrote Governor Martinez on January 17, 1821, that he had obtained its recognition from the deputation.

lay far to the west of the settlements, had no definite place of entry specified, no custom house or officer to issue clearances, no adjacent settlement nearer than Goliad, and was equally inconvenient for importation or exportation.

For the first few years, while the settlers were absorbed in the grim struggle for existence, this did not greatly matter. The few indispensables that they could not produce or manufacture were brought into the Brazos and Colorado, and they had little or nothing to sell. But by the beginning of 1825, to enable the colonists to ship their surplus products, particularly cotton and wool, Austin was asking for the establishment of the port of Galveston, which, he said, was well and favorably known to sailors.[5] He believed that this would be the most convenient port for the settlements on the Colorado, Brazos, and San Jacinto Rivers, but subsequent examination, when he charted the harbor, convinced him that it was less suitable than he had supposed. The water was eleven or twelve feet over the bar, and the harbor was safe, well protected, and easy of access; but the island itself was uninhabited, totally without timber, and subject to inundation, so that he doubted whether a custom house could be maintained there to advantage. Instead, he suggested the provisional establishment of a port at the mouth of the Brazos, where the water varied from seven to ten feet, according to wind-tide and river stage, which would be more convenient both for the port officers and for the colonists. The port of Galveston had now been provisionally established,[6] however, and Congress could not be induced to turn its attention again to the Texas coast. In 1828 the president confirmed the establishment of San Bernard by the Spanish government, but no steps were taken until 1830 to plant a custom house in Texas.[7] Trade with the United States nevertheless developed with immigration, and the first collector appointed for Galveston wrote in 1830 that the colonists had established *de facto* ports on the Colorado, Brazos, and Trinity Rivers.[8]

Austin saw the importance of establishing trade with Mexican

[5] Austin to the Legislature, February 4, 1825.

[6] By act of October 17, 1825. There is no explanation of "provisionally." *Colección de los Decretos y Órdenes del Primero Congreso Constitucional* (Second edition), IV, 6.

[7] Arciniega *et al.* to Campos, November 7, 1830. Bexar Archives.

[8] George Fisher to Zavala, February 10, 1830. On this subject in general see: Bastrop to Austin, April 9, May 6, 1825; Padilla to Austin, June 4, July 2, 1825; Austin to Saucedo, January 10, March 18, 1826.

ports, and wrote the governor as early as 1825 that the colonists wanted to send corn, lard, and cotton to Refugio, Matamoras, and Tampico. But his principal hope of prosperity was in the exportation of cotton to Europe. Year after year, with the rapid increase of immigration to his colony, he tried to make the government understand the economic potentialities of such trade for all Mexico; but, though he seems to have convinced every official who read his arguments, nothing was ever accomplished.

In the United States, he said, the exportation of cotton had increased in thirty years from practically nothing to six hundred thousand bales, with a European value of nearly thirty million dollars. There agriculture supplied the wealth that Mexico drew from its mines, but why not add this fountain of riches to that of the mines? Mexico had the soil, climate, and labor for greater production of cotton than had the United States. All that was needed was an object lesson to show the people its value and teach them how to prepare it for market, and the Texas crop, which he estimated at five hundred bales for 1828, would furnish that, if shipped from Vera Cruz. The colonists would escape the tariff, which operated as a discount against the price in New Orleans, and might profit by cheaper rates from Vera Cruz, because vessels sometimes had difficulty in getting cargoes there for the return voyage. England resented the Tariff of Abominations, was seeking cotton in Egypt and Brazil to enable it to retaliate by the exclusion of the American product, and would welcome the possibility of a new source of supply and do much to encourage and develop it. Thus the rivers and ports of Mexico would soon be filled with traffic, poverty and misery would disappear, and Mexico, exchanging its agricultural products for imported manufactures, could retain its precious metals.

To bring this dream to pass, three concessions must be made to Texas: immigrants must be allowed to introduce duty free for ten years everything that they needed, whether or not forbidden by the general tariff; the port of Brazos must be legalized; and the coasting trade with Mexico opened. Aside from the belief that his colonies merited so much consideration, Austin pointed out that the development of coastwise trade would bring about mutual understanding between colonists and Mexicans, establish commercial ties, and cement the union with bonds of personal friendship and common interest.[9]

The lack of such ties did, in fact, constitute a chief cause of the revolution of 1835. Whether or not the government appreciated the value of Austin's suggestion, it did attempt in the ill-advised law of April 6, 1830, to ameliorate the isolation of Texas from the rest of the Republic by permitting foreign vessels to engage in the coasting trade for four years, when, it was hoped, there would be enough Mexican vessels to carry it on. But the irritation engendered by other features of the law would have counteracted the beneficial influence of this provision, even if foreign tonnage had taken advantage of it.

The capricious administration of the coasting trade—whether from ignorance of port officers or unreasonable instructions of the treasury department—is illustrated by the history of a Texan cargo in 1826. In July of that year, to relieve a famine in Yucatan, President Victoria urged the littoral states to export food-stuffs, particularly grain. Stephen Richardson, of Austin's colony, chartered a vessel (the *Little Zoe*), loaded it with six hundred sacks of corn and a hogshead of lard, and sailed for Campeche. He had a copy of the president's proclamation, a passport from the political chief, and a certificate that the cargo was of domestic production; but the captain of the port refused to let him land and ordered him away within forty-eight hours. Expostulations proving futile, he sailed to Tampico, but after a month's detention there the cargo spoiled and he threw it into the sea.[10]

In the fall of 1828 John and James Austin obtained Mexican registry for the schooner *Eclipse* and made a voyage to Matamoras, but sold it a year later, after some trade to New Orleans.[11]

For a few months during 1830 George Fisher, the first customs

---

[9] Austin to the Governor, February 5, April 4, 1825; to Terán, June 30, September 20, 1828; to Manuel Ceballos, July 28, September 20, 1828; to the president, September 8, and to the minister of foreign and interior relations, October 7, 1828; to Governor Viesca, February 16, 1829; Bustamante to Austin, January 19, February 8, 1828; Músquiz to Austin, April 17, 1828; Terán to Austin, September 29, 1828.

[10] This statement was prepared by Austin, at Saltillo in November, 1827, to support Richardson's claim for damages of $2,450. A note from J. A. Padilla, May 3, 1828, advised Austin to have Richardson employ Victor Blanco as his attorney, but it is doubtful whether the claim was ever paid.

[11] Austin to Ceballos, September 20, 1828; to Bustamante, January 25, 1829; Ceballos to Austin, November 5, 1828; Bustamante to Austin, December 20, 1828; John Austin to Austin, September 16, 1829.

collector appointed for Texas, showed great activity in preparing for trade with the southern ports, and, like Austin, foresaw the development of thriving commerce with Europe, in which Texas cotton would play the principal rôle.[12] But after his suspension, interest in the subject apparently subsided. Austin's energy was now for a time absorbed in efforts to avert the colony's impending ruin rather than in planning its future prosperity. Though there was some trade in lumber from Harrisburg to Matamoras, foreign shipping did not avail itself to any considerable degree of the privilege allowed by the law of April 6, 1830, and down to the time of the revolution the normal route between Texan and Mexican ports lay through New Orleans.[13]

With the United States, on the other hand, trade steadily increased. In July, 1830, Fisher reported for the preceding ten months an average of two vessels a month from New Orleans. These had a total capacity for the period of twelve hundred tons,[14] and vessels from New York and Philadelphia were not uncommon.[15]

An official inspection in 1834 convinced Almonte of the importance of Texan commerce, which he saw in much the same light as Austin and Fisher, and he recommended, without effect, indefinite extension of the permission for foreign ships to engage in the coasting trade.[16] But the real trouble now, as always, was that the rulers of Mexico were too much absorbed in personal plots and schemes to give the necessary attention to a public question of such fundamental, but apparently remote, national concern.

With some of the other problems of this period Austin was more

[12] Fisher to A. M. Voss of Matamoras, July 21, 1830. Transcripts from department of Foreign and Interior Relations, Mexico.

[13] The anonymous writer of *A Visit to Texas* (New York, 1834), records (p. 31) that in April, 1831, three vessels were awaiting cargoes at Harrisburg and that the saw mill had more orders from Matamoras than it could fill. See also *The Texas Gazette,* July 22, 1830.

[14] Fisher to Voss, July 21, 1830, as cited in note 12 above. He says: "According to the official report existing in this custom house." As a matter of fact the custom house had not yet been established, and Fisher's statement may have been merely an estimate of the entries into the Brazos.

[15] James F. Perry, who moved to Texas in 1831, bought a stock of merchandise in Philadelphia for his store. John P. Austin to Austin, October 10, 1831, reported four vessels sailing from New York to Austin's colony.

[16] J. N. Almonte, *Noticia Estadistica sobre Tejas,* etc., 39 (Mexico, 1835). Almonte probably exaggerated the volume of the Texas trade, which he placed at $630,000 worth of imports and $500,000 worth of exports (p. 80). He estimated that two thousand bales of cotton were shipped from Austin's settlements in 1833, though the actual figures could hardly have exceeded a thousand.

successful. The completion of the state constitution in March, 1827, opened the way to the surrender of his extraordinary political powers and to his release, legally and formally, at least, from the burden of governing his collection of "North American frontier republicans." While at Saltillo in the fall of 1827, Austin requested the establishment of constitutional government in his colony, and the governor responded by instructing the political chief to order an election, under Austin's supervision, for an ayuntamiento with jurisdiction from the Lavaca to the watershed east of the Trinity and from the Gulf to the San Antonio road. Saucedo transmitted the order to Austin on December 11, and Austin called the election for February 3–4, 1828.

This, the first constitutional election in Anglo-American Texas, presented little in procedure that was new to the colonists, familiar with the operation of local government in the United States. Polls were opened in the seven old alcalde districts under the presidency of the respective alcaldes, and the voters elected a secretary and two tellers in each. A candidate must, if single, be twenty-five years old, or twenty-one if married; must have resided three years in the municipality, one year immediately preceding the election; must be able to read and write; and must have a capital or occupation sufficient for his subsistence. The voter called the names of his candidates aloud and they were recorded by the secretary; or, if he offered a written list, the names were read aloud by the secretary. All voted for an alcalde, two *regidores,* and a *síndico procurador.* Separate tallies were kept for each office and sent at the close of the election to Austin. A week later the officers of the district polls met at San Felipe, canvassed the vote, and announced the successful candidates.

The duties and functions of officers were prescribed—not entirely clearly to present readers—by the constitution and by a somewhat elaborate law for the government of municipalities, passed on June 15, 1827. The alcalde presided over the ayuntamiento, and was its executive officer; he was a primary judge, or judge of first instance in the phrase of the time, having sole jurisdiction in petty criminal cases and in civil cases under ten dollars, final jurisdiction from ten to one hundred dollars when acting with a representative of each party to a suit, and preliminary, examining jurisdiction in all other cases; and he was the medium of correspondence and administration between the colony on one side and the superior departmental and state authorities on the other. The natural comparison that comes to mind is that of a mayor who has not relinquished his judicial functions to police judges, but the alcalde's part in the state administration was more direct and important than that of a modern mayor. The duties of the *regidores* and of the *síndico procurador* are nowhere clearly defined, the various Spanish and Mexican laws concerning the ayuntamiento assuming, apparently, that their functions were too well known to require statement. In general, the *regidores* may be compared with aldermen or city commissioners. They served on committees and looked after various branches of municipal administration, and in the absence of the alcalde the first *regidor* (ranked according to the number of votes received at election) acted in his place. The *síndico* seems to have been a sort of combination notary and city attorney. In addition to these officers, the alcalde appointed a sheriff, and the ayuntamiento chose a secretary, an official of more than usual importance because he had to serve as interpreter and translator in all relations with the superior authorities.

Taking the place of Austin's district alcaldes were a *comisario* and a *síndico procurador* in each precinct of five hundred inhabitants, elected by the voters of the precinct. They were subject to the ayuntamiento, and might attend its meetings voluntarily or on summons, and have a voice but no vote in its deliberations. The duties of the *comisario* were to take the census of his precinct, keep a record of the families moving into it and of the places from which they came, assist tax collectors, execute the orders of the ayuntamiento, arrest disturbers of the peace and preserve public tranquillity, and report "idle and vicious" persons to the alcalde. In addition, he had minor judicial authority, similar to that of a justice of the peace. The precinct *síndico* seems to have been a sort of constable.

The ayuntamiento was now to assume, in a measure at least, the position previously occupied by Austin as a buffer between the colonists and the government. Knowing the importance of prompt and punctilious performance of every function in relations with the political chief and superior administration and aware of the usual American carelessness and impatience of form, Austin hoped for the election of competent men, living near enough to San Felipe to meet frequently, who would take their duties seriously, avoid snarls, and relieve him of the strain of constant watchfulness which he had so long borne. It is evident that he did some quiet electioneering, but his ticket was defeated.[17]

Greatly to Austin's disappointment, this body held no meeting from the end of March until December 21, when the vote was canvassed for its successor. As usual, it fell to him to explain these shortcomings to the political chief; and he complained that after having exhausted all reasonable excuses that he could invent he had been compelled to draw so largely "upon shadows and frivolous apologies" that he was ashamed. This ayuntamiento did, however, adopt two measures of considerable importance. One was a petition to the legislature to pass a law recognizing labor contracts, which, in effect, would legalize slavery; and the other was a municipal ordinance, or city charter, which the legislature approved on May 30, 1829. This defined the duties, functions, and rules of order of the ayuntamiento, and outlined a scheme of taxation to meet local expenses and build a town hall and jail. It levied specific taxes on land, livestock, and slaves, ranging from four dollars and a half on a league of land to two cents a head on hogs; and occupation taxes on lawyers, merchants, and keepers of "tippling shops." The property taxes aroused much opposition and resentment and were probably never collected. The occupation taxes met with more favor and yielded a little revenue, but never enough to build the hall and jail.

The jurisdiction of the ayuntamiento covered a wide range of subjects, including most of the functions of a modern city commission and some of those belonging to the county commissioners. Study of its minutes after the first year shows the ayuntamiento laying off roads and supervising their construction; regulating ferries and ferriage rates; creating boards of health, boards of medical examiners, and quarantine boards; regulating weights and

---

[17] He wanted Ira Ingram, a man of unusual ability and education, for alcalde, his old and trusted friend, Josiah H. Bell, for one of the *regidores*, and L. R. Kenny, an able lawyer, for *síndico*. Thomas M. Duke, ten leagues distant on the Colorado, was elected alcalde, and Humphrey Jackson, one of the *regidores*, lived on the San Jacinto, seventy-five miles away.

measures; directing militia organization; holding special elections and settling election contests; and serving generally as conservator of public morals. It assisted Austin in keeping the colony free of undesirables, advising when to grant and when to withhold titles to land; and relieved him of no little responsibility in deciding when titles should be forfeited for non-fulfillment of the conditions of the grant. There is evidence throughout of the closest harmony and cooperation between Austin and the ayuntamiento, which always consulted him on matters of state or federal relations.[18]

While the constitution was forming Bastrop was the sole representative of Texas in a unicameral legislature of twelve members, but the law putting the constitution into effect increased the Texan quota to two.[19] This, on the whole, was a reasonable apportionment and for some years caused no dissatisfaction. The judicial system was unsatisfactory from the beginning, however, and became the object of great and ever increasing complaint. The colonists naturally deplored the lack of trial by jury, but the principal defect was the want of a court of last resort short of Saltillo for important civil and criminal cases.

Austin's jurisdiction, which was ample enough in civil cases during the pre-constitutional régime, was inconveniently restricted in criminal cases. He explained the difficulty to Alamán, the minister of foreign relations, in a letter of January, 1824, before the union of Texas and Coahuila. The commandant general had instructed him to employ criminals on public works, pending sentences from the superior government, but, he said,

"We are from forty to fifty leagues from Bexar, and have no jail, no troops to guard prisoners, and a condemnation to hard labor without an adequate guard to enforce the decree is only to exasperate a criminal, make him laugh at the laws and civil authorities and turn him loose on society to commit new depredations, for nothing has a more disorganizing effect than a weak and inefficient administration of the laws, as it discourages and disgusts the good and well disposed and emboldens evil men and renders them arrogant and audacious. I have therefore in some

---

[18] This discussion of the establishment of the ayuntamiento of San Felipe is adapted from an article by the writer on "The Government of Austin's Colony, 1821–1831," in *The Southwestern Historical Quarterly*, XXI, 242–252. For complete bibliographical references see that article.

[19] Gammel, *Laws of Texas*, I, 157.

cases been driven to the painful alternative of either permitting a criminal to escape unpunished or of taking upon myself the responsibility of inflicting corporal punishment. If those difficulties could be removed by vesting authority in some tribunal here to punish by corporal punishment . . . I think it would greatly tend to the harmony and good order of this part of the province." [20]

In December, 1824, Austin had prepared a long memorandum of the needs of his settlements for Bastrop's use in the legislature, and one suggestion was that a *juez de letras*,[21] or professional judge, should be appointed to hear appeals from the alcaldes.

"I am ready and willing to act in any capacity in which the government may deem me useful in this colony [he protested] and that without any pay or salary whatever, . . . but if it can be otherwise arranged I do not wish to have anything to do with judicial proceedings, for I think that a man learned in the Mexican laws ought to be appointed for that purpose. . . . If this colony was divided into as many partidos [districts] as are necessary and one alcalde elected by the people for each partido, from whose decission there should be an appeal to the *juez de letras* of the province, I think it would very much tend to promote good order, and it certainly would be in the highest degree satisfactory to me, as I should then be relieved from the most responsible and disagreeable part of my duties." [22]

His eventual solution of this aspect of the matter was, as we have seen, the creation of the appellate court of alcaldes; but that did not solve the question of jurisdiction nor of the provisional character of the regulations administered by the courts. For some reason —probably because reflection told him that it would be inexpedient at the time—Austin reconsidered and withheld this suggestion for nearly two years. In August, 1826, however, he wrote J. A. Padilla, secretary of state and his confidential friend, that he did not think he could carry the duties of judge longer than the following autumn.

"We ought to have here [he insisted] a subaltern political chief and a judge. This is of great importance. In fine, the prosperity, and perhaps the existence, of the colony demands it. It will be better that both should be Mexicans, and, particularly, the judge ought to be different from those here,[23] and learned in the laws of the country and in the English, French, and Spanish languages. In the district of Nacogdoches they are governed

[20] Austin to Alamán, January 20, 1824.
[21] Literally, judge of letters. There is no precise equivalent of the term in English.
[22] Austin to Bastrop, December 22, 1824.
[23] "El juez debe ser de otra que de aqui."

by various alcaldes, and there, as I have understood from rumor, nothing less than anarchy reigns; and if there are not a sub-chief and a judge here to supervise the alcaldes and instruct them by translations of the laws in operation, it will be the same, or perhaps worse. This is not because the inhabitants in general are of bad character, but they have no knowledge of the language, of the laws, of the customs of the country; nor of the different position which they occupy here with respect to the government and their right as inhabitants from that which they had in their native country. This is due to lack of knowledge and not to evil dispositions." [24]

In November, 1826, Austin wrote Bastrop that "One of the most important subjects to the people of the State of Cuahuila and Texas is a speedy organization of the Judiciary on a system which promises permanency, uniformity in the interpretation of laws, and convenience to the people." He then outlined a system which he thought would be satisfactory: a supreme court, sitting alternately at San Antonio and Saltillo; two circuit courts of appeal in Texas, one with jurisdiction from the Lavaca to the Sabine—the region which included substantially all of the English speaking population—and the other with jurisdiction west of the Lavaca; and, at the bottom, the local alcalde courts. The jurisdiction of the alcaldes should be clearly defined, their fees fixed, and forms provided for uniform procedure. The circuits courts should have final appellate jurisdiction in all cases carried up from the alcaldes, and original jurisdiction in all civil and criminal causes above the alcaldes' range, having charge particularly of probate business and the issuing of licenses. The supreme court should hear appeals from the circuit courts in all civil cases where the amount involved exceeded a certain fixed sum, and in capital criminal cases, if trial by jury was not allowed below. The supreme court should have original jurisdiction in civil cases "of great importance"—a phrase which Austin did not further define. He suggested that the circuit court of the eastern district should sit at San Felipe in October, February, and June, and at Nacogdoches in December, April, and August. At each place there should be a clerk to keep records and issue processes and a sheriff or marshal to serve processes and execute decrees. Judicial proceedings in English should have full validity when officially translated. And a complete digest of the laws in force should be published in book form and furnished

---

[24] Austin to J. A. Padilla, August 12, 1826.

freely to proper officers, and sold to the people at a moderate price.[25]

The constitution was nearly finished when Bastrop received this letter. It contained the outline of a judicial system, and provided that the details should be elaborated by law, which was done by an act of June 21, 1827.[26] The constitution declared that one of the main objects of the attention of congress should be to establish trial by jury in criminal cases, to extend its use gradually, and "even to adopt it in civil cases in proportion as the advantages of this valuable institution [should] become practically known."[27] The law, however, did not touch this subject. It did meet Austin's desire for a definition of the alcaldes' jurisdiction, but for the rest it established an extremely complex procedure which, in effect, left the Texans almost without judicial recourse in important civil and criminal cases. Up to three hundred dollars the alcalde's verdict in civil suits was final, when reached in accordance with certain prescribed formalities easily complied with; but above that amount it was subject to appeal to one of the three chambers of the supreme court, sitting at Saltillo. In the same way, his jurisdiction was plenary in criminal cases when the penalty did not exceed a fine of one hundred dollars or imprisonment for one month. But verdicts of corporal punishment must be referred to the supreme court, whether or not the defendant appealed, and penalties of "death, deportation, perpetual exile, or ten years' confinement at hard labor" had to be confirmed successively by two chambers of the supreme court.[28] In all his decisions the alcalde was expected to be guided by the state's attorney (*asesor general*) at Saltillo.

The occasions for delay in such a system were very great, and its inconvenience to the Texans was enormous. Austin forcefully summarized its defects in 1833, after five years of experience and observation:

"In all civil cases [he said] there is an appeal to the supreme tribunal of the state at Saltillo, a distance of near seven hundred miles from the inhabited parts of Texas. There are but few men in Texas who are quali-

---

[25] Austin to Bastrop, November 3, 1826.

[26] This law (Number 39) is omitted from all compilations known to the writer. There is a copy in pamphlet form in the Bexar Archives.

[27] One wonders whether this was not due to Bastrop's influence, but the journals do not enable one to answer.

[28] The law seems to leave a hiatus between fines of one hundred dollars and penalties of the serious character indicated in this sentence. The procedure is not clear.

fied to prepare cases for the supreme court, and when appeals have been taken, they have generally been sent back several times to be reformed, so that decissions in such cases are seldom had. It has become proverbial in Texas that an appeal to Saltillo is a payment of the debt. It amounts to a total denial of justice, especially to the poor, and this is the frail tenure by which the most important rights of the people of Texas are suspended.

"The manner of trying culprits for high criminal offences is such that it amounts to no tryal at all. The tryal by jury is not sanctioned by law, and the rights of the accused are committed to an alcalde who is ignorant of the formulas of the laws, and of the language in which they are written, who prepares the cause for the judgement of the supreme tribunal in Saltillo. Thus the lives, liberty, and honor of the accused are suspended upon the tardy decission of a distant tribunal which knows not nor cares for his suffering, and the rights of the community to bring offenders to speedy and exemplary punishment are sacrificed to forms equally uncertain and unknown. The formula required by law in the prosecution of criminals is so difficult to be pursued that most of the courts in Texas have long since ceased to attempt its execution. The tryal by jury has been attempted in some of the municipalities, but, being unsupported by the sanction of law, it also has failed of success. A total interregnum in the administration of justice in criminal cases may be said to exist. A total disregard of the laws has become so prevalent, both amongst the officers of justice and the people at large, that reverence for laws or for those who administer them has almost intirely disappeared, and contempt is fast assuming its place; so that the protection of our property, our persons and lives is circumscribed almost exclusively to the moral honesty or virtue of our neighbor." [29]

In serious criminal cases the examining trial was held by the alcalde, who submitted a transcript of all the evidence to the *asesor general* at Saltillo and awaited his advice concerning the penalty. When this arrived he was not bound by it, though he departed from it at some risk; and, having pronounced judgment, he must again send all the documents to Saltillo to be reviewed by the appropriate chamber of the supreme court. The least possible delay occasioned by these long journeys was four months, and the usual time was from six to eight months. In the meantime, the prisoner must be kept secure, which, for want of jails, entailed almost equal inconvenience upon him and the public.[30]

Austin recounts this difficulty in reporting a celebrated case to the political chief in 1830. The case aroused great feeling at the

[29] Draft of address of the Central Committee to Convention, April 1, 1833.
[30] *The Texas Gazette,* August 29, 1830.

time and gave rise later to mean, unfounded insinuations that Austin, for some purpose of his own, was responsible for the hardships of the defendants.[31] On September 2, 1830, Seth Ingram killed John G. Holtham in a street duel. Hosea H. League was implicated as accessory. Holtham was a lawyer who had left an unpleasant reputation in Natchitoches,[32] and Austin spoke of him as a vagabond in Texas, though he had served for a time as secretary of the ayuntamiento. Ingram was one of the earliest settlers, a surveyor, and Austin said there was no better man in the colony. League was a man of upright character and had been elected to the ayuntamiento the year before; but he was irascible, pettish, had the habit, Austin said, of "speaking ill of almost all the world," and was extremely unpopular.[33] Two months passed and the examining trial was not completed. The alcalde pleaded lack of a translator, and said that it probably would not be completed for many months. Since there was no jail, the prisoners must be guarded. The militia declined this duty and could only be compelled to serve by the assessment of heavy fines, which would have had to be forcibly collected. Austin told the political chief that the men could get the best sureties in the country, and asked if they could not have bail.[34]

Evidently the reply was unfavorable, because for sixteen months they continued in desperate straits.[35] They were then released on

---

[31] See below, page 308.

[32] See Dr. John Sibley to Austin, November 21, December 10, 1824.

[33] Austin wrote Josiah H. Bell, April 4, 1829, defending League's course in the ayuntamiento: "There appears to be a great prejudice against Major League and the most scurrilous and unjust abuse is heaped upon him. I believe that all this is unjust and unfounded as far as I can understand or know of his acts—and I am of opinion that it has all originated from personal animosity and nothing else. . . . I belong to no party and will engage in no personal animosities, but I do say, justice compels me to say, that League is an injured and persecuted man or I am more deceived than I ever was before in my life. He has been challenged and threatened with clubs and death—I know not for what. It is said the people will rise and mob him—I cannot understand for what. He has one fault which has injured him greatly—he is too irritable. His personal enemies are if possible more so." That this hostility did not subside is evident from a letter which League wrote Austin on December 19, 1829, asking him to intercede with the political chief to have him excused from service during the remaining two months of his term as *regidor*. The people were so much opposed to him, he said, that "any interference with the public business by me or even an idea that I will interfear infuriates them to madness—it is resolved that the next ayuntamiento shall not be contaminated with my Rascally intrigues (as they say)."

[34] Austin to Ramón Músquiz, November 30, 1830. See also Austin to Perry, September 22, 1830.

[35] See "Minutes of the Ayuntamiento of San Felipe," in *Southwestern Historical Quarterly*, XXII, 84, 188, 354; XXIII, 216, 220, 307. In the session of December 31, 1830, the ayuntamiento refused to pay a bill for ironing and unironing the prisoners on the ground that "the expense was incurred for the special convenience of sd Ingram and League," who should therefore pay; and the session of April 4, 1831, declined to pay their board.

bond, but a murder occurred soon after and they were again imprisoned. A petition from the prisoners to the political chief gives some further features of the case. According to this, seven hundred citizens petitioned the ayuntamiento in the fall of 1831 to settle the case. After their re-arrest the ayuntamiento fixed a day for their trial by jury; but they were told that none of the seven hundred who signed the petition in their behalf would be admitted to the jury, which meant that their enemies would control the trial; and they therefore protested against jury trial as unlegal and begged the political chief to see that they were tried according to law, and at once.[36] On June 12 a meeting at San Felipe, called by the ayuntamiento—evidently to advise about this case—adopted resolutions warning against any departure from the legal procedure "under the pretense that it is necessary to do so from any particular circumstance or because it is naturally just"; but declaring reform necessary and urging the ayuntamiento to obtain from the government either the appointment of a *juez de letras* and the establishment of trial by jury or the appointment of an *asesor general* for Texas alone, which would obviate the tedious references to Saltillo.[37] Here the record of the case is lost. Ingram's brother wrote in July, 1833, that the prisoner was home at last.[38]

The inherent defects of the system were in this instance, no doubt, aggravated in some way by local spleen; but it is evident that Austin did not greatly exaggerate when he declared that an interregnum existed in the administration of justice in criminal cases.

Austin was elected to the legislature in 1830, and while asking his constituents for instructions he suggested that they request appointment of professional judges (*jueces de letras*) and trial by jury. Individual officials recognized the necessity of such reform, and General Terán advised the federal government at this same time that jury trial should be established, with review of the verdict by a trained judge visiting the settlements periodically in circuit.[39] Aside from habitual inertia, the chief obstacle to this re-

[36] League and Ingram to Political Chief, May 19, 1832, Nacogdoches Archives.
[37] The resolutions are in the Nacogdoches Archives.
[38] Ira Ingram to H. H. League, July 29, 1833, Franklin Papers, University of Texas.
[39] Austin to Ayuntamiento of Nacogdoches, September 18, 1830, Nacogdoches Archives; Terán to Austin, January 5, 1831.

form seems to have been the reluctance of the state government to establish a system in Texas different from that in Coahuila. Hence no relief was offered the Texans until the session of 1834, when a system was framed nearly identical with that which Austin outlined for Bastrop in 1826. But this, for reasons which will later appear, did not go into effect.

The circumstances under which many of the colonists left the United States led Austin to propose a stay law, exempting their property in Texas for twelve years from execution to pay debts contracted before immigration.

"This is very important [he wrote in 1824] for if the Settlers can be sued and their property taken here for debts due in the U. States of North America before they have time to establish themselves and make any thing they will be totally ruined. They have some of them spent all they had to move and settle themselves in this uninhabited Country. They will however be able by Cultivating Cotton to pay all their Debts if time is given them, but if their Land and property can be taken for those debts it will ruin them and be of more injury to the improvement of this Country than any thing that Could happen—I therefore take the Liberty of respectfully suggesting whether the interest of the Gov^t would not be greatly promoted by protecting the new Emigrants from all old foreign debts for at least Twelve Years—Many very good Men are unfortunate in business and become involved in Debt by misfortune; some such have removed here and endured all the fatigues, and dangers and losses of settling a wilderness with the hope of bettering their situation and being able in time to pay off all their Debts, and they are now looking to the Government of the State as to a father who will interpose its parental Authority to save them and their wives and Children from the Cruel and Merciless persecution of unfeeling Creditors who may follow them from the U. States—I am not in favor of extending too much protection to any who have defrauded their Creditors but it appears to me that sound policy and the dictates of Justice and Humanity certainly would justify affording the most ample protection to every honest but unfortunate debtor whose hard fate elsewhere has driven him to seek an asylum in the Mexican Republic. Therefore if the Laws do not already afford sufficient protection, I think the Legislature would promote the prosperity of the Country and do an act of humanity and justice by giving at least Twelve years for all who remove and settle in this State to pay their old debts Contracted before they removed here." [40]

As we know, the legislature for the next three years was giving

[40] Austin to Bastrop, December 22, 1824. He asked Bastrop to translate and present this to the governor and legislature.

most of its attention to the formation of the constitution and the passage of various administrative measures, and this subject went unnoticed. In the meantime, Austin's "Civil Regulations" ruled in Texas, one article of which provided that, "In all cases where the cause of action accrued out of this nation, neither party being a citizen or inhabitant of this nation at the time when the debt was contracted, application must be made to the judge of the colony"—that is, to Austin himself—for permission to institute suit.[41] The matter being temporarily, therefore, in his own hands, Austin did not press the subject further with the government until danger seemed to threaten. But the commercial treaty between the United States and Mexico negotiated by Joel R. Poinsett in 1826 contained an article guaranteeing reciprocally to the citizens of the two countries access to "the tribunals of justice for their judicial recourse, on the same terms which are usual and customary with the natives or citizens of the country in which they may be." [42] Consideration of the treaty by the Senate during 1827 and 1828,[43] and a report that the Mexican minister had assured the Washington government that no legal obstacles existed to the collection of foreign debts in Texas, caused a rush of claims which Austin feared would be taken to the legislature in the fall of 1828. He therefore resumed his efforts to obtain the passage of a state law for the protection of debtors.

His first step was an identical letter, presenting the situation fully to the political chief, governor, federal congressman, federal commissioner in Texas, and Lorenzo de Zavala, whose interest, he thought, might be touched by the fact that Zavala was just entering the field of colonization as an empresario. The majority of the colonists, he wrote, owed debts, in the United States; they had emigrated to Texas hoping to become able, with time and industry, to accumulate a capital and pay their debts; upon arrival they had encountered an unpopulated country without trade or resources; and consequently it would be impossible for them to obtain money

---

[41] This article is in Wooten (ed.), *A Comprehensive History of Texas*, I, 486. The Regulations were approved by the political chief on May 24, 1824, and by the governor (see Austin to Saucedo, March 18, 1826) on February 12, 1825.

[42] *American State Papers, Foreign Relations*, VI, 609.

[43] William R. Manning, *Early Diplomatic Relations between the United States and Mexico* (Baltimore, 1916), 205–251, gives the history of this treaty through 1828. Various obstacles delayed its ratification until 1832.

to pay their obligations until the country was more developed. After terrible hardships they were beginning to advance, but at this juncture "some one comes along from the United States with a claim and demands of the unfortunate settler all his land, all his little herd, in fact, everything he has in the world; no arguments [he declared] are necessary to prove the harshness and injustice of such a demand." Land now worth two hundred or three hundred dollars a league would be worth in ten years five or six thousand, and this would be due to the labor and suffering of the original settlers, not to the efforts of the creditor. He thought a law ought to be passed forbidding the forcible collection of foreign debts in the colonies of Texas until 1840, and providing then only for collection of the principal. He had understood that there was precedent for such a law in the Laws of the Indies, but, whether this was true or not, circumstances justified its passage, as they had justified the laws of individual states of the north against British creditors after the Revolutionary War. To the political chief and the governor he added that the attorney general or the supreme court would probably be asked soon whether foreign debts were collectable, and that he hoped the answer would be as favorable as possible to the immigrant debtors.[44]

The Spanish precedent which Austin had vaguely in mind was of very ancient lineage. It originated apparently in a law of Ferdinand and Isabella in 1476 forbidding the seizure of oxen, work animals, or tools of farm laborers, except for debts due the king, overlord, or owner of the land. A hundred years later the exemption included also the sown and fallow land occupied by the tenant, save for crown dues, rent to the landlord, or advances made by him to produce the crop, and even in these three cases a pair of oxen, mules, or other plough animals were totally exempt. In 1683 Carlos II began the protection of artisans by exempting from execution looms, spinning wheels, and other tools of silk workers; and in 1786 Carlos III extended exemption of tools to all workmen.[45] In the absence of legislation to the contrary, which there does not seem

---

[44] Austin to Zavala, June 24, 1828; to Terán, June 30, and "Apuntes relativos a la Colonia de Austin en Texas formados en Junio [30] 1828." Austin says in a note that the letter to Zavala was sent also to Ramón Músquiz, Governor J. M. Viesca, Manuel Ceballos, and General Terán.

[45] *Novísima Recopilación de las Leyes de España* (Madrid, 1805), Tomo V, Libro XI, Titulo XXXI, Leyes XII, XV, XVIII, XIX, pp. 291–294.

to have been, these laws were applicable in the American dominions.[46]

Austin's views met general approval.[47] Governor Viesca promised to present, and did present, at the September session of the legislature a bill covering the emergency. In his discussion supporting the bill, possibly written by Padilla, the governor raised the point that the colonization law prohibited the sale of land until it was fully improved, and that foreclosure by a creditor would in effect violate this restriction.[48] He might also have mentioned that the federal colonization law denied possession to non-residents. Such bars, however, were less real than apparent, and would no doubt have been evaded by creditors' assigning their claims to resident agents.[49] For some reason the first article of the governor's draft met opposition, and the bill went over for consideration in the long session of 1829.[50] Meanwhile, on September 8, Austin embodied his ideas in an informal bill, which he probably furnished to Padilla.[51] This bill, after reciting in the preamble the substance of Austin's original letter on the subject, provided that, "until after 1840 no emigrant colonist legitimately settled in any colonial grant in this state shall be molested in his person or property by any creditor for debts contracted in foreign countries before his emigration to this country; and after the year 1840 the payment of their foreign debts may be exacted of debtors only in installments of ten per cent. of the original each year, without interest or premium whatever."[52]

As passed in January, 1829, the law exempted, without limitation of any kind, lands "acquired by virtue of" a state or federal colonization law from execution to pay a debt contracted before

---

[46] *Recopilación de Leyes de los Reynos de las Indias* (Madrid, 1774, Third edition), Tomo I, Libro II, Título I, Ley II, p. 127.

[47] Terán to Austin, July 8, 1828; Músquiz, July 24; Zavala, August 6; Viesca, August 8; and Padilla, August 9.

[48] Governor's message to the legislature, September 2, 1828. The bill is not available, but, as revealed by the message, it must have followed very closely Austin's letter of June 24.

[49] This procedure is suggested by a public notice of January 11, 1826, in which Alexander Calvit warns settlers not to buy claims against him in the United States, saying that all the property which he brought to the colony belonged to his wife and children.

[50] Músquiz to Austin, November 27, 1828. Músquiz had been in Saltillo during the September session.

[51] Padilla to Austin, January 24, 1829, shows the exchange of letters not now available on the general subject.

[52] "Proyecto de ley, propuesto por E. F. A., 8 de Septiembre, 1828."

the acquisition of the land;[53] provided that colonists and empresarios should not be sued for such debts for twelve years; and declared that after that time they should be obligated to pay only in
money or products "in a manner not to affect their attention to
their families, to their husbandry, or [to the] art they profess."
Lands, farming implements, and tools or machines of their trade
were specifically exempted.[54] The last section suggests influence of
the Spanish precedents. It was more favorable to the debtor than
Austin had requested, because in practice the vague provision that
payment could not be exacted in a way to incommode the family
or the industry of the debtor would probably have outlawed the
debt altogether. Austin was, however, entirely satisfied,[55] and
there are indications that the law relieved a good deal of anxiety
in the colonies.[56] There is abundant evidence, as will be seen later,
that Austin himself never claimed the privilege of the law to evade
or delay the payment of his own debts with interest.

This statute constituted, of course, a sweeping homestead law.
Though the intricacies of judicial procedure were probably sufficient to have relieved them of serious annoyance from their old
creditors, there can be no doubt that the colonists leaned more
comfortably on the safeguard of the law. It was in effect for ten
years, being continued after the separation from Mexico by the
general provision of the first constitution of the Republic of Texas
that laws not inconsistent with the constitution "shall remain in
full force until declared void, repealed, altered, or [until they shall]
expire by their own limitation."[57] It gave place then, January 26,
1839, to the better known, but not more effective, act of Lamar's
administration, which has been regarded as the foundation of the
successive homestead exemption laws that have ruled in Texas

[53] This article had been amended at Austin's suggestion to include federal grants.—
See Padilla to Austin, January 24, 1829.

[54] Gammel, *Laws of Texas*, I, 220. The act is dated January 13, 1829, but Padilla wrote
Austin that the third article was still undergoing revision on January 24.

[55] Austin to Bell, February 24, 1829.

[56] Peter Ellis Bean, for example, acknowledging a copy of the law from Austin on March
18, 1829, said, "it will Give Roome for men to make Property and not be Broke up as it
has bin in the wish of some to Buy in the United Staits at and undervalue those Debts
for specilasion."

[57] Constitution of the Republic of Texas, Schedule, Sec. I, in Gammel, *Laws of Texas,*
I, 1077. An Act of January 20, 1840, repealed all Coahuiltecan laws then in force, except
those relating in any way to land or to water or mineral rights.

since that day and as the prototype of a goodly progeny in other states.[58]

Whatever may be thought of the economic propriety of such an exemption law in the twentieth century, there can be no doubt of its beneficent rôle in the past, nor of Austin's part in its origin. Familiar from childhood with the distress and misery caused by speculation and abuse of credit, Austin came to play half seriously with the idea of establishing a new economic system in which credit would rest solely on personal confidence. While a member of the legislature in 1832, he wrote a letter to Edward Livingston—whether he ever sent it we do not know—asking his opinion of such a system. Admitting its Utopian character and seeing many obstacles to its successful operation, he yet was half convinced that it might be practicable in Texas. The letter reveals a good deal of Austin's mind and character.

"The mass of the settlers [in Texas, he said] are plain, honest farmers, working men. Until within a short time past they have had no lawyers amongst them, and consequently very little litigation. . . . They have had time to contemplate from the peaceful solitudes of their new homes the war of lawyers, the intreagues of speculators; in short, the agonizing throes of neighborhoods, counties, and states under the high pressure of the credit system. Having enjoyed a few years of quietness, they dread a change and [wish to] shield themselves from the evils of the monied mania and the expensive labarinths of the old law systems. But how prevent it? Here sir is the great question which we all wish to have solved. . . . Robert Owen undertook to teach mankind how to govern themselves.[59] He expected to distroy the monied mania by making everything common. This distroyed man's individuality, it confounded him with a common herd; character was therefore of no consequence to him. Would not the reverse of Mr. Owen's basis be a better one? The old systems recognize the individuality of property. To this let us add that of *character,* but entirely divested of the weight which property gives to it—character

---

[58] D. B. Edward, *History of Texas,* 176 (Cincinnati, 1836), quotes Section X, articles 141–144, of a revised judiciary law, passed by the legislature April 17, 1834, which considerably elaborates the act of 1829. This law was known as the Chambers Jury Law, from its author, Thomas Jefferson Chambers. The official publication of this act, however, ends with Section IX, article 140. The most plausible explanation that suggests itself is that Chambers's original bill contained these articles, that the legislature failed to pass them, and that Edward wrote from a translation of the bill instead of the law. Certain unusually awkward expressions indicate that Edward's copy is a translation.

[59] After the failure of his socialistic enterprise at New Harmony, Indiana, Owen in 1828 applied to Mexico for a grant of Texas in which he wished to make another experiment. See Manning, *Early Diplomatic Relations between the United States and Mexico,* 323.

based upon intrinsic moral worth, good faith, and virtue, without any regard whatever to wealth. How is this to be effected? By changing the old laws so as to base the credit system upon moral character alone, and not upon wealth and coersive means—or, in other words, to place the whole credit system upon good faith, and annul all laws (avoiding unjust retroactive effects) for the coersive collection of debts, all landed or personal securities, all imprisonment or process against the person or property for debts."

While he knew that such a system would "cramp the progress of improvement for a time" and be impracticable "in a country that did not abound in natural resources or that depended principally on commerce," and while he realized that it would be a "very bold and perhaps a dangerous experiment," some of his friends, he said, were convinced of its utility and wished the experiment made. Would the victims of misplaced confidence seek redress by personal violence? Could such a system be squared with the federal constitution? How would it affect citizens of other states dealing with Texans, or Texans dealing with other states or with countries having treaties with Mexico? Debts due to the government should, of course, not enjoy this immunity. Ought there to be exceptions in favor of others—for example, in favor of mechanics and laborers for their wages, of carriers and freighters, of minors and widows for property sold on credit to settle an estate?

The subject, he thought, needed the sifting and critical examination of a public discussion, and he hoped that Livingston might use his letter to further that object. "The learned and pious in the United States" had, he said, "devoted much of their time to the discussion of the merits or demerits of the systems of other countries, with a view to enlighten public opinion generally. Why not also take some interest in the happiness of a new and rising country, their close neighbor and a sister republic, a friend?"

The letter contains one of the very few positive declarations from Austin on the subject of religion. He thought a "belief in religion . . . absolutely *indispensable* for the well being and sound organization of all societies."[60]

But even as he wrote, Austin was recalled—he wrote from Matamoras—to quiet an insurrection against the military commandant

---

[60] Austin to ———, June 24, 1832. The letter is unaddressed but it speaks of "your codes designed for the particular use of Louisiana," which identifies Livingston.

on Galveston Bay, and few contemplative moments were left him after that to pursue this subject. Livingston, too, passed from the State Department at Washington to be minister to France under trying conditions, and probably never found the leisure—if he thought it worth attention—to answer the letter.

Austin's agency in securing recognition of slavery by the imperial colonization law, as well as the intense interest of prospective colonists in the legal status of slavery in Texas, has been noticed. It was a subject that refused to stay settled, and, first and last, probably caused Austin more anxiety during the early years of the colony than any other. Mexican statesmen learned their political philosophy from the orators of the French Revolution. "Liberty, Equality, and Fraternity" spoke the language of their emotions. The first member of the fair trinity, especially, diffused about them a pleasurable glow of warm and generous sentiment. They hated slavery and loved liberty. They linked it with God to make a national motto—"God and Liberty." That it was a word without significance in their relations with the Indian peons and mixed-blood dependents around them, they, of course, did not see—or, perhaps, wish to see. In the abstract, and by its proper name, they detested slavery.

Austin's own views of slavery underwent several changes. Until 1830 he thought it indispensable to the rapid progress of Texas and exerted himself to safeguard it. Then for two years he had hopes of large immigration from the free states and Europe, particularly from Switzerland. At the same time the Nat Turner insurrection in Virginia and the harsh repressive laws of southern states turned his attention to the danger from an excessive slave population. Intimate association with his cousin, Mrs. Mary Austin Holley, a woman of rare charm and unusual intellectual gifts, perhaps did something to strengthen his convictions. He inaugurated a discreet propaganda against slavery among the colonists with disappointing results. Even immigrants from the free states discouraged it. Some time in 1832 there seems to have been a definite pronouncement of the colonists on the subject—probably during the convention of October, though it does not appear in the journal—and thereafter Austin reluctantly but finally accepted the inevitable and returned to the earlier doctrine that Texas must be a slave state.

Prior to 1829 the principal expression of the federal government against slavery was a law of July 13, 1824. Its caption reads, "Prohibition of Commerce and Traffic in Slaves." The first two articles prohibited forever "commerce and traffic" in slaves, from whatever country or under whatever flag; and declared slaves introduced contrary to the tenor of this provision free by the mere act of treading Mexican soil. The third and fourth articles fixed heavy penalties for violation of the law, but suspended them for six months in favor of colonists who wished to land slaves on the isthmus of Coazacoalco.[61] Did Congress intend by this to prevent the introduction of slaves by their owners for their own use? The implication of the last article is that it did, and other indications point to the same conclusion. Erasmo Seguin wrote Bastrop in March, 1824, that an abolition law was already passed.[62] If in fact passed, the law was evidently reconsidered, but the report shows intention. On June 3 the committee on petitions presented a request from Jared E. Groce that no new regulation be applied with respect to the slaves that he had introduced when he settled in Texas, or that he be permitted to remove them from the country. Carlos Bustamante thought that "in view of what Congress had resolved concerning slaves" the petition should be returned; but Ramos Arizpe and Father Mier objected that the resolution prohibiting the slave trade (*comercio de esclavos*) was not the same as one affecting slaves already in the country, which would demand great circumspection.[63] Final action on the petition is not disclosed, nor is there any material discussion of the law of July 13 in the broken journals that are accessible. Seguin told Austin that the whole Congress became "electrified when it considered the unhappy condition of that branch of humanity, and was resolved to decree the perpetual extinction in the Republic of the commerce and traffic in slaves; and that their introduction into our territory should not be permitted under any pretext." He thought that no relief could be expected from Congress, and could only hope that the state legislature might be induced to interpret the law favorably.[64]

[61] Dublan y Lozano, *Legislación Mexicana*, I, 710.
[62] Seguin to Bastrop, March 24, 1824.
[63] *Diario de las Sesiones del Congreso Constituyente*, June 3, 1824, p. 1 (Mexico, 1824).
[64] Seguin to Austin, July 24, 1825.

Austin had not been unmindful of the consideration of this law by Congress, and, representing a general meeting of the colony held at San Felipe on June 5, 1824, a committee of which he was chairman had prepared a memorial on the subject. The argument was the first of a numerous brood that Austin launched in the next few years. Briefly, slaves of the first three hundred colonists were introduced with the explicit recognition of the imperial law as confirmed by the Constituent Congress. They were not Africans but family servants, raised by the settlers from infancy. They were not for sale or trade, but to clear the land and open farms. To lose them now, on the heels of the heavy expense of moving to Texas, would ruin the colonists. They begged exemption from the emancipation law, which they understood this to be, or, at the least, time to remove their slaves to the United States.[65] The document went to the provincial deputation at San Antonio to be forwarded through the governor to Congress, but whether it reached its destination we do not know.

Neither the federal colonization law nor the federal constitution mentioned slavery, and the state colonization law of March 24, 1825, merely said that in the introduction of slaves the colonists should subject themselves to existing laws and those that might be passed in future. Austin consulted his friend Padilla about this and received the learned opinion that the state law was too indefinite to mean anything and that the federal act of July 13, 1824, could be reasonably interpreted only as prohibiting the slave trade. Mexican attorneys were fond of quoting the maxim, he said, that "what is not prohibited is to be understood as permitted"; wherefore he believed that colonists could bring in slaves for their own use, and that any emancipation laws of the future must provide compensation to the owners.[66]

This and the letter from Seguin holding out hope of favorable state legislation caused Austin to prepare an elaborate memorial which he forwarded to the governor in August, 1825. He proposed that until 1840 colonists, but no others, should be allowed to bring

[65] Petition concerning Slavery, June 10, 1824. The other members of the committee were James Cummins and John P. Coles, alcaldes respectively of the Colorado and the Brazos districts, and Jared E. Groce, who as the owner of nearly a hundred slaves was particularly interested. At the same time another petition asked the privilege of raising tobacco.

[66] Padilla to Austin, June 18, 1825.

slaves to Texas for their own use and property; that, in accordance with the general law, trading should be strictly forbidden, except that colonists might buy from each other for their own use; that after 1840 introduction should be prohibited under any pretext; and that the grandchildren of slaves thus introduced should be free, the males at twenty-five and the females at fifteen. Minute regulations followed to prevent violation of the law by professional traders, for registration of slave births and deaths, and for preventing exchange of old and infirm for young and vigorous slaves in the United States, or the exportation of the second generation to avoid liberation. In practice, however, much of this machinery would have been rendered useless by the provision that colonists might trade with each other. The right of the first colonists to hold slaves introduced at least prior to July 13, 1824, rested on the firm ground of the imperial colonization law, confirmed by the government that succeeded Iturbide, but the same law declared that children born in the empire to such slaves should be free at fourteen. Austin somewhat disingenuously ignored this and sought to make a virtue of not claiming for the settlers of the first contract the descendants of these slaves *ad perpetuam*. Slavery thus regulated, he thought, would enable Texas to flourish, because its principal products must be cotton and sugar, for which, under the circumstances, slave labor was indispensable. The federal constitution did not prohibit slavery; therefore, on the principle that "what is not prohibited is permitted," he did not doubt the competence of the state to pass such a law as he advised. He anticipated objection to the remoteness of emancipation, but believed that a shorter period of immunity would not invite desirable immigrants.[67]

In July, 1826, Austin was informed that work on the state constitution was approaching a critical stage. The framework of the government was completed and the legislature was occupied with a chapter of general provisions, one article of which dealt with slavery. An illiterate but intelligent correspondent wrote from Mexico City that emancipation would certainly pass at Saltillo but that the colonists could evade its effects by the subterfuge of nominally liberating the slaves at once, taking contracts from them to work for their former owners at stipulated wages until they had

[67] Austin to Governor Gonzales, August 20, 1825, and memorial of August 18.

repaid their value.[68] At the same time Saucedo, from San Antonio, was deploring the slavery article and the article fixing the representation of Texas in the legislature. He had foreseen from the beginning the inconvenience of union with Coahuila, he said, and had tried to stipulate certain conditions before agreeing to the arrangement but had been unable to get the people of Bexar to support him. He advised a protest as soon as possible from all the inhabitants of Texas and pledged himself to do his utmost in its favor. Without such action he thought all was lost.[69]

As reported by the committee on the constitution the slavery article read: "The state prohibits slavery absolutely and forever in all its territory, and slaves now in it shall be free from the day the constitution is published in this capital. A law shall regulate the mode of indemnifying those who owned them at the time of publication." [70] Austin did not need Saucedo's invitation to address the government, but it was encouraging to know that he had the support of the local authorities and native inhabitants. Telling Saucedo that he had sent the document to Bastrop, Austin said,

"I have no words to express the great interest that I feel in this matter. To my own fate I give not a single thought, but the fate of many honest, innocent, and unfortunate families, that of all the new colonies, and I may say that of Texas, is pending; because, if the confidence which up to now all have felt in the good faith of the government is once destroyed, many years and infinite pains will be necessary to reestablish it, and the damage will extend not merely to stopping immigration but will cause doubts of the faith of the government in everything." [71]

The memorial was an expansion of this theme. The law authorizing the settlement of the first three hundred permitted the introduction of slaves and guaranteed property without distinction. To free them now would be an act of bad faith, hardly palliated by recognizing the obligation to indemnify the owners; because,

---

[68] Ellis H. Bean to Austin, July 5, 1826: "But there is a way you settlers can stop it all But the sooner the Better that is Gow in Presens of and Alcalde stating that this nigro cost yo[u] so much and when he Pays it by labor Don you have no charge against him he Discounts so much a month as and other hired Person a small sum so that he will be the same to you as before and it will be no more notised." Comparison of this letter signed Ellis H. Bean with several others written by Peter Ellis Bean shows that they were written by the same hand. Why Bean thus varied his signature is unknown.

[69] Saucedo to Austin, July 14, 27, 1826.

[70] Quoted by Austin in his memorial to the legislature, August 11, 1826.

[71] Austin to Saucedo [August 7, 1826].

where was this indemnity to come from? The value of a slave was from six hundred to fifteen hundred dollars, and some could not be bought for three thousand. It would be unjust to tax the Coahuilans to pay for the slaves of Texas, but equally unjust to take the property of Texans and then levy a heavy tax on them to pay for it. Some families, some widows and orphans, had no other property, and to take their slaves would beggar them. The colonists deserved better than to be buried in the wilderness without laborers, "without consolation for the present or hope for the future"; and the negroes, moreover, if liberated, would become vagabonds, a nuisance and a menace. The ayuntamiento of San Antonio thought the statement *"algo duro,"* very strong, but said that conditions justified it, and forwarded a similar one itself.[72]

Austin's settlements were on the eve of a campaign against the Waco and Tahuacano Indians, and the eastern settlers were harassed by the controversy with Edwards which led to the Fredonian rebellion. Rumor now of the intention to abolish slavery caused the greatest despondency, and many talked of returning to the United States.[73] Austin wrote his brother a letter so depressed and "triste" as to give him the "horrors." Brown Austin was at San Antonio and conversation with Saucedo and others left him more hopeful. They were convinced that slavery was indispensable to the prosperity of Texas; had "sent up a representation couched in the strongest language they could express," asking for its admission to the new colonies; and were confident that, whatever happened, the slaves of the original colony would not be freed, first because they were guaranteed by the federal act of establishment, and second because no means could be found for compensating the owners. "Saucedo showed me a letter from the Baron and the Senator Cevallos on this subject; the viejo [old man] is very warm on the subject. . . . The Old Baron has strove hard for us. I know

[72] Austin to legislature, August 11, to Padilla August 14, and to Ayuntamiento of Bexar, August 14, 1826; J. E. B. Austin to Austin, August 22, 1826.

[73] As an example of the exaggeration of rumor: Jesse Thompson and J. C. Peyton of Austin's colony wrote John Sprowl of Ais Bayou (August 11) under strict injunction of secrecy that emancipation was certain and that the country was in despair. Ten days later (August 21) James Gaines wrote Austin that Sprowl was prophesying "that one half of your Colony and the people here would be out of the Country he was asked if they would be drove out he answered no they would go out of their Own accord I insisted on knowing If It was anything that might Effect the Government or the interest of the people he refused to answer me But told Mr. Thomas It was the subject of Slavery and that no hope Remained on that Subject thereby Creating much Rumor."

not what would have been our fate if he had not been a member of the Legislature. Our situation would have been a deplorable one indeed." [74]

Arrived at Saltillo, Brown Austin became less cheerful. Bastrop stood alone in the legislature, and the other members were so inimical to Texas that the most that could be expected would be permission for the original three hundred to retain their slaves. Two weeks of judicious lobbying, however, materially improved the outlook, so that by October 10 he felt certain that the privilege would be extended to all. Further introduction would undoubtedly be stopped, and children would probably be freed at fourteen, though he had done his best to postpone emancipation until twenty-five or twenty-one. Austin's memorial had been so convincing, he said, that Carillo himself, the author of Article 13, had asked permission to withdraw it. Writing November 18, Bastrop gave Brown Austin full credit for his work with the legislature. The article would be passed the following week, he said—though in fact it was not—and all the members except Carillo were pledged to recognize slaves already in and those introduced for a certain term after publication of the constitution, but neither this term nor the age for emancipating children had been determined. Even as Bastrop wrote, these points were forming the subject of another memorial from Austin to the legislature, asking that five years be allowed for introduction and that twenty-five be fixed for the age of emancipation. Austin tried, with at least some success, to enlist the support of Coahuilan municipalities for this petition, but it failed of effect. The members had reached the limit of concession. As passed, the article provided that children born to slaves after the publication of the constitution in the capital of each district should be free from birth and that further introduction of slaves should cease after six months.[75] The constitution was signed at Saltillo March 11, 1827, and published at San Felipe May 29, which, by local interpretation, permitted immigration with slaves until the end of November.[76] This was not satisfactory, but neither was it ruinous; and Austin was still hopeful

[74] J. E. B. Austin to Austin, August 22, September 3; Saucedo to Austin, August 22, 1826.

[75] J. E. B. Austin to Austin, September 23, October 10; Saucedo to Austin, October 5; Bastrop to Austin, November 18; Austin to legislature, November 20; Governor's message to legislature, November 30; Lewis to Austin, December 8, 1826.

[76] J. E. B. Austin to E. M. Perry, May 24; Austin to J. F. Perry, May 26, 1827.

enough to advise his brother-in-law, James F. Perry, to remove to Texas before the door to slavery was shut.

Machinery for the operation of Article 13 was established by a law of September 15, 1827. This provided for a census by age, name, and sex of slaves in the state six months after publication of the constitution; and required ayuntamientos to keep a register of slave births and deaths and report to the government every three months. At the same time it declared that slaves of a master who died without direct heirs should be liberated and that one-tenth should be freed by lot as a sort of inheritance tax when there were heirs; but manumission should not take place if masters or heirs were murdered by one of the slaves. Penalties of the federal act of July 13, 1824, were expressly applied to those who introduced slaves contrary to the constitution, and presumably the federal law prohibited domestic trading.[77]

This law passed, so far as the Texans were concerned, without premonition, but Austin, who arrived at Saltillo shortly afterwards, pleaded strongly, and with partial success, against it. He said that it was unconstitutional, because both state and federal constitutions guaranteed the protection and equality of property. Slaves were property; and to deprive owners of the right to dispose of them by sale or will destroyed equality and violated the constitution. Even the right of eminent domain was denied the state except in cases of public utility, and then only with indemnification of the owner. Suppose a slave owner died, deeply in debt and without heirs, should his creditors have no recourse? It was contrary to public policy, and would be regarded as a breach of faith, pledged in the national and state colonization laws inviting immigration and in the constitution recognizing slavery. It would stop immigration; Texas would revert to the wilderness and the Indians; and the frontiers of Tamaulipas, Nuevo Leon, and Coahuila, now safe behind the buffer of the colonies, would be exposed and harried as before the coming of the settlers. Finally, it incited the slaves to murder. True, the law declared that the slaves should not be freed when the master was poisoned or assassinated by a slave, but who could detect the secret means or the apparent accidents that might be employed? But on this point he would say no more. "It was a

[77] Decree No. 18, Gammel, *Laws of Texas*, I, 188.

mistake, an act of precipitation, an excess of enthusiasm in the cause of liberty, and not an intention to reward assassins." The law was the result of excitement, of an enthusiasm "just, glorious, and holy," but it was injudicious and injurious; and he did not doubt that when they considered calmly and deliberately members would repeal the law.[78]

The response of the legislature was to pass, on November 24, two supplementary articles to be annexed to the original decree. One of these safe-guarded owners by providing that slaves should not be freed when the master died by an unknown hand or in any unnatural way. The other, in the guise of a benefit to the slave, which, of course, it might well have been, allowed him "to change his master," if the new master would indemnify the old for the value of the slave.[79]

Aside from half-hearted efforts of the political chief to inaugurate the registration of slaves in Texas, no more attention seems to have been paid to the law from any source. Slaves must have passed by inheritance after 1827, but there is no record of any manumissions, nor of the question's being raised.

Settlers on the ground might now accept the *status quo* with reasonable assurance, so far as their own slaves were concerned—might even foresee their rapid rise in value by the exclusion of others—but letters from the United States made it plain that immigration of the better class would cease, unless a way could be found to continue the introduction of slaves.[80] Perhaps the solution of this problem lay in the direction of Bean's suggestion of July 5, 1826. If slaves already in Texas could be retained as indented servants, why could they not be introduced as such? The idea first appears full grown in a laconic minute of the newly organized ayuntamiento of San Felipe: "Considering the paralized state of immigration to this Jurisdiction from the U. S. arrising from the difficulties

---

[78] Austin to members of the legislature, November 8, and to ————, evidently a member of the national senate, November 8, 1827.

[79] Decree No. 35, Gammel, *Laws of Texas*, I, 202. There is no documentary evidence that Austin influenced this second provision. It gave domestic trading an appearance of regularity, but otherwise was hardly needed. A transaction of November 16, 1824, when the shadow of the federal prohibition was heavy, shows how sales could be effected. By it Samuel and Elizabeth Pharr, for a consideration of $625, "hired" to William Pettus for a term of sixty years, Lissy, twenty-eight years old, and her son Willis, seven. The loss was to Pettus if they died or ran away before the term expired.

[80] See, for example, [Richard Ellis] to Austin, from Tuscumbia, Alabama, January 3, 1828, and Henry S. Brown to Austin, New Orleans, March 21, 1828.

encountered by Immigrants in bringing servants and hirelings with them, this Body conceive it their duty to propose to the Legislature of this state through the chief of Depart[ment] a project of a Law whereby Emigrants and inhabitants of this state may be secured in the Contracts made by them with servants or hirelings in for‐ eign countries which project the pres[iden]t will make out in the following terms to wit. 'Are guaranteed the Contracts made by emigrants to this state or Inhabitants of it with the servants or hire‐ lings they introduce' and solicit the said Chief to forward it on to the Legislature with such additional influence as he may think proper to extend to it." [81]

Austin transmitted this to the political chief on April 7, 1828, in a letter which has disappeared. Músquiz replied that the ayunta‐ miento had the right to petition but not to frame a bill, but, not to lose time while the ayuntamiento was recasting the document, he sent the bill to the two Texan representatives, José Antonio Navarro and Miguel Arciniega, so that they could prepare the way for its presentation. Fortunately, because Músquiz's mail was delayed, Austin had already furnished them copies; and Navarro, who was a member of the committee on colonization, introduced the bill and secured its passage during a heated contest over a law suspend‐ ing the executive council, vice-governor, and political chief. Both Navarro and Arciniega believed that under other circumstances it might not have passed, and Arciniega dropped a hint that it might be repealed. [82]

A clean-cut translation of the law by Austin reads:

"The Legislature of the State of Coahuila and Texas taking into con‐ sideration the scarcity of laborers and servants for agricultural purposes, and being desirous to promote the general advancement in all the various branches of industry, have decreed as follows,

"All contracts not contrary to the laws of this State made in foreign countries between emigrants to, or inhabitants of, this State and servants or hirelings introduced by them are guaranteed as valid in this State." [83]

The application of this law was simple and comprehensive. Theoretically master and slave, but often in practice only the mas‐

---

[81] *Southwestern Historical Quarterly*, XXI, 311. The action was taken on April 5, 1828.
[82] Músquiz to Austin, April 17, May 15; Padilla to Austin, May 3; Navarro to Austin, May 17; Arciniega to Austin, May 17, 1828. The law passed on May 5.
[83] Decree No. 56, Gammel, *Laws of Texas*, I, 213.

ter, went before a notary and declared the value of the slave to be a certain sum. The slave wished to be free, and in Texas would be free; but he could not avail himself of this boon unless his master took him there; and the master could not afford to sacrifice his value. Therefore, in recognition of the owner's right and of the privileges which he himself would acquire, the slave contracted to work for the master after removal at stipulated wages until he had repaid his value. Minors and unborn children were included in the contract and the wages were so low that Bean's injunction was fulfilled, and "the slave was the same to the master as before." [84]

As a subterfuge, the law legalizing this evasion of the constitution was reasonably effective, but Austin was not comfortable under the shadow of the constitutional prohibition and of the law regulating the inheritance of slaves. After receiving from Padilla a prophecy that the time would come when both could be repealed, he took up the subject with the governor, combining it opportunely with his campaign for open ports and for domestic and foreign trade. Coahuila and Texas, he declared, must seek its wealth and happiness in the promotion of agriculture, and all the state's laws should be directed to that end. Coahuila could produce in excess of its own consumption wine, olives, wheat, cotton, tobacco, and other products, of which cotton and tobacco would be most profitable for exportation. Texas could produce cotton, corn, tobacco, possibly sugar, and all the vegetables. Cotton would be its most valuable export. The stimulation of cotton culture would encourage all branches of agriculture, which would enrich the state. At present the product of Mexican mines went to Europe to buy merchandise; the merchants bought from manufacturers; and they in turn bought raw materials from the United States; so that in the end the gold and silver of Mexico found its way to the purses of the North American farmers. Why should not Mexico enjoy a part of this fountain of riches?

[84] Copy of a contract prepared by Austin, May —, 1828. Pizarro Martinez, Mexican consul at New Orleans, complained in 1831 that owners made these declarations alone and then embarked, with the slave in ignorance that such a document existed, or that he was "going to breathe the free air of a country where virtue and merit take care of color." (Quoted by Governor Letona to Ramón Músquiz, May 20, 1831, General Land Office of Texas, Vol. 57, p. 139). Martinez gives another form of contract in which the slave receipted for a sum of money and agreed to serve the master for a specified term, from seventy to ninety years.—Transcripts from Department of Fomento, Mexico, Legajo 7, Expediente 56.

Opinions might differ concerning the best method of encouraging and extending the cultivation of cotton, but some measures
were so obvious that they need only be stated. First, encourage the
settlement of Texas by repealing Decree Number 18 and Article 13
of the constitution; by opening the port of the Brazos; and by admitting gins and bagging free. All the colonists were experienced
in the cultivation of cotton and in preparing it for the European
market, and Coahuilans would learn from them by the influence
of example. Second, make a commercial treaty with England,
granting reciprocal privileges to English and Mexican shipping,
and admitting English bagging and coarse fabrics free in return
for the free entrance of Mexican cotton in English ports. Angered
by the protective system of the United States, England was already
casting its eyes over Mexico to find a source of cotton, rice, and tobacco to enable it to break with the North; and, for the same reason, rich planters of the southern states were eager to move to
Texas. Only the prohibition of slavery stood in their way. The stimulation of cotton would react on other branches of agriculture;
canals and roads would follow; and Coahuila would find a market
for its wines, olives, fruits, and flour.

Part of this program depended upon the federal government and
part upon the government of the state. Its adoption would "bind
Texas to Mexico internally by indissoluble bonds of the strongest
character—those of interest and of the individual happiness of
each person." [85]

The fact that Austin's purpose was the advancement of Texas
did not make his argument less true for the rest of Mexico; and
Viesca was friendly enough, and probably intelligent enough, to
realize it. There was little that he could do, however; the legislative
power resented suggestions from the executive; and Austin expected no more from his memorial perhaps than an educative influence.

Austin continued correspondence during the summer of 1829
with the political chief and with Navarro, going so far as to sound
Navarro on the feasibility of suspending the constitutional prohibition for ten years without going through the well-nigh impos-

[85] Austin to Governor Viesca, February 19, 1829. See also Terán to Austin, June 24,
1828; Durst to Austin, July 22, 1828; Padilla to Austin, January 24, 1829.

sible procedure prescribed for amending the constitution.[86] In August his brother died, and in September he himself was on the brink of death. During his illness fell a bolt from the blue. President Guerrero had been invested in August with extraordinary military authority to concentrate all the resources of the nation to repel a Spanish invasion; and General José María Tornel induced him to take advantage of this military dictatorship to issue on September 15 a decree, in commemoration of Mexican independence, abolishing slavery throughout the republic, except in the Isthmus of Tehuantepec. Tornel was frankly hostile to the United States, feared that it was getting a hold on Texas by the colonization policy, and believed that emancipation would check immigration.[87]

The decree reached Texas in a letter from Governor Viesca on October 16.[88] Without waiting to confer with Austin, the political chief resolved to suspend its publication until the president could be urged to except Texas from its operation. He drew up for the governor a statement of the situation that Austin could not have bettered. The right of the first colonists to hold slaves, he declared, was specifically recognized by the act legalizing Austin's contract. Subsequently both the federal and state colonization laws invited immigrants to settle in the country and solemnly guaranteed their property. In the face of these assurances it seemed very hard that those already in the province should be deprived of the one form of property that was indispensable to them in agriculture, cattle raising, and other labors "to which they are dedicated, and which could not be carried on without the aid of the robust and almost indefatigable arms of that race of the human species which is called negroes, and who, to their misfortune, suffer slavery." But it must not be forgotten that they were already slaves before coming to Mexico; neither the government nor the people of the country made them slaves; and, while "philanthropy and the natural sympathies of humanity cry out in favor of liberty, the positive laws which regulate society take the part of property and declare it a

[86] Músquiz to Austin, May 28, 1829, acknowledging letters from Austin of April 15 and 21 and May 5; Austin to Navarro, July 23, 1829.

[87] Dublan y Lozano, *Legislación Mexicana*, II, 151; Tornel, *Breve Reseña Histórica*, (Mexico, 1852), 85. Tornel's recollection in 1852 of his purpose in 1829 may have been shaped in some degree by the recent war with the United States. When he wrote it was a popular exercise of public men to claim to have seen the catastrophe afar and to have tried to avoid it.

[88] Músquiz to Elosua, November 24, 1829, General Land Office of Texas, Vol. 57, p. 115.

sacred and inviolable right." There were more than a thousand slaves in the colonies, Músquiz estimated, and the governor would realize from what he had said the disturbance of public order and the fatal consequences to the settlers that would follow the publication of the decree. He begged, therefore, that the governor would petition the president to exempt Texas from its operation.[89]

Obviously enough Músquiz was not blind to the danger of resistance from the colonists but it is clear beyond doubt that he and the other intelligent inhabitants of Bexar were keenly awake to the importance of protecting the interest of the colonists as the only means of raising Texas from the desolation which the handful of natives at Bexar and Goliad had endured for a hundred years. Even in Coahuila some looked to the fees from Texas to support the government and saw in its prosperity the surest pledge of Coahuilan progress. Navarro wrote Austin, "We have already written very strongly to the government and to friends who can exert great influence for the repeal of such a law. We have also the satisfaction of having received by today's mail letters from some friends of the best deputies of Saltillo in which [they say] they are preparing to notice the decree in print, even before knowing what we have to say about it here. Thus, you may believe that the best men of the state oppose such a law, which betrays justice and good faith." Asking the president to exempt Texas from the decree, Governor Viesca declared that he would have made the request, even without the petition of the political chief, because the advancement of Coahuila was so dependent upon that of Texas. Liberty was, of course, a noble sentiment, but slavery was established in a barbarous age and even the strongest and most enlightened nations had not been able to extinguish it. He feared that the colonists, seeing themselves deprived of their property with only a remote hope of indemnification, would bring upon the state some disturbances that it was in poor condition to withstand. By this he did not mean to imply that the colonists were turbulent or insubordinate, for up to the present there were only proofs to the contrary; "but the nature

[89] Músquiz to the governor, October 25, 1829. This copy is in the General Land Office of Texas, Vol. 57, p. 103ff. Following it is another copy, identical for the most part but toward the end inveighing more strongly against the decree. There is a copy in the Political Chief's Blotter in the Bexar Archives, a translation in the Nacogdoches Archives, and a translation of a "cautiously edited" copy (see Padilla to Austin, November 26, 1829) in *The Texas Gazette*, January 23, 1830.

of man is known and the feelings of which he is capable when he sees himself from day to day in danger of being ruined, as would happen to many of them whose fortune consists entirely of slaves." [90]

In the meantime, Músquiz had written Austin of the decree, enjoining him to the strictest secrecy until the result of his petition for exemption should be known. In some unexplained way, however, a copy of the document reached the alcalde at Nacogdoches and caused consternation, though he, too, withheld it from official publication. Piedras, the military commandant there, wrote his superior at San Antonio that the people, crushed down by destitution, were hoping for assistance from the federal government, and then came the decree abolishing slavery. All the inhabitants of the frontier owned slaves, which they had lost the right to take back to the United States, and they could not be expected to submit. The news had spread with lightning speed, and all day foreigners and some Mexicans had been coming to ask him the truth. John Durst, a prominent citizen of Nacogdoches, wrote in a state of desperation to Austin, "In the name of God what shall we do—for God sake advise me on the subject by the return of mail—we are ruined forever should this measure be adopted." [91]

Though somewhat reassured by the political chief's evident concern,[92] Austin seems to have been determined to resist, if the decree were not withdrawn. To Durst's frenzied appeal he wrote:

"What the people of Texas have to do is to represent to the Government through the Ayuntamientos or some other channel, in a very respectful manner that agreeably to the constitution, and the colonization laws all their property is guaranteed to them without exceptions in the most solemn and sacred manner. That they brought their slave property into the country and have retained it here, under the faith of that guarantee, and in consequence of a special invitation publically given to emigrants by the government in the colonization law to do so. That they have taken an oath to defend the constitution, and are bound to do so. That the constitution of the state expressly recognizes the right of property in slaves by allowing six months after its publication for their intro-

---

[90] J. A. Navarro to Austin, October 29, 1829; Governor Viesca to the president, November 14, 1829—a translation of this was published in the *Texas Gazette,* January 30, 1830.

[91] José de las Piedras to Colonel Elosua, November 9, 1829, Nacogdoches Archives; Durst to Austin, November 10, 1829; José Ignacio Ibarbo (Alcalde of Nacogdoches) to Músquiz, November 10, 1829, General Land Office of Texas, Vol. 57, p. 124.

[92] Músquiz to Austin, November 12, 1829, speaks of a letter of November 2 from Austin arguing against the constitutionality of the decree.

duction into the State. That they *will* defend it, and with *it,* their property.

"There ought to be no vociferous and visionary excitement or noise about this matter. Our course is a very plain one—calm, deliberate, dispationate, inflexible firmness; and not windy and ridiculous blowing and wild threats, and much less anything like opposition to the Mexican Constitution, nothing of this kind will do any good, it will in fact be unjustifiable, and will never be approved of by me but on the contrary opposed most decidedly. I will not violate my duty as a Mexican citizen.

"The constitution must be both our shield, and our arms; under *it,* and with *it,* we must constitutionally defend ourselves and our property.

"The chief of department Dⁿ Ramon Musquiz, has taken a firm and noble stand. He has suspended the publication of said decree, and has represented in a very able manner against it. If he should finally be compelled to publish and circulate it, the Ayuntamientos must then take an unanimous, firm, and *constitutional* stand. The people will unanimously support them.

"I know nothing of the men who compose the Ayuntamiento of Nacogdoches, if they are true patriots and true friends to themselves and to Texas, they will not suffer that decree to be published or circulated in that Municipality and they will take the stand I have indicated or some other that will preserve the constitution and our constitutional rights from open, and direct violation.

"These are my ideas on the matter. I have said the same to my friends in Bexar, and when the decree arrives officially, (which it has not yet) I shall say the same to the Govᵗ. What I do in this matter will be done openly. Mexico has not within its whole dominions a man who would defend its independence, the union of its territory, and all its constitutional rights sooner than I would, or be more ready and willing to discharge his duties as a Mexican citizen; one of the first and most sacred of those duties is to protect my constitutional rights, and I will do it, so far as I am able. I am the owner of one slave only, an old decreped woman, not worth much,[93] but in this matter I should feel that my constitutional rights as a Mexican were just as much infringed, as they would be if I had a thousand, it is the principle and not the amount, the latter makes the violation more agravated, but, not more illegal or unconstitutional." [94]

Several of Austin's letters of this period have disappeared. He was probably too much pressed to take copies, and the originals

[93] Bill of sale from John Gibson to Austin, February 5, 1828, selling a negro woman for $350.

[94] Austin to Durst, November 17, 1829. Durst replied on the 24th that the people would unanimously follow Austin's example. Thus far he had been able to control the ayuntamiento, but had no confidence in its stability—"they are a Boddy without souls and subjects easy worked on by intrigue."

were not preserved in the archives of the political chief. In one of them he evidently asked Músquiz's opinion of the likelihood of Mexico's selling Texas to the United States. Colonel Anthony Butler was then passing through Texas with instructions from President Jackson to Poinsett—later to become his own, after Poinsett's recall —to make an offer for the province; and one of the arguments suggested for Poinsett's use when the instructions were drafted in August was that by selling Texas Mexico could raise enough money to defend the rest of its territory from Spain.[95] Butler evidently disclosed to Austin enough of his mission to prompt the question. Músquiz was too far from the font of political information to have significant knowledge, but his reply is interesting. He thought that if the Spanish invasion had had an initial success, Guerrero would have sold Texas; but that since its failure he would be too much afraid of public opinion to attempt it. At the same time Músquiz acknowledged another letter, and authorized Austin, if he thought it necessary, in order to relieve the apprehensions of the colonists, to publish in the *Texas Gazette* a translation of his memorial to the governor. He had already, the day before, instructed the alcalde at Nacogdoches to publish the document there in the *Mexican Advocate*. The next day he notified Austin of the arrival of a copy of the governor's address to the president.[96]

The Texans were favored by the fact that Agustin Viesca, brother of the governor of Coahuila and Texas, was secretary of relations when their petitions reached the president, so that they received prompt attention.[97] On December 2 he wrote the governor that the president "has been pleased to accede to the solicitation of your Excellency and declare the department of Texas excepted from the general disposition, comprehended in said decree [of September 15, 1829]. Therefore his Excellency declares that no

[95] The instructions are in MSS. of the Department of State (Washington), Special Missions, I, 34–50. Austin introduced Butler to Músquiz in a letter of November 10.

[96] Músquiz to Austin, November 26, 27, 1829. See also Padilla to Austin, November 26; Músquiz to Alcalde of Nacogdoches, November 25, Nacogdoches Archives; Músquiz to Elosua, November 24, General Land Office of Texas, Vol. 57, p. 115; Piedras to Elosua, November 24, Transcripts from Department of Fomento. On November 30 Philip Dimmit wrote Austin that his letter to the political chief in defense of his colony was much admired at Bexar, where all were for him. All the *Gazette's* type was tied up in Austin's *Translation of the Laws, Orders and Contracts on Colonization*, etc., so that it was not until January 23 and January 30, 1830, that the memorials of the political chief and governor were published.

[97] Letters of Músquiz and Padilla to Austin, November 27, 1829.

change must be made as respects the slaves that legally exist in that part of your state." [98] This was forwarded by the governor on December 12 to the political chief, and by him circulated on December 24. [99] At about the same time, perhaps—though possibly much earlier—the president in a private letter (*carta particular*) authorized General Terán, now commandant of the Eastern Interior Provinces, to inform the colonists that the emancipation decree did not include Texas, except that there must be no further introduction of slaves. [100] Some historians—both Mexican and American—emphasizing this private letter to Terán, have been led to deny that an official decree of exemption was ever issued. [101] As a matter of fact, it is doubtful whether it was ever published or circulated except in Texas. [102]

Besides Austin's letters, there is little material on the attitude of his colonists. No doubt they were excited and anxious, but it

[98] This quotation is from a translation in the *Texas Gazette,* January 30, 1830. There is a manuscript copy and a translation in the Nacogdoches Archives. See also General Land Office of Texas, Vol. 57, p. 131.

[99] See General Land Office of Texas, Vol. 57, pp. 131ff. Writing the governor on January 3, 1830, Músquiz said, "I shall never be able to be grateful enough for the consideration with which it was deigned to attend to the explanation which I addressed to you on this subject."—*Ibid.*

[100] Terán reported this to Colonel Elosua, at Bexar, on December 18, 1829 (See General Land Office of Texas, Vol. 57, p. 130), and added, "I immediately communicated it to Colonel Piedras [at Nacogdoches] and to Lieutenant Colonel Austin." The letter to Austin is dated November 20, 1829, and was received by Austin December 29 (See acknowledgment, of that date, to Terán). In the letter to Elosua (December 18) Terán says that the president wrote in response to a letter of his own, and uses the past tense in speaking of his letter to Austin, as he does also in a letter to the war department on December 19 (Transcripts from Department of Fomento, Mexico, legajo 5, expediente 34). If, then, the date to Austin (November 20) is correct, and not an inadvertent slip for December 20, which, in the light of the evidence above seems unlikely, Guerrero's letter to Terán exempting Texas was written before the receipt of the protests from Texas. This, if the fact, would be rather significant.

[101] Lester G. Bugbee's "Slavery in Early Texas," in *Political Science Quarterly,* XIII, 389–412, 648–668, is an excellent treatment of the subject, written with access to most of the documents used in this study. Pages 655–658 discuss the incident of the private letter to Terán.

[102] On February 14, 1830, Terán wrote the war department that the settlers in East Texas were still anxious, notwithstanding the fact that the emancipation decree itself had not been published. He thought it very important "to decide this matter, in order to cut off at the root every pretext for dissatisfaction." The war department referred this to the department of relations, now headed by Lúcas Alamán, which replied on March 6 that a committee was engaged in revising the decrees issued by Guerrero and that one of the questions to be considered was the repeal of the emancipation decree (see Transcripts from Department of Fomento, Mexico, legajo 5, expediente 34). The decision of the new government was probably announced in Article 10 of the Decree of April 6, 1830: "No change shall be made with respect to the colonies already established, nor with respect to the slaves which they now contain"—but prohibition of further introduction must be observed.

was always Austin's policy with them to minimize political dangers and grievances. One can imagine him soothing their fears, assuring them that Texas would certainly be exempted from the operation of the decree, that slaves already in Texas were guaranteed and would be recognized, and that indented servants could still be introduced. And they were ready to believe him. He had been equal to every situation in the past, why not to this? At any rate, he could handle it better than they, and there would be time to take stock and decide on the next step when they knew how badly they were hurt.

Austin's disappointment and distress were the keener because he had been recently allowing himself to enjoy fair visions of the future. He had written William H. Wharton in the spring of 1829 that the hardships of his colonies were all behind them and that a small band of men of the right sort working together could "make Texas the garden of North America."

"Suppose [he said] that 4 or 500 southern men of *talents* and *capital* and *high character* were to emigrate to Texas in a body next fall, what can prevent their future prosperity? I have the legal right to guarantee to them a reception as emigrants in my colony and as such the law grants them land. The door is legally opened to them and they are invited to enter and partake of the fortune and prosperity and happiness which nature has provided with a liberal hand for all who will now advance and receive them. Such an opportunity never offered upon earth, never can offer again, and it will be trifling with fortune to neglect it. But do not misunderstand me [he cautioned] as to the kind of emigrants—ardent, inexperienced, hot headed youths piping from college, or ignorant, self willed, 'mobish' mountaineers and frontiersmen who 'hold to Lynch law' and damning those who are in office merely because they are in office would totally ruin us forever. We need that class of emigrants who deserve the appelation of Southern Gentlemen, whose fortunes are independent but not overgrown, whose judgment has been enlightened by education and matured by experience, and who have families to keep the intemperate, wild, ambitious passions of the human heart within the circle of prudence. I would fearlessly pledge my head that an emigration of 400 *such men* next fall to Texas would permanently ensure the prosperity of this country and the happiness of its inhabitants."

The men then in power in the state, he said, wished to tolerate slavery; Texas was too far and too widely separated from Mexico by barren, desolate wilderness to be much disturbed by revolution; and defects in the constitution and laws could be amended if the Texans were united and harmonious.[103]

The contrast to this, he wrote to Terán: "I could see in the decree [of emancipation] nothing but the overthrow and destruction of all the efforts and painful labors of more than seven years to redeem Texas from the uninhabited and abandoned condition that it was in in 1821—nothing but the ruin of many individuals, the loss of faith in the government, and the surrender of this valuable section of the republic to the Indians." [104]

But the reaction to hope and confidence was rapid. Within a week of learning that the danger had passed he was writing to his brother-in-law, urging him for the first time to move to Texas: "I have never been so thoroughly convinced as I now am of the future rapid rise of this country. . . . This is the most liberal and munificent Gov^t. on earth to emigrants—After being here one year you will oppose a change to Uncle Sam. . . . All the difficulties as to slaves . . . are removed, . . . and I have no doubt that in a few years this will be a slave state."[105]

The close of 1829 and the beginning of 1830 found a great immigration pouring into Texas. On January 3, 1830, Austin wrote his brother-in-law that a hundred and fifty-three families had arrived within the past two months. On the 16th he wrote that two hundred persons had arrived in a month. He made a number of contracts with men of comfortable means in northern Alabama. The Reverend Gideon Blackburn, president of Centre College, at Danville, Kentucky, made inquiries with a view to settling from forty to a hundred families, so that he could spend the evening of his life among friends "in promoting the cause of literature and religion." Judge Joshua Child, in Natchez, Mississippi, proposed a plan for the rapid settlement of the country and said that it was immaterial to him whether slavery was tolerated or not. On March 28 Austin again wrote his brother-in-law, "You have no idea at all of this country, nor of the great emigration that is daily coming to it, nor of the character of the emigrants. We are getting the best men, the best kind of settlers. Pay no attention to rumors and silly

---

[103] Austin to Wharton, April 24, 1829.
[104] Austin to Terán, December 29, 1829.
[105] Austin to James F. Perry, December 31, 1829.

reports."[106] At the same time he was investigating, with what appeared to be encouraging prospects, the feasibility of turning Swiss and German immigrants to Texas.[107]

It seems that Austin concluded from these indications that repeal of the anti-slavery measures of the State was no longer necessary to the rapid development of Texas. When, therefore, the federal act of April 6, 1830, recognized existing slavery, forbade further introduction of slaves, and prohibited, apparently, further settlement of immigrants from the United States in Texas his decision was quickly made. With the federal government reinforcing that of the state, it was obviously unreasonable to contend longer for favorable slavery legislation; and by promptly accepting that situation concessions might be obtained for the continuance of immigration from the United States. There could, of course, be no question of the relative importance of the two—especially so long as the labor contract law was not tampered with. On May 17 and 18 Austin dispatched vigorous protests against the anti-immigration provision to Vice-President Bustamante and General Terán, but said nothing about slavery. In an undated fragment, however, evidently written about the same time, he declared the article excluding slaves to be "founded in justice and in the well-being of the state."[108]

This attitude did no violence to Austin's personal feelings—provided always settlement could go on—and, having taken his stand, he attempted to carry the colonists with him and burn the bridges behind him. On June 1 he wrote his cousin, Henry Austin, who had been discussing the possibility of the transfer of Texas to the United States, that he himself would oppose union with the United States without some previous guarantees, among which would be the perpetual exclusion of slavery from Texas. To another relative, Thomas F. Leaming of Philadelphia, he wrote more strongly. One of the reasons, he said, which were causing him to think of the advantages of Swiss and German immigrants—aside from their character and industry—was that

"they have not in general that horrible *mania* for speculation which is so

---

[106] Austin to Perry, January 3, 16, March 28, 1830; Pettit to Austin, January 6; Blackburn, January 19; J. Child, January 24; Ellis, January 30; Faulkner, February 23.

[107] Archibald Austin acknowledged from New York City on May 31, 1830, a letter from Austin on this subject written February 24. See other letters from Archibald Austin, July 14 and September 15, 1830.

[108] Austin to ———, (about May 18, 1830) interpreting the law of April 6, 1830.

prominent a trait in the English and North American character, *and above all they will oppose slavery.* The idea of seeing such a country as this overrun by a slave population almost makes me weep. It is in vain to tell a North American that the white population will be destroyed some fifty or eighty years hence by the negroes. . . . To say anything to them as to the justice of slavery, or its demoralizing effect on society, is only to draw down ridicule upon the person who attempts it. In the beginning of this settlement [he explained] I was compelled to hold out the idea that slavery would be tolerated, and I succeeded in getting it *tolerated* for a time by the Gov^t. I did this to get a start, for otherwise it would have been next to impossible to have started at all, for I had to draw on Louisiana and Mississippi, slave states, for the first emigrants. Slavery is now most positively prohibited by our Constitution and by a number of Laws, and I do hope it may always be so."

Leaming was neither a slave-holder nor a prospective colonist, and Austin might therefore be suspected of expressing himself for effect more strongly than he felt; but he wrote the same to Richard Ellis, a wealthy planter of Alabama, who was both slave owner and colonist, and to S. Rhoads Fisher, who had returned to Philadelphia, after a reconnaissance, to take his family to Texas. He requested Ellis to publish his letter in the Alabama papers, and suggested that Fisher furnish articles to Pennsylvania papers in a similar tone. The continued introduction of slaves under peonage contracts he did not consider inconsistent with this attitude: "This provision [the contract law] will be highly useful to the country without the least danger of doing any harm for no one will be willing to risk a large capital in negroes under contracts with them, for they are free on their arrival here, and can only be held to labor by contracts, as servants are all over this nation, and in other free countries."[109]

The reply of the Alabama gentlemen is not at hand, though most of them ultimately found their way to Texas; but Fisher was not of two minds about the matter. He thought that Texas must continue to draw its population chiefly from the southern states, and that unrestricted introduction of slaves for at least five years was all important.[110]

No doubt the actual settlers were equally emphatic. In this par-

[109] Austin to Henry Austin, June 1, 1830; to Leaming, June 14 (two letters); to Ellis and others, June 14; to Fisher, June 15. See also Austin to Piedras, June 28, 1830; and to Perry, July 4, 14, 1830.
[110] Fisher to Austin, August 14, 23, 1830.

ticular Austin was a voice crying in the wilderness; and, realizing that a status half slave and half free would in the end be impossible, he again turned to the hopeless task of trying to persuade the government to change its policy.[111] With Terán he opened the subject as early as February, 1831; with Alamán, cautiously, on March 21. Alamán evaded an answer, but Terán replied frankly. The admission of slaves, he had no doubt, would hasten the settlement and development of Texas; ultimately their use in all the coast states was probably inevitable; but the system had many drawbacks; and he thought it unwise to raise the subject during the existing political agitations. Comparing Texas with the rest of Mexico, he saw no great obstacles to its ultimate prosperity, but, as in everything, it was "necessary to have patience and not expect progress to be made in a year which could come only with the fullness of time."[112] There the matter rested. After receiving this letter Austin wrote Williams that his arguments had made a great impression, but he was far from comfortable about it. "I sometimes shudder at the consequences," he declared, "and think that a large part [of] America will be Santo Domingonized in 100 or 200 years—The wishes of my colonists have hurried me into this thing. But I am now in for the cuestion, and there is no retreat, for my rule is to go ahead after once coming to a decissive resolution on a matter of such consequence as this."[113] But he could not refrain from looking back with regret. In December he spoke of slavery as "that curse of curses and worst of reproaches on civilized man; that unanswered and unanswerable inconsistency of free and liberal republicans." As late as the middle of 1832 he expressed satisfaction with the constitutional exclusion of slavery.[114] A year later, however, he had surrendered the ideal. "I have been averse to the principle of slavery in Texas [he wrote in May, 1833]. I have now and for the last six months changed my views on that matter; though my ideas are the same as to the abstract principle. T[exas] *must be* a slave coun-

---

[111] Austin wrote Mrs. Holley, July 19, 1831: "Negroes can be brought here under indentures, as servants, but *not* as *slaves*. This question of slavery is a difficult one to get on with. It will ultimately be admitted, or the free negroes will be formed by law into a separate and distinct class—*the laboring class*. . . . Either this or slavery in full *must* take place. Which is best? Quien sabe? It is a difficult and *dark* question."

[112] Terán to Austin, March ——, April 3, 1831; Austin to Alamán, March 21, 1831, Transcripts from Department of Fomento, Mexico, legajo 2, expediente 5.

[113] Austin to Williams, April 16, 1831, Rosenberg Library.

[114] Austin to Mrs. Holley, December 25, 1821; to Edward Livingston, June 24, 1832.

try. Circumstances and unavoidable necessity compel it. It is the wish of the people there, and it is my duty to do all I can, prudently, in favor of it. I will do so."[115] Austin was then at Matamoras, on his way to Mexico City to present the petition of the convention of the previous month for the separation of Texas from Coahuila and the organization of a local state government. He had presided at another convention in October, 1832; was it there that he became finally convinced of the futility of trying to reconcile the colonists to the government's policy of exclusion?

In April, 1832, the legislature had passed a new colonization law, repealing that of 1825. Two of its provisions concerned slavery. The first declared new immigrants subject to the existing laws and those to be passed thereafter; the second limited to ten years' duration labor contracts with "servants and day laborers whom the colonists introduced." [116] Slaves were now excluded by federal law and state constitution, and the loophole for evasion was narrowed to these contracts for ten years. Austin was a member of the legislature that passed this law, but neither in his writings nor in those of others that have come down to us is there a word of reference to these provisions.[117]

Measured by any standard but that of the success of the colonies and the welfare of the colonists, Austin's attitude appears unstable. That, however, was always his controlling standard. Usually he could lead; but when he could not, he must yield, or compromise, in order to retain his influence over the majority of the colonists, which was always essential to the happiness of them all. As he himself realized, this sometimes gave him the appearance of weakness and inconsistency.[118] There can be no doubt that for a time his feelings combined with his judgment to convince him that success

[115] Austin to Wily Martin, May 30, 1833.

[116] Decree No. 190, Gammel, *Laws of Texas,* I, 299–303.

[117] The journals of the legislature are unenlightening. Benjamin Lundy, who was at San Felipe shortly after the convention of April, 1833, said that members openly declared that an object in desiring to set up a separate state government was to establish slavery by state laws.—*The War in Texas,* etc., 12 (Philadelphia, 1836). There is no reason to doubt this, but it is far from proving Lundy's thesis that the Texas revolution was caused by the determination of the Texans to maintain slavery.

[118] "My native countrymen are blunt republicans, and do not always reflect sufficiently, and some of them have accused me of debility, want of firmness, temporising, etc. It was my duty to steer my precious bark (the Colony) through all the shoals and quicks[ands] regardless of the curses and ridicule of the passengers. I knew what I was about—they did not."—Austin to Williams, February 19, 1831, Rosenberg Library.

could be achieved under the restrictive Mexican laws; that a strong current of anti-slavery immigration could be turned to Texas; and that, in the end, Texas might prosper as a free state. He could not win the settlers to this program—even, apparently, if we are to judge from Fisher's attitude, those from free states—and, consistently with his practice, he reluctantly adapted himself to conditions which he could not change.

The want of religious toleration occupied, as we have seen, a prominent place in the thoughts of the immigrant making up his mind to move to Texas, but, unlike the question of slavery, it seems to have caused him little active worry after his arrival. From time to time, no doubt, he dutifully regretted the fate of his children, condemned to grow up in the wilderness without the beneficent influences of churches and schools; but in sober truth it was a condition to which he reconciled himself with unconscious ease.

To Austin, however, responsible for the successful development of the colony, there were two elements of danger in the situation. One was that the application of a rigid test might exclude or banish many desirable families who had resigned themselves to the formal restriction; the other was that the settlers might be stirred by a peripatetic evangelist to some demonstration that would excite the fanaticism of the government and upset abruptly the whole policy of colonization. If only they could be kept quiet on the subject for a few years, he believed that the liberal tendencies of republican government would break down the monopoly of a state church.[119] He was punctilious, therefore, even beyond his wont to warn the early settlers against offense in that direction. In his first address after returning from Mexico in 1823 he cautioned them, "We must all be particular on this subject and respect the Catholic religion with all that attention due to its sacredness and to the laws of the land." At the same time, to make the injunction as palatable as possible he told them, as we know, that he had asked for the appointment of a curate, Father Francisco Maynes, who had served at Natchitoches, and who spoke English and French, and knew the American character.[120]

[119] Austin to ———, October 20, 1823.
[120] Austin to the Colonists, August 6, 1823; to Luciana García, August 10; Terms of Settlement, October 30.

He particularly feared the Methodists because he knew that the unrestrained emotionalism which then characterized them would draw unfavorable attention of the government. When Brown Austin returned to Missouri in 1824, Austin instructed him to "let the Methodists know the truth relative to religion"; and at the same time he told the Reverend William Stevenson, a Methodist and his friend, that he should be compelled to imprison any preacher who went about the country preaching. Writing some months later to his sister, he said that the Methodists were criticizing him, which he rather welcomed because it would convince the government that the law was being obeyed in the colony. "If they are kept out, or would remain quiet if here for a short time," he added, "we shall succeed in getting a free toleration for all religions."[121]

Austin's confidence in the development of liberal opinion was not based entirely upon his own optimism. Seguin wrote from his seat in Congress that even under the Spanish government Texas had enjoyed toleration in fact, and he did not believe that private worship would now be disturbed, or that the requirement that immigrants must be Catholic would be rigidly enforced, so long as they were Christians. Subsequently he reported that a proposal to restrict immigration exclusively to Catholics had been rejected with only the vote of the proponent in its favor.[122] Despite such encouragement, however, toleration was a subject which Austin found it hard to approach in his correspondence with the authorities. In an early letter to Seguin he had written, only to delete upon second thought, that the colonists were ready to pay for the maintenance of the Catholic church if they could then practice their own religion. And a year later after preparing for the legislature a somewhat elaborate argument upon toleration he wrote in the margin of his file copy, "deemed a dangerous subject to touch and therefore not sent."[123]

After the successful revolution which at the beginning of 1829 put Guerrero in the presidency in spite of the unanimous opposition of the clergy, Austin expected an amendment of the federal constitution to permit toleration; and wrote Josiah H. Bell that

[121] Austin to J. E. B. Austin, May 4, 1824; to Rev. William Stevenson, May 20, in *Jackson* (Tennessee) *Gazette,* October 2, 1824; to Mrs. James F. Perry, December 17, 1824.
[122] Seguin to Bastrop, March 24, 1824; to Austin, August 11.
[123] Austin to Seguin, (about January 1, 1824); Memorial to the Legislature, December 22, 1824.

even without it the government would not object to family or neighborhood worship or to moral lectures circumspectly delivered "in that pure, chaste, and dignified language and manner with which such instructions ought to be imparted to rational beings." Guerrero's brief and stormy career, however, left him no time for such reform.

It is doubtful whether Austin ever ventured a direct discussion of toleration with any Mexican but Terán, whose liberal and practical mind and accurate knowledge of Texas enabled him to see colonial problems objectively. In 1832 Austin wrote him that toleration and the abolition of military privileges were necessary to the peace and advancement of Mexico, and that the man who could bring those reforms to pass would deserve to be called the Washington of Mexico and to be ranked with the great heroes and benefactors of the world. Terán himself favored freedom of religion in Texas because, as he frankly explained, he thought that preferable to practicing no religion at all there, which was the actual situation.[124] Finally, in 1834, with Terán two years dead and Austin in prison in Mexico, the legislature at Monclova thrust incongruously into a law revising the land system of the state the declaration that "No person shall be molested for political and religious opinions, provided he shall not disturb the public order."[125] The object, no doubt, was to stimulate land sales; perhaps it could have been interpreted as legalizing Protestant preaching, but whether advantage was taken of it for that purpose in the short time remaining before the revolution the records do not show.

Austin made repeated efforts to obtain a curate for the colony, but until 1831, when Father Miguel Muldoon became vicar general of Texas, no official appointment was made. In the meantime, the settlers were dependent for marriage and baptism upon occasional visits from the priest at San Antonio. These visits were very infrequent and necessity developed the civil marriage, in which the parties pledged themselve to be remarried upon the arrival of the priest. Father Muldoon commended himself to Austin as an intelligent, liberal, polished man of the world, but he remained in Texas little more than a year, and had no successor. It is certain that a few Protestant ministers practiced their calling discreetly among the

[124] Austin to Terán, June 27, 1832, in Filisola, *Memorias para la Historia de la Guerra de Tejas*, I, 234; Terán to Austin, January 1, 1831.
[125] Decree No. 272, March 26, 1834, Gammel, *Laws of Texas*, I, 358.

settlers, but contemporary records of their activity are extremely rare.[126]

Austin's writings give little clue to his personal religion. He was not sectarian; he disapproved of emotionalism; and in strict privacy he criticized the Catholic church—not altogether justly perhaps, when all the conditions are considered—upon the shortcomings of its work in Mexico. He regarded religion as an indispensable cohesive and uplifting force in society. For the rest, he was silent.

Measured by the standards of his time, Austin had had good educational advantages. By the test of a well-stored mind and ability to use it efficiently in his environment, he does not suffer in comparison with the standards of any time. Naturally, his conception of the agencies necessary for developing an intelligent and congenial society in Texas included a system of public education. He sought to make it the constitutional duty of Congress to establish schools, academies, and colleges throughout the nation.[127] As early as 1825 he was endeavoring to obtain the establishment of a state school in his colony;[128] and while at Saltillo in the fall of 1827 he drafted a bill for the foundation of a "seminary of learning" at San Felipe to teach the "various branches of education." It was to be under the direction of thirteen trustees, appointed annually by the ayuntamiento, and was to be endowed with six leagues of land from the public domain east of the Colorado River.[129] But the population of Texas was still too sparse and scattered for this to be a critical problem, and the bill—if Austin, in fact, presented it—received no action.

By 1829 Austin thought settlement at and near San Felipe sufficiently advanced to justify an attempt to establish a school there by private subscription. This, he thought, would both hasten government aid and, perhaps, fix the location of the capital at San

[126] On this paragraph see marriage contracts of April 29 and May 10, 1824; Austin to Saucedo, June 20, and Saucedo's reply, July 10, 1824; Austin to Peña, February 1, 1825; Buchetti to Austin, April 29, 1826, and to Williams, November 8, 1827; Austin to Williams, January 13, 1831; Barnett to Austin, June 15, 1831; Buckner to Austin, July 2, 1831; Bacon to Austin, July 30, 1831; "Reminiscences of Henry Smith," *Quarterly* of Texas State Historical Association, XIV, 33–37. A half humorous article by Father Muldoon in the *Mexican Citizen*, May 26, 1831, mentions two men who had been in the habit of preaching more or less publicly. This paper is in the Wagner Collection of Yale University.

[127] Project of a Constitution, etc., March 29, 1823.

[128] Padilla to Austin, June 4, 1825.

[129] See a Bill to Establish a Seminary of Learning, (October 11, 1827?).

Felipe when Texas should be separated from Coahuila. Thomas J. Pilgrim, a competent teacher, was ready to undertake the direction of the school, and Austin himself drew a plan for a building to accommodate a hundred pupils. Writing to Josiah H. Bell, on February 24, he said: "This subject is a very important one. It has always been a favorite one with me, and I think an effort should be now made to get the school under way.... I fear that if the present opportunity passes of getting a permanent teacher another may not o[ffer soo]n. I will however unite in support of any general plan to establish schools which will do the most public good." At the same time the ayuntamiento reported subscriptions of eight hundred dollars in hand to be applied to the erection of a building. This seems, in a measure, to have retarded the plan. The ayuntamiento was very unpopular, because it had manifested an intention to give the colony a vigorous administration. The people professed great interest in education in the abstract, but protested that they liked neither San Felipe nor the ayuntamiento. They would support a school in proportion to their means anywhere else, but not there. Austin defended the ayuntamiento, declaring that it was doing no more than its legal duty, and went on with the project but it came to naught.[130]

In the summer of 1830 Austin was elected to represent Texas in the legislature, and wrote Lúcas Alamán soon afterward that he had for a long time wanted to see a college established in Texas for instruction in the Spanish and English languages but that funds, donations of land, and certain legislative measures were necessary which he had little hope of being able to obtain at Saltillo, though he intended to make the effort during the biennium for which he was elected. In case of separation from Coahuila he suggested that fees due the state for land should be appropriated to the establishment and endowment of such an institution. This promise Austin fulfilled to the extent, at least, of preparing a bill. He or his colleague probably presented it, but of this we have no record. It provided for the establishment of an Institute of Modern Languages at San Felipe to teach primarily Spanish, English, and French, and incidentally "arithmetic, geography, mathematics, history, rhetoric, constitutional law, philosophy, astronomy, and chem-

---

[130] Austin to Bell, February 24, March 17, April 16, 1829; Bell to Austin, March 13; William Morton to Austin, March 25; "Minutes of the Ayuntamiento of San Felipe," in *Southwestern Historical Quarterly*, XXI, 405.

istry." The school was to be managed by a board of six trustees appointed by the political chief from a list of twelve nominated by the ayuntamiento; and was to be endowed with eleven leagues of land, which could be leased for terms of five years, but could not be sold without the consent of the legislature.[131] The convention over which Austin presided in 1832 asked for a grant of land to establish a system of primary schools, but the proceedings of this body were never presented to the government.[132]

Abstractly the Mexicans, like the colonists, appreciated the importance of at least primary education. Both the constitution and the statutes attest this; so that the indictment of the Texan declaration of independence, that the government had "failed to establish any public system of education," while literally true, was certainly unfair, because it ignored the willingness of the government to establish such a system, if only the difficulties of poverty and scanty population could have been overcome.[133] In practice, therefore, during all the colonial period the settlers were dependent upon widely scattered and exceedingly intermittent private schools.

Though his efforts were absorbed in other directions, Austin's interest did not flag. From Mexico in 1833, surrounded by desolation and death, and himself recovering from an emergency treatment which barely averted cholera, he instructed Williams to locate for him and not sell a beautiful tract of land on the east bank of the Colorado, at the foot of the mountains, as a retreat to which he could go and get away from trouble. "I mean to go and live there. It is out of the way and will do for an academy scheme with which I can amuse myself and do good to others."[134] With rare appropriateness that tract now contains the Capital City and the University of Texas, and Austin lies buried in the land that he himself chose for his last peaceful years.

[131] This bill is translated by Mrs. Mattie Austin Hatcher, in the *Quarterly* of Texas State Historical Association, XII, 233–239.

[132] The committee which reported the petition to the convention left the amount of the grant blank. Motions were made to insert twenty-five, one hundred, and one hundred and fifty leagues. William H. Wharton moved to table indefinitely, which was lost, seventeen to thirty-four. The petition was then passed, leaving the amount such as the government might think proper to grant.—Gammel, *Laws of Texas,* I, 493.

[133] Eby, *Education in Texas* (University of Texas Bulletin No. 1824), 27–40, reprints the material showing the Mexican legal attitude toward education; it can also be found in Gammel, *Laws of Texas,* I, *passim.*

[134] Austin to Williams, August 21, 1833, Rosenberg Library.

CHAPTER IX

Austin and His Work as Seen by Himself

SELDOM does a man so clearly reveal his mind and character by his works as Austin has done. For a time after his return from Mexico in 1823 his relations with the settlers, as we have seen, gave him some trouble and anxiety. His power was almost unlimited, and he himself was untried. From the end of 1825, however, until the development during 1831 of a small group of radicals who lacked the necessary patience and tact to appreciate his cautious and sometimes temporizing method of steering the colony through the shoals of Mexican jealousy, suspicion, and caprice, there appears to have been little disposition to question his authority, his knowledge, or the essential justice and wisdom of his guidance. His principal task with the settlers during this period was to preserve harmony among them and prevent them, as he expressed it, from destroying themselves. They were years of grinding, unremitting labor, the most critical years in the history of American settlement, because an imprudent policy, a false step then, could have wrecked the whole colonization system. Until the declaration of independence, his influence with the old settlers continued to be decisive, and a trial of strength with the relatively small radical element could have had but one ending. Because he believed unity all important to Texas, however, the aggressiveness of the radicals forced from him some reluctant compromises which his judgment distrusted. His feeling of responsibility for the colonists was intense and personal. He measured success by the substantial improvement of their condition. At the same time he was honestly loyal to Mexico; grateful for its liberality; and, with all his knowledge of its deficiencies, hopeful—at least until 1832—for the evolution of a stable, intelligent, and powerful government. He did not want to annex Texas to the United States, and after 1829 his difficulties in maintaining a good understanding with Mexico were aggravated by the efforts of the Jackson government to buy Texas and by the activities of several companies in the United States speculating in Texas lands.

His devotion to the colonists, his loyalty to Mexico, his aims for Texas, his management of the diverse social and sectional elements that poured into the colonies from the United States, his personal traits, ambitions, and philosophy of life—in short, the man himself —emerge from the record of these middle years, and reveal an able, altogether human, and remarkably interesting personality. To his few intimates and equals Austin must have been a thoroughly lovable man.

Naturally, his original motive in undertaking the colonization of Texas was to retrieve the family fortunes, pay his debts, and acquire a comfortable competence for himself. In this end, honorably and considerately pursued, there need be no incompatibility with the interest and welfare of Mexico and the colonists. But the work once begun, Austin's personal interest was subordinated, if not absorbed, by pure enthusiasm to win from its barbaric wildness a region which held for him surpassing charms and possibilities. His confidence in its economic value and his faith in a proud future sprang full-grown from his first hasty exploration of the country and strengthened with observation and knowledge. He wrote, in 1830, "I was both delighted and astonished to find it the most favor^d region I had ever seen. Its fertility and natural resources, so far exceeding any thing I had imagined, determined me to devote my life to the great object of redeeming it from the wilderness." His methods and some of his difficulties, as he appraised them, are described in the same letter:

"It was a heavy undertaking for a young, inexperienced *and very poor man*. My first step was to study the character of the Mexicans and ascertain their ideas and views as to Texas. I found they knew nothing about it, and were profoundly ignorant of its real value, and also that they considered it next to impracticable to form a settlement in its wilderness without the aid of a very strong military force for garrisons to keep the Indians in check. I also discovered that strong prejudices existed against the North Americans owing to the conduct of some who were engaged in the revolutionary expeditions that had entered Texas at various times since 1811. I saw that all the efforts to get a foothold here by means of such expeditions had failed and ended in defeat and ruin, and I believed they always would fail. These observations convinced me that the only means of redeeming this country from the wilderness was by peaceful, silent, noiseless perseverance and industry, and that the axe, the plough, and the hoe would do more than the rifle or the sword. Under these impressions I began and have pursued the main object with a degree of patience and perseverance which nothing but its vast importance to the civilized world could ever have given me fortitude to continue through so many years of hardships and amidst so many discouraging obstacles. The worst is now over and the few clouds which seem to hang over us are mere shadows when compared with those which have passed. I have laid a sufficient foundation for others to build on, and a prudent course will make this country one of the finest in the world." [1]

To the same correspondent he wrote a year later:

"The principles which have uniformly governed me since I began colonizing in this country in 1821 are so different from those which appear to have influenced others who have attempted colonization in Texas that neither this colony nor myself ought to be confounded with the others. My object, the sole and only desire of my ambition since I first saw Texas, was to redeem it from the wilderness—to settle it with intelligent, honorable, and enterprising people. To make a fortune, a great pecuniary speculation for myself, was and always has been, and now is, a secondary consideration with me. When I left my native Govt. and became a citizen of this I consider^d that all and every kind of political obligation ceased as to the first, and became fully as binding as to the second as if this had been my native country.

"More than this, I considered that the liberality and confidence with which this Govt. treated the emigrants who came here in good faith, and who conducted themselves with anything like ordinary decency or common sense, imposed a moral obligation on them to give in return at least common gratitude. In short, my mottoes have been—*The redemption of Texas from the wilderness, Fidelity and gratitude to my adopted country, and to be inflexibly true to the interests and just rights of my settlers.* It is my boast to say that I have never deviated from these general principles, and it is a matter of proud gratification to me that my colony has always possessed the confidence of this Govt. . . .

"Others who have attempted colonization here have wished to make a matter of great and speedy speculation of it. No one who starts on that plan will succeed in doing anything except to injure this country and throw it back many years. They have fail^d so far, and strange to say, some of them have wished to throw the blame of their failure on me, and have suspected me of an unfriendly disposition towards them or towards their enterprises, on the ground that competition was disagreeable to me. Such a suspicion displays a total want of all correct knowledge of the subject.

[1] Austin to Thomas F. Leaming, June 14, 1830.

There can be no competition to my injury with any others who have attempted or ever may attempt colonizing in Texas. . . .

"It has been my policy to slide along without any noise. I discover^d on examining Texas that in point of soil, climate, and natural advantages it was greatly superior to any other part of North America that I had seen, or had any knowledge of. I saw that its value was unknown to this government or to anybody else. I knew that I would be suffer^d to go on undisturbed, because no one believ^d that there was any thing here worthy of attention and I should thus lay a foundation which could not be broken up by the hungry swarms of speculators who would inundate the country as soon as its value was known. Had all others followed my system and kept Texas out of the newspapers the law of 6 April 1830 would not have been passed prohibiting emigration from the United States. My friends in that country have blamed me for keeping so quiet, and for not adopting the *bellows system,* so much the stile in the north, and making a great blow—by so doing I should have blown away my own foundations as others have done."

The time for silence, however, had passed, said Austin. Speculators had given Texas unsavory advertisement in the United States and sharpened the apprehensions of the Mexican government; his colony might now be benefited by some "judicious paragrafs not too long to go the rounds," showing the prosperity of his own settlers and their attachment to the government.[2]

To his cousin, Mrs. Holley, to whom he wrote most intimately, Austin said:

"I found the country so much more valuable than I expected that the idea of contributing to fill it with a civilized and industrious population filled my soul with enthusiasm. I can with truth, and with a clear conscience, say that none of the sordid and selfish motives . . . had any weight in determining me to attack this wilderness. I commenced on the solid basis of sound and philanthropic intentions and of undeviating integrity. I asked the *favor* of the new government of Mexico—that is, *permission* to settle this country and become one of its citizens. What I asked was granted. I became a Mexican citizen. From that moment honor, the sanctity of an oath, gratitude—all bound me to Mexico and her interests. Never have I for one moment deviated from the line of duty which those obligations imposed on me. And I attribute my success (for I may say with pride I have been successful) to this circumstance. . . .

"A thorough knowledge of the Mexican character, the policy of the government, and the feelings of the mass of the people toward foreigners convinced me at an early day that Texas must be settled *silently* or not at

2 Austin to Leaming, July 23, 1831.

all. Hence it is that I was progressing here for years and rearing a flourishing settlement in this country, and it was unknown even in parts of Louisiana, the adjoining state, that such a thing existed. The circumstances are now changed, and it is time to bring out my *ward* and introduce her to the world."

Again to Mrs. Holley he wrote:

"I labored with faithful intentions, and as disinterested views of general good as circumstances and my capacity permitted. . . . For the first time *Ambition* kindled its fires in my breast, but I think I can with truth say that the flame was a mild and gentle one, consisting more of the wish to build up the fortunes and happiness of others and to realize my dreams of good will to my fellow men than of the overbearing spirit of military fame or domineering power. My ambition was to *redeem this fine country*—our glorious Texas—and convert it into a home for the unfortunate, a refuge from poverty, an asylum for the sufferers from selfish avarice.

"Here the hand of nature had spread her bounties with such profusion that the most indigent, with moderate industry, could make a support. The poor, but honest, man's cottage would not be looked down upon with contempt from the lofty attics of the lordly palace, for in that particular there would be perfect equality.

"I took upon myself the task of getting secure and valid titles for their land, and to furnish each emigrant with solid grounds on which to build the hopes of his family, and his humble 'forest home.' Avarice was as incompatible with such views as I trust it has ever been foreign to my heart. . . . My still youthful imagination (I was but 28 years old) became enthusiastic. I had read of the withering march of the bloodhounds of war over the fairest portions of the old world, spreading fire and famine and desolation and death in their course, and sweeping whole nations from existence—*all to promote the happiness of mankind.* I could not understand it but I *could understand* how that happiness might be promoted by conquering a wilderness by the axe, the plough, and the hoe. . . .

"On reviewing what I have written [he added] I fear you will laugh at my enthusiasm, and think I am suffering my fancy to wander in the Elysian Fields when everything around ought to remind me that before I can enter them the Styx and Infernus are to be passed. It may be so; but even that cannot prevent enjoyment by anticipation." [3]

[3] Austin to Mrs. Holley, November 17, December 29, 1831. To William H. Wharton, April 24, 1829, he wrote in the same vein: "I think I derived more satisfaction from the view of flourishing farms springing up in this wilderness than military or political chieftains do from the retrospect of their victorious campaigns. My object is to build up, for the present as well as for future generation."

To Perry, July 11, 1830: "Instead of running about in other countries to speculate I have devoted my life to the arduous task of trying to redeem this country from the wilderness. . . . I had no capital, and have supplied its defect by personal labor and attention, and by putting my shoulder to the wheel in earnest and in good faith. I have not made a fortune

Except for the "peculiar value of the Mississippi River and the harbors," Austin esteemed Texas of greater intrinsic value than all the Gulf States and Arkansas. It would present to posterity, he said, "a second Eden."[4]

As we have seen, it pleased Austin to regard his settlers as a great family for whose welfare he was personally responsible.[5] The unvarying rule of conduct which he tried to impress upon them was to live in harmony with each other, to be loyal to Mexico and obedient to the laws, and to keep aloof from revolutions and party convulsions. For the rest, he was confident that his own knowledge of Mexican character and his acquaintance with men and conditions would enable him to win safely through all difficulties with shifting governments.

From the time when his own authority was convincingly established, divisions among the settlers did not again threaten the progress of the colony until after the inauguration of the ayuntamiento. People had "growled and grumbled and muttered, without knowing why, or without being able to explain why"; but this arose, as he saw it, "from a principle which is common to all North Americans, a feeling which is the natural offspring of the unbounded republican liberty enjoyed by all classes in the United States; that is, jealousy of undue encroachments on personal rights, and a general repugnance to everything that wore even the semblance of a stretch of power."[6] The same propensity caused them to distrust and criticize the ayuntamiento, which, being elective and changing annually, lacked Austin's experience and prestige as well as his knowledge and ability. The storm against the ayuntamiento arose from its effort to levy a property tax for local improvements

---

for myself (except in lands which now have no value) and probably shall not live to derive much personal benefit, but I have greatly benefitted many others, hundreds of them, and made them and their families rich who were worth nothing before, and I have opened and enlarged a fine field for human enterprise and human happiness. This has always been the main object of my ambition, and not a mere avericious view to personal speculation. I have no fears that my motives or my acts will not receive the reward in public opinion which they merit, or that a few speculators can materially injure me, but they may harrass me. In a democratic republic enemies are sometimes more troublesome than in any other form of government, for popular opinion is as often moved by whim or accident as by reason or justice."

[4] Austin to Perry, March 31, 1828; to W. C. Carr, March 4, 1829.

[5] "I feel almost the same interest for their prosperity that I do for my own family—in fact I look upon them as one great family who are under my care."—Austin to the colonists, August 6, 1823. See also Austin to Bell, January 1, 1828.

[6] Austin to White, March 31, 1829.

and from its method of executing certain duties, which, though prescribed by law, the people regarded as gratuitous meddling. At the same time there seems to have been a sudden increase in litigation which some ascribed to collusion between the alcalde and a group of lawyers at San Felipe. When it seemed to Austin that the discontent was assuming serious proportions, he took pen in hand and indited a forceful and instructive lecture to his old friend Josiah H. Bell, which he trusted him to circulate with soothing effect among his neighbors of the lower Brazos.

As to taxes, he pointed out, the people were laboring under a misapprehension both as to their legality and amount. The colonization law specifically authorized municipal taxes. How otherwise could the local government be maintained? A secretary acquainted with Spanish would cost a thousand dollars; two hundred was needed for blank books, stationery, fuel, and rent; four hundred more was necessary for Indian expenses and post office accounts; a fire-proof room was urgently needed for the land records, now kept in a log cabin; a court room and jail ought to be built. The total budget he estimated at $4,700, of which three thousand would come from property taxes but need not all be paid in one year.[7]

The law required the ayuntamiento to keep a register of births, deaths, and marriages and to report them to the political chief every three months. To avoid the expense of collecting these vital statistics by the sheriff the ayuntamiento instructed the secretary to circulate notices "urging the inhabitants as good citizens to carry into effect as far as possible this necessary requirement" by reporting to the ayuntamiento.[8] This the people resented, and complained that it was simply a scheme "to get fees into the office," though no fees were involved and no fine imposed even for failure to report. Austin said he could not understand how this measure could have been misrepresented, "for it is of the highest importance to children that a legal register of their births should be kept, for it secures to the children beyond the possibility of a doubt important privileges as native born Mexicans that some day or other may be of the

---

[7] For the scale of property taxes, which were specific, see the minutes of the ayuntamiento in *Southwestern Historical Quarterly*, XXI, 400–401. The budget given there (pages 403–404) somewhat exceeds Austin's statement.

[8] See *Ibid.*, 400.

greatest advantage to them. But independent of this it is the law and should be obeyed."

The ayuntamiento's determination to enforce the vagrancy law against habitual drunkards and disturbers was also the subject of criticism. For this Austin shouldered full responsibility; "rioting, drunkenness, and fighting" had become too common. It was regrettable that good citizens allowed themselves to be deceived by men who hoped to avoid punishment by setting them against their officers. "Where is the security of honest men," he asked, "if the people are mere puppets in the hands of artfull demagogues and clamorous factionists?" Much of the trouble he attributed to the fact that the people were ignorant of the laws, but these could not be published in English, and he saw no way of correcting that; much more he attributed to the indifference of the voters at elections. Not one in three had voted at the last election; "in this way the best and dearest interests of the community are wantonly sported with, and are as likely to fall into the hands of a fugitive vagabond or an ignorant fool as into those of an honest or intelligent man. A community that tramples on so sacred a privilege as the elective franchise deserves to suffer, and sooner or later it will suffer." However, he said, "if the people have confidence in me, they are safe. I know the laws and the duties of the ayuntamiento and I also understand what the people of this colony ought to do for their own good . . . Let the people therefore dismiss their unfounded fears and suspicions and repose in me . . . and above all things let them close their ears against the clamors of those who have *more to say* and *less to loose,* either of property or character, than any body else in the country."

There had been too much of personalities at San Felipe, he said; some of the best men had

"displayed a childish pettishness and suffered themselves to be enraged at trifles and at low bred and unprincipled men, when they ought in fact to have paid no attention to them. This is an infirmity of human nature. It is not every man who can command his temper at all times and especially when he is abused and slandered by others. As a general rule which never ought to be departed from a person in office should never, at no time, act officially while under the influence of irritation or passion. He ought to execute the law calmly and firmly, but not pationately—and he should do his duty totally regardless of clamor or abuse. My own temper is hasty to a fault and violent when excited, and I therefore laid down the above rule for my own government when I first began the colony. I have violated it in some instances and have sometimes suffered my temper [to rise?] at the unjust abuse and misrepresentation that has been heaped upon me. I always regretted it afterwards, for a man in a passion most generally says or does things that he ought not to have said or done. My fits of irritation however have been but momentary. Reason and the public good told me that I must bear abuse and clamor and do my duty regardless of what was said and done ... and I am now convinced that the rule which I laid down from the beginning to control my own temper and to bear all things patiently as a dray horse [has] saved the colony from total ruin. There is however reason in all things, and the people of this colony must not expect to find many men who will bear abuse for the sake of public good as I have done."

The lawyers, Austin thought, were responsible for a good deal of the ill feeling that existed, but at bottom the trouble lay, after all, with the people who employed them; it was a national characteristic of Americans to be contentious and litigious; if they wished to correct the evil, let them cut it up by the roots; let every man settle his differences by an arbitration of his neighbors. "An honest consciencious lawyer," he was careful to add, "is a valuable member of society—there is none more so, but a hot headed, fractious, abusing, and contentious lawyer is a curse on any community, and ought to be discountenanced, but I really cannot see any other effectual remedy than the one I have pointed out. . . .

"My whole thoughts and ambition and desires," he concluded, "have been devoted to the advancement of this colony and the happiness of its citizens . . . and I therefore cannot but observe with deep regret any thing like a want of union or of confidence in the people."[9] His most difficult task, he declared, had been to keep the settlers at peace with each other—"I do say that the North Americans are the most obstinate and difficult people to manage that live on earth."[10]

By some it will perhaps be thought that since his own interests were so dependent upon the progress of the colony Austin protested too much his devotion to the colonists. Aside from the fact, however, that no other empresario except DeWitt—who generally acted under Austin's direction—attempted to follow the same road

[9] Austin to Bell, March 17, April 4, 1829.
[10] Austin to Leaming, June 14, 1831.

to success, there is much to indicate that he did not over-state the disinterestedness of his service. Whatever his expectations of sudden fortune when he began, he very soon realized that they were unsubstantial and reconciled himself to years of exacting labor in the full knowledge that much of his reward must consist in the consciousness that he had done very well a work which, as he said to Wharton, was "laudable and honorable and worthy the attention of honorable men."[11] He repeatedly declared that pecuniary interest alone could never carry such an enterprise to success, and if in his intimate correspondence—for he rarely talked about it except to members of his family—he spoke of his patience and perseverance and unselfishness, it was a human weakness which we can easily forgive. He was proud of success where so many had failed, and could not but contrast his own methods and motives with those of others.

It was no doubt the abandonment of the fees of twelve and a half cents an acre which he had expected to collect from the colonists that brought Austin to the realization that his compensation might be meager and would certainly be long delayed. He probably had this in mind when he wrote his sister in December, 1824: "All my plans have been broken in upon and I make no more calculations except to spend my life here: wheither rich or poor, here (that is in this colony) I expect to remain permanently." He hoped to pay his debts and then "sit quietly down on a farm." But as yet he was poor and lived poorly—"corn coffee, corn bread, milk and butter, and a bachelor's household, which is confusion, dirt, and torment." And his house, he added, was "a thoroughfare for the whole country."[12] Most of the letters to Mrs. Perry for the next two years touched this theme—thus: "My labors in this country, altho arduous and in every way perplexing, will not yield me anything for some years and then not the fortune which some have supposed. I shall benefit others much more than myself in proportion—but thank heaven I am not avaricious";[13] again, "The enterprise I undertook is better calculated to enrich those who come after me than to benefit myself. I have the labor to perform and the seed to sow, but my successors will reap the harvest."[14] At another time, "my

[11] Austin to W. H. Wharton, April 24, 1829.
[12] Austin to Mrs. Perry, December 17, 1824.
[13] Austin to Mrs. Perry, (May ——, 1825).
[14] To the same, December 12, 1825.

prospects of making a fortune are bad; I shall be but poorly compensated, though [I] expect to pay my debts and make a comfortable support for my old age." [15] Inviting a cousin, Henry Austin, to visit Texas with a view to settling, Austin warned him:

"If you come here you will find me living in a log cabin—a bachelor's life—poor as to active means, no comforts around me, rather soured with the world, laboriously engaged to serve my settlers, who do not thank me for the care and labor they cost me. When I began this enterprise my ambition was to succeed in forming a flourishing settlement of North Americans, and I sacrificed pecuniary considerations to that object. I shall succeed fully as to the main object and benefit a great many, but no great pecuniary benefit will result to me. I shall not live long enough to enjoy it."

To another correspondent he wrote that he had not even the means of living in comfort and with that decency which his position seemed to require, except by selling his premium lands "so hardly earned, and that I will not do for it is my only stake for my old age." [16]

In 1825 Austin wrote his sister that he hoped to close his second contract in another year and that if he retained his senses he would "never again have anything to do with public business"; if he married, he would settle down as a farmer near the mouth of the Brazos; if not, he would probably travel. [17] This dream of retiring to pastoral ease intrigued him all his life. It is plain enough that the trait of human stubbornness which compels us all to "carry on" in the face of recurrent difficulties would have kept him at the helm; but in his own analysis it was mainly responsibility to the colonists that held him there. He wrote Josiah H. Bell in 1828, "were it not my duty to the settlers who are here never to abandon them, I should give up my last contract with Gov^t for the settling of the new colony, and either settle myself down on a stock farm or seek some other country where I might hope to find harmony, but *it is* my duty to persevere and for that reason, and that alone, I will go on." To Lúcas Alamán, secretary of relations, he wrote in 1830: "I can do no less than feel much interest in the fate of the

---

[15] To the same, August 21, 1826. See also to Mrs. Perry, October 22, 1825, and June 15, 1826.

[16] Austin to Henry Austin August 27, 1829; to Breedlove, October 12, 1829. See also Austin to Leaming June 14, and to Perry, July 14, 1830; and to Mrs. Holley, November 14, 17, 1831.

[17] Austin to Mrs. Perry, October 22, 1825.

colonists of Texas. I was the cause of the emigration of most of them and we have borne years of labor together. I could do no less than feel much interest in the advancement and prosperity of Texas, because it has been the object of my efforts and the sole aim of my ambition to contribute to the redemption of this country from the unpopulated condition in which I found it in 1821 and make it a useful and productive part of the great Mexican republic." [18]

He wrote his brother-in-law repeatedly that he had to devote all his time to the colony and that without somebody to look after his own business he would be poor to the end of his days. His surrender of self to the public interest cannot be seriously questioned. It is misleading, in a way, to support such a statement by particular evidence because it is attested by the whole history of colonial Texas. Still, a few witnesses may be heard. His brother urged in 1828 that a few years of attention to his own affairs would relieve him from embarrassment and enable him to live in ease and comfort. A year later Aylett C. Buckner, whose testimony is the more significant because he had not always supported Austin, wrote:

"Those to whom I have talked with relative to the claims you have against them for what may be owed on their lands consider it high time they were paid. But you know where long indulgence is given and a long laps of time taken place without any demand a great many all most conclude the debt is paid. According to my opinion the most expeditious way of getting or collecting your claims would be to make a demand of each ones debt; if so those who are owing will begin to make preparations to discharge what they owe. You know the nature of a great many; for so long as they can get indulgence so long will they refrain from paying. . . . I have taken the liberty of saying it would be better [to] pay as soon as possible, otherwise they would perhaps be compelled to do it— and with cost to the debtor. Some [he added parenthetically] require it."

John Austin warned Austin in December, 1829, that he was injuring his health by confinement to the office: "Make these men who want land now pay up and those who are oweing you on the

---

[18] Austin to Bell, January 21, 1828; to Alamán, July 13, 1830. To Perry, September 22, 1830: "Nine years ago I enlisted myself as the slave of this colony, and . . . I am bound in honor and duty to labor for it untill its affairs are done." To S. Rhoads Fisher, June 17, 1830: "I am not anxious on my own account— . . . but I have been the means of drawing many families to Texas, and their present and permanent welfare and happiness is very dear to me, and costs me many anxious hours and days." See also Austin to Breedlove, October 12, 1829; to Leaming, June 14, 1830; to Perry, June 16, December 19, 1830; to Mrs. Holley, July 19, November 14, 17, December 29, 1831, and January 4, 14, 1832.

old colony pay; they may grumble some but . . . they will do it at any rate." At the same time his sister-in-law described him as "a mere shadow," and thought that "if he does not quit his desk, ride about and take more exercise, his life will be but short." [19]

In return for his devotion, as has been said, Austin had the confidence of the overwhelming mass of substantial men in the colony, and enjoyed periods of genuine popularity.[20] In fits of depression, which sometimes carried him to the verge of melancholia, he unduly magnified transient criticism and irresponsible abuse, but normally his place in the sober judgment of the colonists gave him no concern. He wrote his sister, who had resented some apparent lack of appreciation for him, "As to the settlers being ungrateful . . . all that is nothing . . . In the end they will be *just* and if I merit a reward from them, they will give it. The settlers of this colony will never forget the man or the family who has made their fortunes." That he had some enemies he philosophically accepted as inevitable, "for none but a miserable and contemptable poor devil could have had as much to do with public matters as I have in Texas without making enemies." [21]

Loyalty and aloofness were the twin doctrines of Austin's creed for avoiding trouble with Mexico. The policy is well stated, though not then for the first time, in a letter to his brother in 1823: "I wrote to the settlers . . . that they ought not to meddle with politics. . . . I hope they have followed my advice—they are as yet too recently established in the country to take an active part in its political affairs. If any questions are asked them as to their opinion of the Gov^t etc., they ought to answer that they moved here to live under the government which the nation may establish. . . . As foreigners we have a good excuse for remaining neutral without being lyable to suspicion and this is the safest course." [22] His motto, as he never

<hr>

[19] J. E. B. Austin, September 16, 1828, Buckner, August 7, 1829, John Austin, December 19, 1829—all to Austin; Eliza Austin to Mrs. Perry, January 6, 1830.

[20] J. E. B. Austin to Austin, March 18, 1829: "I may say with propriety that you are the most popular man in the country." Bell to Austin, March 13, 1829: "I am Convinced that you have much in your power and that you have the intire confidence of the people and that any measure you [approve] would meet their seport and apprebation." Henry Austin to Austin, November 28, 1831: "The substantial part of the community are not disposed to take any steps in public matters without your previous approbation."

[21] Austin to Mrs. Perry, January 26, 1833; to Perry, November 6, 1834, Rosenberg Library.

[22] Austin to J. E. B. Austin, May 10, 1823. See also to Josiah H. Bell, July 26, 1822, and to J. E. B. Austin, December 25, 1822, January 1, 1823.

tired of repeating, was "fidelity and gratitude to Mexico." He possessed the faculty, rare in Americans of any time and in his day almost unknown, of sympathy with an alien race, and willingness and ability to adapt himself to its national mannerisms and sensibilities. There is a sense of unreality, to be sure, about a handful of western backwoodsmen waving a patchwork tricolor and shouting *vivas* for a constitution which they had not seen and could not read;[23] but to the ceremonious mind of the Mexican there was no incongruity; and it is hardly too much to say that studied observance of such punctilio was indispensable to Austin's success.

There was policy here, of course, but it was founded essentially on loyalty and was shaped by sincere sympathy for the Mexican people as well as by the needs of his establishment. "With all the errors and infernal Spanish prejudices and ignorance of these people," he wrote after much provocation in 1833, "I cannot help but feel a great anxiety for their welfare and prosperity. They wish to be free and to be like the rest of the civilized world and I think it is more noble to try and aid them and encourage than to abuse and ridicule." Explaining his policy on another occasion, he wrote:

"You are well aware that in my intercourse with this govt. I have followed a few fixed rules from which I have never deviated since 1821 when I first entered the country. In the first place I came with pure intentions. I bid an everlasting farewell to my native country, and adopted this, and in so doing I determined to fulfill rigidly all the duties and obligations of a *Mexican* citizen. I have endeavored to keep all the officers with whom I was in direct communication in a good humor, and to make friends of them. I have excused and even invented plausible reasons to justify or explain away all the political errors of my adopted countrymen. I have been silent as to all their defects and lavish of praise where there was the least pretext for bestowing it, but at the same time decissive and unbending where a constitutional or vested right of vital importance was directly attacked. Rights of minor consideration I have paid no attention to, for bad feelings might be engendered about *trifles* that would jeopardise an important interest. To sum up all, I have endeavored to do my duty as a Mexican citizen."[24]

To remain aloof from politics became increasingly difficult, however, after 1830, because party conflicts were frequent and violent thereafter and, for reasons that will be made clear, all parties began

[23] Austin to Bell, April 2, 1824.
[24] Austin to Williams, February 19, 1831, August 21, 1833. Rosenberg Library. See also Austin to Mrs. Holley, February 19, 1832.

then to manifest a more searching interest in Texas. Though severely embarrassed by this at times, Austin nevertheless held to the policy until 1832, and abandoned it then only because during a necessary absence from Texas conditions developed there which left him no alternative but to declare for Santa Anna. Commenting in a confidential letter to his secretary on the discomforts of neutrality, Austin said:

"There can scarcely be a more difficult thing than to play a *double game;* it is dangerous, and it is at times a nice point to draw the distinction between such a game and dishonor. We are so situated that we must keep a good understanding with Teran and Alaman, but at the same time all our best friends at Saltillo and in Mexico are very hostile to both those men. Silence, prudence, and vigilance must all be called in requisition. [Parties in Mexico, he explained, were not clearly defined; had no fixed character nor permanency of purpose; and] if we enter into such a scramble we shall be like children in a mob, and as likely to be trodden upon by friends as by foes. Hence it is that situated as we are it is dangerous to be classed as belonging to any party. Our neutrality injures neither, for our weight is of not sufficient importance to injure or benefit either materially, and it may gain us the good will of both, or what is of just as much importance to us, both will let us alone." [25]

At the same time Austin, who was in the legislature at Saltillo, warned Williams that a conflict was imminent in East Texas between the federal military commandant, enforcing the law of April 6, 1830, and the state land commissioner, attempting to give titles to scattered settlers. In that case, he said, "do as I have frequently been compelled to do—play the turtle, head and feet within your own shell. Some of the people may curse and abuse—no matter—they abused *me,* the best friend they ever had." The trouble did develop and was the subject of other letters to Williams. "If anything is said by my colony in favor of one side or the other it will be taken hold of to class us as belonging to one party or the other. This will do an injury—we belong to the *law* and to the Gov^t and will obey when officially called on to do so." Madero, the commissioner, was in the right, he said, and in the end, if prudent, would be vindicated. "But I am compelled to touch that matter cautiously, for the colony has much at stake. . . . In these matters say little or nothing, and nothing definite—as many smooth words

[25] Austin to Williams, December 28, 1830, February 19, 1831, Rosenberg Library.

without meaning as you please." On another occasion he wrote that much propaganda and perhaps some agents might be sent to Texas from Vera Cruz and Tampico advocating Santa Anna; "if so, treat them all *politely*. That is read the papers, and feed and lodge the agents while they stay—but nothing more. No matter which party gains, it would ruin the people of the colony to take any part in any way. They must be mere spectators, and silent ones —hear and see everything, but without taking any part or expressing any opinion." Some men, he said, held it "degrading and corrupt to use policy in anything." Without committing himself one way or the other as to this, he would say that there was "no degradation in prudence and a well tempered and well timed moderation. . . . As a general rule all over the world *Language* and *Acts* must be regulated in a great degree by *circumstances* and *characters.*"[26]

To some, who had neither Austin's knowledge of affairs, his loyalty, nor his burden of responsibility for the colony, such talk was incomprehensible—the disingenuous temporizing of "a half Mexican, half American Jesuit."[27] But they were few in number, and, as Austin said, he relied on "the old standards, the first settlers. They have known me for years. They now know that their destiny was almost entirely in my hands—nay I might say completely in my hands—for several years. . . . They can now look back and see that so long as their affairs were exclusively under my own control they progressed in peace and harmony with the Gov^t."[28] His aversion to tilting with windmills did not, however, prevent him from speaking to officials with astonishing bluntness and finality when he thought the occasion required. And in doing so, moreover, he seldom lost their confidence and esteem.

One product of these years by which Austin sought to ingratiate himself with the government and advance the interest of his colony was a map of Texas.[29] With the exception of some notes furnished by General Terán it was entirely original, made without earlier

[26] Austin to Williams, February 19, March 12, April 2, 1831, April 4, 28, 1832, Rosenberg Library.

[27] Ira Ingram to League, July 29, 1833. Franklin Papers, University of Texas.

[28] Austin to Williams, April 28, 1832, Rosenberg Library.

[29] William Tanner (Philadelphia, 1830) published the English copy. Austin furnished manuscript copies in Spanish to various Mexican officials, ranging from the political chief to the president, and hoped the government might publish it, but it never did.

map or sketch of Texas to guide him. He wrote his kinsman, Thomas F. Leaming of Philadelphia, who made the arrangements for publication, that its purpose was to promote immigration without attracting undue attention from the Mexicans, most of whom did not understand maps.[30]

Notwithstanding their burden of sorrow—he lost his brother in 1829—ill health, fatigue, and anxiety, these middle years from 1828 to 1832 gave Austin his nearest approach to happiness and contentment. He saw that his work was established, and, whatever the Fates held in store for Mexico, he knew that with prudent management Texas must ultimately prosper. He was slowly reducing the accumulation of debt that harassed him for many years. And his family was gradually gathering around him and relieving the loneliness and isolation of his position. First came his cousin, Henry Austin, staunch and dependable, ripe in experience, and unsoured by hard knocks and the vain pursuit of fortune in many lands; next his sister with her crowd of growing boys and steady-going husband; and finally Mrs. Holley, whose charms of mind and person won through the taciturnity and reserve which he had written Perry—not quite accurately, perhaps—were becoming second nature to him.[31]

Austin wrote in 1818 that he would never marry until the family was out of debt. A month later he "plunged" unfortunately on New Madrid certificates in Arkansas and increased his burden. It weighed heavily on him and is one of the themes running through his family letters for years.[32] It would be impossible, obviously, to follow to settlement a multitude of small claims. Austin's correspondence manifests the determination to pay them all and contains evidence of the payment of many. The larger debts, however—there were only three—require a brief notice.

The sum of the New Madrid speculation was nine thousand dollars. Most of this was assumed by James Bryan in a settlement with Austin, but his death returned the obligation to Austin, who wrote his sister in 1828 that he was paying it as rapidly as possible.

[30] There is much correspondence relating to the map. See particularly Leaming to Austin, May 8, 1828; Austin to Navarro, to Músquiz, and to Zavala, July 23, 1829; Austin to Leaming, June 14, 1830.

[31] Austin to Perry, September 22, 1830.

[32] See, for example, Austin to J. E. B. Austin, May 4, 1824; to Mrs. Perry, December 17, 1824, May ——, October 22, 1825, August 21, 1826, July 24, 1828, and others.

Minutes of a settlement, December 10, 1831, with George Tennille, whose original claim was $7,400, showed $1,785.20½ still due him. Tennille was then a resident of Texas and the balance was no doubt paid.[33]

The most annoying debt, and the only one about which Austin ever complained, was to Colonel Anthony Butler. This has an historical significance because of Butler's agency in Jackson's effort to acquire Texas for the United States. The records of the transaction furnish only an outline without details. During 1815 and 1816 Austin and his father and James Bryan, as we have seen, jointly hired from Butler a number of slaves whom they worked in the lead mines. The next year Austin and Butler alone worked the mines in partnership. Austin made a statement for the year showing that "nothing of consequence" was made. In the meantime the rent, or some part of it, for the use of the negroes during the preceding two years was unpaid, and Butler sued and got judgment for this in Jefferson County, Missouri. Subsequently the county records were burned. In 1828 Butler appeared in Texas and demanded some six thousand dollars, part of it on the judgment, apparently, and part on the partnership. Austin refused to recognize the claim in full and wrote for the books of the partnership to prove the production of lead for that year. Whether they, like the court records, had been destroyed is not disclosed; but Butler seems to have made his point. Writing to his attorney in March, 1829, Austin said that he had paid Butler "upwards of two thousand dollars, and arranged the balance in three payments, in 1831, '32, and '33. The interest was all exacted to a cent and in some instances compounded. . . . I still owe considerably over four thousand dollars on it. This has been a cruel affair and has harrassed me very much, more than any event in my life ever did."[34] The notes were duly paid, though again not without unpleasantness. Butler refused to surrender the final note on the ground that his agent in Texas had not had authority to collect the full amount.[35]

Butler held property in Texas—possibly by agent—which ac-

[33] Memorandum of debts to George Tennille and to W. M. O'Hara, January 30, 1819; Austin to Mrs. Perry, July 24, 1828; statement of Tennille's account, December 10, 1831, Rosenberg Library.

[34] Moses Austin to Bryan, September 2, November 25, 1814; Austin to Mrs. Perry, July 24, 1828, and to W. C. Carr, March 4, 1829; Mrs. Perry to Austin, November 29, 1828.

[35] Austin to Williams, April 12, 1832, October 6, 1834, Rosenberg Library.

counts in part for his pertinacious industry in trying to obtain the territory for the United States. Though he and Austin were superficially amicable when brought together by accidents of social intercourse, there was no love lost between them. Butler believed that but for Austin's opposition he would have succeeded in the principal object of his mission;[36] while Austin wrote of Butler in 1835, "I have never known so bad and base a man"; and added, quite correctly, "he has not one friend in Mexico amongst the foreigners and is dispised by most of the Mexicans."[37]

The obligation to Joseph H. Hawkins, was not, as things turned out, a money debt. By the agreement of November 14, 1821, Hawkins, it will be remembered, was to advance four thousand dollars or less toward the expense of settling the first three hundred families, and was to share equally with Austin in the lands and profits derived from the enterprise. How much he actually advanced it is impossible to say. In May, 1822, he wrote that his advances already exceeded seven thousand dollars, "including the provisions shipped, and my interest in the Only Son," a schooner to be used as a transport to Texas. In March, 1823, ten months later, he still wrote that advances and disbursements "now exceed $7,000."[38] He died bankrupt and terribly involved at the end of this year, and a friend, Nathaniel Cox, compiled from his papers, for he kept no books, an estimate that the Texas venture had cost him thirty thousand dollars. This included, Cox explained, "the purchase of Vessels, Cargoes, and disbursements to officers and seamen—Loans to individuals traveling to and from the grant, who are unknown to me, and lost to his Heirs except as a charge to the grant—payments made to you and on your draft—and the dreadfull Item of Usurious Interest to money Brokers for loans." He understood, however, that the only claim of the estate on Austin was "one half of the Grant."[39]

The original agreement acknowledged receipt by Austin of four thousand dollars; but in 1832, writing partly from memory, because he had lost a memorandum book, Austin declared that he had not at the time of signing received that much and that the sum

---

[36] Butler to McLane, July 13, 1834, MSS., Department of State (Washington), Despatches from Agents to Mexico, Vol. 6: "I am very sure that he was the principal cause of my being defeated in the last effort made to obtain a cession of Texas."

[37] Austin to Williams, April 29, 1835, Rosenberg Library.

[38] Hawkins to Austin, May 31, 1822; to Mrs. Austin, March 29, 1833.

[39] Nathaniel Cox to Austin, June 3, August 6, November 16, 1824.

of Hawkins's later advances did not bring the total to that amount.[40] This, however, was not a material question, since, regardless of the amount spent, the debt would be canceled by half the lands and profits obtained from the colony.

Austin felt a very warm affection for Hawkins [41] and correspondence extending over a number of years shows only cordial and confidential feelings between him and Mrs. Hawkins and members of her family. There was no misunderstanding about this claim, and the delay in settlement was not of Austin's seeking.[42] He requested Mrs. Hawkins to appoint a representative for a division of the premium land during the winter of 1824; [43] but she replied that she trusted him completely and asked him to act alone [44]—a commission that he probably found it inadvisable to accept. He renewed the proposal in 1827.[45] In 1829 he suggested taking plats of the land to New Orleans and making the division with Nathaniel Cox, who had represented Mrs. Hawkins in the settlement of the estate in 1824. He wished also, he said, to consult with Cox "as to the best mode of making the estate of some value to the heirs." [46] In the fall of this year Major Robert Carter Nicholas wrote Austin that he intended moving to Texas, and that in the double capacity of uncle and guardian of the Hawkins heirs—Mrs. Hawkins being now dead—he would be ready to divide the lands and make a settlement. When he wrote the newspapers of the United States were making much of the prospect of acquiring Texas from Mexico, in which event he saw the lands of the Brazos rising rapidly to the price of sugar land in Louisiana, which he said was selling at seventy dollars an acre.[47] Perhaps the failure of the United States to buy Texas deterred him. At any rate he did not move to

[40] Austin pointed out that much of the expenditure charged by the executors against the colony was really incurred for goods and slaves which Hawkins's brother and an agent named Botts took to Texas for speculation in 1822. For a full account of the unfortunate venture of Littleberry Hawkins see his letter to Austin, October 7, 1824.

[41] See especially Austin to his mother, January 20, 1821, May 4, 1824; and to Mrs. Hawkins, April 20, 1824.

[42] Nathaniel Cox, acting for Mrs. Hawkins, requested Austin (March 20, June 3, 1824) to hold the title to the partnership land in his own name to avoid having it swallowed up by creditors. Half the grant, he said, would not bring a hundred dollars at auction.

[43] Cox to Austin, August 6, 1824, acknowledges Austin's request of July 12.

[44] Mrs. Hawkins to Austin, October 9, 1824; Cox to Austin, November 16, December 14, 1824.

[45] Mrs. Hawkins to Austin, August 4, 1827, acknowledges his letter of May 4.

[46] Austin to Cox, March 10, 1829.

[47] Ro. C. Nicholas to Austin, October 11, 1829.

Texas. In 1831 General John T. Mason was appointed to represent the Hawkins interests,[48] but settlement was still deferred—and then with another representative—until the fall of 1832.

In preparation for this Austin drew up an elaborate statement of the fiscal history of the first colony. He did this, he explained, to counteract erroneous impressions conveyed by common rumor that he had derived a fortune from the grant. Annulment of his contracts with the settlers to pay the twelve and a half cents an acre for land had, of course, destroyed the principal source of profit upon which he and Hawkins had counted. While his subsequent arrangement with Bastrop for a share of the commissioner's fee had yielded something, it had gone back into the enterprise in the form of unavoidable expense. Much of this, to be sure, should have been paid by the government, but its refusal to recognize the obligation put the burden upon Austin. To reach a "judicial or litigated settlement," he said, "would be the work of many years and of endless expense." He offered an equal division of the premium lands—twenty-two and a half leagues and three *labors*—less the cost of surveying; and this seems to have been the basis of settlement.[49] On September 27 he wrote that he had begun the division of the land, and on November 5 that he was nearly through "the trouble-some business of settling my affairs with the Hawkins estate."[50]

A letter from Austin to Nathaniel Cox, who had been in close touch with the Hawkins interest since 1824, gives the only clue to the contemporary attitude of the family toward the settlement. Acknowledging a letter of March 1, 1833, from Cox, Austin wrote: "It is highly gratifying to me that you and Mr. Sanders[51] approve of my conduct in relation to the settlement of the business of our mutual friend J. H. Hawkins' estate. . . . Edmund [Hawkins], I fear, received incorrect impressions from some persons who are unfriendly to me, but I think they are removed now and that he is very well satisfied."[52] No further details of the settlement are

---

[48] Richard Hawes to Austin, August 29, 1831; Cox to Austin, March 22, 1832; Austin to Williams, April 12, 1832. Rosenberg Library.
[49] Austin to —— Martin, September 14, 1832.
[50] Austin to Perry, September 27, November 4, 1832; to Mrs. Perry, November 5, 1832.
[51] Possibly a brother-in-law of Joseph H. Hawkins. There is a reference to him as an uncle of the Hawkins children. Mrs. Hawkins had been a Nicholas.
[52] Austin to Cox, April 2, 1833.

available. Since land could not be held by non-residents, it is likely that title to the Hawkins lands after the division was vested in a trustee.[53]

There were two other creditors to whom Austin was indebted for small amounts which he used in the inauguration of the colony. They were Edward Lovelace, a Louisiana planter who accompanied him on his exploration of Texas in 1821, and General Arthur Goodall Wavell, an English soldier of fortune whom he met in Mexico in 1822. The loan from Lovelace, in November and December, 1821, was seven hundred dollars. Austin referred to it in his statement concerning the Hawkins settlement; said that he used part of it for the purchase of the *Lively;* and that the debt was still unpaid. It was settled in 1847 by a deed to seven hundred and forty acres of land from Austin's estate.[54]

From his own account, Wavell was a general in the Chilean army of independence when he arrived at the Mexican capital on a government mission in the summer of 1822 and there met Austin. His business with the government ended in his transferring to the Mexican army with the rank he had held in Chile and being sent to London on a mission that he does not explain. He and Austin were strongly and immediately attracted to each other, and his connections and knowledge of Spanish enabled him to give Austin influential assistance. On July 4 they entered into a contract to share equally in all lands granted to either, excepting the half interest in the grant already pledged to Hawkins. On such lands Wavell was to form a company in London to promote colonization, min-

[53] In Tyler's *Quarterly Historical and Genealogical Magazine*, III, 20–23 (July, 1921), A. J. Morrison publishes a sketch of Joseph H. Hawkins compiled from a rare volume by William B. Victor, entitled *Life and Events* (Cincinnati, 1859). Victor wrote from papers of the Nicholas family of Kentucky, a daughter of which Hawkins married. He recites with some errors of proportion the part that Hawkins played in the colonization of Texas and says that "his estate seems not to have been reimbursed." This is seen from the preceding account to be incorrect. In 1859 Victor, who was the husband of the only surviving Hawkins heir, presented a memorial to the Texas Legislature, asking additional compensation for Hawkins's part in establishing the first colony. He acknowledged settlement of the original four thousand dollars which Hawkins was obligated to advance by Austin's division of the premium lands; but contended that Hawkins made large additional advances which were not covered by the premium lands. He quoted numerous letters from Nathaniel Cox; but apparently did not have access to correspondence between Austin and Cox which explained the nature of the "additional advances." They were, in fact, personal speculations by Hawkins, connected with the Texan venture, but having no relation to Austin. See *Memorial to the Legislature of Texas,* by William B. Victor (Cincinnati, 1859), a pamphlet of 35 pages and appendix, in the Library of the University of Texas.

[54] See Austin's account with Edward Lovelace, March 30, 1822.

ing, and commerce. After trying experiences with pirates in the Gulf, Wavell reached England in November. He wrote in May, 1823, that he had made conditional arrangement for flotation of the company, which would be consummated as soon as Austin furnished him with the necessary documents showing title to the grant.[55] In Mexico, as we know, the grant was just then confirmed, but it did not invest Austin with a fee title to any land. Though Wavell might still have made the contract the basis of a speculative organization in London, Austin was evidently not of a mind to try it.

Before leaving Mexico Wavell lent Austin money which Wavell believed later to have been indispensable to him in wearing through the long delay preceding confirmation of the grant.[56] In 1826 he authorized B. R. Milam to act for him in settlement with Austin, but in 1832, after a conference with Austin, revoked the power, saying that he would himself attend to the settlement later. In 1851 he declared that the account was never paid.[57] Neither Austin nor Wavell gives a clue to the amount of the loan, but it was probably not large.[58]

In January, 1833, Austin wrote his sister, who despaired of his living long enough to enjoy the fruits of his labor, that four thousand dollars more would clear him of debt. This—"to have paid off nearly all the old debts," and to have gained for his family by settling Texas credit that would be "permanent and honorable for ages to come"—seemed to him cause for pride and satisfaction. Moreover, as showing the rapid development of the country, he had been offered five dollars an acre for a piece of land and could get eight for it on credit. Why despond? The world was what we made it, "all trouble or not so bad." A puncheon hut or an Indian

[55] Wavell to Austin, May 22, 1823.

[56] Writing Wavell in July, 1824 (probably), Austin says, "I can refund you the money you let me have and will secure a piece of land here for you."

[57] Wavell to Austin, January 14, 1826; to Milam, January 24, 1832, Texas State Library; to Ashbel Smith, February 28, 1851, December 18, 1855. Wavell obtained in 1826 a contract to settle a colony of Europeans in the border reserve between Red River and the Sulphur Fork and appointed Milam his local agent. But for interruptions interposed by the government, Wavell contended, he would have fulfilled the contract and been entitled to premium land; and for many years he sought compensation for his efforts from the government of Texas. Statements made in support of his claims furnish some of the facts for the foregoing account. They are in the Texas State Library and in the Ashbel Smith papers at the University of Texas.

[58] Austin's statement (to Martin, September 14, 1832) of the resources, besides those advanced by Hawkins which he used in Mexico does not mention a loan from Wavell.

camp was but a trifle when only a stepping stone to "a comfortable home and farm for life." [59]

This gives us the essence of Austin's personal philosophy of life. He did not desire great wealth. At times his thoughts turned to travel, but for the most part he looked forward to a quiet life on a farm adjoining his sister's, free of public cares, and spending his leisure in the enjoyment of books, friends, music, and conversation. "Let us unite a few choice families and make a neighborhood," he wrote. "Abundance of such substantial and wholesome food as sound health and useful exercise require will never be wanting. Most of the things called luxuries are inventions or phantasms of the imagination. We can invent and give reins to the fancy in this country as well as anywhere else; and can supply our own luxuries in case we cannot get a regular supply of them from Paris, London, or New York. In short, I think we can live happily if we choose to do so." Sometimes he even grew poetic. "We will . . . arrange our cottages—rural—comfortable—and splendid—the splendor of nature's simplicity. Gardens and rosy bowers, and ever verdant groves and Music, books, and intellectual amusements can all be ours; and that confidence and community of feeling and tastes which none but congenial minds can ever know; all these without excessive wealth we can have. Millions could not buy them, but the right disposition, with competence, insures them." He denied that such a life would bore him. He would set his colony an example of plainness and economy, and the poor would not be mortified and the middle class ruined by the extravagant example of the rich. Envy and jealousy could never be banished from the human heart, but something at least could be done toward reducing the cause which excited and fed them.[60]

In 1830 Austin had occasion to explain to his brother-in-law, who had complained of his silence and reserve, that the habit of taciturnity had grown upon him and that he no longer found in conversation the pleasure of earlier years. Fortunately it did not affect his writing. His letters reveal a studious, thoughtful mind, accurately informed and extensive in range. He wrote with fluency and precision and with noteworthy simplicity and ingenuousness.

[59] Austin to Mrs. Perry, January 26, 1833. See also November 5, 1832.
[60] Austin to Mrs. Holley, July 19, December 29, 1831, January 14, 1832. See also Austin to Carr, March 4, 1829, and to Perry, July 14, 1830, December 27, 1831.

It would be interesting to be able to compile a list of his reading. A letter to his brother-in-law deplores the want of money to buy "a few good Spanish and English books of a literary and historical character." Few books, he added, had come within his reach in Texas. Most of them we may be sure were related to his work. Politics, economics, diplomacy, law, international law, history, contemporary essays on political subjects, and a few novels held his principal interest. Such general scientific knowledge as he had was obtained mainly from Rees's Encyclopaedia.

Temperamentally and by his methods Austin belonged to the statesman-diplomat type. On a less isolated stage and under different conditions his work would have attracted more attention from contemporaries. But he deliberately sought to avoid notice; and to the casual observer, familiar from childhood with the restless westward surge of emigration in the United States, the problems of establishing and nursing to robust stature a colony of American pioneers in a frontier Mexican province did not differ obviously from those of maintaining elsewhere an advanced post on the western fringe of Anglo-American settlement. Thus his work has not yet enjoyed its full meed of appreciation.

CHAPTER X

The Law of April 6, 1830

THE law of April 6, 1830, was to accomplish frankly and without disguise what Guerrero's emancipation decree sought by indirection—to stop the flood of emigration from the United States to Texas. It was an emergency measure to avert a supposed crisis, and from the national point of view was justifiable and proper. Mexican statesmen read the record of American expansion with profound uneasiness and distrust. Wherever it had met the Spanish boundary with a determined push, the Spanish line had receded. The expectation of the framers of the colonization policy to balance native and European settlements against Anglo-American colonists was plainly doomed to disappointment, and the safeguard of the border and coast reserves was both insufficient and unenforceable. Preservation of the province might still lie, however, in that other reservation of the federal colonization law allowing Congress to stop immigration at its discretion from any particular nation.

A number of influences converged at this time to sharpen the fears of the government. The first of these was the attitude of the government of the United States toward the Red River-Sabine boundary. While recognizing its validity, the Adams administration hoped by a new treaty of limits to gain advantageous adjustments, and in 1825 and again in 1827 instructed Poinsett, the American representative at Mexico, to suggest such a negotiation. The Mexicans as a matter of fact had entertained the same hope of pushing the boundary eastward that the Americans had of moving it westward, so that Poinsett found them unyielding; and, as the subject stood in the way of concluding a commercial treaty, he signed on January 12, 1828, an agreement confirming the line described by the Florida treaty and providing for its survey by a joint commission. This was promptly ratified by the Senate of the United States and in due time by the Mexican Congress but the lassitude of the Mexican Foreign Office prevented exchange of ratifications at Washington within the stipulated term, and this made it necessary to submit the treaty again to the Senate. Poinsett's conduct of the negotiation was straightforward and above reproach; but Mexican representatives at Washington since 1822 had magnified the popular desire for Texas and condemnation of the Florida treaty which abandoned it; had filled the ears of their government with imaginary plots and invasions for its acquisition; and had emphasized a connection that did not exist between the colonization of Texas and the efforts of Adams to buy it. Forgetting, therefore, their own longing for a slice of Louisiana and Arkansas, Mexicans at home regarded Poinsett's overtures as proof of cupidity and lack of scruple.

In 1824 the Mexican chargé at Washington reported that he had heard General Jackson say that the United States ought not to have surrendered its claims to Texas, that it ought to regain it, and that the way to get a territory was to take it and then negotiate for it, as had been done with Florida. Whether or not the report was accurate, Jackson did want Texas; and on March 4, 1829, he became President of the United States. Adams had not re-submitted to the Senate the treaty of limits, nor did Jackson. On the contrary, he instructed Poinsett to renew the negotiation for Texas and authorized him to offer five million dollars for a line west of the Nueces. Colonel Anthony Butler was the bearer of these instructions. He traveled overland through Texas, and before he reached Mexico Jackson acceded to the request of the Mexican government and recalled Poinsett. Unfortunately he appointed Butler to the vacant post, and his persistent and unscrupulous intrigues for the next six years removed from the Mexican mind the last lingering doubt of Jackson's willingness to balk at nothing to obtain Texas.[1]

Simultaneously with the preparation of Poinsett's instructions in August a widespread propaganda was launched by the pro-Jack-

[1] William R. Manning, "Texas and the Boundary Issue, 1822–1829," in *Southwestern Historical Quarterly*, XVII, 217–261, gives a very detailed and excellent account of Poinsett's negotiations and of the agitations and rumors which fed Mexican anxiety. See by the writer "President Jackson and the Texas Revolution" in *American Historical Review*, XII, 788–798, for Butler's negotiations.

son press urging and foretelling the early acquisition of Texas.[2] Naturally, therefore, the Mexican press was forewarned, and, though objection was not needed, lost no time in planting obstacles in Butler's way, announcing the purpose of his mission and declaring that the cession of Texas would degrade the republic and disgrace the minister who consented to it. At the same time Colonel Piedras, commanding the garrison at Nacogdoches, reported that the United States was moving troops to the frontier, that hundreds of Americans were entering Texas—and not all of them to settle—that it was reported that men were being recruited in New Orleans to revolutionize Texas, and that there was "no other subject of conversation on the frontier but the views of President Jackson to take possession of Texas."[3]

Opportunely riding the crest of the wave of popular attention which the newspapers of the United States were gratuitously turning towards Texas, the first of several more or less fraudulent companies speculating in Texas lands began a scrip selling campaign in the summer of 1829. On July 8 *The National Intelligencer* carried a column and a half advertisement explaining a "proposal for disposing of 48,000,000 acres of land in the provinces of Coahuila and Texas."[4] The basis of the project was an empresario contract granted to Stephen J. Wilson in 1826 to settle two hundred families between the thirty-second parallel and the Arkansas River west of the hundred and second meridian. The territory is now included in Texas, New Mexico, Oklahoma, Colorado, and Kansas. In September, 1828, the grant was enlarged and Richard Exter was associated with Wilson.[5] They were British subjects, with Mexican citizenship, and lived in Mexico City. The advertisement declared that they had authorized Dennis A. Smith, a Baltimore broker, "to sell and dispose of the

---

[2] Among the first articles to appear were two by Benton, contributed to the *St. Louis Beacon* over the pseudonym of *Americanus*. In October and November, 1829, Benton contributed nine more to the same paper, signed *La Salle*. See William M. Meigs, *The Life of Thomas Hart Benton* (Philadelphia, 1904), 340. *The National Intelligencer* (Washington), an anti-Jackson paper, published in its issues of September 26, October 5, 10, 20, 1829, extracts from a large number of papers of various shades of opinion. McMaster, *History of the People of the United States* (Philadelphia, 1905), V, 543–550, gives a good summary of the newspaper discussion.

[3] Piedras to Terán, December 8, 1829, Translations of Empresario Contracts, p. 343, General Land Office of Texas.

[4] The advertisement ran daily from July 8 to 17, and probably appeared in other papers.

[5] Translations of Empresario Contracts, 102, 163, General Land Office of Texas; Transcripts from Department of Fomento, Mexico, legajo 4, expedientes 7, 24.

lands ... together with all the privileges and advantages possessed by them to such person or persons as may be disposed to purchase the same and comply with the terms of the grant." The rest of the plan was no doubt Smith's. He proposed to form a stock company of $400,000 paid in capital to take over the grant from the Mexican proprietors, and offered stock to the public in blocks of ten to one hundred dollars, plus two and a half per cent brokerage fees. When $200,000 had been paid there would be a meeting of the stockholders, seven trustees would be appointed, and they would hand the money to the "proprietors, first taking care to procure a good and *bona fide* title or transfer, to be approved by the United States minister or charge de affaires resident in the Republic of Mexico." Each ten dollars entitled the subscriber to a thousand acres of land, and the first two hundred families who moved to the grant would receive a bonus. If as many as two hundred failed to settle, it was the duty of the trustees to make up the deficiency, thereby fulfilling the contract. If the original grantees could not make title, subscriptions, less the brokerage fee, would be returned.

This, of course, was a palpable fraud. The empresarios had no title to transfer. They had merely the right to settle the two hundred families within a designated area and receive therefor a stipulated reward when the work was done. The Mexican government probably did not object to seeing the American public mulcted by a fraudulent speculation, but the result of this would inevitably sharpen popular interest in Texas and swell immigration, and to that it did object. As Austin explained, the general discussion and agitation of Texas "roused the attention of the Mexican Gov^t and excited their jealousy that the U. S. were determined to take this country by force right or wrong," and it was this, he said, which produced the law of April 6, 1830.[6]

Smith's advertisement reached Austin's eyes on September 21 and the next day he wrote his cousin, Henry Austin, explaining the nature of an empresario contract and warning him not to be taken in by it. A few days later, in response to a request from James W. Breedlove, vice-consul for Mexico at New Orleans, he wrote a detailed description of the method of acquiring land in Texas and predicted the annulment of Exter and Wilson's contract; and "if that

[6] Austin to Leaming, June 14, 1830.

is done," he added, "those men, to justify themselves, will in all probability lay the blame on the government and complain that they have been robbed of 48,000,000 acres of land." All this was very unjust and the public ought to be disabused concerning it, but he was unwilling for his name to appear in any way connected with it; because, he said, "I have heretofore given frank and honest advice to persons on the same subject, and have never yet failed to make an enemy by doing so." Subsequently, however, a letter to his kinsman in Philadelphia, Thomas F. Leaming, was published in the *National Gazette,* and, naturally, roused the resentment of the speculators, who sought to revenge themselves by injuring Austin in Mexico. "They will find themselves gnawing a file," he grimly remarked. His own interest was twofold. In the first place, the speculations turned the attention of the government unnecessarily to Texas; and, in the second place, they tended to undermine confidence in the legitimate colonization enterprises.[7]

Austin's analysis of public opinion in Mexico, as gathered from the newspapers, was that Poinsett's unpopularity was extended to the American people and government.

"The charges ... are that Mr. P. intermed[dled] with the internal affairs of Mexico—that he formed and organized political parties—that he fomented disunion—that his object in doing so was to defraud the Gov^t out of Texas. In proof of this they say that as soon as all Mexico was thrown into convulsions by the virulence of the Yorkino (founded as is said by P.) and the Escoses parties the Jackson papers of the U. S. simultaneously, vociferated 'we must have Texas'—That P. was concerned in the grants of Exter and Zavala for colonizing Texas. This caused a suspicion by inference that as he was the agent and representative of the U. S. that Gov^t was also secretly a colonizer, and had improper views of this country. To all this the little imprudences and silly expressions of some of the settlers on the frontiers of Texas and elsewhere have been added, greatly magnified, and construed by some into disobedience, or a wish to be disobedient, etc., etc. To these matters have also been superadded reports that the present representative of the U. S. Gov^t to Mexico was sent especially to purchase Texas from Guerrero while he had dictatorial powers, and was under the influence of Zavala, who it is known was under that of Poinsett. The time when this offer is said to have been made is also noticed, that is when the nation was pressed for money and

[7] Austin to Henry Austin, September 22, and to Breedlove, October 12, 1829; to Leaming, June 14, and to Perry, July 11, 1830.

in distress, owing to the Spanish invasion, internal divisions, etc. Perhaps [Austin added] I hazard nothing in saying that causes may be discovered in this train of circumstances, in connection with others, which would have roused the suspicions of any people, and more particularly when it is remembered that the North is a giant and Mexico a new and not firmly organized Gov^t, and also that the U. S. have silently, as it were, extended their dominion over the vast regions of Louisiana, Missouri, Oregon, etc." [8]

Undoubtedly, however, the decisive influence in bringing about the law of April 6, 1830, was the advice of General Manuel de Mier y Terán. He was the head of a scientific commission which spent a good part of 1828 at Nacogdoches making observations and gathering information in preparation for the boundary survey.[9] On the way he and Austin had become well acquainted at San Felipe, and formed for each other a mutual respect and esteem. For the next four years, until Terán's untimely death in 1832, their relations were intimate and for the most part cordial.

Conditions on the frontier, as he bluntly described them to President Victoria, filled Terán with depression and foreboding. "The whole population here," he said, "is a mixture of strange and incoherent parts without parallel in our federation; numerous tribes of Indians, now at peace, but armed and at any moment ready for war, whose steps toward civilization should be taken under the close supervision of a strong and intelligent government; colonists of another people, more aggressive and better informed than the Mexican inhabitants, but also more shrewd and unruly; among these foreigners are fugitives from justice, honest laborers, vagabonds and criminals, but honorable and dishonorable alike travel with their political constitution in their pockets, demanding the privileges, authority, and officers which such a constitution guarantees." Added to this motley mixture were the slaves, "beginning to learn the favorable intent of the Mexican law toward their unfortunate condition" and held with an iron hand to keep them in a state of subjection. The Mexican natives were poor and ignorant, and the local civil officers venal and corrupt; and the colonists, imagining that they were typical, despised all Mexicans.

[8] Austin to Fisher, June 17, 1830.
[9] Berlandier and Chovel, *Diario de Viage de la Commision de Límites,* etc. (Mexico, 1850), 1–110, follows the march of the party from Mexico on November 10, 1827, to Bexar, which they reached on March 1, 1828.

"The incoming stream of new settlers was unceasing; and the first news of them came by discovering them on land which they had already long occupied; the old inhabitants would then set up a claim of doubtful validity, a law suit would ensue, and the alcalde had a chance to come out with some money." Both Mexicans and colonists complained of the union with Coahuila and favored the organization of Texas as a federal territory. He thought there was much justice in their complaints, but believed that the establishment of a sub-political chief and a court of appeals in the colonies to avoid the tedious references to Saltillo would sufficiently meet their needs. He was confident that repeal of the laws against slavery would make of Texas in a few years a powerful state, able to compete in productions and wealth with Louisiana; but God forbid the payment of such a price for prosperity.[10]

In September, 1829, Terán became commandant general of the Eastern Interior Provinces, and responsible, therefore, for the defence of Texas. The newspaper agitation in the United States for the purchase of Texas coupled with his own observations caused him to devise a program for the preservation of the province. A portion of this he submitted to the minister of war in November, together with a denunciation of the methods employed by the United States in absorbing the territory of its neighbors.

"Instead [he said] of armies, battles, or invasions, which make a great noise and for the most part are unsuccessful, these men lay hands on means which, if considered one by one, would be rejected as slow, ineffective, and at times palpably absurd. They begin by assuming rights, as in Texas, which it is impossible to sustain in a serious discussion, making ridiculous pretensions based on historical incidents which no one admits —such as the voyage of La Salle, which was an absurd fiasco, but serves as a basis for their claim to Texas. Such extravagant claims as these are now being presented for the first time to the public by dissembling writers.[11] The efforts that others make to submit proofs and reasons are by these men employed in reiterations and in enlarging upon matters of administration in order to attract the attention of their fellow countrymen, not to the justice of the claim, but to the profit to be gained from admitting it. At this stage it is alleged that there is a national demand for the

[10] Terán to Victoria, June 30, 1828, in Howren, "The Causes and Origin of the Decree of April 6, 1830," *Southwestern Historical Quarterly,* XVI, 395–398.

[11] Knowledge of the facts gives one a good deal of sympathy with Mexican impatience of American claims to Texas, but of course Terán was in error in saying that the claim was now first presented.

step which the government meditates. In the meantime, the territory against which these machinations are directed, and which has usually remained unsettled, begins to be visited by adventurers and empresarios; some of these take up their residence in the country, pretending that their location has no bearing upon the question of their government's claim or the boundary disputes; shortly, some of these forerunners develop an interest which complicates the political administration of the coveted territory; complaints, even threats, begin to be heard, working on the loyalty of the legitimate settlers, discrediting the efficiency of the existing authority and administration; and the matter having arrived at this stage —which is precisely that of Texas at this moment—diplomatic manoeuvers begin." [12]

Terán's full plan, with arguments, was presented by his *aide*, Colonel Constantino Tarnava, in a report to the war department on January 6, 1830. Briefly, it included three features: (1) military occupation of Texas; (2) counter-colonization by Mexicans and Europeans, particularly by Swiss and German immigrants; (3) the development of an economic bond between Texas and the rest of Mexico by establishing coastwise trade.

The military recommendations were: to strengthen the garrisons at Bexar, Goliad, and Nacogdoches; to establish new garrisons at the head of Galveston Bay, at the mouth of the Brazos, and at the Brazos crossing of the Bexar-Nacogdoches road; to move the troops usually stationed on the Rio Grande up to the Nueces; and to commission a war schooner for regular transport service. The Mexican colonists were to be of two classes—convict soldiers, who at the expiration of their service should receive farms and means to support themselves, and poor families who might be induced to settle in return for land and government maintenance for a limited period. "Whatever obstacle may be encountered must be overcome," he insisted, "for these measures involve the safety of the nation and the integrity of our territory. Indeed, there is no choice of measures in this matter. Either the government occupies Texas *now*, or it is lost forever, for there can be no possibility of a reconquest when our base of operations would be three hundred leagues distant while our enemies would be carrying on their struggle close to their base and in possession of the sea." It was of the greatest importance to settle Mexican colonies on the coast, which would require alteration of one of Austin's contracts. He anticipated difficulty in drawing Swiss and German immigrants, but had no suggestion to overcome it. The proposal for coasting trade emphasized the potential importance of Texas cotton in trade with England, and shows the influence of arguments which Austin had been pouring into Terán's ears for the past eighteen months. It is evident that Jackson's failure to resubmit the boundary treaty to the Senate strengthened Terán's suspicions of the United States, and one end that he hoped to accomplish by his program was to bring about ratification of the treaty by showing that Mexico was determined to defend Texas.[13]

To a copy of this report which he transmitted to Alamán, secretary of relations, Tarnava added other reflections and suggestions. The plan of colonization proposed must be continued for many years, he said, "and always with the same urgency: To-day we shall only try to populate the banks of the Brazos; to-morrow it will be necessary to think of colonizing the territory bathed by the Red River of the Natchitoches; and before long that of the Arkansas"; for the Americans were expanding to the northwest with amazing rapidity and the Mexican frontier must keep pace with them. He asked if England could not be induced to make a declaration against designs of the United States on Texas; and suggested that Mexican newspapers begin to talk of the possibility of inciting a slave insurrection in Louisiana in the event of a war with the United States.[14]

Terán's proposals met the immediate approval of the government. Bustamante was now acting president. He had long been commandant general of the Interior Provinces and was already informed of conditions in Texas. On February 8 Alamán presented to a secret session of Congress his famous *iniciativa,* or recommendation, for a law to carry out Terán's views. Incorporating in his message literally, but without quotation marks, Terán's denunciation of the methods by which the United States promoted its spurious claims to the territory of its neighbors and the means by which he hoped to thwart its designs on Texas,[15] Alamán, unnecessarily

---

[13] *Ibid.,* 406–413.

[14] Tarnava to Alamán, January 14, 1830, University of Texas Transcripts from Department of Fomento, Mexico, legajo 5, expediente 30.

[15] Alamán to Terán, March 2, 1830, University of Texas Transcripts from Department of Fomento, Mexico, legajo 5, expediente 30: "You will perceive that . . . nothing has been done but to make extracts from and coordinate different paragraphs of your communications on this subject."

perhaps, dwelt on the disaffection of the colonists and their evasion of all laws that interfered with their convenience. He referred particularly to the evasion of the religious restriction, requiring colonists to be Catholics, and to the introduction of slaves contrary to the federal law of July 13, 1824, which he contended—probably correctly, as we have seen—forbade immigration as well as their importation for sale. To Terán's military occupation, counter-colonization, and coasting trade he added a fourth measure for the preservation of Texas. Let Congress repeal the national colonization law in its application to Coahuila and Texas, take from the state the right to make new contracts, suspend the execution of existing contracts, and vest in the federal government the further direction and supervision of colonization in Texas.[16] The supreme object, he said, was to overcome as quickly as possible the preponderance of Anglo-American population there by the settlement of Europeans, whose religion, language, customs, and habits set them apart from the North Americans.[17]

Material is not available to follow the passage of the law through Congress. A joint committee of the two houses framed the bill, and presented it about the beginning of March. By the 10th the house of deputies had passed twelve articles.[18] On April 6 the law was signed.

It enacted Terán's proposals unchanged and sought to provide the means for carrying them out. That is, it authorized a loan, secured by the duty on cotton and woolen imports, to meet the cost of transporting Mexican colonists; and, to cover the deficiency of Mexican shipping, opened the coasting trade to foreign vessels for four years. Without annulling the state's right to make new contracts, as Alamán had advised, the law vested authority in a federal

---

[16] "It is desirable that the right of the state to make contracts be ended, and that those which it has already made, whether with Mexican or with North American empresarios, should remain in their present state [of fulfillment] without permitting the said empresarios to introduce families or to cede, sell, or alienate under any form of title the lands which have been conceded to them, without the previous approbation of the general government." Though this was not included in his formal recommendations, Terán had written on December 14, 1829, "if the colonization contracts in Texas by North Americans are not suspended, and if the conditions of the establishments are not watched, it is necessary to say that the province is already delivered to the foreigners."—University of Texas Transcripts from Department of Fomento, Mexico, legajo 5, expediente 34.

[17] The copy of the *iniciativa* used for this summary is an appendix to Filisola, *Memorias para la Historia de la Guerra de Tejas* (Mexico, 1849), II, 590–612.

[18] Alamán to Terán, March 2, 10, 1830, University of Texas Transcripts from Department of Fomento, Mexico, legajo 5, expediente 30. The debates of Congress are not available.

commissioner to supervise the execution of the contracts and see that they did not violate the limitations of the general colonization law. For the rest, it apparently intended to suspend existing contracts and put an abrupt end to further colonization from the United States. Existing slavery was recognized, but further introduction was strictly forbidden. To facilitate enforcement of these provisions foreigners entering by the northern frontier must show passports issued by Mexican representatives at their place of residence.[19]

Much depended on the interpretation of two critical paragraphs. A contemporary translation published by Austin[20] reads as follows:

Article "10. No change shall be made with respect to the colonies already established, nor with respect to the slaves which they contain—but the general government and that of each particular state, shall exact, under the strictest responsibilities, the observance of the colonization laws and the prevention of further introduction of slaves."

Article "11. In exercise of the right reserved to the general congress by the 7th article of the law of 18th August, 1824, the citizens of foreign countries lying adjacent to the Mexican territory are prohibited from settling as colonists in the states or territories of the republic adjoining such countries. Those contracts of colonization, the terms of which are opposed to the present article, and which are not yet complied with, shall consequently be suspended."

In the Spanish the last sentence reads, *"En consecuencia se suspenderán las contratas que no hayan tenido su cumplimiento y sean opuestas a esta ley."* [21] It is somewhat ambiguous in both translation and original. In the light of the practical interpretation, a better translation would be, "Those contracts which have not become effective . . . shall be suspended." But that comes later.

Terán did not entirely approve these emendations. The passport requirement could not be enforced without a much larger military force at Nacogdoches. He feared that the United States, which, in his opinion was hunting pretexts for taking possession of Texas, would seize upon that of self-defense and declare that the purpose of the law was to establish a frontier of Mexican settlements on its border; he would have preferred to reserve the frontier to Mexican

[19] This was simply a special application of the general passport law of March 12, 1828.—Dublan y Lozano, *Legislación Mexicana*, II, 64.

[20] *Texas Gazette*, July 3, 1830.

[21] Dublan y Lozano, *Legislación Mexicana*, II, 239.

empresarios and permit them to fill one-fourth of their contracts with foreigners, at the discretion of the government, without specifying any particular nation. But his chief objection was to the slavery provision. It could not be enforced, he said, because slaves would be brought in under contracts of indenture. Moreover, it was not desirable that it should be enforced. Nothing but a strong barrier of Mexican and foreign population could prevent the North American advance as far as Vera Cruz; and to establish this slavery was indispensable. He spoke from observation and study; in the abstract he hated slavery as much as any Mexican; but this was a practical matter upon which the integrity of the national territory depended; and it was his duty, without shrinking from the condemnation of public opinion, to give the government the facts. Indeed, he said, a large slave population in Texas would be a safeguard against disorder; the colonists knew that slave insurrections were promoted by turbulence and for that reason would hesitate to launch a revolution.[22] He had traveled far since 1828.

Terán was chosen to administer the law, and had added to his duties as commandant general those of federal commissioner of colonization.

It is evident that Austin's reception of the law was a matter of concern. On March 20 Bustamante wrote to assure him of his continued interest, and determination to exert his official influence, as in the past, for the advancement and happiness of "those worthy colonists." He forwarded the letter by Terán, no doubt for his information, but as he explained to insure its safe delivery.[23] Terán forwarded it with a letter of his own on April 24, innocently remarking that he supposed Austin was informed concerning the bill which Congress was discussing for the development of Texas; some friends in Mexico had asked his opinion, but he wanted to hear what Austin had to say about it before replying.

Rumors of Terán's military plan had been reaching Texas since early March, and, true to his practice of trying to forestall or ameliorate popular excitement, Austin had published editorials extolling

[22] Terán to Alamán, June 6, 1830, University of Texas Transcripts from Department of Fomento, Mexico, legajo 5, expediente 30.

[23] Alamán also writing to Terán on April 7, 1830 (University of Texas Transcripts from Department of Fomento, Mexico, legajo 5, expediente 30) cautioned him to move with prudence and tact, so as to avoid occasion for disturbances.

the generosity of the government to the colonists and its paternal interest in their welfare. Besides protecting them from the Indians, the soldiers would furnish a convenient market for their products. On April 5 a correspondent wrote him from New Orleans that Congress was considering a bill to stop immigration from the United States.[24] Austin was not, therefore, unprepared for the letters from Bustamante and Terán, though he wrote with a good deal of the force and impetuosity of surprise. He thanked the vice-president with a touch of sarcasm for his "manifestation of friendship and protection, especially agreeable under the circumstances, since the object of the law of April 6 appeared to be to destroy at one stroke, and at the sacrifice of the national faith, the happiness and prosperity of the colony which His Excellency had always protected and which he promised now to continue to protect." Many individuals, he said, were already on the way to his colony; others had made improvements and returned to the United States for their families. To exclude these would give the law a retroactive effect and be most cruel and unjust. Moreover, the law itself declared that "no change shall be made with respect to the colonies already established." His colony was established, and he hoped by return of mail to be able to publish a striking proof of the vice-president's protection in the form of a declaration that his colony was not comprehended in the law and that immigration to it would not be embarrassed. To Terán he wrote in the same vein; repeated that his colony should not be affected; and insisted that Terán, as commissioner, should so interpret the law.[25]

Austin said that the first clause of Article 10 was crowded in by his friends to save his colony;[26] that his colony was "established"; and that there should be therefore no change in it. What did he mean by "established"? And how did he meet the last sentence of Article 11: "Those contracts which are not yet complied with[27] (*que no hayan tenido su cumplimiento*) shall consequently be suspended"? The natural interpretation of the language, and the one in all probability intended, would seem to be that a colony was

<hr />

[24] *Texas Gazette,* March 13, 27, 1830; Austin to Músquiz, March 29, and Pettit to Austin, April 5, 1830.

[25] Austin to Bustamante, May 17, to Terán, May 18, 1830.

[26] Austin to Leaming, June 14, 1830.

[27] This is Austin's translation, and is possible. Perhaps the natural translation would be: "which have not yet been completed," or "which have not had their fulfillment."

established when the contract authorizing it was filled, in which case no more families could be settled; and that contracts that were not completed were suspended, which equally closed them to further immigration. Briefly, Austin's idea of "established" was a colony in which settlement was well advanced. He made no effort to fix a numerical standard for this, but the orthodox opinion which later developed in Texas was that the settlement of a hundred families constituted the validation of an empresario's contract and brought it under the protection of Article 10.[28] The basis of this was the provision of the state colonization law that empresarios must settle one hundred families before being entitled to premium land. Austin stood flatly on Article 10; there should be no change; therefore Article 11 did not apply to his contracts, or, at the least, could not exclude families already on the road or under agreement to immigrate. A letter to the governor states his position very clearly at the end of May; later his claims were enlarged.

"I understand [he wrote] that Article 10 of the law of the 6th of April . . . covers my colony, because it is already 'established,' and 'no change will be made' with respect to it. With this understanding I have advised the colonists engaged to emigrate in the autumn, winter, and spring next ensuing that the prohibition in Article 11 does not extend to them, and that there is no legal obstacle to hinder their entry as colonists of my colony. Those colonists have made all preparations to emigrate, have sold their lands and possessions where they lived, many of them are already on the way, and some have built their houses, selected their lands, paid the expenses of surveying, etc., all as the necessary preparation for the permanent removal of their families. To hinder their entrance now by a law of the general government will be to give retroactive effect to the law. It will be highly unjust . . . and will be treating with contempt the authority of the state, under which the contracts were made. Besides all this the law ought not to include contracts already concluded, and whose fulfillment has begun."

He urged the governor to try to obtain from Bustamante an order directing the military authorities "not to hinder the entry of colon-

[28] Contesting the annulment of his contract under this law, Sterling C. Robertson introduced witnesses before the ayuntamiento of San Felipe to prove that he had brought at least a hundred families before passage of the law. See below, pages 300–304. Transcripts from Archivo General de Coahuila, Saltillo, legajo 28, 1833, expediente 1293. The ayuntamiento expressed the opinion that he had introduced "at least one hundred families, which . . . was a fulfillment of the contract as far as said one hundred families were concerned." Brown, *History of Texas*, I, 319. In 1847 the Supreme Court of Texas assumed that the validity of Robertson's contract depended on his having introduced one hundred families before the passage of the law. 2 Texas Reports, 3.

ists included in my colony, and it will be just likewise to include the colony of Green DeWitt on the Guadalupe, which is already begun and has about a hundred and fifty families settled." Aside from presenting his point of view the letter was cleverly designed to stir the governor to the defense of state rights.[29]

Without waiting for a reply from Terán, Austin next transmitted his views to Colonel José de las Piedras, who commanded the garrison at Nacogdoches and upon whom would fall, for the most part, the enforcement of the law. He approached the subject somewhat obliquely. He understood, he said, that there had been some unpleasantness and personalities at Nacogdoches and offered his assistance in restoring and maintaining harmony. In accord, he and Piedras could render an important service to their government and country; civil war was kindled in Mexico, and God knew how far it would extend, but he thought it the duty of the local authorities to save Texas from similar misfortune. He closed with an apparently innocent paragraph that may have meant more than it said: "There is no news here. All is peace. The physical force of this colony exceeds six hundred men subject to militia duty, and for the past year the Indians have left us in peace." Piedras replied, also without awaiting Terán's instructions, that he concurred in Austin's views.[30]

Fortunately Terán also concurred, going even further, perhaps, than Austin had dared hope. He wrote the commandants at San Antonio and Nacogdoches that all the orders received by him from the government were "aimed to guarantee the colonies already established on the terms in which their contracts were granted; so that they have the right to conclude all matters pending in the part which has not yet been fulfilled."[31] He was expecting instructions concerning certain details, but these would require time, and meanwhile they were to act according to this declaration. Sending Austin a copy of this, he added: "For the present I can say to you that you should advise those families which are lacking to fulfill your contracts that there is no obstacle to your receiving them. To facilitate their removal you should send each one a certificate. This, pre-

---

[29] Austin to Viesca, May 31, 1830.
[30] Austin to Piedras, June 12, Piedras to Austin, June 21, 1830. Piedras had one hundred and fifty men at Nacogdoches.
[31] "De modo que tienen derecho a concluir todas las dependencias en la parte que aun no hayan tenido efecto."

sented to the authorities on the frontier, will serve as a passport." At the same time he suggested that Austin should try to get the scattered settlers in East Texas to move into his colony, "for to me it is all the same whether you bring a family from Tennessee or from the Sabine." In fact, the government would have been very glad to get these squatters away from the border.[32]

This was equivalent to ruling that Article 11 suspended only the contracts that had not become effective by the progress of settlement. But the government, which without doubt had intended to stop all colonization in Texas from the United States,[33] had read Austin's arguments with greater discrimination than Terán had done, and seeing that he seemed to insist only on the right of those already under contract to enter, instructed Terán to ask Austin for a list of these and to admit no others. Even these, the government hoped, might be induced to continue their journey to Coazacoalco, and accept land there. In all that he did, however, Terán was to be careful not to disturb the confidence and loyalty of Austin, whose steadying influence was recognized.[34]

Terán protested that his interpretation had been according to his understanding. He thought it particularly necessary to draw the scattered settlers to Austin's colony, "in which," he said, "there will be no difficulty while he lives and retains his influence, because he is a very reasonable man." On this subject he seems to have written Austin at length on August 20, but not to have informed him, either then or later, of the government's interpretation.[35] On the contrary, he reiterated his order to military commanders to admit immigrants without distinction if they gave evidence of destination to Austin's colony; and instructed the vice-consul at New Orleans to issue passports to those only who were going to Austin's or DeWitt's colony.[36]

The intensity of Austin's initial disappointment and chagrin

[32] Terán to Piedras and Elosua, June 14, and to Austin, June 15, 1830.

[33] Alamán to Terán, to vice-consuls at New Orleans and New York, and to chargé d'affaires at Washington, April 7, 1830: "In consequence, no individual of that country may pass to Texas with the view of colonizing." University of Texas Transcripts from Department of Fomento, Mexico, legajo 5, expediente 30.

[34] Alamán to Terán, July 14, 1830. University of Texas Transcripts from Department of Fomento, Mexico, legajo 5, expediente 32.

[35] Terán to Alamán, July 30, 31, 1830. University of Texas Transcripts from Department of Fomento, Mexico, legajo 5, expedientes 34 and 32. The substance of Terán's letter of August 20 is clear from Austin's reply of September 17, 1830.

[36] Terán to Elosua, August 21, 1830, Translations of Empresario Contracts, 347, General Land Office of Texas; to James W. Breedlove, October 6, *Ibid.*, 348.

upon hearing of the law of April 6 can best be measured in the light of his enthusiastic reaction from the threat of Guerrero's emancipation decree. With the lifting of that cloud he saw only a clear track ahead. Urging the removal of his brother-in-law from Missouri, he wrote: "I have never been so thoroughly convinced as I now am of the future rapid rise of this country. You have no idea of it, or you would be *here before* April, family and all. This is the most liberal and munificent government on earth to emigrants—after being here one year you will oppose a change even to Uncle Sam." A hundred and fifty-three families had arrived in the past two months, he wrote a few days later; in a year more his contracts would be filled. Again, just a week before the passage of the law:

"You have no idea at all of this country, nor of the great emigration that is daily coming to it, nor of the *character* of the emigrants. We are getting the best men, the best kind of settlers. Pay no attention to rumors and silly reports. . . . We have nothing to fear from this Gov^t nor from any other quarter except from the United States of the North. If that Gov^t should get hold of us and introduce its *land system* etc., etc., thousands who are now on the move and who have not yet secured their titles, would be totally ruined. The greatest misfortune that could befall Texas at this moment [he went on] would be a sudden change by which many of the emigrants would be thrown upon the liberality of the Congress of the United States of the North—*theirs would be a most forlorn hope.*" [37]

The *Texas Gazette* of January 30, 1830, reported that during the preceding two months Austin had issued two hundred and thirty certificates of reception to settlers and prospective settlers. On March 13 it declared that probably a thousand people had entered Texas during the past "season"—meaning the past fall and winter. Every fortnight vessels brought from sixty to a hundred passengers, mostly families, for settlement in Austin's colony; even the abundant food crop of the recent harvest would scarcely suffice for "the extraordinary emigration that has poured in upon us." [38]

Even before receiving Terán's favorable interpretation of the law, however, Austin's confidence revived. On June 1 he wrote Henry

[37] Austin to Perry, December 31, 1829, January 3 and March 28, 1830.
[38] Issue of April 24. The same issue announced the docking of the *Pocahontas* at Brazoria with sixty-four passengers and a full cargo of freight; that of May 7 reported the *Emeline Watlington* with "upwards of sixty passengers"; and on May 15 the *Nelson Brown* had arrived with sixty-two, and reported several other vessels at New Orleans booked for "this colony."

Austin at Matamoras: "That law will be a *dead letter* in Texas so far as regards my colony for the 10th Article covers me entirely.... The timorous will hesitate about immigrating here, but all who are fully informed on the subject will not—for the fact is there is nothing to fear, neither will any embarrassments be interposed to stop emigration to my colony." From the standpoint of the government, however, he thought the law a grave mistake; the settlers were opposed to the sale of Texas to the United States, and were becoming sincerely attached to the government. It is significant of Austin's accurate information in everything that concerned Texas that he knew thus early the real authorship of the law. Terán had committed a capital error in advising it, he said, "for the fact is he is the author ... although he has no idea that I am apprised of that fact —*I have always known it.*" With the same assurance he wrote prospective colonists in the United States: "My colony is established, and no legal impediment will of course be interposed to the removal to it of those who have contracted to become settlers; for they properly belong to the colony as much as those who are here. ... Those who bring their families here, and can produce evidence that they belong to a contract on colonization which is in legal operation, and who can also bring unequivocal evidences of good character, have nothing to fear." [39]

To one of his correspondents in the United States Austin wrote that the people were quiet and settled, but that "one imprudent measure on the part of Gov^t would have a dreadful effect. This must be closely watched and guarded against if possible and harmony and peace preserved." Besides this there is very little to indicate the attitude of the people. They probably wrote little, and we may be sure that the newspaper was carefully censored. Apologizing to Terán for the harshness of his letter of May 18, Austin explained that he had just returned from a month in the field with surveyors and "found the people restless and uneasy on account of a thousand false rumors. ... Many of the colonists expected their relatives—brothers and fathers—in the autumn and winter. They were frightened, and all beset me." But be sure, he added, that "if I wrote excitedly to you, I have tried to smother excitement in others." A memorandum that he wrote some time later says that

[39] Austin to Henry Austin, and to Perry, June 16, and to Fisher, June 17, 1830.

the excitement on the Nacogdoches frontier "was so violent as to be on the point of breaking out." [40]

By a series of extremely clever editorials in the *Texas Gazette* Austin sought to relieve the apprehensions of the colonists by directing attention to the beneficial aspects of the law: military protection to the frontier by the establishment of a garrison, commanded by an officer known and liked by the settlers; relief from militia duty; promotion of commerce by opening the coasting trade to foreigners; encouragement of woolen and cotton manufactures. And withal, immigration was not forbidden, as was erroneously reported: Article 10 guaranteed the rights "of all emigrants who are comprehended in the contracts of empresarios whose colonies are established, and permits the full completion of such contracts to the full number contracted for." At the same time, for Mexican consideration, he dwelt upon the development of the province from a wilderness to a flourishing member of the confederation at no cost to the nation; and upon the importance of a strong population in Texas to protect the states to the south from the hordes of Indians that the United States was pushing west of the Mississippi. [41]

While relieved, naturally, and expressing gratification that the law was no worse, Austin left the government in no doubt that he thought it bad. It would check the immigration of substantial colonists, but would hardly affect the entrance of undesirables. As for himself, the idea of passing all his life as he had passed the preceding nine years was terrible: "Better to adopt a system of free immigration to Texas or condemn it at once to the wilderness, the Indians, and the presidials. You know the difficulty of populating this country with Mexicans," he wrote Terán, "and to do so with Europeans is the work of a century. The English will not come because of the religious restriction, and they are the best colonists because they are the most enterprising. I have had the idea that it was the interest and the policy of Mexico to make Texas a state in order to have a bulwark on its northern frontier; and I have had an

---

[40] Austin to Fisher, June 17, and to Terán, June 28, 1830. The memorandum, in the Rosenberg Library, is dated "May, 1830," but was written at least as late as August. In it Austin says that "inflamatory" resolutions were adopted by the Ais Bayou settlement and that an unidentified "J.J.C." came to consult him. "I advised peace and quietness; he coïnsided with me. I was of opinion that a popular commotion amongst the people would totally ruin the whole country and destroy those who had anything to loose."

[41] *Texas Gazette*, June 26, July 3, 10, 1830. In the issue of July 3 he published a translation of the law and of Terán's letter of June 14 interpreting it.

ambition to assist in the advancement of this country to the extent of my ability. But I confess that I am beginning to doubt whether Texas will for a great many years be more than a depopulated waste." He spoke frankly of the possibility of separation from Mexico to save Texas from utter ruin; he did not want to separate; and in any case would not want to unite with the north. The true system for the nation was to settle Texas with men of character and property, regardless of the country from which they came, and organize it as a state. A territorial organization might be acceptable if a stable system of control could be established, but the frequent changes in the federal government made him fearful of the experiment.

To the suggestion that he fill his contracts with the settlers on the eastern border, he replied that it could not be done. They had invested years of labor in the improvement of their lands and would not leave them. Moreover, they should not be asked to leave; both federal and state governments had duly approved these settlements, and the people should be put at rest by giving them titles without further delay.[42]

Toward the end of September the consulate at New Orleans informed Terán that great numbers were applying for passports to Texas and asked instructions, to which he replied, as we have seen, that none but those going to Austin's or DeWitt's colony should be given passports. Terán forwarded a copy of this to military commanders in Texas with orders to turn back all who did not show such passports.[43] The effect of this at Nacogdoches was soon apparent. On October 29 Frost Thorn wrote Austin from there that Colonel Piedras was admitting none without passports or documentary evidence that they were under contract with Austin. He suggested that Austin give Piedras a list of immigrants whom he knew to be on the road; but instead Austin appointed an agent at Nacogdoches and instructed him to certify to Piedras all applicants who, upon examination, seemed to him to fulfill the requirements of the colonization law. This was not an effort at evasion, for the agent was to show his powers to Piedras "and have a friendly un-

[42] Austin to Terán, September 17, 1830. He wrote substantially the same to Alamán on the 20th.
[43] Breedlove to Terán, September 26, and Terán's reply, October 6, 1830. University of Texas Transcripts from Department of Fomento, Mexico, legajo 5, expediente 34.

derstanding with him"; after which he was to 'trouble him as little as possible, but was to call on him enough to show respect and a desire to act in concert with him.' After some hesitation, however, Piedras vetoed this arrangement, saying that Austin himself could undoubtedly issue such certificates but that he could not delegate the authority. Austin then explained the situation to Terán and asked him to instruct Piedras to honor the agent's certificates; " but before a reply could have been received he seems to have made a different arrangement. Briefly, this was to deposit certificates signed by himself at convenient points on the frontier, where immigrants lacking passports could obtain them without difficulty. All that we know about this is in a letter from Austin to his secretary, written while on his way to Saltillo to attend the legislature.

"I send you," he said, "two hundred signatures. Have certificates printed over them verbatim like the others and fill them up, all except the name. Give as many to R. Williamson as he wants and send some to McGuffin and some to Piedrass and some to Col. Thorn. Try and have them printed at night when no one is present and take care that none of the blanks get into other hands. Let none know of this but Lesassier and Williamson." There is an air of furtiveness here, but it was the signatures and not the certificates that gave uneasiness—"Do take care of my signatures," he cautioned, "don't put me in the power of the printer or his boys." That there was no desire to deceive the authorities is evident from the fact that Piedras was to have a supply of the certificates. DeWitt could admit settlers in the same way, Austin said, and ought to send two hundred certificates to Natchitoches and places in Arkansas—"aid the poor fellow along with it." [45]

[44] Thorn to Austin, October 29, 1830; Austin to M. B. Menard (the agent), November 13, and Menard to Austin, November 27; Austin to Terán, December 7, 1830. At the same time that Piedras refused to recognize Menard as Austin's proxy he allowed a number of families to proceed to San Felipe under bond to return if Austin did not receive them. See Durst to Austin, November 27, 1830. This came to be a fairly common practice.

[45] Austin to Williams, December 28, 1830, Rosenberg Library. The certificates simply declared the bearer, whose name was to be inserted, one of the colonists belonging to Austin's contracts. As opportunity offered Austin had been sending such passports to the United States for some time. For example, on August 2 he sent sixteen authorizing families to move within eighteen months, and on December 10 a James R. Phillips took sixteen for families to emigrate from Alabama within a year. See Register of Families in Austin's colonies, Book B, pages 14–15, General Land Office of Texas. It is possible that Williamson intended to use the certificates provided by Austin to smuggle settlers into Milam's colony on the Guadalupe, for which he was agent; but, on the other hand, he may merely have had friends in the United States whom he did not want to be excluded from Texas and to whom he would send the documents. He had asked the political chief on November 10 whether settlers were barred from Milam's colony. See letter in Nacogdoches Archives.

In the meantime, the Mexican chargé at Washington, Tornel, had published in the newspapers of the United States a translation of Article 11 with the warning that all further settlement of Americans in Texas and New Mexico was absolutely prohibited. Breedlove wrote Austin that, unless explained, this would "prevent thousands from emigrating this Winter and Spring that have intended doing so until they saw or heard of this publication." [46] But Austin made no effort to remedy this. It was hardly worth while. DeWitt's contract and one of his own would expire by limitation in a few months; his other contracts were nearly filled, and there was certainly no possibility of making new ones; so that for their own good it was well for emigrants to be warned from Texas. Even Tornel's further announcement that those who had entered Texas since the publication of the law were "liable to be expelled" brought no response from him. [47]

The application of the law suspended two enterprises that gave promise of some activity. One of these was the Leftwich or Nashville Company contract, which had been taken over in part by Sterling C. Robertson; this will be discussed in the next chapter. The other was that of the Galveston Bay and Texas Land Company, which was organized to exploit the contracts of Burnet, Zavala, and Vehlein. These contracts as we have seen, [48] authorized the settlement of twelve hundred families: Burnet's to be "foreigners," without specification; and Zavala's to be Mexicans and "foreigners," excepting Spaniards; while one of Vehlein's contracts was for Swiss and Germans and the other for Swiss, Germans, and Americans in no specified ratio. No settlement had taken place under any of the contracts, but, except to exclude Americans, the law did not necessarily affect them.

The company completed its organization in New York on October 16, 1830. Legally it conceived itself to be the agent of the empresarios to promote the fulfillment of the contracts, and made no preliminary effort to obtain the approval of the Mexican government. A public announcement of the company stated frankly

[46] Archibald Austin to Austin, November 11, 1830, forwarded a copy of Tornel's notice from New York. It was dated, Baltimore, November 5. Breedlove's letter from New Orleans was written December 4.
[47] Henry Austin to Austin, March 30, 1831, gives an account of this and of the more reasonable, but still strict, attitude of Pizarro Martinez, who had succeeded Breedlove in the consulate at New Orleans.
[48] See above, pages 126–127.

that "several persons have connected themselves with the original Empresarios, for the performance of their contracts, in the full belief that if engaged in with spirit, the terms of the grants might be complied with out of the means the contracts themselves furnish, and something be left as a reward for the disbursements and trouble of the undertaking." This was to be accomplished in two ways, by the sale of stock in the company and by the sale of land scrip. It was here that the public was expected to contribute, and yet there appears to have been no effort to deceive. On the contrary, the company circulated a pamphlet of more than a hundred pages[49] explaining the undertaking and faithfully setting forth all the documents necessary for an understanding of the essential facts— the "Articles of Association" and the contract between the company and the empresarios, the contracts of the empresarios with the government, the federal and state colonization laws, the instructions to the land commissioners (showing how titles were obtained), and even the law of April 6, 1830. The hope was expressed that this law would be temporary, but there was no slurring of the fact that Americans could not settle in the grants while it operated. The scrip showed on its face that it was merely a permit to settle, and that in order to obtain title the settler must fulfill and comply with all the requirements of the laws.

Why, then, should Americans buy the scrip? It did not convey title; they could not occupy the land and obtain title—and few wanted to occupy it. It carried no priority or pre-emption privileges; and could have no possible value except in the remote event of such a rush of immigrants that the empresarios would be compelled to make selective grants. The answer is that for the most part buyers never saw the pamphlet and did not read the scrip. They paid from five to ten cents an acre for it[50] and believed that they held a deed. Families actually sent to Texas by the company—presumably not scrip holders—were to receive a league of land and re-convey most of it, by which it was thought the company would acquire a fee

[49] *Address to the Reader of the Documents Relating to the Galveston Bay and Texas Land Company, which are contained in the Appendix,* New York, January 1, 1831.

[50] Langworthy to Austin, January 5, 1831. John P. Austin (New York) to Austin, December 20, 1830, said the price was ten cents an acre and was going to twenty cents soon. Henry Austin (New Orleans) to Austin, March 15, 1831: "The Galveston Bay land company in New York are running wild in their operations. Selling land by hundreds of thousands of acres at 5 cents p^r acre, etc. Sending out steam machinery for mills, boats etc. I fear they will do much harm by calling the attention of Gov^t too much to that quarter."

title to a vast area.[51] This, of course, was illegal, but it is not certain that the company so understood. It is likely that the members trusted to the influence which Zavala was supposed to be able to exert to remove difficulties.

Austin's cooperation, or at least his neutrality, was greatly desired. It was feared that he might regard the company as a competitor. Anthony Dey, president and trustee,[52] wrote: "There is much may be done if your views and ours accord that will aid us and add tenfold value to your Colony and increase the value of Texas in every point of view, whether social, agricultural, political, or otherwise." Zavala also wrote to bespeak assistance. He was on the eve of sailing for France to enlist German, Swiss, and French colonists. Other agents were to work in England, Scotland, and Ireland.[53]

The troubles of the company began with the arrival of fifty-seven immigrants in Galveston Bay. They had sailed from New York on December 29. Most of them were hired to prepare temporary quarters and raise food for the Europeans, who were expected later.[54] They were said to be Swiss and Germans, but they embarked in New York, and some at least were Americans. The commandant of the garrison on Galveston Bay refused to let them land, and Terán sustained him. From Saltillo Austin sensed the rising storm and warned Williams, as we saw, to keep out: "Have nothing to do with these collisions. Do as I have frequently been compelled to do—play the turtle, head and feet within your own shell. . . . That colony [Austin's] is the heart of Texas; keep all sound there, and we shall gain the confidence of Gov^t and save the country."[55]

The further history of the company need not be followed here. It was able to enlist many powerful agencies in Mexico. In due time it obtained extension of time for the fulfillment of the em-

[51] Langworthy to Austin, January 5, 1831; Austin to Leaming, July 23, 1831.
[52] William H. Sumner of Boston and George Curtis of New York were the other trustees. Lynde Catlin, George Griswold, John Haggerty, Stephen Whitney, William G. Buckner, Barney Corse, and Dudley Selden were directors. John P. Austin wrote December 16, 1830: "Its board of directors is composed of the most respectable and influential men among us, with the President of one of our first banks at its head."
[53] Dey to Austin, December 16, 1830, January 5, 1831; Zavala, December 17; John P. Austin, January 5.
[54] Dey to Austin, December 16, 1830; Langworthy to Austin, January 5, 1831.
[55] Austin to Williams, February 19, 1832, Rosenberg Library.

presario contracts, thereby extending its own lease of life;[56] and after the repeal of the law of April 6, 1830, it proceeded with the settlement of Americans.[57]

Austin's attitude must not be misunderstood. It was not jealousy, nor fear of competition that made him stand aloof; it was self-preservation and consideration for his colonists and the ultimate development of Texas. In the letter to Williams just cited he went on:

"Whether the Genl Gov^t has authority to annul Zavala's grant or not is no question for *us* to interfere with . . . those are matters between the interested parties and the Gov^t with which my colony ought to have nothing to do, in any shape manner or form. My colony has cleared away the rude asperities of the wilderness—made Texas known—given it a station in geography—a place, and a distinguished one, in the class of *desirable countries,* and has demonstrated its value by developing its resources. In doing *this,* it has done enough to aid others who now wish to settle in that country, and they ought not to expect that we will unite with them in projects for forcing their way against the will of the Gov^t, or that we are to make common cause of their quarrels and collisions, and if they do expect it I hope they will be deceived. Hope! I know they will, for there is too much common sense and too much honest patriotism in the people of Austin's colony for them to be misled, or to deviate from the line of their duty as Mexican citizens, and besides they have a *great deal* to loose, the others have much to gain but *nothing* to loose." [58]

But, on the other hand, they were to take no active part against the new settlers:

"Be mere lookers on—say nothing—give no opinions—no advice—take no part—have nothing to do with the matter at all—refer them to the Gov^t, but if Genl Terán issues any orders *obey them.* He is our main stay. You may rely upon it and he is worthy of our confidence and sup-

[56] Burnet's and Vehlein's contracts were extended April 28, 1832, for three years; Zavala's on January 27, 1834, for four years. Gammel, *Laws of Texas,* I, 305, 339.

[57] Besides the *Address to the Reader of the Documents Relating to the Galveston Bay and Texas Land Company,* already cited, two other booklets deal extensively with the operations of the company. One of these (anonymous) is *A Visit to Texas* (New York, 1834); the other is David Woodman, Jr., *Guide to Texas Emigrants* (Boston, 1835). The University of Texas has many Transcripts from the Department of Fomento, Mexico, which throw a good deal of light on the company's negotiations in Mexico. But the internal history of the company can probably never be written. The papers of General John T. Mason, who represented the company in Mexico and Texas, would no doubt have revealed much of this; but after a pursuit of several years the writer, in the summer of 1922, overtook the ashes of these papers in Detroit, Michigan, just six weeks after they were thrown into the furnace.

[58] Austin added in a postscript: "If times get very bad and public opinion should seem to waver, it might be well to publish the paragraph marked thus [that is, the paragraph quoted] as an extract from me."

port. . . . All will come round right. Many of the most influential men of all parties, in office and out, in the City of Mexico and elsewhere have procured grants in Texas and more are daily making. *All these* are true friends to the *real* prosperity of that country. We can make them *our* friends by adopting the policy I have indicated, or rather by following the policy I have always followed."

The company had started *"wrong foot ahead"* through ignorance, he wrote Mrs. Holley in July, 1831, but, with prudence, he thought their difficulties would be overcome. "He could not afford to involve himself and the interests of his colonists, however, with the views of any company or individual that was in any manner in collision with the Mexican government." [59]

Discussing with Williams his method of procedure in this crisis, he said:

"The law of 6 April was founded in error and unjust suspicions, but to have said so would have been very impolitic and highly injurious, for it would have wounded *self love, pride,* etc. (dangerous things to touch among any people) and it would have strengthened the suspicions which produced the law, for everything said against it would have been taken as evidence of disaffection. For these reasons in the remarks which were made in the *Texas* [*Gazette*] in June, July, etc. the policy of the Gov^t was rather defended than condemned, and circumstances were stated to show that there were reasons for that measure which justified it. This gratified the *self love* of its authors on the one hand (a great point gained) and they were very much surprised on the other to see that the very people who were most injured by the measure were the first to excuse and defend it. This caused inquiries to be made through various channels as to the real characters of the settlers and their feelings towards the Gov^t and the result has been very favorable as to my colony. This at once explains the reasons why so many more favors have been extended to my colony than to any other. The people at large know of no favors they have rec^d . . . but *you* and *I* know that emigration to that colony could have been stopped." [60]

The military dispositions contemplated by the law, being more or less under Terán's own control, were carried out promptly. The

[59] Austin to Mrs. Holley, July 19, 1831; to Leaming, July 23, 1831.

[60] The little *Texas Gazette,* said Austin, "badly as it has been conducted has been a great service to [Texas] and has had an agency in warding off some blows that were meditated against that country. . . . You have no idea there what importance is attached, even to trifles, coming from the Austinians." The *Gazette* had suspended publication in January, 1831, and was succeeded by *The Mexican Citizen,* of which Austin was part owner and R. M. Williamson was editor. It must be managed with great prudence, said Austin.

forces at San Antonio, Goliad, and Nacogdoches were increased; garrisons were established on the Brazos some twelve miles west of the crossing of the upper Bexar-Nacogdoches road, at the head of Galveston Bay, and near the mouth of the Nueces; and smaller detachments were placed on the Neches and the Lavaca. The time-honored Aztec names of the new posts were perhaps significant of Terán's determination to Mexicanize the province. That on the Brazos was Tenoxtitlan, that on Galveston Bay Anahuac, and that on the Nueces Lipantitlan. The little establishment on the Neches was Terán, while the one on the Lavaca simply took the name of that stream. Subsequently a strong garrison was stationed near the mouth of the Brazos at Velasco. The purpose of the maritime posts was to prevent smuggling, as well as to enforce the immigration regulations; and as Terán expected a Mexican settlement to grow up around each, they were strategically placed to hem in the American colonies and prevent their further spread. Thus, blocking the way to the south would be San Antonio, Goliad, Lavaca, and Lipantitlan; the door to the west would be closed by Tenoxtitlan; while Necogdoches, Terán, Anahuac, and Velasco would ultimately guard the eastern frontier and the coast.[61]

But the counter-colonization project could never be started. The governor of Coahuila and Texas threw some obstacles in the way by insisting that Terán should specify the number of families he expected to introduce and subject himself in general to the provisions of the state colonization law. Terán, on the other hand, resented the idea of the federal government's having to buy back from the state land that it ought never to have relinquished. The insuperable difficulty, however, was in getting Mexican colonists. In June, 1830, Alamán addressed a circular to the governors of Mexico, Puebla, Vera Cruz, Zacatecas, Jalisco, Guanajuato, Michoacan, and San Luis Potosi, asking them to make known to the poor of their states the generous provisions of the law; but there was no response. The effort to collect criminals from the jails was hardly more successful. Though the plan was not formally aban-

---

[61] For this paragraph see, among other sources, Terán to Elosua, April 24, and to Chovel, June 1, 1830, General Land Office of Texas, Vol. 53, pp. 126 and 112; Terán to Alamán, July 31 and December 15, 1830, and Piedras to Terán, November ——, 1831, University of Texas Transcripts from Department of Fomento, Mexico, legajo 5, expediente 34. This file contains much material on this topic.

doned, Terán confessed to Austin before the law was a year on the books that Mexican colonists could not be drawn to Texas.[62]

In June, 1830, Austin wrote: "I shall be able with good management to keep open the door for some time longer, and perhaps untill a new order of things takes place." In February, 1831, he wrote Williams from Saltillo that the government was then convinced that its suspicions had been unfounded and that it would repeal the law as soon as a pretext could be found for doing so without a seeming loss of dignity. He wished his settlers to furnish "such a reason by proof of fidelity and attachment to Mexico." If Austin believed this, he was over-sanguine; but it was good policy to put the colonists on their good behavior, for in that direction lay the only hope of repeal. In the meantime, this policy would continue to hold the door ajar.[63]

Because Austin's contracts were not annulled it was maliciously asserted later that he himself secured the passage of the law to block competition. The statement seems too absurd to require refutation. From the standpoint of selfishness alone—though it was not a motive that had much influence with him—nobody had a greater interest in the rapid settlement of Texas; for population, by whomever introduced, would give value to his vast possessions and bring those amenities of civilized society for which he longed. The law was undoubtedly intended to stop immigration from the United States. By a clever twist Austin stretched the loophole offered by the ambiguity of Article 10 and saved his own and DeWitt's contracts. Under no pretext could he make the loophole larger. Should he therefore have allowed it to close?

[62] Terán to Austin, March 21, 1831. See also on this paragraph many documents in University of Texas Transcripts from Department of Fomento, Mexico, legajo 6, expedientes 51, 52.

[63] Austin to Leaming, June 14, 1830; to Williams, February 19, 1831.

CHAPTER XI

The Robertson Colony Controversy

AS we saw in the preceding chapter, several contracts that had long been dormant were showing signs of activity when suspended by the law of April 6, 1830. One of these was the Leftwich contract. Its history is involved, and beclouded by bitter controversy, but the following preliminary summary will serve to clarify Austin's connection with the subject: (1) Austin welcomed the grant to Leftwich, because it promised to erect a protective barrier on his western frontier against the inroads of hostile Indians. (2) When Leftwich transferred the contract to the Nashville Company, which in fact he represented, Austin induced the government to recognize and validate the transfer. (3) The company had not begun to settle the grant, though five years of its term had expired, when the federal act annulled the contract. (4) Two months after the passage of the federal law, however, the company authorized Sterling C. Robertson, one of its members, to settle two hundred families. (5) Robertson, with nine families, arrived in Texas in October, 1830, only to be told that the contract was abrogated and that he must leave the country. (6) In his extremity he appealed to Austin, who had consistently befriended the company. (7) Austin tried to assist him; but could make no headway against the law of April 6, 1830. He learned, on the contrary, that the grant was about to be re-let to a French company, and to prevent that he applied for and obtained it and other extensive areas in partnership with Samuel M. Williams. (8) Austin's explanation, which, in connection with his previous history in Texan colonization, is convincing to the candid student, was: that the grant was irretrievably lost to Robertson and the Nashville Company; that no European company had ever attempted to settle a grant, and that there was no reason, therefore, to expect the French company to do more than speculate on its contract; that granting the region to the French company would have blocked extension of the frontier for six years; and that he obtained the grant to prevent this long delay and the consequent injury to existing settlements. Naturally enough, perhaps, Robertson refused to see the altruism of Austin's motives and with much abuse and vituperation charged Austin with betraying his trust for personal profit. Robertson's statements teem with error and misrepresentation. Austin's explanation, on the other hand, is consistent with all the known facts. The story must now be told in detail—regrettable detail, perhaps—and with minute attention to chronology.

On March 2, 1822, "The Texas Association" of Davidson County, Tennessee, addressed to the new national government of Mexico an application for a grant of land and permission to settle a colony in Texas.[1] The company originally consisted of fifty-two members and was subsequently increased to seventy-four.[2] Most of the members were business and professional men of Nashville. Their interest had been aroused in part, no doubt, by newspaper accounts of Austin's grant and his preparations to introduce settlers. Robert Leftwich and Andrew Erwin carried the petition to Mexico, where they arrived about the end of April, just as Austin reached the capital seeking confirmation of his own grant.[3] The tedious delays that prevented the dispatch of all colonization business have already been recounted. Erwin soon returned to take his seat in the legislature of Tennessee,[4] but Leftwich remained to push the application[5] and to become the recipient of many kindnesses from Austin.[6] After the passage of the national colonization law the

---

[1] The date is from Herbert E. Bolton, *Guide to Materials for the History of the United States in the Principal Archives of Mexico* (Washington, 1913), 355.

[2] League to Austin, September 1, 1827. League names the original members, among whom were Sam Houston, Ira Ingram, and Sterling C. Robertson, later prominent in the history of Texas.

[3] Austin to Hawkins [about May 1, 1822] mentions meeting them.

[4] Petition of the stockholders to governor, March 7, 1827, Translations of Empresario Contracts, 28–31. MS., General Land Office of Texas.

[5] For his activity see Mateos, *Historia Parlamentaria de los Congresos Mexicanos*, II, 377, 379, 477, 482, 648—May 23, 26, 1822; June 10, August 18, 1823; January 13, 1824.

[6] Acknowledging on April 30, 1823, a letter of introduction from Austin to J. B. Arizpe, Leftwich said: "This is adding one more favour to the many hundreds already received. I read your letter to Major Edwards . . . and we are both pleased with the advise you have given for us to pursue in getting our business closed. As the highest proof that we could give you of our intense approbation of your plan I need only say to you that we lost no time in presenting your letter to El Señor Arispe, who appeared much pleased at receiving a line from you. On reading it he gave the highest assurances of his friendship and promised to use his exertions on our behalf, in which I believe him to be sincere."

scene of his vigils shifted to Saltillo, where on October 20, 1824, he presented a petition to the legislature of Coahuila and Texas asking for a contract to settle eight hundred families in the Brazos River basin west of the Bexar-Nacogdoches road.[7] On April 15, 1825, his application was granted. He had dealt with the state government as a principal and not as agent of the "Texas Association," and the contract was in his name; but the colonization law made no provision for a corporate empresario, and it is doubtful whether he could have obtained the grant in the name of the company.[8]

The region chosen by Leftwich, though exposed to the fierce Tahuacano, Waco, and Comanche Indians, was well watered and immensely fertile. He had not explored the country, and how he came to select it we do not know; probably by the advice of Austin.[9] Certainly Austin was gratified by the prospect of a strong settlement there to serve as a protective buffer for his own colony. Submitting a referendum in the fall of 1825 on a campaign against the Wacos, he advised delay, reminding the colonists that by the following April many immigrants would be finding their way to the frontier, with whose aid the war could be waged with greater certainty of success. His attitude is more circumstantially disclosed by a letter from Brown Austin to his sister.

"This Gov^t [he wrote] have authorized four new colonies to be settled which will be done immediately. One lies above this on the Rivers Colorado and Brazos which if settled will be a perfect safeguard to us against the Indians. The other three are East and West of us, so that this Colony will be nearly the center. None of the other Colonys are so rich in land as this. Neither have they such an outlet for their produce as this so that it is of much importance to us that they should settle as soon as possible." [10]

Hopes of the rapid fulfillment of these contracts were, however, doomed to disappointment. Thorn's colony was never begun; that of Edwards we have followed to its disastrous end in the Fredonian rebellion; DeWitt's, to the west, instead of assisting Austin's settlers

---

[7] Translation of Empresario Contracts, 22, MS., General Land Office of Texas. More explicitly, the boundary described began at the intersection of the Navasota River and the Bexar-Nacogdoches road, followed the road westward to the watershed between the Brazos and Colorado, followed the watershed northwestward to the Comanche trace, ran eastward with this to the Navasota, and down that stream to the point of beginning.

[8] Translations of Empresario Contracts, 23, General Land Office of Texas.

[9] Austin took to Mexico in 1822 a crude map, compiled from observation and report, which showed all the landmarks used by Leftwich in his description. See this map facing page 53.

[10] Austin to colonists, September 28, 1825; J. E. B. Austin to Mrs. J. F. Perry, October 28, 1825.

drew heavily on them for protection; while the Leftwich grant, through untoward circumstances now to be narrated, retarded the extension of the frontier in that direction for a number of years.

The associates of Leftwich were surprised and disappointed on his return to Nashville, to find that the grant was not in the name of the company. Next a dispute arose over Leftwich's claim for compensation for his three years in Mexico. They had furnished him and Erwin four thousand dollars in 1822 and understood that he was to charge nothing for services beyond expenses. Finally they agreed to pay him an additional fourteen thousand dollars, which, as Erwin wrote Austin, was equivalent to expenses plus two hundred dollars a month. In return Leftwich conveyed his contract to the company and agreed to serve as empresario in a'l relations with the government which could not be performed by an agent. To pay Leftwich, an assessment was levied on the stock and to distribute this in easy amounts each of the original shares was subdivided into eight "fractions" which the owners could offer for sale. Thus there came to be five hundred and ninety-two shares, which at the end of August, 1825, were selling at "about 100 p^r c^t advance"—meaning, perhaps, about fifty dollars a share.[11]

Having adjusted these difficulties, the president of the company, Dr. Felix Robertson, accompanied by "several gentlemen," set out to explore the grant and make preliminary arrangements for its settlement. Leftwich seems to have been expected to join him in Texas, but was prevented by ill health.[12] John P. Coles, alcalde of the adjacent district of Bravo in Austin's colony, wrote Austin on April 6, 1826, that Robertson had returned to Tennessee "without effecting any considerable object in the country above," and went on to say that Robertson had expressed in writing the wish for Austin's authority to extend over his grant until forty families were settled there. One of those who accompanied Dr. Robertson

[11] Erwin to Austin, August 29, 1825; Leftwich's relinquishment to the company, no date, Translations of Empresario Contracts, 29, General Land Office of Texas; Memorial of the company to government of Coahuila and Texas, March 7, 1827, *ibid.*, 25–28; League to Austin, September 1, 1827. The Franklin manuscripts of the University of Texas contain thirty-nine of the 592 stock certificates, issued October 15, 1825, and signed by Felix Robertson, President, and J. P. Erwin, Secretary, of the Texas Association. They simply certify that "—— is entitled to fraction No. —— being the one [eighth] of share No. —— of the original stock of the Texas Association." They were transferable by endorsement.

[12] The company's memorial to the government, March 7, 1827, Translations of Empresario Contracts, 25–28, General Land Office of Texas.

—the only one we know—was a man of the same name, perhaps a kinsman, Sterling C. Robertson. He was one of the first fifty-two stockholders. He lingered in Texas after the departure of his chief and selected a piece of land occupied by a squatter named Early, whom he requested Coles to remove.[13] In the fall the company sent out Benjamin F. Foster, W. R. Winn, "and three or four other young men of worth" to begin settlement. Foster was to be the company's agent.[14] According to the statement of the company, which is all we know about the matter, Foster and his companions were discouraged from making a settlement by the confusion incident to the Fredonian rebellion.[15]

The company seems now to have determined to get its relations with the government on a more regular footing. At any rate, on March 7, 1827, the directors set forth the pertinent facts in the history of the grant; asked recognition of the company as the true owner of the contract, and the substitution of Hosea H. League as empresario and agent of the company instead of Leftwich; and begged for extension of the boundaries of the grant and of the term for making the settlement. Up to that time they had spent in the enterprise, they said, $22,000. What they asked, in effect, was the annulment of the contract with Leftwich and the formation of a new contract with the company good for six years.[16] Bespeaking Austin's support for this petition, Dr. Felix Robertson wrote: "To comply with the letter of the colonization law in the settling of their Colony presents so many and serious difficulties to the view of the Company that they have become very much disheartened, and will I believe cause them to entirely abandon the enterprise unless they can obtain some modification of the grant more favorable to its settlement." A short time before this League had written Austin from Nashville: "With regards to the prospects of the

---

[13] Coles to Austin, April 6, 1826: "I am Now Requested to Remove Early who has put them all at defiance and says that he will hold his place in spite of them and threatens the Life of the Barrer of this who is the owner of the Tract of Land that he is on, Maj. Sterling C. Robertson. What should I doo in this case shall I put Early off or not." Sterling C. Robertson's presence in Texas is attested also by a deposition concerning the character of P. E. Bean. See Austin to Saucedo, August 28, 1826. Bexar Archives.

[14] Martin to Austin, November 1, and Felix Robertson to Austin, November 5, 1826, introducing Foster.

[15] Translation of Empresario Contracts, 25–28, General Land Office of Texas.
[16] *Ibid.*

upper colony I am at a los[s] but upon the whole must say they are dull. . . . Before your last communication a Texas Scrip was not worth a Dollar. Since that I have known of two selling for $20 each. They are very dull and price uncertain." [17] Two years of the contract had now expired. Some reconnaissance of the grant had been made and perhaps some locations selected, but it seems evident that no settlements had been made and certainly no titles had issued, nor could they issue until there was a local empresario and a land commissioner.

It is important now to know something of League. He had visited Texas in the summer of 1826, accompanied by a party from the neighborhood of Nashville. They may have held stock in the "Texas Association," but it does not so appear. League was much impressed by Austin's colony and contracted with Austin to introduce ten families, for which no doubt he was to receive a premium in land. He had a similar agreement with DeWitt; and it was on the eve of his return to Texas with these twenty families that Robertson made with him the arrangement just described. Obviously his connection with Austin's colony must have been known. Far from its being objectionable, one can even imagine that it was the recommendation that drew the attention of the company to League. They had tried without success to establish an agent on the grant; here at least was a man who would live near by and attend to the necessary local formalities, provided the government would consent to the transfer of the contract from Leftwich to the company.[18]

League returned to Texas in April, 1827, with the families for Austin's colony. He was to go on to Saltillo in the fall with the company's petition, but in the end he empowered Austin to act for him, and on October 11 Austin presented the papers to the governor, reinforced by a memorial of his own begging that the petition be granted. One the 15th a new contract allowed all that the company had requested, except the extension of time.[19] The boundary exten-

[17] League to Austin, January 18, and Robertson to Austin, March 8, 1827.

[18] League to Austin, September 20, 1826, January 18, 1827.

[19] League to Austin, April 11, August 28, September 10, 1827; League's power of attorney to Austin, September 8, Austin's address to the governor, October 11, and the new contract, October 15, 1827, in Translations of Empresario Contracts, 31–35, General Land Office of Texas.

sion added to the original grant the Brazos valley to a point considerably above the present city of Waco.[20]

With legal obstacles out of the way and an agent-empresario in Texas to seat colonists and execute the directions of the company, settlement should have begun without delay and progressed rapidly; but still nothing was done. The fact seems beyond dispute. In July, 1828, Amos Edwards, applying for land in Austin's colony, wrote:

"I have considerable interest in the Nashville Company's Grant and it would probably be more to my interest to settle in that Grant than any other part of the province, as I could induce a great many families to emigrate to the section of country that I select for my residence, but I begin to think the Grant will never be colonized by the present Company, unless some three or four of us will take all the trouble upon us, pay all the expense, and undergo all the privations, dangers and difficulties of colonizing the Grant and then give the balance of the company their full share of the lands without any charge. I was in Nashville in March last and prevailed on the Directors . . . to have a meeting and try to make the necessary arrangements for colonizing the Grant and forward instructions forthwith to Maj^r. League on that subject, call in their old scrip, and make new scrip agreeably to the form you gave them. They promised me that they would do so and call^d a meeting which was attended by a bare majority and they only talked of what they would do and concluded to call another meeting in a short time, when they expected to have a full Board, and then would do everything necessary for colonising and promised to inform me what they did before I left Kentucky, where I remained untill the 3^d of May and heard nothing more from them. Most of the Directors hold very small interests in the Grant, viz. ⅛ of a share and they care very little about it, as scarcely one of them ever intend emigrating to the Country. I should probably have settled in that Grant if the Company had done what they ought to colonize it, but as they have not, I have determined to locate myself where my judgment induces me to believe is the best place for my private interest." [21]

Several months later William H. Wharton wrote League from Nashville that he did not expect the company to do anything before the expiration of the contract.

[20] As now defined the line followed the Bexar-Nacogdoches road westward from the crossing of the Navasota River to the watershed west of the Brazos, along this northwestward to the most northern source of the San Andrés or San Gabriel River, thence northeastward to the "Cross Timbers" east of the Brazos, thence southward to the Navasota, and down it to the road and point of beginning.

[21] Amos Edwards to Austin, July 7, 1828. Though he was the brother of Haden Edwards, the writer declared that he had heartily disapproved of the Fredonian rebellion.

"I have postponed writing until this late period [he explained] in order to get the company to take some prompt, energetic steps in relation to the settlement of their grant, but all to no effect. The Texas fever seems to have died with Pattison. No meeting of the board has taken place since his death. I have circulated your letters and endeavored to procure a meeting but could not succeed. Notwithstanding this apparent apathy they value highly their Texas stock and yet hope to realize fortunes from it they know not how. Talk to them of relinquishing their grant and they hoot at the idea. My own opinion is that nothing will be done before the expiration of the time and that their grant will be forfeited. . . . They say they mean to apply for a prolongation of the time. I tell them it will be useless and that every American in Texas will remonstrate against it, it being to their interest that the grant should fall into the hands of some one that will settle it. Sterling Robertson will bring on twenty or thirty families this fall to settle his scrip and they are all that may be expected." [22]

Three and a half years of the contract had now expired. Whether Robertson did go out in the fall of 1828 is doubtful. Wharton expressed very aptly the feelings of the Texans. They wanted the colony settled. Population would increase the value of their own lands, and would, moreover, in a measure protect them from the western Indians. Together Wharton and Edwards explained clearly enough the reasons for the company's failure to act. Many of the stockholders—perhaps the most of them—regarded the enterprise as a speculation. They had never intended to become colonists themselves, but it was understood that each fractional share of stock entitled the holder to a league of land, and in some way they seem to have expected to be able to hold it as absentees. [23] In the mass there was great ignorance of the colonization law. As a settler, each stockholder could, of course, if he were married, obtain a league of land; but his stock would entitle him only to his proportionate equity in such premium land as the company earned. If all the

---

[22] Wharton to League, September 12, 1828, Franklin Papers, University of Texas.

[23] The *Kentucky Reporter* of August 1, 1825, quoted from the *Nashville Whig* an article on the "Texas Association." Many members of the company, it said, never intended to go to Texas; but others would go, "and should the anticipations of many be realized in any reasonable time, that the province of Texas will, by treaty, purchase, or otherwise be annexed to the territories of the United States, the acquisition would then prove to the holders of immense value." Acquisition by the United States was suggested by President Adams's recent overture for readjustment of the boundary. Felix Robertson wrote Austin (March 8, 1827), "I think it at present would greatly benefit your country for it to be generally understood (and be lawful) that foreigners should hold landed estates in it." League wrote Austin (September 10, 1827) that the company wished stockholders to have "a preference of settlement . . . until the 592 is setled and then the ballance of the 800 families to be setled in the ordinary way."

eight hundred families contracted for were settled, this would amount to slightly more than forty-one leagues, equivalent to less than three hundred acres a share. Some, perhaps, expected to plant a settler on a league and have him convey to them a portion of it for the privilege of holding the rest; but in practice such a settler would have found soon after arrival that in Austin's and DeWitt's grants he could retain an entire league at probably no greater cost.

The story now approaches a bitterly controversial stage, but it can still be followed without reference to partisan documents. In December, 1828, League was elected a member of the ayuntamiento in Austin's colony and held the office well through 1830.[24] William H. Wharton, who was certainly interested in the company, visited Texas in 1829, but, like Amos Edwards, was attracted to Austin's colony.[25] In the light of the preceding evidence, it seems unlikely that settlement was going on or that emigrants were being sent to Texas to settle on the company's grant. During 1830, however, promise of activity developed. League, on August 30, notified the political chief that he had heard of the formation of a sub-company in Nashville to settle three hundred families during the following autumn and winter.[26] He gave no further particulars, but we know that the new company consisted of Sterling C. Robertson and Alexander Thomson;[27] what terms they made with the old company we are not informed. On October 1 ,1830, League as empresario and agent of the original company, executed a power of attorney authorizing Sterling C. Robertson, then at San Felipe, to act as his agent in the settlement of the colony.[28] On the 25th, Robertson, with six companions, reported to Colonel Francisco Ruiz, commanding the post of Tenoxtitlan, on the Brazos twelve miles above the Bexar-Nacogdoches road.[29]

[24] "Minutes of the ayuntamiento of San Felipe de Austin," *Southwestern Historical Quarterly*, XXI, 325, XXII, 194.

[25] Austin to Wharton, April 20, 1829.

[26] League to Músquiz, August 30, 1830, Nacogdoches Archives, Texas State Library.

[27] Contract of Robertson and Thomson with Jeremiah Tinnin, June 21, 1830, in Archives of Coahuila (Saltillo), 1835, expediente 1313. For the relation between Robertson and Thomson see also papers in the suit of Alexander Thomson *vs*. E. S. C. Robertson, March 12, 1851, District Court of Travis County, Texas, File 98. The contract with Tinnin was signed in Tennessee and was renewed in the "Nashville Company" colony, December 2, 1830. It bound Tinnin to settle and remain on the land "so as to enable the said Robertson and Thomson to obtain and perfect a title to a league of land in virtue of said settlement," in return for which Tinnin would receive nine hundred acres and a town lot.

[28] Archives of Coahuila (Saltillo), legajo 28, 1833, expediente 1293.

[29] Ruiz to Elosua, October 30, 1830, General Land Office of Texas, Vol. 54, page 279.

The chronology of this post will presently become important. Terán issued the order for its establishment on April 24, 1830.[30] Ruiz set out from San Antonio on June 25, reached the Brazos July 13, and selected the site for the fort about the end of that month.[31]

After explaining his purpose to Ruiz, Robertson set about exploring the country. On November 12 he returned and told Ruiz that nine families were encamped at the crossing below, and that "many others ought to arrive in a few days at the same place." By now, however, Ruiz had received a general order not to admit Americans within his jurisdiction without passports. Robertson showed his papers, and pleaded the heavy expense of the journey from Tennessee and the necessity of settling his families without delay. Ruiz was favorably impressed and most sympathetic and wrote to Elosua for instructions.[32] At the same time he wrote Samuel M. Williams, asking if Austin could not smooth the way by commending the families to him.[33]

In the same mail Robertson laid his case before the political chief, protesting that the passport law and the decree of April 6, 1830, did not apply to him;[34] and Thomson, who had joined him at Tenoxtitlan, wrote Austin, detailing an unpleasant experience that he had encountered at Nacogdoches. He had arrived there without passports, not knowing that they were necessary, and had been stopped by Colonel Piedras. Since his character certificates and other papers seemed in order, however, Piedras consented for him and four companions to press on to Austin's colony, and suggested that Austin might give them passports, but he exacted a condition that the men should leave their families near Nacogdoches to ensure their return. The sequel had better be told in Thomson's own words: "We had traveled better than eight weeks," he said, "had spent a great deal of money, and was much fatigued, we could not feel willing to remain in that part of the country on expenses so long. We therefore came round, which caused us to lose 2½ days

---

[30] Terán to Elosua, April 24, 1830, General Land Office of Texas, Vol. 53, page 126.
[31] Elosua to Terán, June 28, 1830, Ruiz to Elosua, July 19, 23, August 7, 1830, Bexar Archives.
[32] Ruiz to Elosua, November 13, 1830, General Land Office of Texas, Vol. 54, page 281.
[33] Ruiz to Williams, November 13, 1830, Rosenberg Library, Galveston.
[34] Robertson's letter to Músquiz, November 13, 1830, is in the Nacogdoches Archives, Texas State Library. Its substance is recited in Músquiz to Elosua, December 10, 1830, General Land Office, Vol. 54, page 284.

travel." He seemed unconscious of having committed an impropriety, and wrote Austin not for assistance but to suggest that he place an agent at Nacogdoches to issue passports and thereby avert in future such interruptions to immigration.[35]

In the meantime, Piedras had reported the incident to his superior at San Antonio,[36] who, in turn, relayed it to Terán. Thinking that Thomson was headed for settlement in Austin's colony, Piedras warned Austin that by violating the law and breaking his parole Thomson had proved himself unworthy of admission as a colonist.[37] Knowing Thomson's side of the story, Austin was able to write Piedras a very earnest and tactful defense of the evasion. He understood, he said, that these families had emigrated from Tennessee to settle in the Leftwich grant; that they had started without knowing that their entrance was prohibited; had come in good faith; and had had no thought of violating any law or insulting any authority. He was certain that they were innocent of any intention to break the law. Of course, they could not plead ignorance after receiving Piedras's warning, but consider the circumstances—having traveled five hundred leagues, their resources were almost exhausted; they had sold their possessions in Tennessee and made all their preparations and calculations to settle in this country; all their hopes were fixed on reaching their destination, erecting houses before the rigors of winter set in, and preparing land for the cultivation of a crop the following year. Under such conditions, to return to the north or to remain at Nacogdoches was alike ruinous, and it was probable that they continued their march because they were convinced that there was no other remedy or recourse and because they hoped, from Piedras's humanity and justice and that of the government, for a pardon which would cover their offense.[38]

The situation was by now, however, beyond local control. Terán instructed Ruiz to notify Robertson that the law of April 6 had suspended all contracts except those of colonies already established, and wrote the governor that titles were not to be issued to families

[35] Thomson to Austin, November 13, 1830.

[36] Piedras to Elosua, November 7, 1830, Nacogdoches Archives, Texas State Library.

[37] Piedras to Austin, November 12, 1830. Piedras gave as the names of Thomson's companions James Ledbetter, Thomas J. Wooton, John Sherman, and Everton Kennedy.

[38] Austin to Piedras, November 29, 1830, in file of June 5.

introduced by Robertson and Thomson.[39] A little while later he ordered both civil and military authorities to expel Robertson and the families that he had introduced.[40] Now began a tedious epistolary pursuit of these families.[41] In the end, Terán suggested to Austin that he request permission for them to settle in his grant.[42] This Austin did,[43] and on September 26, 1831, Terán officially approved the request.[44] In the meantime, Thomson returned to Tennessee, still ignorant, apparently, that the contract was suspended, and in April of 1831 was back in Texas with additional families, for whom he asked land in Austin's colony. In the light of Robertson's subsequent charge that Austin made a practice of enticing his colonists away from him, Thomson's letter is important.

"I am sorry to be compelled to trouble you with a few lines [he wrote] but necessity forces me to do it. I arrived with my own and eight more families on the 2nd Inst. at Harrisburgh, at which place I learned that the families that I had brought out last fall were ordered below the St. Antonia road, and that they had all mov'd down, the most of them to Mr. Milligan's. I immediately went to St. Phillippi, to know the particulars. While there an order arrived that all the families, and myself, should return to the U. S.[45] I at first concluded to go immediately, but all with whom I convers'd at St. Phillippi advised me to wait and peti[ti]on for privilege to remain in this colony and become settlers here.[46] I have arranged all my business in the U. S. and came with view to become a per-

---

[39] Elosua to Ruiz, November 9, 1830, Bexar Archives; Terán to Elosua, December 20, 1830, General Land Office of Texas, Vol. 54, page 283; Terán to Austin, January 5, 1831.
[40] Terán to Elosua, December 31, 1830; Músquiz to Elosua, February 9, 1831; Ruiz to Elosua, February 16, 1831, acknowledging order of January 18—General Land Office, Vol. 54, pages 285–287; Músquiz to alcaldes of Nacogdoches and San Felipe, February 16, 1831, Nacogdoches Archives, Texas State Library.
[41] Ruiz to Elosua, March 1, 4, 1831, and Músquiz to Elosua, March 29, August 31, 1831, General Land Office, Vol. 54, pages 287–292; Ruiz to Elosua, September 16, 1831, General Land Office, Translations of Empresario Contracts, 349; Governor Letona to Músquiz, August 3, 1831, Nacogdoches Archives, Texas State Library.
[42] "No hay ningun embarazo pᵃ qᵉ establesca V. en su colonia las ocho familias qᵉ vinieron de Tenesee pʳ cuenta de la compᵃ. de Nashville, y aun creo qᵉ es el mejor auxilio qᵉ puede darseles si quieren quedar en el pais. Si V. lo cre conveniente puede ponerme un oficio pᵃ contestar como ahora lo hago en lo particular."—Terán to Austin, June 30, 1831.
[43] Austin to Terán, August 6, 1831.
[44] Translations of Empresario Contracts, 226, General Land Office.
[45] On March 29, 1831, the political chief transmitted to the alcalde of San Felipe a copy of the order to Ruiz to expel the families.—Archives of Coahuila (Saltillo), legajo 28, 1833, expediente 1293. It was to this, no doubt, that Thomson referred.
[46] Williams, on April 8, 1831, wrote the alcalde of San Felipe a letter, intended for transmission to the superior authorities, describing the hardships of the unfortunate immigrants and saying that if permission could be obtained land would be given them in Austin's colony.—Archives of Coahuila (Saltillo), legajo 28, 1833, expediente 1293.

manent residentor in this country . . . and if we have to return, it will break us all prety well. . . .

"As I believe it is in your power to do more with the government, and with Gen'l Teran, than any one else, and believing that you are disposed to be friendly toward us, I now take the liberty to request you to interceed for us in any way your discretion may point out. . . . Now is the time, sir, for you to do me perhaps a greater kindness than you may ever have an opportunity to do me again." [47]

In all probability they obtained land in Austin's colony, but, as Thomson did not give the names of the eight families, this cannot be determined.

We return now to Robertson. Finding relief, despite the sympathy of Ruiz, beyond the power of the local authorities, he appealed to Austin, who was leaving for Saltillo to take his seat in the legislature. Austin agreed, more or less perfunctorily, one may imagine, to present the case to the governor—perfunctorily because, as he knew, the only thing that could clear the way for Robertson was to establish the fact that a hundred families were settled in the grant before the law of April 6, 1830, was passed. This, as the preceding narrative has shown, could not be done. Austin knew, too, that the Nashville Company's grant was already the subject of an application from a European company, and, in view of the government's desire to balance European and Mexican colonists against the Anglo-Americans, this might be expected to have strong attractions for it.

The application was from Gabriel Laisné de Villaveque, a Frenchman, residing in Mexico City. As early as January, 1830, he addressed a questionnaire to the minister of foreign relations concerning vacant lands in Texas, and enclosed a map showing three areas in which he was particularly interested. One of these was west of the Lavaca River and the other two, for the most part, east of the Trinity. [48] The minister forwarded copies of these documents to General Terán and to the governor of Coahuila and Texas, and urged prompt reply, that the policy of counter-colonization against the Americans might not be delayed. The letter to Terán indicates that the government had taken the initiative with Villa-

[47] Thomson to Austin, April 9, 1831. Austin was then in Saltillo as a member of the legislature.

[48] Villaveque to minister, January 30, 1830, University of Texas Transcripts from Department of Fomento, Mexico, legajo 4, expediente 14.

veque, because of his influential connections in Europe, and that his application was in response to its proposal.[49] The governor referred the questions to the general land commissioner, Juan Antonio Padilla, then in Texas,[50] and the matter slept through the summer. In October the federal government again addressed the governor, transmitting with the urgent approval of Bustamante a second application from Villaveque. In this Villaveque asked for two grants, aggregating fourteen or fifteen hundred leagues of land—more than six million acres. One, of three hundred leagues, he wished east of Austin's colony and south of the Bexar-Nacogdoches road, in the name of Villaveque and Company, of Paris. The other, of eleven or twelve hundred leagues, he wanted somewhere in the immense rectangle bounded north and south by the thirty-second parallel and the Bexar-Nacogdoches road and east and west by the ninety-fifth and ninety-eighth meridians of longitude. This was to be in the name of Villaveque Brothers.[51] On November 12, Acting-Governor Eca y Músquiz forwarded these documents to Austin with a request for information concerning previous grants in the regions designated. Austin replied, December 14, that neither time nor the information at hand permitted him to answer with the necessary detail, but that he expected to reach Saltillo by the first of January and would reply there after examining the records in the official archives.[52] On February 3, 1831, he wrote formally that the first area indicated by Villaveque was included in the grants to Vehlein and Zavala and the second in the contracts of Burnet and the Nashville Company, but he suggested other territory bordering on the Red River which might be available.[53]

Austin took with him to Saltillo a power of attorney from Samuel M. Williams to apply in his name for a contract to colonize "foreign families or others." No number was specified nor was any region

[49] Minister to Terán and to Governor of Coahuila and Texas, February 13, 1830, *ibid.*
[50] Governor to minister, March 5, 1830, *ibid.*
[51] Villaveque to Governor, October 5, and minister of relations to governor, October 6, 1830, *ibid.*
[52] Autograph copy of the letter in Austin's blotter, filed as June 5, 1830. The original is in the archives at Saltillo, 1830, legajo 24, expediente 1046.
[53] Copy transmitted by governor to minister of foreign relations, February 6, 1831, University of Texas Transcripts from Department of Fomento, Mexico, legajo 4, expediente 14. Part of the land suggested by Austin, as he pointed out, was in Frost Thorn's grant, but Thorn had taken no steps to settle it, and his contract would expire the following April.

suggested.[54] On February 4, in behalf of himself and Williams, Austin asked for a contract to settle eight hundred Mexican and foreign families in a vast area including: (1) the vacant lands remaining in his own previous grants, when his existing contracts should expire, (2) the Nashville Company (Robertson) grant, and (3) a great extension west and northwest of the Nashville Company.[55] On February 25 Governor Viesca granted this application.

Announcing the contract to Williams, Austin wrote: "The power of attorney is effected in union with myself—the lower line is ten leagues from the coast, the upper on the heads of the Brazos and Colorado. I wish the [B]oss to take a part in this. If he will, all is safe. I am operating on a pretty large scale for a taciturn and noiseless man, but I have no other object in view than the gen¹. prosperity of *us all* and particularly of this nation and government." [56] The "Boss" was Terán. Subsequently Austin repeatedly said, and there is no reason to doubt his statement, that he besought both the secretary of state and the governor to admit Robertson and reinstate his contract; that they declared this impossible, and were impatient with him for suggesting such a violation of the law of April 6, 1830; that the governor was disposed to grant the territory to Villaveque, which he felt sure would have delayed the peopling of the frontier for another six years; and that to prevent this he obtained the contract for himself and Williams.[57] No one who has accurately gauged the sentiment behind the law of April 6, 1830, can believe that it would have been possible for Robertson to gain recognition and extension of time at Saltillo in the spring of 1831;

[54] Archives of Coahuila (Saltillo), legajo 25, 1831, expediente 1061. The document was signed before the alcalde of San Felipe on December 17, 1830. Inadvertently or maliciously John Henry Brown (*History of Texas*, I, 314) says that it authorized Austin to represent Williams "in getting a colonial grant above Austin's colony."

[55] As defined by Austin's application, the boundary began on the left bank of the Lavaca ten leagues from the coast, ascended that stream to its westernmost source, ran thence northwestward to the Bexar-Nacogdoches road, which it followed eastward to the Colorado, ascended that to the "Salt or Red Fork," thence in a straight line northeastward to the watershed between the Brazos and Trinity, down this southeastwardly to the head of the San Jacinto, along this to a point ten leagues from the coast, and thence parallel with the coast line to the point of beginning. Archives of Coahuila (Saltillo), legajo 25, 1831, expediente 1061; also Translations of Empresario Contracts, 190–191, General Land Office of Texas.

[56] Austin to Williams, March 5, 1831, Rosenberg Library, Galveston.

[57] Austin to the Senate, December 5, 1836, Translations of Empresario Contracts, 236–241, General Land Office of Texas. See also Austin to McKinney, October 18, 1834; and Austin to Williams, March 14, 21, 1835, Rosenberg Library, Galveston.

and, even if it had been possible there, he must still have run the gauntlet of Terán and the federal government. Obviously Robertson lost nothing by the grant to Austin and Williams, because he had nothing to lose; and as between Austin and the French company there can be no hesitation in seeing where the public interest lay.[58]

Nevertheless, it was natural enough, perhaps, for Robertson to feel aggrieved and to believe that Austin had injured him. He had played in hard luck. After five years of the contract had expired with nothing done, he apparently had galvanized a part of the company into a semblance of life and had arranged to start the work that ought then to have been drawing to a close. This shows enterprise. What progress he might have made but for the interposition of the law of April 6 it is impossible to guess; but it is well to remember that the contract had but five months to run when Ruiz stopped the settlement of his first nine families in November.

Rumors of the disposition of the grant preceded Austin from Saltillo, and upon Austin's arrival Robertson lost no time in inquiring whether the rumors were true. His letter to Austin is dignified and somewhat touching:

"I have just learned [he wrote] that you have arrived. I expect your house is crowded with those that are wanting to know the news from the interior. Therefore I dont wish to call on you at the early hour. I and my friend Alexander Thomson has been ordered forthwith to the place from whence we came and all those that we brought with us. . . . I am anxious to know our fate. My own I dont much care for although I have spent a fortune in what is called the Nashville Colony—but [for] Esqr. Thomson and the unfortunate setlers who we have brought with us I have great anxiety. I expect you can give me all the information on the subject. . . . Report says our colony is given to Mr. Williams—please wright to me

[58] That it was very well understood in Texas that Robertson had no chance is indicated by a letter from Amos Edwards to Austin (March 7, 1831) asking Austin to make a contract for him to settle a thousand families in the former Nashville Company grant. In advances to Leftwich and subsequent expenses that colony had cost him, he said, "upwards of $12,000." He had emigrated to Texas "for the purpose of aiding in colonizing s^d grant ... and they have done nothing towards colonizing but have sold out their shares to speculators who will probably try to get the grant for themselves." Concerning the public importance of promptly settling the territory, Edwards wrote: "It will be of great importance to the country and great advantage to your colony and all the lower country to have that section of the country settled as early as possible by agricultural people, as they will soon be able to supply the lower country with flour etc. which we are now compelled to import . . . and it will also be the means of driving back all the tribes of hostile Indians who are now constantly committing some depredations on the settlements of yours and Dewit's colonys."

on the subject and the fate of our setlers, also the fate of Esqr. Thomson—whether we have to leave the country or not." [59]

What Austin may have replied we do not know. Eighteen months later, in a sworn statement, to be more fully noticed presently, William Pettus declared that Austin denied to him that he had obtained the Nashville colony grant. If true, this was a piece of stupidity and dishonesty utterly inconsistent with what we know of Austin.

In December, 1831, Robertson appeared before the alcalde's court with a petition. Except that Austin had secured the revocation of the order for expulsion of his first nine families, we are ignorant of what had transpired since June. Robertson said he was informed that the government was deceived concerning the families that he introduced, both as to their number and their conduct after arrival; and, in order to establish the truth, he asked the court to examine certain witnesses who would present themselves. In the absence of the alcalde,[60] who was ill, the first *regidor,* Walter C. White, granted the petition and questioned two witnesses, one on December 7 and the other on the 22d. The alcalde of the following year, Horatio Chriesman, examined nine on January 2 and two more December 10 and 15, 1832. Though, according to the record, the witnesses were sworn, the examination was *ex parte.* Austin and Williams were unrepresented; there was no cross-questioning; and, inexplicable as it seems, Austin appears not to have heard of the proceedings until long afterwards.[61]

The first witness to be examined gave his name as Diadem Millican, aged twenty-five, a resident of Austin's colony, and a farmer.[62] He said that he knew Robertson well, and, from current report and documents he had seen, knew that he was a member of the Nashville Company, the object of which was to plant a colony in Texas. Asked if he knew whether Robertson had contracted with any persons to settle in the colony, he said that Robertson informed

---

[59] Robertson to Austin, June 7, 1831.

[60] Frank W. Johnson was alcalde.

[61] Writing to Williams from Mexico, August 21, 1833 (Rosenberg Library, Galveston), Austin said: "Sterling Robertson has presented to the State Govt a long memorial about his business in which there are depositions taken before Chrisman to prove that he introduced a great number of settlers which I took from him, etc. How he could get men to state such falsehoods or agents to advocate and arrange them I am at a loss to imagine."

[62] Possibly a son of William Millican, who lived in Austin's colony, near the Bexar-Nacogdoches road. Diadem held no land in his own name.

him that he had contracted with a matter of three hundred; and that he himself knew and had seen and talked to sixty-three men— whose names he gave—who told him that they had contracted with Robertson. Asked whether Robertson had introduced any settlers prior to April 15 "of the current year" (1831), he replied that the first forty-nine of those he named told him that they arrived before that time. Of those he listed some were now in Austin's colony, he said, and others were scattered, so that he did not know their where- abouts. In addition to the sixty-three named, he said that there were fifteen others actually settled on the ground. Answering a further question, he said that Robertson had at first provided supplies for his colonists but that after the order of expulsion came they had suffered great privation. This, in substance, was the story repeated by eleven witnesses.[63] The first two witnesses listed ninety-three names; the other nine added fifty-seven, of which four were re- peated, making a net total of a hundred and forty-six.[64] It is to be observed that much of the testimony was hearsay. And it is partic- ularly important to notice the date of introduction. Uniformly, when the question was asked, the witnesses testified that the im- migrants arrived prior to April 15, 1831, when the Leftwich con- tract expired by limitation. As we know, however, contracts were suspended in which a hundred families were not settled before the passage of the Law of April 6, 1830, and colonists subsequently in- troduced could not be seated.[65]

Two other witnesses remain to be heard—one at tedious length.[66]

[63] Diadem Millican, Daniel Millican, John S. Black, Levi Bostick, J. Scott, D. Arnold, Alexander Thomson, Samuel Humm, Jesse E. Evans, Henry Applewhite, and Socrates Moseley. Arnold, Thomson, and Humm were sworn and testified together. Besides their own, they mentioned but three names; and were not questioned concerning the date of introduction. The original of this testimony, retained in the alcalde's office at San Felipe, has disappeared. The Spanish translation, certified by Horatio Chriesman, December 20, 1832, is in the Archives of Coahuila (Saltillo), legajo 28, 1833, expediente 1293. John Henry Brown (*History of Texas*, I, 316), who used an English translation of this certified Spanish copy, gives the names of eight other witnesses who, he says, confirmed this testi- mony; but the copy in the archives, which seems complete, does not mention these other witnesses.

[64] The fact of so little repetition suggests careful preparation of the witnesses before examination.

[65] Brown (*History of Texas*, I, 316) knew the importance of this point, and makes one witness say that forty-nine settlers were introduced before the passage of the law of April 6, 1830, and leaves the inference that other witnesses testified to the same effect concerning additional families. He says (page 316) that "in the aggregate Robertson had introduced over two hundred families."

[66] It would be a pleasure to abbreviate this controversy, but Brown (*History of Texas*, I, 312–340) has published Robertson's side of it so fully, with gratuitous interpolations and distortions, that a detailed analysis of the case is unavoidable.

William Pettus offered himself for examination on December 15, 1832. Austin was then engaged in a tour of the Mexican settlements endeavoring to persuade them to inaugurate a movement for reforms thought to be essential to prevent a violent outbreak in the colonies.[67] Pettus said that he was acquainted with Robertson and knew a great deal about the business of the Nashville Company's grant; that "a considerable number of families" settled there as early as 1826 and told him that they did so by authority of the company; that afterwards they moved down to Austin's colony, and, "as they informed him, by Austin's persuasions." In 1830 Robertson came, "bringing with him a great number of families," and he told the witness that he had contracted with nearly three hundred who would be on very shortly; later witness saw "a great number of families, who informed him that they had come to settle in the grant, but afterwards they had settled in Austin's colony." He was, he said, anxious to see the upper country populated as a protection to the older settlements, and had therefore gone with Robertson to see Austin and ask him to intercede with the government for an extension of the term of the contract,[68] which Austin agreed to do. Austin then went to Saltillo as a member of the legislature, and before his return the rumor spread that Austin had had the contract transferred to himself. "Not believing that Austin would commit an act of such perfidy," the witness took the liberty of denying the rumor positively; and on Austin's return told him that he had done so, to which Austin replied that he had done well. "Austin continued denying it," he said, "until the following autumn, when the truth came to light in an announcement from Colonel Austin for himself and his secretary, Samuel M. Williams." At the same time it was said that orders had arrived from the government for the expulsion of Robertson from the country. Witness asked whether this was true, and both Austin and Williams assured him that it was, and Austin again pledged his word to use all his influence to get the order revoked; but afterwards the witness learned that no such order had ever existed, that it referred

---

[67] See below, pages 353–356.

[68] The witness dates this visit in 1829, but in the preceding paragraph he dates Robertson's arrival in 1830. Austin was not elected to the legislature until the fall of 1830, and the visit could not have been earlier. The date of Robertson's arrival is discussed more fully below, page 308.

only to eight or ten families that Robertson had brought in.[69] When the transfer of the colony to Austin became public, he asked Austin, he said, why he had previously denied it, and Austin replied that he had "feared that [the admission] would cause difficulties and that he had hoped Robertson would abandon the country, and that he could then serve the families better." Asked if he knew that Austin had introduced any colonists at his own expense or whether he "had not always made a practice of selling land to the settlers," Pettus replied that he did not know a single man whose expenses had been paid by Austin; recited the old story of the fees that Austin originally planned to charge for land;[70] and said that the price was still sixty dollars a league, exclusive of fees to surveyor and commissioner and the cost of sealed paper, and that "many times after the money was received from the colonists and certain lands promised them they were swindled and the same land sold to others —these facts [he added] could be proved by hundreds of persons."

The animus of Pettus is obvious but its cause is not clear. Two years before this Austin had written, "Pettus and myself parted in such terms as I wish to be with all the settlers. I have confidence in him now, and I think he has in me." [71] Remember that he offered this testimony of his own motion, without process, and that the proceedings were *ex parte*. As we have seen, there is no contemporary evidence of settlement in the grant in 1826, but if there were such settlements, inability of the settlers to get titles, and exposure to the Indians, would account for their removal to Austin's colony without persuasion. Under the circumstances Pettus's report of his searching personal questions and Austin's answers do not carry conviction. Austin was not the man to receive such questions or to give such answers.

[69] The facts are given above. Several orders mentioned Robertson by name—both he and his colonists were to be expelled. See Terán to Elosua, December 31, 1830; Músquiz to Elosua, February 9, March 29, 1831—General Land Office of Texas, Vol. 54, pages 285, 286, 292. Also Músquiz to alcaldes of San Felipe and Nacogdoches, February 16, 1831, Nacogdoches Archives, Texas State Library.

[70] See pages 97–105.

[71] Austin to Williams, writing from San Antonio, December 28, 1830. Rosenberg Library, Galveston. On Pettus see Pettus to Royall, May 16, 1825; Royall to Austin, August 23, 1825, and Ellis to Austin, January 3, 1828. The last, Judge Richard Ellis of Tuscumbia, Alabama, later president of the convention that declared the independence of Texas, wrote of Pettus: "I believe I might use the same language to you, Sir, John Falstaff did to prince Henry (of Poins), 'he is the most omnipotent villain that ever cried stand to a true man.' "

Finally, R. Williams testified concerning Austin's disposition of the grant. He said that John Austin claimed to have bought Austin's interest for six thousand dollars; that one Benjamin Smith had bought from John Austin an interest of twelve hundred leagues on which he was to plant settlers; and that he heard they were selling the privilege of locating claims in the colony at the rate of fifty dollars a league. This seems to be confirmed in general by letters from Austin. On the eve of his mission to Mexico in April, 1833, Austin wrote his brother-in-law: "I made an arrangement with John Austin and Williams as to the upper colony, above the San Antonio road, and what is made out of that colony is to be equally divided between us. Williams is to attend to the business, but nothing is to be done contrary to law or the true interests of the country. That is, there is to be no kind of wild speculation. My object in this is more to have the business attended to and that wilderness country settled, than to make a speculation." [72] And from Matamoras, on this same trip, he wrote Williams some weeks later:

"You are engaging in one business [before the] other is finished and may spoil [everything] Rush the records of the office . . . the testimonios and surveys etc., then give it up *in toto* and go to the merchant's occupation, but finish first and keep clear of land jobbing. I am of opinion that the upper colony will totally ruin *me,* in fact I have but little doubt of it, for such men as Bowie etc. will lead you and John too far into speculations. B. F. Smith's cursed foolish trip has done great harm,[73] and I am sorry he ever came to Texas. Keep clear of speculations for the future. They are a *curse* to any country and will be a very *sore curse* to me individually. I believe they will ruin me if they have not already done it. Cursed be the hour I ever thought of applying for that upper colony." [74]

Interpretations of this will inevitably differ. Some will regard it as admission of wrong-doing in obtaining the Nashville grant.

---

[72] Austin to Perry, April 20, 1833, quoted by Brown, *History of Texas*, I, 335. Since this was written the University of Texas has acquired a photostat copy of this letter from the original, which belongs to Judge Norman G. Kittrell, of Houston.

[73] This is not explained and can only be guessed at. Smith was known to early Texans as the owner of some African slaves. The convention of April, 1833, adopted resolutions condemning the African slave trade, and the occasion of the resolutions was said to be the appearance of a vessel off the coast with a cargo of negroes. According to the testimony of Williams, Smith made some sort of arrangement with John Austin for twelve hundred leagues of land. Was it Smith's cargo that offended the humanity of the convention, was he to develop a great slave plantation on the upper Brazos, and was it this to which Austin referred?

[74] Austin to Williams, May 31, 1833, Rosenberg Library, Galveston.

To the writer, on the other hand, it means simply the recognition of certain regrettable consequences that he had not foreseen. Austin's abhorrence of speculation and speculators was ingrained and frequently expressed. It runs through all his correspondence from the assumption of his father's contract until his own death. "I had rather herd with vermin than with that class of human beings," he wrote Williams.[75] And yet his acquisition of this grant threatened to involve him in just such company.

In Mexico, after a grisly summer in the city stricken with cholera, from which he himself escaped by the narrowest margin,[76] Austin secured the repeal of the immigration restriction of the law of April 6, 1830. Before his return to Texas he was arrested and was detained until July, 1835. He was thus absent from Texas for more than two years—from May, 1833. John Austin died of cholera in Texas in August, 1833, and Williams was left with the management of the colony.

Robertson now moved to make use of the testimony that he had collected. He notified Williams that he intended, on the first Monday of November, 1833, to present his papers to the ayuntamiento to obtain "an expression of that body with regard to their opinions and views upon the validity and justness of my claim." Williams could appear, if he wished, and offer a counter-claim.[77] For some reason this procedure was delayed until the following February.[78] Then the ayuntamiento gave Robertson what he wished: "Resolved by this Ayuntamiento," read its report to the governor, "that from the facts laid before us by Sterling C. Robertson in relation to the Nashville Company, that they *are of opinion*[79] that said contract was never forfeited by the Nashville Company. That anterior to the passage of the law of the 6th of April, 1830, the aforesaid Sterling C. Robertson had introduced, for the purpose of establishing or settling in the Nashville Colony, at least one hundred families, which in our opinion under Article 8th of the Colonization Law of March the 24th, 1825, of the State, was a saving of the contract

[75] Austin to Williams, August 21, 1833, Rosenberg Library, Galveston.
[76] *Ibid.*
[77] Robertson to Williams, October 29, 1833, in collection of Dr. Alex. Dienst, Temple, Texas.
[78] Robertson again notified Williams of his intentions. See letter of January 24, 1834 (?), Rosenberg Library, Galveston.
[79] The Italics are the author's.

so far as related to the one hundred families thus introduced." It was the opinion of the ayuntamiento, therefore, that Robertson should be reinstated when the repeal of the law of April 6 became effective, and that his contract should be extended one year from the date of such repeal, because, by misapprehension of the facts, the original contract had been shortened by that much. "The zeal, industry, and untiring perseverance of Sterling C. Robertson in endeavoring to settle the Nashville Colony," said the document, "is a matter of general and universal admiration, and we are further satisfied that a very large majority of the people of Texas anxiously desire that he should be recognized as the Empresario of said Colony."[80] This was signed by R. M. Williamson, president, and William B. Travis, secretary, of the ayuntamiento.

In fact, as we have seen, neither Robertson nor the company had made any settlements prior to April 6, 1830; and the testimony on which the ayuntamiento based its opinion contained nothing whatever to indicate the introduction of a hundred families before that date.[81]

Robertson now proceeded to the capital, and on April 2, 1834, delivered his documents to the governor. He declared that his company introduced "some families as early as 1826" and that before the passage of the prohibitory law of April 6, 1830, they had introduced more than a hundred families, "as is shown by the documents which I duly submit and swear to."[82] Afterwards, he proceeded, they brought in "many more families," but neither these nor those who came before the passage of the law were seated; some had now returned to the United States, but others, without homes or property, were scattered through the country awaiting the gov-

---

[80] From the original in the Archives of Coahuila (Saltillo), legajo 28, 1833, expediente 1293. Brown, *History of Texas*, I, 319–320, prints a slightly variant copy in full. Brown's copy is probably a re-translation into English of a Spanish translation of the original.

[81] Diadem Millican, examined on December 7, 1831, was asked "si sabia que dicho Robertson habia introducido algunos pobladores en este departamento anteriormente al dia quince de Abril del corriente año." John S. Black, questioned January 2, 1832, was asked whether Robertson had introduced any families "antes del mes de Abril ultimo." Levi Bostick on the same day was asked whether colonists were introduced "antes de Abril del año pasado." Jesse E. Evans, Henry Applewhite, and Socrates Moseley, testifying together on January 2, 1832, were asked if settlers were introduced "antes del quince de Abril del corriente año"—evidently a slip in the question for "año pasado." Daniel Millican, J. Scott, Daniel Arnold, Alexander Thomson, and Samuel Humm, R. Williams, and Pettus, according to the record, were not given this question.

[82] "Como consta de los documentos que debidamente acompaño y juro." The documents were those that we have already examined.

ernor's final decision. Austin had agreed to intercede for the settlement of the families and for extension of the term of his contract, but "lacking good faith, which is indispensable to men of character, and rejecting those principles of honor which none but wicked and perfidious men forget, he deceived the government with false statements, making it believe that we had never taken the first step to carry out our contract; and the object which he had in view by this falsehood was to secure our colony for himself and his partner in iniquity, Samuel M. Williams." He considered the contract of Austin and Williams illegal, because it was granted "one month and eighteen days" before that of the Nashville Company expired, "and even if we had not introduced a single family until the last day of our term, and on that day had introduced the eight hundred families contracted for—or any part of them—they would have entered within the legal term, and consequently, as it seems to me, the government could not contract with others until that day was passed." Moreover, the contract of the partners was null because they obtained it by fraud and the government granted it upon false information which they gave it, "acting upon the wholly mistaken and erroneous supposition that we had never taken the first step toward fulfilling our contract." [83] In consideration of these statements would the governor not appoint a commissioner to extend titles to the immigrants still in Texas and submit the accompanying documents to the legislature with a request that it declare the contract with Austin and Williams void? [84]

The facts of Austin's intervention, so far as they are known, have already been given. Robertson's argument for the validity of his contract until the day of its expiration would be conclusive but for its suspension by the federal act on April 6, 1830.

With his documents Robertson transmitted to the legislature a most vituperative attack on Austin, which it would be a grateful privilege to ignore if John Henry Brown had not published a translation with his hearty approval and endorsement. [85] After reciting,

[83] Robertson's basis for this statement was a clause in Austin and Williams's contract saying that up to that time no part of the Leftwich contract had been complied with— "y a Leftwich se le cumple en 15 de Abril del presente año el termino que se le concedio al efecto cuando celebro su contrata y hasta ahora no ha complido ni con una parte de ella."

[84] Archives of Coahuila (Saltillo), 1833, legajo 28, expediente 1293. The document is in Spanish and is signed by Robertson.

[85] Brown, *History of Texas*, I, 320–328. Though Brown's translation is somewhat sketchy, it omits no abuse of Austin.

accurately enough, the early history of the grant and the desire of the company to settle the colony, Robertson goes on to say: "But after having spent a matter of thirty thousand dollars [86] in the business, its energies and efforts have been blocked and frustrated by an uninterrupted course of mishaps, intrigues, and unforeseen misfortunes—now by exigencies which the company could not control or direct, again by the perfidy and deceptions of agents and insidious and pretended friends." Great hopes had been founded on the agency of League, "but another misfortune befell: The agent *was accused in the colony of Austin* as an accomplice in a homicide and incarcerated in jail and loaded with irons for the long period of sixteen months, suffering during all this period a persecution so severe, so rigorous, and so implacable, that, in the end, the people themselves, outraged in their ideas of law and justice . . . to the number of six or seven hundred petitioned the alcalde that justice be done him without delay and that he be released from imprisonment. This persecution was so bitter and distressing that the petitioner [87] cannot regard it as less than *very strange and notable.*" The evident implication is that League's arrest and persecution explain in part the failure of the company to settle the colony, and that Austin, no doubt, had a hand in it. The facts in this celebrated case have already been given.[88] The homicide occurred on September 2, 1830, too late to have any influence on the success of the company. The contract had long been suspended, and Robertson himself was already on the way to Texas to supplant League, which he did on October 1,[89] three weeks after League's arrest. Austin's defense of League has been noted.

In the meantime, Robertson says he himself went to Texas "in the autumn of 1829 with a considerable number of families." He then describes what really took place in the autumn of 1830—the trouble with Piedras about passports at Nacogdoches, his explorations by consent of Ruiz, while his colonists remained encamped below the Bexar-Nacogdoches road in Austin's colony, and Ruiz's appeal to his superiors for instructions. Why, he pauses to ask, should passports be required of his colonists, when "a simple cer-

[86] Brown, *ibid.*, 320, says $32,000.
[87] That is, Robertson. Brown's translation says "alcalde."
[88] Above, page 192.
[89] Brown, *History of Texas*, I, 316, misreads the Spanish "1º" for 10.

tificate from Señor Austin was sufficient to admit settlers going to his colonies"? Did he not have a right to expect the laws to operate equally for all? Returning from his explorations, Robertson was informed by Ruiz, he claims, "that he had received the government's reply and that it was very happy to see at last that our colony would be settled—a thing which it greatly desired. Thus flattering myself with the protection of the government and the good offices of the commandant of that post [Tenoxtitlan], I made every arrangement for the comfort of the families I had introduced and returned to the United States in December of the same year, 1829."

Here Robertson's memory played him strangely false. He may have been in Texas in 1829—there is no record of it except this statement—but none of these experiences that he recites could have happened then. Ruiz's post at Tenoxtitlan was not established until July, 1830;[90] the trouble over passports began in October of that year; and Robertson's explorations and Ruiz's correspondence followed in November. Robertson himself wrote Músquiz that he had been unable until June of 1830 to gain the consent of the company to make the settlement and that on November 13, when he wrote, only ten families had arrived.[91] If the government ever expressed satisfaction at Robertson's arrival, the record has disappeared. Its reply to Ruiz in 1830 was that Robertson and the families introduced by him must return to the United States. Austin's authority to give passports to his colonists has been sufficiently explained.[92] Certainly, so far as he was responsible, there was no discrimination against Robertson.

Early in the following year, to resume Robertson's story—that is in 1830, he would have us understand—he "introduced into the country directly or indirectly more than three hundred families" and contracted with many others, so that, if no obstacle had intervened, he would have settled, before the expiration of the contract,

---

[90] See above, page 292.

[91] Robertson to Músquiz, November 13, 1830, Nacogdoches Archives, Texas State Library. "Hase como tres anos que he solicitado una entrevista [con los] directores pᵃ haber un orden de ellos en que me autorisen venir a establecer docientos familias y no pude conseguir otras mas hasta en Junio atiempo ₍que la estendieron despues de cuyo tiempo he hecho quantos diligᵃˢ han estado en mi poder pᵃ colectar familias, y por ultimo tuve el exito de enganchar las docientas que me comprometi reunir, dies de las cuales han arrivado sobre los Brazos sobre el camino de San Antonio, parte del balanse se hallan en camino y el resto arrivaran aqui en este ynvierno y la proxima primavera."

[92] See preceding chapter.

almost all of the eight hundred families originally stipulated. He admitted hearing of the law of April 6, 1830, before his return, but his colonists had already burned their bridges behind them. Confiding in the benevolence of the government, in the validity of their contract, and in the constitutional principle prohibiting the passage of a retroactive law or a law impairing the obligation of contracts, "they came to the country with all their property and their hopes." [93] Their rejection upon arrival was to him incomprehensible. "Considering that we had a contract with the government in almost the same terms as that of Señor Austin, and seeing many new settlers admitted to his colony daily from the United States, on the principle that his contract was dated prior to the law; seeing also that the date of our contract was anterior to the date of his, and that we had begun to settle as early as 1826, I was confounded, and it was not until long afterwards that I learned that it was because of the infamous falsehoods told the government about the matter." He explained this by saying that General Terán said the government was informed that the company had never settled more than eight families. The falsity of this, Robertson added, could be readily seen from the documents submitted. As we already know, of course, it was not the date of Austin's contract that enabled him to continue settling colonists from the United States, but the fact that he had secured his contracts by settling at least a hundred in each before the troublesome restriction was passed.

In his distress, said Robertson, he appealed to Austin. "That gentleman, employing the same insidious and jesuitical policy that has ever marked with black footprints the tortuous path by which he has skulked to the execution of his nefarious and perfidious ends, received me with false and smiling countenance and pledged his word of honor, before witnesses," etc., etc. [94] For the rest, "perfidy," "wicked practices," "false and lying statements" are terms applied to Austin. The more serious additional charges, stripped of vitu-

---

[93] Robertson probably stated the real facts here. He trusted to the validity of his contract and the constitutional practice of the United States. He was ignorant of the strong anti-American sentiment in Mexico and either did not know of or did not understand the reservation of the federal colonization law, under which the state administered the public lands, which permitted Congress to forbid immigration from the United States without a technical breach of contract.

[94] "Usando este Señor de la misma politica jesuitica e ensidiosa que siempre ha señalado con huellas negras la senda tortuosa por donde ha caminado a sombra de tejado a cumplimiento de sus nefarios y perfidiosos designos, me recibio" etc., etc.

peration, are: that Austin tried to procure the banishment of Robertson; that he ever advanced his own interests by the labor and misfortune of others; that he filled his contracts with settlers who migrated at their own expense or were introduced by other empresarios; that he was allowed—through dishonorable machinations, it is implied—to receive colonists denied to Robertson; that Austin had already arranged to sell the colony before obtaining it, that he later did sell his interest for six thousand dollars, and that he was still making a speculation of it by selling location rights for fifty dollars a league. At every step Robertson supported his abuse by reference to the testimony which we have already examined.

There is no documentary evidence one way or the other, except Pettus's extremely questionable deposition, that Austin tried to secure the expulsion of Robertson from the country. It is perfectly true that Austin did not bear the traveling expenses of his colonists. How could he have reimbursed himself for such an outlay? Certainly not by his premium lands. If Robertson did, as he implied, introduce immigrants at his own cost, the reason is perhaps to be found in the contract with Jeremiah Tinnin, by which Tinnin after receiving a league of land was to convey thirty-five hundred acres of it to Robertson and Thomson.[95] It was not exploitation of the misfortunes of others when Austin incorporated scattered settlers in his colony. It was an act of practical beneficence—though reciprocally beneficial—that they keenly appreciated, because otherwise they remained squatters and tenants at will, without hope of obtaining titles.[96] The apparent discrimination which allowed Austin to continue introducing American colonists and denied the same privilege to Robertson rested on the interpretation of the law of April 6, 1830, as we know; and although Austin was responsible for the establishment of that interpretation, it was without reference to Robertson. While it benefited himself and DeWitt and their colonists, it injured no one.[97] The assertion that Austin had planned the disposition of the grant before obtaining it is unsupported. All that is known of the arrangement with John Austin has been told. The sale of location privileges, as we shall see, was perhaps abused by Williams; but, in effect, it was the same

[95] See above, page 292.
[96] See above, pages 96–97, 149, 324, and Cooke to Austin, December 3, 1824.
[97] See above, preceding chapter.

thing as the empresario's fee exacted of colonists for each league of land, and this fee was recognized and permitted by the colonization law.[98]

On April 11 the legislature acknowledged receipt of Robertson's documents and referred them to the committee on jurisprudence. On the 26th the committee's report was adopted. It authorized the governor to decide the case as seemed to him appropriate (*conveniente*) and provided that should the decision be favorable to Robertson, he should be allowed premium lands for the families introduced at his expense and denied settlement on account of the law of April 6, 1830, and that his contract should be extended four years from date.[99] The governor gave his decision on May 22. He said that the contract of Austin and Williams was "merely conditional," though what he meant by that it would be hard to guess. In consequence of this and of the report of the ayuntamiento of San Felipe "that Robertson had introduced a hundred families before April 6, 1830," he declared the contract of Austin and Williams void in so far as it covered Robertson's grant. Settlers introduced by Austin and Williams should retain the lands with which they were invested but should not be counted by any empresario in claims for premium land. Families previously introduced by Robertson should be seated. This could now be done without federal complications, because the repeal of the law of April 6, 1830, would soon be effective.[100]

Austin was a prisoner, *incomunicado,* and ignorant of Robertson's movements. Williams, however, had tried to defend his case. He started an attorney, T. McQueen, to Monclova early in February with documents and instructions to refute Robertson's plea, but a day's journey beyond San Antonio McQueen was severely wounded by Indians and had to return. Then, after considerable delay, Williams engaged Juan Antonio Padilla to represent him; but for several years Padilla had been deprived of the rights of citizenship for killing a man in Texas, and upon his arrival at the capital was unable to take any steps until the legislature removed his

[98] See above, pages 104–105, 121–122.

[99] Journals of the legislature of Coahuila and Texas, pages 1820, 1835–1836, transcript at University of Texas. Part of the decree is published in Gammel, *Laws of Texas,* I, 385.

[100] Translation by Thomas Jefferson Chambers, published in a broadside by Robertson, November 29, 1834. Austin Papers.

disabilities. In the meantime, Robertson's business was concluded without opposition.[101]

The information that Williams furnished McQueen adds something to our knowledge of the case. For the most part, it is confirmed by what we have already learned and bears the stamp of accuracy:

"I find myself considerably at a loss [he began] how to frame anything like instructions for you. . . . Presuming, however, that an attempt will be made to convince the Government that the Nashville Company complied on their part to a certain extent in the introduction of families, I will briefly state to you facts which have come under my own observation and knowledge, having been during the progress of the total matter on the scene of action.

"After Mr. Leftwich returned to the United States from this country with his contract, and the Company purchased it from him, they employed Doctor Robertson[102] to visit the country for the double object of examining the colony for information as to its extent, fertility of soil, etc., etc., and also to become acquainted with the true nature of the contract or grant, as it was termed. The Company was under the impression, although with some doubts, that it was a grant in fee simple. Doctor Robertson during his stay at this place altho short, must have been convinced that it was in no manner a grant but a contract, and that all the land the Company would obtain from the Gov't would be simply 40 leagues and Labors after introducing 800 families. The Company previous to making themselves acquainted with the true character of the grant had issued to shareholders, and had sold, large amounts of scrip, some of which called for eight leagues of land. Under the law there was no way that the holder of the scrip could obtain a title to that quantity except by introducing 8 families, and then the title would be made for one league to each distinct family, and the scrip holder obliged to take from the family a bond for a certain portion of the land as might be stipulated. A title could not be made because the colonization law prohibited the sale of land. One other way an increased quantity could have been obtained; that is, by special petition to the Governor—then the scrip was of no use, because the holder would be obliged to pay the Government for the land.

"Not exactly satisfied with Doctor Robertson's visit, and the matter of too much importance to be lost without exertions, the Company in the

---

[101] Williams to McQueen, February 4, 8, 1834; Padilla to Williams, February 26, 1834; Spencer H. Jack to Williams, September 16, 1834—all in Rosenberg Library, Galveston. Journals of legislature of Coahuila and Texas, Transcript at University of Texas. Williams wrote also to the political chief at San Antonio and to Ex-governor J. M. Viesca, who was then a member of the legislature. The first, March 26, 1834, is in the General Land Office of Texas, Vol. 54, page 301; the other, April 1, 1834, is in the Austin Papers.

[102] That is, Felix Robertson.

close of 1826 sent out Colonel Foster: he was not able to do anything for the Company, but returned to the United States fully convinced that the contract was a very different thing from what the Company wished it, even if they did not know it."

Williams then told of the transfer of the contract, through Austin's intervention, from Leftwich to the company, and the appointment of League to act as empresario in Texas.

"Two or three times Major League applied to the Company for permission to admit settlers as there were a good many families that had emigrated to Texas and were anxious to settle in that colony, but no permission could be had, and nothing was done; and no families could go there with the hope of getting land, as they might at any time be removed to give place to the families of the company—thus passed on time regardless of Company or its views and wishes, and the colony, to the general injury of Texas, a perfect wilderness.

"Here I will remark that it must be evident to every discerning mind that had the Nashville Company used exertions and placed a few hundred good laborious families within the limits of their colony, very different would be the present aspect and prospect of Texas.

"In the fall of 1829 there was some stir made that Texas was to be sold to the U. States. Hardly had the Company time to arouse from the apathy of a long sleep and get the directors together before the idea blew over and they returned again to their slumbers. Then came the law of the 6th of April 1830 after the Company had trifled away five years without hardly an exertion. Then it was they were prepared to give up the ship, and did so with the exception of granting permission to Sterling Robertson to introduce 100 or 150 families, offering him the premium lands on that number.

"Robertson made contracts with some families and introduced some 8 or 10 in the fall of 1830 and Mr. Thomson introduced some which did not arrive until after the term granted had expired.

"It really appears to me as idle and irrelevant to the question, whether or not the Company complied, to gather up certificates from families in the country setting forth as having been their intention on emigrating to the country to settle in the Colony, when they could not do so without the approbation of the Company and at the same time the agent of the Company residing in this town. If they were authorized to go there by the Company they should have made it known to the agent and have gone and settled there; no law or obstruction existed further than the one created by the Company. And for my part I look upon the course of attempting to throw censure on Colonel Austin as humiliating and unmanly, to say that Colonel Austin wanted the settlers to fill his contracts, when the facts are the very reverse. Why did he not prevent any leaving the country who came out and returned dissatisfied? Why not prevent any going to DeWitt's colony? And why not compel all within the limits of the country to settle here? I have often heard of stage trick for stage effect but it truly appears to me as poor and mean to endeavor to operate on the feelings of a community by holding a man up as a bugaboo of arbitrary power and authority in a country where every man does as he pleases."

Passing to a summary of his argument, Williams questioned the authority of Robertson to act as agent of the company; and denied the competence of his evidence to establish a validation of the contract before its annulment by the act of April 6, 1830. On the contrary, he said, the declaration of certain families that it had been their intention to settle in the grant "should justly operate against the company, because they prevented them from carrying their intentions into effect and kept the country a wilderness, to the injury of Texas." Moreover, the depositions were "procured by private examination of individuals in the office of Lewis and Chambers, not in open court, and without the knowledge or a citation of the other party." [103]

Robertson's success seems to have been due to influence with Acting Governor Viduarri y Villaseñor. Oliver Jones, one of the Texan representatives in the legislature, wrote Williams that the governor was disposed to favor Robertson; and some months later Spencer H. Jack, on his way to Mexico in behalf of Austin, wrote after a conference with Padilla that the legislature's authorizing the governor to decide the case "amounted to giving the Colony to Robertson, for it was well known by every person that the governor was disposed to do every[thing] for him"—"for the reasons," Jack added, "which you no doubt heard before this." [104] The contemporary interpretation of the last clause was that other than strictly legal considerations entered into the governor's decision. [105]

Robertson announced the restoration of his contract in a broadside published by the *Texas Republican* at Brazoria. Justice had at

[103] For McQueen's information and use Williams provided various documents, some of which have been used in the preceding narrative and some of which have disappeared. Among those no longer available was a letter from League to Robertson, August 31, 1830, "declaring the then situation of affairs." Williams indicates the nature of this letter in his instructions. "Offer to prove," he said, "that no introduction whatever was made by or in behalf of the Company until the close of 1830 and then only 9 families. The best evidence exists in the letter of the acknowledged agent of the Company, dated 31 Augt 1830, which you have."

[104] Jones to Williams, April 2, and Jack to Williams, September 16, 1834, Rosenberg Library, Galveston.

[105] See Jones to Perry, June 10, 1834.

last triumphed over perfidy, he said, and his colony, though long
kept a wilderness by fraud and chicanery, could now be settled.[106]
The governor had appointed a commissioner to issue titles—William H. Steele—and work began without delay.[107]

At the same time Williams set about preparations to reopen the
case. From the new ayuntamiento of San Felipe he got a statement
endorsing his claims,[108] and no doubt the documents previously
furnished McQueen and Padilla were still available. Toward the
end of January, 1835, he started for the capital, very optimistic,
and determined, as he wrote Perry, to pay in their own coin some
to whom he and Austin were deeply indebted for injuries.[109] On
March 31 he filed with Marcial Borrego, acting governor, a general complaint against Robertson's commissioner, Steele, and asked
for his suspension pending an investigation.[110] With this the governor complied, but he based his action on a letter from Steele
which he said showed that Steele was violating his instructions and
the terms on which Robertson's contract was reinstated.[111] Williams
wrote Austin that Borrego, who had been Robertson's chief supporter in the preceding legislature, admitted that they had been
deceived, but said the matter must be remedied in such a way as to
save the face of the government.[112] This proved to be a more puzzling problem than was anticipated. The first impulse of the legislature was simply to repeal the governor's decree restoring the
colony to Robertson, but John Durst, of Nacogdoches, quoted a
section of the constitution that seemed to preclude that solution.[113]

---

[106] *Texas Republican*, November 29, 1834. This copy was filed by Williams in the state archives and is now there, expediente 1313, año 1835.

[107] Austin's brother-in-law, who naturally did not regard Robertson with much tolerance, wrote Austin on December 7, 1834: "Sterling C. Robinson is cavolting about in the upper colony at a great rate. He is tareing up all that was done by Austin and Williams. He will hardly let the hills and rivers stand that they happened to have crossed with a chain. While Chambers was up the country he wrote an expose for Robinson in which he makes heavy charges against you—but all these things are now pretty generally understood and if Williams goes on and has that business straightened all these assertions will go back on themselves."

[108] Williams to Perry, January 7, 1835. The statement of the ayuntamiento has not survived, nor is there any further indication of the content.

[109] Williams to Perry, January 14, 1835.

[110] Archives of Coahuila (Saltillo), año de 1835, expediente 1313.

[111] Governor to Political Chief of Department of Brazos, April 1, 1835, General Land Office of Texas, Translations of Empresario Contracts, page 234.

[112] Williams to Austin, March 31, 1835.

[113] "Art. 169. Neither Congress nor the governor can remove cases pending from an inferior to a superior court; nor can the tribunals and courts of justice themselves open those already concluded."

Finally the end was accomplished by a species of verbal gymnastics: the resolution, it was declared, on which Viduarri had acted in Robertson's favor had been misinterpreted; it should have been understood to say that the determination of the case belonged to the judicial power.[114] Therefore any decision by any other authority was null, and the colony should be returned to Austin and Williams. But rights of settlers acquired under Robertson should be respected.[115] The governor, Agustin Viesca, who had now relieved Borrego, published the decree without delay, and it was formally transmitted to Robertson by the political chief of the Brazos department just at the beginning of the Texas revolution.[116] The revolution, rather than the governor's order, ended the issuing of titles by Steele.[117]

How many colonists did Robertson introduce? In 1841 the district court of Travis County awarded him premium lands for six hundred families. The government appealed, and the supreme court in 1847 reduced the count to three hundred and seven families. Chief Justice Hemphill, who wrote the decree of the court, reached this number by the following process: (1) The jury in the lower court had found that Robertson introduced 100 families *prior to renewal of his contract in 1834.* This he did not question. (2) Steele had issued, according to the record, 279 titles,[118] of which 108 were to single men. Counting three unmarried men as a family, Judge Hemphill deducted 72 from the total, leaving 207. (3) Adding to this the 100 families found by the jury to have been introduced before May 22, 1834, when Robertson's contract was renewed, gave the total of 307.[119] (4) The court refused to count 221 families because they were introduced after the pro-

---

[114] "La resolucion de que hablo el decreto de 6 [26] de Abril de 1834, en el asunto que promovio el extrangero D. Sterling Robertson debio entenderse propia como lo es del poder judicial." Journals of the Legislature, Transcript, page 1919, University of Texas.

[115] Durst was responsible for this safeguard to individuals. At the same time he declared it an act of justice to return the colony to Austin and Williams.

[116] General Land Office of Texas, Translations of Empresario Contracts, page 234.

[117] Robertson testified before a joint committee of the Texan Congress in 1840 that he received a "reputed copy" of the governor's decree declaring his contract void, "yet I was informed that the Congress making the decree had not a legal quorum."—*Evidence in Relation to Land Titles,* etc. (Austin, 1856), 18.

[118] The Land Office files, Vols. 14–15, show two hundred and seventy individuals receiving titles from Steele, but the total number of titles issued by him is considerably larger, because some persons obtained land in two parcels.

[119] The court did not raise the question of whether those introduced before 1834 might also be included in those who received titles.

visional government closed the land offices in November, 1835.[120]

The law of April 6, 1830, excluded from the Austin and Williams contract colonists from the United States, and Austin expected to settle it with Irish, Scotch, German, Swiss, and French immigrants. For a time, at least, he contemplated a voyage to Europe for this purpose[121] and prepared the manuscript for an elaborate pamphlet on Texas which he evidently intended to circulate abroad.[122] The disturbances of 1832–1833 and the mission to Mexico with its disastrous sequel compelled abandonment of the idea. No doubt, too, dawning hope of repealing the restrictive law would have deferred the undertaking.[123]

During 1833 Williams permitted the location of a number of large claims in the grant, ranging from three to eleven leagues each; and charged for the privilege a fee of fifty dollars a league. He explained this by saying: "The law and the contract gave me the right of approving or disapproving. No man was compelled to locate his land within the limits of the contract. We could not compel any one to do so. If he desired to do so, it cost him $50 per league for permission. In no instance has any native Mexican been charged anything—but solely those persons who had bo't them up as speculation." [124] As a legal defense this leaves nothing to be said. Nevertheless, the subsequent history of these grants brought great bitterness on Austin's memory. They became, in time, the basis of much litigation extending over many years, and in general the courts sustained them. The losers in these suits, frequently small holders, blamed Austin as the original cause of their losses and gave full sway to a sense of wrong and injury the consequences of which have survived to the present day.

Requesting the appointment of a land commissioner in February,

---

[120] 2 Texas Reports, 1–34. The style of the case is Houston *vs.* Robertson. Both the original record of this case in the district court and the transcript which should be in the supreme court have disappeared.

[121] Colonel Francisco Ruiz, writing Austin December 11, 1831, expressed regret that Austin had to go to Europe in order to fulfill the new contract; it would entail great labor and much expense and would perhaps yield small results. He prayed God that better times might come and avert such a voyage.

[122] Address to European Immigrants, December [31], 1831, in *The Southwestern Historical Quarterly*, XXVIII, 103–118; also Austin to Mrs. Holley, November 17, 1831.

[123] The ayuntamiento of San Felipe petitioned for such repeal on February 18, 1832, and Austin wrote Williams (Rosenberg Library, Galveston) April 28 that there was a prospect of modifying the law.

[124] Williams to McQueen, February 14, 1834, Rosenberg Library, Galveston.

1834, Williams claimed that there were twenty or thirty Mexican families settled in the colony and enough German and Swiss to make up a hundred, while he was daily expecting, he said, a hundred and twenty-five more German, Swiss, and Irish families.[125] This was probably an over-statement. The commissioner was not appointed until May, 1835, and of the titles thereafter issued—eighty-eight in October, 1835, and seventy-eight in January and February of the following year—few contain foreign names.[126]

Unfortunately, while at Monclova, Williams engaged in gigantic land speculations which aroused keen resentment in Texas.[127] Austin, still a prisoner on bail in Mexico, had with them no connection whatever; but his relations with Williams and his interest in the annulment of Robertson's contract brought suspicion upon him and probably cost him the presidency of Texas in the election of 1836.[128] Moreover, the odium of this transaction, reacting upon undiscriminating public opinion, tended to confirm Robertson's violent charges against Austin—since Williams had acted with grave impropriety, Austin also must be guilty.

The pertinent facts of this unpleasant controversy are now before the reader: (1) Austin welcomed the grant to Leftwich and the prospect of a settlement to the west as a protection for his own colony. (2) By his intervention, the government was induced to transfer the contract from Leftwich to the company and recognize the agent-empresario that the company nominated. In this he gave the company freely and gladly all the assistance in his power. (3) Notwithstanding the fact that this removed all legal obstacles, the company still did nothing toward fulfillment of the contract. (4) In June, 1830, however, the company finally authorized Sterling C. Robertson to settle two hundred families in the grant. This is according to the contemporary statement of Robertson himself. (5) But prior to this, the law of April 6, 1830, had annulled all contracts in which a hundred families were not already settled. This meaning was established by interpretation; the intent of the law was evidently to annul all contracts for the settlement of emigrants

---

[125] Williams to McQueen, February 8, 1834.

[126] Settlers from the United States were then, of course, no longer excluded.

[127] See an article by the writer in *Quarterly* of Texas State Historical Association, X, 76–95.

[128] Gail Borden, Jr., to Austin, August 15; and Austin to Borden, August 21, 1836.

from the United States. (6) Robertson arrived in Texas in October, 1830, with nine families, and others were to follow; but the federal act had vacated his contract and he was forbidden to proceed. (7) The grant, being vacant, was about to be awarded to the French company, and to prevent this, which in all probability would have postponed the expansion of the frontier another six years, Austin applied for the territory and obtained it. (8) Robertson's protest that his own contract had not yet expired by limitation when Austin's was granted is beside the mark, because his contract had been annulled nearly a year before by the federal law.

Opinion concerning the purity and public-spiritedness of Austin's motives in taking over the Robertson, or Nashville Company, grant will no doubt continue to vary directly with individual estimate of his general character. Certainly the contract could not have been renewed to Robertson in 1831, but, as events developed, public interest would have suffered little injury if Villaveque had obtained the colony; and Austin would have been saved much embarrassment and misunderstanding. But Austin laid no greater claim to the gift of prophecy than belongs to any intelligent man acquainted with his environment and its history. He did not know that the Texas revolution would sponge the slate clean less than five years from the date of his application; and from all the knowable facts he had every reason to believe that the grant to such a company would be detrimental to the true interest of Texas. That his personal interests were bound up in the public interest does not necessarily weaken the sincerity of his belief or the cleanness of his motives.

In a statement to the Texan Senate, of which Robertson was a member, in December, 1836, Austin recounted the history of the Leftwich contract and his connection with it. He wrote, as he explained, from memory, because his papers were scattered by the confusion of the Mexican invasion and his own long absence from the country; yet most of his statements of fact can be checked by independent documents which have been used in the preceding narrative. Concerning his motives he said:

"It is well known that nothing but injury to this country has resulted from the companies who have had colonization contracts in Texas. They have uniformly made it a matter of illegal speculation by selling 'Land

Scrip' and deceiving the ignorant and credulous in foreign countries. The credit of Texas and all faith in any of our land titles has been destroyed in the United States by such proceedings and emigration has been retarded rather than promoted by them. Besides this, it was very evident that the upper colony, if granted to a foreign company, would be again hung up for six years, as it had been by the Nashville Company, and thus have left the settlers in my colonies below exposed to the Indians; and what would have been still worse, that nothing but anarchy and perhaps civil war would have been produced within the limits of my old colonies, if a Foreign Empresario or Company were permitted to have anything to do with the distribution of the vacant land remaining there. . . .

"Under these circumstances it was a solemn and paramount duty in me to keep the land business within and adjoining my colonies as much under my own control as was possible. I should have failed in my obligations to the settlers if I had not done it, and should have merited censure from them. . . .

"I have performed many services to the people of my colonies and to Texas in general, and I consider that few of them was of more essential and vital importance than this one of procuring this colonization contract, and keeping off the foreign companies." [129]

[129] Austin to the Senate, December 5, 1836, Translations of Empresario Contracts, 236–241, General Land Office of Texas.

CHAPTER XII

Popular Disturbances of 1832

ERÁN'S military measures, as we have seen, scattered garrisons at strategic points to prevent the spread of the Anglo-American colonies and promote counter-colonization by Mexicans. With the most prudent and tactful conduct the commanders of these garrisons were likely to encounter friction, and without it trouble was certain. Unfortunately an American, Colonel John Davis Bradburn, was stationed at the head of Galveston Bay, an important post because it controlled the entrance to the unorganized East Texas settlements. Bradburn was irascible, arbitrary, and injudicious. His pretentiousness made him the butt of practical jokes and ridicule, which, lacking the good sense to ignore, he sought to punish with undue severity and very questionable authority. Expressing himself privately to Williams, Austin said of him, "The fact is he is incompetent to such a command and is half crazy part of his time." [1] Terán thoroughly understood the delicacy of the situation and instructed him with the greatest care. He was to establish himself and erect barracks on the bay shore at the mouth of the Trinity River. This was not within the limits of any active empresario contract and no one had a right to object. Galveston Island or Point Bolivar would be preferable for the location of a custom house, but they were subject to inundation and had no timber, which fact rendered them unsuitable for habitation. In the building of the barracks Bradburn would employ carpenters and workmen from the adjacent settlement of Atascosito, some fifteen miles distant, and would make every effort to establish cordial relations with all the inhabitants, assuring them that his object was to protect the colonies, pointing out that the troops would provide a market for much of their surplus production and urging them to avail themselves of the commercial

---

[1] Austin to Williams, June 20, 1832, Rosenberg Library, Galveston.

privileges of the law of April 6, 1830, by engaging in coasting trade to the south. He was to notify the alcaldes of his arrival, and was to prevent the soldiers from interfering in any way with the civil administration. The settlement at Atascosito, Terán explained, was built by accretions from the United States. It was originally unauthorized, but had been often assured of approval, and Bradburn was to convince the inhabitants that their interests were safe and invite them to act through him, without expense, in negotiations for their titles, which they had not yet obtained.[2]

These unauthorized settlements in East Texas, of which the one at Atascosito was typical, have appeared from time to time in this narrative, but, since they were to become the seat of much of the resentment aroused by Bradburn and were to be instrumental in precipitating an insurrection that threatened to hasten the Texas revolution by several years, a more comprehensive summary of their history is now necessary. As to their origin we need not bother much. There seems to have been a gradual infiltration of Anglo-Americans from the end of the eighteenth century. Their number was increased by the filibustering expeditions of 1812–1820. In 1823 the minister of relations wrote Saucedo that the government had credible information that "a multitude of Anglo-American families" had entered Texas "under pretext of the inundations which they have suffered on the banks of the Mississippi." Saucedo was to send some one to make an inspection, settle them provisionally until the passage of the colonization law, and exclude vagrants, idlers, and adventurers. Bastrop made the inspection and reported two hundred families between the San Jacinto and the Sabine, but most of them, he explained, were Spanish creoles.[3] In the spring of 1827, after the subsidence of the Fredonian rebellion, Colonel Ahumada visited the settlements east of Nacogdoches and heard another explanation of their origin. The settlers, he was told, had read Austin's advertisements in the New Orleans papers of October and November, 1821, and had started to join him. On arriving in East Texas they learned of his journey to Mexico. Then

[2] Terán to Bradburn, October 4, 1830, University of Texas Transcripts from Department of Guerra, Mexico, legajo 14, operaciones militares. There is also a copy, dated November 25.

[3] General Land Office of Texas, applications for land; *ibid.*, minister to political chief, August 20, 1823, Vol. 53, page 194; Bastrop to political chief, December 2, 1823, Nacogdoches Archives, Texas State Library.

followed various rumors—Austin was dead, his petition was rejected, the government was in confusion. In the meantime they stopped, made small clearings, and planted crops, obtaining for this a semblance of approval from James Dill, alcalde and commandant at Nacogdoches. With the passage of the imperial colonization law they felt secure and intended to apply for the land that they had occupied. Before they could act, however, the law was annulled, and the national law of 1824 reserved the border from foreign settlement; but by that time they had made valuable improvements and could not afford to move.[4] In its main outlines there is no reason to doubt the integrity of this version.

The principal border settlements, as we have seen, were at Ais, Tenaha, and Sabine, while to the westward lay Atascosito, on the Trinity River, and an unnamed settlement on the San Jacinto. The last, to the great gratification of the settlers, was incorporated in Austin's first colony.[5] That on the Trinity more than once petitioned for the same privilege, but never obtained it. Through Austin's efforts, however, it was approved by both state and federal government in 1828, and the inhabitants were promised titles.[6] The heartfelt gratitude of the settlement to Austin is expressed by George Orr: It was a "Grate Satisfaction to hear the Good Tidings that thrue your feling and kind Gratitud that you have persevered

---

[4] Ahumada to Bustamante, April 1, 1827, University of Texas Transcripts from Department of Fomento, Mexico, legajo 5, expediente 28.

[5] Austin to Saucedo, August 26, 1824; to Flores, November 6; Saucedo to Austin, September 21, 1824 (General Land Office of Texas, Translation of Records of Austin's first Colony, Vol. 1, page 18). John Cooke to Austin, December 3, 1824: "The settlers are all well pleased with being included in your colony."

[6] Humphrey Jackson wrote Austin, April 3, 1825: "The settlers on the east of San Jacinto is unanimous to Continue in your Collony. They are willing to sine any peti[ti]on for that purpose." On September 28, 1826, George Orr and Henry W. Munson transmitted to the political chief the result of a vote of the district and a petition praying the extension of the boundary of Austin's colony over it. They seem to have thought this all that was necessary, for they wrote Austin: "As we are now to be under your wing we hope you will find it convenient to call on us with the commissioner and put us quickly in a way to know where our lands are . . . we shall be grievously disappointed if the Commissioner does not visit us and set us to rights." In due time their petition was denied by the governor, because the land was covered by one of Vehlein's grants. (February 7, 1827, General Land Office of Texas, Translations, 351–352). Nothing daunted, they next addressed a petition to the commandant general, Bustamante, alleging as a claim to his attention their service in suppressing the Fredonian rebellion. Ahumada and Austin testified to their service and endorsed the petition (Land Office, Translations, 135–137; Austin to Bustamante, Transcripts from Department of Fomento, Mexico, legajo 4, expediente 8). On July 28, 1828, the governor approved the application and recommended it to the president, who must also approve because the Atascosito settlement was in the ten league coast reserve. The president approved August 27, 1828 (Land Office, Translations, 135–137, 224).

in obtaining a Grant for the Lands in this Sacsion of Contra from the honarable Government and I think the Setlers on this River should never forget you as their faithful friend."[7]

The border settlers passed through a similar period of suspense. They first presented themselves officially to the government in February, 1824, when they protested against the claim of Edmund Quirk to sixteen leagues of land covering all their improvements.[8] The question was not then determined, but they continued to occupy the land and extended their improvements. Following the Fredonian rebellion, which they opposed, they petitioned for titles. They were too compactly settled to allow each to have a league, but married men could receive four *labors* and unmarried men one without overlapping, and for this they asked. Colonel Ahumada, who inspected the settlements at this time, was very favorably impressed with their development, reporting wagon roads and ferries, mills for grinding wheat and corn, five gins—each capable of ginning two bales of cotton a day—herds of cattle and hogs, and houses ranging in cost from $200 to $800. The year before, he said, they had sold two hundred bales of cotton in Natchitoches. Not to follow in detail the hopes and disappointments of the settlers, on April 22, 1828, the president approved their settlements. The governor had previously approved, and thus the requirements of the national colonization law were complied with. It only remained to receive their titles from the commissioner.[9] This, too, was the apparently happy condition of the settlers on the Trinity, and from this point the two groups can be considered together.

In 1828 Juan Antonio Padilla, secretary of state, was appointed general land commissioner for Texas. Various delays prevented his arrival at San Antonio until November, 1829.[10] In February, 1830,

[7] Orr to Austin, February 18, 1829.

[8] John A. Williams and others to Saucedo, February 10, 1824, General Land Office of Texas, Vol. 53, page 197.

[9] Most of the documents for this paragraph are in University of Texas Transcripts from Department of Fomento, Mexico, legajo 5, expediente 28. The more important are: Saucedo to governor, March 19, April 18, 1827; Ahumada to Bustamante, April 1, 1827; and various statistical reports from the alcaldes of Ais, Tenaha, and Sabine. See also General Land Office of Texas, Translations, 357.

[10] His letters to Austin explain these delays. First he wants Austin to send him a carriage for the transportation of his family from Saltillo, next he finds it difficult to get a man to relieve him in the state department, and finally there is sickness in his family. See Padilla to Austin, April 9, June 14, July 12, November 29, December 13, 1828, January 24, November 26, 1829.

he was at Nacogdoches, and Thomas F. McKinney wrote Austin that his arrival had greatly improved conditions in East Texas. Before he could organize his office, however, and begin surveys and the granting of titles, he was arrested for embezzlement and murder, and his commission was suspended. This produced much excitement and alarm among the border settlers, who suspected that the arrest was merely a pretext to avoid giving them titles. To allay this feeling the political chief urged the governor to appoint a successor to Padilla without delay, and he responded with the appointment of J. Francisco Madero on September 27.[11]

Madero reached San Felipe January 14, 1831, and published in the *Texas Gazette* a notice of his plans. His intention was to begin on the Trinity, making his headquarters at George Orr's, and after concluding surveys and issuing titles there to proceed to the border settlements.[12] Bradburn saw the notice and wrote to inform Madero that it would be a violation of the law of April 6, 1830, as well as of that provision of the national colonization law reserving the coast and border leagues for him to issue such titles. Madero replied that it was his intention to seat only those settlers who had entered before the passage of the law of April 6, 1830, and that their settlements had been approved by both state and federal governments as the colonization law required; therefore he would proceed with his commission. The correspondence continued and became increasingly sharp until February 13, when Bradburn arrested Madero and his surveyor, José María Carbajal. Bradburn held that the law of April 6, 1830, being subsequent to the approval of the settlements, annulled the permission to grant titles, and in this Terán upheld him.[13]

Presently Madero was released. He made no further effort to issue titles, merely notifying the border settlements of what had befallen him; but before returning home he established an ayuntamiento at Atascosito, which he renamed, "village of the most holy Trinity of Liberty"—immediately shortened to Liberty. Bradburn

---

[11] Padilla to Austin, April 27, July 5, 1830, and to Viesca, May 11, Chambers to Austin, May 12, Austin to Viesca, May 31, McKinney to Austin, June 24; Viesca to Músquiz, April 28 and Músquiz to Viesca, June 6 (General Land Office of Texas, Translations, 296, 358); Madero to Músquiz (*ibid.,* Vol. 44, pages 1–3).

[12] *Texas Gazette,* January 15, 1831.

[13] Terán to minister of relations, March 24, 1831, University of Texas Transcripts from Department of Fomento, Mexico, legajo 6, expediente 36. The correspondence of Madero and Bradburn is in General Land Office of Texas, Vol. 44, pages 1–70.

annulled this in November, 1831, declaring that the town was within the ten league coast reserve and therefore outside Madero's jurisdiction. In its place he established, with Terán's approval, an ayuntamiento at Anahuac.[14] In the meantime, he had engaged in altercations with various inhabitants of the district, threatening arrest and creating a general feeling of alarm and exasperation.[15]

Austin, as we saw, had foreseen the clash between Madero and Bradburn, and exerted himself to keep his colonists free of trouble.[16] He tried also to prepare the settlers at Atascosito, sending from Saltillo a message which Williams was to forward. "What the people on the Trinity ought to say," he advised, "is that they cannot and ought not to take any part in any quarrel between any two officers or authorities, unless officially called on to do so by the competent superior authorities. If they take sides, they will in the end be kicked by both sides as a person who intermeddles in a quarrel between man and wife"[17]—hard advice to men so long in suspense, so often disappointed, who felt that Bradburn's interference had snatched from their very hands titles to their lands and security for the accumulations of years of laborious effort.

It is necessary to leave Bradburn now, for the moment, and turn to another source of friction—the establishment of the customs administration.[18] An editorial notice, probably written by Austin, in the *Texas Gazette* of May 8, 1830, announced the arrival of "Colonel Fisher, administrator of the port of Galveston." In the issue of the 22d Fisher spoke for himself, announcing that he had assumed the duties of his office, that he would establish the custom house temporarily at the mouth of the Brazos and place a deputy on Galveston Island, that vessels entering the port must show manifests of cargo, and that passengers must have passports. At the same time he asked Austin for a statement of the privileges enjoyed by his colonists and a list of the commodities whose importation was forbidden, such as tobacco. In the paper of June 5 he was more circumstantial: the "manifest must specify each bale, barrel, box,

[14] The principal documents for this paragraph are in the General Land Office of Texas, Vol. 44, page 75, and Vol. 53, pages 178–183.

[15] John A. Williams to Bradburn, February 25, 1831, and to Músquiz, no date, Nacogdoches Archives, Texas State Library.

[16] Above, pages 283, 324, and Austin to Williams, February 19, 1831, Rosenberg Library, Galveston.

[17] Austin to Williams, March 12, 1831, Rosenberg Library.

[18] For the early history of the Texas ports see above, pages 179–183.

package, or parcel, with its respective mark and number, describing the quantity and quality of the goods it contains, by specifying the number of pieces, measures, or weights of each parcel or package." Goods not so described or differing from the manifest would be seized, and passengers without passports would not be allowed to land.[19] In mid-stride Fisher was suspended. Terán postponed the establishment of the custom house because he thought the admission of foreign vessels to the coasting trade by the law of April 6, 1830, rendered it unnecessary.[20] Fisher, however, was not to be saved from a clash with the colonists by such a providence. The ayuntamiento of San Felipe employed him as secretary and dismissed him, after an unpleasant scene, for trying, as the record declares, to involve it in national politics by misrepresenting its acts and intentions.[21] In September, 1831, Terán again ordered Fisher to duty. Temporarily he was to establish the custom house at Anahuac but as soon as possible would erect buildings at Point Bolivar and at the mouth of the Brazos. Meantime, he would appoint a deputy for the Brazos at Brazoria.[22] With his passion for proclamations, Fisher issued an order on November 24 that caused a riot. No copy has come to light, but it is evident that the objectionable provision required

[19] *Texas Gazette*, May 8, 22, June 5, 1830. Fisher to Austin, May 18, 1830. Fisher was an interesting adventurer, a Serbian, who became a naturalized citizen of the United States in 1822, drifted to Mexico, and received this appointment apparently early in 1830. The first notice that we have of his appointment is a letter that he wrote Lorenzo de Zavala from New Orleans on February 10, 1830. He was a man of vivacious temperament, rather egotistical, and, at this stage of his career, certainly officious. His bustling self-importance is revealed by a letter in which he describes his multitudinous duties. He was presumably writing in English (to Andres Mauricio Voss of Vera Cruz, July 21, 1830, Mexico, Department of Relaciones, Asuntos Varios, 1830–1834, caja 2): "the office [is] laborious, for I am a compleat slave, attending to all the business connected with this aduana [custom house], viz, Administrador, Contador, Tesorero, Vista Guardo Almacen, Alcaide, and Resguardo, and allways on wings to attend to distant points on this coast, viz. Galveston Bay, Rio Trinidad, San Jacinto and Brazos, beside carry on immense correspondence, viz: Ministerio de Relaciones, de Hacienda, Commisaria General de San Luis Potosi, Commandancia General, Consulados Mejicanos [etc., etc.] . . . and to keep the following books, viz: Manual de Cargo, id. Data, id. Entrados y salidas de Caudales, id. de Buques, making out manifests and passenger lists in Spanish to be forwarded [etc.] . . . I assure you that since my arrival in this country I was as busy as I possibly could be; in day time travelling through a hot sun over large plains (prairie) destitute of shade or water, and sometimes even of provisions in passing from one point to another; and in the night despatching my correspondence, which I always carry with me in my portmanteau in a tin tube (at least the most necessary)," etc., etc.

[20] Terán to Fisher, May 24, 1830.

[21] "Minutes of the Ayuntamiento of San Felipe de Austin," *Southwestern Historical Quarterly*, XXII, 275–278.

[22] Terán to Fisher, September 27, November 19, 1831, University of Texas Transcripts from Department of Guerra, Mexico, operaciones militares, 1835, legajo 1.

vessels landing in the Brazos to obtain clearances from Fisher's office at Anahuac.[23] Austin wrote Bradburn that the regulations "as to their views are utterly impracticable and their execution is impossible." He advised the officer on the Brazos not to try to enforce them.[24]

The details of what happened we do not know. Evidently some vessels at Brazoria forced their way to sea despite the efforts of a small guard to detain them, and a soldier was wounded. Austin described the excitement as "terrible," and admitted that it carried him beyond himself and drew expressions from him that were given a much wider meaning by others than he intended.[25] Knowing that reports would soon reach Terán, he wrote to forestall them. The trouble was all due, he said, to Fisher's impracticable order, and signified no disloyalty to the government. He asked for a conference with Terán and begged him not to act hastily.[26] Terán was thoroughly angry and replied with a lecture on gratitude and obedience to the laws. He had strained his authority, he said, to favor the colonists. Only Congress could establish ports, but, knowing what use was made of the Brazos, he had intended from the beginning to have a deputy collector there. The arrival of this officer was delayed by contrary winds, which, after he embarked at Matamoras, took him to Tampico instead of Velasco. But why could they not have exercised a little patience? All Mexicans were subject to the tariff; duties were paid from Hudson's Bay to the Horn; and only at Brazoria were they considered cause for violence. He evidently felt that Austin was largely responsible, and particularly resented his letter of December 30 to Bradburn. But his conclusion was not rash. Tonnage duties of the delinquent vessels must be paid by the owners of goods that they had landed; and if the vessels again entered a Texas port with the same crews and registry, they were to be detained until they surrendered for trial those guilty of wound-

[23] Austin to Terán, January 8, February 5, 1832.

[24] Austin to Bradburn, December 30, 1831, Wagner collection, Yale University.

[25] Austin to Mrs. Holley, January 4, 14, February 19, 1832. P. E. Pearson, in the *Quarterly* of the Texas State Historical Association, IV, 33–35, tells of two vessels forcing their way past the fort at the mouth of the Brazos, but at this time there was no fort there, and it is not certain that the whole incident which he relates does not belong to a later disturbance. Pearson gives the name of one vessel as the *Sabine;* the other he does not name. Austin refers several times to the *Boston Packet.* Yoakum (*History of Texas,* I, 281) mentions a meeting at Brazoria on December 16, which he says sent commissioners to Bradburn to demand revocation of Fisher's order.

[26] Austin to Terán, January 8, 1832, Wagner collection, Yale University.

ing the soldier.[27] At the same time, though he did not admit it to Austin, Terán wrote Fisher that he had been unreasonable. A few months later, at Fisher's request, he relieved him and turned over to Fisher's deputy, Francisco Duclor, the administration of the custom house.[28]

In this action Terán was probably influenced by Austin, who urged the removal of Fisher as one of the essentials to avoiding a recurrence of friction. The people distrusted him, Austin explained, and believed that he was using his office to retaliate for his humiliation the year before by the ayuntamiento of San Felipe. In the same letter Austin recurred to his own position. He had entered into the excitement and had advised the soldiers not to try to enforce the objectionable order. "I knew very well that in a certain degree I compromised myself. My object was to preserve the public tranquillity and avert the ruin of the country, which would surely be the result of disorders. It was very important to calm their minds for the moment, and I was convinced that a few days of reflection would restore them all to their senses. This has happened. . . . It would be a lamentable misfortune," he continued, "if a man like George Fisher should destroy all that has been done in ten years to redeem this country from the wilderness. Every man who has anything to lose or who has three grains of common sense is opposed to separation from Mexico, and to all disorder, and I believe that it is very important to allow the momentary excitement to die of itself, as in effect it has already done; and if possible to remove Fisher, it would, in my mind, be conducive to the preservation of harmony."[29] Whatever Terán may have believed of the loyalty of the colonists, he harbored no lasting grievance against Austin. A few days before his death he wrote, in a tone of lament, one feels, "the affairs of Texas are understood by none but you and me, and we alone can regulate them"; but there was time, he said, to do no more than temporize.[30]

Austin was now long over-due at Saltillo. The legislature had

[27] Terán to Austin, January 27, 1832.
[28] Terán to Fisher, February 9, April 14, 1832, University of Texas Transcripts from Department of Guerra, Mexico, operaciones militares, 1835, legajo 1.
[29] Austin to Terán, February 5, 1832.
[30] Terán to Austin, June 25, 1832.

passed an urgent resolution requesting him to attend the session, and toward the middle of March he started. Had he been able to remain in Texas, the further developments of this year might have been different.[31] He took with him a memorial from the ayuntamiento of San Felipe praying for exemption from the tariff of 1827, for modification of the law of April 6, 1830, so as to permit immigration of good character from all nations, and suggesting the granting of titles to the settlers in East Texas.[32] Austin stopped at San Antonio to get the support of that ayuntamiento, which it gave rather grudgingly on condition that its address should be antedated so as to make it appear that the movement had originated there.[33]

Austin's anxiety is apparent in all his letters of this period. The burden of their message was patience and loyalty. Time would cure all evils. Thus: "If things can be kept quiet in the colony all will end right and prosperously, of this I have no doubt. What is needed there is a *dead calm*. All reflecting men will become convinced that the true interest of Texas is never to separate from Mexico, and that it is the true interest of this nation to encourage the population of Texas and make a state of it. This being the case, the government will remove the restrictions and the country will prosper." Moreover, there were more than a thousand soldiers in Texas, besides seven hundred at Matamoras, and a large garrison at Tampico; all could be thrown into Texas by sea in a few days, and further disturbance would be disastrous. From Saltillo he wrote that the memorial would reach the federal authorities with the endorsement of the state and would almost surely be granted. "The object is a very important one, and it is best to bear almost anything rather than jeopardize *all* by rashness and ill timed passion and imprudence.... Do try and impress this on every one, and especially on those in Brazoria who are rather warmer than they ought to be, tho perhaps not much more so than rigid justice requires." Again: "Prudence and a *dead calm* in the colony will insure a favorable answer to the memorial—imprudence and rashness, even if just cause is given,

---

[31] Governor Letona to Austin, January 21, 1832; Austin to Perry, March 6; to Williams, March 21, from Bexar (Rosenberg Library, Galveston).

[32] The memorial is dated February 18, 1832. There is a copy in the Austin Papers and another in the Bexar Archives.

[33] Austin to Williams, March 21, 1832, Rosenberg Library, Galveston.

will totally defeat everything and ruin all. My motto, 'Fidelity to Mexico,' ought to be in every man's mouth, and repeated instead of many other things that are said over cups and in moments of heat." The removal of Fisher was the text of a final sermon: "How silly and imprudent the best of us will talk and act sometimes when under excitement. . . . I can assure the whole colony and all Texas that nothing but the outrageous imprudence of the people themselves will bring trouble on that country. If the whole of the settlers will adopt my motto, *Fidelity to Mexico,* and act and talk in conformity, they will flourish beyond their own expectations." [34]

Two cannon at Brazoria gave him particular uneasiness. The authorities would misunderstand their presence there, and in a measure they would encourage truculence in the colonists. Anticipating an investigation by the government, he reminded Williams of their history. They had been removed from the steamboat *Ariel* in 1829, with other heavy ballast, to enable the boat to get over the Brazos bar. He urged their sale to Bradburn, who had offered to buy them; and later offered himself to pay for them if the inhabitants would donate them to the custom house at Velasco. [35]

Assuming that the crisis had passed with the removal of Fisher, Austin determined to visit Terán at Victoria and not return to Texas until after the short session of the legislature in September. This plan, however, did not take into account the growing unpopularity of Bradburn. From the mass of contemporary material on Bradburn's imprudences certain charges stand out: (1) He pressed supplies for his troops, and used slave labor without compensation in the erection of military buildings; (2) he encouraged a spirit of revolt among the slaves by telling them that it was the intent of the law to make them free, and harbored and refused to surrender two runaway slaves from Louisiana; (3) he arrested a number of the colonists at various times and held them for military trial. It was the last that brought the storm upon him. Patrick C. Jack organized a militia company, and was arrested on some charge that is not clear. William B. Travis, as an attorney, undertook to recover two fugitive slaves from Bradburn, and found himself in the guard

---

[34] Austin to Williams, March 21, April 9, 12, 28, 1832, Rosenberg Library, Galveston.
[35] Austin to Williams, March 21, April 28, 1832, Rosenberg Library.

house with Jack.[36] Other arrests followed. The detention of Travis and Jack seems to have been long and aggravated, and on June 4 a force started from Brazoria to release them. On the way it grew to a hundred and sixty men, and the men of the Sabine border were ready to join. Colonel Ugartechea, commanding the garrison at Velasco, realized the gravity of the situation and sent Lieutenant Dominguez with John Austin to urge Bradburn to release the prisoners. After some skirmishing Bradburn agreed to this, and the attackers withdrew, but he seized the opportunity to strengthen his position and then defied them. Thinking it unwise to attack again without artillery, the insurgents went into camp and sent for the two cannon at Brazoria. They employed their leisure by declaring their adherence to Santa Anna, who was leading a liberal revolution against Bustamante's administration.

Meantime, Piedras was marching from Nacogdoches, but he had a better conception of the situation than Bradburn had, and his object was peace, not war. Arriving in the vicinity of the camp, he entered into negotiations and signed an agreement to turn the prisoners over to the civil authority for trial, to pay for the private property used by Bradburn, and to endeavor to obtain Bradburn's removal from the command—a pledge which he redeemed by tactfully inducing Bradburn to ask to be relieved. Though he had no confidence in the loyalty of the colonists, Piedras was convinced that hostility to Bradburn was the motive of the uprising. Bradburn he said, had committed grave imprudences under the influence of a convict clerk named Ugarte, "a mean and meddlesome man." Appointing Bradburn's adjutant, Juan Cortina, to command at Anahuac, Piedras returned to Nacogdoches, and the colonists dispersed.[37]

The settlement was not effected in time, however, to prevent serious fighting at Velasco, because Ugartechea refused to let a

[36] Terán wrote Governor Letona, May 21, 1832 (General Land Office of Texas, Vol. 53, page 163), that he understood there were some men "with the title of lawyers" stirring up civil and political discord at Anahuac, and asked if the state laws permitted "wandering foreigners, without domicile, and some even without a country, to practice law without a license."

[37] Edna Rowe, "The Disturbances at Anahuac in 1832," *Quarterly* of Texas State Historical Association, IV, 265–299, follows Bradburn's actions in considerable detail. Besides the sources that she uses, there are some important documents in General Land Office of Texas, Vol. 53.

vessel leave the Brazos with the cannon to be used against Anahuac. Both sides suffered considerable loss in a battle on June 26, and on the 29th Ugartechea signed a capitulation allowing the garrison the honors of war and providing for the transportation of the soldiers to Matamoras.[38]

News of the movement against Bradburn reached San Antonio on June 18 in letters from Ugartechea. The next day Ramón Músquiz received letters from Miguel Arciniega, Williams, and Thomas Jefferson Chambers at San Felipe. All expressed the belief that the uprising had no political significance, that it was directed against Bradburn personally, and that the presence of the political chief and the prestige of his authority would quickly restore order. The ayuntamiento of San Felipe officially invited him to come, which he did without delay, arriving on June 24. His observations on the way convinced him of the peaceful disposition of most of the colonists, and with the assistance of the ayuntamiento, Williams, and others, the greatest exertions began to prevent excitement from spreading. A joint meeting of the ayuntamiento and sixty citizens of San Felipe adopted resolutions expressing "regret, sorrow, and disapprobation for the imprudent and precipitate action at Anahuac and Brazoria," and urging those in arms to return to their homes and await investigation of their complaints by the civil authorities. This, with an address from Músquiz, was circulated through all the settlements and sent by the ayuntamiento to the insurgents at Anahuac and Velasco.[39] Músquiz was reassured, and, though rumors of the movement against Velasco had reached him, wrote Colonel Elosua that "the opinion of the colonists is generally in favor of the government." On June 30 the ayuntamiento, with Músquiz presiding, sent out a call for a convention at San Felipe on July 7. This, signed by Horatio Chriesman, Josiah H. Bell, Martin Allen, Henry Cheves, and Rawson Alley, exhorted the people to remember the hardships of 1821–1822 and the liberality of the Mexican government in admitting them to the territory and giving

---

[38] The principal sources for this engagement are to be found in the Nacogdoches Archives and in the Lamar Papers in the Texas State Library, and in Holley, *Texas* (1833), 141–167.

[39] Proceedings of the ayuntamiento, June 25, and the proclamation of Músquiz of the same day are in Nacogdoches Archives, Texas State Library, as are the other documents used in this paragraph. The address of the ayuntamiento "To the Citizens and Inhabitants of Austin's Colony under arms against the military post of Anahuac," June 26, 1832, is in the Lamar Papers, Texas State Library.

them land; let them now repay that generosity by inducing "our deluded and unfortunate fellow citizens to return to their homes." This summons was spread by fast riders instructed to "spare neither horseflesh nor labor"; every man must stick to the government. The meeting, duly held, was attended by several hundred men, and adopted resolutions declaring loyalty and obedience to the federal and state constitutions and laws.[40]

Before this many districts had already held meetings—Bastrop, the lower Colorado and Lavaca settlements, the lower Brazos, Liberty, and Ais.[41] Though the feeling was general that Bradburn had been harsh and indiscreet and had unwarrantedly interfered with civil authority, it is evident that the people did not want the trouble to spread. Only at Brazoria was there a belligerent spirit, and that was quick to feel the chill of disapproval from the rest of Texas. William H. Wharton railed at the "toryish spirit" of San Felipe, and complained that the insurgents were receiving as much opposition from their own countrymen as from the Mexicans. He wished that he might spend a few days at San Felipe; and thought that he could "reason some of these fellows into sense and cowhide the balance into rags."[42] But a careful observer, Thomas J. Pilgrim, wrote that the people of Brazoria were "decidedly opposed to any further hostile operations and anxious to enjoy peace and repose. . . . They have been excited thus far, I believe, by false representations and could the truth come before them I think it would allay the excitement and restore order."[43] Undoubtedly the desire to avoid further trouble was sincere, but the expressions of loyalty to the government may be dismissed as little more than lip service to that end. There was no positive approval or veneration for the government—hardly more than toleration. Músquiz seems, however, to have been satisfied, and wrote the governor on July 9 that peace and order were restored. The suppression of the disturbance had aroused some personal ill feeling among the colonists, however, which he thought only the influence of Austin could remove, and for that reason he asked the governor to excuse Austin from

---

[40] Proceedings of the meetings of June 30, July 7, Nacogdoches Archives, and Williams to Sims, July 1, 1832, Lamar Papers.

[41] The proceedings of these meetings are partly in the Nacogdoches Archives and partly in the Lamar Papers.

[42] Wharton to Brazoria Committee, July 4, 1832, Lamar Papers.

[43] Pilgrim to Williams, June 30, 1832, Nacogdoches Archives.

attendance upon the legislature, and, if he were in Saltillo, to send him home "to exert his influence to prevent any personal conflict and a renewal of disturbances." [44]

Austin was now at Matamoras. He had left Saltillo on May 12 and traveled by Monterey, Pelon, Linares, and Victoria through heat and drought to Terán's headquarters at the Hacienda del Cojo, twenty leagues back of Tampico. He wrote Williams on June 15. It was his intention then to return to Saltillo to rest and recuperate in that delightful climate until after the session of the legislature in September. He enclosed a copy of a federal act extending for two years the privilege of importing certain articles into Texas free of duty. The law was not as liberal as he desired, and contained some queer anomalies—why, for example, should whisky be admitted free? He wanted the ayuntamiento to frame another petition, asking tariff exemption for tools, furniture, carts and wagons, iron and steel, and cotton bagging and bale rope, and that whisky and lumber be removed from the free list. It would not do to go further, he said, and nothing else ought to be mentioned. He had found Terán in the midst of his army, ill, perplexed, and overwhelmed with business, having just retreated from Tampico before Santa Anna forces. Nevertheless, they had had considerable conversation about Texas, and Terán was friendly. He favored repeal of the eleventh article of the law of April 6, 1830, and the further extension of commercial privileges. He had returned Fisher to Texas and established the custom house the year before, he explained, because he was informed that more goods entered Brazoria for the interior than paid duty at Matamoras. "He says," Austin reported, "that what the settlers need for their own use is of no consequence, and if goods could be prevented from being taken from Texas to the interior, no custom house would be established there for many years ... that every indulgence would be allowed on all articles for the necessary use of the settlers, but that the utmost rigor would be used as to light and fancy dry goods suitable for the interior trade." "By the by," Austin added, "this interior trade has never been carried on from Brazoria or Galveston[45] ... and I hope for the future our merchants will let it alone. It is more important at this time to encourage

---

[44] The letter is in the Nacogdoches Archives.
[45] It had gone mostly, though Austin does not say so, through Goliad.

the farmers than the merchants." On his return through Monterey he would try, he said, to enlist the influence of friends who could move the new ministry in Mexico to modify the law of April 6, 1830. The tone of the letter is optimistic, even cheerful: "These long trips in the sun through such a wilderness as this country, totally destitute of every comfort for the traveller, are truly wearisome to the body, to the health, to the patience, and to the mind, but if I can do any good to the colony I shall feel myself well compensated for all." [46]

On the 19th Austin wrote a long letter to Horatio Chriesman, the alcalde of San Felipe. He intended it for the colony, but did not want it published. He did not hear of the trouble with Bradburn until the next day, but the letter is almost prophetic in its anticipation of contingencies that arose. After expressing the belief that the republicans would triumph in the next election and place civil power "where it ought to be in all republics"—above the military —he voiced the fear that a conflict might develop on the Trinity before the reformation could be effected. The thing to do in that event was to act with great circumspection. Let the ayuntamiento make a formal record of any misdoings of the military and file it with a complaint in the hands of the political chief. "But should acts occur of so flagrant a nature that public indignation could not be restrained, a thing which my knowledge of military operations generally in Texas causes me to fear may happen, great care must be taken not to do or say anything against the government—*take great care and use great prudence* on this point. If any public act, or publication is made, head it with 'Fidelity and obedience to the laws and the constitution and nation,' or something of that kind. ... Let all be done calmly, not one rash or abusive word ought to be used—nothing that indicates passion or excitement or *personal* feelings or animosity of a *personal* nature against any one. Let all be mild, decorous, and respectful, but clear and firm—in short, let it be a plain, open, and unvarnished statement of facts"—and all in both Spanish and English. That such a publication, if one became necessary, might be dignified and forceful, Austin suggested a committee—P. W. Grayson and Dr. Branch T. Archer for the English and T. J. Chambers, Alexander Greaves, and Father Mul-

[46] Austin to Williams, June 15, 1832, Rosenberg Library, Galveston.

doon for the Spanish. His own motto of *"adherence and fidelity to Mexico"* had gained great benefits for the colonists; and he recommended it for "the standing popular toast." It would remove unjust Mexican prejudice and would exert a restraining influence and keep down impetuous outbursts of impatience in the colonies.

One of his fixed rules of action for Texas, Austin said, had been "that with respect to her rights *she must always act on the defensive and never on the offensive.*" This really explained what no doubt seemed to some inconsistency in his attitude toward the events at Brazoria in December and January. He then at first believed that they would be attacked: "Mexico was at peace; the whole force of the country could have been turned against them; the press was muzzled; there was no liberal party to raise its voice in favor of justice; and the masses were prejudiced against all foreigners." He therefore thought it necessary to prepare for defense, but in the midst of the excitement the mail arrived with news of Santa Anna's rising at Vera Cruz, and the development of liberal principles; he had also "some information of a peculiar nature" which influenced him; he became convinced that the government could not move against Texas; and then, true to his principle, he stopped the preparations. "But," he went on, "much had been said, something had been done, and much had been written; to unsay, undo, and unwrite all this was awkward and embarrassing, for at a superficial view it looked like inconsistency. [Nevertheless] I did not [hesitate to set] *to work undoing* [*and unwriting*]." The memorial of the ayuntamiento for tariff exemption was a step in this direction, "to allay public feeling by *giving* something for hope and expectation to feed upon." He was sure they had acted wisely; conditions in Mexico had now greatly changed, and with patience and loyalty in Texas all would come right, "and this country will be a flourishing state of the Mexican confederation and a firm and efficient supporter of Mexican liberty and of its national rights. This is the station I wish to see that country occupy and the one which I have no doubt it will occupy."

On one point Austin thought it particularly necessary to warn the alcalde: the military were a privileged class; no matter what the offense, a soldier could not be tried by a civil judge—"a most infamous and unrepublican principle," he thought, but one sanctioned by the constitution and the laws. "Take great care," he enjoined, "and have all the law as well as all the justice on your side, for you see that under this military system what is law is sometimes very far from justice." [47]

The same day Austin wrote Ugartechea — a cordial, newsy, friendly letter, but, as always, one with a purpose—seeking to give him, very subtly and indirectly, the clue to handling the colonists. If they could be once convinced of the government's sympathetic interest in the progress of Texas—which he now believed it felt— the laws, even the tariff laws, would execute themselves. It was Ugartechea's problem, by his conduct, to effect this understanding.[48]

No better illustration could be found of Austin's never-ceasing labor for Texas—and, it must be said, for Mexico. Mutual understanding and forbearance were indispensable to the welfare of both. Prudence, patience under provocation, and strict adherence to the law the colonists must practice; but at the same time intelligent Mexican officers must know the nature of the elements they were dealing with and be prepared to make allowances.

The next day news of the attack on Bradburn reached Matamoras, and Austin elaborated his first letter to Ugartechea: 'With the constitution and the law in hand, the colonists could be led by a thread, but nothing could be done with them by illegal means or means they believed to be illegal; it was Bradburn's disregard of this characteristic, and not disloyalty to the government, that had caused the outbreak.' Therefore, Ugartechea was to infer, though Austin was much too shrewd to say it, that no drastic measures would be required to restore order.[49] At the same time he wrote Williams, who was to be the mouthpiece for his counsel to the colonists: "We have a wild account of difficulties at Anahuac. The course to be taken is a very simple and plain one. Let a full statement of all the facts be made out judicially, keeping certified judicial records, and send them on to the chief of department. This is the only legal and correct course, and it will put all things right.

---

[47] Austin to Horatio Chriesman, June 19, 1832, Rosenberg Library, Galveston. This letter is in a very fragmentary condition, and much of what is quoted here is supplied by the context—parts of words and sometimes phrases—but to indicate these reconstructions would needlessly confuse the reader. The letter will be published elsewhere in full, in a comprehensive collection of Austin's writings.

[48] Austin to Ugartechea, June 19, 1832.

[49] Austin to Ugartechea, June 20, 1832.

The reign of military power is over I think, and justice may now speak openly and plainly. Let a copy of the facts be published in the paper, but treat the government and the officers with respect. Even when the latter have to be censured, let it be in mild and very decorous language—nothing inflammatory or passionate. But above all things, keep down popular commotions and all acts of violence." The compelling reason for this he explained: "Now is a critical time. It is said that a new and liberal party are getting up. Pray try and keep the people there from any acts that may be construed into opposition to the government, for *that will turn all parties against us.*"[50]

That Austin did not consider the situation particularly threatening is evident from the fact that he still intended to return to Saltillo. Terán, too, took it calmly, ordering Ugartechea to relieve Bradburn of his command and asking Austin to use his influence to allay excitement.[51] In furtherance of this request Austin wrote Ugartechea on the 27th a frank statement of his views.[52] On the 29th he wrote again, saying that Bradburn's arbitrary course had convinced the settlers that there was no law but that of the strongest; and that Ugartechea must cooperate with the political chief in proving that the rule of the constitution was restored. Specifically, he advised reestablishment of the ayuntamiento of Liberty, immediate provision for giving the eastern settlers the titles they had been promised, and assurance that the régime of arbitrary arrests and imprisonment was at an end. Ugartechea must not be offended by his bluntness, Austin pleaded: he had devoted the best years of his life to the development of Texas, and felt for each person there, whether colonist or native Mexican, the interest of a father for his family.[53]

At the same time Austin wrote Terán a fearless criticism of the government's policy toward Texas. Only a great respect and mutual understanding between the two men could have made such plain speaking possible without offense. Starting with the tariff, he said that it demonstrated the utter ignorance of the government of the sort of protection needed by a purely agricultural country. Iron, steel, tools, wagons, carts, household and kitchen furniture, and

[50] Austin to Williams, June 20, 1832, Rosenberg Library, Galveston.
[51] Terán to Austin, June 25, 1832; to Ugartechea, June 29.
[52] This letter has not been found. Austin refers to it in his letter of the 29th.
[53] Austin to Ugartechea, June 29, 1832.

cotton bagging and baling rope must pay duty, but whisky was admitted free—what a benefit to industry, good morals, peace, and harmony! On the contrary, whisky was a curse to the country; the price in New Orleans was so low that, with admission free, everybody could intoxicate himself at little cost. Fisher should be removed from the custom house and never returned to Texas in any public employment; the law of April 6, 1830, should be reformed; and all troops ought to be withdrawn, except barely enough to guard the frontier. Every additional soldier would endanger the tranquillity of the country; in fact, he believed firmly that until the army was reduced and military privilege abolished there could be no hope of peace, stability, and advancement in Mexico. This and religious toleration were two reforms that were indispensable, and the man who could bring them about would deserve to be called the Washington of Mexico.[54]

The significance of this letter is heightened by a glance at the political condition of Mexico. In December, 1831, a quiet, well conducted revolt had been launched from Vera Cruz, having for its object the removal of Bustamante's ministers, who were held responsible for the centralistic policy of his administration. Santa Anna emerged from retirement at Manga de Clavo to lead the movement. Liberals in all parts of the country pricked up their ears. Bustamante refused to dismiss the ministers or, at first, to accept their resignations. In May, however, they did retire, but by that time it was no longer possible to control the revolt. The presidential election was due in the fall, and moderates of both parties began to look toward Terán as a compromise candidate. Nothing would have pleased Austin better than to have seen Terán elected to the presidency. He had confidence in Terán's honesty; and believed that, so far as the ignorance and prejudices of his people permitted, Terán would govern liberally. Terán's loyalty to Bustamante and his distrust of Santa Anna prevented him from lending himself to this program, and with one source of his hesitation Austin ventured to argue.

"I think [he wrote] that the party that has risen against the ministry is very badly named the party of Santa Anna. As I understand the situation,

---

[54] Austin to Terán, June 27, 1832, in Filisola, *Memorias para la Historia de la Guerra de Tejas*, I, 231–236.

it ought to be called the *democratic republican federal party*. It appears to have made use of Santa Anna for lack of another leader and this has given his name to the party, which seems to me to be a misfortune, because it gives a *personal* character when it ought to be named for principles. It appears that this party is very strong and that sooner or later it will embrace the great mass of the nation and triumph as it has done in the north and also in England and France, with a difference of form and men; and I do not doubt that in the end it will triumph over all Europe and the Americas. It is the natural order. Water flows down hill; and man rises from a state of nature to civilization and the sciences, from slavery to freedom, advancing as by the steps of a ladder. These are laws of nature, at times retarded and slow in their operation, but certain in their results."

No finer confession of faith in democracy can be imagined. Nor can Austin's earnestness and sincerity be doubted. He had little faith in Santa Anna and did not believe that his party would follow him beyond the overthrow of the existing government. Perhaps the party itself would fail now because it lacked leadership, but the nation would learn by its failures and ultimately a real republic would develop.[55]

It is characteristic of Austin's thoroughness and attention to every detail that might affect the fortunes of Texas that, though he had little expectation of Santa Anna's remaining at the head of the Liberal party, he took the trouble to explain to him the condition of Texas and to expound incidentally some of the obligations of a republic. One of these obligations was to foster a free press, another to govern by constitution and not by military force. A free press was the battery, pen and ink the small arms, and sound principles the balls and shells with which well disseminated and united public opinion beat down aristocratic privilege and abuse. Through it constitutional democracy had triumphed in the United States; why should it not have the same effect in Mexico? Perhaps it might be answered that the masses there were too backward, too lacking in education; that their judgment must be trained before they would be qualified to enjoy the advantages of a free press; but this would be equivalent to sealing up in a dark room without a ray of light a man with weak eyes in order to prepare him for the brilliant

[55] Austin to Williams, April 9, 28, 1832; and to Chriesman, June 19, 1832, Rosenberg Library, Galveston.

light of the sun, and so weakening his eyes still further under pretext of strengthening them. As for the military, was it not they who insulted the Mexican flag by disregarding the constitution, rather than those who endeavored to maintain the constitution by resisting them? Yet the colonists had been suspected and misunderstood for doing this very thing. They had in fact, he declared, no other desire than to remain firmly united to Mexico under the federal system, and would never think of separation except as a last resort to save themselves from utter ruin.[56]

Finally Austin wrote to Governor Letona,[57] and with this the circle of his labors was for the time complete. He had planted his explanations in every quarter where misunderstanding could accrue to the injury of Texas, and, so far as it could be done, had impressed upon the colonists the importance of further patience and forbearance, so as not to prejudice themselves with the rising Liberal party. His well-tried policy of aloofness was not to be abandoned. He wrote Williams on July 1:

"The course for the people there to take in the present distracted state of the nation is to declare *that they will take no part in the civil war at all; that they will do their duty strictly as Mexican citizens; that they will adhere to Mexico and to the general and state constitution, and resist any unjust attacks upon either by any or by all parties no matter who they may be.* This must be the basis of all they do, or say—that is, should they find themselves bound to do or say anything to protect their personal security and property from unjust and arbitrary attacks. But should there be no such necessity they ought not to say, or do, anything. A dead calm is the best."

The vessel that was to have taken this letter was lost on the bar before getting to sea, and the next day Austin wrote again. To sustain the constitution and authority of the state and to adhere firmly to Mexico and the Mexican confederation should be the burden of all their actions and declarations. If the conditions required it, but not otherwise, they should approve "the principles of the democratic constitutional federal party."

Austin's plan when he wrote was still to return to Saltillo, visiting Terán on the way with the object of getting "such orders as

[56] Austin to Santa Anna, July 6, 1832.
[57] July 9, 1832.

will put all matters in Texas at rest." But events at Matamoras compelled a reversal of this plan.

On June 28 Colonel José Antonio Mexia had entered Matamoras with several hundred soldiers of the Liberal army and Colonel Guerra with the government forces had retired. Austin wrote Williams that he had never seen anything conducted with such good order—"one party quietly marched off towards San Fernando, and the other as quietly marched in and took up quarters in the barracks." On July 2 General Terán, in a spell of despondency, killed himself; and, as reports from Texas became more and more alarming, Mexia and Guerra on July 6 agreed to an armistice so that Mexia could sail to Texas, look into the situation, relieve the garrisons, and prevent the dismemberment of the province. By the desire of both, Austin agreed to accompany Mexia to assist in restoring order, though he was careful to explain very emphatically that he knew there was no insurrection against the government and that the integrity of the national territory was not in danger. Indeed he wrote Guerra—what was probably still true—that if the government should proclaim the freedom of Texas to secede at will, the answer of the people would be: "Let the constitution of the nation and state be observed, and we will never consent to such a secession." [58]

Mexia arrived at the mouth of the Brazos July 16, and the history of the next few days reads like *opéra bouffe*. After a conference with John Austin—supervised we may be sure by Stephen F. Austin—Mexia wrote a formal statement of the object of his visit: it was to preserve the integrity of the national territory; if secession was the purpose of the uprising, it would be his duty to suppress it; but if, as he was informed, its purpose was to support the plan of Vera Cruz, he would unite with and protect the colonists. To this there could be but one reply: that the people were loyal to Mexico and to the liberal cause upheld by Santa Anna. [59] Mexia and Austin were escorted to Brazoria, where they were received with speeches and salute of cannon and entertained at a "Santa Ana dinner and

[58] Austin to Williams, July 1, 1832, Rosenberg Library, Galveston; Guerra to Austin, July 7, Mexia to Austin, July 8, Austin to Mexia, July 9 and to Guerra, July 10, Nacogdoches Archives, Texas State Library.

[59] Mexia to John Austin, July 16, 1832, and Austin's reply, July 18, in Holley, *Texas,* etc. (1833), 155. There is a draft of John Austin's reply in the hand of Stephen F. Austin.

ball." [60] On the 24th Mexia sailed to Anahuac to spread the doctrine of liberalism there, only to find that the garrison had already declared for Santa Anna and embarked for Tampico. The same day Colonel Piedras wrote from Nacogdoches that a declaration for Santa Anna was brewing there, and a week later, after a sharp battle and considerable loss, he was compelled to evacuate the garrison. The soldiers thereupon declared for Santa Anna and were escorted from the country.[61] Toward the end of August Ruiz retired to San Antonio, much against the wishes of the settlers around Tenoxtitlan, and the military measures of General Terán were completely undone. Only the ancient garrisons at San Antonio and Goliad remained.

Circumstances had finally driven Austin from his settled policy of aloofness. The civil war had reached Texas, and it was no longer possible to avoid taking sides. Fortunately he had already formed a high opinion of the sincerity and patriotism of the Liberal party, and public adoption of its cause now did no violence to his personal convictions. On July 18 he wrote the political chief that the happiness and peace of the nation demanded adherence to the plan of Santa Anna, and he advised an immediate pronunciamento to that effect, emphasizing the fact that the movements in Texas were not directed against the integrity of the national territory but to the maintenance of the constitutional rights of the people. On the 28th he wrote again—the party of Santa Anna was truly the liberal republican and constitutional party and should be supported; there was no secession sentiment in Texas, no disloyalty, no hostility to any Mexican officers except Bradburn and Fisher; but there was a strong desire for separation from Coahuila, and until it was obtained neither peace, progress, nor efficient government could be expected. Bexar must take the lead. It must pronounce for Santa Anna, protest against the law of April 6, 1830, and against the tariff and the abuses of the military power, and, above all, it must be the first to urge separation from Coahuila. Lukewarm measures would now be ruinous; they must adopt a party and publicly support it. On the 26th and 27th, under Austin's direction, the ayuntamiento

[60] An invitation to this affair on July 21 is preserved in the Nacogdoches Archives, Texas State Library.
[61] The documents covering the events at Nacogdoches are in the Nacogdoches Archives, Texas State Library.

and people of San Felipe adopted resolutions to this effect and forwarded them through the political chief to the governor. Músquiz, however, was extremely doubtful about a declaration, fearing that it would be misunderstood even by the Liberals. The colonists must be even more circumspect than native citizens, he said, and while he endorsed the objects of the resolutions, he thought this an unseasonable time to advance them.

On August 15 Austin wrote again to Músquiz. The people were convinced, he said, that the Liberals were trying in good faith to restore constitutional government without distinction of persons, parties, or names, and he did not believe that they would recede from their declaration. They had never desired separation from Mexico, but they had "with their toil and labor redeemed the country from a state of wilderness, without one dollar of expense to the nation, and they expect in return to be governed according to the spirit of the constitution and the federal system and in a manner adequate to the necessities of the country and their own interest." "Man," he continued, "seeks happiness in the improvement of his condition. This is a natural and invariable law—a law that will bind Texas to Mexico with stronger ties than the force of large armies. With a due regard to this law and the true spirit of the system of government that rules the nation, no one could harbor a suspicion that Texas would ever secede." [62] Finally the strain was relieved by the adhesion of San Antonio, on August 30, to the Santa Anna cause, but there is evidence that the authorities there—and we may suppose those higher up—continued to look with suspicion and distrust upon the movements in the colonies. [63]

One is tempted to speculate on what would have been the course of events had Austin not been absent during the development of the clash at Anahuac. Before leaving for the legislature he had had a conference with Bradburn and exacted a pledge that he would respect the civil authorities and conciliate the people, as in fact Terán had instructed him to do. Had Austin been on the ground, he might have influenced Bradburn to greater moderation or the

[62] Austin to Músquiz, July 18, 28, August 15, 1832, Músquiz to ayuntamiento of San Felipe and to Austin, August 4, Nacogdoches Archives, Texas State Library.

[63] Austin to Elosua, August 21 and Elosua's reply, August 30, 1832. See also Músquiz to the governor, August 27, Nacogdoches Archives. The declaration of Goliad for the Plan of Santa Anna is described by Thomas G. Western to Austin, August 24, 25, 1832.

people to greater forbearance. Pretty certainly he would have controlled John Austin and thereby have prevented the battle at Velasco. This alone would have been sufficient to hold back the Mexia expedition and thus would have avoided the necessity for abandoning the policy of aloofness. That, however, was now passed. Much water had flowed under the bridge, and Austin wrote Williams, "We must now all pull at the same end of the rope . . . right or wrong, we must all pull together."

The sudden turn of events caused by Mexia's arrival created a very uncomfortable situation for those who had been working feverishly to restore tranquillity on the old basis of loyalty and obedience to the existing government. At Brazoria the resentment against Williams and Chambers, who had been most active, was manifested by hanging them in effigy. Austin's counsel to Williams in these circumstances sheds a good deal of light on his own philosophy of conduct: "These things [are] to be expected everywhere and amongst all people under excitement. They have their hour and pass away and are forgotten. All that is necessary for you to do or say is, that you wished to do for the best—may have been mistaken as to the means, that nothing but an anxious desire to serve the common cause of the country actuated you, without personal feeling against any one. . . . Something of this nature, and in a good humored way, without any display of passion or irritation will soon put it all at rest. . . . It will do you no harm unless you get into a passion about it—so keep quite cool and let it all pass away. . . . In short, vale mas reir que maldecir"—it is better to laugh than curse.[64]

[64] Austin to Williams, July 19, 20, 1832, Rosenberg Library, Galveston.

CHAPTER XIII

The Conventions of 1832 and 1833

THE convention of 1832 was no doubt a natural outgrowth of the conditions that we have just been following. By good luck the settlers seemed to be on the crest of the Santa Anna wave; what could be more reasonable, therefore, than a formal statement of their grievances and a petition for liberal reforms? No contemporary discussion of the propriety of a convention has survived. The official call was issued on August 22 and was signed by Horatio Chriesman and John Austin, first and second alcaldes of San Felipe. It is doubtful whether Stephen F. Austin fully approved the meeting, but the language of the call is probably his, trying to present the movement to the authorities with the best face possible. The civil wars and violations of the constitution that had plagued Mexico so long had finally reached Texas, said the announcement, and the spontaneous, unorganized resistance of the scattered districts had been misunderstood and misrepresented, so that a convention was necessary to proclaim the loyalty of the people to Mexico and to the liberal cause represented by Santa Anna. Besides, the restlessness of the Indians on all the frontiers required the formulation of a system of defense. Therefore the various settlements were requested to send five representatives each to a meeting at San Felipe on October 1. Of the local elections we have no account, but at the appointed time fifty-eight delegates assembled, representing sixteen districts. In a brief address John Austin outlined the reasons for the meeting, adding to the reasons previously given the necessity of petitioning for repeal of the exclusion article of the law of April 6, 1830, for reform of the tariff, and for the extension of land titles to the settlers in East Texas. The convention then organized by electing Stephen F. Austin president over William H. Wharton, and F. W. Johnson secretary over Charles S. Taylor of Nacogdoches.

The work of the convention moved with a rapidity that suggests considerable preparation before the meeting. A committee of which Jared E. Groce was chairman reported, and the convention adopted, a brief petition on the tariff, embodying the substance of the memorial sent up by the ayuntamiento of San Felipe the preceding February. It requested, for three more years, duty-free admission of farming implements and machinery, clothing, household and kitchen furniture, tobacco, ammunition, medicine, books, and stationery, explaining that these were the principal imports needed in Texas and that some of them were excluded and others in effect prohibited by the exorbitant duties of the recent tariff. William H. Wharton wrote the report of the committee on amendment of the act of April 6, 1830.[1] Though less tactfully phrased than Austin might have desired, it was respectful in tone. It declared the effect of the eleventh article of the law to be the exclusion of substantial immigrants who could not afford to violate the law, while irresponsible and undesirable squatters drifted in at will; protested the loyalty of the colonists; and denied any desire for independence. On the subject of Indian relations the convention urged the ayuntamiento of Nacogdoches to prevent white encroachment on the claims of the partly civilized tribes of the eastern border, provided for the organization of the militia of Austin's settlements into a regiment of two battalions of six companies each, and suggested the employment of forty men to range the frontiers of Austin's and DeWitt's colonies. The committee on East Texas lands simply recited the history of the claims in that quarter as we already know them and asked for the appointment of a commissioner to put the settlers in possession. John Austin reported that Francisco Duclor, who was left by Fisher in charge of the customs office at Brazoria, had abandoned his post,[2] and the convention ordered the continued collection of tonnage duties at Matagorda, Brazoria, and Galveston Bay by bonded officers subject to the respective ayuntamientos. On the fifth day of the session Luke Lesassier of San Felipe, an intimate friend of Austin's, reported a petition to the state government for a donation of land for the maintenance of primary schools to teach English and Spanish. After vain efforts to specify

[1] Four pages of Wharton's manuscript are preserved in the county records of Austin County at Bellville.
[2] See Duclor to John Austin, September 27, 1832.

the amount of land at twenty-five, one hundred, and a hundred and fifty leagues, and after rejecting a motion by Wharton to table indefinitely, the convention finally adopted the report, leaving to the judgment of the legislature the amount of land to be appropriated. On none of these subjects could misapprehension easily arise, but at one point the convention touched sensitive ground. Upon taking the chair Austin had suggested an address on the defects of local government, particularly in the administration of justice. No attention seems to have been paid to this, but Silas Dinsmore of Bastrop moved the consideration of a petition to Congress for separate state government for Texas. His motion was first tabled and then withdrawn, but the next day by a vote of thirty-six to twelve a motion was adopted for the appointment of a grand committee of two from each delegation to report on the expediency of such a petition. Austin did not vote, but John Austin, who probably reflected his attitude, opposed. The committee reported favorably with the draft of a petition, which, upon motion of Wharton, was referred to a select committee for revision. Austin was added to this committee. As adopted, the petition expressed the belief that separation from Coahuila would be to the mutual advantage of the two provinces and to the ultimate interest of the republic. Dissimilarity of Coahuila and Texas in soil, climate, and productions, and inequality of representation rendered suitable legislation for the needs of Texas impossible, it was said, besides which the rapid immigration of Indians from the United States made it desirable for Texas in self-defense to control its resources as a sovereign state. Despite the solidity of these reasons, it would, of course, be difficult for the government to believe, under the circumstances, that separation from Coahuila was not desired simply as a preliminary to secession from Mexico.

William H. Wharton was elected by acclamation to present the work of the convention to the state and federal governments, and arrangements were made to collect two thousand dollars for his expenses. Subscriptions were to be paid by the first of December, but whether Wharton's mission was to be deferred until that time is not clear.

Before adjournment the convention provided for the creation of a central standing committee with local sub-committees in each community. The committees were to correspond with each other on all matters relating to the peace and safety of the frontier, and on all relating to the tranquillity of the interior. For, it was explained, "united our strength and resources are more than adequate to our defense in any possible event. Disunited, we may become an easy prey, even to a handful of cowardly invaders." In addition, the central committee was empowered to call a convention whenever, in its judgment, conditions seemed to warrant. The functions of the committee indicate that the convention was controlled by a group not in sympathy with Austin's conciliatory methods, but Austin was included among the seven members chosen for the central committee.[3]

After adjournment of the convention delegates arrived from Goliad, approved what had been done—especially the petitions for amendment of the law of April 6, 1830, and for separation from Coahuila—and selected one of their number, Rafael Manchola, to accompany Wharton to Mexico.[4]

The Mexicans of San Antonio admitted that the reforms requested were founded in justice, but declined to participate in the convention. They explained that such meetings were forbidden by law, and that this one, besides, was ill-timed because by declaring for Santa Anna, who was not yet in power and could therefore do nothing for them, the colonists had naturally cut themselves off from the favorable action of the Bustamante government. They stated very clearly, however, their readiness to cooperate in lawful ways when order should be restored. This also was the tone of the political chief. He wrote Austin that the ayuntamiento of San Felipe had acted illegally in calling the convention, but "you are not to understand from this," he added, "that I am opposed to the objects which that ayuntamiento has in mind. Altogether to the contrary, I should have wished to further them to the limit of my legal power. I am a citizen of Texas, and have the greatest interest in every betterment that can advance the welfare of the country and its inhabitants, notwithstanding that some, as I have heard, do not think me the same Ramón Músquiz that I was in 1830 and 1831." As in duty bound, however, he ordered the annulment of all the proceedings of the convention and the dissolution of the

---

[3] Other members of the committee were F. W. Johnson, James B. Miller, Lewis L. Veeder, Robert Peebles, Wily Martin, and William Pettus.

[4] The journal of the convention, published at Brazoria in 1832, is reprinted in Gammel, *Laws of Texas*, I, 475–503.

central and sub-committees, but promised to do what he could to advance reforms properly requested through the ayuntamiento. Músquiz was, in fact, doubtful of the loyalty of the colonists and expressed to the governor the conviction that the recent disorder was the forerunner of secession.[5]

The political chief's disapproval brought apologies and disavowals, certainly insincere in some cases, from the ayuntamientos of Gonzales, Liberty, San Felipe, and Nacogdoches;[6] and for reasons that can be inferred Wharton's mission was abandoned. Reforms from the state and federal governments could obviously not be expected in the face of the political chief's opposition; there is, besides, some indication that the settlers themselves were not wholly satisfied with the convention;[7] and, finally, there was the hope of cooperation from the Mexicans of Bexar when order should be re-established in the government. On the whole, it seemed wise to wait.

Austin's thoughts are hard to follow for the next few months. Of his agreement with most of the demands of the convention there is no question; and, though it is doubtful whether he considered the meeting opportune, he wrote Músquiz in November that he believed some good had already come of it, that the people were quieter and better satisfied than they had been. At the same time he disclosed the plan by which he certainly would have preferred to proceed and to which he seems now to have bent his energies. This was to have the Mexican population take the lead in the movement for reform and, if possible, in the organization of a state government.

"There is little probability [he wrote Músquiz] that we shall soon have a stable and peaceable order of public affairs, and I give it as my deliberate judgment that Texas is lost if she take no measures of her own for her welfare. I incline to the opinion that it is your duty, as chief magistrate, to call a convention to take into consideration the condition of the coun-

---

[5] Ayuntamiento of San Felipe to ayuntamiento of Bexar, September 4, 1832; central committee to ayuntamiento of Bexar, October 16; reply of the ayuntamiento, November 2; Músquiz to Austin, October 11 (Austin Papers), to the governor, November 5, and to the ayuntamiento of San Felipe, November 7—all in Nacogdoches Archives, Texas State Library, except the letter to Austin.

[6] Gonzales December 16, 1832, Liberty December 27, San Felipe January 8, and Nacogdoches January 29, 1833, all in Nacogdoches Archives.

[7] The preface to the journal protests too much the spirit of compromise that pervaded the convention and suggests dissatisfaction because too little time had been allowed for the elections.

try. I do not know how the state or general government can presume to say that the people of Texas have violated the constitution, when the acts of both governments have long since killed the constitution and when the confederation itself has hardly any life left." [8]

A few days after writing this letter Austin started on a tour of the Mexican settlements, and from Goliad wrote Músquiz again, suggesting that as the people at Bexar agreed upon the substance of the convention's demands it ought to be easy to avoid misunderstanding. Forms were of little importance and ought not to engender discord; let Bexar take the lead and thereby establish union and harmony in Texas. To accomplish this was the object of his journey, which was undertaken at considerable inconvenience, he added, because of the bad condition of the roads, the danger from Indians, and the loss of time from his personal business. [9] A letter from an American resident of Goliad some weeks later indicates the other half of Austin's mission during this journey. "Our friends here," said the writer, think the political chief "is not as warm in the cause as your letter led us to anticipate." [10] Obviously Austin was trying to tranquillize the settlers.

From Goliad he went to San Antonio, and the effect of his visit there is seen in a most vigorous arraignment of the government framed by a joint committee of the citizens and of the ayuntamiento. On December 19 the ayuntamiento forwarded a copy of this document to the other ayuntamientos of Texas, suggesting that they also send remonstrances to the state and federal authorities praying for relief. The memorial began with a startling picture of the desolation and distress said to be attributable to the indifference and neglect of the central government. Various settlements and military establishments founded in Texas had entirely disappeared. In some the inhabitants had perished to a man. San Antonio had been in existence a hundred and forty years; Goliad and Nacogdoches a hundred and sixteen; [11] and yet a glance at the census and a review of the unwritten history of these settlements were sufficient to reveal the neglect which had sacrificed so many of the primitive

---

[8] Austin to Músquiz (translation), November 15, 1832, Nacogdoches Archives.
[9] Austin to Músquiz, November 30, 1832, Nacogdoches Archives.
[10] Western to Austin, December 21, 1832.
[11] This was an exaggeration. San Antonio was founded in 1718, Nacogdoches in 1716, and Goliad about 1746.

inhabitants and their descendants to savages, starvation, and pestilence. Only since 1821, it was asserted, ninety-seven persons had been murdered by Indians in San Antonio, Goliad, and the new settlement of DeWitt on the Guadalupe, and during most of that time the Indians were nominally at peace. Civil wars had paralyzed the national resources, and soldiers in Texas, unpaid and unsupported, were compelled to work for a livelihood. Little protection could be had from such a force, and no industrial progress was possible. For the past two years there had been a loom in San Antonio, but in the other native settlements that ingenious machine was unknown, and even the simple manufacture of blankets, hats, and shoes was undeveloped, so that such articles must be obtained from foreigners or from the interior two hundred leagues away. As for the union with Coahuila, it had been little short of a curse. Laws discriminated deliberately against the development of Texas, and it had come about that want of a separate state government was the fountain of most of the ills from which the people then suffered. And what should be said of the federal law of April 6, 1830? It could not be enforced, but desirable immigration was stopped by it, while vagabonds with nothing to lose poured in unchecked. A fine tribute was paid to the "honest, industrious North American settlers," who in seven or eight years had developed plantations of cotton, corn, and cane, established gins and mills, and made themselves comfortable and prosperous. The welfare of the native settlements was declared to be dependent upon the continued introduction of such colonists. They furnished a source of supply for the natives, protected them from Indians, and would develop roads and commerce which in time would divert the Santa Fé trade from Missouri to Texas. Recapitulating, the memorial insisted on the revision of various state laws, the establishment of an adequate judiciary system, provision for public schools, reapportionment of representation so as to allow Texas four representatives in the legislature, suspension of the law of April 6, 1830, tariff exemption for ten years on imports "for the consumption of the inhabitants," and guarantees against future encroachment of federal officers on the rights of the State.[12]

[12] The document is printed in Filisola, *Memorias para la Historia de la Guerra de Tejas,* I, 273–293 (Mexico, 1849), and briefly summarized by Brown, *History of Texas,* I, 233–235.

Austin's part in the passage of this protest, with sidelights on the temper of the Mexican population, appears in a letter to Williams. Writing from San Antonio on December 6 Austin said:

"I arrived here on the 3 inst. Yesterday there was a meeting of the principal citizens—that is, the Chief, Erasmo, the Navarros, Col. Elosua, Balmaceda, Garza, etc., and I gave them an exact discription of the evils that are retarding the progress of Texas. Stated in plain terms the necessity of separating from Coahuila and the desire of the people generally to do so, and said everything I could to induce them to concur in taking that step at once.

"The matter was discussed and talked over with great calmness and interest. There was not a dissenting voice as to the necessity of a remidy and all agreed that a separation from Coahuila was the best."

They would take no steps to this end, however, without first petitioning for reform, which led Austin to urge that an immediate statement of all grievances must be made through the ayuntamiento, with the plain declaration that they would proceed to organize a local government if abuses were not fully redressed by March 1. To this they agreed in substance, said Austin, but demurred at the date of the ultimatum and suggested April 1, which he thought would be adopted. The ayuntamiento was in session when Austin wrote and had asked him to furnish the heads of the contemplated protest, a request to which he responded with great fullness.

"The object [he explained] is to form a list of all the insults offered to Texas, and all her grievances and to demand full satisfaction. . . . [If I succeed] in getting this ayto to [pass] this remonstrance as I have proposed and as was agreed to in the conference yesterday, it will place Texas on much better ground than to go into the measure now, and it will unite this place and La Bahia firmly with the balance of Texas, for they will be so compromised that there will be no backing out, even if they wished to do so, which they will not, for they are as anxious for a separation as we are, but wish to show to the world that they are right and stand on just ground in case force must ultimately be resorted to." [13]

While the memorial as adopted avoided an ultimatum, in other respects it met Austin's suggestions. Besides forwarding copies to the other ayuntamientos, the framers formally transmitted a copy to the political chief, which he sent on to the governor with an

[13] Austin to Williams, December 6, 1832, Rosenberg Library, Galveston.

apology. Conditions really had been intolerable in Texas, he said, and the ayuntamiento was compelled to take this action to avoid a revolution.[14] The ayuntamientos of Goliad, San Felipe, and Nacogdoches endorsed the Bexar remonstrance and framed similar documents, but there is no record of action by other communities.[15]

In the meantime, besides traveling actively, Austin was carrying on an extensive correspondence with leaders in all sections. From the replies received—we have none of his letters of this period—it is evident that it was determined as early as the middle of November to hold a second convention; that Austin had undertaken to gain the support of the Mexican inhabitants for a separate state organization; and that he was trying to unite the colonists on this program and avert a more radical step, perhaps an ill-timed movement for independence, by a small group of impatient radicals. Jonas Harrison wrote from Tenaha acknowledging a letter of November 18. He had shown it, he said, to representative citizens of his own neighborhood and of Ais Bayou and all concurred in its sentiments and in the project that it presented—"they want a local government, they want a judiciary proceeding according to the principles of the common law, so far at least as respects the mode of trial, and one that will protect their property and persons. . . . The principles in the state constitution are in the main excellent; but the thread is too fine spun. Much is lost in detail. It resembles the works of the famous Abbe Sieyes." The people, he continued, "deprecate the idea of being independent of the Mexican republic. . . . Neither do they wish nor would they consent to become a part of or belong to the states of the North." The illiberal land system of the United States was the reason assigned for this. Reciting his own experiences, Harrison suggested that the second convention should have but two representatives from each district and that their expenses should be paid. In going, returning, and attending the convention in October his expenses had been fifty dollars; he had lost a valuable horse; and he could not make enough in a year to recoup his losses. His explanation throws a flood of light on the

---

[14] Músquiz to the governor, January 10, 1833.
[15] The proceedings of Goliad and San Felipe (January 14) and of Nacogdoches (January 30) are in the Nacogdoches Archives, Texas State Library. On the Goliad document, which was even more vigorous than that of San Felipe, see Western to Austin, January 19, 1832.

economic condition of the East Texas frontier. "Strange as it may appear," he said, "to those that are in the habit of handling money there are in these districts many good citizens, many good livers, men of property, who do not handle five dollars in a year." Thomas M. Duke, of the Brazos, wrote that his views coincided exactly with Austin's and that he hoped the people would unite to carry out the plan proposed, which was the "safest course" that could be adopted. John A. Williams, however, on the Trinity, could not agree with Austin. He said that the inhabitants in his quarter had no grievances and that there was no need of a second convention.[16]

Austin was now in a situation that might easily become embarrassing. With the settlers he was consenting to, if not promoting, a second convention, while with the Mexicans he was committed to the more conservative procedure of protest and petition through the ayuntamientos. Probably he had in the background of his mind the conviction that the reforms would not be effected by this means and that the Mexicans must then join the colonists in setting up a provisional state government. Indeed, he implied as much in the letter to Williams already quoted,[17] but unless the movement for the convention could be checked until action on the petitions was had the Mexicans would feel that he had misled them. On the other hand, suppose by chance all the demands should be granted except that for the separate state organization, what then would become of the convention? D. W. Anthony, editor of the *Brazoria Advertiser*,[18] put the matter squarely to Austin.

"I do not see much harmony [he said] in the design of a remonstrance, which must include the idea of submission on conditions of redress, and contain the request of the people to govt to grant a mitigation and redress of grievances, and at the same time that there should be going forward a solemn and firm determination of the same people to form a separate government and remedy the evils of which they complain. . . . Such I understand to be the actual state of things. The Central Committee have ordered a positive and unconditional call of a convention. The people with whom you have been in communication have remonstrated, and expect the same thing to be performed by the people and authorities of

[16] Harrison to Austin, November 30, December 8, 1832; Williams, December 21; Duke, December 22. See also Western to Austin, December 21, 1832, and January 19, 1833, and Ingram, January 20, 1833.

[17] Above, page 355.

[18] See by the writer, "Notes on Early Texas Newspapers," *Southwestern Historical Quarterly*, XXI, 137–139.

the whole country. Should what is complained of be listened to and acted upon favorably by the present state government, how will we stand or how will we proceed?" [19]

Austin's solution of such a dilemma would probably have been to surrender the demand for state government and depend upon the practical good sense of the settlers to be content with the gains obtained.[20] The precipitate calling of the convention was a severe blow. It put him in a false light with his Mexican friends and destroyed all hope of making the movement ultimately appear to emanate from them. The whole situation is fully discussed in a letter from Austin to Williams of January 12, 1834.[21]

"Ever since I returned from Bexar a year ago last December [he wrote] and found the convention called in my absence I have consider'd myself as suspended over the altar of sacrifice. That measure placed me in an awkward position. It compromised me in the highest degree with the people and authorities of Bexar, on the one hand, and with my friends at San Felipe on the other, for altho I had agreed to the calling of a convention before I went to Bexar, I did not expect it would have been done in my absence. I went there to consult with the authorities of that place. I considered that very great respect and deference was justly due to them as native Mexicans, as the capital of Texas, and as the oldest and most populous town in the country, and I knew the importance of getting them to take the lead in all the politics of Texas. Besides this, I was personally attached to those people as a sincere friend and wished to act in concert with them. I wished the convention to meet in Bexar, but at that time it was death to any man's popularity to speak in favor of the Mexicans. These things are all passed and had best be forgotten. Probably I have no just cause to blame any one but myself, for in some things that occurred then I was a mere *passive actor* when I ought to have been a firm and unbending *director*. My object was to smother the party spirit and violent and ruinous divisions which I saw brewing in the colony; and as my friendship for the Mexicans and opposition to violent measures was to have been used by my enemies (who were in fact also the only real enemies to Texas) as the kindling materials, the oil and brimstone to set the flame of discord and confusion ablazing, I thought it best to deprive them of the kindling matter by a passive course. I mistook the means, and committed a great error, but I have learned this lesson in politics,

---

[19] Anthony to Austin, December 26, 1832. Anthony's paper would be invaluable for this period, but no copy is known to exist.

[20] Acknowledging on January 20, 1833, a letter from Austin, the date of which he does not give, Anthony expressed regret at the call for the convention, saying that he should have preferred to await the result of the Bexar remonstrance, and in case its requisitions or its principal objects should have been complied with, "I should undoubtedly have decided for a postponement of such a measure as that now adopted."

[21] Rosenberg Library, Galveston.

that there is no medium with envy and party spirit between victory and defeat.

"I was always in favor of the state question, but I feared, especially after my trip to Bexar, that it would not succeed unless the people of that place took the lead, and it was arranged for them to do so. The representation and remonstrance of 19 December was the first step, and would have led to all the others, and Texas by this time would have been a state, or nearly so, and the discord that I fear has arisen between Bexar and a part of Texas would have been avoided. All was defeated and deranged and Bexar was offended and turned against a measure that it was in favor of."

Despite chagrin and disappointment, Austin resumed the labors of Sisyphus with such resignation as he might. He published a translation of the Bexar remonstrance, and, working through Anthony, sought to create an atmosphere of moderation that might still leave ajar the door to cooperation from Bexar. At the same time he reiterated his own loyalty and that of the colonists to Mexico and tried to convince the political chief that the organization of a state government was the utmost to which the colonists aspired. He was assisted in this endeavor by Miguel Arciniega, the land commissioner residing at San Felipe, but Músquiz was only half persuaded and wrote the governor that he feared the colonists were aiming at independence and that Arciniega had not penetration enough to see it.[22]

Of the actual calling of the second convention we know very little. That the call was issued by the central committee is clear, and a notice posted by Thomas Hastings, chairman of the sub-committee of Nacogdoches, declared that the call was issued only after it had been approved by the sub-committees, but this may be doubted. According to this notice, elections were to be held on March 1 for the meeting on April 1—five delegates from each district—and the purpose was to form a constitution for the state of Texas with the approval of the general government.[23] The ayuntamiento of San Felipe exerted itself to induce the inhabitants of

[22] Anthony to Austin, January 25, February 3, 1833; Músquiz to Governor, January 11, 1833, University of Texas Transcripts from Department of Fomento, Mexico, legajo 7, expediente 55.

[23] Hastings's "notice to the public" is dated January 3, 1833, Nacogdoches Archives, Texas State Library. For efforts of the local officials to suppress the notice see in the same collection Durst to Músquiz, January 12, and ayuntamiento of Nacogdoches to Músquiz, January 29, 1833.

Bexar to endorse the convention, and even proposed that the meeting be held at Bexar, but without avail.[24] Músquiz replied that the Mexican inhabitants were well aware of the evils that Texas suffered and knew the remedies that should be applied, but that nothing could be accomplished until peace and order were restored. He suggested that the colonists in the meantime should ask permission to hold the convention. This would, if granted, legalize the meeting, and the request would have a tendency to restore confidence in the good faith of the colonists.[25]

The convention was in session two weeks, from April 1 to April 13. There is no journal of its proceedings, but the essential facts of its history can be reconstructed with reasonable confidence.[26] It seems to have been attended by from fifty-three to fifty-five delegates, of whom only fourteen had served in the previous convention.[27] Of the new members Sam Houston, ex-member of Congress, ex-governor of Tennessee, and friend of President Jackson, was the most notable. He had arrived in Texas the year before, and now represented Nacogdoches. William H. Wharton was president of the convention and Thomas Hastings was secretary. Austin has left us three drafts of the address of the central committee to the convention explaining why the meeting was called.[28] In brief, he explained, it seemed necessary to call this convention because at first, on account of the continued disorder and civil war in Mexico, the petitions of its predecessor were not presented to the government,

[24] Addresses of January 14 and February 8, 1833, Nacogdoches Archives.

[25] Músquiz to Ayuntamiento of San Felipe, February 27, and to that of Nacogdoches, March 7, 1833, Nacogdoches Archives.

[26] If the journal was ever compiled, it disappeared early. No historian of Texas acknowledges access to it.

[27] A copy of the provisional constitution adopted by this body and printed at the office of the New Orleans *Commercial Bulletin* in 1833 carries a list of the signers. A manuscript translation of the constitution by Austin in the Gómez Farías papers of the García Library of the University of Texas contains the same list, written in the same order except for the omission of two names, William English and Charlton Thompson, which are in the printed list. Brown, *History of Texas*, I, 227–229, gives fifty-six names compiled from the notes of James Kerr, who, he says, was a member; but on the two contemporary lists appear only twenty-two of Brown's names and Kerr's name is not among them. That some of the men whom Brown names were members who failed to sign the constitution is rendered unlikely by Austin's statement in 1835 that there were in round numbers fifty members.—See his "Explanation to the Public concerning the Affairs of Texas," *Quarterly* of Texas State Historical Association, VIII, 240.

[28] These papers illustrate in a striking way the painstaking labor with which Austin prepared for the meeting. The first draft is a mere outline of points; the second is an expansion of these points in direct, straightforward language without obvious restraint or effort to soften words; the third, the finished form of the address, elaborates the outline with great fullness but with the apparent desire to make the statement as conciliatory as the facts would allow.

and then, later, all the work of the first convention was annulled and the central and sub-committees which it had created were ordered dissolved. Nevertheless, it was the right, even the duty, of the settlers to inform the government of the obstacles that were retarding the welfare of Texas, and the chief of these obstacles was the enforced union with Coahuila. Only the wisdom of the convention could determine the best method of obtaining relief.

The work of the convention as we know it consisted in the formation of a provisional constitution and in the adoption of petitions to Congress for approval of the constitution, for the repeal of the eleventh article of the law of April 6, 1830, for an extension of tariff exemption, and for improvement of the mail service.

The constitution was drawn by a committee of which Houston was chairman.[29] By a curious quirk of fate it was closely modeled upon the Massachusetts constitution of 1780—possibly because a copy of that happened to be at hand—and there was scarcely a perceptible effort to adapt it to the requirements of a Mexican state.[30] The governor was to be elected for two years and should serve not more than four years in six. He had the right of veto, but laws might be passed over the veto by a simple majority of all the members elected to the legislature. The legislature was bi-cameral—an anomaly in the Mexican system—and judges were to be elected by the legislature and were subject to removal by vote of two-thirds of the two houses. In certain provisions the constitution reflected political questions that were agitating the United States. The legislature was authorized to establish a system of internal improvements, but no bank or banking institution should ever be established, and nothing but gold, silver, and copper coin could be made a legal tender.[31]

David G. Burnet was chairman of the committee that prepared the memorial arguing for approval of the constitution and the

[29] Brown, *History of Texas*, I, 228, says that the other members of the committee were Nestor Clay, Luke Lesassier, R. M. Williamson, James Kerr, Oliver Jones, and Henry Smith; but the last three are not named by contemporary lists as members of the convention.

[30] There is a touch of almost ludicrous irony in thus transplanting the handiwork of John Adams to make it the fundamental law of a Mexican state, the principal object of whose creation, according to John Quincy Adams, was to be the evasion by sovereign state authority of federal anti-slavery laws.

[31] The constitution is printed in D. B. Edward, *History of Texas*, etc. (Cincinnati, 1836) 196–205; and in a pamphlet printed in 1833 at the office of the *Commercial Bulletin* (New Orleans, 1833). There is a Spanish translation by Austin in the Gómez Farías manuscripts of the University of Texas.

organization of state government. Unquestionably it was written by him. It insisted that the union with Coahuila by the constituent Congress in 1824 was intended to be temporary and that the erection of Texas into a state did not require the approval of three-fourths of the states, which was the constitutional procedure laid down for the admission of new states. The reasons for separation were elaborated with force and eloquence but with no great originality. The first convention and the Bexar remonstrance of December, 1832, had, in fact, said all that could be said on the subject. Anticipating that the government might counter with a proposal for territorial organization, the convention insisted that that would not meet the situation.[32]

The committee on repeal of the eleventh article of the law of April 6, 1830, was headed by Wily Martin. Whether Austin was a member of the committee we do not know.[33] The report of the committee was more conciliatory than that of the first convention and emphasized, as proof that the Texans did not desire independence, the great advantages that they might enjoy as citizens when commercial relations with the rest of Mexico should be properly developed. Otherwise it did not differ in substance from its predecessor.

To put these documents before the government, the convention elected Austin, Dr. James B. Miller, and Erasmo Seguin of San Antonio. The election of Seguin implied the hope, of course, that the Mexican inhabitants might still be induced to endorse the work of the convention, though they had refused to participate in it. Seguin was a staunch friend of the colonists and, as we know, had represented Texas in the constituent Congress of 1823–1824. He would have made on this occasion an excellent commissioner. In the end, however, Austin went alone. He left San Felipe a week after the adjournment of the convention and expected to return in a few months, but was detained for more than two years.[34]

---

[32] The memorial is published in Yoakum, *History of Texas*, I, 469–482.

[33] There is, however, in the Austin Papers in Austin's hand a rough draft of a petition for repeal that seems to have influenced the report of the committee. There is a Spanish translation of the committee's report in the Austin Papers.

[34] The ayuntamiento of San Felipe wrote that of San Antonio, April 18, 1833 (Bexar Archives, University of Texas), telling of the work of the convention. Miller could not arrange his business for a long absence, it was explained, Austin insisted on paying his own expenses, and the ayuntamiento would be willing therefore to assume six hundred dollars of Seguin's expenses, if he would consent to serve.

Some uneasiness seems to have been felt lest Austin might not represent with sufficient firmness the convention's attitude toward separation from Coahuila.[35] As a matter of fact the subject had been much in his mind for years, and he was now convinced that separation could not with safety be longer deferred. Well down to the end of 1831 he looked forward to release from the union with Coahuila by the organization of Texas as a federal territory.[36] He suggested this to Terán in 1828 in a comprehensive statement of the needs of Texas, in which he described, without naming it, the territorial system of the United States, with governor, secretary, and judges appointed by the president and territorial legislature and delegate to Congress elected by the people.[37] This seems to have been always the condition, expressed or implied, upon which he advocated territorial organization. In September, 1830, he wrote Alamán that a system like that of the United States would be hailed with acclaim, "for the truth is," he explained, "that Texas united with Coahuila is in a bad way." In 1831, with a member of the legislature, he wrote Alamán from Saltillo that every day's experience convinced him more thoroughly that Texas could never obtain adequate legislation until the union with Coahuila was dissolved, but that before entering into a territorial status the people must know what their political rights would be. He then proceeded to sketch with much detail the basis for a federal law which should establish the practice of the United States. Without committing himself as to the law, which in the main, however, he probably would have approved, Alamán replied very frankly that he, too, was persuaded that Texas could not develop and prosper until separated from Coahuila and that he believed also that separation would be best for Coahuila. He suggested that, in order to ease his own difficulty in getting the subject through Congress, Austin should first get the legislature to recommend it. This perhaps would have been impossible in any event, because the disposal of the deferred payments on Texas lands, not to mention other obstacles, would have arisen, but the session was too far advanced for Austin

---

[35] Austin to Perry, April 22, 1833.

[36] However, it should be said in connection with this statement that on May 18, 1830, Austin wrote Terán that he thought the people would then unanimously oppose a territorial organization for Texas.

[37] Austin to Terán, May 24 and June 30, 1828.

to attempt action in 1831, and by the next session the revolution against Bustamante and the ministers had rendered any action useless.[38] Moreover, Austin did not care to move blindly. "Much depends on the organic law for the territories," he wrote Williams; and again, after receiving Alamán's reply, "The arms of the Genl. Govt. are *wide open* to receive us as a territory (but no basis is stated with the absolute precision which I think necessary, agreeing in general terms to the plan of Arkansas or something like it)."[39] As time passed his hope of relief by the territorial route declined and he turned to the necessity for a state organization.[40]

Sometimes Austin's thoughts dwelt upon the eventual necessity of separation from Mexico. Such a contingency must have occurred to any intelligent man in his situation, but it was not one that he desired. His numerous protestations of loyalty to Mexico were sincere. He was actually grateful for the benefits which he and his colonists had enjoyed; he saw many potential advantages in the connection with Mexico, provided only the government could be established on a stable basis and an enlightened commercial policy be developed; and he perceived some real disadvantages in union with the United States. Therefore, until the close of 1832 at least, it was always to independence that he looked in case the chronic tumult and disorder of Mexico should finally compel secession for self-preservation. His earliest discussion of this theme is in a remarkably interesting letter to William H. Wharton in 1829.[41]

"If the Gov^t stands and prospers [he said] Texas must prosper under it. If the Gov^t falls the bonds which bind Texas and Mexico will of course be severed by that fall, and in this event Texas can either unite herself to the North under the necessary guarantees from that Gov^t or become an independent speck in the galaxy of nations. Europe will gladly receive our cotton and sugar, etc., on advantageous terms for 'untariffed' manufactured articles. We should be too contemptible to excite the jealousy of the Northern Mammoth, and policy and interest would induce Europe to let us alone. I deem it to be more than probable that the great powers

---

[38] Austin to Alamán, September 20, 1830, and March 21, 1831; Alamán's reply is dated April 6, 1831. See also Austin to Terán, September 17, 1830, and to Henry Austin, October 14, 1830.

[39] Austin to Williams, April 2 and 16, 1831, Rosenberg Library, Galveston.

[40] On January 14, 1832, he wrote Mrs. Holley that the government must be made to see that "the only true policy is to make Texas a state, and bind it to the nation by the ties of interest."

[41] April 24, 1829.

would all unite in guaranteeing the independence of little Texas. There are many powerful reasons why it would be to their interest to do it."

During the summer of 1829 the newspapers of the United States carried on an active discussion of President Jackson's determination to obtain Texas for his government, and in November of that year Colonel Anthony Butler passed through Texas with dispatches for the American minister at Mexico.[42] Austin evidently felt that there was an imminent possibility of Mexico's selling the province and protested that it had no right to do this without the consent of the people; that under no circumstances did they want to be transferred to the United States without guarantees; and that independence would be preferable. But he did not believe that the country yet had the resources that independence would require. As late as December, 1831, he wrote, "We have not the right kind of material for an independent government. . . . I think the government will yield and give us what we ought to have. If not, we shall go for *independence,* and put our trust in ourselves, our rifles, and our God."[43]

Just after the adjournment of the convention of 1832 Austin wrote to General William H. Ashley, member of Congress from Missouri, a letter that is hard to interpret. It may have been no more than a casual overture to renew an earlier friendship, but one suspects a design to sound Ashley concerning the attitude that might be expected from the people of the United States if Texas should attempt to set up for itself. After describing the improvement of Texas since 1821 and telling of recent events Austin went on to say:

"Should the future drive us into an attitude of hostility in defense of what we have so dearly earned . . . we shall *then* expect that the sympathies which cheered the struggling Greeks and Poles . . . will also cheer the humble watch fires of our undisciplined militia, and if necessary soon swell their ranks to a respectable army. . . . The sons of the North may be buried in Texas, but they cannot be driven from it. Neither do I think such a thing will be attempted. It would be a blind and mistaken policy. This country, as a state of Mexico, would prosper. It would be of great service to the nation, and add much to the national strength and resources. It is not our interest to separate if such a thing can be avoided,

---

[42] Austin wrote to Ramón Músquiz November 10, 1829, introducing Butler.
[43] Austin to Músquiz, March 29, 1830, and to Mrs. Holley, December 29, 1831. See also Austin to Leaming, June 14, 1830; to S. Rhoads Fisher, June 17, 1830; and to Terán, September 17, 1830, and February 5, 1832.

unless we should float into the Northern Republic with the consent of all parties, ourselves included." [44]

What did this mean? That statehood under Mexico was still preferable surely, but that revolution might perhaps become inevitable, in which event incorporation with the United States on terms might be acceptable.

It is certain that the nullification movement in South Carolina occupied a passing thought of the Texans. They hoped to profit by it, but in what way is not quite clear. As early as 1830 S. Rhoads Fisher wrote Austin from Northumberland, Pennsylvania, "How far you may have been the means of laying the basis of a new republic time will show. I think it not chimerical that Texas may yet have a sensible influence on the views of the Southern Nullifiers, that she may prove a powerful lever in the political machinery of their *adherence to their rights,* and ultimately weigh so heavily in the balance as to be one mean of dismembering them from the northern States. I am in great hopes to see the importance of our country [Texas] taken up by some Carolina writer." [45] And Austin wrote Ashley in the letter just quoted, "Perhaps the nullifiers on one side and the spirit of revolution on the other may split matters into fragments and leave us to ourselves here in the centre." Perhaps, too, it was significant that in the summer of 1832 Austin found occasion to renew correspondence with Joel R. Poinsett, who was leading the Unionist forces in South Carolina. [46]

If doubt of Austin's attitude could remain, it would be dispelled by intimate letters to members of his family on the eve of his departure for Mexico. Though he believed that the convention was called prematurely and regretted the abandonment of his passive policy, he approved of its work. He wrote Henry Austin that the memorial for admission to statehood was respectful and dignified and that he saw no reason why it should give offense. If, after this application, relief was denied, he should advise immediate organization of a provisional state government and then a second application for admission as organized. "That also failing, we shall have to do the best we can." Both in this letter and in one to Mrs. Holley written the next day he made it clear that he believed revolution

---

[44] Austin to Ashley, October 10, 1832.
[45] Fisher to Austin, August 14, 1830.
[46] On October 14, 1832, Poinsett acknowledged letters of August 13 and 29 from Austin.

must follow a rejection of the present petition, and that he would favor it, provided always the political situation in Mexico showed no promise of improvement. *"Texas is determined to have a state government,"* he wrote Mrs. Holley. "There is a decided opposition to separating from the M[exican] confederacy. The people do not desire it and would not agree to it, if they could get a state government, but anything would be better than to remain as we are." In both letters he expressed confident hopes of success, but to Perry, his brother-in-law, he was less optimistic. "I shall try and get the law of April 6, 1830, repealed and a *declaration that the people of Texas may legally convene in convention to make a constitution.* This much I expect to effect and no more." This probably meant that he should not feel it necessary to insist on approval without amendment of the constitution submitted by the convention.[47]

Leaving San Felipe on April 22, Austin went to San Antonio to make a final effort to obtain the cooperation of the Mexican inhabitants. Rain and high water delayed his arrival until the 29th. Then Seguin, whom the convention had elected to accompany him, had to be summoned from his ranch. For three days the notables debated what should be done, the meeting of May 4 adjourning after midnight. Only Seguin would sign the application for separation from Coahuila. All were willing to ask for the removal of the state capital to San Antonio, but a recent law forbade the signing of a petition by more than three persons, and, in the end, it was impossible to find three to sponsor the demand which *en masse* perhaps all would have signed. Austin believed that they would welcome state government, but was convinced that they could be induced to do nothing to further it. There is independent evidence that he gauged their sentiments accurately.[48]

[47] Austin to Henry Austin, April 19, 1833, to Mrs. Holley, April 20, and to Perry, April 22. At about the same time Austin must have written to J. Francisco Madero: "With only two measures Texas would be satisfied, judges who understand English . . . and trial by jury. The colonists would gladly pay the judges if they were given the right to nominate them. . . . I must speak frankly, and I tell you that the inhabitants of Texas must have either a state government or judges and trial by jury. . . . Of the two alternatives the best for Coahuila and for all Mexico is to erect Texas into a state." Madero quoted this to Acting Governor Berramendi, May 13, 1833, Transcripts from Department of Fomento, Mexico, legajo 7, expediente 57.

[48] Austin to Lesassier, May 6, 1833, gives a full account of the proceedings at Bexar, for confirmation of which see Manuel Ximenes, acting political chief, to Elosua, May 9, and to the governor, May 19, Bexar Archives. See also Austin to Williams, May 9, Rosenberg Library, Galveston.

From San Antonio Austin proceeded to Matamoras by way of Goliad, still retarded by rains and flood. Apparently he was not more successful with the Mexicans at Goliad than he had been at San Antonio. At Matamoras he found, as he wrote Williams, a darker squall gathering than he had lately seen. General Filisola, Terán's successor, believed that a revolt was under way and was preparing to meet it. Austin hastened to set him right. "The public tranquillity is not disturbed in Texas," he wrote. "Not a single hand's breadth of Mexican territory in that country is in danger; there are no gatherings there to oppose Mexican soldiers; and there is neither desire nor sentiment, as I understand that rumor has it here, in favor of separation from the Mexican federation." But concerning the just grievances of Texas he did not mince words, dwelling particularly on the need of judicial reform, and supporting his statements by a copy of the Bexar remonstrance of December 19, 1832. The remedy, he said equally plainly, must be the establishment of a state government. Filisola expressed himself as satisfied with the explanation, and Austin believed that he was.[49]

Weak and ill from dysentery and cholerina when he reached Matamoras, Austin there learned that Congress would adjourn before he could reach the capital; and shrinking from the discomfort of the long journey through the hot country, he at first determined to return home and watch the course of events until fall. With this in mind, he sent a copy of the constitution and of the petition for statehood by Filisola's mail to the secretary of relations to show what the Texans had in mind, and then an opportunity offered for passage to Vera Cruz, and he decided to embrace it. On the first of June he embarked on a voyage much longer than he anticipated and filled with more discomforts than that by land would have been, and here for a moment we shall leave him.

After Austin's visit to San Antonio, Manuel Ximenes, the acting political chief, tried with partial success to get the ayuntamientos of the colonies to repudiate the convention,[50] and the governor ap-

[49] Austin to Filisola, May 24, 30, 1833, in Filisola, *Memorias para la Historia de la Guerra de Tejas,* I, 347–353, 355–359; to Martin, May 30; and to Williams, May 31, Rosenberg Library, Galveston.

[50] For repudiation by Gonzales see the ayuntamiento's explanation to Ximenes, May 27 and June 22, 1833, Bexar Archives. Brown, *History of Texas,* I, 232, lauds the alcalde of Gonzales without stint for the firmness of an earlier declaration, but was unaware of this later apology. For the disavowal by Liberty see Madero to political chief, July 15, 1833, General Land Office of Texas, Vol. 44, page 80, and compare John A. Williams to Austin, December 18, 1832.

pointed J. Francisco Madero and Ramón Músquiz to investigate conditions and try to restore tranquillity. Madero was more or less popular in the colonies because of his clash with Bradburn the year before, and he proved his moderation now by declaring that he should favor the elevation of Texas to statehood as soon as it possessed the necessary resources. Músquiz for some reason was absent when Madero arrived, so that Madero conducted the mission alone; but beyond the fact that he invited the various districts to send representatives to San Antonio for a conference we know nothing of its results.[51] A devastating cholera epidemic was already sweeping the settlements near the coast, and when that subsided public interest did not readily shift again to politics. Moreover, there was nothing to do but wait for the results of Austin's mission. But Austin, ignorant of the lessened tension, continued to think of the people as on the brink of revolt, a misapprehension that greatly influenced his course in Mexico.

[51] See Berramendi to Madero, May 20, 1833, Transcripts from Department of Fomento, Mexico, legajo 7, expediente 57, and Madero to ayuntamiento of San Felipe, June 15, 1833, Nacogdoches Archives.

CHAPTER XIV

The Mission to Mexico: Arrest and Imprisonment

USTIN sailed from Matamoras expecting to reach Vera Cruz
in six days. He described the voyage laconically in a letter
to his brother-in-law: "I had a wretched trip. *One month
from Matamoras to Vera Cruz in a little schooner*—ten days on
short allowance of water—none but salt provisions—and sea sick
all the time."[1] From Vera Cruz to Mexico City other delays awaited
him,[2] so that he did not reach the capital until July 18. The next
day he called on the ministers of relations and justice and on the
vice-president, Gómez Farías, who, in the absence of Santa Anna
on campaign, was serving as executive. They appointed the 23d for
the formal presentation of his mission, when, after listening cordially and with apparent sympathy, they asked him to repeat his
statement in writing. Austin was encouraged by the tone of the
interview and wrote that he believed the application for statehood
would be approved.[3]

On August 1 he filed with the minister of relations, Carlos García,
a vigorous argument in support of the Texan application. The
principal theses upon which he based this were: that Texas possessed the necessary qualifications, the people wanted statehood,
and the act of union with Coahuila guaranteed it; that Texas as
a separate province at the establishment of Mexican independence
had, like any other original member of the federation, the right
to local autonomy; that the federal system, by implication, guaranteed adequate local government to all its citizens; that it was the
duty of the people to remove every obstacle that interfered with

[1] Austin to Perry, July 30, 1833. He had written the central committee a full account of
the voyage on July 3 in a letter that is not preserved.
[2] The road was blocked by rebels led by Generals Arista and Duran, which caused a
halt at Jalapa, and when this obstacle was removed further delay occurred because General
Vásquez had neglected to endorse Austin's passport at Vera Cruz.
[3] Austin to the central committee, July 24, 1833.

their loyalty to the nation and that the union with Coahuila was such an obstacle; and, finally, that the right of self-preservation, the right of any people to save themselves from anarchy and ruin, compelled the Texans to insist on state organization. He elaborated these points at length and with great frankness, even with downright bluntness. Texas did not admit, he said, that its right of admission to the Mexican federation depended upon the consent of Coahuila and the vote of three-fourths of the states. Admission was a natural right, unaffected by the fact that for a while the people had held it in abeyance. Separation from Mexico would be a real calamity, but it must be understood that Coahuila could not govern Texas and that Texas could not and would not remain quiet united with Coahuila. Nor could Texas be coerced; it must be governed by moral force. Austin offered to submit a supplementary argument to prove that it was contrary to the interest of Texas to separate from Mexico, and he did submit a statement of the economic condition of the country to show that it had the necessary resources to maintain a state government. It is impossible to check this statement with any confidence. Undoubtedly it greatly exaggerated the resources of Texas. The population was represented as 46,500, exclusive of wandering tribes of Indians. It could have been hardly more than half that number. The products of Texas were said to be, accurately enough, cotton, sugar, tobacco, grain, vegetables, cattle and swine, lumber, and hides. In Austin's colonies there were thirty cotton gins, two steam saw mills and two grist mills, six water-power mills, and many others propelled by horse power and oxen; there was a water-power saw mill at Gonzales; and the East Texas settlements were well supplied with gins and mills. Seven thousand bales of cotton would be harvested the coming season; cattle and hogs had increased with such rapidity that their numbers could not be estimated; and the raising of horses and mules was well advanced. Fat beeves of from five hundred to seven hundred and fifty pounds brought from eight to ten dollars, and hogs of two and three hundred pounds brought from three and a half to five dollars. The inhabitants were intelligent, enterprising, and industrious, with few illiterates among them; and this greatly augmented the natural capacity of the country to support a state government. On August 12 Austin submitted the appeal for amendment of the law of April 6, 1830. These subjects were of the greatest importance to the nation as well as to Texas, and he urged their settlement by special order without delay.[4]

Haste, however, was not possible. Cholera had already reached the city and assumed the proportions of a terrible plague. Austin estimated forty-three thousand cases in the city at one time, and from eighteen to twenty thousand deaths in six weeks. Feeling the premonitory symptoms of the disease himself on August 14, he exhausted himself trying to present in the most effective form the argument for repeal of the law of April 6, 1830. This brought his case to a crisis, and only the successful application of a popular remedy, he thought, saved his life. In the meantime, Congress had recessed and held no session until near the end of September. In the interval hope fluctuated. On August 6 Austin wrote John Austin that he hoped Texas would before another year be a state of Mexico or of the United States, "for I am so weary that life is hardly worth having situated as we now are." On the 14th he wrote Williams that the objectionable article of the law of April 6, 1830, would soon be repealed but that the question of state government must follow the constitutional course and be approved by three-fourths of the states. A week later he thought the outlook for statehood was more favorable but admitted that he might be deceived. On the 28th he was "very doubtful"; but by September 5 optimism was again in the ascendant. "I am in better spirits as to the result of our Texas matters," he wrote, "than I have been in since my arrival. . . . I have confidence in the result which I now anticipate, because this matter has been the subject of much and very mature deliberations, and the conclusions which I think the government and leading men in congress have come to are therefore not hastily formed and may be relied on with the more confidence for that reason. Upon the whole I am of opinion that my trip to Mexico in 1833 will do as much and perhaps more good for Texas than my trip in 1822 did. The latter laid a foundation to build upon, the former [will] raise the superstructure by removing the obstacles that have impeded its progress and Texas will then become a state of this republic, in harmony with the constitution and with the

---

[4] Austin to García, August 1, 2, 12, Transcripts from Department of Fomento, legajo 2, expediente 5.

other states. . . . Nothing is now wanting but a meeting of congress to dispatch all favorably. These matters were not sufficiently matured and understood for congress to act safely on them untill within a week past, so that on the whole, the cholera has done no harm in preventing the meeting of congress. *There is nothing like patience and perseverance.*" Specifically, Austin now expected prompt amendment of the law of April 6, 1830, suspension of the tariff for at least a year, improvement in the mail service, and submission of statehood in a way to insure prompt approval by the states. Repudiation of the convention by the ayuntamientos of Gonzales and Liberty had proved beneficial by showing that the Texans were not united and bent on secession.[5] Austin's varying impressions reflected in a measure, of course, the attitude of the men with whom he talked.

After his departure from Texas at the end of April Austin received but one letter from there until well past the middle of September. Then came news of the distressing ravages of cholera and of the death of John Austin and many friends. At the same time Congress resumed its sessions and failed to show the expected disposition to settle the Texas business promptly. Grief-stricken and desperate, Austin told Farías, still acting as president, that his people would not submit to further delay. Farías was deeply angered at what he conceived to be a threat, and Austin was further discouraged by what he interpreted as a determination to evade the demands of Texas. Returning to his quarters, he wrote the ayuntamiento of San Antonio under the spell of his disappointment and urged it to take the lead in effecting a provisional state organization.

"Up to the present [he wrote] nothing has been done, and I regret to say that in my opinion nothing will be done, and that it is difficult to form an idea of the result of the civil war. In this state of affairs, I recommend that the ayuntamientos of Texas place themselves in communication with each other without a moment's delay for the purpose of organizing a local government for Texas as a state of the Mexican federation according to the law of May 7, 1824, so as to have everything in readiness to effect the organization in union and harmony as soon as it is known that congress has refused its approval. This step is indispensable as a preparatory measure for there is no doubt but that the fate of Texas

[5] Austin to John Austin, August 6, 1833, and to Williams, August 14, 21, 28, September 5 and 11, Rosenberg Library, Galveston. See also Austin to Perry, September 11.

depends upon itself and not upon this government; nor that that country is lost if its inhabitants do not take its affairs into their own hands. I am firmly persuaded that what I recommend is the only means of saving us from anarchy and total ruin. In this belief I hope that you will not lose a moment in urging all the ayuntamientos of Texas to unite in organizing a local government independent of Coahuila, even though the general government refuses its consent." [6]

Again, however, the outlook brightened. Farías was mollified. The civil war ended in complete victory for the government. The chamber of deputies amended the law of April 6, 1830, and although the senate hesitated, Austin was confident that it, too, would pass the amendment. Of statehood, however, he remained extremely doubtful and repeated his advice to the ayuntamiento of Bexar to initiate a provisional organization. To his brother-in-law he wrote about the same time that Mexico ought either to make a state of Texas or transfer it to the United States without delay, and added that there was a possibility that one or the other would be done. At the end of October he declared that Congress had done more for real liberty in the last ten days than in the preceding ten years, explaining, in part, that it had repealed all laws authorizing civil officers to enforce the collection of tithes or to compel observance of monastic vows. Santa Anna's return to the capital at the beginning of November gave an unexpected twist to the amendment of the law of April 6, 1830, because he wished the repeal of article eleven to be suspended until six months after passage. He opposed state government but suggested territorial organization for Texas, and, upon Austin's rejecting that, promised to urge reforms on the legislature of Coahuila and Texas. Austin was the more readily reconciled to the final decision of the state question because Lesassier had written that the Texans were less inflamed on the subject than they had been when he left home. On December 7 the secretary of relations informed him that the repeal of the immigration restriction in the law of April 6, 1830, was formally approved; that tariff exemption and improvement of the mail service were referred to the treasury department; that revision of the judiciary system so as to allow trial by jury had been recommended to the state legislature; and that the government would do everything

[6] Austin to Ayuntamiento of San Antonio, October 2, 1833, Transcripts from Department of Fomento, Mexico, legajo 2, expediente 5; and Austin to Perry of same date.

possible to hasten the development of Texas in preparation for statehood or territorial government. Nothing more seemed obtainable, and on December 10 Austin set forth on the journey home. If his opinions have seemed vacillating, the explanation is to be found, no doubt, in a letter to Williams—"In these ticklish times almost every day brings in unexpected change."[7]

The letter of October 2 to the ayuntamiento of San Antonio now becomes important. Why did Austin write it? The answer must be partly conjectural. The ayuntamiento and citizens of San Antonio, as we saw, condemned the union with Coahuila in unmeasured terms in the memorial of December 19, 1832, and though they later declined to endorse the demands of the convention, Austin believed that they would rejoice to see them granted, and that, if the government rejected a respectful petition for reforms, they might be induced to support a local organization. At the end of September Austin received a letter from John P. Coles describing conditions in Texas as desperate. He understood from it that an outbreak of popular impatience was imminent, and it was then that he had his unfortunate interview with Farías.[8] If the Mexican inhabitants would take the lead in forming a state organization, more radical action might be averted, and the government's resentment would certainly be less bitter.[9]

But the ayuntamiento declined to act. On the contrary, it wrote Austin a lecture on the folly of trying to cure one revolution by another, a prescription from which Mexico had already suffered too much, and sent a copy to the governor at Monclova, who forwarded it to the minister of relations.[10] Finally it reached Gómez Farías, and he, gravely outraged, issued an order for Austin's arrest. The order was executed at Saltillo on January 3, 1834, when Austin walked into the office of the commandant general to confer with him concerning additional reforms for Texas.[11]

[7] Austin to Ayuntamiento of San Antonio, October 16, 1833, and to that of Nacogdoches, October 30; to Perry, October 23; to Williams, November 5, 26, Rosenberg Library; Blanco to governor (printed), November 6, Bexar Archives.

[8] Austin to Williams, November 5, 1833, tells of the letter from Coles.

[9] For Austin's own statement of his reasons for writing the letter see *Quarterly* of Texas State Historical Association, VIII, 247.

[10] Benjamin Lundy recorded in his diary the interest aroused by the communication at Monclova. See *Life, Travels and Opinions of Benjamin Lundy*, 77, 79, 85, 129.

[11] The ayuntamiento of San Antonio to Austin, October 31, 1833, and other documents for this paragraph are in Transcripts from Department of Fomento, Mexico.

Austin's first thought was to prevent turbulence when the news should reach Texas, and from Monterey, where for some reason he was taken before returning to Mexico, he wrote many letters with that end in view. "I hope there will be no excitement about my arrest," he wrote Williams, and repeated 'in substance to all others. "All I can be accused of is that I have labored arduously, faithfully, and perhaps at particular moments pationately and with more impatience and irritation than I ought to have shown, to have Texas made a state of the Mexican Confederation separate from Coahuila. This is all, and this is no crime." "I do not in any manner blame the government for arresting me," he wrote to the ayuntamiento of San Felipe, "and I particularly request that there be no excitement about it. I give the advice to the people there that I have always given, keep quiet, discountenance all revolutionary measures or men, obey the state authorities and laws so long as you are attached to Coahuila, have no more conventions, petition through the legal channels, that is through the ayuntamiento and chief of department, harmonize fully with the people of Bexar and Goliad, and act with them." The condition of national politics was more favorable to constitutional government than it had been for years, he said, some relief had already been granted, and he thought the people could well afford to wait patiently for the fulfillment of their other demands.[12]

If Austin in the rôle of peacemaker to the colonists may be thought to have painted too brightly blessings already received and the hope of others yet to come, he cannot be accused of sparing the somber colors when describing the needs of Texas to Mexicans. He wrote Williams, "I have said openly to all persons in Mexico, and to the government itself, that the local government of Texas ought to be organized, or that country ought to be transferred to the United States." And he now wrote to a number of Mexican friends, notifying them of his arrest and discussing its cause. His letter to Rafael Llanos, senator from Nuevo Leon and an old and intimate friend, is a passionate statement of dreams disappointed and plans thwarted by the ignorance and prejudice of the government. He had labored thirteen years, a lifetime of weariness, in

[12] Austin to Williams, January 12, 1834, Rosenberg Library; to Perry, January 14, 16; and to ayuntamiento of San Felipe, January 17.

peopling the wilderness of Texas, he said. As a consequence the frontiers of Coahuila, Nuevo Leon, and Tamaulipas had been protected against the destructive raids of northern Indians that they had previously suffered and the foundation had been laid for the security and prosperity of those states. He had gone to Mexico at his own expense as the representative of his people, seeking to obtain timely reforms that would avert revolution and possible loss of the province. If this were crime, then he was a great criminal.

"I have been accused [he went on] of having magnificent schemes for Texas, and I confess that I have had them. . . . It is depopulated; I wish to people it. The population that is there is backward; I wish it to be advanced and improved by the introduction of industrious farmers, liberal republicans. I want the savage Indians subdued, the frontier protected, the lands cultivated, roads and canals opened, river navigation developed and the rivers covered with boats and barges carrying the produce of the interior to the coast for export in exchange for foreign products. . . . I wish to take from my native land and from every other country the best that they contain and plant it in my adopted land—that is to say, their inhabitants, their industry, and their enlightenment, so that the eastern frontier, which is now without population and in its greater part almost without government, might present an example worthy of imitation. These are the magnificent and, as it now appears, visionary plans that I have had for Texas; and if there is a Mexican who does not wish to see them realized, I must say that he does not love his country—neither wants to see her emerge from the darkness of the fifteenth century nor shake off the chains of superstition and monastic ignorance that she is still dragging along."

He had seen in the United States a vast wilderness covered with dense population in a few years and new states erected where at the time of his birth there was not a single civilized person. He had believed that it would be the same with Mexico, but now realized that he was mistaken, because before Mexico could develop in that way "she must pay the price by a moral revolution in which shall be overthrown all the customs and the Gothic politico-religious system set up by Rome and Spain to hold the people in subjection like beasts of burden." Such a revolution she would have in a century but not in the lifetime of a single man. He ended with a note of bitterness: "I was not born in a wilderness, and have not the patience of the Bexareños and other inhabitants of this frontier, who are daily enduring the same dangers and annoyances that their fathers and grandfathers and perhaps their great-grandfathers suffered without advancing or thinking of advancing. Death is preferable to such stagnant existence, such stupid life."

In a long postscript he continued more calmly. It was not to the interest of Texas to separate from Mexico; nevertheless, he reminded Llanos, "it is well known that men are influenced more by petty local annoyances or grievances in the present, even though temporary, than by the hope of great benefits in the future." The grievances of Texas were not petty but very serious, and it was from this that opinion arose that continued union with Mexico was inconsistent with the progress and happiness of Texas. The conflict could be removed by remedying the abuses that the Texans complained of; but if they were not removed, then Mexico ought to sell the province to the United States "so as to get some profit from it before losing it," because the duty of self-preservation would drive the settlers inevitably to union with that country or to independence. He had said this repeatedly, he added, and "Mexicans with whom I have talked and who thoroughly understand the matter are of the same opinion." [13] One could not write a more fearless straightforward statement, but its effect on Llanos may perhaps be inferred from the fact that it ultimately found its way into the file of the evidence against Austin.

Austin knew the vagaries of court procedure too well to take his arrest lightly. He wrote Perry that he might be "hammered and pummeled about for a year," and asked Williams to arrange for his expenses. His anticipations were justified. Leaving Monterey under escort on January 20, he reached Mexico on February 13 and was lodged in a cell of the old Inquisition prison, solitary and *incommunicado*. Father Muldoon and William S. Parrott, an American merchant, had tried to arrange for him to stay at the *Casa Mexicana,* a boarding house, under bond, but to no avail. The vice-president, on the contrary, had issued orders that he was to be prevented from talking or writing after his arrest.[14]

---

[13] Austin to Llanos, January 14, 1834, Transcripts from Department of Fomento, Mexico. At the same time and no doubt in the same strain Austin wrote to the governor of Coahuila and Texas and to another old friend, José María Viesca, but these letters are not available.

[14] Austin to Williams, January 12, 1834, Rosenberg Library, and to Perry, January 14; the proposal for bond by Muldoon and Parrott is in Transcripts from Department of Guerra, Mexico, legajo 1, expediente 23.

In retrospect Austin wrote of this experience philosophically enough, but the journal that he kept in prison reveals the strain of terrible monotony. His cell was thirteen by sixteen feet, without windows. A slot in the door admitted food, and a skylight in the ceiling afforded light enough on fair days for reading between ten o'clock and three, but for the first month he had no books. For two hours a day he was allowed to take the sun on the roof, and in going to and from the *soledero* he sometimes saw other prisoners but was not permitted to speak to them. Indeed, except with the sergeant who brought his meals, he seems to have conversed with but two men during the three months of this rigorous confinement. One of these was Father Muldoon, who with great difficulty, and, as he said, by the use of "priestcraft," [15] gained permission to see him shortly after his arrival, and the other was the attorney assigned to his case. Father Muldoon promised to send books and food but was apparently not permitted to send the books, and it was not until the second of March, when he bribed his attendant to carry an appeal to Victor Blanco, that Austin obtained anything to read. The first book was "a tale called Yes and No," concerning which he makes no comment, except that he preferred "bread and water with books to the best of eating without them." Two weeks later the diary records the receipt of "The History of Philip II, King of Spain," and a month later again of two volumes of Plato's works, translated into French by Victor Cousin. What else he may have had we do not know. For a time he had an allowance of a dollar a day for expenses, but, after receiving twenty dollars, the commandant general notified him that he must return it, "because," as the diary explains, "I ought to receive my daily allowance from another quarter—but he did not say from what quarter or authority." Austin returned the advance and made a loan to the sergeant, and must have begun to feel the pinch of economy, for he entered in the diary, "This day I also sent away my servant, Medina, and ceased to receive my meals from Offutt's." [16]

[15] Quoted by Oliver Jones to Perry, June 10, 1834.

[16] There is nothing more in the journal concerning this subject, but on April 19 the minister of war wrote the minister of relations that Austin and the other prisoners demanded an allowance. He knew, he said, that Austin was able to bear his own expenses and he did not think the public treasury should be burdened with his support. The state department ruled, nevertheless, that he was entitled to an allowance, but before the question was settled Austin was removed to another prison. This correspondence is in Transcripts from the Department of Fomento.

In the meantime Austin's case, so far as he knew, was making no progress. On February 18 Lieutenant-Colonel J. M. Bermudor called promptly enough to say that he had been appointed counsel for the prisoner. The next day he called to have Austin sign an "act." On the 23d he reported that he had been recalled from the case. On the 25th a new attorney appeared but left neither name nor address, and his client seems not to have heard of him again. On April 29 Austin poured out his feelings in the diary.

"What a system of jurisprudence is this of confining those accused or suspected without permitting them to take any steps to make manifest their innocence or to procure proofs for their trial. . . . I do not know of what I am accused—How can I prepare my defense? . . . This system may be in conformity with law, but I am ignorant of which law, or of what rights the party accused has, but it is very certain that such a system is in no wise in conformity with justice, reason, or common sense."

Toward the end of April Santa Anna resumed the reins of government, and with the retirement of Gómez Farías, Austin's condition improved. On May 9 the decree of solitary confinement was revoked, and he was allowed to converse with the other prisoners, all of whom were educated men being held for political offenses. On June 12 the military court decided that it did not have jurisdiction, and Austin was transferred to another prison, the Acordada, and his case given to a civil court. There it slept for two months— in fact, until Santa Anna took a hand and wrote the judge that while he favored the punishment of crime, he believed also that the innocent should be acquitted.[17] This brought a prompt disclaimer of jurisdiction. The judge of the Federal District in turn quickly disclaimed authority because Austin did not reside in his district, and the case then went to the supreme court to determine where jurisdiction lay; so that, as Austin wrote Perry, after eight months he did not know what court was to try his case. Finally it was assigned to the court of the Federal District and he hoped that it might then proceed more rapidly, but in this hope, as we shall presently see, he was disappointed.[18]

[17] Santa Anna's letter of August 6, 1834, to Judge Cayetano Ibarra is in Transcripts from Department of Fomento, Mexico.

[18] Austin's "Prison Journal" is in *Quarterly* of Texas State Historical Association, II, 183–210. For his life in prison and procedure of his case see his letters to Perry, May 10 and August 25, 1834; to Oliver Jones, May 30, and to Williams, June 3 and September 7.

In telling Williams of his arrest Austin had suggested that it might expedite his release if the ayuntamientos would write the government what they knew of his character and conduct, but he hastened to add, "I do not ask it; if it is done I wish it of their own accord." His letter to the ayuntamiento of San Felipe probably outlined what he wanted said—that is, that he went to Mexico as an agent and represented accurately and faithfully the attitude of the people as it appeared when he left Texas. But the emphatic matter in all his correspondence of this time was that there must be no excitement about his arrest. "It will do me harm, and great harm to Texas. Keep quiet and let me perish if such is to be my fate." [19] Actually there was great excitement when the news first reached Texas,[20] but his friends took his advice literally and quieted it. The adoption of such a statement as he had in mind need not have conflicted with the course that he advised; but the colonists made no pretense of understanding the Mexican mind; so far as they could see, it was likely to misinterpret the most innocent measure; Austin wanted quiet, and quiet there should be.

Submission and loyalty continued to be the theme of Austin's letters, but with this came to be mingled a feeling of disappointment and injury at what looked like the indifference of the people and the persecution of his enemies. He rarely received letters, but of rumors there was no end. He resisted, but the conviction grew that he was abandoned by the people he had served; and he sometimes yielded to terrible fits of depression like those that had given his brother the "horrors" in the early days of the colony. His reluctant surrender to the feeling is evident, and, indeed, he never resigned himself to it. A respectful statement from the ayuntamientos would have opened his dungeon at any time, "and would do it now," he wrote at the end of May, "but perhaps this is too much to be done for S. F. Austin." Nevertheless, he would not believe that the people were, as rumors said, abusing him and rejoicing in his misfortune—"A few may do so, but not the mass, not the farmers, the honest and sound part of the community. They have always been correct, sound, and honest in their feelings, intentions and principles, and I have no doubt that all their sym-

[19] Austin to Perry, January 16, 1834.
[20] Bryan to Perry, February 1, 1834.

pathies are in my favor. I will not calumniate them even in my thoughts by believing otherwise." And even his enemies, he was sure, must be fair in the end; they could not be "so base as to calumniate the man who has served them faithfully and is suffering for their benefit. Personal feelings are momentary in their influence but justice will ultimately prevail." [21]

At the end of August, however, he was greatly distressed by circumstantial reports that only the active hostility of men in Texas was keeping him in prison and that "if he was not totally ruined in property and reputation it would not be for the want of exertion on their part." Thomas Jefferson Chambers and William H. Wharton were named to him, and John A. Wharton was said to have established a newspaper for the purpose of abusing him. [22] If these men were really aggravating his misfortunes—which he was loath to believe—he felt that it was particularly shameful, because they had been most active in the agitation of public opinion which had led to the convention, to the demand for state government, and to his own mission to Mexico, where his only offense, if he had committed one, was in representing too faithfully the public sentiment that they had created. The letter expressed intense feeling, but was not abusive. Moreover, it was a family letter written to his brother-in-law and intended to be seen by a few friends whom he named. But Perry published it, and stung William H. Wharton thereby to uncontrollable rage. [23]

On October 6 Austin wrote Williams a desperate letter. He had been transferred to yet a third prison, the *Carcel* of the city. The investigation of his case had begun, but was making no progress; and still no word of help or sympathy came from Texas. On the contrary, it was said that agents were there collecting evidence to convict him.

"In the meantime [he bitterly continued] I am languishing here, and when at the end of six months or a year it is thought that sufficient evidence is collected, I shall then be called on to disprove what is against me and of course shall have to send to Texas.

"In short, to sum up a long story in a few words, my friends in that country may look on me as dead for a long time to come and probably

[21] Austin to Oliver Jones, May 30, 1834, and to Williams, June 3.
[22] Wharton had established *The Advocate of the People's Rights* at Brazoria. See "Notes on Early Texas Newspapers," *Southwestern Historical Quarterly*, XXI, 139.
[23] See below, pages 389–390.

forever. A frank, manly, but mild and respectful representation from the people of Texas in my favor would have set me at liberty long since and would do it now. The president, Genl Santana, is friendly to me. So is the judge, but what can they do against a host of bitter enemies which I made by opposing a territory, and others because I am a foreigner, and hundreds because I have been active and successful in settling Texas, and others from envy, and others because I am in misfortune. What can the president and judge do against all this host, with the Minister Lombardo at their head, and especially when Texas is silent as to me, or worse than silent, for I am told that everything that comes from there is against me. My situation is desolate—almost destitute of friends and money, in a prison, amidst foes who are active to destroy me, and forgotten at home by those I have faithfully labored to serve. I have been true and faithful to this government and nation; have served them laboriously; have tried to do all the good I could to individuals and to the country; have been a philanthropist, and I am now meeting my reward. I expect to die in this prison. I have no reason to make any other calculation. It is hard and unjust and cruel. When I am dead justice will be done me. I have performed my duty and my conscience is at rest. Even the things that my enemies say were errors were evidently intended to benefit the public interest and advance the country and not to benefit myself. But so be it. I have been the means of distributing many millions of acres to make the fortunes of others, and I now doubt whether I shall not have to depend on Charity for six feet of ground to sleep in at rest. This is man and mankind—a picture of human life."

If he had eight or ten thousand dollars, he said, he might gain his liberty; but there was no way to obtain such a sum, and his chief hope now was in an expected change of government that would increase the power of Santa Anna.[24]

Austin dwells in this letter on the hostility of various groups that he had antagonized in Mexico. As to enemies in Texas, he wrote Perry at the same time, "I must confess frankly that I do not believe the hundredth part of what is said about the efforts of my enemies in Texas to ruin me. . . . I begin to think that most of what is said . . . comes from persons who are either blinded by passion or prejudice or who are real enemies of mine and of everybody else who lives in Texas and that the real object is to try and darken the North American character." Here he was interrupted by a Mexican friend who told him that a report had been received from Almonte, in Texas, which would do him great harm and probably increase

[24] Austin to Williams, October 6, 1834, Rosenberg Library.

the severity of his imprisonment; but Austin was inclined to dismiss the rumor as a device to make him offer a bribe for his liberty. In fact, he added, "all these reports about my enemies may be nothing more than management to try and draw out cash." [25] Nevertheless, it went hard with him that no intervention came from Texas in his behalf. "Whether my enemies have been active or not," he wrote Perry, "my friends ought to be so if they wish to relieve me." It had even been suggested, he said, that he held no appointment from the people; that he was not their agent. This should be corrected by official statements from the ayuntamientos avowing responsibility for the convention and for his mission. It could be done without offense, for "the strongest kind of ideas and principles," he explained, "are better expressed in mild, polite and even *flattering* language than in any other way, and such language never gives offense or mortifies self dignity or self pride." [26]

But from this source at least his anxiety and humiliation were soon to end. That they had not been relieved long before was due in part to lack of leadership in Texas and in part, as was said before, to fear that any action whatever might be misconstrued to Austin's injury. In fact, the ayuntamientos of San Felipe, Matagorda, and Liberty adopted resolutions in April and May declaring full popular responsibility for the convention and praying for his release, but they were not forwarded, and for a time no others were adopted. Possibly Almonte's arrival at Nacogdoches on a confidential mission from the government checked this beginning. Then came Austin's letters from the Inquisition. It was clear that he expected something done, and the movement was resumed with great activity, but it took time. The ayuntamientos of Bastrop, Gonzales, and Brazoria adopted resolutions; that of Matagorda substituted a second set for those adopted in May; and steps were taken to obtain the endorsement of the ayuntamiento of San Antonio. Peter W. Grayson and Spencer H. Jack, both competent lawyers, agreed to take the documents to Mexico and do what could be done for Austin's release.

---

[25] Almonte had written the secretary of relations from Nacogdoches on May 20, 1834, advising that Austin be held until the government could place two thousand troops in Texas. It was possibly a rumor of this that now reached Austin. See Transcripts from Department of Fomento, Mexico, legajo 8, expediente 66.

[26] Austin to Perry, October 6, 1834, Rosenberg Library.

The petitions declared that the convention met in response to irresistible popular demand; that Austin only half-heartedly supported it; that he was sent to Mexico because of his wide acquaintance with public men and not because he was an outstanding advocate of the convention's demands;[27] and that he acted, therefore, as the agent of the people and faithfully represented public opinion as it then existed, though it had since been changed by the reforms of the state and federal governments. They probably exaggerated, as was natural, both the unanimity of the demand for the convention and Austin's lukewarmness; but, on the whole, they presented the situation fairly and with a considerable degree of tact.[28] The sincerity of the regard that they expressed for Austin seemed attested by his election now to represent the newly created department of the Brazos in the legislature; and Williams, in fact, wrote that there was a wonderful reaction in his favor.[29]

Picking up on the way a petition from the ayuntamiento of San Antonio and a cordial letter from the governor at Monclova, where Padilla's influence was useful, Grayson and Jack reached Mexico on October 14.[30] Notice of the election in Texas followed immediately. It was only a week before that Austin had poured out his heart in desperation to Williams and Perry, and his rebound now to hope and gratitude was in proportion to his previous despondency. Never in his life, he declared, had any event afforded him greater gratification. He was now convinced that no unfriendly influence had ever been exerted from Texas and that even the hostility said to be felt against him in Mexico had been exaggerated.

Austin was particularly rejoiced by the memorial from Brazoria, signed by William H. Wharton. Of the coolness that had developed between these two since Austin was so charmed by Wharton on his

[27] R. M. Williamson, who wrote the San Felipe resolutions, declared that Austin was defeated for the presidency of the second convention because of his known lack of sympathy with its objects.

[28] The resolutions of the ayuntamiento of San Felipe, April 28, 1834, are in the Bexar Archives. All others are in the Austin Papers—Matagorda, May 17, July 28; Liberty, May 31; Bastrop, July 23; Gonzales, July 28; and Brazoria, July 31. See also Perry to Austin, May 13; Williamson to political chief, June 11 (Bexar Archives); ayuntamiento of San Felipe to that of San Antonio, July 14 (Nacogdoches Archives); and letters to Perry from Jones, June 10; Bell, July 15 and 29; McKinney, July 17; Grayson, July 25; Henry Austin, July 28; and W. H. Jack to McKinney, July 24.

[29] Election report, September 7, 1834, and Williams to Perry, September 9.

[30] Bryan to Perry, August 7, 1834, and Grayson to Perry, August 9 and September 16; election returns, September 7.

first visit to Texas we have little information.[31] Wharton recognizes
its existence in a letter of July 14, 1831, expressing a wish for an
understanding that was apparently not attained. Each defeated the
other for the presidency of the conventions of 1832 and 1833. The
two differed fundamentally in temperament. Wharton was master-
ful, quick to anger, uncontrolled—somewhat domineering, one
imagines—made no allowances for the blundering interference of
Mexican authority, and was ready at all times to try to right a real
or fancied grievance by the most direct means, regardless of the
consequences of failure either to himself or to others. Austin was
almost the opposite in every respect. He regarded Wharton as the
leader of the group of reckless spirits that since 1830 had aggravated
the difficulty of maintaining his policy of compromise and conciliation, and there can be no doubt that at times he thought of him
with considerable bitterness. To Williams he wrote soon after arriving in Mexico in 1833, "as to the man you talked with at Orleans
who said he would take a different course and induce his brother
to do so—I can only say that God can certainly change the negro
to a white man, but that is a miracle not common in our days.
What I mean is that envy, jealousy, malignity when once deeply
fixed in the human heart and fostered by boyish and silly vanity
are not easily rooted out, nor easily controuled." [32] This no doubt
referred to the Whartons. But the Brazoria memorial made ample
amends. It "is calculated to benefit me," Austin wrote, "and was
evidently intended to do so and I therefore thank him so far as
he had any agency in it." If they were not friends on his return,
it would be Wharton's fault, he said, not his.[33]

Of the charges and procedure against him Austin had written
a very accurate description in his letter of October 6 to his brother-
in-law.

"So far as I can judge [he said] all seem to agree that my letter of 2d
October to the ayuntamiento of Bexar was nothing more than an imprudent opinion, but not a criminal act in the eye of the law, because it was
merely an opinion, unaccompanied by any overt act. But as I am informed—for I know nothing certain—the intention is to try and convict

[31] Austin to Wharton, April 24, 1829.
[32] Austin to Williams, August 21, 1833, Rosenberg Library.
[33] Austin to McKinney, October 18, 1834. Perry explained in a letter of December 7
that the Brazoria document was written by William H. Jack and signed by Wharton
pro forma.

me of a design to separate Texas from Mexico and unite it to the United States, and that letter is used as an incident or link in the plot which it is pretended there was. . . . Everything I have said or done with pure intentions and in good faith. All my honest and republican frankness in explaining to the government the true situation of Texas. Everything that has passed in Texas since I went there in 1821. All the events of the last four years. All that is said there now and since my imprisonment. All that has been published about my colony in newspapers, books, etc., even the population and advancement of Texas in agriculture, arts, exports, and resources. In short, everything seems to be construed and perverted against me."

Grayson, apparently to his surprise, found this to be substantially the case. He was accustomed to the formal, specific indictment of English procedure and the situation baffled him. However, he employed a Mexican lawyer and filed an answer, and at last, on Christmas day, Austin was admitted to bail, bond was accepted, and he was set at large within the generous bounds of the Federal District.[34]

Seven suspenseful but not unhappy months were yet to pass before complete liberation. On December 31 Austin thought that the rest of his trial could not consume more than a month—his friends thought much less. On January 21 acquittal was still two or three weeks in the future. By February 6 further thought of completing the trial was abandoned; he was awaiting publication of a general amnesty law, and hoped to leave for Monclova and a meeting with Williams in ten or fifteen days. A week later he might be released by the first of March. By March 10 he no longer ventured a guess. The amnesty law had finally gone to the president for approval, but it was rumored that he would return it to Congress for alterations. "This," said Austin, "is a measure in which many thousands are deeply interested and one that the government and three-fourths or more of both houses and all the influential men are anxious should pass, and yet it has to travel the usual snail's pace of public matters. This example ought, of itself, to be proof to some of those who are so ready to blame me at home for the delay and difficulty of effecting anything here." On April 4 he hoped to be free by the end of the month, but by the 15th there had been no change, and he made no calculations. The law was finally approved and published

[34] Grayson wrote an account of his mission for Lamar in 1837. *Quarterly* of Texas State Historical Association, XIV, 155–163. See also Parrott to Perry, December 24, 1834, and Austin to Williams, December 31.

on May 3, and he hoped to have his bond canceled in time to start homeward with Don Victor Blanco on the 26th. But the matter was not so simple. A ruling must first be obtained that Austin's offense was comprehended in the amnesty law. This was settled on June 22, and on July 11 his passport was issued and he left within a week for Vera Cruz to return to Texas by New Orleans.[35]

In the meantime, Austin busied himself with many things in the interest of Texas, the most important of which, perhaps, was the preparation and publication of his *Explanation to the Public Concerning the Affairs of Texas*.[36] He was confident that this had a great influence in convincing intelligent Mexican opinion that the true economic interest of Texas was opposed to separation from Mexico and that its complaints were entitled to considerate examination and redress.[37] He now had leisure, too, to work at a plan that had been in his mind for years for diverting to Texan ports the important trade that had grown up between St. Louis, Missouri, and northern Mexico through the gateway of Santa Fé. He had written in 1829 that "the whole trade of the Chihuahua and Sonora and New Mexico region must ultimately enter in one of the ports of Texas, either Galveston or Matagorda," [38] and he reverted to the subject now in his *Explanation to the Public*. His plan for accomplishing this was a road through Texas from the Gulf to Chihuahua. He thought that the idea was well received, admitted that it had become "a great hobby" with him, and, characteristically, wrote and talked about it to everybody who might help to put it through —to the federal government, to the governments of Coahuila and Chihuahua, and to many individuals. There is reason to believe that Austin's vision looked beyond immediate commercial profits and saw in the road a bond that might bring the northern states of Mexico into a firm political union. This is indicated in a letter to his brother-in-law. "In this matter," he wrote, "and probably in others, Chihuahua and Texas have the same interest. . . . The Chi-

---

[35] Letters from Austin to Williams, January 21, 1835, February 14, April 1, 4, 15, 29, and May 6 (all of these except the letters of January 21 and April 1 are in the Rosenberg Library); to Perry, February 6, March 4, 10, 28, and July 13; to Fisher, March 30; to Miller and Grayson, May 13; interpretation of amnesty law, June 22; and passport, July 11.

[36] *Exposicion al Público sobre los Asuntos de Texas* (Mexico, January, 1835) translated by Ethel Z. Rather, in *Quarterly* of Texas State Historical Association, VIII, 232–258. Four hundred and fifty copies were printed. See receipt of C. C. Sebring, July, 1835.

[37] Austin to Perry, February 6 and March 4 and 10, 1835.

[38] Austin to Henry Austin, August 27, 1829.

huahua road is a great object for Texas, a vast link in its prosperity. ... Its influence will be known *after* it is opened, and not before." If all the unquiet spirits in Texas would organize themselves into a corps and explore a satisfactory route for such a road, they would be much more useful to Texas, he added, than they or anybody else suspected.[39] Another subject to which he gave much attention was the promotion of cotton trade with Vera Cruz and Tampico. Numerous mills were being established in Mexico, and, foreseeing the demand for raw cotton that this would create, he urged the government to grant a premium on Texas shipments. At the same time he wrote that Spain was expected soon to recognize the independence of Mexico and that the Cuban market would then be open to Texan cattle, oxen, hogs, horses, mules, corn, lard, beans, and peas.[40]

On the whole, this was a happy half-year for Austin, filled with much labor, but brightened by pleasures that he greatly enjoyed. He lived comfortably; mingled with educated men of affairs; attended balls, theaters, and operas; and wrote Williams that he was happier than he had been for fourteen years—"for during all that period my mind has been laboring and worrying for the benefit of others and for the common good. My thoughts are now confined, or I should say are beginning to confine themselves, to a narrower space, myself, my family, my own individual affairs. It is a novelty, a new life to me ... but I shall soon get accustomed to it and be much happier. I want some money to travel with next year. This at present is all my cuidado [care]." He wished, he added, to spend "a year or two in a ramble."

Austin's belief that his imprisonment was prolonged by the management of enemies requires examination. In the first place, it must be remembered that this was the period of Robertson's unbridled abuse of Austin, rumors of which reached Austin and left the impression that a campaign of vilification and distortion was being waged against him. Robertson's attorney, Thomas Jefferson Chambers, was thought by Williams at least to have injured Austin very gravely.[41] In the second place, John A. Wharton established *The*

---

[39] Austin to Williams, February 14, 1835, Rosenberg Library; and to Perry, March 4 and 10.

[40] See letters to Williams and Perry already cited.

[41] Williams to Perry, April 1, 1835.

Advocate of the People's Rights in the fall of 1833 for the purpose, as he explained, of liberating opinion and unshackling the press, and Austin was given to understand that the paper attacked him as the chief obstacle to freedom. Whether true or not,[42] this was plausible, because the Wharton brothers headed the party of opposition—so far as there was one—to Austin's policy of forbearance and conciliation with Mexico. William H. Wharton poured out a veritable tornado of wrath in reply to Austin's letter of August 25, denying that he had done anything whatever to aggravate Austin's misfortunes;[43] and as to intention this must be accepted as final. The attitude of Wharton's group, however, in itself inevitably harmful, is well illustrated by a letter from Sam Houston. Writing to John A. Wharton, Houston said: "William showed me his *card* in answer to Austin's ridiculous letter of last August from Mexico. I think he has left the little Gentleman very few crumbs of comfort. I was provoked at his first letter, when he *broke into prison,* but when I read his letter of August I must confess that it awakened no other emotion in my breast than *pity* mingled with *contempt.* He showed the disposition of the viper without its fangs. The first was very imprudent, the second pusillanimous."[44] These men, though impetuous and at times intemperate, were not mean, and certainly did not deliberately persecute Austin in prison—a fact that he himself was ready to recognize before the arrival of Grayson and Jack for his relief.[45]

There are indications, however, that from another source influence was exerted to discredit Austin with the government and to keep him out of Texas. The details are not clear. Colonel José Antonio Mexia, whose expedition to Texas in 1832 we have already noticed, became an important man in Mexico after Santa Anna's

---

[42] For what is known of this paper see the writer's "Notes on Early Texas Newspapers," in *Southwestern Historical Quarterly,* XXI, 139.

[43] Wharton's "card," dated November 9, 1834, was apparently circulated first as a broadside, but upon his insistence was later printed in the *Texas Republican* of December 13. See his letter of December 8 to the editor. Lamar Papers, Texas State Library.

[44] Houston to Wharton, April 14, 1835, Lamar Papers. Houston adds, "He aimed at me a few thrusts, but I will wait an interview with him before I make any public expose of his want of understanding, or his political inconsistencies." Careful examination of Austin's letter fails to discover anything that might apply to Houston unless it is a reference to "a silly, gasconading letter," published in the New Orleans *Commercial Bulletin* and reprinted in the Mexican *Telégrafo,* which Austin said had injured him. Austin speaks of "inflammatory men, political adventurers, would-be great men, vain talkers, and visionary fools"; but in none of these would Houston have admitted a reference to himself.

[45] Austin to Perry, October 6, 1834, Rosenberg Library, Galveston.

election. At the same time he was an agent and lobbyist for the Galveston Bay and Texas Land Company, working with General John T. Mason. Zavala, one of the principals of the company, was there, too, in high favor. For a time capital gossip cast both him and Mexia for portfolios in Santa Anna's cabinet. These men had a keen interest in Texas, particularly after the repeal of the law of April 6, 1830, which had shut out immigrants from their grant. They apparently recognized the futility of trying to obtain a state government and labored for a territorial organization, which Austin opposed. And weaving in and out of the background was Colonel Anthony Butler, grasping at straws and plotting incessantly for the transfer of Texas to the United States, to the accomplishment of which he considered Austin the most serious obstacle.[46] Austin learned of Zavala's support of the territorial plan in a conference with Santa Anna on November 5, 1833, and wrote Williams anxiously about it the same day. Thereafter he repeated in many letters that he had made powerful enemies by opposing territorial government. Becoming more specific, he said that he had reason to believe that Mason and Mexia had worked to perpetuate his imprisonment—"they never forgave me for opposing their schemes to make a territory of Texas and their monopolies of land, etc." They and Butler, he declared, were birds of a feather. In the end, however, ascribing his earlier suspicions to the machinations of Butler, he questioned whether Mason, at least, had done anything to injure him.[47] All this, of course, is extremely tenuous and might be dismissed as conjecture excited by the plot-laden atmosphere of the Mexican capital. But from Texas at least one letter was sent to Mexia expressing the hope that Austin might be detained for years;[48] and Henry Meigs, who strove zealously to obtain the intervention of the United States for Austin's release, wrote from New York after Austin returned to Texas that a great interest was

[46] Butler wrote of Austin to his government, July 13, 1834 (MSS., Department of State, Despatches from Agents to Mexico, Vol. 6): "He is unquestionably one of the bitterest foes of our government and people that is to be found in Mexico, and has done more to embarrass our negotiations upon a certain subject than all the rest put together; and I am very sure that he was the principal cause of my being defeated in the last effort made to obtain a cession of Texas."

[47] See particularly Austin's letters to Williams, November 5, 26, 1833, and February 14, April 29, and May 6, 1835, Rosenberg Library; and to Perry, March 3, 10, 1835.

[48] Alexander Calvit to Mexia, August 29, 1833, Transcripts from Department of Fomento, Mexico. Calvit had lived in Texas for some years. What his connection with Mexia was is unknown.

exerted to destroy him. "Truly your escape is most fortunate." [49]
Evidently there was sinister fact behind the rumors that came to
Austin, but as yet we can barely glimpse it.

These two years at the capital, observing politics at close range
and seeing Santa Anna re-enact the rôle that Iturbide played a decade earlier—using a platform of liberalism merely as a stepping
stone to a *de facto* dictatorship—profoundly influenced Austin's
views concerning the future of Texas. What these views were requires explanation, because, on their face, Austin's letters of this
period are inconsistent and conflicting. This was caused by the
kaleidoscopic aspect of politics. The welfare of Texas was Austin's
fundamental guiding principle. With a stable government, having
a reasonable regard for the interests of Texas, there would be many
advantages under Mexican rule. But in the last resort the welfare
of Texas might demand a breach with Mexico. What then? In such
thought as he gave to this contingency prior to 1832 Austin certainly favored independence; after that date the contemplation of union
with the United States became more acceptable. This may have been
because he realized that events were tending toward a break before
the resources of Texas could maintain an independent government.
The breach, however, whenever it should come, must be hazardous;
and good policy would always postpone it, either until grievances
could no longer be endured or until local resources guaranteed the
success of resistance. So his feelings varied directly with the activity
of the political caldron. When it seemed about to grow quiet, giving
promise of peace and reform, hope revived and he talked of loyalty
and the benefits of Mexican citizenship; when it boiled furiously he
thought of the inevitable break—but always in his public letters he
urged tranquil aloofness from the dissensions of national politics
and industrious attention to the development of Texas. In effect,
Austin stood at the parting of the ways, and his advice was equally
good for either road that he should finally elect to travel. Which
road it must in all probability be was clear to him before he left
Mexico. We may now follow the fluctuations of his decision with
some degree of certainty.

When he started to Mexico in the spring of 1833 Austin had undoubtedly been brought to a condition of desperation by the con-

---

[49] Meigs to Austin, September 29, 1835. Meigs was the husband of Austin's cousin, a
daughter of the elder Stephen Austin. He speaks of John Forsyth, Secretary of State in
Jackson's cabinet, as his brother-in-law.

stant strain of combating the agitations of the discontented element in Texas. "I am so weary," he said, "that life is hardly worth having, situated as we now are." Taken alone, the annoyances incident to weak and capricious government could still have been endured with a measure of resignation, but not when they continually stimulated the violent nagging of the local radicals. "Ben Franklin or Job would have had their moments of ruffled temper in some situations I have been placed [in]," Austin once wrote;[50] and his patience was now at the breaking point. His letters to Perry, his brother-in-law, and to Williams were generally not for publication, and reveal, therefore, his real thoughts. He wrote Perry soon after reaching Mexico, "I am totally done with conciliatory measures, and for the future shall be uncompromising as [to] Texas matters." Just after the stormy interview with Farías he wrote again, "I am tired of this government. They are always in revolution and I believe always will be. I have had much more respect for them than they deserve. But I am done with all that." And then he spoke of the last resort, "The fact is, this government ought to make a state of Texas or transfer her to the United States without delay, and there is some probability at this time that one or the other will be done."[51] A few days after writing this letter he had his very satisfactory conference with Santa Anna, at which Victor Blanco informed him that excitement in Texas had subsided. While the news was gratifying, a feeling of exasperation against the unquiet spirits who had compelled him to risk a departure from his well-tried policy of isolation and conciliation was natural. This found expression in several letters after his arrest, in which he advised returning to the policy of patient waiting.[52] Nevertheless, as we know,

[50] Austin to McKinney, October 18, 1834.

[51] Austin to Perry, July 30, and October 2 and 23, 1833.

[52] Austin wrote Williams on January 12, 1834, for example: "It has been intimated to me that some enemy, I know not who, had accused me of designs to unite Texas with the United States of the North. Such an assertion is false, and I disregard it. I have said openly to all persons in Mexico, and to the Government itself, that I was of opinion the local government of Texas ought to be organized, or that country ought to be transferred to the United States, for situated as it now is, it is liable to revolutions and anarchy which may do much harm to the frontiers of both nations, and finally loose Texas and ruin the poor and honest settlers who have labored in good faith to redeem it from the wilderness and make it a valuable portion of the Mexican republic. The real fact is that at this time Texas does not belong to Mexico, nor to Coahuila, nor to the settlers who have redeemed it—it belongs to them in justice and in right; that is, to the Mexican republic and to the inhabitants of Texas. But in point of fact, it belongs to demagogues, pettyfoggers, visionary speculators and scheamers, to Indians, to anarchy and discord and confusion—to comprehend all in one word, it is without government." See also letters to Perry, January 16, 17, May 10, and August 25, 1834.

and as he himself intimated to Perry, this policy looked two ways. "I have always been of the opinion," he wrote, "that a silent and quiet course was the true one for Texas. I wished to see it grow up in tranquility like an oak sapling in the midst of a thick forest, which protects it while slender and weak from the storm, until it rears its head above the rest with a sturdy trunk and firmly rooted foundation that enables it to defy the storms and rely upon its own matured strength." There had been a painful conflict in his mind for the past three years, he said, between abstract right and "what I believe to be the true policy and interest of Texas. This conflict, added to the influence which my friends had over me, has caused me much unhappiness, and perhaps it has at times given to me the appearance of wavering. I have felt for Texas as a parent feels for its only child when he believes it to be in danger." [53]

Toward the end of 1834 Austin became convinced that the transfer of Texas to the United States within two years was probable, because men who were thought to be in the secrets of the government were trying to buy Texas lands. The course of Mexican politics gave him no cause to regret the prospect; but whatever the issue, the future of Texas would be secure if only its development went on unchecked; its prosperity "should flow onward like the silent current of a river." As to politics, he no longer made any pretense of trying to understand them. "Who does? Keep quiet and still in that state —look on ... at present everybody is *looking on,* for something— no one knows what." Santa Anna was obviously preparing to revise the constitution, but as yet Austin did not believe that he would abandon the federal system. On the eve of his return to Texas, however, he wrote that the federal system would surely fall. And from this point one feels that Austin knew the road that Texas must ultimately travel. There would be no hope of political tranquility for it under a despotic central government. On the way home he wrote Mrs. Holley from New Orleans that it was now only a matter of "a great immigration of good and efficient families this fall and winter. Should we get such an emigration, especially from the Western States, all is done." The violent political convulsions of Mexico would finally have shaken Texas off. [54]

[53] Austin to Perry, November 6, 1834.

[54] Austin to Mrs. Holley, August 31, 1835, and the letters to Perry and Williams during 1834 and 1835 previously cited.

CHAPTER XV

Texas During Austin's Absence

FOLLOWING Austin's departure the Texans settled down, as we saw, to await the results of his mission. Arciniega, acting political chief, wrote from San Antonio that the colonists were tranquil and that their adherence to the existing government could be safely relied upon, because "as long as they live they can never cease to be republicans." In the same letter he gave an account of the ravages of cholera. This was confined principally to the coast settlements. Eighty died at Brazoria, and Velasco was nearly depopulated. Malaria, too, was unusually virulent, due no doubt to overflow and continuous rains; and Perry wrote that Austin would find on his return "a great vacuum" among his friends.[1]

Under such conditions political irritation would naturally sink into the background and Austin's advice in October, 1833, to proceed with a provisional organization of state government found even Brazoria unwilling to move.[2] After Austin's arrest this attitude continued, despite the efforts of Anthony Butler and others to "stampede" the colonists into an act of insurrection from which it would be difficult to withdraw.[3] It was encouraged by Austin's ad-

---

[1] Arciniega to Secretary of State, August 26, 1833, Nacogdoches Archives; Perry to Austin, October 26. See also Lesassier to political chief, September 2, Bexar Archives. In 1834 cholera visited Goliad and San Antonio, but the American settlements seem to have escaped.

[2] A printed address of the ayuntamiento of Brazoria, January 1, 1834 (Bexar Archives), warned the people that organization without the consent of the general government would mean war. This they did not want. If, as Austin gave reason to hope, the law of April 6, 1830, should be amended, they would be inclined to wait a year or two before applying again for a state organization—provided they were not in the meantime oppressed "by planting law-despising garrisons, custom houses, etc, etc, amongst us." This was signed by Edwin Waller, William H. Wharton, Henry S. Brown, and Peyton R. Splane. On the somewhat irregular history of the ayuntamiento of Brazoria see Decree No. 196, Gammel, *Laws of Texas,* I, 307, and documents in the Bexar Archives dated May 8, August 26, September 30, December 16, 1833, and June 16, 1834.

[3] For Butler's efforts see letters of January 28 and February 8, 1834, signed O. P. Q., in *Mississippi Valley Historical Review,* XI, 109–118. An intemperate, bombastic letter from Matagorda, dated February 17, 1834, and published in the New Orleans *Commercial Bulletin,* declared that "the low rumble of an earthquake was being heard and felt in Texas; it might be repressed for some years or break out suddenly with fury, fire, and destruction." But if Austin's blood were shed "five thousand swords would leap from

vice to remain calm, and was greatly strengthened by the important reforms now put through the legislature in behalf of Texas. The law forbidding foreign born citizens to engage in retail trade was repealed; local self-government was extended by the creation of the department of the Brazos and of four new municipalities— Matagorda, San Augustine, San Patricio, and Mina; Texas was allowed an additional representative in the legislature, making three to Coahuila's nine; the use of English in official documents was legalized; religious toleration was established; and a special judiciary act, though it never went into effect, promised removal of an abuse of long standing.[4] This last provided for an appellate circuit court in Texas, subject to the supreme court, created a sufficient number of local courts, and authorized jury trial in both civil and criminal cases. The jury was to consist of twelve men, but a verdict could be rendered by eight. The judge of the superior or appellate court was to be appointed by the legislature from nominations by the governor, held office during good behavior, and received a salary of three thousand dollars, which for the first year was to be paid with thirty leagues of land. Thomas Jefferson Chambers, who was appointed judge of the Texas circuit, wrote in December, 1834, that the mere passage of these laws had had a political effect which nothing but their repeal could ever destroy.[5]

The generally peaceful condition of Texas during this year is attested by a competent official investigation. About the time that Austin was arrested the vice-president ordered Colonel Juan Nepomuceno Almonte to Texas on a special mission. He was to explain that the confusion arising from plague and civil war had prevented attention to the needs of the colonists; that the government was now firmly established, however; and that he was to hear their complaints and transmit them for consideration. He was to try to reconcile the colonists to a territorial government; and if questioned about Austin was to say that he was accused of attempting to incite revolution but that he would no doubt soon be released and return to Texas a peaceful citizen. Almonte's private instructions were more enlightening. He was to observe the number and distribution of the

---

their scabbards." Beyond injuring Austin, however, by furnishing evidence of a spirit of recalcitrance in Texas, this effusion had no effect.

[4] Gammel, *Laws of Texas,* I, 281, 318, 352, 355, 356, 360, 364, 384.

[5] Chambers to Secretary of State, December 14, 1834, Bexar Archives.

colonists, with their arms and resources for defense; cultivate loyal leaders and consult with them upon the best means of defeating the aims of the independence party, if there was one, as reported; and do everything possible to paralyze menacing preparations of the colonists in order to gain time for the government to free itself from its other difficulties and turn attention to Texas. Much time might be consumed by a census, he was reminded, if the inhabitants insisted that they were ready for a state organization. In some prudent way he was to get information to the negroes that the laws of Mexico made them free, and was to make tentative selection of vacant lands for colonies of free negroes from the United States.[6] It is evident that Farías believed that Texas was on the verge of revolt and that he impressed his belief on Almonte.

From Vera Cruz Almonte reported on February 12 that he would sail for New Orleans the next day and go thence to Texas. The original plan had been to send him on a war ship but none was available, and direct passage to Texas in a merchant vessel could not be obtained. At New Orleans he received conflicting reports about Texas. Some predicted a revolt and seizure of all the Mexican settlements as a result of Austin's arrest; others declared that Austin's arrest was already known and that the colonists were still quiet. He decided therefore to delay his journey by going through Natchitoches and Nacogdoches, where he could learn from Bean the actual condition of the country. In the meantime, correspondents in New Orleans would reassure the colonists and prepare them for his arrival. He found free negroes well disposed to emigrate to Texas, but wisely took no steps to inaugurate such a movement. At Natchitoches people conveniently assumed that he was connected with the boundary commission and he did not undeceive them. He visited Fort Jessup at the invitation of General Leavenworth and was convinced by his observations that the United States contemplated no hostile movement against Mexico. But a great emigration was pouring into Texas—more than three thousand, he estimated, would enter during the year—and two thousand troops should be placed

[6] There are several different drafts of these instructions in Transcripts from the Department of Fomento, Mexico, legajo 8, expediente 66. They are undated, but the covering letter to Almonte is dated January 17, 1834. On the project of colonizing free negroes in Texas see: "Influence of Slavery in the Colonization of Texas" in *Mississippi Valley Historical Review*, XI, 3–36, and correspondence between Almonte and David Lee Child in Fomento Transcripts, University of Texas.

in Texas to prevent the loss of the country. Reports of the tranquility of the colonies continued to reach him.[7]

May, June, and half of July Almonte spent at Nacogdoches gathering statistics and readjusting his conception of the settlers. He noted little desire for state government and no excitement over Austin's imprisonment. Contrary to expectation, he found the settlers "well disposed and friendly"; and it is evident that he began to study their needs without prejudice. As a consequence, he recommended a considerable part of the program that had taken Austin to Mexico—the establishment of weekly mail service between Nacogdoches and Natchitoches to connect with the postal system of the United States; and tariff exemption until 1838 on iron, tools, wagons, agricultural implements, bagging, and household furniture. For the improvement of local government he urged precisely the measures that the state government had already enacted—increase in the number of ayuntamientos, appointment of political chiefs for the departments of Nacogdoches and Brazos, and trial by jury. He conferred with the friendly Indians around Nacogdoches and advised granting them land and using them as a buffer against the United States.[8]

Almonte arrived at San Felipe on July 19 in some uneasiness still, because he had been told that Austin's friends might try to hold him as a hostage. On the contrary, he was cordially received. William H. Jack wrote of him that he was "intelligent, agreeable, and apparently candid"; and Josiah H. Bell introduced him to Perry as "much of a gentleman." He visited Brazoria, Velasco, Matagorda, and Harrisburg; was convinced that the colonists had been misunderstood; and said that his report would be "of the most favorable character"—which in fact it was, so far as we know. He wrote the government that all was quiet in Texas and that it would remain so, if the civil convulsions of Mexico could be stopped. At the same time he urged the release of Austin as a political measure.[9]

Almonte summed up his recommendations to the state govern-

[7] Almonte to minister of relations, February 12, March 4, April 12 and 13, 1834, Transcripts from Department of Fomento as cited, expediente 65.

[8] Almonte to minister of relations, May 4, 5, 20 (four letters of this date), June 16 (two letters), and June 30, 1834, *ibid.;* to governor of Coahuila and Texas, May 6, June 16, Saltillo, legajo 29, expediente 1269; and Lemus to minister of war, quoting Almonte, June 4, Transcript from War Department archive, op. mil. Texas, 1834, legajo 1, expediente 158.

[9] Letters of Almonte to minister of relations, July 22 and August 7, Transcripts as cited; Jack, Grayson, and Bell to Perry, July 24, 25, and 29, 1834.

ment in a letter written at Monclova on September 23. He described Texas as a veritable paradise of fertile land, fine rivers, noble forests, good ports, and abundant productions; but the land system, he said, had been improvidently lax and speculators had taken advantage of it to enrich themselves without corresponding benefit to the state. To remedy this and prevent further dissipation of the state's resources he suggested the appointment of five special commissioners—the first to investigate the execution of empresario contracts and hear complaints of the colonists; the second to supervise the purchase of lands by Mexicans and prevent the illegal sale of such lands to unnaturalized foreigners; the third to extend titles to colonists who had settled at their own expense, whether on vacant lands or on those of an empresario; the fourth to collect dues on the lands already granted and to take possession of lands that had lapsed to the state; and the fifth to prepare a classified exhibit of the vacant lands to enable the government to value them. English should be legalized for five years, the laws should be officially translated and circulated, and public interpreters should be appointed for the courts and paid by fees. Properly qualified lawyers should be licensed without examination by the supreme court. The law allowing the superior judge of Texas thirty leagues of land for a year's service should be repealed, because even ten leagues would be an exorbitant equivalent for three thousand dollars, the amount of the salary in money. He repeated his previous advice to settle agricultural Indians on the East Texas frontier, and emphasized the general need of schools and of a priest in the department of Brazos.[10] After his return to Mexico Almonte published the results of his observations in his *Noticia Estadistica sobre Tejas*. It is a valuable supplement to Austin's pamphlet, which appeared a few weeks earlier.[11] It gives a picture, in some respects too flattering, of the progress and prosperity of Texas, but it is a significant testimonial to the character and industry of the mass of the settlers, as well as to Almonte's impartial effort to get at the bottom of conditions. What oral reports he may have made we do not know, but in his available writings he recognized and condemned most of the

[10] Almonte to Governor Elguezabal, September 23, 1834, Saltillo, legajo 29, expediente 1292. Almonte found some evidence of slave trade with Cuba, and of course introduction of slaves from the United States was common.
[11] A translation of Almonte's *Noticia* by Carlos E. Castañeda is published in *The Southwestern Historical Quarterly*, XXVIII, 177–222. Date of the original publication is obtained from Almonte to Williams, March 25, 1835, Rosenberg Library, Galveston.

abuses of which the colonists had complained, and seems to have believed that the removal of these and the establishment of political order in Mexico were the conditions most essential to the content- ment and continued loyalty of the colonists.

When Farías sent Almonte to Texas he dispatched José María Diaz Noriega on a supplementary mission to the state capital. The state's dues to the federal government were long in arrears. Noriega was to obtain a settlement of these, taking land in Texas at the public price and agreeing, on behalf of the general government, to colonize it according to law. Part of the plan contemplated settle- ment of Indians in the coast and border reserves. Though frankly skeptical of this feature of the plan, Governor Villaseñor interposed no objection, and Noriega's business seemed on the eve of satis- factory adjustment when he became involved in a controversy with the permanent deputation over a proclamation that it issued against Santa Anna and was ordered from the state, an act of discourtesy which Austin thought reacted injuriously upon himself.[12]

Shortly after this, and while Almonte was still at San Felipe, a feud developed between Monclova and Saltillo which left the state for some months without constitutional government. This conflict had its origin in the removal of the capital to Monclova by a decree of the legislature passed March 9, 1833.[13] On June 24, 1834, after adjournment of the legislature, the permanent deputation and the executive council issued jointly a protest against the reactionary program championed by Santa Anna in the Plan of Cuernavaca, and called a special session of the legislature to take steps for the "safety of the confederation [and] for the permanent restoration of the public tranquillity, at present interrupted by collisions of the supreme national authorities."[14] A month later they retracted and

[12] Noriega's correspondence—from January to August, 1834—is in Transcripts of the University of Texas from Department of Fomento, Mexico, legajo 8, expediente 66.

[13] Decree No. 214, Gammel, *Laws of Texas,* I, 317; Journals of the legislature of Coahuila and Texas, 1678–1682, transcripts of University of Texas. The change was officially initiated by petitions from the alcaldes of Bexar, Goliad, and Parras and was voted by all the deputies except those from Saltillo.

[14] Gammel, *Laws of Texas,* I, 388. On May 31 Santa Anna had dismissed Congress, and a copy of the legislature's protest (in transcripts of the University of Texas, Fomento, legajo 9, expediente 68) declared that the legislature would recognize none of his acts as legal since that date, nor until Congress was again free. In his letter of August 25, 1834, to Perry Austin explained very clearly that Santa Anna—whatever his motives— had acted within his constitutional functions. The constitution provided that the regular sessions of Congress should close on April 15 but might be extended for thirty days if the members or the president thought it desirable. If, at the end of the thirty days,

announced their readiness to accept any measure approved by a majority of the states.[15] On July 19, however, four days earlier, the city of Saltillo, seeing a chance to regain its former prestige, declared unequivocally for Santa Anna, repudiated the government at Monclova, set up a rival governor, and declared void all laws passed by the legislature since the removal of the capital from Saltillo.[16] Thereupon the ayuntamiento of Monclova, three deputies, and two members of the executive council, with the local garrison, set aside the constitutional acting governor, who was old and infirm, and, without a shadow of authority, appointed in his place Colonel Juan José Elguezabal of the regular army.[17] They obviously expected an attempt to reestablish the supremacy of Saltillo in the state and were preparing for defense.

Thomas Jefferson Chambers and two of the Texan deputies, Oliver Jones and Antonio Vásquez, were in Monclova when this *coup* occurred, and joined in an address describing what had been done and recommending that a convention be held at Bexar, either to organize a provisional government or to decide what other steps should be taken. The reception of this document reveals a complete reversal of the attitude of Bexar since the ayuntamiento declined to follow the same advice from Austin. With the approval of Juan N. Seguin, who was now chief of the department, a public meeting on October 7 endorsed the proposal, and Seguin wrote to the chiefs of the Brazos and Nacogdoches departments requesting them to have delegates elected for a meeting on November 15.[18] Henry Rueg, of

---

further prolongation was necessary, extra sessions might be called by the president and executive council. Congress was attempting to continue its session beyond the constitutional thirty days despite the fact that no extra session had been called. "Men of judgment," said Austin, "can easily decide, I think, by examining these constitutional points whether the president or congress were in error. I fear these things have not been understood in Texas, and that the people have been excited to take part against the president. What they ought to have done, and ought to do in future, is to take no part at all in such matters and to preserve a *dead silence*. Neither yea nor nay, pro nor con. Stick to the constitution and close their eyes and ears against all kinds of Plans and pronunciamentos and against *all inflamatory advice, from all* quarters."

[15] Gammel, *Laws of Texas*, I, 390.

[16] J. Antonio Vásquez, Oliver Jones, and Thomas Jefferson Chambers to the Texans, September 1, 1834, Bexar Archives. Vásquez and Jones were members of the legislature from Texas and probably went to Monclova in response to the call for a special session.

[17] *Ibid*.

[18] The address of Jones, Chambers and Vásquez, September 1, 1834, Seguin to ayuntamiento of Bexar, October 13, and to the other chiefs, October 14, are in the Bexar Archives. Chambers, now at Bexar, reinforced Seguin's request by an address on October 15 in which he explained that the recent judiciary act was fatally defective and could not be amended on account of the prevailing anarchy. Bexar Archives.

Nacogdoches, took no action; but Henry Smith, of the Brazos, violently prejudiced against all Mexicans, issued an address before receiving Seguin's communication, advocating substantially what Seguin proposed. The conflict between the rival cities had destroyed the government, he said, and in fact dissolved the union of Coahuila and Texas; let a convention recognize this, declare the separation permanent, and set up a constitutional government.[19] The central committee, composed now of James B. Miller, Wily Martin, Robert Peebles, William Pettus, William B. Travis, William H. Jack, and F. W. Johnson, publicly opposed Smith. They reminded the people of the remedial legislation just enacted and denied both the legality and the necessity of the course that he proposed. Smith replied in a long tirade and ordered an election for November 8 to decide whether delegates should be sent to Bexar on the 15th. He had received on October 28 Seguin's invitation to cooperate, and, anticipating that there would not be time to hold elections and get representatives to San Antonio by November 15, had urged him to adjourn the convention from day to day until they arrived.[20]

Aside from the fact that they did not think conditions justified such a measure, friends of Austin feared the effect of another convention on the movement for his release and set themselves to defeat Smith's efforts. The address of the central committee was, of course, a part of their work. This was written by William H. Jack, and Williams, describing it to Austin, prophesied that it would "kill Smith and his friends and check this present exertion for a state." He was glad to see, he added, that men formerly opposed to Austin were now foremost in declaring themselves his friends, "and the old three hundred almost to a man are warm in your cause." Thomas F. McKinney, whose language was seldom restrained, thought the time had come "to put an end to the demagogues and scoundrels who wish to view and use us as mere appendages to their highness and instruments for their convenience." In fact, the people felt none of the indignation that Smith professed. They were prosperous, unprecedented immigration was pouring in, and, what-

[19] Rueg to Governor Elguezabal, December 3, 1834, Bexar Archives; Smith's broadside, "Security for Texas," October 20, 1834, Lamar Papers, Texas State Library.

[20] Address of the central committee, October 28, 1834, Edward, *History of Texas,* 225–231; Smith's "Explanatory Remarks on . . . 'Security for Texas,' " no date, Lamar Papers; Smith to Seguin, November 6, 1834, Domestic Correspondence, Texas State Library.

ever irritations the future might hold, they had as yet experienced no inconvenience from the clash between Saltillo and Monclova. The few precincts that held elections therefore voted against sending delegates to San Antonio.[21]

In the meantime, Saltillo and Monclova were approaching an adjustment. Commissioners from the two cities agreed on November 6 to submit their claims to Santa Anna and abide by his decision. After conferring with Victor Blanco and with Almonte, who had little patience with the Saltillo party, he decreed that Monclova should remain the capital; that a new election should be held for governor, vice-governor, legislature, and Congress; and that Elguezabal should continue to act as governor until the elections were held.[22]

The conflict and resultant confusion at Monclova were, however, far from ended. In addressing the newly elected legislature on March 1 Elguezabal expressed the conventional wish to be relieved soon of the burdens of office, and to his great chagrin the members chose to consider this a resignation, and elected José M. Cantú in his stead. Elguezabal declined to publish the decree announcing this action, but otherwise did not protest, and retired from the capital on March 12, 1835. Cantú yielded the office after two weeks to Marcial Borrego, head of the executive council, and Borrego was relieved on April 15 by the inauguration of the elected governor, Agustin Viesca.[23] Saltillo, in the meantime, encouraged by the *comandante general* of the Eastern Interior States, Martin Perfecto de Cós, had taken with ill grace Santa Anna's decision leaving the capital at Monclova.[24] On March 12 the Saltillo deputies, for reasons that are not clear, withdrew from the legislature.[25] On the 14th the

[21] Perry to Austin, December 7, 1834, gives the result of the election at Brazoria, Columbia, and Velasco—the only precincts in the Brazos department so far as we know that opened the polls. See also Chambers to Governor Elguezabal, December 14 (Bexar Archives); McKinney to Perry, November 4; and Henry Austin to Perry, November 14. Isidro Benavides to Seguin, November 11 (Bexar Archives), indicates that an election was held at Victoria but does not give the results.

[22] See a decree of Elguezabal, December 26, 1834, Bexar Archives; and Almonte to secretary of relations, October 10, 1834, Transcripts from Department of Fomento, Mexico, legajo 8, expediente 65.

[23] Gammel, *Laws of Texas,* I, 390–392; Journals of the legislature of Coahuila and Texas, transcript, pages 1846, 1856, 1860.

[24] Filisola, *Memorias para la Historia de la Guerra de Tejas,* II, 112.

[25] They last appeared in a debate opposing the removal of Acting Governor Elguezabal by accepting his imputed resignation. Cantú wrote the political chief of Bexar (March 14) that they protested *"frivolos motivos,"* but he did not specify what the motives were.

legislature passed a law authorizing the governor to sell four hundred leagues of public land and to fix conditions of settlement thereon without regard to the general law of March 26, 1834. The avowed purpose of the law was to obtain money for the current expenses of the government, but the use made of it suggests that other motives were behind it. Cós, watching for a pretext to strike a blow for Saltillo, declared it contrary to the federal colonization law; instructed the political chief at San Antonio to prevent the location of any land purchased under it; and ordered troops to Monclova, with the intention, no doubt, of using them against the governor and legislature as occasion offered.[26]

This act of March 14 was one of a series of laws that opened the way to gigantic speculations. Samuel M. Williams and John Durst, who introduced the law, shared largely in the sales under it. Upon learning that Cós had ordered troops to the capital, the legislature on April 7 passed another law authorizing the governor to collect the militia for its defense and to pay for the service by a loan based on the state's revenues. Since the state was chronically bankrupt for the want of revenue, the law would have gone, no doubt, without effect had Governor Viesca not generously found authority in it for a huge sale to James Grant, a member of the legislature from Parras. Finally Williams and two associates—Robert Peebles and F. W. Johnson—resuscitated a law passed the year before, April 19, 1834, and obtained four hundred leagues under it. This law authorized the governor to use the public domain to pay for defense of the frontier, but no use had been made of it. The contractors now agreed to furnish a thousand men for a year, fully armed and equipped for service, except that the government was to provide food and horses—an obligation that it was totally unable to discharge, and one that relieved the contractors, in effect, from making any return for the land.[27]

These transactions caused intense indignation in Texas and alienated from the state authorities the interest and support that they might otherwise have had in the approaching clash with the federal government. The Anglo-American inhabitants in the de-

[26] Gammel, *Laws of Texas*, I, 391; Cós to political chief, March 21, 1835, General Land Office of Texas, Vol. 53, page 266.
[27] For a detailed study of these speculations see an article by the writer in *Quarterly of Texas State Historical Association*, X, 76–96.

partments of Brazos and Nacogdoches refused to obey Governor Viesca's call for militia to defend the capital against Cós's troops, and frankly assigned the legislature's prodigal, if not corrupt, waste of public land as the reason. In a measure they misunderstood the actual situation. Congress, by a decree of April 25, annulled the state law of March 14, 1835, declaring it contrary to the federal colonization law and the act of April 6, 1830; and the pretext for the movement of troops against Monclova was to prevent the state law from going into effect. In all probability the real reason for the movement was that the legislature had vigorously denounced Santa Anna's evident design to centralize the national government. The presence of soldiers would smother the spirit of independence and perhaps forestall the development of such an insurrection as Santa Anna was then engaged in crushing in Zacatecas.

The legislature adjourned on May 21 after authorizing Governor Viesca to move the seat of government at his discretion to prevent its falling into the hands of General Cós. Days passed in indecision. Finally Viesca was persuaded to move the capital to Bexar, only to be intercepted and arrested on June 8. Texans returning from Monclova in great excitement sought in vain to convince the people that Santa Anna intended to establish military government in the state and that Viesca's arrest and the consequent interruption of the civil government was the first step to that end. The speculations were a stench in the nostrils of the average citizen, and to his mind all the alarmists were tarred with the same stick. His conviction that their solicitude for the public weal was calculated in some way to advance their own interests blinded him for a time to the real significance of what was going on in Mexico City.[28]

For Santa Anna really was engaged in maneuvers that the Texans would normally have viewed with apprehension. Austin confided to Williams at the end of 1834 that the political horizon was dark and that little good could be said of Santa Anna's personal politics. On January 28, 1835, Congress, in full accord with Santa Anna, summarily removed Gómez Farías from the vice-

[28] Williams, for example, was said to have tried to stir up an excitement that would send men to the defense of the governor and then claim them as a part of the thousand due in payment for his lands.—Austin to Williams, October 12, 1836, quoting W. H. Jack.

presidency. His rugged republican record was a guaranty that he would be an obstacle to radical alteration of the government; hence his removal. Writing to his brother-in-law, Austin deplored the fact that the country seemed destined to take its political character from its volcanic geological origin. On March 31 Congress passed a law reducing the militia to one man for every five hundred inhabitants. No explanation was offered, but the obvious purpose was to forestall opposition from the states. At the same time Santa Anna put himself at the head of the army to compel Zacatecas to accept the Plan of Cuernavaca. Austin wrote Williams that civil war was beginning and no one knew where it would end; men were simply waiting; some change was to be made in the government, but he did not believe the federal system would be abandoned. On May 2 Congress promulgated the remarkable declaration that it possessed in itself the "necessary 'extra-constitutional powers' to make such changes in the constitution of 1824 as it thought to be for the good of the nation, without subjecting itself to the obstacles and delays that the constitution prescribed." Austin reported that well-informed men still believed the federal system would be spared. Before leaving Mexico in July, however, he knew that it would fall.[29]

It was inevitable that any administration strong enough to extricate itself from difficulties nearer home must turn its attention sooner or later to Texas. The tariff exemptions granted for two years in 1832 had expired and the custom houses and their accompanying guards must be revived. This was not merely to collect the duty on imports consumed by the colonists. Almonte reported an enormous smuggling trade to the interior that should have paid duty at Matamoras and gone to maintain the military chest of the Eastern Provinces. He probably did not exaggerate. Official correspondence from San Antonio contains many complaints of the practice,[30] which was casually admitted by the Texans.[31] The first step toward a firmer régime in Texas was the appointment of Gen-

[29] Dublan y Lozano, *Legislación Mexicana*, III, 15, 38, 43, 75; Gammel, *Laws of Texas*, I, 398, 400; letters of Austin previously cited, December 31, 1834, and March 10, April 15, May 13, July 13, 1835.

[30] See, for example, Colonel Ugartechea's letters to Cós during December, 1834, and following months, in the Bexar Archives.

[31] For example, Austin's letter of June 15, 1832, to Williams, previously quoted: "This interior trade . . . is a loosing business at best, and I hope for the future our merchants will leave it alone."

eral Cós to be commandant of the Eastern Interior Provinces. He, in turn, made Colonel Ugartechea commandant of Texas. Ugartechea was an honorable, sensible, and tactful officer, but one not likely to minimize the importance of any obligation due the national government. Then, in January, 1835, Captain Antonio Tenorio with a detachment of soldiers and a collector arrived at Anahuac to reopen the custom house. A deputy collector was stationed at Brazoria; and immediately, to all outward appearance, the hand of time moved back three years, with Tenorio and Gonzales now playing the rôle of Bradburn and Fisher, and Andrew Briscoe and Travis, that of Patrick Jack and John Austin.

Briscoe was a merchant at Anahuac. He particularly resented the enforcement of the tariff there because he believed that it was not being enforced in other Texan ports. Irritation led to practical jokes on the guards, and these, in turn, to retaliation on the jokers. In the end Briscoe and a friend were arrested and lodged in the guard house.

News of this reached San Felipe about the time that a military courier arrived in the village with mail. He delivered a letter from General Cós to James B. Miller, the political chief, telling him of the arrest of the governor and the suspension of civil government at Monclova. It was court week and the town was crowded. Despite the fact that the people had recently refused to obey the governor's call for militia and had expressed their keen disgust at the wasteful land legislation, there was now great excitement. A group quickly gathered around the courier and seized other letters that he was bearing to Tenorio. Among these was a letter from Cós assuring Tenorio that heavy reinforcements would sail shortly to his relief and another from Ugartechea saying that the troops that had crushed Zacatecas were then at Saltillo on the way to Texas. The details of what followed are not entirely clear. Apparently a meeting collected and elected the political chief to preside.[32] According to Travis it adopted a resolution "that, in connection with the general defense of the country against military sway, the troops of Anahuac should be disarmed and ordered to leave Texas." On the same day—presumably influenced by the meeting—Miller issued a proclamation calling upon the men of his department to march

[32] In *The Texas Republican* of August 8, 1835, Miller admitted and apologized for this.

to the governor's rescue and bring him to Texas to reestablish the state government.[33]

The next day another meeting, presided over by R. M. Williamson, adopted resolutions reviewing Santa Anna's violations of the federal and state constitutions and declaring their intention ,to maintain these instruments in their original republican character. An address by Williamson on the Fourth of July following gives the additional information that the meeting resolved to capture San Antonio, take possession of the military equipment collected there, and install the vice-governor, Ramón Músquiz, at the head of a provisional government, pending the release of Governor Viesca. The meeting was attended, said Williamson, by some of the oldest citizens of Texas, men in no way concerned with the speculations; "upon investigation [they] declared the country in danger and that no time should be lost in preparing for war."

Travis, in the meantime, was enlisting volunteers to expel Tenorio from Anahuac, an enterprise that certain friends of his at that place had previously begged him to undertake. On June 29, with twenty-five men and a small cannon, he appeared before the garrison and demanded its surrender. The next day Tenorio gave up his arms and agreed to lead his men from Texas.[34]

Travis returned to San Felipe to find himself and the meeting of the 22d the target of severe criticism. People resented the apparent effort to "stampede" them into precipitate action. A large meeting at Columbia, on June 28, condemned the "acts and conduct of any set of individuals (less than a majority) calculated to involve the citizens of Texas in a conflict with the federal government of Mexico." It declared that separation from Mexico was neither the wish nor the interest of the people. At the same time it exhorted the people to adhere strictly to the constitution and laws, and urged the political chief to take steps to defend the frontier from Indian depredations. Militia organized to fight Indians would be equally effective against Mexicans, and, since Santa Anna was then remaking the constitution, adherence to the original instrument would be equivalent to rebellion; but, despite this apparent ambiguity, there is strong evidence of the pacific intent of

[33] *The Texas Republican*, June 27, 1835.
[34] For a fuller account of Tenorio's experiences see the writer's "Difficulties of a Mexican Revenue Officer," in *Quarterly* of Texas State Historical Association, IV, 190–202.

the meeting. Other communities followed Columbia's lead, declaring their loyalty and their desire to remain at peace. Some specifically condemned the attack on Anahuac. Miller apologized for the meeting of the 21st. Travis declared that he had acted with the most patriotic motive, which no doubt he had, and asked the public to suspend judgment until he could publish an explanation. By the middle of July observers of all shades of opinion agreed that the people wanted peace and would maintain it, unless some extraordinary provocation occurred.

Provocation did not tarry. Cós issued a requisition for the arrest of Travis, Williamson, and others who had been conspicuous in the recent agitations and ordered Ugartechea to enforce it. He declined to receive a peace commission until the men were delivered. At the same time it became certain that Cós, with large reinforcements, intended to assume command in person at San Antonio. Why was he coming if not, as the alarmists argued, to establish military rule?

In any event, the colonists could no longer afford to drift. A deliberate policy was desirable, if not essential. Therefore, on August 20 a committee of fifteen, appointed by a meeting at Columbia on the 15th, issued an urgent call for a convention, or consultation. Only by such means, said the committee, could the people be united, either for peace or war. Cursing the land speculators and the war party would avail nothing. The situation was menacing and must be faced. The plan, in brief, was for each precinct to elect five delegates—"selected for their wisdom and honesty and their deep interest in the welfare of their country"—to meet on October 15 at Washington on the Brazos. There was wisdom in the proposal, but it came from the war party and would probably have failed had Austin not arrived opportunely and approved it without hesitation or qualification.[35]

---

[35] This chapter is condensed from several papers previously published by the writer with full bibliographical references. In addition to papers already cited see "The Organization of the Texas Revolution," *Publications* of Southern History Association, November, 1901; and "Public Opinion in Texas Preceding the Revolution," *Report* of American Historical Association, 1911, I, 217–228.

CHAPTER XVI

Austin Again at the Helm: Beginning of the Revolution

USTIN arrived at Velasco on September 1, and a wave of relief swept quickly over the country. There was great anxiety concerning the propriety of another convention. Past conventions had not been successful either in obtaining reforms or in uniting the people. Were the Columbia radicals not trying to precipitate a crisis that could still be avoided? San Felipe was now controlled by the peace party, and opposed the meeting. As the capital of the department of the Brazos, championing the policy that Austin had always advocated, its attitude would go far toward defeating the convention. Though popular meetings at Nacogdoches and San Augustine had endorsed the meeting, the ayuntamiento of Nacogdoches forbade the election of delegates.[1] Uncertainty ended, or ceased to trouble, with Austin's return. The pilot was again at the helm and responsibility for the course to be steered was joyously shifted to him.

The very hyperbole of contemporary expressions reveals the intensity of the general relief. "It is with feelings inexpressible that I write you this," said F. W. Johnson. "Your return has been long wished for, but little expected at this time, but the God of Nature seems to have arranged all things better than even man could have desired. Your coming would always have been hailed by the people as the coming of a father, but your coming at this time is doubly dear to the people of all Texas. Never was there a time in the events

---

[1] John Rice Jones, Jr., wrote from San Felipe on September 1 of a visit from a Columbia committee, "A few of the individuals of Columbia have come to this place and held their meetings. It was termed by several, in fact numbers, that it was a Columbia meeting, and not a San Felipe meeting. . . . The principal part of the people of San Felipe are opposed to a convention or any thing resembling it." See also F. W. Johnson to Austin, September 5, 1835. Resolutions adopted at Nacogdoches and San Augustine are in *The Texas Republican*, September 26, 1835, and those of the ayuntamiento of Nacogdoches, forbidding the election, are in "Acts" of the ayuntamiento, Texas State Library.

of Texas that so much required the joint action of the people as the present. Union of sentiment and action is the one thing alone can save the country." And Johnson believed that only Austin could bring about such unity. Many years later, Gail Borden wrote that the congratulatory addresses of committees and popular meetings could "but faintly express . . . the feelings of joy and pleasure on the return of Austin. They looked upon the event as one which would settle all their doubts as to what should be done, and as one which would, as it proved, unite all parties. . . . Even his enemies, and some who had threatened in his absence to brand him with infamy,[2] were constrained to greet him as the only physician that could correct the disorganized system and restore a healthy action to the body corporate."[3] Towns vied with each other to do him honor, and members of the war party no doubt tried to win him to their side. A committee from Brazoria invited him to a public dinner, where the people could "express their approval of his public services and their respect for his private virtues." A similar committee from San Felipe inquired when they might escort him into the town where all were "prepared to receive him with open arms and acclamations of joy."[4]

The Brazoria dinner was set for September 8, and the day must have been awaited with keen suspense, for it was well understood that Austin would deliver a "keynote" speech, charting the course that must be immediately followed. If he approved the consultation, elections would go forward with no further doubts; if he opposed, the plan would certainly fail, and would probably be abandoned. He had peace or war in his hands and the people would unquestioningly accept what he gave. He spoke unequivocally for the consultation. Whether the people were to accept or reject the change from republican to centralized government could only be determined by such a meeting. Santa Anna had repeatedly assured him that he wished to give the Texans "a special organization suited to their education, habits, and situation"; but only by such a meeting could Santa Anna be informed of the sort of or-

---

[2] This refers to William H. Wharton's publication of November 9, 1834.

[3] Johnson to Austin, September 1, 1835; notes by Borden, February 6, 1844.

[4] B. F. Smith, Edmund Andrews, John W. Cloud, and R. J. Calder represented Brazoria, September 4; and Wily Martin, J. H. Money, A. W. Ewing, George Erving, Joshua Fletcher, Thomas Gay, and John P. Borden spoke for San Felipe, September 5.

ganization that would suit their "education, habits and situation."
He had uniformly warned Santa Anna, he said, that "the inevitable
consequence of sending an armed force to this country would be
war"; yet troops were coming in large numbers and a Mexican
war vessel had already been ravaging the coast. The people were
not responsible for this condition, but they must decide what to
do about it, and for that a convention was necessary. It was plain
enough to Austin that war was all but inevitable and that, if disaster
was to be avoided, the people must be united.[5]

Austin threw himself now with the utmost energy into the task
of securing a fully representative convention. A public meeting at
San Felipe made him a member of the local committee of correspondence on September 12; and thereafter, by common consent,
the direction of events passed definitely to him.[6] On the 13th the
committee inaugurated its work with a circular letter urging the
prompt election of delegates and defining its conception of the
functions of the consultation. These were simply to organize a
local provisional government under the republican constitution
of 1824 and to decide whether a plenary convention should meet.
If it thought such a meeting necessary, then it was to choose the
time and place and make provision for representation in proportion to population. The committee proposed to substitute San
Felipe for Washington as the meeting place of the consultation
because there was a printing press at San Felipe. It suggested that
"just and legal rights of the civilized Indians be protected," and
asked delegates to bring to the meeting an exact census of the
population and militia strength of their respective districts. On the
19th Austin, as chairman of the committee, issued a second circular, saying that Cós was probably already at San Antonio with a
large body of troops and that he would march immediately against
the colonies.[7] Conciliatory measures would now be useless, and,
moreover, they would be ruinous, because by holding out to the
colonists hope of a peaceable adjustment they would prevent union
and preparation. "War," he concluded, "is our only resource. There

---

[5] Austin's speech was published in *The Texas Republican,* September 19, 1835.

[6] By the 19th Austin was signing himself chairman, having been elected, no doubt,
by the committee.

[7] This information was derived from a report of September 8 from Edward Gritten.
He had been dispatched by the San Felipe authorities in August to make peace with
Cós and was stopped by Ugartechea at San Antonio.

is no other remedy but to defend our rights, ourselves, and our country by force of arms. To do this we must unite, and, in order to unite, the delegates of the people must meet in general consultation and organize a system of defense." In the meantime, every district should muster its militia and report its force, arms, and ammunition to the political chief at San Felipe. The avowed object of all these movements should be the maintenance of rights under the federal constitution of 1824, and "union with the Mexican confederation." On the 21st he received information that Cós had landed at Copano and that a force of colonists was gathering to prevent his uniting with Ugartechea. This, of course, meant war. He had already seen that it was inevitable and now accepted it cheerfully. He believed that the Texans were in the right—and also, no doubt, that they were probably strong enough to win. There must be no "half way measures," he wrote, but "war in full." He relayed the news by fast riders to all parts of the settlements, with suggestions for prompt mobilization.[8]

The indispensable quality of Austin's influence is evident to us from facts rather than words, but his contemporaries, too, acknowledged it promptly and ungrudgingly. Travis wrote, "all eyes are turned towards you. . . . Texas can be wielded by you and *you alone;* and her destiny is now completely in your hands. This is not the base flattery of a servile mind, but is the reasoning of one ardent in his country's cause and who wishes to unite his feeble efforts with those who have the power and inclination to lead us in safety to the desired end." Another writer declared: "The people hail your appearance in Texas at this time as one of the happiest events, because they believe you are capable of managing our difficult affairs better than we could without you. We wish you to head the preasant expedition against General Coss in person, believing your presance will be neaded to unite the people, enforce obedience, and to plan the movements of the troops. Believe me, Sir, I use no flattery with you but speak what I believe to be the truth."[9]

One of those vivid letters that Austin could write with such self-detached intimacy describes his life at this time. He had set up

[8] Austin's circulars of September 13, 19, and 21 are in *The Texas Republican,* September 19, 26, 1835. See also his letters of the 19th to D. W. C. Hall and P. W. Grayson.
[9] Travis, September 22, and Eli Mercer, September 23, to Austin. See also Martin Allen to Perry, September 22, and Gail Borden's statement already quoted.

bachelor quarters on his return to San Felipe, but his belongings were scattered, the house was unfurnished, his man-servant was sick, and he would have been hardly more devoid of comforts in a primitive camp. Bare as it was, though, his house must be host to the public.

"I want a barrel of salt beef [he wrote Perry] one of salt pork—some flour—some boxes of wine that Williams sent to McKinney for me . . . two beds and bedding—a barrel of good whiskey—some spoons—some rice—some beans—send them by steamboat. Also if Mrs. Williams can spare the oxen and wagon I wish to keep it to haul wood until I can buy one—and some cows for milk, for I have nothing. I want a brick layer to build the kitchen chimney, which has fallen down in the great rain. I would like to have one set of bed curtains. I must receive visitors and must be a little decent to receive them. I want hand irons for the fireplace and shovel and tongs—in fact, as housekeeping is a new thing, I hardly know what I want—I never think of such things until I need them. I have no blankets or bedding at all. . . . Show this to McKinney and Jack and the ladies, and among you fit me out with something. . . . As to the cost, it must go where the cost of my trip to Mexico went, and where I expect much more will go—that is to serve the country. If *that* is well served we shall all of us have enough, for we shall all prosper in common."

To the remonstrances of his sister and friends that he should live more comfortably and take more thought to his own affairs, he replied that the situation was necessary, that circumstances had made him a center for public opinion, and that he was "not yet a free man. I must be here to finish the land business and to try and systematise our political affairs; otherwise we shall all go overboard."

That Austin fully realized whither his labors were now taking Texas is beyond doubt. "The formation of a government (perhaps of a nation) is to be sketched out," he explained. "The dayly progress of events is to be watched over, and public excitement kept from going too fast or too slow." And to David G. Burnet he wrote more plainly, "No more doubts—no submission. *I hope to see Texas forever free from Mexican domination of any kind.* It is yet too soon to say this publically, but that is the point we shall end at—and it is the one I am aiming at. But we must arrive at it by steps and not all at one jump." [10]

[10] Austin to Perry, September 13, 14, 30, 1835; to Burnet, October 5; and Allen to Perry, September 26.

Not the least, nor the least important, of Austin's tasks was to allay party feeling and induce hard-headed conservatives to forget the past and cooperate now with the leaders of the war party. A letter to Thomas F. McKinney well illustrates this aspect of his work.

"I believe you know and understand the principles that have always influenced me [he wrote]. I was in times past opposed to mixing war measures with our affairs. . . . Now our position is quite different—our all is at stake. . . . I now believe that our *rights* are attacked, and that war is our only remidy. . . . There was, as you know better than I do, great divisions and that it required some prudence to unite so many discordant materials. I have done all I could. I have not suffered the past to have any influence upon me as to any person whatever. I do think this rule ought to govern every one. We are now all united, but anything like *party* or intolerance will create new divisions. There ought to be no divisions in the ranks of those who are fighting for the same cause. Even personalities should be laid on one side. It is a sacrifice which every one owes to the country." [11]

Colonel Ugartechea's demand for a cannon at Gonzales and the refusal of the inhabitants to surrender it diverted attention from Cós and finally enabled him to slip into San Antonio unopposed. The situation quickly developed into a crisis, and a skirmish at Gonzales on October 2 inaugurated the Texas revolution. Austin had already taken steps to form a provisional government, pending the meeting of the consultation, by requesting each local committee of correspondence to send one of its number to form with his committee at San Felipe what he called a "permanent council." This proved to be extremely fortunate, because Austin was soon called to command the forces gathering at Gonzales. [12]

The men at Gonzales were loosely organized in groups of varying size, according to the section from which they had come. Each group had company officers and there was nominally a general commander, but the weakness of his authority can be inferred from the fact that a "board of war," made up of a representative from each company, had to be created "to advise with and direct the commanding officers." Many felt the need of Austin's judg-

[11] Austin to McKinney, September 26, 1835. See also letters of Josiah H. Bell and Thomas J. Pilgrim to Austin, October 6.
[12] For the "Permanent Council" see *Quarterly* of Texas State Historical Association, VII, 249–278.

ment and personal authority, and, on October 6, a committee of officers requested him to join the army. Meantime, volunteers continued arriving at Gonzales, and, responding to an urgent demand, the "board of war," on October 11, ordered the election of a commander-in-chief. Instantly personal and sectional rivalry flamed high, and there was danger that the election, instead of uniting, would dissolve the army. In the end, however, all agreed on Austin and he was unanimously elected.[13] He addressed the army—about three hundred in number—upon the absolute necessity of obedience; a regimental organization was effected, and staff officers appointed; and on October 12 the march against San Antonio began.[14]

Austin remained in command until November 24, when the provisional government found more important work for him to do. The details of the campaign need not be followed. On the march the force increased to six hundred, but the organization continued extremely loose. Companies varied in size from thirteen to seventy privates, some officered by a captain and three lieutenants, and some commanded by a sergeant. The men were undrilled and almost without discipline. Time and again Austin was compelled to issue orders against promiscuous shooting in and out of ranks, and with food scarce for men and beasts stringent measures were required to prevent its reckless waste. As there was no regular enlistment, and no oath, men felt themselves free to withdraw at will, and sometimes left in squads. Austin reported on November 4 that within the past few days a hundred and fifty men had gone home for winter clothing, leaving but four hundred and fifty effective men in camp. Cós had entered Bexar on October 7 and Austin now estimated his strength at seven hundred men, strongly fortified and equipped with heavy artillery. Concerning his own force Austin wrote the president of the consultation, which was now in session, "This force, it is known to all, is but undisciplined militia and in some respects of very discordant materials. The officers, from the commander in chief down, are inexperienced in military service. With such a force Bexar cannot be effectually invested."

---

[13] William T. Austin, who wrote in 1844, mainly from contemporary documents, tells circumstantially how Austin reached camp at one o'clock on October 11 and was elected at four (Wooten, ed., *A Comprehensive History of Texas*, I, 539). This chronology seems to be contradicted, however, by a letter from Austin dated at Gonzales on the 10th.

[14] Austin's Order Book for the campaign of 1835 is in *Quarterly* of Texas State Historical Association, XI, 1–56.

Nor could the enemy be prudently stormed. Men of all shades of opinion agreed on that, and so advised the commander. Upon Austin's election at Gonzales an old friend admonished him "please to recollect we have not a man to lose. . . . I think the only chance in our situation is to fight them from the Brush; fight them from the Brush all the time. Never take our Boys to an open fight. . . . All must be deciplend before we can fight in the open field." At the same time William H. Jack wrote: "You will pardon me for expressing my views and opinions to you *freely, fully* and frankly. . . . I understand your force does not possibly exceed four hundred. I cannot conceive that it is seriously contemplated to attack Bexar with that number. The fate of Texas must not be risked upon one battle unless the advantages are so decidedly in our favor as to place the result beyond a shadow of doubt. . . . They have the numerical strength. They have artillery, cavalry, muskets, bayonets, lances. Against all these you present a band (brave perhaps to a fault) of untrained militia with such arms only as could be procured in the immediate emergency." Houston thought the Texans "ought never to have passed the Guadalupe without proper munitions of war to reduce San Antonio." To attack without heavy cannon would be folly, he declared, and the siege was merely "nominal"; therefore he advocated falling back from Bexar, leaving a sufficient force at Gonzales and Goliad to protect the frontier—"which, by the by, will not be invaded," he added—and furloughing the rest to comfortable homes. Fannin reluctantly agreed with Houston, though he believed that "with two hundred and fifty men well chosen and properly drilled so as to rely upon each other the place can be taken by storm, and not much loss to the party." Rusk declared that to attack without cannon and mortars "would be the death of very many worthy men." On November 2 and again on the 22d Austin submitted to a council of war the question of assaulting the works, and both times the decision was against it.[15]

[15] On the last two paragraphs see "The Texan Revolutionary Army," by the writer, in *Quarterly* of Texas State Historical Association, IX, 247–250; Austin's Order Book, as cited in preceding note; letters from Austin, October 25, 26, 28 (to the permanent council), November 2 (to Bowie and Fannin), November 4 and 8 (to president of the consultation) —all in Texas State Library—and November 22 (to Perry); Bryan to Perry, October 26, 28, November 7, 18; letters to Austin from Mercer, October 12, and W. H. Jack, October 13; S. H. Jack and George Huff to permanent council, October 28, McFarland to Houston, November 9, Fannin to Houston, November 18, and Rusk to Robinson, November 25— Texas State Library; Houston to Fannin, November 13 (copy by Frank W. Johnson).

That there was much dissatisfaction with conditions and some with the commander-in-chief is evident. Bowie and Fannin for a time commanded what in effect was an independent division. The report spread eastward that Bowie was, in fact, at the head of the army, and Houston wrote to congratulate both him and the army.[16] Austin's nephew wrote on November 7 that his uncle had had a trying time with dissatisfaction, disorganization, and aspiring men. On the 8th William H. Wharton resigned the appointment of judge advocate general, saying that he was compelled to believe, "from a failure to enforce general orders and from an entire disregard of grave decisions of councils of war . . . that no good will be atchieved by this army except by the merest accident under heaven." Travis resigned—though he later reconsidered—because he could not "be longer useful to the army without complaints being made."[17] Added to all this, volunteers from the east believed that they were bearing an undue burden in the campaign and complained that while they were suffering "from cold, wet, and the want both of provisions and the implements of war," the inhabitants of the exposed western frontier "by letters written from those comfortable firesides" urged them to keep up the siege.[18]

Perhaps, under the circumstances, the most experienced commander could have accomplished no more, nor have enforced better discipline. Fannin, at least, who had had two years at West Point, thought it imprudent to attack without heavy guns, and Houston, who had had much military experience, would have withdrawn the force. Austin succeeded in maintaining a skeleton organization and a nucleus of fairly uniform strength. He favored an assault, and believed the post could be taken with little loss—a judgment that the event justified. In the meantime, the siege was more effective than it seemed. While the enemy could enter and leave at will, it was always at the cost of a skirmish and possible loss; cattle and corn could not be freely gathered; and the menace of vanishing stores played a part in the final surrender.[19]

[16] Minutes of Council of War and Austin to Bowie and Fannin, November 2, 1835, Army Papers, Texas State Library; Houston to Fannin, November 13 (copy by F. W. Johnson).

[17] Travis and Wharton to Austin, November 6, 8, and Bryan to Perry, November 7, 1835.

[18] Chessher and McHanks to provisional government, November 30, 1835, Army Papers, Texas State Library.

[19] Filisola, *Memorias para la Historia de la Guerra de Tejas,* II, 199, says that it was the arrival of reinforcements on December 9 without supplies that caused the surrender.

At the same time lack of provisions was at the bottom of much restlessness and dissatisfaction in the Texan ranks. On November 4 Austin notified the provisional government that there were no medical supplies in camp, nor, so far as he knew, on the road. He authorized the government to mortgage all his property, if necessary, for the public service. By the 22d food was scarce and all the corn in the San Antonio valley had been exhausted. Besides, the men needed clothing, shoes, and ammunition.[20]

Most of the blame for this condition was laid at the door of the provisional government. However, the condition was really the inevitable consequence of the sudden emergency, slow communication, and lack of organization. Before joining the army Austin, as we saw, took steps to form a central committee at San Felipe to serve until the meeting of the consultation. This body elected R. R. Royall chairman and was as efficient as circumstances permitted in disseminating information, collecting and forwarding supplies, and directing volunteers. Some of the delegates elected to the consultation went to the camp at Gonzales instead, and, being unwilling to return when the advance to San Antonio began, requested the other members either to join them at San Antonio or to adjourn from day to day until November 1. This necessarily prolonged the service of Royall's committee—the "permanent council"—but it also delayed the establishment of an authoritative provisional government and the adoption of a systematic plan of procedure. Meantime there was danger that those who assembled at San Felipe would disperse without waiting for the absent members and thereby make an end of the meeting altogether. Royall wrote Austin on October 16: "The members here are like volunteers in camp (very restless) and much is said about going home. One by one each plead their necessities. Some from the frontier are afraid of the Indians on the Brazos; others to the eastward are not fully into the spirit of our times and are yet wanting explanation. . . . I think we can detain all but a few until about the 1st of Nov[r]. After that it will require positive assurances of a meeting and that in a few days to stop them." The situation was plainly critical, and members in camp—there were thirty or more—prepared to return only to find that their companions, for some reason, were unwilling

---

[20] Austin to provisional government, November 4, 22, 1835; Rusk to Robinson, November 25, Army Papers, Texas State Library.

to let them go. Austin's nephew, Moses Austin Bryan, wrote on October 26, "when the thing was first talked of I thought it would be the means of disbanding the army, as I heard most every one say that he would return if the members of the convention left." After speeches by Branch T. Archer, Houston, William H. Jack, and Austin explaining the urgent necessity of holding the consultation, the excitement subsided and a vote of the army determined that all the members except staff officers might return.[21]

The consultation finally organized on November 3. Had Austin followed his inclination, he would have been present. He was fearful that the members might go too fast and too far, and sent to San Felipe a program of the utmost that he thought they should attempt. In this he advised that a declaration be made in favor of the constitution of 1824; that a provisional local government be organized, with the statement that existing laws of Coahuila and Texas would be retained provisionally until more deliberate action could be taken; that the faith of the state be pledged to obtain means for pushing the war "in defence of the constitution and Federal System"; that land claims of agricultural Indians be guaranteed, in order to keep them quiet; that fraudulent grants of land made by the legislature since 1833 be annulled; and that the militia be organized and steps taken to raise a regular army. Dr. Branch T. Archer was elected president of the consultation, and, in an inaugural address, elaborated this document article by article; and the consultation rigidly adhered to Archer's outline. Archer had been one of the delegates serving at San Antonio, and had evidently been deeply impressed by Austin's program. The first article of Austin's plan, suggesting, in effect, a declaration of causes for taking up arms, involved determination of the fundamental question of whether the Texans were fighting for independence or for the maintenance of the constitution of 1824. This held the exclusive attention of the members until November 6, when, by the decisive vote of thirty-three to fourteen, they agreed to organize a provisional government "upon the principles of the constitution of 1824," and to declare accordingly. The declaration, adopted the next day, was equivocally phrased and looked, perhaps, as much toward in-

---

[21] "Journal of the Permanent Council," *Quarterly* of Texas State Historical Association, VII, 249–278; Austin to Consultation, October 11, 25, 1835, and Royall to Austin, October 16, Texas State Library; Bryan to Perry, October 26.

dependence as toward continuing the connection with Mexico. That, however, was probably due to the logic of events rather than to deliberate intention.[22] For the rest, the work of the consultation was quickly done. It created a provisional government, consisting of governor, lieutenant governor, and general legislative council; and formulated a plan for the organization of a regular army—providing at the same time, as far as it could, for the necessities of the volunteers already in the field. On November 12 it elected Austin, Archer, and William H. Wharton commissioners to the United States to enlist aid and sympathy.[23]

The declaration for the constitution of 1824 was simply an expression of Austin's characteristic caution. That he foresaw and accepted—with mingled feelings of regret and relief—the inevitable outcome of the situation hardly admits of doubt. He had written Mrs. Holley in August that nothing was wanting but a great immigration during the fall and winter; that Texas would then be ripe to be shaken off by the political convulsions of Mexico. His significant letter to Burnet has already been quoted—"*I hope to see Texas forever free from Mexican domination of any kind. . . . That is the point we shall end at.*" On November 22 he wrote Perry from San Antonio, "We ought to get united to the U. S. as soon as possible. It is the best we can do." And his nephew thought that he would not accept the mission to the United States if he were not authorized to work for annexation.[24] The reason for temporizing, too, is plain. The crisis developed prematurely, forestalling the desired immigration and rendering it necessary to obtain the support, or at least the neutrality, of Mexican Liberals.

The hope of Liberal support was not fantastic. Zavala was actively aligned with the Texans. Colonel Mexia was fitting out an expedition at New Orleans to lead against Tampico. Tamaulipas was reported to be friendly to Texas, and in the event of Mexia's success Santa Anna would have need of his army nearer home than Texas. Juan N. Seguin and Salvador Flores led detachments of

[22] For this aspect of the consultation's work see, by the writer, "The Texan Declaration of Causes for Taking up Arms against Mexico," *Southwestern Historical Quarterly,* XV, 173–185.

[23] The journal and the decrees of the consultation are conveniently reprinted in Gammel, *Laws of Texas,* I, 507–548, 907–917.

[24] Austin to Mrs. Holley, August 21, to Burnet, October 5, and to Perry, November 22, 1835; Bryan to Perry, November 30.

Mexicans at Bexar. Governor Viesca escaped from his captors and fled to Texas. And Colonel José María Gonzales, who had commanded some of the cavalry then in Bexar, was ready to urge them to desert to the Liberal cause. With the issue of the struggle so extremely doubtful, it would have seemed rank folly to turn the back on such promises of succor.[25]

On November 18 Austin received the announcement of his selection by the consultation to go to the United States. He submitted to a council once more the question of storming Cós. The proposal was voted down; and he then set about preparing the army for his departure. On the 24th four hundred men pledged themselves to remain at San Antonio, and elected Edward Burleson to the chief command in Austin's stead. The next day Austin started for San Felipe, where he arrived on the 29th.[26]

Three long and interesting letters reveal Austin's mind at this time. Congress had given the final stroke to the destruction of the federal system by the decree of October 3, and the government was trying, with some success, to give the war in Texas the character of a national crusade against rebellious foreigners. For that reason Austin found fault with the ambiguous declaration of November 7. The true policy of the Texans had been, he said, to effect, if possible, "the most close and perfect and unequivocal union and co-operation with the remnants of the federal party." Whether this could still be done, he doubted, but thought the only alternative to it was "a direct declaration of independence." And to choose decisively between the two policies he believed that another convention, with plenary power, must be elected on a rigidly proportional basis after the people were fully informed of the situation. Submission to the decree of October 3 he thought inconceivable. That such a government as it contemplated "would destroy the people of Texas must be evident to all when they consider its geographical situation and its population, so different in education, habits, customs, language, and local wants from all the rest of the nation." He had labored faithfully for years, Austin truly said, "to unite Texas permanently to the Mexican confederation by separating its local government and internal administration, so far as practicable, from

---

[25] On this paragraph see, by the writer, "The Tampico Expedition," *Quarterly* of Texas State Historical Association, VI, 169–186; Austin's Order Book, *ibid.*, XI, 26, 39, 47; —— to McKinney, October 19, 1835.
[26] Austin's Order Book, as cited, 50–54.

every other part of Mexico and placing it in the hands of the people of Texas. . . . There was but one way to effect this union with any hopes of permanency or harmony, which was by enacting Texas into a state of the Mexican confederation." That Austin expected such a convention as he proposed to declare independence when it met is fairly evident from his conception of the situation.

"The character of the struggle in which Texas is engaged [he said] is now clearly developed: it evidently is one of life or death, 'to be, or not to be.' It is no longer a mere question about the forms of political institutions; it is one of self preservation. Texas is menaced with a war of extermination; the government of Mexico has so proclaimed it. The people now understand their situation, and, consequently, are much better prepared to elect public agents to provide against such a danger than they were at the time of the last election. At that time the form of government was not changed by any act which had the influence or the character of law; it now is by the decree of 3d October last. At that time the state government existed; at this, no such thing as a state exists, not even in name. The decree of the 3d of October has converted them into *departments,* without any legislative powers whatever, and entirely subject to the orders of the president and central government."

Texas, he concluded, "must either be a state of the Mexican confederation"—which he now plainly thought to be all but impossible—"or must separate *in toto* as an independent community or seek protection from some power that recognizes the principles of self government. I can see no remedy between one of these three positions and total ruin." The same day Austin's nephew and confidential secretary wrote concerning the mission to the United States, "If he is not vested with the power of attaching Texas to the U. S. . . . I think he won't go." [27] Taking the two statements together, it seems evident that Austin had then abandoned hope of effective assistance from the Mexican Federalists. Later, hope was to revive for a moment and unsettle his conviction of the expediency of declaring independence.

Austin dwelt at length in the first of these letters on the services and achievements of the volunteers, and upon the importance of sustaining them. "Had this army never crossed the River Guadalupe," he wrote, "a movement which some have condemned, the war would have been carried by the centralists into the colonies,

[27] Austin to provisional government, November 30, December 2, 1835, and to Barrett, December 3; Bryan to Perry, November 30, 1835.

and the settlements on Guadalupe and Lavaca would probably
have suffered and perhaps been broken up. The town of Gonzales
had already been attacked and many of the settlers were about
to remove. What effect such a state of things would have had
upon the moral standing and prospects of the country, although a
matter of opinion, is worthy of mature consideration; and more
especially when it is remembered that at that time the opinions
of many were vacillating and uncertain, and much division prevailed." Continuing, he pointed out that Cós's forces had been
shut within the fortifications of Bexar; that the confidence of the
volunteers had been strengthened by victory in every skirmish;
that Goliad had been taken, with many valuable supplies, and the
port of Copano closed so that reinforcements and provisions could
not enter by sea; that a post on the Nueces had fallen; that three
hundred horses had been captured; "and the resources for sustaining an army in Bexar all destroyed or exhausted." [28]

On December 9 the volunteers justified Austin's confidence by
the capture of San Antonio, and the next day the general council
adopted a resolution providing for the election of a plenary convention to meet on March 1.

In the meantime, Austin became convinced—perhaps by conversation with Colonel Gonzales, whom the council outfitted and
dispatched to Bexar on December 3; perhaps from Captain Julian
Miracle, representative of the Liberals in Tamaulipas and Nuevo
Leon—that an effective alliance with the Federalists was still possible; and by Mexia, who retired to Texas after the disastrous Tampico raid, he was led to believe that the Federalists might gain all
the North Mexican states and secede from the Centralist south.
This was a contingency that Austin had long contemplated,[29] so
that Mexia's information did not seem improbable. At any rate, it
seemed to him advantageous still to play for the Federalist alliance.
If the party won, Texas would become a state in the smaller and
more homogeneous confederation, with greater autonomy than
it could have as a member of the United States. If the Federalists
failed, then the fifth article of the declaration of November 7 [30]

---

[28] Austin to provisional government, November 30, 1835.

[29] Remember, for example, his advocacy of the Chihuahua road.

[30] "They hold it to be their right, during the disorganization of the Federal system,
and the reign of despotism, to withdraw from the Union, to establish an independent
Government, or to adopt such measures as they may deem best calculated to protect their

would become automatically a declaration of independence. He therefore prepared, and the council adopted, an address to the Federalists designed to convince them that the Texans were sincere in their defense of the constitution of 1824, and that they preferred union with Mexico as a state under it to independence or union with the United States.[31] Consequently the new convention, which he still thought necessary, should confine itself, when it met, to the organization of a state government in conformity with this exposition.

It is evident enough now that the Federalists were a broken reed to lean upon; but as Austin pondered, the alternative appeared more and more desperate. McKinney, his old and intimate friend, estimated the cost of independence at ten or twelve million dollars. Where was such a sum to be found; and, if obtained, how could it be repaid? So, on the eve of his departure for the United States, Austin reiterated emphatically to friends in the general council his belief that Texas should rest for the time on the declaration of November 7. To do otherwise would bring back to Texas the war which the surrender of Cós had removed.[32]

Immediately after Christmas—probably on December 26—the commissioners sailed. They were authorized to negotiate a million dollar loan, fit out a navy, procure supplies for the army, and receive donations; to enlist aid and sympathy; and, finally, to proceed to Washington and learn the attitude of the government there toward annexation.

Austin went in great despondency. He was ill from exposure in camp, and was out of harmony with his colleagues, especially Wharton, whom he thought too violently committed to independence. A few days at New Orleans, however, convinced him both that the Federalists could not be relied upon and that popular opinion in the United States would strongly support a declaration of independence. Without hesitation he reverted to his earlier judgment, and henceforth exerted his influence to remove all obstacles to such a declaration. "I advise you to take an open and

---

rights and liberties; but that they will continue faithful to the Mexican Government so long as that nation is governed by the Constitution and laws that were formed for the government of the political association."

[31] For this document see Gammel, *Laws of Texas*, I, 651.

[32] Letters from Austin to provisional government, December 11, 14, 22, 1835; to McKinney, December 16; to Johnson *et al.*, December 22; to Royall, December 25; McKinney to Austin, December 17.

bold stand for independence at once," he wrote Henry Austin on January 7. "I hope all my friends will do the same, and that the question will be decided unanimously."

It would be easy to mistake the means for the end and condemn Austin for instability and timidity, as some of his contemporaries did; but the test of his consistency is in the steadiness of his aim. That was to secure the permanent welfare of his people at the least cost of suffering and sorrow to them. His feeling of responsibility for Texas, and particularly for the old settlers, was too keen and too personal for him to risk their happiness and prosperity as long as the hazard could be postponed. If defense were needed for Austin's sentiment—which reached the fervor of a passion—he himself has left, in two brief paragraphs, all that need be said:

"I have felt it to be my duty [he wrote in all sincerity] to be very cautious in involving the pioneers and actual settlers ... by any act of mine until I was fully and clearly convinced of its necessity, and of the capabilities of our resources to sustain it. Hence it is that I have been censured by some for being over cautious. Where the fate of a whole people is in question it is difficult to be over cautious or to be too prudent. Besides these general considerations, there are others which ought to have weight with me individually. I have been, either directly or indirectly, the cause of drawing many families to Texas; also, the situation and circumstances in which I have been placed have given considerable weight to my opinions. This has thrown a heavy responsibility upon me, so much so that I have considered it to be my duty to be prudent, and even to control my own impulses and feelings. These have long been impatient under the state of things which has existed in Texas, and in favor of a speedy and radical change. But I have never approved of the course of forestalling public opinion by party or partial meetings, or by management of any kind. ...

"A question of vital importance is yet to be decided by Texas, which is a declaration of independence. When I left Texas I was of opinion that it was premature to stir this question and that we ought to be very cautious of taking any steps that would make the Texas war purely a national war, which would unite all parties against us. ... In this I acted contrary to my own impulses, for I wish to see Texas free from the trammels of religious intolerance and other anti-republican restrictions, and independent at once; and as an individual have always been ready to risk my all to obtain it; but I could not feel justified in precipitating and involving others until I was fully satisfied that they would be sustained." [33]

[33] Austin to Houston, January 7, 1836.

CHAPTER XVII

The Independence of Texas: The End of the Voyage

HOPE of the Texans for assistance from the people of the United States was spontaneous, and the response was prompt and liberal. As early as October 7 a Texas committee organized at New Orleans to solicit volunteers and donations. Partly through its effort three companies reached San Antonio in time to share in its capture from Cós, and it was instrumental in fitting out Mexia's unfortunate expedition against Tampico. Before the end of November similar committees were active in most southern and western states and in Pennsylvania and New York.[1]

The appointment of a commission by the provisional government to make the most of this popular enthusiasm was therefore natural and obvious. The commissioners landed at New Orleans on New Year's Day. Their first task, in which they thought themselves reasonably successful, was to obtain money. They readily found two groups of capitalists who were eager to speculate in Texas lands under the guise of loans, and closed contracts for two hundred and fifty thousand dollars, upon which sixty thousand dollars was paid. The lenders were to receive eight per cent interest, and had the option—which they intended to use—of taking land in repayment at fifty cents an acre. The government was to survey the land in six hundred and forty acre tracts, and was to withhold all public land from sale until the lenders made their selection. These were hard terms, but the commissioners were elated and thought that "rather than have missed the loan, we had better have borrowed the money for five years and given them the land in the bargain." At the same time the commissioners ar-

---

[1] For details and bibliography of popular interest in the United States see the writer's "The United States and Mexico, 1835–1837," *Mississippi Valley Historical Review*, I, 3–10.

ranged with William Bryan, a merchant of the city, to execute orders for the government and to accept drafts on the government "so far as prudence will justify." This proved equivalent to an additional loan for nearly a hundred thousand dollars, because in the next few months Bryan used his own credit for Texas to that amount. Reserving from the proceeds of the first loans enough for their own subsequent expenses, the commissioners laid out the balance in medical and quartermaster supplies, in purchasing and equipping a vessel, and in financing various agents whom they appointed to execute special commissions.[2]

The itinerary of the commissioners furnishes a convenient thread upon which to hang their labors after leaving New Orleans. On February 12 they were at Nashville, where they were detained for some time by unseasonable cold and ice. On March 3 they were at Louisville; and on March 30 at Washington. There they separated, Austin and Archer going respectively to New York and Richmond and Wharton remaining at Washington. Later Wharton and Archer joined Austin in New York, and they were again reunited at Washington in May. There they closed their joint labors on the 24th, Austin and Archer starting to Texas by different routes, leaving Wharton in Washington as before. The Mississippi Valley was ablaze with interest, and the commissioners left in their wake active committees and recruiting agencies but placed no loans. This was due in part to reports of the paralysis of the Texan government by the disastrous quarrel between Governor Smith and the Council and in part to the uncertainty of a declaration of independence when the new convention should meet. Potential lenders seemed uniformly agreed on the necessity of a declaration. Though this obstacle was removed on March 2, the commissioners were never officially notified, and unofficial reports in the papers were immediately followed by news of the tragedies of the Alamo and Goliad and of Houston's retreat and the panic-stricken flight of the people, known in Texas history as the "runaway scrape." The news aroused horror, indignation, and ardent sympathy, but was a poor exhibition of assets upon which to float a loan.

[2] See the writer's "Finances of the Texas Revolution," *Political Science Quarterly*, XIX, 612-635; and the correspondence of the commissioners in Garrison, *Diplomatic Correspondence of the Republic of Texas*, I, 55-70.

The commissioners were empowered to negotiate ten bonds of a hundred thousand dollars each on the best terms obtainable, not exceeding ten per cent, and it was with the hope of disposing of some bonds that they separated after reaching Washington and learning of the declaration of independence. At Philadelphia Austin submitted a proposal to Nicholas Biddle, President of the United States Bank. Briefly, the bank was to hold half a million dollars of the bonds in trust and issue stock upon them in shares of a hundred dollars each, payable in ten years at eight per cent, or currently redeemable at the custom houses and land offices of Texas in part payment of dues. Subscriptions could be paid in installments, with one-fourth cash and the balance in notes of two, three, and four months; and the bank was to discount the notes and make the proceeds of the subscription immediately available. Without waiting for Biddle's reply, which, so far as we know, was never given, Austin pushed on to New York and there arranged a loan for a hundred thousand dollars—or, more accurately, another sale of land, since the lenders, as at New Orleans, had the option of taking land in payment. Ten thousand dollars was paid, but no more, because the government refused to ratify the contract. This also was the case with the New Orleans loans.

The commissioners took their mission with desperate seriousness, feeling that the fate of Texas depended upon their obtaining money. Wharton wrote that they offered lenders the pledge of their personal property; and Austin, heart-sick and frantic over the tale of desolation from Santa Anna's initial victories, entertained for a moment the impossible hope of obtaining a loan from the surplus revenue that was embarrassing the treasury of the United States.[3]

The failure of the Texan government to correspond with the commissioners was most harmful, perhaps, in their relations with the government of the United States. Governor Smith had instructed them to ascertain whether any interposition of the United States could be expected; whether by "any fair and honorable means Texas could become a member of that republic," and finally whether, in case of a declaration of independence, the United

---

[3] "Finances of the Texas Revolution," by the writer, *Political Science Quarterly*, XIX, 633–635; Garrison, *Diplomatic Correspondence of the Republic of Texas*, I, 66, 71, 72, 80.

States would immediately recognize Texas and make a defensive and offensive alliance with it. Toward the end of April petitions began to reach Congress asking for the recognition of Texas, and on May 23 a considerable debate on the subject took place in the Senate, when resolutions and petitions were referred to the committee on foreign relations. Robert J. Walker, Webster, Calhoun, and others declared themselves in favor of recognition as soon as the United States should be officially informed that the Texans had a *de facto* government in operation. The newspapers had published accounts of the battle of San Jacinto (April 21) and the capture of Santa Anna, but official confirmation was lacking; nor was there yet any official notification of the declaration of independence.[4]

The commissioners had been greatly disappointed in finding no dispatches awaiting them at Washington and wrote the Texan government that official reports and new powers, since the declaration of independence, were indispensable; but apparently the only communication they ever received from the new government was a letter of recall dated May 29. Acknowledging a letter from William Bryan on April 24, Austin wrote, "You, and *you alone,* have written to us; from the government of Texas we have not received one word." Bryan's letter was a messenger of desolation and death, carrying the terrible news of Fannin's massacre, Houston's retreat, and the flight of the inhabitants before the Mexican army, but Austin's confidence in the ultimate outcome did not waver. "My heart and soul are sick," he wrote, "but my spirit is unbroken.... Texas will rise again." After the battle of San Jacinto nothing, in the judgment of the commissioners, prevented recognition by the United States but the want of official reports of the battle and of the existence of a *de facto* government. "If such documents . . . had been received . . . before I left Washington, I believe," Austin declared, "that I could have brought on our recognition. The feeling there is decided and ardent in our favor." Simply a report from Houston of the battle of San Jacinto, he thought, would have been sufficient. Austin's belief was fully shared by Wharton and gains confirmation from Wharton's re-

[4] Garrison, *Diplomatic Correspondence of the Republic of Texas,* I, 53; *Congressional Globe,* 24th Cong., 1 Sess., Vol. 3, pages 331–479 *passim,* particularly 393.

port of an extremely interesting conference with President Jackson. Wharton said that he had spent several hours alone with the President on May 31 and that

"the sole subject of conversation was *Texas*. He asked, where are your letters from your Government? Where Houston's official account of the victory? Where your President's proclamation calling upon the inhabitants to return to their homes and attend to their crops? Where an official annunciation of the fact that the inhabitants are at their homes and in possession of the most of Texas? Where the publication opening your ports and fixing your tariff and tonnage? Sir, says he, your President should send an express once a week to New Orleans to his agent and have published by authority the true situation of your country and everything that goes to show you are a *de facto* government. This is indispensable."

Jackson himself finally dispatched a confidential agent to Texas to report conditions, and both houses of Congress on the eve of adjournment committed themselves to recognition of the new nation whenever satisfactory information should be received that it had "in operation a civil government capable of performing the duties and fulfilling the obligations of an independent power." [5]

The neglect of the commissioners can be explained in a measure by conditions in Texas, but not excused. Ultimately the responsibility must rest on the shoulders of one man, David G. Burnet. The convention which met on March 1 and declared independence framed a constitution, but the Mexican advance made it impossible to submit it for ratification. The convention therefore elected an *ad interim* government, consisting of a president, vice-president, and cabinet, and vested it with full executive and administrative authority, including "ample and plenary powers to enter into negotiations and treaties with foreign powers." Burnet was elected president *ad interim*. Immediately after the election the convention adjourned, and the government established itself at Harrisburg only to be driven from there to Galveston Island by Santa Anna's advance. Domestic conditions were desperate enough to have absorbed the whole attention of the government, and had Bur-

[5] Wharton to Austin ("strictly confidential"), June 2, 1836, Austin to Burnet, June 10, in Garrison, *Diplomatic Correspondence*, I, 98; Austin to Houston, June 16, in Yoakum, *History of Texas*, II, 177; *Congressional Globe*, Vol. 3, pages 453, 479, 486. Jackson's agent, Henry M. Morfit, reported his observations in a series of ten letters from August 13 to September 14, 24th Cong., 2 Sess. *House Exec. Doc.* No. 35.

net neglected foreign affairs altogether some excuse could be found for him. But he did not. On the contrary, on March 19 he appointed George C. Childress, associated with Robert Hamilton, "with plenary powers to open a negotiation with the cabinet at Washington, touching the political rights of the Republic; inviting on the part of that cabinet a recognition of the sovereignty and independence of Texas." Childress had lived at Nashville and was supposed to have means of reaching Jackson; but Wharton also was from Nashville, and he and Austin and Archer might have been expected to have experience and connections which it would take the new agents some time to acquire. Actually Childress and Hamilton made a leisurely journey to Washington and were superseded before they arrived by two other commissioners—James W. Collinsworth and Peter W. Grayson. And then Austin and his colleagues were recalled by the first and only communication that they received from Burnet's government.[6]

Returning to Texas, Austin arrived at the mouth of the Brazos on June 27 and immediately visited President Burnet and exacted a promise from him to write regularly to Collinsworth and Grayson. On the way down the Mississippi from New Orleans he had spoken a vessel from Matamoras and received circumstantial reports of preparations making by the Mexican government to renew the invasion. These reports seemed to be confirmed by news that Burnet had, and before retiring—though he had landed late in the afternoon—Austin wrote a characteristic letter to Henry Austin, who had been in New Orleans for several months on business, urging him to return.

"Texas [he wrote] needs every man who belongs here—the war is not ended. . . . My sister came down here the other day to embark for Orleans, but the vessel did not sail. I have not yet seen her. I shall advise her to stay at home and abide the fate of Texas. You will say to this that she can be of no avail here—not so—it was the panic caused by the flight of families last spring which came so near losing Texas, and if *my* sister goes, it will have its influence on many others. I wish all of my name or connection to stay in Texas and abide the issue be it what it may." [7]

[6] Ethel Zivley Rather, "Recognition of the Republic of Texas by the United States," *Quarterly* of Texas State Historical Association, XIII, 155–256, follows the history of the several commissions in detail. See also Garrison, *Diplomatic Correspondence of the Republic of Texas,* I, 73–91, 111.

[7] Austin's memorandum book (1836), page 24; Austin to Henry Austin, June 27, 1836, copy in file of August 27, 1829.

The next morning Austin wrote General Lamar, whom President Burnet and the cabinet had appointed to command the Texan army, asking for a conference on a subject which he thought could not fail "to have great influence in settling the affairs of Texas." Beyond saying that it would require "unity of action and dispatch" he gave in the letter no intimation of the nature of the subject. What he had in mind was an appeal by Santa Anna to President Jackson asking him to mediate between Mexico and Texas. In describing to Austin his long conversation with Jackson on May 31, Wharton reported the President as saying, "and Sir, be not surprised if I yet soon announce a cession by Mexico of Texas to the United States." Wharton interpreted this to mean that Jackson was negotiating a treaty with Gorostiza, the Mexican plenipotentiary, and protested that Texas would not recognize a sale by Mexico to the United States. Jackson replied, according to Wharton's report, that in any case no more than a quit-claim would be obtained from Mexico and that the final arrangements could be settled by the United States and Texas.[8] Whether Austin had received Wharton's report of this interview is doubtful. If he had, it perhaps suggested the plan that he now conceived; if not, his plan was probably original. If the plan should develop so as to require the liberation of Santa Anna, opposition might be expected from Lamar and the army. Lamar had opposed treating with the prisoner after the battle of San Jacinto, arguing passionately that he ought to be hanged, and the volunteers on June 3 had prevented the government from sending him to Vera Cruz in accordance with the treaty signed at Velasco on May 14. Hence the anxiety to have the concurrence of Lamar.

Santa Anna naturally grasped at Austin's proposal as affording escape perhaps from a situation of great discomfort and danger to himself, and wrote to President Jackson on July 4. He recited events since the battle of San Jacinto—the treaty of Velasco, that is, and the mutiny of Texan troops that prevented its execution; the retreat of the Mexican army from Texas by his order; the removal of Filisola from the command and the reversal of his order by the government; and the preparations to renew the war under

---

[8] Austin to Lamar, June 28, 1836, Lamar Papers, Texas State Library; Wharton to Austin, June 2.

Urrea—and declared that "the continuation of the war and its disasters would be inevitable if some powerful hand were not outstretched to compel the voice of reason to be heard." Jackson, he said, could perform this humane service by interposing to procure the execution of the treaty by the Texans, and on his own part he promised faithfully to comply with it. He was convinced when he signed the treaty, he said, that it would be useless for his government to continue the war, and explained with unconscious humor that he had acquired exact information about Texas that he had been ignorant of four months before. He alone could impart this to the government, hence the necessity for his return.[9]

Austin transmitted this letter to Jackson through General Gaines, who, by order of the United States government, had collected troops on the Sabine to forestall Indian hostilities which it was anticipated might be excited by the war in Texas. Austin also wrote to Jackson, explaining at length why Santa Anna might be depended on to try to fulfill his pledge to end the war and obtain the recognition of Texan independence, but not enlarging upon what was desired of Jackson. The fact was, perhaps, that he did not wish to say quite all that he had in mind. The gist of it was that Texas through Collinsworth and Grayson had already asked Jackson to intercede and that Santa Anna's request would now give him ample ground for doing so. At the same time, however, intervention could certainly not succeed unless Santa Anna were in Mexico to influence the government and people; and public sentiment in Texas—or at least the sentiment of the army—would not consent to his release without a satisfactory guaranty that he would exert his influence in behalf of peace. Jackson was therefore to guarantee that Santa Anna would fulfill his pledges; this would secure his release; Jackson would then offer mediation; and Santa Anna would induce its acceptance. But suppose Santa Anna should violate his promises? This was the very heart of Austin's project, but he touched it very lightly—such an act of "perfidy and baseness . . . would justify the United States government in interposing *by force*," he said, "in favor of a people who had been thus deceived, more especially when Santa Anna's letter . . . is con-

[9] The copy of Santa Anna's letter used here is in Ramón Martinez Caro, *Verdadera Idea de la Primera Campaña de Tejas*, etc. (Mexico, 1837), 129–131. It is translated in Richardson, *Messages and Papers of the Presidents*, III, 274.

sidered and brought into public view, as it would be in the event of his treachery." Austin protested that he believed Santa Anna was sincere, but he could hardly do less in a letter requesting the President of the United States to mediate. As a matter of fact he did not expect Jackson to interfere and gave himself little concern about Santa Anna's good faith—Santa Anna's mere acknowledgment that Mexico could not reconquer Texas and his request for intervention, Austin thought, would benefit Texas abroad and hasten recognition by foreign powers. He explained himself clearly enough in other letters of the time. "I am of the opinion," he wrote on July 9, "that no material good will result from this matter. . . . Santa Anna, however, still says that he can end the war on the basis agreed upon, provided he was set at liberty; but he cannot be set at liberty without such guarantees as are considered to be undoubted. Gen. Jackson's would be of this character, and without it I am of opinion nothing can be done." He advised Santa Anna to write Jackson, he said, "believing that it would, at least, be a kind of opening of the subject, which would lead to a correspondence of some character between the United States and Mexico that might result favorably for Texas. . . . I consider it quite immaterial whether he is sincere or not, if through his promises the guarantee of the United States can be obtained, for that very guarantee would *make* him secure by compelling him to comply, as he well knows." [10]

In any event, however, action could not be expected from Jackson soon, Nine weeks were required, under the most favorable conditions, to get a letter to and from Washington. General Gaines could act more quickly and perhaps as effectively. He was known to have authority to cross the Sabine and take a position as far west as Nacogdoches, if he thought the attitude of the Indians required it, and the Texans had already been at some pains to convince him that the Indians were very threatening. Austin now wrote him, at the same time that he forwarded his own and Santa Anna's letter to Jackson, that Indian hostilities had begun all along the frontier of the San Antonio road and that the Mexican advance had probably reached the Nueces. This would further encourage the Indians, but they could be stopped without a war if

[10] Austin to Jackson, July 4, 1836; to Collinsworth and Grayson, July 9, to Gaines, July 27.

Gaines would move his forces to Nacogdoches. Austin then approached the main point. Explaining the necessity for Santa Anna's release and the obstacle to it in the opposition of the Texan army, unless Jackson would undertake to guarantee his sincerity, he continued, "I believe that your guarantee, in conjunction with the establishment of your headquarters at Nacogdoches, would be sufficient. In this event General Santa Anna would be liberated. I mean in the event of your guaranteeing in the name of the United States the fulfillment of the treaty made by Santa Anna with the government of Texas. . . . Should your instructions admit of the course without waiting for an answer to General Santa Anna's letter to President Jackson, I am of the opinion it will lead to an immediate cessation of hostilities and to a termination of the war." Through delays of the courier Gaines did not receive this letter until July 27, when he replied that his instructions did not empower him to offer such a guaranty. He had by that time, however, anticipated Austin's request to occupy Nacogdoches, having apparently ordered troops there as early as July 10, though we do not know that they arrived before the end of the month. They remained until December, but as the Mexican invasion did not arrive and the Indians did not rise, they served only to involve the United States in an acrimonious diplomatic correspondence with Mexico.[11]

On July 20, Austin, Archer, and Wharton met at Velasco to prepare a report of their mission to the United States. A pleasant personal effect of their common exertions and anxieties had been to bring them to a state of mutual confidence and esteem. That this was true of Austin and Wharton is a fine testimonial to the innate genuineness of the two men. Austin expressed his appreciation of his colleagues in numerous letters, but the completeness of the understanding between himself and Wharton is best evidenced by a letter from Wharton describing his dismay at the rumor—probably false—which reached him in Washington that Houston was opposed to annexation. "If this be so," he declared,

[11] Austin to Gaines, July 4, 1836; Gaines to Austin, August 4; Digges to Austin, September 28; Barker, "The United States and Mexico, 1835–1837," *Mississippi Valley Historical Review*, I, 18–27; T. M. Marshall, *The Western Boundary of the Louisiana Purchase* (Berkeley, 1914), 141–185; G. L. Rives, *The United States and Mexico, 1821–1848* (New York, 1913), I, 372–382.

"it is truly and deeply to be deplored. Like all triumphant conquerors he will be omnipotent for a time at least. I plainly see before me the turmoil and confusion and injustice and the demagogueism which must ensue in Texas after the war is over before we can establish an orderly and harmonious independent government." In tone this might have been written by Austin. "I trust in God that it is a mistake," he added, "about Houston's being opposed to annexation. . . . Do hurry home without a moment's delay." The letter is signed, "With a perfect oblivion of all the past . . . truly your friend." Now at Velasco Wharton and Archer, with other friends, requested Austin to become a candidate for the presidency of Texas.[12] A few days later President Burnet called the election for September 5, and Austin published a dignified statement saying that he would serve if elected—

"Influenced by the governing principle which has regulated my actions since I came to Texas, fifteen years ago, which is to serve the country in any capacity in which the people might think proper to employ me, I shall not decline the highly responsible and difficult one now proposed, should the majority of my fellow citizens elect me. My labors and exertions to settle this country and promote its welfare are well known. My object has been the general good and the permanent liberty and prosperity of Texas. In the pursuit of this object I can say with a clear conscience that I have been honest and sincere in my exertions, and shall continue to be so whether I am acting as a private citizen or a public officer."

At the same time he wrote General Rusk that he consented to run "for only one reason, which is that I believe I can be of material service in procuring the annexation of Texas to the United States." [13]

Henry Smith, governor of Texas during the period of the provisional government, was also a candidate, and the campaign developed quickly after the manner of political contests. In his letter to Rusk Austin denied two charges that were already circulated against himself—one that he was concerned in the land speculations at Monclova in 1835, and the other that he had been the means of saving Santa Anna. Other charges followed—that he had opposed independence, and that he had gone to the United

[12] Austin's Memorandum Book, entry of July 20, in file of July 4, 1836; Archer to editor, in *Telegraph and Texas Register,* August 16, 1836.
[13] Letter of August 4 in *Telegraph and Texas Register,* August 9, 1836; Austin to Rusk, August 9, in Memorandum Book, filed July 4, 1836.

States in the midst of the war and done nothing there but "eat fine dinners and drink wine." On August 15 his good friend Gail Borden wrote that he could not be elected unless the people could be convinced that he had had no hand in the speculations. "I have, when speaking of this affair," said Borden, "offered to pledge my life on the question; that is, I would give my life, if at any time it should be found that you were engaged in the affair." Borden suggested a "circular to the people," and Austin prepared a statement which was published as a broadside and reprinted in the *Telegraph,* of which Borden was owner and editor. Except for the natural human desire to win the game when once begun, Austin was nearly indifferent to the result of the election. His personal affairs had always been neglected; the past three years had been devoted exclusively to public service; and the transition to independence made urgent the conclusion of all business that was in any way dependent upon or related to the former government —as much of Austin's business was. He therefore wrote the candid truth when he said, "I feel but little anxiety, of a personal character, whether I am elected or not." But he did resent the injustice of the charges and imputations against him, and, after explaining the historical background out of which they grew, categorically denied them all.

"I have been connected with the public affairs of Texas in one way or another [he reminded his readers] for fifteen years, and under circumstances during the whole of that period the most difficult, perplexing, and embarrassing. I was for many years the principal organ of the local administration and of communication between the settlers of this colony (who, be it remembered, came direct from a free and well organized government . . . with all their political ideas and habits fresh upon their mind) and the Mexican government, which then was, as it still is, in that state of chaos produced by a sudden transition from extreme slavery and ignorance, to extreme republican liberty. The difficulty of such a position is evident. The dangers of premature and ruinous collisions, produced by a difference of language, forms, laws, habits, etc., were almost insurmountable. The very nature of things opened an almost boundless field for demagogues and personalities, and the country was placed during the whole of that eventful period upon a volcano, subject to be ruined by popular excitements on the one hand or by the jealousy of the Mexicans on the other. I was individually liable to suspicion, and to fancied or real complaints from all quarters, and a mark for the shafts of envy and personal animosity, as well as for the attacks of those who honestly differed in opinion with me, or were misinformed. That period was more difficult and dangerous to the settlement of Texas, and to its ultimate emancipation and liberty, than any which has subsequently threatened, or which now threatens its destinies; for had its colonization failed, there would have been no foundation to plant independence or anything else upon. We passed through that period, however, in safety. A *foundation* was then laid which I believed, and am now convinced, could not, and cannot, be broken up. No one knows or can appreciate so well as I do the labor it has cost, and perhaps but few have maturely considered its strength and results—they are co-durable with the English language and with the Anglo-American race."

As to the present charges, he denied connection with the land speculations; he had supported the declaration of November 7 in the hope of keeping the war out of Texas and gaining strength to make success secure when the struggle became inevitable; finally the mission to the United States had been not of his choosing or devising but in response to the call of the country expressed by the consultation, and though the services of the commissioners had been of a character hard to describe or appreciate, he thought they had been beneficial. In the letter to Rusk he had already answered the criticism that he saved the life of Santa Anna. The answer was that the armistice at San Jacinto and the treaty of Velasco saved Santa Anna, and that he had merely tried to use him to bring about intervention from the United States.[14]

The same issue of the *Telegraph* that contained Austin's statement announced Houston's entrance into the campaign. He was nominated simultaneously by public meetings in different places, the nomination from Columbia being signed, according to the *Telegraph,* by more than six hundred names.[15] The principal reason given for the nomination was that he was well known to President Jackson and the cabinet and could influence annexation. Houston's apology for accepting the nomination was the cryptic statement that "the crisis required it." [16] Many years later he explained that the feeling between the Austin and Wharton parties was so bitter that the election of either Austin or Smith (who he

---

[14] Borden to Austin, August 9, 1836; Austin to Borden, August 20, in *Telegraph and Texas Register,* August 23, 1836.

[15] The names are not published.

[16] *Telegraph and Texas Register,* August 31, 1836.

said headed the Wharton party) would have destroyed all chance of harmony, so necessary to the auspicious inauguration of the new government.[17] This would indicate, perhaps, that Wharton could not carry his friends with him in his support of Austin.

Houston was elected by a great majority. Austin was not surprised at the result, and certainly did not long regret it. Three days before the election he wrote his brother-in-law that he planned to devote the coming winter to closing all his business and requested him to erect a cabin to be used for office and sleeping quarters—

"I must have one clerk at least, and perhaps two, and there ought to be three rooms, one for a sleeping room for the clerks and visitors. I also wish you to make out an order on N. Orleans for the necessary mattresses, chairs, tables, etc. ... I can sell some land and have the money ready for these purposes and for all the necessary supplies of provisions, etc. ... These arrangements are made on the supposition that I shall not be elected. Houston will, I am told, get all the East and Red River now. Many of the old settlers who are too blind to see or understand their interest will vote for him, and the army I believe will go for him, at least a majority of them. So that I have a good prospect of some rest this year, and time to regulate my private affairs, which need regulating very much."

How the election was regarded by some of Austin's friends was tersely expressed by Edmund Andrews. "The body politic," he wrote, "is unlike every other machine that ever existed. Other machines may be thrown out of order by some accident, but this is only right by accident." [18]

Essentially indifferent though he was to the result, the election threatened, nevertheless, to leave in Austin's heart a deep and permanent scar. The unjust charge that he had shared in the land speculations festered, and the barb was twisted in the wound by the malicious insinuation that in the event of his election, Williams would use him to protect the speculators. For twelve years Austin's relations with Williams had been most intimate and confidential. He was a lonely man and could ill afford the loss of such a friend, because he had so few. Yet now, aside from his abhorrence of the speculations, he came to feel that Williams had betrayed his friend-

[17] Houston to Guy M. Bryan, November 15, 1852, in Yoakum, *History of Texas*, II, 193.
[18] Austin to Perry, September 2; Andrews to Austin, September 8, 1836.

ship—that he should have known his actions would involve Austin, in the popular mind, and knowing, that he should have refrained. Williams learned of Austin's feeling, but not clearly of the cause, and wrote from New Orleans a letter that does him honor and testifies to Austin's capacity to inspire warm and lasting affection. He had been proud, Williams declared, to connect in Austin the titles of friend and benefactor; he could never have been disregardful of his fair name; and he desired his election for public, not selfish, reasons.

"Too well am I acquainted with your principles of justice and your integrity to believe for a moment that your office will be held for personal benefit of friends, or for the destruction of enemies—and too well ever to ask or sue from you as president a favor not to be extended to the humblest individual.... As Stephen F. Austin I would have applied for favors which I would not have asked of any living man, for the reason that to Stephen F. Austin will I grant and concede that which I will not concede to any [other] man that lives.... I should like to hear from you. I should like to know what beyond a morbid feeling has aroused you (for it may be two months before I can get back) and of what it is you complain in me. And be assured great as is my affliction under your censure, greater is my esteem for you.... Therefore write to me and do so freely."

"I hope [Williams continued] a better state of feelings will take place between you and McKinney [Williams's partner, who had been alienated by Austin's avowal for independence]. He does not know you so well as I do; nor has he perhaps the same obligation that I have on me to bear your rebukes, and even your injuries if I am doomed to receive them. But I feel persuaded that under less excited feelings he is desirous of doing you justice. Nothing would afford me more true satisfaction than to learn that all misunderstanding between you and him was buried in oblivion." [19]

Austin received this after long delay, when, as he said, he was "barely able to crawl about" from an attack of malaria. He declared that he read it "with such feelings as a drowning man would seize a plank," because Williams was wound round his heart as no other man had ever been or could ever be again, and he wanted to be convinced that Williams had been true to the public interest and to his own friendship. One feels that he did not rise to the fine generosity of Williams's affection, but he was disappointed, ill, and depressed, and happily this was not his last word. He wrote

[19] Williams to Austin, August 29, 1836; McKinney to Austin, February 22, 1836.

again when the horizon was more fair; and the letter illustrates much of his public and personal philosophy.

"This is my birthday [he wrote]. My health is much improved, tho still bad, and I am still tormented with dispepsia, a most cursed disease for body and mind. The public matters are getting on well. A state of things which I have long labored to bring about is gradually coming round, which is union and the disappearance of those old parties and nonsense which in times past have distracted and almost ruined this country. I believe that I have contributed something towards bringing about this state [of] things—tho at the loss perhaps of some [men who] *called* themselves *old friends*. I am [as rapidly as] I can gradually preparing [to relieve] myself in toto from all kinds [of public business] and shall do so permanently as soon as I can.

"Come home Williams . . . You have greatly vexed and worried and distressed me. So much so that my brain has been greatly fevered. I am in a considerable degree getting over it. It is no easy matter to admit anything like *permanent estrangement* from a person who has been united to us by close friendship for years and in times of trouble. . . . That cursed Monclova trip of yours has indeed been a *curse* to you and to me and to the country and to everybody else. I am trying to banish even the recollection of it from my mind, and when I fully recover my health, hope [I] shall be able to do so. In future I never mean to speak of it or allude to it, if I can avoid it. I have cursed it in so many forms and shapes that my anger is becoming almost exhausted and will, I sincerely hope, finally wear away. Williams, you have wounded me very deeply, but you are so deeply rooted in my affections that, with all your faults, you are at heart too much like a wild and heedless brother to be entirely banished. Come home." [20]

Austin's desire to be relieved from public service was not to be realized with his defeat for the presidency. Houston offered him the state department—the most responsible and burdensome post in the cabinet, in view of the importance of presenting the new republic to the society of nations with proper decorum. He declined, pleading bad health and the necessity to close the land business; but Houston submitted his name to the Senate; he was confirmed; and true to his principle of serving when called, he accepted the office. He apparently intended to resign after a few months but hoped before doing so to contribute toward two ends —harmony at home, and the recognition and annexation of Texas by the United States. The first he might accomplish by example; the second by his innate ability and his knowledge of conditions in Mexico, the United States, and Texas.[21]

Santa Anna again was thought to afford a possible means of facilitating annexation by paving the way for recognition of Texan independence by Mexico. Jackson had answered his letter of July 4 saying that he could not intervene on the basis of the treaty of Velasco, but that he would make Santa Anna's appeal the occasion for conversations with the Mexican minister. The effect of Jackson's letter in Texas was incidentally described by Austin in writing to his brother-in-law—"Those who cursed and were for hanging me for going to see Santa Anna at all or getting him to write Jackson, now say that I was right. That measure then so bad is now looked to as one of the best modes of bringing about a peace." He added that Houston's ideas about Santa Anna agreed with his own. These were that Santa Anna, though in temporary eclipse, would still be a power in Mexico and might—if Jackson would cooperate —be able to put through a quit-claim cession to the United States. Public opinion would now permit his release without guaranties and Austin believed that his presence in Mexico, if it accomplished nothing else, would incite party wrangling and intrigue, which would divert attention from Texas. This, as it happened, was exactly Jackson's view of the matter, as we know from Major William B. Lewis. Lewis reported on October 27—though of course Austin had not yet received the letter—that the President thought Santa Anna should be permitted to return to Mexico without delay, that "he had no doubt but it was the best thing the Government of Texas could do, as it would give the Mexicans employment at home instead of making war upon their neighbors."[22]

Santa Anna was released shortly after Houston's inauguration. He wished to visit Washington before returning to Mexico and was sent there under the escort of Colonels George W. Hockley and Barnard E. Bee. Whatever Jackson's attitude might be, Austin expected the visit to benefit Texas, and took pains to have Santa

[21] Austin to Perry, October 25, 1836; to Houston, October 31; to Meigs, November 7; to Merle and Company, December 10; Houston to Austin, October 28.

[22] Austin to Perry, October 25, 1836; to Ficklin, October 30; to Meigs, November 7; Lewis to Austin, October 27. Jackson's letter to Santa Anna, September 4, 1836, is in Richardson, *Messages and Papers of the Presidents*, III, 275.

Anna say in writing, in asking for an interview with the President, that he thought the best interests of the United States, Mexico, and Texas demanded "the separation of Texas from Mexico, either as an independent nation or [by] its annexation to the United States." Jackson answered with scrupulous propriety that he could not act on the basis of anything that Santa Anna might propose, because the Mexican government had disavowed his authority; but for Santa Anna's use in Mexico he outlined an adjustment that the United States might accept and undertake to make acceptable to Texas. This was for Mexico to cede to the United States all claims to territory north and east of a line beginning at the mouth of the Rio Grande, following that stream to the thirty-eighth parallel, and extending thence to the Pacific Ocean. The United States would pay Mexico three and a half million dollars "and deal then as it respected Texas as a magnanimous nation ought." This ended the negotiation with and through Santa Anna. It had been hardly more than jockeying for position, and each of the three parties had gained perhaps all that he expected. Santa Anna had obtained his freedom, and Austin and Jackson the admission from the Mexican statesman best qualified to know that Mexico could not conquer Texas and ought therefore to recognize its independence.[23]

Direct negotiation was expected to be more fruitful than the circuitous approach through Santa Anna, and Austin prepared credentials and instructions with the greatest care for Wharton, whom Houston was returning to Washington as minister plenipotentiary. His object was the annexation of Texas to the United States, but this might depend on recognition, and Wharton was therefore to claim independence both *de jure* and *de facto*. As to the right of independence, which Austin correctly assumed the United States would not question, the argument was unconvincing —simply that the union with Mexico had been dissolved by the overthrow of the federal system without the acquiescence of Texas. The fact of independence, however, was on firm ground and was proved, said Austin, by the failure of Santa Anna's invasion and his admission that Texas was able to maintain itself. The people

---

[23] Austin to Hockley and Bee, November 25, 1836; Jackson to Santa Anna, memorandum without date, Jackson MSS., Library of Congress.

were united and confident in their strength, had an army and a navy, and the government was in undisturbed operation. The treaty of annexation, if the negotiation progressed so far, should provide for the admission of Texas, with boundary extending to the Rio Grande, on an equality with existing states; should recognize slavery with no other limitations than those imposed by the federal constitution; and should guarantee land titles without regard to the fulfillment of formal conditions, such as complete cultivation or adoption of the Catholic faith. If the state were to pay its public debt—that is, if the debt were not to be assumed by the United States—then the state must retain its public land; and, if possible, a moratorium should be established for a reasonable time on debts owing to foreigners.

These were public instructions, to be shown to Jackson and Forsyth, secretary of state. In his private instructions Wharton was reminded that the Texan desire for annexation was less pronounced than the recent vote indicated; that many voted for annexation without reflection and others from a sense of expediency; and that conditions might develop which would render independence preferable. European recognition and British intervention for recognition by Mexico might create such conditions. "England, France and Mexico therefore have it in their power," said Austin, "to influence very materially in fixing the political position of Texas." If Wharton discovered any coolness on the part of the United States, he was to hold "full and free conversations" with the foreign ministers at Washington and endeavor through them to establish relations with their governments. Finally Wharton was to ascertain the "real view" of the United States in occupying Nacogdoches, and if he found a disposition to claim the Neches instead of the Sabine as the boundary prescribed by the Florida treaty, he was to protest.[24]

This was Austin's last important public service. For another month he busied himself in equipping his office, drafting a proclamation against the slave trade, and preparing a comprehensive report on the colonization business.[25] On December 27 he died. His own words are a fitting epitaph. He had written a short time

[24] Wharton's instructions, November 18, are in Garrison, *Diplomatic Correspondence of the Republic of Texas,* I, 127–140.
[25] Austin to Toby, November 19, 1836; Proclamation, December 1.

before: "I am nothing more than an individual citizen of this country, but I feel a more lively interest for its welfare than can be expressed—one that is greatly superior to all pecuniary or personal views of any kind. The prosperity of Texas has been the object of my labors, the idol of my existence. It has assumed the character of a *religion,* for the guidance of my thoughts and actions, for fifteen years." And characteristically his last conscious thought was of its welfare. He waked from a dream thinking that the United States had recognized its independence, and died happy in that belief. His last words were: "Texas recognized. Archer told me so. Did you see it in the papers?" [26]

[26] Austin to Gaines, July 27, 1836; Hammeken, "Recollections of Stephen F. Austin," *Southwestern Historical Quarterly,* XX, 380.

CHAPTER XVIII

Epilogue: Significance and Personality

NO other of the forty-eight commonwealths composing the United States—with the possible exception of Utah— owes its position so completely to one man as Texas does to Austin. Without Penn and Baltimore the history of Pennsylvania and Maryland would still be the story of Englishmen wresting the territory from nature and the Indians and becoming Americans in the process. The same may be said of Georgia without Oglethorpe. But without Austin there is no reason to believe that Texas would differ today from the Mexican states south of the Rio Grande.

That form of prophecy which seeks to determine what the past might have been with some of its elements changed is, to be sure, little more dependable in its results than that which tries to penetrate the future. Both are subject to the infinite variability of a multitude of individuals reacting in a changing environment. Still, one may review the facts and draw such conclusions as they seem to indicate. From Aaron Burr to James Long the efforts to open Texas to Americans by force had failed; and, even if the establishment of Mexican independence had not removed the stock pretext for such invasions, it is not likely that others would have been more successful. The planting of an Anglo-American population in Texas had to be accomplished, therefore, by peaceful, lawful colonization. Undoubtedly Mexico would have adopted an immigration policy sooner or later; but it seems pretty evident that nothing but Austin's unremitting pressure caused the passage of the imperial colonization law. Without that law, even upon the unlikely assumption that everything else might have happened as and when it did, Austin's original contract would not have been confirmed; he would have remained in the ruck of empresarios hanging on at Mexico and Saltillo; his first colony would not have been established to proclaim the potential loyalty of American settlers when the Fredonian rebellion seemed to prove the reverse; and the federal law excluding emigrants from the United States would have been passed, with no loophole for evasion, at the beginning of 1827 instead of three years later. There would have been no settlement of Texas, no revolution, no annexation, no Mexican War; and the Louisiana Purchase, in all probability, would still define the western boundary of the United States.

It would be a deplorable misconception of the truth, however, as it is hoped these pages have shown, to believe that Austin and his settlers foresaw and desired these ends—to say nothing of having worked for them. Austin's success was due, in fact, to his complete and whole-hearted adoption of the obligations of a Mexican citizen. He strove honestly to make Texas a model state in the Mexican system—a Utopian dream, as he came to realize, but how reluctantly and for what reasons he abandoned it we have seen. The causes of failure were inherent in Mexican character and experience, and are not chargeable to lack of sincerity, of sympathetic forbearance, or of patient, thoughtful labor on Austin's part.

Besides honest intentions, which were fundamental and indispensable, there were two other elements in Austin's successful dealings with the government as an empresario. One was his understanding of and adaptation to Mexican psychology, and the other was tireless industry. The Mexican loves indirection, and Austin made himself a master of the oblique approach. A topic could scarcely be too remote to be coaxed by him into becoming the apparently casual vehicle for an argument to further a favorite reform. But this is not to say that he never employed the method direct. He had rare ability for vigorous and unambiguous expression in both English and Spanish, and the blunt directness of some of his official documents is startling.

The most obvious proof of Austin's ceaseless industry is the mass of his collected writing. The land records alone—shared though they were by Williams—were an enormous burden. Besides these, the correspondence and documents that have been preserved would fill several thousand printed pages. When Austin had an important project in mind he wrote to every one who could influence its fate, and then, having dropped his pen to ease his cramped fingers, he immediately seized it again to iterate and re-iterate the same arguments from new angles. He was tenacious and persistent, but was never nagging and rarely offended. Some documents were written many times, and we can trace their evolution from the first crude memorandum to the finished draft. It is in these successive editions that the mind of the writer is often most clearly revealed.

Little can be added by restatement to the impression of Austin's character and personality gained from the preceding pages. He was a successful leader with none of the tricks of the demagogue. His influence, it is true, may be attributed in part to his great authority and large power; but at bottom it rested on the solid basis of recognized knowledge, wisdom, and character. He was judicial and honest and fair, and the colonists knew that he was. Though he has labored doggedly through these pages, overcoming one mountain of difficulties only to find himself at the base of another, he sometimes dropped the habit of seriousness in sheer self-defense and joined in the mild pleasures of the time. He appreciated music, liked dancing, and enjoyed social intercourse. In the manner of lonely men, he was given to self-analysis; he thought himself reserved, but he does not appear so in his letters. He was singularly clean in thought and speech, and the language of his writings is uniformly dignified and chaste. In physique he was small of stature, lean and wiry, with fine features and the head of a scholar.

How much of himself he spent the preceding pages have shown; how little of reward he reaped in pecuniary gain and ordinary human comfort may be seen from a letter that he wrote a few weeks before his death. The report had reached him that some of the volunteers from Kentucky complained that he had treated them inhospitably. He was mortified and hurt:

"For I do not merit it [he wrote]. I have no house, not a roof in all Texas that I can call my own. The only one I had was burned at San Felipe during the late invasion of the enemy. I make my home where the business of the country calls me. There is none here at the farm of my brother-in-law, who only began to open up this place three years ago, and is still in the primitive log cabbins and wild shrubbery of the forest. I have no farm, no cotton plantation, no income, no money, no comforts. I have spent the prime of my life and worn out my constitution in trying to colonize this country. Many persons boast of their 300 and 400 leagues acquired by speculation without personal labor or the sacrifice of years or even days; I shall be content to save twenty leagues or about ninety thousand acres, *acquired very hard and very dear indeed*. All my wealth is prospective and contingent upon the events of the future. What I have been able from time to time to realize in active means has gone as fast as realized, and much faster (for I am still in debt for the expenses of my trip to Mexico in 1833, '34, and '35) where my health and strength and time have gone, which is in the service of Texas, and I am therefore not ashamed of my present poverty." [1]

He was a man of warm affections, and loved the idea of home, but he never married. Texas was home and wife and family to him. He died on a pallet on the floor of a two-room clapboard shack, a month and twenty-four days past his forty-third birthday. His work was done, but he was denied the years so hardly earned for the enjoyment of its fruits. There is a certain poetic completeness in this, but the prosaic mind rebels. Austin sowed unselfishly and abundantly, and he deserved also to reap.

[1] Austin to Ficklin, October 30, 1836.

CHAPTER XIX

Bibliography

MANUSCRIPTS

The Austin Papers were accumulated by Moses and Stephen F. Austin. For more than sixty years they were reverently preserved by Colonel Guy M. Bryan, grandson of Moses Austin, and after his death were given by his children to the University of Texas. They tell much of the life of the Austins in Virginia, Missouri, and Arkansas, but about seven-eighths of the collection relates to the younger Austin's work in and for Texas. The papers consist of business memoranda, petitions and memorials to local and superior governments, political addresses and proclamations, and personal and official correspondence. The official correspondence consisting of letters written to Austin and autograph copies of many of those written by him, covers every phase of the history of Austin's colony and is, of course, the foundation of this study. Letters from prospective colonists illustrate their motives and describe conditions in the United States that stimulated emigration. In general, copies of Austin's replies to these writers are not available, but such as we have illuminate conditions in Texas. In mass this collection probably totals four thousand printed pages. The American Historical Association published in its *Report* for 1919, Volume II, *The Austin Papers,* I, through 1827 (Government Printing Office, Washington, 1924), edited by Eugene C. Barker. A subsequent volume by this Association is expected to carry the publication from 1828 through 1834, and plans are under way for publishing the papers of the remaining years, 1834–1836.

There is a considerable mass of manuscripts, originally a part of this collection, of which Mrs. Hally Bryan Perry, of Houston, Texas, is custodian for the children of her father, Colonel Guy M. Bryan. For the most part they concern the early history of the Austins and were originally separated from the main collection for personal reasons. The University of Texas has transcripts of the more pertinent documents, and since this statement was written Mrs. Perry has given it the originals.

The Bexar Archives are the manuscript and printed records that accumulated at San Antonio de Bexar during the Spanish-Mexican régime. San Antonio was the capital of the province of Texas, and the archives are both local and general, covering the operation of the local municipality, but containing also much material on the civil and military administration of the province. From 1820 to 1834 the governor and his successor, the political chief, residing at San Antonio, had jurisdiction over all Texas. The records contain, therefore, some of Austin's correspondence, and are otherwise invaluable for this study. They are at the University of Texas. The Nacogdoches Archives in the Texas State Library contain many important documents, with some translations, which originally belonged to this collection. Records of the Department of San Felipe seem for the most part to have perished when the town was burned during Santa Anna's invasion of 1836.

Besides numerous lesser collections of originals, valuable in the aggregate for this study, the University of Texas has from twelve to fifteen thousand pages of transcripts from the Mexican departments of Fomento, Guerra y Marina, and Relaciones Exteriores y Interiores, all relating more or less directly to the subject. The Archivo General of the State of Coahuila, at Saltillo, contains much for 1824–1835 that is not elsewhere available, but much that is there is duplicated by material in the General Land Office of Texas.

The Texas State Library contains a number of large collections, the most important of which are the Lamar Papers, the Nacogdoches Archives, the official records of the provisional government of Texas during 1835 and 1836, the diplomatic correspondence of the Republic of Texas, and letters of George Fisher and of Anthony Butler. Letters from and to Austin form a generous portion of these collections and as a whole they deal mainly with conditions and events of Austin's time. Lamar's collection in particular was begun with a view to writing a biography of Austin. This collection is in process of publication by the Library. The *Diplomatic Correspondence of the Republic of Texas* (George P. Garrison, ed.) was published by the American Historical Association, *Report,* 1907, II, and *Report,* 1908, II (Government Printing Office, Washington, 1908, 1911). The State Library has become the repository of many records that formerly were preserved by the Texan department of state; but some materials for this period still remain in the vaults of the department.

Perhaps the most important single collection owned by the state outside the University of Texas is that of the General Land Office at Austin. Texas retained its domain when it was annexed to the United States and developed its own land system on the model of that of the United States. It was early necessary to assemble all documents relating to empresario contracts and land grants, and these, constituting more than sixty volumes of what are called *Spanish Records,* are a most comprehensive source for the history of colonial Texas.

The Rosenberg Library, at Galveston, Texas, has a voluminous collection of manuscripts, presented by Mrs. Mary D. League and her son, Thomas D. League—daughter and grandson of Samuel M. Williams, Austin's secretary and confidential friend. Much of the collection has been useful for this study, but some sixty letters from Austin to Williams have been invaluable for their intimate revelation of Austin and their explanation of various important movements. The Rosenberg Library is also the trustee for a mass of manuscripts dealing with this period derived from the extinct Galveston Historical Society.

The records of the American legation in Mexico City, and the correspondence between the State Department and its agents in Mexico, the Jackson and Van Buren manuscripts, and the records of the Adjutant General's Office in Washington have been explored and have contributed specifically or atmospherically to the study. The Poinsett Papers, belonging to the Pennsylvania Historical Society, were examined cursorily with, in the main, negative results.

LAWS AND LEGISLATIVE SOURCES

H. P. N. Gammel, *Laws of Texas,* I (Austin, 1898), and *Laws and Decrees of Coahuila and Texas* (Houston, 1839) are comprehensive but incomplete compilations of the state laws and certain federal laws and constitutions affecting Texas prior to its declaration of independence. The laws of the state were originally printed in separate sheets or pamphlets, according to the length of the decree, and published by mailing copies to the various departments and municipalities, and most of those omitted from the two compilations just mentioned can be found in the original form in the Bexar Archives. The manuscript journals of the legislature of Coahuila and Texas, 1824–1835, were preserved as late as 1922 in the legislative archive (*Archivo del Poder Legislativo*) at Saltillo. They were never printed, but the University of Texas owns a transcript. Committee reports and debates would be invaluable at many points but are not available.

Manuel Dublan and José María Lozano, *Legislación Mexicana ó Colección Completa de las Disposiciones Legislativas Expedidas desde la Independencia de la República* (Mexico, 1876), is incomplete, notwithstanding the title, but is adequate for most uses. The first three volumes cover the period of this book. Basilio José Arrillaga, *Recopilación de Leyes, Decretos, Bandos, Reglamentos, Circulares y Providencias de los Supremos Poderes y Otras Autoridades de la República Mexicana* (Mexico, 1836), supplements Dublan and Lozano after 1827 and includes much material not comprehended in the plan of those editors. The García collection in the Library of the University of Texas contains contemporary editions of the Federal laws from 1821 to 1835, but it seems hardly necessary here to cite the several volumes by title.

The García collection contains broken files of the *Actas,* or journals, of Congress as follows: *Diario de las Sesiones de la Soberana Junta Provisional Gubernativa del Imperio Mexicano* (printed by Alejandro Valdés), September 22, 1821–February 25, 1822; *Actas del Congreso Constituyente Mexicano,* Volumes I-IV (printed by Valdés), February 24, 1822–May 13, 1823; *Diario de la Junta Nacional Instituyente del Imperio Mexicano* (printed by Valdés), November 2, 1822–March 6, 1823; *Diario de las Sesiones del Congreso Constituyente de la Federación Mexicana* (Government print), April–June, 1824 (three volumes); *Estracto de las Sesiones de la Cámara de Representantes del Congreso de la Union,* volumes for parts of 1830 and 1831. The volume for 1830 was printed by José Ximeno and that for 1831 by the *Águila.* The journals for July, 1824, and February–April, 1830, when important legislation affecting Texas was enacted, have not been found in any collection in the United States. Juan A. Mateos, *Historia Parlamentaria de los Congresos Mexicanos de 1821 a 1857* (Mexico, 1877), covers the period of this book in its first two volumes. It is very thin, however, after 1824.

For Missouri the laws of this period are in *United States Statutes at Large,* I and II, and *Laws of a Public and General Nature of the District of Louisiana . . . of the Territory of Missouri . . . up to the Year 1836* (Jefferson City, 1842). *The Annals of Congress* and the *Congressional Globe* furnish scattering material supplementing the Missouri period of the Austins.

NEWSPAPERS

The writer has discussed Texan newspapers of the 1819–1836 period in *The Southwestern Historical Quarterly,* XXI, 127–144. The University of Texas has nearly all of the first volume of the *Texas Gazette,* 1829–1830; a considerable run of the *Texas Republican,* 1834; and the *Telegraph and Texas Register,* 1835–1836; besides scattering issues of other papers from 1831 to 1836. It seems hardly practicable to list other papers. I have explored *Niles' Register* and western files of the 1816–1836 period in the Library of Congress, the Library of the Wisconsin Historical Society, the Missouri Historical Society, and the Durrett Collection of the University of Chicago. My primary purpose in the exploration was to discover such material as there might be upon the motives for migration. How was migration affected by political, economic, and social conditions; how influenced, for example, by the panic of 1819, by the establishment and operation of the Second United States Bank, and by the application of the cash system to the public land business of the United States?

GENERAL WORKS

There is little material on the Connecticut and Virginia aspects of this volume except that in the Austin Papers. J. H. Trumbull, *Collections of the Connecticut Historical Society,* II-VII (Hartford, 1870–1899), contains some documents on lead mining at Middletown. William P. Palmer and Sherwin McRae, *Calendar of Virginia State Papers* (Richmond, 1885); *The Virginia Magazine of*

History and Biography (Richmond, 1898–1924); *William and Mary College Quarterly* (Williamsburg, 1892–1923); and *Tyler's Quarterly, Historical and Genealogical* (Richmond, 1920–1924)— all contain Austin items, particularly concerning lead mining in Virginia. Local histories of southwestern Virginia seem consistently misleading in their references to the Wythe County mines.

For Missouri valuable works are relatively numerous. Louis Houck's books are outstanding—*A History of Missouri* (Chicago, 1908), three volumes, and *The Spanish Régime in Missouri* (Chicago, 1909), two volumes. Floyd C. Shoemaker, *Missouri's Struggle for Statehood, 1804–1821* (Jefferson City, 1916), gives the general political history of the Austin period. Local aspects and social and economic conditions are described by H. M. Brackenridge, *Views of Louisiana, together with a Journal of a Voyage up the Missouri River in 1811* (Pittsburgh, 1814); by Amos Stoddard, *Sketches, Historical and Descriptive, of Louisiana* (Philadelphia, 1812); and by Henry R. Schoolcraft, *A View of the Lead Mines of Missouri,* etc. (New York, 1819), *Journal of a Tour to the Interior of Missouri and Arkansaw . . . Performed in the Years 1818 and 1819* (London, 1821), and *Travels in the Central Portions of the Mississippi Valley* (New York, 1825). *The Missouri Historical Review* contains many illuminating articles on this period, of which Breckenridge Jones's "One Hundred Years of Banking in Missouri," Volume 15, pages 345–392, has been especially useful. John Ray Cable, *The State Bank of Missouri* (Columbia University Studies in History, Economics and Public Law, Volume CII, No. 2, New York, 1923), adds nothing to Jones's article on the Bank of St. Louis. E. M. Violette's "Spanish Land Claims in Missouri," Washington University, Studies, VIII, Humanistic Series No. 2, pages 167–200, is an exceptionally clear treatment of an unusually difficult subject. Valuable material on the same subject is scattered through *American State Papers, Public Lands,* Volumes I–VI (Washington, 1834–1860). My references are to the set published by Gales and Seaton.[1]

Dallas T. Herndon (ed.), *Centennial History of Arkansas* (Chicago, 1922), is a good guide to the period of Arkansas history

[1] For this and another set, published by Duff Green, see *Check list of United States Public Documents, 1789–1909* (Washington, 1911), 3, 4.

touched by the Austins. I have also found useful two gossipy volumes of reminiscences: William F. Pope, *Early Days in Arkansas* (Little Rock, 1895): and Josiah H. Shinn, *Pioneers and Makers of Arkansas* (Little Rock, copyright dated 1908). The *Publications* of the Arkansas Historical Association, I-IV (Fayetteville, 1907–1910), contains a goodly number of pertinent items.

It could serve no useful purpose, even if it were practicable, to enumerate all the printed works on Mexico and Texas that have influenced this book. C. W. Raines, *A Bibliography of Texas* (Austin, 1896), lists the more important of them with well considered evaluations. Vicente Filisola, *Memorias para la Historia de la Guerra de Tejas,* two volumes (Mexico, 1848, 1849), is the only comprehensive history of the colonization of Texas and the Texas revolution from the Mexican point of view. Filisola was second in command under Santa Anna in 1836 and led the army in retreat from Texas after Santa Anna's capture. The book is reasonably objective in method, incorporates numerous documents in the text, and each volume includes a documentary appendix. Lorenzo de Zavala, *Ensayo Histórico de las Revoluciones de Mégico,* two volumes (Paris, 1831), is a vivid account in elegant style of the political and constitutional problems of the various parliamentary bodies following the declaration of Mexican independence. The disjointed, fragmentary writings of Carlos María Bustamante which deal more or less journalistically with the same subject are: *Cuadro Histórico de la Revolución* ... five volumes (Mexico, 1843–1846), *Historia del Emperador D. Agustin de Iturbide* ... (Mexico, 1846), and *El Gabinete Mexicana durante el Segundo Período de la Administración del Exmo Presidente D. Anastasio Bustamante* (Mexico, 1842). Lúcas Alamán, *Historia de Mégico desde ... el Año de 1808 hasta la Epoca presente,* five volumes (Mexico, 1849–1852), is the principal source for all Mexican historians who have since written on his period. His fifth volume deals with the period following 1821 and does not greatly supplement Zavala. Hubert Howe Bancroft, *History of Mexico,* six volumes—*Works,* IX–XIV (San Francisco, 1883–1888), is perhaps the best work in its field in either English or Spanish. Like all Bancroft's writings, it is based on exhaustive acquaintance with bibliography and is profusely documented. Volumes IV and V cover the period of this book.

Writings on Texas history prior to 1856 were for the most part frankly intended for propaganda, but this does not seriously militate against their value, if they are used with discrimination. Numerous contemporary documents, in text or appendix, are a common characteristic. Those which need be seriously considered are: Mrs. Mary Austin Holley, *Texas: Observations, Historical, Geographical, and Descriptive, in a Series of Letters* . . . etc. (Philadelphia, 1833). The writer was Stephen F. Austin's cousin, and she wrote the book partly to promote emigration to his colony. Her *Texas* (Lexington, 1836) and David B. Edward, *The History of Texas; or, The Emigrant's, Farmer's and Politician's Guide* . . . etc. (Cincinnati, 1836), were influenced by the timeliness of the Texas revolution. Edward is mildly pro-Mexican, but Mrs. Holley hoped to encourage early recognition of Texas by the United States. Henry Stuart Foote's *Texas and the Texans; or Advance of the Anglo-Americans to the Southwest* . . . etc. (Philadelphia, 1841), in rotund oratorical style, was expected to stimulate interest in annexation. It is chiefly valuable for its documents. William Kennedy, *Texas: The Rise, Progress, and Prospects of the Republic of Texas* (London, 1841; reprint edition by Molyneaux Craftsmen, Fort Worth, Texas, 1925), wrote to stimulate British interest in Texas. Though friendly to the Texans, he wrote with real historical spirit, and, in some respects, his book has not been superseded. N. Doran Maillard, *The History of the Republic of Texas* . . . etc. (London, 1842), is a complete antidote to the pro-Texan bent of Kennedy. In 1856 (New York) appeared Henderson Yoakum, *History of Texas from its first Settlement in 1685 to its Annexation to the United States in 1846*. Yoakum, who was a lawyer, knew the value of evidence, wrote with critical sense, and equipped his volumes with bibliographical notes and documentary appendices. He used material which has since disappeared, and for that reason as well as for its intrinsic merit his book is of permanent value. The text without notes and appendices was reprinted in Wooten (ed.), *A Comprehensive History of Texas* (Dallas, 1898). Colonel Guy M. Bryan contributed to this work several valuable chapters made up chiefly of documentary material from the Austin Papers. Homer S. Thrall, *A Pictorial History of Texas from the Earliest Visits of Europeans to A.D. 1885* (New York and St. Louis, 1885), makes no contribution to the history of Texas, but contains a useful biographical section. Hubert Howe Bancroft, *History of the North Mexican States and Texas* (San Francisco, 1884, 1889), is written with critical objectivity and a wealth of bibliographical equipment, and is the most satisfactory comprehensive history of Texas available. John Henry Brown, *History of Texas from 1685 to 1892* (St. Louis, copyright dated 1892), is bitterly hostile to Austin, is uncritical, and is not always honest, but the book contains many documents and is useful when used with care. George P. Garrison, *Texas: A Contest of Civilizations* (Boston, 1903), is a satisfactory compendium, written with a comprehensive knowledge of the sources, but it necessarily gives little attention to Austin. Louis J. Wortham, *A History of Texas: from Wilderness to Commonwealth* (Fort Worth, 1924), is a serviceable and interesting journalistic synthesis of much monographic and documentary material that has appeared in the past twenty years. The first three volumes cover Austin's period. Most monographic studies in Texas history during the past quarter-century have appeared in the *Quarterly* of the Texas State Historical Association or in its successor, *The Southwestern Historical Quarterly* (Austin, 1897–1925).

Index

Index